The Princeton Review®

P9-BZQ-811

Cracking the

ACT®

WITH DVD

2014 Edition

Geoff Martz, Kim Magloire, and
Theodore Silver

Updated by Melissa Hendrix and
the Staff of The Princeton Review

PrincetonReview.com

Random House, Inc. New York

The Princeton Review, Inc.
111 Speen Street, Suite 550
Framingham, MA 01701
E-mail: editorialsupport@review.com

Copyright © 2013 by TPR Education IP Holdings, LLC

All rights reserved. Published in the United States by
Random House LLC, New York, a Penguin Random
House Company, and in Canada by Random House
of Canada Limited, Toronto, Penguin Random House
Companies.

Terms of Service: The Princeton Review Online
Companion Tools ("Online Companion Tools") for the
Cracking book series and *11 Practice Tests for the SAT
& PSAT* are available for the two most recent editions
of each book title. Online Companion Tools may be
activated only once per eligible book purchased.
Activation of Online Companion Tools more than once
per book is in direct violation of these Terms of Service
and may result in discontinuation of access to Online
Companion Tools services.

Some of the content in the "ACT Insider" has previously
appeared in *Paying for College Without Going Broke*,
published as a trade paperback by Random House in
2012; *College Essays That Made a Difference*, published
as a trade paperback by Random House in 2012;
Planning the Perfect College Visit, published as an eBook
by Random House in 2012; and *The Right College for
You*, published as an eBook by Random House in 2012.

ISBN: 978-0-8041-2440-9
ISSN: 1934-4171

ACT is a registered trademark of ACT, Inc., which does
not sponsor or endorse this product.

The Princeton Review is not affiliated with
Princeton University.

Editor: Meave Shelton
Production Editor: Liz Rutzel
Production Artist: Craig Patches

Printed in the United States of America on partially
recycled paper.

10 9 8 7 6 5 4 3 2 1

2014 Edition

Editorial
Rob Franek, Senior VP, Publisher
Mary Beth Garrick, Director of Production
Selena Coppock, Senior Editor
Calvin Cato, Editor
Kristen O'Toole, Editor
Meave Shelton, Editor
Alyssa Wolff, Editorial Assistant

Random House Publishing Team
Tom Russell, Publisher
Nicole Benhabib, Publishing Director
Ellen L. Reed, Production Manager
Alison Stoltzfus, Managing Editor
Erika Pepe, Associate Production Manager
Kristin Lindner, Production Supervisor
Andrea Lau, Designer

Acknowledgments

A test-preparation course is much more than clever techniques and powerful computer score reports; the reason our results are so great is that our teachers really care. A small group of Princeton Review instructors enthusiastically created a program to prepare students for the previous version of the ACT. We would like to thank John Cauman, Judy Moreland, Bill Lindsley, and Jim Reynolds for their commitment to the original ACT project.

The completion of this book would not have been possible without the help and dedication of several individuals. In particular, we would like to thank Melissa Hendrix for her hard work revising and updating this edition, and Jonathan Chiu, National Content Director for ACT.

Special thanks to Adam Robinson, who conceived of and perfected the Joe Bloggs approach to standardized tests and many other successful techniques used by The Princeton Review.

Contents

...So Much More Online!

More Lessons...

- Step-by-step guide to solving difficult problems
- Tutorials that put our strategies into action
- Useful information about ACT scores, college admissions, and score improvement strategies
- Interactive, click-through learning for English, Math, Reading, and Science
- Overview of the question types you will find on the ACT
- Two full-length practice tests

...then College!

- Detailed profiles for hundreds of colleges help you find the school that is right for you
- Information about financial aid and scholarships
- Dozens of Top 10 ranking lists including Quality of Professors, Worst Campus Food, Most Beautiful Campus, Party Schools, Diverse Student Population, and tons more from our annually revised book, *Best 378 Colleges*.

Register your book now!

- Go to PrincetonReview.com/cracking
- You'll see a Welcome page where you should register your book using the ISBN printed on the back cover of your book, right underneath the price. It's a 13 digit number, starting with "978." Type this number into the window.
- Next you will see a Sign Up/Sign In page where you will type in your E-mail address (username) and choose a password.
- Now you're good to go!

princetonreview.com/cracking

Look For These Icons Throughout The Book

Go Online   More Great Books

Part I
Orientation

Chapter 1
Introduction to
the ACT

So, you have to take the ACT? What will you need to do first? This chapter presents an overview of the ACT as a whole and discusses registration requirements, when to take the test, how to have your scores reported to colleges (or how not to), and the ways in which colleges use your scores.

THE ACT

The ACT is a standardized test used for college admissions. But you probably already knew that. In this book, we'll tell you all the things you didn't know about the ACT, all to show you how to crack the test and get your best score.

The ACT is a pencil-and-paper exam, usually taken on Saturday mornings. Some states offer a special state-administration during the school day. Non-Saturday testing is available but only for students who live in remote areas or who can't test on Saturdays for religious reasons.

The ACT on Computer
Beginning in the spring of 2015, the ACT should be available on computer at those schools and test centers that can accommodate a computer format, but it will still be available in paper format. We expect to learn more about the computer format in the next year, but as of this time, we do not expect the content or scoring to change.

Where Does the ACT Come From?

The ACT is written by a non-profit organization that used to call itself American College Testing but now just calls itself ACT. The company has been producing the ACT since 1959, introducing it as an alternative to the College Board's SAT. ACT also writes ACT Aspire, ACT Explore, and ACT Plan, which are tests you may have taken earlier in your academic career. The organization also provides a broad range of services to educational agencies and business institutions.

What Does the ACT Test?

The nice people who write the ACT—we'll refer to them as "ACT" from now on—describe it as an assessment of college readiness, "a curriculum- and standards-based educational and career planning tool that assesses students' academic readiness for college."

We at The Princeton Review have always been skeptical when any standardized test makes broad claims of what it can measure. In our opinion, a standardized test is just a measure of how well you take that test. Granted, ACT has spent an extraordinary amount of time analyzing data and providing the results of their research to various educational institutions and agencies. In fact, ACT has contributed to the development of the Common Core Standards Initiative, an educational reform that aligns diverse state curricula into national uniform standards.

With all due respect to ACT and the various state and federal agencies working on the Common Core, we still think the ACT is just a measure of how well you take the ACT. Many factors other than mastery of the "curriculum-based" content determine your performance on a standardized test. That's why we'll teach you both the content you need as well as crucial test-taking strategies.

Power Booking
If you were getting ready to take a history test, you'd study history. If you were preparing for a basketball game, you'd practice basketball. So if you're preparing for the ACT, study the ACT!

What's On the ACT?

The ACT consists of four multiple-choice, timed tests: English, Math, Reading, and Science, always given in that order. The ACT Plus Writing also includes an essay, with the Writing test given after the Science test. (ACT calls them tests, but we may also use the term "sections" in this book to avoid confusion.) In Parts II–VI, we'll thoroughly review the content and strategies you need for each test.

Watch it on your DVD

1. English Test (45 minutes—75 questions)

In this section, you will see five essays on the left side of the page. Some words or phrases will be underlined. On the right side of the page, you will be asked whether the underlined portion is correct as written or whether one of the three alternatives listed would be better. This is a test of grammar, punctuation, sentence structure, and rhetorical skills. Throughout each essay, commonly known as a "passage," there will also be questions about overall organization and style or perhaps about how the writing could be revised or strengthened.

**More great titles by
The Princeton Review**
English and Reading Workout for the ACT and *Math and Science Workout for the ACT*

2. Math Test (60 minutes—60 questions)

These are the regular, multiple-choice math questions you've been doing all your life. The easier questions, which test basic math proficiency, *tend* to come first, but the folks at ACT can mix in easy, medium, and difficult problems throughout the Math test. A good third of the test covers pre-algebra and elementary algebra. Slightly less than a third covers intermediate algebra and coordinate geometry (graphing). Regular geometry accounts for less than a quarter of the questions, and there are four questions that cover trigonometry.

3. Reading Test (35 minutes—40 questions)

In this test, there will be four reading passages of about 800 words each—the average length of a *People* magazine article but maybe not as interesting. There is always one prose fiction passage, one social science passage, one humanities passage, and one natural science passage, and they are always in that order. After reading each passage, you have to answer 10 questions.

4. Science Test (35 minutes—40 questions)

No specific scientific knowledge is necessary for the Science test. You won't need to know the chemical makeup of hydrochloric acid or any formulas. Instead, you will be asked to understand six sets of scientific information presented in graphs, charts, tables, and research summaries, and you will have to make sense of one disagreement between two or three scientists. (Occasionally, there are more than three scientists.)

5. Optional Writing Test (30 minutes)

The ACT Plus Writing contains an "optional" writing test featuring a single essay. We recommend you take the "ACT Plus Writing," version of the test because many if not most schools require it. While on test day you may think you don't need it, you might later decide to apply to a school that requires a writing score. The last thing you want is to be forced into taking the whole ACT all over again…this time *with* the Writing test. The essay consists of a prompt "relevant" to high school students on which you will be asked to write an essay stating your position on the prompt. Two people will then grade your essay on a scale of 1 to 6 for a total score of 2 to 12. In this book, we will teach you how to write the best possible essay for the ACT.

How Is the ACT Scored?

Scores for each of the four multiple-choice tests are reported on a scale of 1 to 36 (36 being the highest score possible). The four scores are averaged to yield your composite score, which is the score colleges and universities primarily use to determine admission. Next to each score is a percentile ranking. Percentile ranking refers to how you performed on the test relative to other people who took it at the same time. For instance, a percentile ranking of 87 indicates that you scored higher than 87 percent of the people who took the test and 13 percent scored higher than you.

Closed Loop
The ACT tests how well you take the ACT.

Some of the scores have subcategories. English is broken down into Usage/Mechanics and Rhetorical Skills. In these subcategories, scores are reported on a scale of 1 to 18 (18 being the highest score possible). They are also reported as percentiles.

If you decide to take the ACT Plus Writing test, you will receive standard ACT scores plus two additional scores. One will be a scaled score from 1 to 36, which combines your performance on the Writing test and the English test. The other will be a subscore, ranging from 2 to 12, which reflects how you did on your essay. Neither score contributes to your composite score.

On your score report, ACT also indicates if you met their "College Readiness Benchmark Scores:" 18 in English, 22 in Math, 21 in Reading, and 24 in Science. ACT maintains that these benchmarks can predict college "success," defined by a "50% or higher probability of earning a B or higher in the corresponding college course or courses." These scores and their meaning have been determined by ACT's own research and data, not by any studies done by colleges and universities themselves.

When Should You Take the ACT?

If you haven't already, go to ACTStudent.org and create your free ACT Web Account. You can register for tests, view your scores, and request score reports for colleges through this account. You can also view the specific test dates and centers for the upcoming academic year.

In the United States, U.S. Territories, and Canada, the ACT is given six times a year: September, October, December, February, April, and June. Internationally, the September test date is not offered, and in New York State the February administration is not available.

Many states also offer an additional ACT as part of their state testing. Check with your high school to see if and when your state offers a special ACT. Your school will register you automatically for a state ACT. You must register yourself for all other administrations.

Traditionally, most students have waited until the spring of their junior year to take the ACT. Many high schools still recommend spring of junior year because the content of the Math test includes topics some curricula do not cover before then. However, these topics appear in only a handful of questions, and many juniors take their first ACT in the fall or winter.

We recommend that you consider your own schedule when picking your test dates. Do you play a fall sport and carry a heavier load of extra-curricular activities in the fall? Is winter a quiet time in between semesters? Do you act in the spring musical and plan to take several AP exams? Have you been dreaming of attending Big State University since you were a toddler and already plan to apply early decision? Let the answers to these questions determine your test dates. But we recommend taking your first test as early as your schedule allows.

How Many Times Should You Take the ACT?

For security reasons, ACT will not let you take the exam more than twelve times. But we certainly hope no one is dismayed by this restriction. There are certainly better things to do with your time on a Saturday morning, and we don't believe any college will accept "taking the ACT" as an extra-curricular activity!

The Princeton Review recommends that you plan to take the ACT 2–3 times. If you achieve your goal score in your first administration, great. Take the money and run. On the other hand, if after three tests you have reason and motivation to take the ACT again, do it. On your first day of college, you will neither remember nor care how many times you had to take the ACT.

Does ACT "Super Score"?

The term "super score" or "super composite" is used by students, maybe even colleges, but not by ACT. ACT sends a separate score report for each test date and will send reports only for the dates you request. ACT does not combine scores from different test dates.

However, many schools (and the common app) will ask you to list the score and test date of your best English, best Math, best Reading, and best Science and then calculate a "super composite" based on these scores. Therefore, if you worry that some scores will rise as others fall when you take the ACT again, the "super composite" will reflect your best results.

The Princeton Review recommends strongly that you consult each school you're applying to. While ACT will send only the test dates you request, you should decide which and how many dates to send based on your scores and the school's guidelines about super scoring. Moreover, some schools require that you submit all test scores from every administration, and you should abide by any such requirements.

How Do You Register for the ACT?

The fastest way to register is online, through your ACT Web Account. You can also obtain a registration packet at your high school guidance office, online at ACTStudent.org/forms/stud_req, or by writing or calling ACT at the address and phone number below.

> ACT Student Services
> 2727 Scott Blvd
> PO Box 414
> Iowa City, IA 52243-0414
> 319.337.1270

Registration Tip #1

The registration includes ACT's survey on your grades and interests, but you are not required to answer these questions. To save time, you can provide only the required information, marked by an asterisk.

Registration Tip #2

If you take the December, April, or June test, sign up for the Test Information Release. Six to eight weeks after the test, you'll receive a copy of the test and your answers. This service costs an additional fee and is available only on these test dates. You can order the Test Information Release up to 3 months after the test date, but it's easier to order it at the time you register. It's a great tool to help you prepare for your next ACT.

Bookmark ACTStudent.org. You will start at this portal to view test dates, fees, and registration deadlines. You can also research the requirements and processes to apply for extended time or other accommodations. You will also start at ACTStudent.org to access your account to register, view your scores, and order score reports.

Check the site for the latest information about fees. The ACT Plus Writing costs more than the ACT (No Writing), but ACT also offers a fee waiver service. While you can choose four schools to send a score report to at no charge, there are fees for score reports sent to additional schools.

Test Security Changes

As part of the registration process, you have to upload or mail a photograph that will be printed on your admissions ticket. On test day, you have to bring the ticket and acceptable photo identification with you.

Standby testing is available, but you have to register in advance, usually before the prior Monday. Check actstudent.org for more information.

HOW TO PREPARE FOR THE ACT

The Princeton Review materials and test-taking techniques contained in this book should give you all the information you need to improve your score on the ACT. For more practice materials, The Princeton Review also publishes *1,296 Practice ACT Questions*, which includes six tests' worth of material.

Other popular coaching books contain several complete practice ACT exams. We strongly advise you *not* to waste your time taking these tests. In some cases, the questions in these books are not modeled on real ACT questions. Some of them cover material that is not even on the real ACT. Others give the impression that the ACT is much easier or more difficult than it really is. Taking the practice tests offered in these books could actually hurt your score.

One reason these coaching books do not use real ACT questions is that the folks at ACT won't let them. They have refused to let anyone (including us) license actual questions from old tests. You may have chosen our book because it contains two practice ACT exams. Rest assured that these tests are *modeled very closely after actual ACT exams*, with the proper balance of questions reflective of what the ACT actually tests.

Cynics might suggest that no one else can license ACT exams because ACT sells its own review book called *The Real ACT Prep Guide*. We think *The Real ACT Prep Guide* is well worth the price for the five real tests it contains (make sure you buy the third edition). We recommend that you either buy the book or ask your high school to send away to ACT for actual ACT tests. You can also buy real ACT tests on ACT.org. You should get a copy of *Preparing for the ACT Assessment* from your counselor. It's free, and it contains a complete, real ACT. The same test can be downloaded for free from ACT's website.

While we advise you to obtain these practice tests to further your preparation for the ACT, it is important that you use them properly. Many students like to think that they can prepare by simply taking test after test until they get the scores they want. Unfortunately, this doesn't work all that well. Why? Well, in many instances, repetitive test-taking only reinforces some of the bad test-taking habits that we address in this book. You should use practice tests for the following three key purposes:

- to build up familiarity with the exam
- to learn how to avoid the types of mistakes you are currently making
- to master our techniques and strategies so you can save time and earn more points

More great titles by The Princeton Review
1,296 ACT Practice Questions

Do I Need to Prepare if I Have Good Grades?

Let's take the hypothetical case of Sid. Sid is valedictorian of his class, editor of the school paper, and the only teenager ever to win the Nobel Prize. To support his widowed mother, he sold more seeds from the back of comic books than any other person in recorded history. He speaks eight languages in addition to being able to communicate with dolphins and wolves. He has recommendations from Colin Powell *and* Bill Gates. So if Sid had a bad day when he took the ACT (the plane bringing him back from his Medal of Freedom award presentation was late), we are pretty sure that he is going to be just fine anyway. But Sid wants to ensure that when his colleges look at his ACT score, they see the same high-caliber student they see when they look at the rest of his application, so he carefully reviews the types of questions asked and learns some useful test-taking strategies.

I Have Lousy Grades in School. Is There Any Hope?

Watch it on your DVD

Let's take the case of Tom. Tom didn't do particularly well in high school. In fact, he has been on academic probation since kindergarten. He has caused four of his teachers to give up teaching as a profession, and he prides himself on his perfect homework record: He's never done any, not ever. But if Tom aces his ACT, a college might decide that he is actually a misunderstood genius and give him a full scholarship. Tom decides to learn as much as he can about the ACT.

Most of us, of course, fall between these two extremes. So is it important to prepare for the ACT?

If you were to look in the information bulletin of any of the colleges in which you are interested, we can pretty much guarantee that somewhere you would find the following paragraph:

> Many factors go into the acceptance of a student by a college. Test scores are *only one* of these factors. Grades in high school, extracurricular activities, essays, and recommendations are also important and may in some cases outweigh test scores.
>
> (2014 University of Anywhere Bulletin)

Size Matters
Large schools process more applications, so they rely heavily on standardized test scores. Small schools have the time to read the rest of your application.

Truer words were never spoken. In our opinion, just about *every* other element in your application "package" is more important than your test scores. The Princeton Review (among other organizations) has been telling colleges for years that scores on the ACT or the SAT are pretty incomplete measures of a student's overall academic abilities. Some colleges have stopped looking at test scores entirely, and others are downplaying their importance.

So Why Should You Spend Any Time Preparing for the ACT?

Out of all the elements in your application "package," your ACT score is the easiest to change. The grades you've received up to now are written in stone. You aren't going to become captain of the football team or editor of the school paper overnight. Your essays will be only as good as you can write them, and recommendations are only as good as your teachers' memories of you.

On the contrary, in a few weeks you can substantially change your score on the ACT (and the way colleges look at your applications). The test does not pretend to measure analytic ability or intelligence. It measures your knowledge of specific skills such as grammar, algebra, and reading comprehension. Mostly, it measures how good you are at taking this test.

THE ACT VS. THE SAT

You may have to take the ACT anyway, but most of the schools in which you're interested also accept the SAT. We think the SAT is nowhere near as fair a test as the ACT. Whereas the ACT says it measures "achievement" (which we believe *can* be measured), the SAT says it measures "ability" (which we don't think can be measured at all; and if it can, the SAT sure isn't doing it).

More great titles by
The Princeton Review
ACT or SAT? Choosing the Right Exam For You

What Exactly Are the Differences?

The SAT tends to be less time-pressured than the ACT. However, many of the questions on the SAT are trickier than those on the ACT. The SAT Verbal sections have a stronger emphasis on vocabulary than do the ACT English and Reading tests. The SAT Math section tests primarily algebra and plane geometry and includes no trigonometry at all.

Both tests include an Essay section, although ACT has made the Writing Test optional because some colleges require it while others do not. ACT doesn't want to force students to take (and pay for) a test they don't need. The implication then is that many students can ignore the new Writing Test altogether depending on what the schools to which they are applying require.

To find out if the schools in which you are interested require the ACT essay, visit the ACT Writing test page at ACTstudent.org/writing or contact the schools directly.

While we are obviously not tremendously fond of the SAT, you should know that some students end up scoring substantially higher on the SAT than they do on the ACT and vice versa. It may be to your advantage to take a practice test for each one and see which is more likely to get you a better score.

More great titles by The Princeton Review
The Best 378 Colleges, The Complete Book of Colleges

Check out the Best Fit College Search at
PrincetonReview.com

WHAT IS THE PRINCETON REVIEW?

The Princeton Review is the world's leading test-preparation and educational services company. We run courses at hundreds of locations worldwide and offer Web-based instruction at PrincetonReview.com. Our test-taking techniques and review strategies are unique and powerful. We developed them after studying all the real ACTs we could get our hands on and analyzed them with the most sophisticated software available. For more information about our programs and services, feel free to call us at **800-2Review.**

A FINAL THOUGHT BEFORE YOU BEGIN

The ACT does not measure intelligence, nor does it predict your ultimate success or failure as a human being. No matter how high or how low you score on this test initially, and no matter how much you may increase your score through preparation, you should *never* consider the score you receive on this or any other test a final judgment of your abilities.

Chapter 2
ACT Strategy

You will raise your ACT score by working smarter, not harder, and a smart test-taker is a strategic test-taker. You will target specific content to review, you will apply an effective and efficient approach, and you will employ common sense.

Each test on the ACT demands a specific approach, and even the most universal strategies vary in their applications. In Parts II–VI, we'll discuss these strategies in greater detail customized to English, Math, Reading, Science, and Writing.

THE BASIC APPROACH

The ACT test is different from the tests you take in school, and therefore you need to approach it differently. The Princeton Review's strategies are not arbitrary. To be effective, ACT strategies have to be based on the ACT and not just any test.

You need to know how the ACT is scored and how it's constructed.

Scoring

When students and schools talk about ACT scores, they typically mean the composite score, a range of 1–36. The composite is an average of the four multiple-choice tests, each scored on the same 1–36 scale. Neither the Writing test score nor the combined English plus Writing score affect the composite.

The Composite

Whether you look at your score online or wait to get it in the mail, the biggest number on the page is always the composite. While admissions' offices will certainly see the individual scores of all five tests (and their subscores), schools will use the composite to evaluate your application, and that's why in the end it's the only one that matters.

The composite is an average. Add the scores for the English, Math, Reading, and Science tests, and divide the total by four. Do you add one test twice? Um, no. Do you omit one of the tests in the total? Er, no again. The four tests are weighted equally to calculate the composite. But do you need to bring up all four equally to raise your composite? Do you need to be a super star in all four tests? Should you focus more on your weakest tests than your strongest tests? No, no, and absolutely not. The best way to improve your composite is to shore up your weaknesses but exploit your strengths as much as possible.

> To lift the composite score as high as possible,
> maximize the scores of your strongest tests.

You don't need to be a rock star on all four tests. Identify two, maybe three tests, and focus on raising those scores as much as you can to raise your composite score. Work on your weakest scores to keep them from pulling you down. Are you strongest in English and Math, or maybe in English, Reading, and Science? Then work to raise those scores as high as you can. You won't ignore your weaknesses, but recognize that the work you put in on your strengths will yield greater dividends. Think of it this way. If you had only one hour to devote to practice the week before the ACT, you would put that hour to your best subjects.

Structure

Let's review quickly the structure of the ACT. The five tests are always given in the same order.

English	Math	Reading	Science	Writing
45 minutes	60 minutes	35 minutes	35 minutes	30 minutes
75 questions	60 questions	40 questions	40 questions	1 Essay

Enemy #1: Time

How much time do you have per question on the Math test? You have just one minute, and that's generous compared to the time given per question on the English, Reading, and Science tests. But how often do you take a test in school with a minute or less per question? If you do at all, it's maybe on a multiple-choice quiz but probably not on a major exam or final. Time is your enemy on the ACT, and you have to use it wisely and be aware of how that time pressure can bring out your worst instincts as a test-taker.

Enemy #2: Yourself

Many people struggle with test anxiety in school and on standardized tests. But there is something particularly evil about tests like the ACT and SAT. The skills you've been rewarded for throughout your academic year can easily work against you on the ACT. You've been taught since birth to follow directions, go in order, and finish everything. But that approach won't necessarily earn you your highest ACT score.

On the other hand, treating the ACT as a scary, alien beast can leave our brains blank and useless and can incite irrational, self-defeating behavior. When we pick up a #2 pencil, all of us tend to leave our common sense at the door. Test nerves and anxieties can make you misread a question, commit a careless error, see something that isn't there, blind you to what is there, talk you into a bad answer, and worst of all, convince you to spend good time after bad.

You can—and will—crack the ACT. You will learn how to approach it differently than you would a test in school, and you won't let the test crack you.

Watch it on
your DVD

ACT STRATEGIES

Personal Order of Difficulty (POOD)

If time is going to run out, would you rather it run out on the hardest questions or the easiest? Of course, you want it to run out on the points you are less likely to get right.

You can easily fall into the trap of spending too much time on the hardest problems and either never getting to or rushing through the easiest. You shouldn't work in the order ACT provides just because it's in that order. Instead, find your own Personal Order of Difficulty (POOD).

Make smart decisions quickly for good reasons as you move through each test.

The Best Way to Bubble In

Work a page at a time, circling your answers right on the booklet. Transfer a page's worth of answers to the scantron at one time. It's better to stay focused on working questions rather than disrupt your concentration to find where you left off on the scantron. You'll be more accurate at both tasks. Do not wait to the end, however, to transfer all the answers of that test on your scantron. Go a page at a time on English and Math, a passage at a time on Reading and Science.

Letter of the Day (LOTD)

Just because you don't *work* a question doesn't mean you don't *answer* it. There is no penalty for wrong answers on the ACT, so you should never leave any blanks on your scantron. When you guess on Never questions, pick your favorite two-letter combo of answers and stick with it. For example, always choose A/F or C/H. If you're consistent, you're statistically more likely to pick up more points.

Now

Does a question look okay? Do you know how to do it? Do it *Now*.

Later

Will this question take a long time to work? Leave it and come back to it *Later*. Circle the question number for easy reference to return.

Never

Test-taker, know thyself. Know the topics that are your worst and learn the signs that flash danger. Don't waste time on questions you should *Never* do. Instead, use more time to answer the Now and Later questions accurately.

Pacing

The ACT may be designed for you to run out of time, but you can't rush through it as fast as possible. All you'll do is make careless errors on easy questions you should get right and spend way too much time on difficult ones you're unlikely to get right. Let your (POOD) help determine your pacing. Go slowly enough to answer correctly all the Now questions but quickly enough to get to the number of Later questions you need to reach your goal score.

In Chapter 3, we'll teach you how to identify the number of questions you need to reach your goal score. You'll practice your pacing in practice tests, going slowly enough to avoid careless errors and quickly enough to reach your goal scores.

Process of Elimination (POE)

Multiple-choice tests offer one great advantage: They provide the correct answer right there on the page. Of course, they hide the correct answer amid 3–4 incorrect answers. It's often easier to spot the wrong answers than it is to identify the right ones, particularly when you apply a smart Process of Elimination (POE).

POE works differently on each test on the ACT, but it's a powerful strategy on all of them. For some question types, you'll always use POE rather than wasting time trying to figure out the answer on your own. For other questions, you'll use POE when you're stuck. ACT hides the correct answer behind wrong ones, but when you cross off just one or two wrong answers, the correct answer can become more obvious, sometimes jumping right off the page.

POOD, Pacing, and POE all work together to help you spend your time where it does the most good: on the questions you can and should get right.

Be Ruthless

The worst mistake a test-taker can make is to throw good time after bad. You read a question, don't understand it, so read it again. And again. If you stare at it really hard, you know you're going to just *see* the answer. And you can't move on, because really, after spending all that time it would be a waste not to keep at it, right?

Wrong. You can't let one tough question drag you down, and you can't let your worst instincts tempt you into self-defeating behavior. Instead, the best way to improve your ACT score is to follow our advice.

- Use the techniques and strategies in the lessons to work efficiently and accurately through all your Now and Later questions.
- Know your Never questions, and use your LOTD.
- Know when to move on. Use POE, and guess from what's left.

In Parts II–VI, you'll learn how POOD, Pacing, and POE work on each test. In Chapter 3, we'll discuss in greater detail how to use your Pacing to hit your target scores.

Use Your Pencil
You own the test booklet, and you should write where and when it helps you. Use your pencil to literally cross off wrong answers on the page.

For more help check out our academic tutoring offers at PrincetonReview.com.

Chapter 3
Score Goals

To hit your target score, you have to know how many raw points you need. Your goals and pacing for English, Math, Reading, and Science will vary depending on the test and your own individual strengths.

SCORE GRIDS

On each test of the ACT, the number of correct answers converts to a scaled score 1–36. ACT works hard to adjust the scale of each test at each administration as necessary to make all scaled scores comparable, smoothing out any differences in level of difficulty across test dates. There is thus no truth to any one test date being "easier" than the others, but you can expect to see slight variations in the scale from test to test.

This is the score grid from the free test ACT makes available on its website, ACT.org. We're going to use it to explain how to pick a target score and pace yourself.

Scale Score	English	Math	Reading	Science	Scale Score
36	75	59–60	40	40	36
35	73–74	57–58	39	39	35
34	71–72	55–56	38	38	34
33	70	54	—	37	33
32	69	53	37	—	32
31	68	52	36	36	31
30	67	50–51	35	35	30
29	66	49	34	34	29
28	64–65	47–48	33	33	28
27	62–63	45–46	32	31–32	27
26	60–61	43–44	31	30	26
25	58–59	41–42	30	28–29	25
24	56–57	38–40	29	26–27	24
23	53–55	36–37	27–28	24–25	23
22	51–52	34–35	26	23	22
21	48–50	33	25	21–22	21
20	45–47	31–32	23–24	19–20	20
19	42–44	29–30	22	17–18	19
18	40–41	27–28	20–21	16	18
17	38–39	24–26	19	14–15	17
16	35–37	19–23	18	13	16
15	33–34	15–18	16–17	12	15
14	30–32	12–14	14–15	11	14
13	29	10–11	13	10	13
12	27–28	8–9	11–12	9	12
11	25–26	6–7	9–10	8	11
10	23–24	5	8	7	10

PACING STRATEGIES

Focus on the number of questions you need to hit your goal scores.

English

For English, there is no order of difficulty of the passages or their questions. The most important thing is to finish, finding all the Now questions you can throughout the whole test.

Math

Spend more time to do fewer questions, and you'll raise your accuracy. Let's say your goal on Math is a 24. Find 24 under the scaled score column, and you'll see that you need 38–40 raw points. Take all 60 minutes and work 45 questions, using your Letter of the Day (LOTD) on 15 Never questions. You'll get most of the questions you work right, some wrong, and pick up a couple points on the LOTDs.

Look at this way: How many *more* questions do you need to answer correctly to move from a 24 to a 27? As few as five. Do you think you could find five careless errors on a practice test that you *should* have gotten right?

Reading

When it comes to picking a pacing strategy for Reading, you have to practice extensively and figure out what works best for you.

Some students are slow but good readers. If you take 35 minutes to do fewer passages, you could get all of the questions right for each passage you do. Use your LOTD for the passages you don't work, and you should pick up a few additional points.

Other students could take hours to work each passage and never get all the questions right. But if you find all the questions you can do on many passages, using your LOTD on all those Never questions, you could hit your target score.

Which is better? There is no answer to that. True ACT score improvement will come with a willingness to experiment and analyze what works best for you.

Science

In the Science lessons, you'll learn how to identify your Now, Later, and Never passages.

Our advice is to be aggressive. Spend the time needed on the easiest passages first, but keep moving to get to your targeted raw score. Identify Never questions on Now Passages and use your LOTD. Alternatively, find the Now questions on as many Later passages as you can get to.

PACING CHARTS

Revisit this page as you practice. Record your scores from practice. Set a goal of 1–3 points in your scaled score for the next practice test. Identify the number of questions you need to answer correctly to reach that goal. The score grids provided in Part VIII come with their specific scales. You can use those, or use the score grids in this chapter.

English Pacing

Scale Score	Raw Score	Scale Score	Raw Score	Scale Score	Raw Score
36	75	27	62–63	18	40–4
35	73–74	26	60–61	17	38–39
34	71–72	25	58–59	16	35–37
33	70	24	56–57	15	33–34
32	69	23	53–55	14	30–32
31	68	22	51–52	13	29
30	67	21	48–50	12	27–28
29	66	20	45–47	11	25–26
28	64–65	19	42–44	10	23–24

Remember that in English, your pacing goal is to finish.

Prior Score (if applicable): _____

Practice Test 1 Goal: _____   Practice Test 2 Goal: _____

# of Questions Needed: _____   # of Questions Needed: _____

Practice Test 1 Score: _____   Practice Test 2 Score: _____

Math Pacing

Scale Score	Raw Score	Scale Score	Raw Score	Scale Score	Raw Score
36	59–60	27	45–46	18	27–28
35	57–58	26	43–44	17	24–26
34	55–56	25	41–42	16	19–23
33	54	24	38–40	15	15–18
32	53	23	36–37	14	12–14
31	52	22	34–35	13	10–11
30	50–51	21	33	12	8–9
29	49	20	31–32	11	6–7
28	47–48	19	29–30	10	5

Our advice is to add 5 questions to your targeted raw score. You have a cushion to get a few wrong—nobody's perfect—and you're likely to pick up at least a few points from your LOTDs. Track your progress on practice tests to pinpoint your target score.

Prior Score (if applicable): _____

Practice Test 1 Goal: _____   Practice Test 2 Goal: _____

# of Questions Needed: _____   # of Questions Needed: _____

                                    +5   +5

= # of Questions to Work:_____   = # of Questions to Work:_____

Practice Test 1 Score: _____   Practice Test 2 Score: _____

Reading Pacing

Scale Score	Raw Score	Scale Score	Raw Score	Scale Score	Raw Score
36	40	27	32	18	20–21
35	39	26	31	17	19
34	38	25	30	16	18
33	—	24	29	15	16–17
32	37	23	27–28	14	14–15
31	36	22	26	13	13
30	35	21	25	12	11–12
29	34	20	23–24	11	9–10
28	33	19	22	10	8

Experiment with Reading with fewer passages, more time per passage and then with more passages, more questions. Identify first how many questions you need.

Prior Score (if applicable): _____

Practice Test 1 Goal: _____   Practice Test 2 Goal: _____

# of Questions Needed: _____   # of Questions Needed: _____

How many passages to work: _____   How many passages to work: _____

Practice Test 1 Score: _____   Practice Test 2 Score: _____

Science Pacing

Scale Score	Raw Score	Scale Score	Raw Score	Scale Score	Raw Score
36	40	27	31–32	18	16
35	39	26	30	17	14–15
34	38	25	28–29	16	13
33	37	24	26–27	15	12
32	—	23	24–25	14	11
31	36	22	23	13	10
30	35	21	21–22	12	9
29	34	20	19–20	11	8
28	33	19	17–18	10	7

Use this chart below to figure out how many passages to work.

Target Score	# of passages to attempt
< 20	5 passages
20–23	5–6 passages
24–27	6–7 passages
> 27	7 passages

Prior Score (if applicable): _____

Practice Test 1 Goal: _____   Practice Test 2 Goal: _____

# of Questions Needed: _____   # of Questions Needed: _____

How many passages to work: _____   How many passages to work: _____

Practice Test 1 Score: _____   Practice Test 2 Score: _____

Chapter 4
Taking the ACT

Preparing yourself both mentally and physically to take the ACT is important. This chapter helps you learn exactly what you're in for, so you can plan ahead and be as comfortable as possible on test day. We not only talk about what to do but also what *not* to do.

PREPARING FOR THE ACT

The best way to prepare for any test is to find out exactly what is going to be on it. This book provides you with just that information. In the following chapters, you will find a comprehensive review of all the question types on the ACT, complete information on all the subjects covered by the ACT, and some powerful test-taking strategies developed specifically for the ACT.

To take full advantage of the review and techniques, you should practice on the tests in this book as well as on real ACT questions. We've already told you how to obtain copies of real ACT exams. Taking full practice exams allows you to chart your progress (with accurate scores for each test), gives you confidence in our techniques, and develops your stamina.

The Night Before the Test

Unless you are the kind of person who remains calm only by staying up all night to do last-minute studying, we recommend that you take the evening off. Go see a movie or read a good book (besides this one), and make sure you get to bed at a normal hour. No final, frantically memorized math formula or grammatical rule is going to make or break your score. A positive mental attitude comes from treating yourself decently. If you've prepared over the last several weeks or months, then you're ready.

If you haven't really prepared, there will be other opportunities to take the test, so get some rest and do the best you can. Remember, colleges will see only the score you choose to let them see. No *single* ACT is going to be crucial. We don't think night-before-the-test cramming is very effective. For example, we would not recommend that you try going through this book in one night.

On the Day of the Test

Don't Leave Home Without 'Em
Here are some items you'll want to have on test day.
- Admissions ticket
- Photo ID or letter of identification
- Plenty of sharpened No. 2 pencils
- A watch
- An acceptable calculator with new batteries

It's important that you eat a real breakfast, even if you normally don't. We find that about two-thirds of the way through the test, people who didn't eat something beforehand suddenly lose their will to live. Equally important, bring a snack to the test center. You will get a break during which food is allowed. Some people spend the break out in the hallways comparing answers and getting upset when their answers don't match. Ignore the people around you and eat your snack. Why assume they know any more than you do?

Warming Up

While you're having breakfast, do a couple of questions from an ACT on which you've already worked to get your mind going. You don't want to use the first test on the real exam to warm up. And please don't try a hard question you've never done before. If you miss it, your confidence will be diminished, and that's not something you want on the day of the test.

At the test center, you'll be asked to show some form of picture ID or provide a note from your school—on school stationery—describing what you look like. The time or time remaining is often *not* announced during the test sections, so you should also bring a reliable watch—not the beeping kind—and, of course, several No. 2 pencils, an eraser, and a calculator. Check ACTStudent.org/faq to see if your calculator model is permitted. If you haven't changed the batteries recently (or ever), you should do that before the test or bring a back-up calculator.

When you get into the actual room in which you'll be taking the exam, make sure you're comfortable. Is there enough light? Is your desk sturdy? Don't be afraid to speak up; after all, you're going to be spending three and a half hours at that desk. And it's not a bad idea to go to the bathroom *before* you get to the room. It's a long haul to that first break.

ZEN AND THE ART OF TEST TAKING

Once the exam begins, tune out the rest of the world. That girl with the annoying cough in the next row? You don't hear her. That guy who is fidgeting in the seat ahead of you? You don't see him. It's just you and the exam. Everything else should be a blur.

As soon as one test ends, erase it completely from your mind. It no longer exists. The only test that counts is the one you are taking right now. Even if you are upset about a particular test, erase it from your mind. If you are busy thinking about the last test, you cannot focus on the one on which you are currently working, and that's a surefire way to make costly mistakes. Most people aren't very good at assessing how they performed on a given section of the exam, especially while they're still taking it, so don't waste your time and energy trying.

Some Things to Remember

- Make sure you know where the test center is located and where you need to go once you are at the test center.
- Show up early; you can't show up right when the test is scheduled to begin and expect to get in.
- Lay out your pencils, calculator, watch, admission ticket, and photo identification the night before the test. The last thing you want to be doing on the morning of the test is running around looking for a calculator. Also, it's important to have your own watch because there's no requirement that the room you're in have a working clock.
- Bring a snack and a bottle of water just in case you get hungry. There's nothing worse than testing on an empty stomach.

Keep Your Answers to Yourself

Please don't let anyone cheat off you. Test companies have developed sophisticated anti-cheating measures that go way beyond having a proctor walk around the room. We know of one test company that gets seating charts of each testing room. Its computers scan the score sheets of people sitting in the immediate vicinity for correlations of wrong answer choices. Innocent and guilty are invited to take the exam over again, and their scores from the first exam are invalidated.

Beware of Misbubbling Your Answer Sheet

Probably the most painful kind of mistake you can make on the ACT is to bubble in choice (A) with your pencil when you really mean choice (B), or to have your answers be one question number off (perhaps because you skipped one question on the test but forgot to skip it on the answer sheet). Aargh! The proctor isn't allowed to let you change your answers after a section is over, so it is critical that you either catch yourself before a test section ends or—even better—that you don't make a mistake in the first place.

Write Now
Feel free to write all over your test booklet. Don't do computations in your head. Put them in the booklet; you paid for it. Go nuts!

We suggest to our students that they write down their answers in their test booklets. This way, whenever you finish a page of questions in the test booklet, you can transfer all your answers from that page in a group. We find that this method minimizes the possibility of misbubbling and it also saves time. Of course, as you get near the end of a test, you should go back to bubbling question by question.

If you get back your ACT scores and they seem completely out of line, you can ask the ACT examiners to look over your answer sheet for what are called "gridding errors." If you want to, you can even be there while they look. If it is clear that there has been an error, ACT will change your score. An example of a gridding error would be a test in which, if you moved all the responses over by one, they would suddenly all be correct.

Should I Ever Cancel My Scores?

We recommend against canceling your scores, even if you feel you've done poorly. If you have registered as we recommended and not sent the scores to any colleges and possibly not to your high school, then the score you receive won't go anywhere unless you send it on later. There is no need to panic and cancel your score without knowing what it is if no one will ever see it. You never know—perhaps you did better than you think. Furthermore, if you've taken the ACT two or more times (something we heartily recommend), you can choose which score you want colleges to see when you request reports from ACT.

If you do decide to cancel your scores, ACT allows you to do it only at the test center itself. However, you can stop scores from reaching colleges if you call ACT by 12:00 P.M., Central Time on the *Thursday* following the test. The number to call is 319-337-1270.

Part II
How to
Crack the ACT
English Test

Chapter 5
Introduction to the ACT English Test

The English test is not a grammar test. It's also not a test of how well you write. In fact, it tests your editing skills: your ability to fix errors in grammar and punctuation and to improve the organization and style of five different passages. In this chapter, you'll learn the basic strategy of how to crack the passages and review the grammar you need to know.

WHAT'S ON THE ENGLISH TEST

Before we dive into the details of the content and strategy, let's review what the English test looks like. Remember, the five tests on the ACT are always given in the same order and English is always first.

There are five prose passages on topics ranging from historical essays to personal narratives. Each passage is typically accompanied by 15 questions for a total of 75 questions that you must answer in 45 minutes. Portions of each passage are underlined, and you must decide if these are correct as written, or if one of the other answers would fix or improve the selection. Other questions will ask you to add, cut, or re-order text, while still others will ask you to evaluate the passage as a whole.

WRITING

While the idea of English grammar makes most of us think of persnickety, picky rules long since outdated, English is actually a dynamic, adaptive language. We add new vocabulary all the time, and we let common usage influence and change many rules. Pick up a handful of style books, and you'll find very few rules that everyone agrees upon. This is actually good news for studying for the ACT: You're unlikely to see questions testing the most obscure or most disputed rules. However, few of us follow ALL of even the most basic, universally accepted rules when we speak, much less when we e-mail, text, or tweet.

The 4 C's: Complete, Consistent, Clear, and Concise

ACT test writers will never make you name a particular error. But with 75 questions, they can certainly test a lot of different rules—and yes, that's leaving out the obscure and debated rules. You would drive yourself crazy if you tried to learn, just for the ACT, all of the grammar you never knew in the first place. You're much better off with a common sense approach. We'll teach you the rules that show up the most often, and we'll show you how to crack the questions that test them. What about all the rest of the questions? That's where the 4 C's come in.

Good writing should be in *complete* sentences; everything should be *consistent*; the meaning should be *clear*. The best answer, free of any errors, will be the most *concise*. All of the rules we'll review fall under one or more of the 4 C's. But even when you can't identify what a question is testing, apply the 4 C's, and you'll be able to answer even the most difficult questions.

We'll explain in greater detail what the 4 C's mean in the grammar review and in the following lessons. But first, let's discuss your general strategies and overall approach to the English test.

HOW TO CRACK THE ENGLISH TEST

The Passages

As always on the ACT, time is your enemy. With only 45 minutes to review five passages and answer 75 questions, you can't read a passage in its entirety and then go back to do the questions. For each passage, work the questions as you make your way through the passage. Read from the beginning until you get to an underlined selection, work that question, and then resume reading until the next underlined portion and the next question.

The Questions

Not all questions are created equally. In fact, ACT divides the questions on the English test into two categories: usage and mechanics, and rhetorical skills. These designations will mean very little to you when you're taking the test. All questions are worth the same amount of points, after all, and you'll crack most of the questions the same way, regardless of what ACT calls them. Many of the rhetorical skills questions, however, are those on organization and style, and some take longer to answer than other questions do. Since there is no order of difficulty of the passages or of the questions, all that matters is that you identify your *Now, Later, Never* questions and make sure you finish.

The best way to make sure you finish with as many correct answers as possible is to use our 5-step Basic Approach.

Step 1: Identify the Topic

For each underlined portion, finish the sentence, and then look at the answers. The answers are your clues to identifying what the question is testing. Let's start off with this first question.

American <u>author Junot Diaz, was born in</u>
the Dominican Republic.

1. **A.** NO CHANGE
   B. author, Junot Diaz
   C. author Junot Diaz
   D. author, Junot Diaz,

Watch it on your DVD

Do any of the words change? No. What is the only thing that does change? Commas. So what must be the topic of the question? Commas.

Always identify the topic of the question first. Pay attention to what changes versus what stays the same in the answers.

Step
2

Step 2: Use POE

You may have chosen an answer for #1 already. If you haven't, don't worry: We'll review all the rules of commas in the next lesson. But let's use #1 to learn the next step, POE. To go from good to great on the English test, you can't just fix a question in your head and then find an answer that matches. Instead, after you've identified what's wrong, eliminate all the choices that do not fix the error.

For question #1, the comma after *Diaz* is unnecessary and should be deleted. Cross off the answers that leave it in, choices (A) and (D).

> 1. A. ~~NO CHANGE~~
>   B. author, Junot Diaz
>   C. author Junot Diaz
>   D. ~~author, Junot Diaz,~~

Now compare the two that remain, choices (B) and (C). Do you need the comma after *author*? No, you don't need any commas, so choice (C) is the correct answer. Here's where you could have messed up if you didn't use POE: If you knew all along you didn't need any commas, you could have easily missed that new comma in choice (B) and chosen incorrectly. POE on English isn't optional or a backup when you're stuck. You have to first eliminate wrong answers and then compare what's left.

Let's go onto the next step.

Step
3

Step 3: Use the Context

Even though you may struggle with time on the English test, you can't skip the non-underlined text in between questions in order to save yourself a few minutes. Take a look at this next question.

> After Diaz won the 2008 Pulitzer Prize,
> many college literary courses will add his
> <u>   </u>
>   2
> works to the curriculum.
>
> 2. F. NO CHANGE
>   G. added
>   H. were adding
>   J. add

Don't forget to apply the first two steps. The verb in the answer choices is changing, specifically verb tense. How do you know which tense to use? Look at the beginning of the sentence: The phrase *After Diaz won* tells us we want past tense, so eliminate the choices that don't use past tense.

> 2. F. ~~NO CHANGE~~
>   G. added
>   H. were adding
>   J. ~~add~~

This is the 4 C's in action, or at least two of them: Between choices (G) and (H), choice (G) is most *concise*. The correct tense has to be *consistent* with the clues in the non-underlined portion. Between two choices that are technically grammatically correct, the more *concise* choice wins.

Don't skip from question to question. The non-underlined text provides context you need.

Let's move on to the next step.

Step 4: Trust Your Ear, But Verify

For question #2, you may have never even considered choice (H) as serious competition for choice (G). It just sounds wrong, doesn't it? Well, it turned out you were right. In fact, your ear is pretty reliable at raising the alarm for outright errors and clunky, awkward phrasing.

You should, however, always verify what your ear signals by confirming the actual error. Steps 1 and 2 will help with that: Use the answers to identify the topic, and use POE heavily.

But remember to be careful for errors your ear *won't* catch. Using the answers to identify the topic will save you there as well.

Let's try another question.

One college class chose Diaz's *The Brief Wondrous Life of Oscar Wao* as their favorite book of the semester.
3

3. **A.** NO CHANGE
   B. it's favorite book
   C. they're favorite book
   D. its favorite book

That sounded pretty good to us, how about you? But before we circle NO CHANGE and go on our merry way, look at the answers to identify the topic and confirm there is no error. Only the pronoun changes, so the question is testing pronouns. We'll go over all the rules about pronouns in Chapter 7, so we'll just give a short explanation here. *Their* is a plural pronoun, but *class* is singular. Cross off choices (A) and (C)—choice (C) isn't even the right type of pronoun, plural or not. Since we need a possessive pronoun, cross off choice (B) as well. Choice (D) is the correct answer.

Let's move on to our last step.

Step 5: Don't Fix What Isn't Broken
Read the next question.

Among a generation of new American writers, Diaz has <u>emerged as one of the</u> freshest, most original voices.
₄

4. **F.** NO CHANGE
   G. been distinguished and deemed
   H. come on the scene as
   J. made a strong case to be called

Sounds okay, so go to Step 1, identify the topic. Remember that saved us with question #3. *Everything* seems to be changing in the answers for #4: What the question is testing isn't obvious at all. You can't confirm what you can't identify, so leave "NO CHANGE," and apply the 4 C's.

Does one of the answers fix something you missed?

Does one of the answers make the sentence better by making it more concise?

If the answer to both questions is No for all three other answers, the correct answer is choice (A), NO CHANGE.

NO CHANGE *is* a legitimate answer choice. Don't make the mistake of assuming that all questions have an error that you just can't spot. If you use the five steps of our Basic Approach, you'll catch errors your ear would miss, and you'll confidently choose NO CHANGE when it's the correct answer.

Pace Yourself
Repeat Steps 1–5 as you make your way through all the questions on all five passages. Since there is no order of difficulty in the passages or questions, your pacing goal is to finish.

Goal Score
Use the pacing strategies and score grid on page 22 to find your goal score for each practice test and, eventually, the ACT.

GRAMMAR REVIEW

This is not an exhaustive review of English grammar. It is an overview of the most common rules tested on the English test. We focus on the rules that show up the most AND that we know you can easily identify. In the next two chapters, we'll teach you how to crack those questions on the ACT. For now, we'll introduce you to the terms and rules you need to know.

Verbs

What's wrong with the following sentences?

1. Ryan play soccer.
   plays
2. Mary and Allison practices every day.
   practice
3. Next week, the team traveled to play its bitter rival.
   will travel
4. Shivani has became the star of the team.
   become

If you read thoughtfully, your ear probably caught all of the verb errors in these sentences. Remember, your ear will pretty reliably raise the alarm with many errors you'll encounter on the English test. You don't always need to know why a sentence is wrong to get the right answer, but the more you know why, the more you can count on getting that question right the next time it appears, and every time after that. Know the likely errors for verbs.

Subject-Verb Agreement

First, know your terms. A *subject* is the performer of an action. A *verb* is an action, feeling, or state of being. Verbs have to be consistent with their subjects. Singular subjects take the singular form of the verb, and plural subjects take plural forms of the verb.

> ### The Rule
> Your ear can alert you to many, if not most, subject-verb agreement errors. **As a general rule, singular verbs end with *s* and plural verbs do not.**

*Ryan **plays** soccer.*

*Mary and Allison **practice** every day.*

Verb Tense

The tense of the verb changes with the time of the event.

Simple Tense

ACT tests your ability to choose from among the three simple tenses.

Past: *Last year, the team **finished** in last place.*

Present: *This year, the team **plays** a demanding schedule.*

Future: *Next week, the team **will travel** to play its bitter rival.*

Perfect Tenses

The perfect tenses provide additional ways to place an event in time. On the ACT, the perfect tenses appear less often than do the simple tenses.

Past perfect: *Before I went to the performance with Kelly, I **had** never **appreciated** ballet before.*

Use the past perfect to make clear the chronology of two events completed at a definite time in the past, one before the other.

Present perfect: *I **have lived** in Chicago for 10 years. I **have read** all the Harry Potter books.*

Use the present perfect to describe an event that began in the past and continues into the present, or to describe an event that was completed at some indefinite time before the present.

Future perfect: *Jim **will have left** by the time I arrive.*

Use the future perfect to describe an event that will be completed at a definite later time.

Irregular Verbs

ACT tests heavily the correct past *participle* of irregular verbs. Participle refers to the form the verb takes when it's paired with the helping verb *to have* to form a perfect tense. For regular verbs, the simple past tense and the past participle are the same.

I **called** you last night. I **have called** you several times today.

For irregular verbs, the two are different.

Shivani **became** *the star of the team,* or *Shivani* **has become** *the star of the team.*

Here is a list of some common irregular verbs.

Infinitive	Simple Past	Past Participle
become	became	become
begin	began	begun
blow	blew	blown
break	broke	broken
bring	brought	brought
choose	chose	chosen
come	came	come
drink	drank	drunk
drive	drove	driven
eat	ate	eaten
fall	fell	fallen
fly	flew	flown
forbid	forbade	forbidden
forget	forgot	forgotten
forgive	forgave	forgiven
freeze	froze	frozen
get	got	gotten
give	gave	given
go	went	gone
grow	grew	grown
hide	hid	hidden
know	knew	known
lay	laid	laid
lead	led	led
lie	lay	lain

Infinitive	Simple Past	Past Participle
ride	rode	ridden
ring	rang	rung
rise	rose	risen
run	ran	run
see	saw	seen
shake	shook	shaken
sing	sang	sung
speak	spoke	spoken
spring	sprang	sprung
steal	stole	stolen
swim	swam	swum
take	took	taken
teach	taught	taught
tear	tore	torn
throw	threw	thrown
wear	wore	worn
write	wrote	written

Pronouns

What's wrong with the following sentences?

1. The team nominated their goalie the most valuable player.
   its

2. My friends and me took the train downtown.
   I

3. Her and I worked on the group project together.
   She

4. The crowd pushed Cesar and I onto the stage.
   me

Pronoun Agreement

First, know your terms. *Pronouns* take the place of nouns. Pronouns have to be consistent with the nouns they replace in number and in gender.

	Female	Male	Things
Singular	she, her, hers	he, him, his	it, its
Plural	they, them, their	they, them, their	they, them, their

*The team nominated **its** goalie the most valuable player.*

Pronoun Case

Pronouns also need to be consistent with the function they perform in a sentence. There are three different cases of pronouns: *subject*, *object*, and *possessive*.

	1st person	2nd person	3rd person
Subject	I, we	you	she, he, it, they
Object	me, us	you	her, him, it, them
Possessive	my, mine, our, ours	your	her, hers, his, its, their, theirs

*My friends and **I** took the train downtown.*

***She** and I worked on the group project together.*

*The crowd pushed Cesar and **me** onto the stage.*

Modifiers

What's wrong with these sentences?

1. No one took her warnings serious/y.

2. Blizzard is a charmingly energetically puppy.

3. Farid is ~~more busy~~ busier than Wesley is.

4. Lara was the ~~beautifulest~~ most beautiful girl at the prom.

Adjectives and Adverbs

Adjectives modify nouns. *Adverbs* modify everything else, including verbs, adjectives, and other adverbs. Most adverbs are formed by adding *-ly* to the end of an adjective.

*No one took her warnings **seriously**.*

*Blizzard is a charmingly **energetic** puppy.*

Comparisons and Superlatives

For most adjectives, an *-er* at the end makes a comparison, and an *-est* makes a superlative. But some adjectives need instead the word *more* for a comparison and the word *most* for a superlative.

*Farid is **busier** than Wesley is.*

*Lara was the **most beautiful** girl at the prom.*

In the following chapters, we'll show you how these rules appear on the ACT and how to crack those questions. We'll also discuss some of the more difficult and challenging concepts that you may face.

Summary

o   Identify what the question is testing by changes in the answer choices.

o   Use POE heavily.

o   Don't skip the non-underlined text: Use it for context.

o   Trust your ear, but verify by the rules.

o   NO CHANGE is a legitimate answer choice.

o   Good writing should be complete, consistent, clear, and concise.

Chapter 6
Complete

The ACT English test contains a number of questions that test sentence structure and punctuation. This chapter discusses how to identify ideas as complete or incomplete and then explains how to punctuate different ideas. In addition to covering punctuation, the chapter also covers how to change ideas with the addition or removal of conjunctions.

COMPLETE AND INCOMPLETE IDEAS

Many questions on the English test involve sentence structure and punctuation. The correct structure and punctuation all depend on whether the ideas are complete or incomplete.

A complete idea can stand on its own, whether it's the entire sentence or just one part. Let's look at some examples.

1. *Amanda throws strikes.*
2. *Go Bears!*
3. *Who won the game?*
4. *The team celebrated after they won the game.*

Think of a complete idea as one part of a conversation. You don't have to say a lot to hold up one side of a conversation, but you can't leave your listener hanging. You have to finish your sentence. You can give commands, and you can ask questions, too. Your listeners don't have to know what you're talking about: They just have to wait for you to finish to ask questions of their own. *What game are you asking me about? How did the team celebrate?*

In grammar terms, a complete idea must have a subject and a verb. Let's break down the examples above.

	Subject	Verb
1	*Amanda*	*throws*
2	You (understood)	*Go*
3	*Who*	*won*
4	*team* and *they*	*celebrated* and *won*

An incomplete idea can't stand on its own. Look at the following examples.

1. *The batter who hit second*
2. *Since you bought the hotdogs*
3. *To get a batter out*
4. *The team grabbed*

If anyone began a conversation with any of these, you would be waiting for the speaker to finish before you could speak. That's a sure sign all of the examples are incomplete: None of them is finished, and all would leave you hanging as a listener.

Now, in real life terms, we may think some of those examples could be fine as answers to these questions: *Who got the run? Why did you buy the sodas? Why did he pitch a fastball?* Remember, however, that in real life we don't always follow the conventional rules when we speak. So let's define an incomplete idea in grammatical terms.

An incomplete idea is always missing something, whether a subject and verb (example #3), the main idea (example #2), or the rest of an idea (examples #1 and #4). None of these could stand on its own, and each would need to link up with another idea to make a sentence. ACT tests heavily how to link ideas with punctuation and conjunctions, so let's see how that works.

For the Record
Semicolons can be used to separate items on a very complicated list, but ACT almost never tests this. Exclamation points and question marks show up only occasionally.

STOP PUNCTUATION

Imagine two trucks heading toward a busy intersection, one from the south and one from the west. If there were no traffic signals at the intersection, the two trucks would crash. Writing is just like traffic, depending on punctuation to prevent ideas from crashing into each other.

Two complete ideas are like two trucks and need the strongest punctuation to separate them. All of the punctuation in the box below can come in between only two complete ideas.

> STOP Punctuation
> Period (.) Semicolon (;) Question mark (?) Exclamation mark (!)

Let's see how this works in a question.

Use the 4 C's: Be *Concise*.

After the thumping music started. The bird began to dance.

1. **A.** NO CHANGE
   B. started, the bird began,
   C. started; the bird began
   D. started, the bird began

Here's How to Crack It

Begin with Step 1 of the Basic Approach you learned in Chapter 5. Use the differences and similarities in the answer choices to identify the topic. Whenever a question is testing Stop punctuation, use the Vertical Line Test. Draw a vertical line where the Stop punctuation is to help you determine if the ideas before and after the line are complete or incomplete.

After the thumping music started. The bird began to dance.

After the thumping music started is incomplete. *The bird began to dance* is complete.

Since Stop punctuation can come in between *only* two complete ideas, go to Step

2 and use POE. Eliminate all the answers that don't fix the error, and compare those that are left.

1. **A.** ~~NO CHANGE~~
   B. started, the bird began,
   C. ~~started; the bird began~~
   D. started, the bird began

Using Steps 3 and 4, we can use the context of the rest of the sentence to confirm that we don't need the second comma that choice (B) offers. Choice (D) is the correct answer.

GO PUNCTUATION

Let's go back to the traffic analogy. Imagine a road with a stop sign at every block. Those stop signs prevent accidents, but when rush hour hits, traffic backs up. Stop signs need to be used strategically, so that they don't cause more problems than they solve. Punctuation functions the same way: Use it to prevent accidents, but don't slow down ideas and make the sentence longer than necessary, or just plain incomprehensible.

A sentence is a complete idea, regardless of how many complete and incomplete ideas it's made up of, so it will always end with Stop punctuation. Within a sentence, use punctuation only to avoid an error or to make your meaning clear. Use Stop punctuation in between two complete ideas. Use a comma to slow down, but not stop, ideas. If you don't need to stop or slow down, don't use any punctuation. Keep traffic moving, and keep ideas flowing.

Here's another example.

I wondered how Snowball had learned to
dance, and asked his trainer.
2

2. **F.** NO CHANGE
   G. to dance and asked his trainer.
   H. to dance; and asked his trainer.
   J. to dance. And asked his trainer.

Use the Vertical Line Test whenever you see Stop punctuation, either in the sentence as written or among the answer choices. When you draw your line in between *dance* and *and*, the first idea is complete, and the second idea is incomplete. Eliminate choices (H) and (J). There is no reason to slow down the ideas at all, so eliminate choice (F). The correct answer is choice (G). By the way, this question isn't testing whether you can start a sentence with *and*—that's a good example of an outdated rule few enforce anymore, so ACT doesn't test it. Choices (H) and (J) are wrong because the idea to the right of the Stop punctuation is incomplete.

Check for Commas

Look out for
- words and phrases in a series
- introductory phrases and words
- mid-sentence phrases that are not essential to the sentence

Commas

Commas work like blinking yellow lights: They slow down but do not stop ideas. Since the goal is to be concise, use a comma only for a specific reason. On the ACT, there are only four reasons to use a comma.

Stop

A comma by itself can't come in between two complete ideas, but it can when it's paired with what we call FANBOYS: *for, and, nor, but, or, yet, so*. A comma plus any of these is the equivalent of Stop punctuation. These words also impact direction, which might influence the correct answer.

> *The music changed suddenly, but Snowball picked up the new beat.*

Draw a vertical line on either side of *but* to help break the sentence into separate ideas. *The music changed suddenly* is complete. *Snowball picked up the new beat* is complete.

For the record, all conjunctions link things, but coordinating conjunctions—that is, FANBOYS—specifically come in between two ideas and are never a part of either idea.

Go

A comma can link an incomplete idea to a complete idea, in either order.

> *After Snowball stopped dancing, the trainer gave the bird another treat.*

> *Snowball rocked out to Lady Gaga, oblivious to the growing crowd of fans.*

Lists

Use a comma to separate items on a list.

> *Snowball prefers songs with a regular, funky beat.*

Regular and *funky* are both describing *beat*. If you would say *regular and funky* then you can say *regular, funky*.

> *Snowball seems to like best the music of The Backstreet Boys, Lady Gaga, and Queen.*

Whenever you have three or more items on a list, always use a comma before the "and" preceding the final item. This is a rule that not everyone agrees on, but if you apply the 4 C's, the extra comma makes your meaning *Clear*. On the ACT, always use the comma before the "and."

Unnecessary Info

Use a pair of commas around unnecessary information.

> *Further research has shown that parrots, including cockatoos, can dance in perfect synch to music.*

If information is necessary to the sentence in either meaning or structure, don't use the commas. If the meaning would be exactly the same but the additional information makes the sentence more interesting, use a pair of commas—or a pair of dashes—around the information.

Try the next questions.

Many people point to dog dancing competitions to <u>argue that birds are not the only animals</u> that can dance.
3

3. **A.** NO CHANGE
   B. argue, that birds are not the only animals,
   C. argue, that birds are not the only animals
   D. argue that birds are not the only animals,

Here's How to Crack It

The changes in the answers identify the topic of the question: commas. Remember, there are only four reasons to use a comma on the ACT, and if you can't name the reason you shouldn't use one. If you thought the sentence was fine, leave NO CHANGE, and confirm none of the answers fixed something you missed. Think of ACT's comma rules, and determine if any apply here. With neither STOP punctuation nor FANBOYS in play, it can't be two complete ideas or a list. If the Unnecessary Info rule is in play, choice (B) would mean that *that birds are not the only animals* isn't necessary, but the sentence would make no sense, so eliminate choice (B). The only other possible rule is GO, linking a complete idea to an incomplete idea. Neither choice (C) nor (D) offers a complete idea on one side of a comma, so eliminate both. The correct answer is choice (A), NO CHANGE.

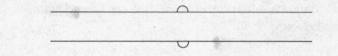

Scientists now believe that the ability to

mimic, which requires complex circuitry, for

vocal learning, is necessary for an animal to

keep a synchronized beat.

4. F. NO CHANGE
   G. mimic, which requires complex circuitry
   H. mimic, which, requires complex circuitry
   J. mimic which requires complex circuitry

Here's How to Crack It

The changes in the answers identify the topic of the question: commas. By reading to the end of the sentence, you catch the comma that isn't underlined. Since the Unnecessary Info rule requires two commas, not three, check that rule first. The extra information is *which requires complex circuitry for vocal learning,* and thus the correct answer is choice (G).

Let's see how this works in a few questions.

The African grey parrot, which also
mimics human speech and therefore can
dance.

7. **A.** NO CHANGE
   B. parrot which
   C. parrot that
   D. parrot

Here's How to Crack It

If conjunctions change in the answer choices, it is likely testing Complete. When you read to the end of the sentence, you're left hanging, waiting for the main point about African grey parrots. The sentence is incomplete, and the only way to fix it is to take out the conjunction. Choice (D) is correct. It's no coincidence that it's the most concise.

Try another.

The videos of Snowball dancing have
sparked a serious area of study, researchers
admit they appreciate the sheer entertainment
value.

8. **F.** NO CHANGE
   G. Although the videos of Snowball
   H. The videos appearing all over the Internet of Snowball
   J. Since the videos of Snowball

Here's How to Crack It

If it sounded fine to your ear, using the answers to identify the topic will help you spot something you missed or verify that NO CHANGE is correct. If conjunctions change in the answer choices, it is likely testing Complete. Check if the entire sentence makes a complete idea and that all ideas within are joined correctly. There are two complete ideas in the sentence, separated only by a comma. A comma alone is GO punctuation, so eliminate choices (F) and (H). You need a choice with a conjunction added to the first idea, making it incomplete. Conjunctions vary by direction, which we'll discuss in the next lesson. The two ideas show a contrast—*serious* and *entertainment*—so choice (G) is correct.

Complete Drill

In the drill below, you will find only questions that focus on sentence construction. Before you start, take a few moments to go back over the review material and techniques. Use the basic approach explained in Chapter 5. Answers are in Chapter 24.

When you see the gingerbread houses of Roskilde with their neatly thatched roofs, the gardens filled with flowers, blooms, and the happy smiles on the fresh-faced inhabitants, it is difficult to believe that this town was once the home of a more warlike people—the Vikings. Roskilde's main museum is devoted to those early inhabitants, the Vikings once wandered throughout Europe, and by some reports, may have traveled all the way to North America as well. The museum sits on a site at the edge of Roskilde fiord. Where the Viking ships were once launched on voyages of conquest and plunder. Until 20 years ago used only by the fishermen who still ply their trade in the fiord, since the craggy shoreline must now be shared with tourists who arrive in buses to watch local artisans build the Viking ships in the traditional manner.

My most memorable vacation as a child was a trip I took to the Grand Canyon with my grandfather. I was only eleven at the time, and had never been outside the city of Boston. My romantic picture of the West complete with cowboys and Indians was a little out of date, but the incredible scenery took my breath away. On our first day we decided that the best way to explore the vast beauty of the canyon would be to take a

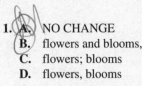

1. **A.** NO CHANGE
   B. flowers and blooms,
   C. flowers; blooms
   D. flowers, blooms

2. **F.** NO CHANGE
   G. inhabitants the Vikings
   H. inhabitants. The Vikings
   J. inhabitants, the Vikings,

3. **A.** NO CHANGE
   B. fiord. Where,
   C. fiord, where
   D. fiord; where

4. **F.** NO CHANGE
   G. the craggy shoreline must now be shared with tourists who arrive in buses
   H. since the craggy shoreline must now be shared with tourists, who arrive in buses,
   J. the craggy shoreline must now be shared with tourists, who arrive in buses

5. **A.** NO CHANGE
   B. the time and had never been
   C. the time; never been
   D. the time. Never been

6. **F.** NO CHANGE
   G. West—complete with cowboys and Indians—
   H. West—complete with cowboys and Indians
   J. West; complete with cowboys and Indians,

7. **A.** NO CHANGE
   B. On our first day we,
   C. On our first day, we
   D. On, our first day, we

mule-packed trip down one of the trails. I rode along, on my
8

mules back, I noticed that each rock stratum displayed a
8

distinctive hue; gray and violet in some places, dark brown and
9

green in others. The rock layers of the Grand Canyon are

mostly made of limestone, freshwater shale and sandstone.
10

8. F. NO CHANGE
   G. I rode along on my mule's back,
   H. I was riding along on my mule's back,
   J. As I rode along on my mule's back,

9. A. NO CHANGE
   B. hue. Gray
   C. hue, gray
   D. hue: gray

10. F. NO CHANGE
    G. limestone, freshwater, shale, and sandstone.
    H. limestone, freshwater shale, and sandstone.
    J. limestone freshwater shale and sandstone

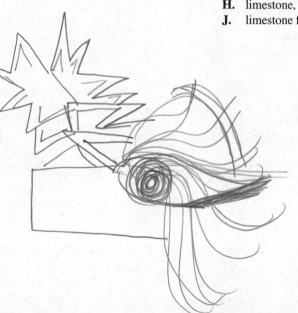

Summary

o ACT writers like to test your knowledge of whether sentences are put together and punctuated correctly.

o A complete idea can stand on its own as a complete sentence even though it may be part of a longer sentence. An incomplete idea can't stand on its own as a complete sentence and must be appropriately linked to a complete idea.

o Stop punctuation includes a period, a semicolon, an exclamation mark, a question mark, and a comma plus FANBOYS. Stop punctuation can come in between only complete ideas.

o Go punctuation includes a comma and nothing at all. Go punctuation can link anything except for two complete ideas.

o Always put a comma before "and" at the end of a list with three or more items.

o Always put a pair of commas around unnecessary info.

o Colons and single dashes must follow a complete idea, but can precede a complete or incomplete idea.

o Conjunctions make an idea incomplete.

Chapter 7
Consistent, Clear, and Concise

The key to an outstanding ACT English score is to focus on the topics that show up the most often *and* which are both easy to identify and simple to fix. In this chapter, we'll teach you how to crack questions on verbs, pronouns, apostrophes, and transitions. For each topic, following the rules makes good writing consistent, clear, and concise.

VERBS

A verb expresses an action, feeling, or state of being. The form of a verb depends on the number of the subject—singular or plural—the time of the event, and the presence of helping verbs. Whenever you spot the verb changing among the answer choices, use these three steps along with your Basic Approach.

1. Identify the subject. The verb must be consistent with its subject. Singular subject with a singular verb, and plural subject with a plural verb.
2. Check the tense. The tense must be consistent with the setting and the participle. Use the context of the non-underlined portion to determine if the verb should be past, present, or future.
3. Be concise. Pick the shortest answer free of any errors.

Here's an example.

───────────────○───────────────

Each of the first three taxis I saw were
                                    ‾‾‾‾
                                      1
too far away to hail.
‾‾‾‾‾‾‾‾‾‾‾‾‾
     1

1. **A.** NO CHANGE
   B. are too far away
   C. is too far away
   D. was too far away

Here's How to Crack It

Use the changes in the answers to identify verbs as the topic ACT is testing. Both tense and number seem to be changing, so find the subject first. What was too far away? *Each* of the taxis. *Each* is singular, so eliminate the plural forms of the verb, choices (A) and (B). Now check the tense. *Saw* is past tense, so choose the past tense, choice (D).

───────────────○───────────────

Tricky Pronouns

Question #1 wasn't testing pronouns directly—the changes among the answer choices were verbs. To answer correctly, however, you had to know that the pronoun *each* is singular. The following pronouns are all singular.

anybody	either	nobody
anyone	everybody	somebody
each	everyone	someone

Your ear should reliably raise the alarm over a subject-verb agreement error, both for tricky pronouns and regular nouns. Consider the following examples.

*Somebody **love** me.*
*Everyone **like** ice cream.*
*Each **are** beautiful.*
*Nobody **do** it better.*

Your ear probably automatically fixed these.

*Somebody **loves** me.*
*Everyone **likes** ice cream.*
*Each **is** beautiful.*
*Nobody **does** it better.*

This is why your ear can frequently help you eliminate the wrong answers on verb questions. But remember Step 4 of the Basic Approach: Trust, but verify your ear. Confirm the error by making sure you have correctly identified the subject. Another way ACT can make identifying the subject difficult is with prepositional phrases, another trap in question #1.

Prepositional Phrases

Another way ACT made question #1 confusing was by burying the subject to the left of the prepositional phrase. *Each **of the first three taxis** I saw were too far away to hail.* Prepositions are little words that show a relationship between nouns. Some examples are *at, between, by, in, of, on, to,* and *with*. A prepositional phrase modifies—that is, describes—a noun. ACT will add prepositional phrases to distract you from the subject, so be on the lookout for them. Always look to the left of the preposition to find your subject. Try the following examples. Does the subject agree with its verb?

Only one of the dresses fit me.
A selection of fruit, cheese, and nuts were served at the party.
The argument between Pat and Ron sadden all of us.
The books on the table is due back to the library.

Cross out the prepositional phrases to find the subject and confirm the verb.

*Only **one** ~~of the dresses~~ **fits** me.*
*A **selection** ~~of fruit, cheese, and nuts~~ **was** served at the party.*
*The **argument** ~~between Pat and Ron~~ **saddens** all of us.*
*The **books** ~~on the table~~ **are** due back to the library.*

Irregular Verb Participles

ACT can make verb tense difficult as well. Most tense questions are straightforward choices of past, present, or future. However, ACT loves to test the correct past participle for irregular verbs.

Let's try another ACT question.

I woken up at 10:30 to find that my
———
        2
alarm clock had failed to go off.

2. **F.** NO CHANGE
   G. had woke up
   H. woke up
   J. waked up

Here's How to Crack It

The changes in the answers identify verbs as the topic. The subject, *I*, doesn't change the form, and all of the choices are in past tense. Use POE to get rid of all the wrong answers that do not use the correct form of the irregular verb, *to wake*. Use *woke* on its own but *woken* with *had* in front. Choice (H) is the only correct form.

Regular verbs follow a predictable pattern.

*Present: I **study** for the ACT every day.*
*Present perfect: I **have studied** for months.*
*Simple past: I **studied** all day yesterday.*
*Past perfect: I **had studied** for the SAT.*

Irregular verbs are the problem. While you can usually use your ear to find the correct participle, here is a small sample of some common irregular verbs. The *infinitive* is the form of the verb used with *to*; the simple past works on its own, without a helping verb; the *past participle* works with a form of the helping verb *to have*.

*Infinitive: Jacob would like **to become** a biotech engineer.*
*Present perfect: Hannah **has become** a star swimmer.*
*Simple past: Samara **became** a voracious reader.*
*Past perfect: Jonah **had become** tired of practicing.*

Let's try another ACT question.

My boss was mad that I <u>had forgot to bring the report I had been preparing at home.</u>
₃

3. **A.** NO CHANGE
   B. had forgotten to bring the report that I had prepared at home.
   C. had forgotten to bring the report that had been prepared at home by me.
   D. had forgotten to bring the report I had been preparing at home.

Here's How to Crack It

The changes in the answer choices identify verbs as the topic, specifically past participles. Choice (A) incorrectly uses the simple past *forgot* with the helping verb *had*, so you can eliminate it right away. Choices (B), (C), and (D) all fix that error, so compare the differences among them. Choice (B) is the most concise, and neither choices (C) nor (D) fixed something choice (B) missed. Both just made the sentence longer, so the correct answer is choice (B).

> ## You Don't Have to Be Perfect
> The perfect tenses change the time of an event in subtle ways. You will never need to identify by name a particular tense on the ACT, nor choose between the present and present perfect. Choose the past perfect to establish an order of one event happening in the past before another.

Need a refresher on irregular verbs? Check out the table in Chapter 5.

Consistent, Clear, and Concise | **65**

Passive Voice

In question #3, choice (B) was the most concise in part because it uses the active voice. Choice (C) is passive, which make the sentence much longer. Both active and passive voice are grammatically correct, they just describe one event in two different ways. Compare the following sentences:

Beatrice prepared the fine meal.

The fine meal was prepared by Beatrice.

Beatrice makes the meal in both sentences. Active voice preserves the performer of the action, *Beatrice*, as the subject. Passive voice promotes the receiver of the action, in this case *the meal*, to subject and changes the verb by adding the helping verb *was*.

How to Spot Passive Voice

Look for forms of the verb *to be* and the preposition *by*.

How to Crack It

Choose passive voice *only* when you're confident that the other three choices contain a grammatical error.

PRONOUNS

Pronouns take the place of nouns and make your writing more concise. On the ACT, several questions will test the correct usage of pronouns. Whenever you spot pronouns changing among the answers, use these two steps with your Basic Approach.

Revisit Chapter 5 for lists of different types of pronouns.

1. Find the original. The pronoun has to be consistent in number and gender with the noun it replaces and other related pronouns.
2. Check the case. Choose the correct pronoun based on its specific function in the sentence.

Let's try a few examples.

Have you ever had a day when you wished <u>you could have</u> just stayed in bed?
4
4. F. NO CHANGE
   G. you could of
   H. one could of
   J. one could have

Here's How to Crack It
Nothing seems obviously wrong, so leave choice (F) and use the answers to see if you missed something. Pronouns and verbs are changing—sort of; *of* is not a verb, even if it sounds like *have*. Eliminate choices (G) and (H). The pronoun should be consistent with the *you* in the non-underlined portion, so eliminate choice (J). Choice (F) is correct.

Try another.

The taxi driver <u>who finally picked up my boss and I</u> wouldn't take credit cards.
5
5. A. NO CHANGE
   B. whom finally picked up my boss and I
   C. who finally picked up my boss and me
   D. which finally picked up my boss and myself

Here's How to Crack It

The changes in the answers identify pronouns as the topic of the sentence. There are two pronouns in the underlined portion, so consider both and follow your two steps. *Taxi driver* is a person, and which is only for things. *Myself* is correct only for emphasis (I myself don't know the answer) or when the subject and object are the same (I corrected myself). Cross off choice (D). Check the case for *who* and *I,* and don't worry—it's perfectly okay to check *I* first since everyone is scared of "who" versus "whom" (see "Who Versus Whom" below). For case, cross off everything except for the pronoun and the verb. *Picked up I* is incorrect, because *I* is a subject pronoun, so eliminate choices (A) and (B). The correct choice is (C), and you didn't even have to worry about "who" and "whom." Now go learn about them so you don't have to depend on luck the next time.

Who Versus Whom

Who is the subject pronoun. *Whom* is the object pronoun. Why do they seem so hard to all of us? Very few movies and television shows use *whom* when it's needed, and most of us do the same in our regular conversations.

How to Crack It

Whenever you see *who* and *whom* tested on the ACT, try *he* and *him* in their place. If you would say *he called me*, you would say *who called me*. If you would say *I called him*, you would say *whom I called*. Don't worry about how the words flip: Just match your "m" pronouns and you're fine.

APOSTROPHES

Similar to pronouns, apostrophes make your writing more concise. They have two uses, possession and contraction.

Possession

To show possession with single nouns, add *'s*, and with plural nouns, add just the apostrophe. For tricky plurals that do not end in *s*, add *'s*.

Consider the following examples.

The new car of Peter = Peter's new car
The room of the girls = the girls' room.
The room of the men = the men's room.

To show possession with pronouns, never use apostrophes. Use the appropriate possessive pronoun.

His car.
Their room.
Its door.

Revisit Chapter 5 to review a list of possessive pronouns.

Contractions

Whenever you see a pronoun with an apostrophe, it's (it is) a contraction, which means the apostrophe takes the place of at least one letter.

Consider the following examples.

It is important. = It's important.
They are happy to help. = They're happy to help.
Who is the leader of the group? = Who's the leader of the group?

Because these particular contractions sound the same as some possessive pronouns, these questions can be very tricky on the ACT. You can't use your ear—you have to know the above rules. Let's look at some sample ACT questions.

Pronouns Most Frequently Misused
The ACT test writers will sometimes try to confuse you by presenting both a possessive pronoun and the same pronoun in a contraction as answer choices. Do you know the difference between these words: *whose, who's, its, it's?*

I watched in dismay as my laptop was

crushed beneath the taxis wheels'.
6

6. F. NO CHANGE
   G. taxis' wheels.
   H. taxi's wheels'.
   J. taxi's wheels.

Here's How to Crack It

The changes in the answer choices identify apostrophes as the topic. Use POE heavily with apostrophes: Eliminate all the answers that are wrong. If you just try to fix it in your head and find a match, you'll likely miss something. *Wheels* don't "possess" anything, so eliminate choices (F) and (H). There is only one taxi, so choose the singular, choice (J).

Its' screen was smashed to pieces.
7

7. A. NO CHANGE
   B. Their screen
   C. It's screen
   D. Its screen

Here's How to Crack It

The changes in the answer choices identify apostrophes/pronouns as the topic. There is no such word as *its'*, so eliminate choice (A). The *laptop* (context from non-underlined portion in prior question) is singular, so eliminate choice (B). To determine if you need the possessive or a contraction, expand out to *it is*. *It is screen* makes no sense, so choose the possessive pronoun, choice (D).

TRANSITIONS

In Chapter 6, we used traffic as an analogy to explain punctuation. If good writing is like a pleasant drive, then transitions are road signs, preventing you from getting lost and helping you make important turns. Good transitions are consistent with the flow of ideas.

Many words can act as transitions. Some are specific to the context, where only one word will fit the precise meaning. But others are just slight variations, giving you directions: *turn around* or *keep going*. Here's a partial list.

Turn Around
although, but, despite, even though, however, nonetheless, nevertheless, or, yet

Keep Going
and, because, finally, furthermore, moreover, since, so, thus, therefore

---

Try an example.

I apologized for not having the report ready, <u>since she</u> had told me the report wasn't
                        8
due for another week.

8. F. NO CHANGE
   G. even though she
   H. because she
   J. and she

Here's How to Crack It

The changes in the answer choices are transition words, but they are also FAN-BOYS and conjunctions. Before you consider direction, make sure the sentence is complete and that all ideas within the sentence are joined correctly. All are correct and complete, but the sentence doesn't make sense because the direction is wrong. It is a transitions question. The two ideas on either side of the transition word disagree, so choose a *turn around* word. Only choice (G) makes sense.

CONCISE

All the 4 C's are important on the ACT. They are your framework for understanding the topics that you can identify and your strategy to conquer the questions whose topics you can't identify. But concise isn't just a strategy or a tool used to understand certain grammar rules. Sometimes, ACT tests it directly.

Try the following examples.

Next, my boss was furious that I was late.
₉

9. **A.** NO CHANGE
   B. My boss
   C. Then, my boss
   D. Next my boss

Here's How to Crack It

The changes in the answer choices identify transitions as the topic, with possibly commas as well. Use POE. The words *then* and *next* mean the same thing used in this context. If both could be right, both must be wrong. Eliminate choices (A) and (C). *Next* should have a comma after it because it's an introductory idea, so eliminate choice (D) also. The correct answer is choice (B) because you do not need a transition word here.

ACT will frequently test concise in a transitions question. If you don't need a transition word for your sentence to be either complete or clear, don't use it. In the answer choices for question #9, note how *my boss* appeared in each, and one choice featured only *my boss* (and was correct). That is a reliable sign ACT is testing concise.

Try these additional questions.

I was already an hour and a half late for

work and not on time.
10

10. F. NO CHANGE
  G. work, and behind schedule.
  H. work and delayed in getting the morning started.
  J. work.

Here's How to Crack It

The appearance of *work* in every choice and by itself in one identifies the topic as concise. Use POE and pay attention to the non-underlined portion of the sentence for context. The narrator has already established she's late, so all of the other choices are unnecessarily wordy. The correct answer is choice (J).

I had left the lights on the previous

evening, and my car wouldn't start. Many
11
new cars have separate electrical boards for
11
the lights, so the battery won't drain.
11

11. A. NO CHANGE
  B. Batteries should be replaced every five years.
  C. I plan to buy a new car next year.
  D. DELETE the underlined portion.

Here's How to Crack It

The presence of DELETE is a sign the question might be testing concise, but it doesn't guarantee choice (D) is the answer. Read the answer choices through before making a decision. None of the other sentences add any useful info to the first sentence. Cross off the first three choices. In fact, the sentence *is* irrelevant to the passage, and Choice (D) is the correct answer.

There is no reliable pattern of how many times DELETE will be the correct answer on any given ACT. Always be biased toward DELETE. Unless deleting the under-lined portion would create an error or drastically change the meaning, choose it.

Consistent, Clear, and Concise Drill

In the drill below, you will find questions focusing only on consistent, clear, and concise. Before you start, take a few moments to go back over the review material and techniques. Use the basic approach explained in Chapter 5. Answers are in Chapter 24.

Our Family Has Chemistry

There was always one big difference between my twin brother and I. He was good at subjects such as English and

1. **A.** NO CHANGE
   B. and me.
   C. and me were.
   D. and I had.

history, while I was better at math and science. We were always thoughtful; he would be a professor and I would be a doctor. Because of this, I never felt particularly competitive with him and was unconcerned when we accepted offers from the same college. However, once we started, we would find that things did

2. **F.** NO CHANGE
   G. Thoughtful as we were,
   H. I always thought that
   J. Although we were thoughtful,

3. **A.** NO CHANGE
   B. he found
   C. one had found
   D. I found

not work out quite as I would expect.

4. **F.** NO CHANGE
   G. had expected.
   H. was expecting.
   J. expect.

I would never believe it if he hadn't told me himself, but all of a sudden, my brother wanted to be a doctor, too. I can't say that I was too happy about the situation, and I told him so. It was fine if he wanted to "make a difference" and "help humanity," but as far as I was concerned, he could find his own way to do it. Not surprisingly, he didn't see things that way; the next day, he was sitting beside me in the front row of the lecture hall, waiting for biology class to begin.

5. **A.** NO CHANGE
   B. of believed
   C. believed
   D. have believed

I wasn't too worried because I thought that a few days of lectures on stoichiometry and the Krebs cycle would be enough to send him running back to the English department for good.

6. **F.** NO CHANGE
   G. worried, but
   H. worried, although
   J. worried, despite the fact that

However, as the weeks passed, this did not happen. I found that while we were struggling to maintain a B+ average, my brother was getting straight A's. To make matters worse, he seemed to be enjoying himself.

Determined to outdo him, I was thrown into my work. I went to the library every night, smuggling in big cups of coffee, and stayed until closing time.

I took a summer job working in a professors chemistry lab. By the end of the summer, I decided to apply to graduate school in chemistry instead of medical school.

7. A. NO CHANGE
    B. he was
    C. I was
    D. they were

8. F. NO CHANGE
    G. threw it
    H. threw myself
    J. was throwing everything

9. A. NO CHANGE
    B. professor's chemistry lab.
    C. professors chemistry's lab.
    D. professors' chemistry lab.

Summary

o   Verbs, pronouns, apostrophes, and transitions are heavily tested on the ACT.

o   All four are readily identifiable from changes in the answer choices, and all have relatively few rules to use to evaluate the question.

o   The 4 C's can be applied to evaluate any question whose topic you can't identify. ACT also tests concise as its own topic.

o   Be biased toward the choice that says DELETE, but do not assume it will be the correct answer all or even half the time.

Chapter 8
Rhetorical Skills

ACT categorizes the questions on the English test as either Rhetorical Skills or Usage and Mechanics. For most questions, the Basic Approach used to crack them is the same, regardless of how ACT labels them. Some questions, however, require a different approach. In this chapter, we'll teach you how to crack questions that ask for wrong answers, as well as questions on strategy and order.

EXCEPT/LEAST/NOT

You know a question is tricky when the right answer is wrong. That is, if the question asks you to identify the choice that is "NOT acceptable," you have to cross off three answers that work and choose the one that doesn't.

The EXCEPT/LEAST/NOT questions, or E/L/N for short, hide in plain sight, posing a challenge to spot. When most "questions" on the ACT feature only four answer choices, you could easily miss the presence of a bona fide question. Moreover, many of the topics on E/L/N will look familiar: Stop/Go punctuation and transition questions are two topics heavily tested in this format, so the four answers look pretty much the same way they always do.

For the Record
Not all EXCEPT/LEAST/NOT questions are Rhetorical Skills questions by ACT standards. Our argument is that when most of the "questions" are just four answer choices, the presence of a true question demands a different category and different approach.

POE provides your key to cracking these: Eliminate all choices that *could* work. Cross off the EXCEPT/LEAST/NOT word and then use POE to cross off the answers that do work. NO CHANGE is almost never an option on these. Use the sentence as it is written as your standard of comparison for the answer choices. Let's try an example.

Be on the look out for E/L/N questions: Expect as many as 3–4 *per passage*.

I gave my information to the director of the animal shelter. She promised to contact me if any French Bulldogs came in.

1. Which of the following alternatives to the underlined portion would be NOT acceptable?

   A. shelter; she promised
   B. shelter, and she promised
   C. shelter, she promised
   D. shelter, who promised

Here's How to Crack It

Cross out NOT. Since the sentence used Stop punctuation, use POE to eliminate first all answers that are Stop punctuation, choices (A) and (B). Before you worry about choice (D), which changes the wording, focus on the remaining choice with the exact same wording as the original sentence. Remember that a comma alone can never be Stop Punctuation, so choice (C) is grammatically wrong—and therefore the correct answer here.

Word Choice and Idioms

Two of the most popular and challenging topics ACT tests are word choice and idioms, either in regular or E/L/N format. Word choice refers to selecting the precise word that fits with the context. An idiom is an expression that requires a specific preposition. Idioms follow no grammatical rules—they are what they are.

Both word choice and idioms will be easy to spot by the changes in the answers, but neither fits our standards for being easy to fix. While they tend to be fairly common words and expressions, you'll either know them or you won't. ACT rarely, if ever, repeats any words or idioms, so there is no way to prepare for the particular ones that will show up on your ACT. Use POE heavily with these, and don't let them drag you down in your pacing.

Try additional examples.

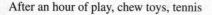

I remember well the day I first saw

Wheezie at the animal shelter. In truth, I think

Wheezie is the one who <u>adopted</u> me.
₂

2. Which of the following alternatives to the underlined word would be LEAST acceptable?

   F. selected
   G. assumed
   H. picked
   J. chose

Here's How to Crack It

Cross out LEAST. Use POE, trying each answer choice in place of *adopted*. Choices (F), (H), and (J) could all mean the same thing, but *assume* just doesn't work and is therefore the correct choice.

After an hour of play, chew toys, tennis

balls, and stuffed animals were strewn <u>around</u>
₃
the living room.

3. Which of the following alternatives to the underlined word would be LEAST acceptable?

   A. on
   B. throughout
   C. all over
   D. about

Here's How to Crack It

Cross out LEAST. This is testing an idiom, specifically which prepositions work with *strewn*. Use POE, trying each answer choice in place of *around*. Choices (B), (C), and (D) could all work with *strewn*, but *on* doesn't work and is therefore the correct choice.

———○———

STRATEGY QUESTIONS

Strategy questions come in many different forms, but they all revolve around the *purpose* of the text. Among the different types of Strategy questions, expect to see questions asking you to add and replace text, determine if text should be added or deleted, evaluate the impact on the passage if text is deleted, or judge the overall effect of the passage on the reader.

Let's see some examples.

———○———

Many dog owners turn to animal trainers when they find they can no longer control their pets. Most experts find that a poorly-trained dog has received plenty of affection but not enough discipline or exercise. [4]

4. Which of the following sentences provides new, specific guidelines about the proper training of a dog?

   F. Behavior that was cute in a twenty-pound puppy is alarming in a one hundred-pound adult dog.
   G. Would-be dog owners should consider their own lifestyles and the temperament of a specific breed before adopting the animal.
   H. Dogs should be walked at least three times a day and should never be given a treat without first obeying a command.
   J. Small children should never be left unsupervised with a dog.

Here's How to Crack It

Identify the purpose of the proposed text. According to the question, one of these choices *provides new, specific guidance about the proper training of a dog*. We don't even need to go back into the passage: Find an answer choice that fulfills the purpose. Choices (F), (G), and (J) all may be true, but they do not offer any *specific* information about training a dog. Only choice (H) does that, and it is our correct answer.

Try another.

Wheezie's puppy playfulness masked the steely determination of a true French bulldog, and she stubbornly resisted all the lessons from our obedience class. [5]

5. At this point, the writer is considering adding the following true statement:

> My nephews trained Blizzard, a black lab with a sweet disposition, very easily.

Should the writer add this sentence here?

A. Yes, because it explains why the author felt so insecure about her difficulties training her dog.
B. Yes, because it provides an important detail about another breed of dog.
C. No, because it doesn't explain how Blizzard was trained.
D. No, because it distracts the reader from the main point of this paragraph.

Here's How to Crack It

Whenever a strategy question asks if you should add or delete new text, evaluate the reasons in the answer choices carefully. The reason should correctly explain the purpose of the selected text. Here, choice (D) is correct because there is no reason to add text that is irrelevant to the topic.

Most puppy books no longer recommend
using newspapers to housebreak dogs. I
_____
                        6
bought three safety gates to block off the
kitchen from the rest of the house. I also
brought home a crate, baby blankets to make
it cozy, a stylish collar and matching leash,
several bags of food, and of course, plenty of
toys.

6. Given that all choices are true, which one provides the best opening to this paragraph?

   F. NO CHANGE
   G. When I was growing up, my family had an Irish Setter and four cats.
   H. I made sure I had all the supplies we'd need before bringing Wheezie home.
   J. Many people prefer cats as pets.

Here's How to Crack It
In many strategy questions, the purpose is to add a sentence to open or close a paragraph, or tie two paragraphs together. Use the context of the paragraph and read through to the end before deciding. Since the author mentions several things she's bought in preparation, choice (H) provides the best introduction to the paragraph.

ORDER

There are also several types of Order questions, but they all involve the correct placement of ideas. Some order questions will ask you to place correctly a modifier or additional text. Other questions will ask you to evaluate and possibly correct the order of sentences within a paragraph or the paragraphs themselves.

All order questions work best with POE. Ideas should be consistent and the meaning should be clear, but that meaning can be difficult to understand until ideas are in their proper place.

Let's look at a few examples.

French bulldogs can face a serious(7) number of health issues affecting the respiratory system, knees, and eyesight.

7. The best placement for the underlined word would be:
   A. where it is now.
   B. before the word *French* (revising the capitalization accordingly).
   C. before the word *health*.
   D. before the word *respiratory*.

Here's How to Crack It

Use POE, trying the word in the places suggested by each answer choice. The best answer is choice (C) because it modifies health issues and therefore includes all three listed. "Serious" to mean "a lot of" is slang, and thus appeals to your ear. But "large" is not a definition of serious, literally or figuratively, and none of the other definitions really apply to the figurative meaning of "large."

Order of Sentences

If there is a question on order of the sentences or placement of new text within a paragraph, all of the sentences in the passage will be numbered. NO CHANGE could be the answer to order of the sentences, but if you're reading along and get confused by a sudden shift in the action, that's a good sign the sentences are in fact out of order. Do not go back and reread, but instead wait until you get to the question.

Don't waste time trying to re-order all of the sentences yourself. Look for transition words that indicate an introduction, a conclusion, or a pair of sentences that should go back to back, and use POE.

Try an example.

---

[4]

[1] He recommended an excellent specialist to perform the surgery. [2] When the day came, I drove to the hospital, dreading the moment I'd need to leave her behind. [3] While we waited for her to be admitted, Wheezie sensed something was wrong and curled on my lap, trembling. [4] My vet broke the bad news that Wheezie would have to have surgery to correct the problems in her nasal passage and vocal chords.

8. Which of the following order of sentences will make the paragraph most logical?
   F. NO CHANGE
   G. 2, 3, 1, 4
   H. 4, 3, 2, 1
   J. 4, 1, 2, 3

Here's How to Crack It

Use POE. The surgery isn't properly introduced until the end, which means sentence 4 should be the introduction. Eliminate choices (F) and (G) and determine if sentence 3 or 1 should be next. Sentence 1 makes more sense, so the answer is choice (J).

Order of the Paragraphs

If there is a question on the order of the paragraphs, there will be a warning at the beginning of the passage, alerting you that the passages may or may not be in the correct order and identifying which question will ask about which paragraph.

Almost no one ever spots this warning. Treat these the same way you treat the order of the sentences. If you suddenly find yourself confused by an inexplicable shift in the action, check above the title if the warning is there. Alternatively, continue reading and working the questions and bet safely you'll encounter a question on the order of the paragraphs at the end of the passage.

AND IN THE END. . .

> Questions 9 and 10 ask about the passage as a whole.

Other than order of the paragraphs, two other questions routinely appear at the end and are always preceded by the announcement above.

Placement of New Info

The paragraphs will also be numbered for a question testing the placement of additional info.

9. Upon reviewing this essay and concluding some information has been left out, the writer composes the following sentence:

   After a night spent winning the hearts of all of the attendants, Wheezie bounded out of the recovery room and into my waiting arms.

   This sentence should be:

   A. placed at the end of paragraph 4.
   B. placed at the end of paragraph 3.
   C. placed at the end of paragraph 2.
   D. placed at the end of paragraph 1.

Here's How to Crack It

Okay, so this is a little unfair: We didn't give you the entire passage, and only the correct paragraph (4) was numbered. But we couldn't leave you hanging about Wheezie's fate. Even with a little bit of cheating on our part, the new information is consistent with the rest of the information in that paragraph, and choice (A) is the correct answer.

Grading the Passage

Questions at the end that ask you to evaluate the passage are another version of a strategy question. The question identifies the purpose of the passage and asks you to determine if the author succeeded. These are always at the end, so we waited to show you here.

10. Suppose that one of the writer's goals has been to address the role obedience classes can play in the healthy development of dogs. Would this essay fulfill that goal?

   F. Yes, because the essay implies the writer and her dog benefited from obedience classes.
   G. Yes, because the essay indicates French Bulldogs are not easily trained.
   H. No, because the essay is focused on one anecdote about one dog.
   J. No, because the essay indicates the dog displayed aggressive and territorial behavior.

Here's How to Crack It

With all strategy questions, identify the purpose in the question. With questions that use a Yes/No format, connect the purpose in the question to the reasons given in the answer choices. Choice (H) is the correct answer.

Rhetorical Skills Drill

In the drill below, you will find questions focusing only on Rhetorical Skills. Before you start, take a few moments to go back over the review material and techniques. Answers are in Chapter 24.

> The following paragraphs may or may not be in the most logical order. Each paragraph is numbered, and question 9 will ask you to choose where Paragraph 2 should most logically be placed.

[1]

The golden age of television means many things to many people, but to the small band of actors, writers, and directors who would rise to prominence in the late 50s and early 60s, without a doubt it meant the televisions shows such as

Playhouse 90, on which many of them worked for the first live time.

[2]

Despite the undeniable risks of live performances—or perhaps because of—the results rank among the greatest achievements in American entertainment. Many of its productions were later remade, both for television and film, including *Requiem for a Heavyweight, Judgment at Nuremberg,* and *Days of Wine and Roses.* [3] Many critics maintain none of the remakes could match the brilliance and electricity of the live performances displayed in *Playhouse 90*.

[3]

[1] Each week, a new "teleplay" was created from scratch—written, cast, rehearsed, and performed. [2] *Playhouse 90* was truly a remarkable training ground for the young talents. [3] Such future luminaries as Rod Serling, Sidney Lumet, Paddy Chayefsky, Marlon Brando, and Patricia Neal worked

1. Which of the following alternatives to the underlined word would be LEAST acceptable?
   A. fame
   B. projection
   C. stardom
   D. greatness

2. The best placement for the underlined word would be:
   F. where it is now.
   G. before the word *actors*.
   H. before the word *doubt*.
   J. before the word *television*.

3. The writer is considering deleting the preceding sentence. Should the sentence be kept or deleted?
   A. Kept, because it provides context for the reference to remakes in the next sentence.
   B. Kept, because it is crucial to understanding why *Playhouse 90* was a success.
   C. Deleted, because it does not match the objective tone of the essay.
   D. Deleted, because it contains information that has already been provided in the essay.

long hours reading scripts. [4] In some cases, when there were problems with the censors, it would have to be created

twice. 5

[4]

Due to the frantic pace, accidents happened frequently. David Niven once revealed that, during an early show, he inadvertently locked his costume in his dressing room two minutes before air time. As the announcer read the opening credits, the sound of axes splintering the door to Niven's dressing room could be heard in the background. 7

4. Which choice would most clearly indicate that the actors, writers, and directors became extremely skilled?

   F. memorizing their lines.
   G. honing their craft.
   H. constructing the set.
   J. skimming the want-ads.

5. Which of the following order of sentences will make the paragraph most logical?

   A. NO CHANGE
   B. 1, 2, 4, 3
   C. 2, 1, 4, 3
   D. 2, 3, 1, 4

6. Given that all choices are true, which one most effectively introduces this paragraph?

   F. NO CHANGE
   G. The ratings for *Playhouse 90* were unimpressive.
   H. Broadway has produced many famous actors as well.
   J. *Playhouse 90* ran on CBS from 1956 to 1961.

7. The writer is considering deleting the preceding sentence. If the writer were to make this deletion, the essay would primarily lose a statement that:

   A. explains the organization of the last paragraph.
   B. adds a much needed touch of humor to the essay.
   C. information that explains how one accident was resolved.
   D. nothing, since the information is provided elsewhere in the essay.

Questions 8 and 9 ask about the preceding passage as a whole.

8. Suppose that one of the writer's goals had been to write a brief essay describing an influential program in television's history. Would this essay fulfill that goal?

   F. Yes, because it explains that many future stars underwent valuable training working on *Playhouse 90*.
   G. Yes, because it mentions that *Playhouse 90* had the greatest number of viewers in its time slot.
   H. No, because it fails to mention any future stars by name.
   J. No, because even though many future stars received their start on *Playhouse 90*, few ever returned to television.

9. For the sake of the logic and coherence of this essay, Paragraph 2 should be placed:

   A. where it is now.
   B. before Paragraph 1.
   C. after Paragraph 3.
   D. after Paragraph 4.

Summary

- The official categories of Usage and Mechanics and Rhetorical Skills do not matter if you use the same approach to crack.

- Questions that come with actual questions—not just answer choices—do need a different approach.

- For EXCEPT/LEAST/NOT questions, cross off the E/L/N word and use POE.

- Strategy questions all involve a purpose.

- Order questions involve the correct placement of words, sentences, and paragraphs.

Part III
How to
Crack the ACT
Mathematics
Test

Chapter 9
Introduction to the ACT Mathematics Test

The second section of the ACT will always be the Math test. To perform your best, you'll need to become familiar with the structure and strategy of the ACT Math test. In this chapter, we discuss the types of questions you can expect to see and how you can use organizational strategy, estimation, and elimination skills to improve your Math score.

Watch it on
your DVD

WHAT TO EXPECT ON THE MATH TEST

You will have 60 minutes to answer 60 multiple-choice questions based on "…topics covered in typical high school classes." For those of you who aren't sure if you went to a typical high school, these questions break down into rather precise areas of knowledge.

There are usually

33 Algebra questions
- 14 pre-algebra questions based on math terminology (integers, prime numbers, etc.), basic number theory (rules of zero, order of operations etc.), and manipulation of fractions and decimals
- 10 elementary algebra questions based on inequalities, linear equations, ratios, percents, and averages
- 9 intermediate algebra questions based on exponents, roots, simultaneous equations, and quadratic equations

23 Geometry questions
- 14 plane geometry questions based on angles, lengths, triangles, quadrilaterals, circles, perimeter, area, and volume
- 9 coordinate geometry questions based on slope, distance, midpoint, parallel and perpendicular lines, points of intersection, and graphing

4 Trigonometry questions
- 4 questions based on basic sine, cosine, and tangent functions, trig identities, and graphing

What Not to Expect on the Math Test

The ACT does not provide any formulas at the beginning of the Math test. Before you panic, take a second look at the chart on the previous page. Because the ACT is so specific about the types of questions it expects you to answer, preparing to tackle ACT Math takes a few simple steps.

A NOTE ON CALCULATORS

Not all standardized tests allow calculators. Fortunately, ACT does. We're not about to give you the stodgy advice that you shouldn't use your calculator—quite the opposite, in fact. Your calculator can help to save a ton of time on operations that you may have forgotten how to do or that are easy to mess up. Adding fractions, multiplying decimals, doing operations with big numbers: Why not use a calculator on these? The place where you have to be really careful with your calculator, though, is on the easy ones. Let's see an example.

---

1. What is the value of $3x^2 + 5x - 7$ when $x = -1$?
    A. −15
    B. −9
    C. −1
    D.   5
    E.   15

Here's How to Crack It

If you've got your calculator handy, use it. This problem is pretty straightforward, but a calculator can help to put everything together. BUT, make sure you're treating the −1 with the respect it deserves. What you punch into your calculator should look something like this:

$$3(-1)^2 + 5(-1) - 7$$

When working with negative numbers or fractions, make doubly sure that you use parentheses. If not, a lot of weird stuff can happen, and unfortunately all of the weird, wrong stuff that can happen is reflected in the wrong answer choices. If you computed this equation and found −9, choice (B), you got the right answer. Well done. If not, try to go back and figure out where you made your calculator mistake.

Types of Calculators

Throughout the rest of the Math chapters, we discuss ways to solve calculator-friendly questions in an accurate and manageable way. Because TI-89 and TI-92 calculators are not allowed on the ACT, we will show you how to solve problems on the TI-83. If you don't plan to use a TI-83 on the test, we recommend you make sure your calculator is acceptable for use on the test and that it can do the following:

- handle positive, negative, and fractional exponents
- use parentheses
- graph simple functions

> Use your calculator, but use it wisely. Be careful with negative numbers and fractions.

- convert fractions to decimals and vice versa
- change a linear equation into $y = mx + b$ form

THE PRINCETON REVIEW APPROACH

Because the test is so predictable, the best way to prepare for ACT Math is with

1. a thorough review of the very specific information and question types that come up repeatedly.
2. an understanding of The Princeton Review's test-taking strategies and techniques.

In each Math chapter in this book, you'll find a mixture of review and technique, with a sprinkling of ACT-like problems. At the end of each chapter, there is a summary of the chapter and a drill designed to pinpoint your math test-taking strengths and weaknesses. In addition to working through the problems in this book, we strongly suggest you practice our techniques on some real ACT practice tests. Let's begin with some general strategies.

Order of Difficulty: Still Personal

The Math test is the only part of the ACT that is in Order of Difficulty (OOD). What this means is that the easier questions tend to be a bit earlier in the exam, and the harder questions are later. Usually, this means that #1 is a freebie and #60 is a doozy. None of the other tests have an OOD, unfortunately, so they are all about Personal Order of Difficulty (POOD). This OOD in and of itself is great to know when planning how you will attack this part of the ACT.

Now we all love easy questions, but hold on for a second. If you and I both get a B on a math test at school, is it necessarily because we got exactly the same questions right or wrong? Unfortunately, no. What makes for a hard question? Is it hard because it's a long word problem, or is it hard because it tests some arcane concept that your teacher went over for like five seconds? Only the very hardest questions will be both. So even on the Math test of the ACT, you still need to use your POOD. The things you might find easy or hard won't necessarily jibe with ACT's.

The Princeton Review's *1,296 ACT Practice Questions* offers the equivalent of 6 whole ACT practice tests.

Now, Later, Never

Now

Do the problems you're sure you can do quickly and accurately.

Later

If a problem looks time-consuming, save it for later. Do the Nows first.

Never.

Sometimes it's better to just walk away. If a problem has you totally stumped, answer with your Letter of the Day and move on.

Hard questions take a long time. Easy ones take a short time. That's obvious, but as we've seen, the definition of an "Easy" question is a tough one to pin down. That's why you'll want to be careful trusting ACT's Order of Difficulty on the Math test. The no-brainer approach is to open the test booklet and work questions 1 through 60 in order, but you can get a lot of extra points by out-thinking this test. You'll have a lot easier time drawing your own road map for this test than letting ACT guide you.

Clearly, a lot of the easy questions will be right in the beginning, but they won't all be. This is why when you arrive at each question, you'll want to first determine whether it is a Now, Later, or Never question. Do the Now questions immediately: They're the freebies—the ones you know how to do and can do quickly and accurately. Skip any questions you think might take you a bit longer, or which test unfamiliar concepts—save them for Later. Make sure you get all the points you can on the problems you know you can do, no matter what the question number.

Once you've done all the Now questions, go back to all the ones you left for Later. But here you should be careful as well. For both Now and Later questions, don't rush and make careless errors. On the other hand, don't get stuck on a particular problem. In a 60-minute exam, think of how much spending 5 minutes on a single problem can cost you!

Finally, there's no problem with leaving a few questions behind in the Never category. The good news here is that these problems are not necessarily totally lost. Fill them in with a Letter of the Day: Choose one pair of letters and bubble in all the blanks this way. For example, always bubble in A or F, B or G, etc. ACT doesn't have a guessing penalty, so there's nothing to lose, and you can even get lucky and get a few free points.

USE PROCESS OF ELIMINATION (POE)

Remember the major technique we introduced in Chapter 3: POE, or Process of Elimination. ACT doesn't take away points for wrong answers, so you should always guess, and POE can help you improve those chances of guessing. Don't make the mistake of thinking that POE is a strategy reserved only for English, Reading, and Science. Math has its own kind of POE, one facet of which we like to call Ballparking.

BALLPARK

You can frequently get rid of several answer choices in an ACT math problem without doing any complicated math. Narrow down the choices by estimating your answer. We call this ballparking. Let's look at an example:

---

3. There are 600 school children in the Lakeville district. If 54 of them are high school seniors, what is the percentage of high school seniors in the Lakeville district?

   A. .9%
   B. 2.32%
   C. 9%
   D. 11%
   E. 90%

Here's How to Crack It

Before we do any serious math on this problem, let's see if we can get rid of some answer choices by ballparking.

First, we need to figure out what percent 54 is of 600. It's pretty small, definitely way less than 50%, so we can eliminate choice (E) right off the bat. Now, think about easy percentages that you know—10 and 25%—and start from there. What's 10% of 600? Just move the decimal one place to the right to get it, and you'll find that 10% of 600 is 60. Therefore, if the number from the problem is 54, the answer must be less than 10%. Let's get rid of choice (D). Now, we know that 54 is pretty close to 60, so we want something close to 10% but slightly less, and the only possible answer is choice (C).

It may feel like we somehow cheated the system by doing the problem that way, but here's what ACT doesn't want you to know: The quick, easy way and the "real" way get you the same amount of points. Not all problems will be so easily ballparkable, but if you think before you start frantically figuring, you can usually eliminate at least an answer choice or two.

Cross Out the Crazy Answers
What's the average of 100 and 200?
A. 500
B. 150
C. a billion

WORD PROBLEMS

You've seen the breakdown of the topics that are tested on the ACT Math test. At a glance, it actually looks like the ACT should be kind of an easy test: You've definitely learned a lot of this stuff in school, a lot of it by the end of middle school. So what's the deal? Well, part of the deal is that ACT makes familiar stuff really unfamiliar by putting it into word problems. Word problems add some confusing steps that mask the often simple concepts trapped in the problems. Trap answers, partial answers, and weird phrasing abound in word problems. Is anyone else getting the feeling that this whole exam is about reading comprehension?

Word problems look a lot of different ways and test a lot of different math concepts, but if you keep these three steps in mind, you should be able to get started on most word problems:

> When dealing with word problems on the ACT Math test
> 1. **Know the question.** Read the whole problem before calculating anything, and underline the actual question.
> 2. **Let the answers help.** Look for clues on how to solve and ways to use POE (Process of Elimination).
> 3. **Break the problem into bite-sized pieces.** When you read the problem a second time, calculate at each step necessary and watch out for tricky phrasing.

Let's try a problem:

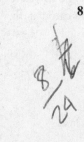

8. Each member in a club had to choose an activity for a day of volunteer work. $\frac{1}{3}$ of the members chose to pick up trash. $\frac{1}{4}$ of the remaining members chose to paint fences. $\frac{5}{6}$ of the members still without tasks chose to clean school buses. The rest of the members chose to plant trees. If the club has 36 members, how many of the members chose to plant trees?

F.   3
G.   6
H.   9
J.   12
K.   15

Here's How to Crack It

Step 1: Know the Question

This is actually a slightly tricky step on this one. First of all, the problem doesn't tell you until the very end that there are 36 students in this class. Without this piece of information, the fractions don't mean much of anything. Second, the question is asking for the number of members who chose to plant trees, and we're going to have to figure out a bunch of other things before we figure that out.

Step 2: Let the Answers Help

There aren't any crazy answers in this one, though if you noticed how much we're subtracting from 36, you're probably thinking that the answer will be one of the smaller numbers.

Step 3: Break the problem into bite-sized pieces

The starting point of this word problem actually comes at the end: This club has 36 members. Once you've got that, work the problem sentence by sentence, and pay particular attention to the language of the problem.

$\frac{1}{3}$ of the members chose to pick up trash.

A nice easy way to start. There are 36 members, and $\frac{1}{3}$ of 36 is 12, so 12 members pick up trash.

$\frac{1}{4}$ of the remaining members chose to paint fences.

This is just like the last piece, except for one HUGE exception, which comes from the word *remaining*. First, we'll need to figure out how many remaining members there are from the first step. There are 36 total members and 12 of them are picking up trash, so there are 24 members remaining. $\frac{1}{4}$ of 24 is 6, so 6 members paint fences.

$\frac{5}{6}$ of the remaining members still without tasks chose to clean school buses.

There's that word remaining again. There were 24 members in the last step, but 6 of them chose to paint fences, so now there are 18 *remaining* members. $\frac{5}{6}$ of 18 is 15, so 15 members clean school buses.

The rest of the members chose to plant trees.

There were 18 members left over in the last step, and 15 of them chose to clean school buses, which means there must be 3 students left to plant trees. Choice (F) is the correct answer. Look at those other answers, then look at the numbers you were dealing with in the problem: What a mess of partial answers!

If it seems like this took kind of a long time to do, don't worry, they won't all take this long. Most of these steps will come naturally after a while, and you'll have a solid base with which to begin any ACT Math problem in such a way that enables you to get to the answer as efficiently as possible.

PACING

As you work through the following lessons, revisit your POOD. The more content you review and the more you practice, you may find more Now questions and fewer Never questions.

GOAL SCORE

Use the pacing strategies and score grid on page 23 to find your goal score for each practice test and, eventually, the ACT.

Summary

- On the ACT Math test, you have 60 minutes to attempt 60 questions. The questions fall into the following categories:
  - 33 Algebra questions (14 pre-algebra, 10 elementary algebra, 9 intermediate algebra)
  - 23 Geometry questions (14 plane geometry, 9 coordinate geometry)
  - 4 Trigonometry questions

- Use your Personal Order of Difficulty to determine if a question is for Now, Later, or Never.
  - Just because the Math is technically in order of difficulty doesn't mean you need to do it in order.
  - Never leave any blanks! Fill in the Never questions with your Letter of the Day.

- Remember the basic approach for Word Problems.
  - **Know the question.** Read the problem all the way through and underline the question.
  - **Let the answers help.** Look for clues on how to solve. Use POE and ballparking.
  - **Break the problem into bite-sized pieces.** Every problem has lots of information: Process each piece one at a time and be careful of tricky phrasing.

- Finally, use your calculator liberally but wisely!

Chapter 10
Fundamentals

A solid base in the fundamentals of the math tested on the ACT is essential to getting a good score. We'll see a number of strategies that will help to work around some of the more advanced concepts, but there's often no way to work around questions that test the fundamentals.

VOCABULARY

Calculators can solve a lot of problems, but Vocabulary is one aspect of the math with which a calculator can't help. Let's review some of the main terms.

A Note on Calculators

This chapter will deal mainly with concepts rather than operations. As mentioned in the previous chapter, we encourage you to use your calculator liberally but wisely. The operations discussed in this chapter will be those for which a calculator might be unhelpful or extra confusing.

Basics

Use the numbers below to answer questions 1 through 6 that follow. Check your answers against the Answer Key at the end of this chapter on page 122.

$$-81, -19, -9, -6, -\frac{1}{4}, -0.15, 0, 1.75, 2, 3, 12, 16, 81$$

1. List all the *positive numbers*. _~~1~~ 1.75, 2, 3, 12, 16, 81_
2. List all the *negative integers*. _−81, −19, −9, −6, ~~−1~~_
3. List all the *odd* integers. _−81, −19, −9, 3, 81_
4. List all the *even* integers. _−6, ~~0~~ 2, 12, 16, 0_
5. List all the *positive*, *even* integers in *consecutive* order. ___
   _~~1~~ 2, 12, 16_
6. List all the numbers that are neither *positive* nor *negative*. ___
   _0_

Now try these questions.

7. What is the *reciprocal* of $-\frac{1}{4}$? _−4_

8. What is the *opposite reciprocal* of 2? _$-\frac{1}{2}$_
9. When a number and its reciprocal are multiplied, what is the product? ___

10. How many times does 2 go into 15 evenly? _7_
11. How much is left over? _1_
12. What is 15 divided by 2? _7.5_

Let's try it the other way. Use the following list of terms to answer questions 13 through 18.

> Number, Integer, Positive, Negative, Even, Odd,
> Consecutive, Reciprocal, Remainder

13. Which terms describe the number 6? _number, integer, positive, even_

14. Which terms describe the number $-\dfrac{1}{5}$? _number, negative_

15. Which terms describe the number 0? _number, integer, even_

16. When 14 is divided by 3, it has a _remainder_ of 2.

17. The _reciprocal_ of $-\dfrac{1}{4}$ is -4.

18. The numbers 2, 4, 6 are listed in _consecutive_ order, but the numbers 3, 1, 14 are not.

Factors and Multiples

Factors and multiples are all about numbers that are divisible by other numbers. Start with examples, and the definitions will become easier.

> Example
> - The factors of 10 are 1, 2, 5, 10.
> - The first four positive multiples of 10 are 10, 20, 30, 40.

A Good Rule of Thumb
- The factors of a number are always equivalent to that number or *smaller*.
- The multiples of a number are always equivalent to that number or *larger*.

1. List the factors of 12. _____
2. List the first four multiples of 12. _____
3. List the factors of 30. _____
4. List the first four multiples of 30. _____
5. Is 12 a multiple or factor of 24? _____
6. Is 8 one of the factors of 64? _____
7. What is the greatest common factor of 27 and 45? _____
8. What is the greatest common factor of 9 and 36? _____
9. What is the least common multiple of 9 and 12? _____
10. What is the least common multiple of 24 and 48? _____

Prime

A prime number is any number with only two distinct factors:
1 and itself.

1. What are the single digit prime numbers? _____
2. What is the only even prime number? _2_
3. Is 1 a prime number? ~~Yes~~ No not 2 distinct factors

The prime factorization of a number is the reduction of a number to its prime factors. Find the prime factorization of a number by using a factor tree. Example:

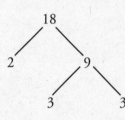

The prime factorization of 18 is $2 \times 3 \times 3$ or 2×3^2.

4. What is the prime factorization of 36?

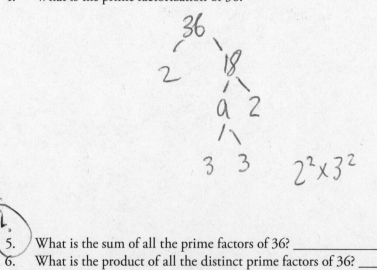

5. What is the sum of all the prime factors of 36? _____
6. What is the product of all the distinct prime factors of 36? _____

ADVANCED TERMS

Real Numbers and Their Imaginary Friends

ACT uses the term "real" a lot, but it's usually only there to scare you. Sometimes, though, ACT will test it directly, so it's good to have at least a sense of what the term means.

1. How much would you like to earn in your eventual job? _____
2. How much scholarship money do you want from your eventual college? _____
3. What's the temperature in the Bahamas right now? (Ballpark it!) _____
4. How many slices of pizza could you eat in a single sitting? _____

Unless you have some interesting ideas about money and/or pizza, ALL of the numbers above are real. The only numbers that aren't real are imaginary—a negative number under an even root.

5. What is $\sqrt{1}$? _____real_____
6. What is -1×-1? _____real_____
7. What is $-1 \times -1 \times -1$? _____real -1_____
8. What is $\sqrt{-1}$? _____imaginary_____
9. What real number could you square to get a product of -1? _____

That last question was a trick: There is no real number that you can square and get a negative product. The only way to get the square root (or any even root) of a negative number is to *imagine* it.

> $\sqrt{-1}$ is defined as the imaginary number i. All other imaginary numbers are something multiplied by i.

Rational Numbers and Their Irrational Friends

1. Write 0.5 as a fraction. $\frac{1}{2}$
2. Write 3 as a fraction. $\frac{3}{1}$
3. In the number 0.1666, what digit is coming next? 6
4. In the number, 0.191919, what digit is coming next? 1

> A *rational* number is any number that can be written as a fraction: that includes integers and repeating decimals. An *irrational* is a number that cannot be written as a fraction because it goes on unpredictably. *Both* types of numbers are *real*.

Love Your Calculator for Real, but Be Rational

Your calculator can be a really handy tool for problems dealing with imaginary and irrational numbers. If you have a Texas Instruments calculator, the second function of the decimal is *i*. Use this function to solve the following problems.

5. $(2 + i)(2 - i)$? 5
6. $(3 + i)^2$? $8 + 6i$

To determine if a number is rational or irrational, it can help to try to convert it into a fraction. In the MATH menu, the first item is >*Frac*. This will convert a decimal to a fraction if the number is rational. For each question below, after you have typed in the number provided hit ENTER, then MATH>ENTER>ENTER. Give the result in the blank and identify whether it is rational or irrational.

7. 0.375 $\frac{3}{8}$ rat
8. 0.16666666666 (until the end of the screen) $\frac{1}{6}$ rat
9. π   3.14   irr
10. 0.479109801431   rational

Exponents

Exponents are a shorthand way of indicating that a number is multiplied by itself. The exponent tells you how many times (for example, $5^4 = 5 \times 5 \times 5 \times 5$). Exponents are tricky when you have to combine them in some way. Here's a great way to remember all the rules.

Remember MADSPM!

- When you *multiply* two numbers with common bases, *add* the exponents.
- When you *divide* two numbers with common bases, *subtract* the exponents.
- When you raise an exponential number to a *power*, *multiply* the exponents.

Basic Rules

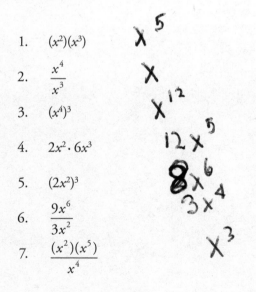

1. $(x^2)(x^3)$

2. $\dfrac{x^4}{x^3}$

3. $(x^4)^3$

4. $2x^2 \cdot 6x^3$

5. $(2x^2)^3$

6. $\dfrac{9x^6}{3x^2}$

7. $\dfrac{(x^2)(x^5)}{x^4}$

Special Rules

Follow the basic rules to see how some of these special rules are derived.

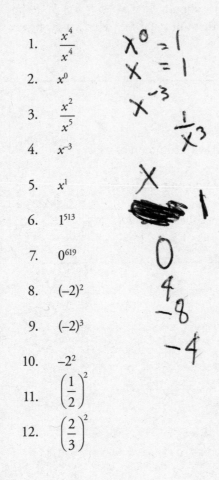

1. $\dfrac{x^4}{x^4}$

2. x^0

3. $\dfrac{x^2}{x^5}$

4. x^{-3}

5. x^1

6. 1^{513}

7. 0^{619}

8. $(-2)^2$

9. $(-2)^3$

10. -2^2

11. $\left(\dfrac{1}{2}\right)^2$

12. $\left(\dfrac{2}{3}\right)^2$

Odd: _____

_____

Opposite: _____

_____

Order of Operations: _____

_____

Positive: _____

_____

Prime: _____

_____

Product: _____

_____

Quotient: _____

_____

Real: _____

_____

Radical: _____

_____

Rational: _____

_____

Reciprocal: _____

_____

Remainder: _____

_____

Sum: _____

_____

GLOSSARY

Absolute Value:	The distance from zero on the number line
Consecutive:	In increasing order
Decimal:	A way of expressing a fraction in which numbers are divided by ten, hundred, thousand, and other powers of ten
Difference:	The result of subtraction
★ **Digits:**	The integers 0 through 9
Distinct:	Different
Divisible:	An integer can be divided by another integer evenly, with no fraction or decimal left over
Even:	Divisible by 2
Exponent/Power:	A number that indicates how many times to multiply a base by itself
Factor:	Integers that multiply together to make a given product
Fraction:	A way of expressing the division of numbers by stacking one over the other
Greatest Common Factor:	The largest factor common to two numbers
★ **Imaginary:**	The square (or any other even) root of a negative number
Integers:	All real numbers other than decimals or fractions
Irrational:	A number that can be expressed as a decimal but not a fraction
Least Common Multiple:	The smallest multiple common to two numbers
Multiple:	The product of an integer and another integer
Negative:	Less than 0
Number:	Everything
Odd:	NOT divisible by 2
Opposite:	Two numbers that have the same magnitude but are opposite in signs. That is, two numbers with the same distance from zero on the number line, but one is positive and the other negative.
...der of Operations:	Parentheses, Exponents, Multiplication, Division, Addition, Subtraction

Positive:	Greater than 0
Prime:	A number that has itself and 1 as its only factors
Product:	The result of multiplication
Quotient:	The result of division
✱ **Real:**	Zero, all positive and negative integers, fractions, decimals, and roots
Radical:	Another word for the $\sqrt{}$ sign
Rational:	A number that can be expressed as the ratio of two other numbers, making a fraction
Reciprocal:	The inverse of a number—flip the numerator and denominator
Remainder:	The number left over when a number is not divisible by another number
Sum:	The result of addition

Fundamentals Drill

In the drill below, you will find questions focusing only on fundamental skills. Before you start, take a few moments to go back over the review material and techniques. Answers are in Chapter 24.

1. What is the product of the distinct prime factors of 54 ?
   A. 2
   B. 3
   C. 6
   D. 11
   E. 54

(handwritten: 2, 27, 3, 9, 3 3)

2. If x is the least odd prime number and y is the least positive integer multiple of 10, what is the difference between x and y ?
   F. 3
   G. 7
   H. 11
   J. 15
   K. 17

(handwritten: 10 - 3)

3. For all x and y, $(x^{-1}y^{-3})^{-2}(x^4y^7)^3 = $?
   A. $x^{10}y^{15}$
   B. x^5y^{10}
   C. x^3y^4
   D. $x^{14}y^{27}$
   E. $x^{-6}y^{18}$

(handwritten: $(x^2y^6)(x^{12}y^{21})$)

4. In the complex numbers, where $i^2 = -1$, which of the following is equal to the result of squaring the expression $(i + 4)$?
   F. $4i$
   G. $16i$
   H. $15 + 8i$
   J. $i + 16$
   K. $17 - 18i$

5. What is the least possible sum of three distinct prime numbers between 10 and 20 ?
   A. 30
   B. 39
   C. 41
   D. 45
   E. 60

(handwritten: 11 13 17 19)

Summary

o   Learn the basics on the ACT Math test before you move on to more difficult concepts. The Fundamentals are the one thing on the ACT that you can't fake!

o   Know your vocabulary. The Math test requires its own Reading Comprehension.

o   Know your rules for 0.
   - 0 is an even number.
   - 0 is neither positive nor negative.
   - Anything multiplied by 0 is 0.
   - 0 raised to any power is 0.
   - Anything raised to the 0 power is 1.

o   A number's factors are always *smaller than* or the *same as* that number.

o   A number's multiples are always *larger than* or the *same as* that number.

o   A prime number has only two distinct factors: 1 and itself.
   - 1 is NOT a prime number.
   - 2 is the only even prime number.

o   Use your calculator well and wisely. A calculator is particularly helpful with
   - Imaginary numbers (represented as i in problems).
   - Square roots that don't contain variables (and often those that do).
   - Converting decimals or other expressions into fractions.
   - Multiplying and dividing large numbers.

o   When combining numbers with exponents, remember MADSPM.

FUNDAMENTALS LESSON ANSWER KEY

Basics (page 106)

1. 1.75, 2, 3, 12, 16, 81
2. −81, −19, −9, −6
3. −81, −19, −9, 3, 81
4. −6, 0, 2, 12, 16
5. 2, 12, 16
6. 0
7. −4
8. $-\dfrac{1}{2}$
9. 1
10. 7
11. 1
12. 7 R 1 (7 *remainder* 1)
13. Number, Integer, Positive, Even
14. Number, Negative
15. Number, Integer, Even
16. Remainder
17. Reciprocal
18. Consecutive

Factors and Multiples (page 109)

1. 1, 2, 3, 4 , 6, 12
2. 12, 24, 36, 48
3. 1, 2, 3, 5, 6, 10, 15, 30
4. 30, 60, 90, 120
5. Factor
6. Yes
7. 9
8. 9
9. 36
10. 48

Prime (page 110)

1. 2, 3, 5, 7
2. 2
3. No, it does not have two *distinct* factors.
4. $2 \times 2 \times 3 \times 3$ or $2^2 \times 3^2$
5. 10 (2 + 2 + 3 + 3)
6. 6 (2 × 3)

Real Numbers and their Imaginary Friends (page 111)

5. 1
6. 1
7. −1
8. No answer, or Imaginary
9. None

Rational Numbers and their Irrational Friends (page 112)

1. $\dfrac{1}{2}$

2. $\dfrac{3}{1}$

3. 6
4. 1

Love Your Calculator for Real, but Be Rational (page 112)

5. 5
6. $8 + 6i$

7. $\dfrac{3}{8}$ Rational.

8. $\dfrac{1}{6}$ Rational.

9. No result. Irrational.

10. $\dfrac{479109801431}{10000000000000}$ Rational.

Basic Rules (page 113)

1. x^5
2. x^1, or x
3. x^{12}
4. $12x^5$. Don't forget the coefficients!
5. $8x^6$
6. $3x^4$
7. x^3

Special Rules (page 114)

1. x^0, or 1
2. 1
3. x^{-3}, or $\dfrac{1}{x^3}$
4. $\dfrac{1}{x^3}$
5. x
6. 1
7. 0
8. 4
9. -8
10. -4
11. $\dfrac{1}{4}$
12. $\dfrac{4}{9}$

Roots (page 115)

1. $2\sqrt{x}$

2. $8\sqrt{x}$

3. Can't be combined!

4. $\sqrt{2xy}$

5. $\sqrt{x^2 y} = x\sqrt{y}$

6. $8\sqrt{36} = 8(6) = 48$

7. $\sqrt{36} = 6$

8. $\left(\sqrt{529} - \sqrt{361}\right)^{\frac{1}{2}} = (23 - 19)^{\frac{1}{2}} = (4)^{\frac{1}{2}} = 2$

Chapter 11
No More Algebra

Once you have a solid foundation in basic operations
and vocabulary, you are well-equipped to do a wide
variety of problems. This chapter will look at some of
the problems that test concepts you may have seen in
Algebra classes, and it will show how to work around
some of the toughest algebra problems.

ALGEBRA AND THE ACT

We've already seen in Chapter 10 some of the easier plug-and-chug algebra problems. Most questions that ACT considers "algebra" questions won't be so straightforward. ACT expects you to use algebra to solve word problems as well as plug-and-chug questions. Let's see how you can make this work in your favor.

HOW I LEARNED TO STOP WORRYING AND LOVE VARIABLES

Let's look at the following problem:

21. John has x red pencils, and three times as many red pencils as blue pencils. If he has four more yellow pencils than blue pencils, then in terms of x, how many yellow pencils does John have?

    A. $x + 4$

    B. $x + 7$

    C. $\dfrac{x}{6}$

    D. $\dfrac{x + 12}{6}$

    E. $\dfrac{x + 12}{3}$

Let's think about the bigger picture for a second here. We're all familiar with these x values from algebra class, but what we often forget is that x is substituting for some real value. Equations use x because that value is an unknown. The variable x could be 5 or 105 or 0.36491. In fact, the ACT writers are asking you to create an expression that will answer this question to find what that "certain number" is. And they want you to make it even harder on yourself by forgetting that x is a number at all.

PLUGGING IN

If you had \$1 dollar and you bought 2 pieces of candy at 25 cents apiece, how much change would you have? 50 cents, of course. If you had *d* dollars and bought *p* pieces of candy at *c* cents apiece, how much change would you have? Um, Letter of the Day.

Numbers are a lot easier to work with than variables. Therefore, when you see variables on the ACT, you can usually make things a lot easier on yourself by using numbers instead. Whenever there are variables in the answer choices or the problem, you can use Plugging In.

> Use Plugging In
>
> - when there are variables in the answer choices
> - when solving word problems or plug-and-chug questions
> - for questions of any difficulty level

Let's go back to #21:

———————————————

21. John has x red pencils and three times as many red pencils as blue pencils. If he has four more yellow pencils than blue pencils, then in terms of x, how many yellow pencils does John have?

   A. $x + 4$

   B. $x + 7$

   C. $\dfrac{x}{6}$

   D. $\dfrac{x + 12}{6}$

   E. $\dfrac{x + 12}{3}$

$3x +$

$\dfrac{1}{3}x + 4$

Here's How to Crack It

1. Know the Question. Underline "how many yellow pencils does John have?" We're not solving for x here, but for the number of yellow pencils. ACT just wants us to name the value "in terms of x."

2. Let the answers help. The answers help a lot here: Each contains the variable x, which means we can Plug In.

3. Break the problem into bite-sized pieces. We know we can Plug In. Let's take it step by step from there:

We want to make the math easy on ourselves, so let's say $x = 3$, so John has 3 red pencils. Now that we've dispensed with the variable, let's work the rest of the problem.

John has 3 red pencils and *three times as many red pencils as blue pencils*. He therefore must have 1 blue pencil. He has *four more yellow pencils than blue pencils*, so he must have 5 yellow pencils.

So now we can answer the question with what is called our *target answer*. The question asks *How many yellow pencils does John have?*, to which our answer is 5. Circle this answer on your paper. Let's go to the answer choices and see which one gives us our target. Remember, $x = 3$.

Make sure to keep your work organized when Plugging In! Always circle your target answer.

A.	$(3) + 4 = 7$	Not our target answer. Cross it off.
B.	$(3) + 7 = 10$	Not our target answer. Cross it off.
C.	$\dfrac{(3)}{6} = \dfrac{1}{2}$	Not our target answer. Cross it off.
D.	$\dfrac{(3) + 12}{6} = \dfrac{15}{6}$	Not our target answer. Cross it off.
E.	$\dfrac{(3) + 12}{3} = 5$	✔

Only choice (E) works, so this is our correct answer. Look how easy that was, and not a bit of algebra necessary! Let's try another.

17. For all $x \neq 3$, which of the following is equivalent to the expression $\dfrac{3x^2 - 7x - 6}{x - 3}$?

A. $3x + 2$

B. $3x - 2$

C. $3(x - 2)$

D. $3(x + 2)$

E. $x^2 - 2$

Here's How to Crack It

This looks a lot more like a standard plug-and-chug than the last problem did, but remember, we can always plug in when there are variables in the answer choices. This will be a tough problem to factor, so Plugging In will probably be your best bet, even if you're an ace with quadratic equations. The only thing the problem tells us is that $x \neq 3$, so let's say $x = 2$:

$$\frac{3(2)^2 - 7(2) - 6}{(2) - 3}$$

$$\frac{3(4) - 14 - 6}{-1}$$

$$\frac{-8}{-1} = 8$$

We now know that for the value we've chosen, the value of this expression is 8. That means **8** is our target answer. Let's plug our x value into the answer choices and find the one that matches the target:

A.	$3(2) + 2 = 8$	✔	This matches our target answer, but when you Plug In, always check all 5 answers.
B.	$3(2) - 2 = 6 - 2 = 4$		Not our target answer. Cross it off.
C.	$3((2) - 2) = 3\,(0) = 0$		Not our target answer. Cross it off.
D.	$3((2) + 2) = 3\,(4) = 12$		Not our target answer. Cross it off.
E.	$(2)^2 - 2 = 2$		Not our target answer. Cross it off.

Only choice (A) worked, and it is the correct answer. So as we can see, Plugging In works for all kinds of algebra problems. Let's review what we've done so far.

What To Do When You Plug In

1. Identify the opportunity. Can you plug in on this question?

2. Choose a good number. Make the math easy on yourself.

3. Find a target answer. Answer the question posed in the problem with your number, and circle your target answer.

4. Test all the answer choices. If two of them work, try a new number.

Let's try a tougher one.

—————————○—————————

36. In my dear Aunt Sally's math class, there are four exams. The first three exam scores are averaged, and the resulting score is averaged with the final exam score. If a, b, and c are the first three exam scores, and f is the final exam score, which of the following examples gives a student's final score in the class?

    F. $\dfrac{a+b+c}{3}+f$

    G. $\dfrac{a+b+c+3f}{6}$

    H. $\dfrac{a+b+c+f}{4}$

    J. $\dfrac{a+b+c+3f}{4}$

    K. $a+b+c+f$

Here's How to Crack It

This is a word problem, so remember the basic approach.

1. Know the question. Underline the question in this problem: *which of the following gives a student's final score in this class?*

2. Let the answers help. There are variables in each of these answer choices, which means we can Plug In, so these answers will help a lot. If you want to do a bit of POE, you might notice that the problem is asking for an average, so choice (K) can't work. Also, something funny will need to happen with the f variable, so you can eliminate choice (H).

3. Break the problem into bite-sized pieces. If you rush through this problem, it's very easy to mess up. Let's go piece by piece as we did in the earlier problem.

The first three exam scores are averaged.

There's no reason to give realistic exam scores here: We can pick whatever numbers we want, so let's use numbers that make the math easy. We know from this problem that the first three exam scores are represented by a, b, and c, so let's say $a = 2$, $b = 3$, and $c = 4$. The average of these three numbers can be found as follows: $\dfrac{2 + 3 + 4}{3} = \dfrac{9}{3} = 3$.

The resulting score is then averaged with the final score.

The resulting score is 3, and we need to plug in some final score, f. Let's use another easy number and say $f = 5$. In averaging these two numbers together, we find $\dfrac{3 + 5}{2} = \dfrac{8}{2} = 4$. Thus we have our target answer: A student's final score with these exam scores will be 4.

Let's go to the answer choices and look for the one that matches the target. Remember, $a = 2$, $b = 3$, $c = 4$, and $f = 5$.

F. $\dfrac{2 + 3 + 4}{3} + 5 = \dfrac{9}{3} + 5 = 8$ ✗

G. $\dfrac{2 + 3 + 4 + 3(5)}{6} = \dfrac{24}{6} = 4$ ✔

H. $\dfrac{2 + 3 + 4 + 5}{4} = \dfrac{14}{4} = 3.5$ ✗

J. $\dfrac{2 + 3 + 4 + 3(5)}{4} = \dfrac{24}{4} = 6$ ✗

K. $2 + 3 + 4 + 5 = 14$ ✗

Choice (G) is the correct answer, and no tough algebra necessary!

Hidden Plug-Ins

Both of the above questions have had variables in the answer choices, which is a dead giveaway that we can Plug In. The good news is that that's not the only time. In any problem in which there are hypothetical values or values relative to each other, Plugging In will work. Let's have a look at a problem.

25. If $x - z = 6$ and $y = 3x - 2 - 3z$, then $y = $?

    A.   2
    B.   4
    C. 14
    D. 16
    E. 18

Here's How to Crack It

There aren't any variables in the answer choices, but notice all values in the problem are defined relative to one another. Let's Plug In.

Using the first equation in the problem, let's make the numbers easy on ourselves and say $x = 8$ and $z = 2$. Using these values, let's find the value for the expression given in the problem: $y = 3(8) - 2 - 3(2) = 24 - 2 - 6 = 16$, choice (D).

It may feel like we just pulled these numbers out of thin air, but try any two numbers that work in the equation $x - z = 6$, and you'll find that it always works.

PLUGGING IN THE ANSWERS

So we've seen that Plugging In is a great strategy when there are variables in the question or the answers. How about when there aren't? Does that mean we have to go back to algebra? Of course not! On most problems on the ACT, there are a variety of ways to solve. Let's look at another one that helps to simplify the math in algebra-related problems.

2. If $600 were deposited in a bank account for one year and earned interest of $42, what was the interest rate?

   F. 6.26%
   G. 7.00%
   H. 8.00%
   J. 9.00%
   K. 9.50%

Before we get started cracking this problem, we should note a few things about it. First of all, there aren't any variables, but you get the feeling that you're going to have to put the $600 and the $42 in relationship to some other number by means of an algebraic expression. Then, notice that the problem is asking for a very specific number, the interest rate, and that the answer choices give possibilities for that specific number in ascending order. All of this taken together means that we can Plug In the Answers.

Plug In the Answers (PITA) when

- answer choices are numbers in ascending or descending order
- the question asks for a specific amount. Questions will usually be "what?" or "how many?"
- you get the urge to do algebra even when there are no variables in the problem

Let's see what this looks like.

---

2. If $600 were deposited in a bank account for one year and earned interest of $42, what was the interest rate?

    F. 6.26%
    G. 7.00%
    H. 8.00%
    J. 9.00%
    K. 9.50%

Here's How to Crack It

1. Know the question. As we've already identified, we need to find the *interest rate*.

2. Let the answers help. The way the answer choices are listed has already indicated that we'll be able to PITA on this problem, so we'll be using the answers a lot in this question.

3. Break the problem into bite-sized pieces. We're going to use the answer choices to walk through each step of the problem, working it in bite-sized pieces.

Because these answer choices are listed in ascending order, it will be best to start with the middle choice. That way, if it's too high or too low, we'll be able to use POE more efficiently.

Therefore, if we start with 8.00% as our interest rate, we can find what the annual interest on a $600 deposit would be by multiplying $600 × 0.08 = $48. Because the problem tells us that the deposit earned $42 of interest, we know choice (H) is too high, which also eliminates choices (J) and (K).

Let's try choice (G): You may find it helpful to keep your work organized in columns as shown below.

	Interest Rate	Rate per $600	= $42?	
F.	6.26%			
G.	7.00%	$42	Yes!	✔
H.	8.00%	$48	X	
J.	9.00%			
K.	9.50%			

We haven't introduced any of our own numbers into this problem, so once we find the correct answer, we can stop. The correct answer is choice (G).

Let's try a harder one.

---

49. In a piggy bank, there are pennies, nickels, dimes, and quarters that total $2.17 in value. If there are 3 times as many pennies as there are dimes, 1 more dime than nickels, and 2 more quarters than dimes, then how many pennies are in the piggy bank?

A. 12
B. 15
C. 18
D. 21
E. 24

Here's How to Crack It

1. Know the question. *How many pennies are in the bank?*

2. Let the answers help. There are no variables, but the very specific question coupled with the numerical answers in ascending order gives a pretty good indication that we can PITA.

3. Break the problem into bite-sized pieces. Make sure you take your time with this problem, because you'll need to multiply the number of each coin by its monetary value. In other words, don't forget that 1 nickel will count for 5 cents, 1 dime will count for 10 cents, and 1 quarter will count for 25 cents. As in the previous problem, let's set up some columns to keep our work organized and begin with choice (C).

Since ACT has already given us the answers, we will plug those answers in and work backwards. Each of the answers listed gives a possible value for the number of pennies. Using the information in the problem, we can work backwards from that number of pennies to find the number of nickels, dimes, and quarters. When the values for the number of coins adds up to $2.17, we know we're done.

If we begin with the assumption that there are 18 pennies, then there must be 6 dimes (*3 times as many pennies as there are dimes*). 6 dimes means 5 nickels (*1 more dime than nickels*) and 8 quarters (*2 more quarters than dimes*).

Now multiply the number of coins by the monetary value of each and see if they total $2.17.

	Pennies ($P)	Dimes ($D)	Nickels ($N)	Quarters ($Q)	Total = $2.17?
C.	18 ($0.18)	6 ($0.60)	5 ($0.25)	8 ($2.00)	Total = $3.03

That's too high, so not only is choice (C) incorrect, but also choices (D) and (E). Cross them off and try choice (B).

	Pennies ($P)	Dimes ($D)	Nickels ($N)	Quarters ($Q)	Total = $2.17?
A.	12 ($0.12)	4 ($0.40)	3 ($0.15)	6 ($1.50)	Total = $2.17 ✔
B.	15 ($0.15)	5 ($0.50)	4 ($0.20)	7 ($1.75)	Total = $2.60 X
C.	18 ($0.18)	6 ($0.60)	5 ($0.25)	8 ($2.00)	Total = $3.03 X
D.	21	Eliminated through POE			
E.	24	Eliminated through POE			

Only choice (A) works. No algebra necessary!

_____

A NOTE ON PLUGGING IN AND PITA

Plugging In and PITA are not the only ways to solve these problems, and it may feel weird using these methods instead of trying to do these problems "the real way." You may have even found that you knew how to work with the variables in Plugging In problems or how to write the appropriate equations for the PITA problems. If you can do either of those things, you're already on your way to a great Math score.

But think about it this way. We've already said that ACT doesn't give any partial credit. So do you think doing it "the real way" gets you any extra points? It doesn't: On the ACT, a right answer is a right answer, no matter how you get it. "The real way" is great, but unfortunately, it's often a lot more complex and offers a lot more opportunities to make careless errors.

The biggest problem with doing things the real way, though, is that it essentially requires that you invent a new approach for every problem. Instead, notice what we've given you here: two strategies that will work toward getting you the right answer on any number of questions. You may have heard the saying, "Give a man a fish and you've fed him for a day, but teach a man to fish and you've fed him for a lifetime." Now, don't worry, our delusions of grandeur are not quite so extreme, but Plugging In and PITA are useful in a similar way. Rather than giving you a detailed description of how to create formulas and work through them for these problems that won't themselves ever appear on an ACT again, we're giving you a strategy that will help you to work through any number of similar problems in future ACTs.

Try these strategies on your own in the drill that concludes this chapter.

Algebra Drill

For the answers to this drill, please go to Chapter 24.

1. What is the largest value of x that solves the equation $x^2 - 4x + 3 = 0$?

A. 1
B. 2
C. 3
~~D. 4~~
~~E. 5~~

2. For all $\dfrac{x^2 + 6x - 27}{(x+9)} = ?$

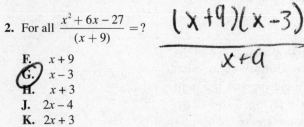

$$\dfrac{(x+9)(x-3)}{x+9}$$

F. $x + 9$
G. $x - 3$
H. $x + 3$
J. $2x - 4$
K. $2x + 3$

3. If 2 less than 3 times a certain number is the same as 4 more than the product of 5 and 3, what is the number?

A. 7
B. 10
C. 11
D. 14
E. 15

$$3x - 2 = 4 + 15$$

19

21

4. A certain number of books are to be given away at a promotion. If $\dfrac{2}{5}$ of the books are distributed in the morning and $\dfrac{1}{3}$ of the remaining books are distributed in the afternoon, what fraction of the books remains to be distributed the next day?

F. $\dfrac{1}{5}$
G. $\dfrac{2}{5}$
H. $\dfrac{1}{3}$
J. $\dfrac{5}{7}$
K. $\dfrac{8}{9}$

5. In the equation $a = \dfrac{3}{b}$, b is a positive, real number. As the value of b is increased so it becomes closer and closer to infinity, what happens to the value of a ?

A. It remains constant.
B. It gets closer and closer to zero.
C. It gets closer and closer to one.
D. It gets closer and closer to three.
E. It gets closer and closer to infinity.

Summary

o   Remember the basic approach for Word Problems.
  • Know the question.
  • Let the answers help.
  • Break the problem into bite-sized pieces.

o   Use Plugging In when there are variables in the answer choices or the problem. Keep the following pointers in mind:
  • Choose numbers that make the math easy.
  • Try all the answer choices.
  • On more complex problems, keep your variables straight!

o   Use Plugging In the Answers (PITA) when answer choices are listed in ascending or descending order and when the question is asking for a specific number. Keep the following pointers in mind:
  • Start with choice (C) or (H) to help with POE.
  • When you find the correct answer, STOP!

Chapter 12
Plane Geometry

The ACT test writers tell us there will be 23 geometry questions on the Math test, 14 of which supposedly cover plane geometry. It's better, however, to think of the topic breakdown in broader terms rather than these specific numbers. For one thing, many problems incorporate several concepts: You even need algebra to solve many geometry questions, so would the ACT test writers count a question like that in the algebra or plane geometry column?

What matters most is that you can identify the topics that can make a question Now, Later, or Never for you.

While occasionally ACT test writers may throw in a more advanced formula or complex shape, the majority of the questions test the basic rules on the basic shapes. This chapter will review a cross-section of those formulas and concepts, and give you a strategic approach to apply those rules on the ACT.

CRACKING THE GEOMETRY ON THE ACT

Plug-and-chug geometry questions can have so much information in them that they feel like word problems. So treat them like word problems. Let's review the basic approach to word problems. We'll then add some points specific to geometry.

Step 1: Know the Question

Know the question. Read the whole problem before calculating anything, and underline the actual question.

Step 2: Let the Answers Help

Let the answers help. Look for clues on how to solve and ways to use POE (Process of Elimination).

Step 3: Break the Problem into Bite-Sized Pieces

Break the problem into bite-sized pieces. When you read the problem a second time, calculate at each step necessary and watch out for tricky phrasing.

For geometry questions, Step 3 has two specific additions:

> **Step 3a:** Write all the information given in the problem on the figure. If there is no figure, draw your own.
>
> **Step 3b:** Write down any formulas you need and fill in any information you have.

Geometry BFFs: POE and Ballparking

Step 2 of the basic approach is particularly important to geometry questions. In the last few chapters, we've seen how POE and Ballparking can help to narrow down the answer choices when you're confused. Before you rush to calculate, Ballparking in particular will help you a ton on geometry problems because most figures are drawn to scale.

To Scale or Not to Scale?

That is the question. The ACT makes a big deal in the instructions about the fact that their figures are "NOT necessarily drawn to scale." Here's the thing, though: They usually are drawn to scale, or at least enough to use them in broad strokes. Use Ballparking to eliminate answers that are too big or too small, rather than to determine a precise value. Questions on angles and area especially lend themselves to Ballparking. The main place to be skeptical is on those problems that ask questions like, "Which of the following must be true?" Those are the ones whose figures can be purposely misleading.

In most other cases, if you know how to use the figures that are given (or how to draw your own), you can eliminate several wrong answers before doing any math at all. Let's see how this works.

How Big Is Angle *NLM* ?

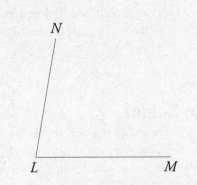

Obviously, you don't know exactly how big this angle is, but it would be easy to compare it with an angle whose measure you *do* know exactly. Let's compare it with a 90-degree angle.

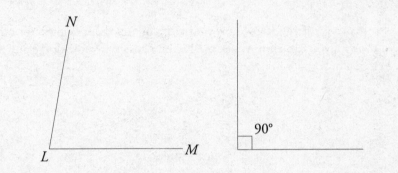

Angle *NLM* is clearly a bit less than 90°. Now look at the following problem, which asks about the same angle *NLM*.

1. In the figure below, *O*, *N*, and *M* are collinear. If the lengths of *ON* and *NL* are the same, and the measure of angle *LON* is 30° and angle *LMN* is 40°, what is the measure of angle *NLM*?

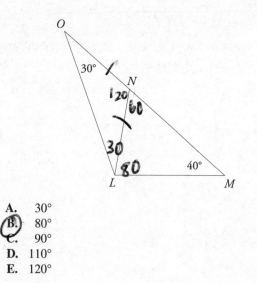

A.   30°
B.   80°
C.   90°
D.   110°
E.   120°

Here's How to Crack It

Start with Step 1: Know the question. Underline "what is the measure of angle *NLM*?" and even mark the angle on your figure. You don't want to answer for the wrong angle. Now move to Step 2 and let's focus on eliminating answer choices that don't make sense. We've already decided that ∠*NLM* is a little less than 90°, which means we can eliminate choices (C), (D), and (E). How much less than 90°? 30° is a third of 90. Could ∠*NLM* be that small? No way! The answer to this question must be choice (B).

In this case, it wasn't necessary to do any "real" geometry at all to get the question right, but it took about half the time. ACT has to give you credit for right answers no matter how you get them. Revenge is sweet. What's more, if you worked this problem the "real" way, you might have picked one of the other answers: As you can imagine, every answer choice gives some partial answer that you would've seen as you worked the problem.

Let's Do It Again

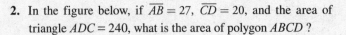

2. In the figure below, if $\overline{AB} = 27$, $\overline{CD} = 20$, and the area of triangle $ADC = 240$, what is the area of polygon $ABCD$?

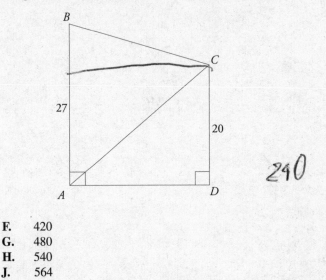

240

F. 420
G. 480
H. 540
J. 564
K. 1,128

Here's How to Crack It

Start with Step 1: Know the question. Underline "what is the area of polygon *ABCD*?" This polygon is not a conventional figure, but if we had to choose one figure that the polygon resembled, we might pick a rectangle. Try drawing a line at a right angle from the line segment $\overline{AB}$ so that it touches point *C*, thus creating a rectangle. It should look like this:

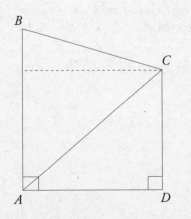

The area of polygon *ABCD* is equal to the area of the rectangle you've just formed, plus a little bit at the top. The problem tells you that the area of triangle *ADC* is 240. What is the area of the rectangle you just created? If you said 480, you are exactly right, whether you knew the geometric rules that applied or whether you just measured it with your eyes.

So the area of the rectangle is 480. Roughly speaking, then, what should the area of the polygon be? A little more. Let's look at the answer choices.

> ### What Should I Do If There Is No Diagram?
> Draw one! It's always easier to understand a problem when you can see it in front of you. If possible, draw your figure to scale so that you can estimate the answer as well.

Choices (F) and (G) are either less than or equal to 480; get rid of them. Choices (H) and (J) both seem possible; they are both a little more than 480; let's hold on to them. Choice (K) seems pretty crazy. We want more than 480, but 1,128 is ridiculous.

The answer to this question is choice (J). To get this final answer, you'll need to use a variety of area formulas, which we'll explore later in this chapter. For now, though, notice that your chances of guessing have increased from 20% to 50% with a little bit of quick thinking. Now what should you do? If you know how to do the problem, you do it. If you don't or if you are running out of time, you guess and move on.

However, even as we move in to the "real" geometry in the remainder of this chapter, don't forget:

> Always look for opportunities to Ballpark on geometry problems even if you know how to do them the "real" way.

GEOMETRY REVIEW

By using the diagrams ACT has so thoughtfully provided, and by making your own diagrams when they are not provided, you can often eliminate several of the answer choices. In some cases, you'll be able to eliminate every choice but one. Of course, you will also need to know the actual geometry concepts that ACT is testing. We've divided our review into the following four topics:

1. Angles and lines
2. Triangles
3. Four-sided figures
4. Circles

ANGLES AND LINES

Here is a line.

$$A \qquad B \qquad C$$
$$\rule{6cm}{0.4pt} \, l_1$$

A line extends forever in either direction. This line, called l_1, has three points on it: *A, B,* and *C.* These three points are said to be **collinear** because they are all on the same line. The piece of the line in between points *A* and *B* is called a line **segment**. ACT will refer to it as segment *AB* or simply $\overline{AB}$. *A* and *B* are the **endpoints** of segment *AB*.

A line forms an angle of 180°. If that line is cut by another line, it divides that 180° into two pieces that together add up to 180°.

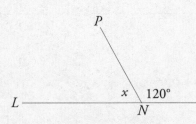

In the above diagram, what is the value of *x*? If you said 60°, you are correct. To find ∠*x*, just subtract 120° from 180°.

An angle can also be described by points on the lines that intersect to form the angle and the point of intersection itself, with the middle letter corresponding to the point of intersection. For example, in the previous diagram, $\angle x$ could also be described as $\angle LNP$. On the ACT, instead of writing out "angle LNP," they'll use math shorthand and put $\angle LNP$ instead. So "angle x" becomes $\angle x$.

If there are 180° above a line, there are also 180° below the line, for a total of 360°.

When two lines intersect, they form four angles, represented below by letters A, B, C, and D. $\angle A$ and $\angle B$ together form a straight line, so they add up to 180°.

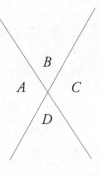

Angles that add up to 180° are called **supplementary** angles. $\angle A$ and $\angle C$ are opposite from each other and always equal each other, as do $\angle B$ and $\angle D$. Angles like these are called **vertical** angles.

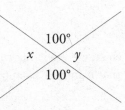

In the previous figure, what is the value of $\angle x$? If you said 80°, you're right. Together with the 100° angle, x forms a straight line. What is the value of $\angle y$? If you said 80°, you're right again. These two angles are vertical and must equal each other. The four angles together add up to 360°.

When two lines meet in such a way that 90° angles are formed, the lines are called **perpendicular**. The little box at the point of the intersection of the two lines below indicates that they are perpendicular. It stands to reason that all four of these angles have a value of 90°.

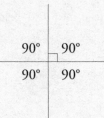

When two lines in the same plane are drawn so that they could extend into infinity without ever meeting, they are called **parallel**. In the figure below, l_1 is parallel to l_2. The symbol for parallel is ||.

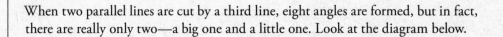

When two parallel lines are cut by a third line, eight angles are formed, but in fact, there are really only two—a big one and a little one. Look at the diagram below.

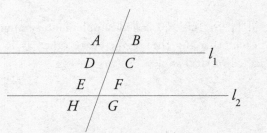

If $\angle A = 110°$, then $\angle B$ must equal 70° (together they form a straight line). $\angle D$ is vertical to $\angle B$, which means that it must also equal 70°. $\angle C$ is vertical to $\angle A$, so it must equal 110°.

The four angles $\angle E$, $\angle F$, $\angle G$, and $\angle H$ are in exactly the same proportion as the angles above. The little angles are both 70°. The big angles are both 110°.

Try the following problem.

1. In the figure below, line L is parallel to line M. Line N intersects both L and M, with angles a, b, c, d, e, f, g, and h as shown. Which of the following lists includes all the angles that are supplementary to $\angle a$?

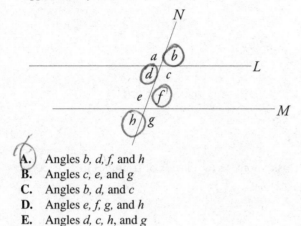

A. Angles b, d, f, and h
B. Angles c, e, and g
C. Angles b, d, and c
D. Angles e, f, g, and h
E. Angles d, c, h, and g

Here's How to Crack It

An angle is supplementary to another angle if the two angles together add up to 180°. Because $\angle a$ is one of the eight angles formed by the intersection of a line with two parallel lines, we know that there are really only two angles: a big one and a little one. $\angle a$ is a big one. Thus only the small angles would be supplementary to it. Which angles are those? The correct answer is choice (A). By the way, if you think back to the last chapter and apply what you learned there, could you have Plugged In on this problem? Of course you could have. After all, there are variables in the answer choices. Sometimes it is easier to see the correct answer if you substitute real values for the angles instead of just looking at them as a series of variables. Just because a problem involves geometry doesn't mean that you can't Plug In on it.

$$N$$

$$a = 100° \quad b = 80°$$
$$d = 80° \quad c = 100° \qquad L$$

$$e = 100° \quad f = 80°$$
$$h = 80° \quad g = 100° \qquad M$$

TRIANGLES

A triangle is a three-sided figure whose inside angles always add up to 180°. The largest angle of a triangle is always opposite its largest side. Thus, in triangle *XYZ* below, *XY* would be the largest side, followed by *YZ*, followed by *XZ*. On the ACT, "triangle *XYZ*" will be written as Δ*XYZ*.

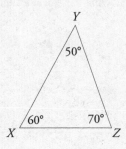

The ACT likes to ask about certain kinds of triangles in particular.

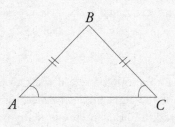

An **isosceles** triangle has two equal sides. The angles opposite those sides are also equal. In the isosceles triangle above, if ∠*A* = 50°, then so does ∠*C*. If $\overline{AB}$ = 6, then so does $\overline{BC}$.

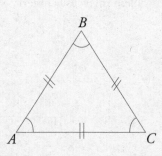

An **equilateral** triangle has three equal sides and three equal angles. Because the three equal angles must add up to 180°, all three angles of an equilateral triangle are always equal to 60°.

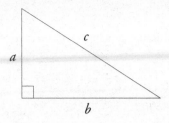

A **right triangle** has one inside angle that is equal to 90°. The longest side of a right triangle (the one opposite the 90° angle) is called the **hypotenuse**.

Pythagoras, a Greek mathematician, discovered that the sides of a right triangle are always in a particular proportion, which can be expressed by the formula $a^2 + b^2 = c^2$, where a and b are the shorter sides of the triangle, and c is the hypotenuse. This formula is called the **Pythagorean theorem**.

There are certain right triangles that the test writers at ACT find endlessly fascinating. Let's test out the Pythagorean theorem on the first of these.

$$3^2 + 4^2 = c^2$$
$$9 + 16 = 25$$
$$c^2 = 25, \text{ so } c = 5$$

The ACT writers adore the 3-4-5 triangle and use it frequently, along with its multiples, such as the 6-8-10 triangle and the 9-12-15 triangle. Of course, you can always use the Pythagorean theorem to figure out the third side of a right triangle, as long as you have the other two sides, but because ACT problems almost invariably use "triples" like the ones we've just mentioned, it makes sense just to memorize them.

The ACT has three commonly used right-triangle triples.

3-4-5 (and its multiples)

5-12-13 (and its multiples)

7-24-25 (not as common as the other two)

Pythagoras's *Other* Theorem

Pythagoras also developed a theory about the transmigration of souls. So far, this has not been proven, nor will it help you on this exam.

Don't Get Snared

- Is this a 3-4-5 triangle?

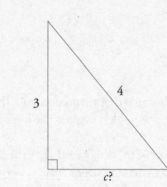

No, because the hypotenuse of a right triangle must be its *longest* side—the one opposite the 90° angle. In this case, we must use the Pythagorean theorem to discover side c: $3^2 + c^2 = 16$. $c = \sqrt{7}$.

- Is this a 5-12-13 triangle?

No, because the Pythagorean theorem—and triples—apply only to *right* triangles. We can't determine definitively the third side of this triangle based on the angles.

The Isosceles Right Triangle

As fond as the ACT test writers are of triples, they are even fonder of two other right triangles. The first is called the **isosceles right triangle**. The sides and angles of the isosceles right triangle are always in a particular proportion.

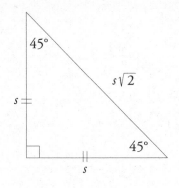

You could use the Pythagorean theorem to prove this (or you could just take our word for it). Whatever the value of the two equal sides of the isosceles right triangle, the hypotenuse is always equal to one of those sides times $\sqrt{2}$. Here are two examples.

> ### Be on the Lookout...
> for problems in which the application of the Pythagorean theorem is not obvious. For example, every rectangle contains two right triangles. That means that if you know the length and width of the rectangle, you also know the length of the diagonal, which is the hypotenuse of both triangles created by the diagonal.

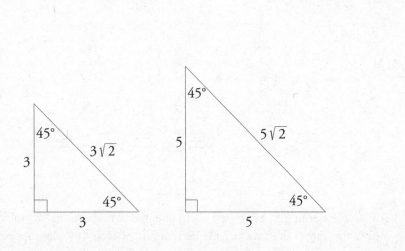

The 30-60-90 Triangle

The other right triangle tested frequently on the ACT is the **30-60-90 triangle**, which also always has the same proportions.

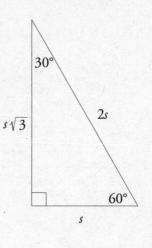

You can use the Pythagorean theorem to prove this (or you can just take our word for it). Whatever the value of the short side of the 30-60-90 triangle, the hypotenuse is always twice as large. The medium side is always equal to the short side times $\sqrt{3}$. Here are two examples.

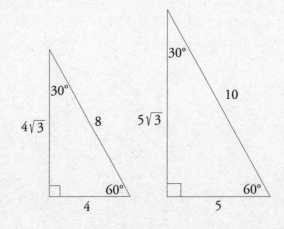

Because these triangles are tested so frequently, it makes sense to memorize the proportions, rather than waste time deriving them each time they appear.

Don't Get Snared

- In the isosceles right triangle below, are the sides equal to $3\sqrt{2}$?

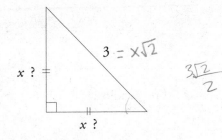

No. Remember, in an isosceles right triangle, hypotenuse = the side $\sqrt{2}$. In this case, 3 = the side $\sqrt{2}$. If we solve for the side, we get $\dfrac{3}{\sqrt{2}}$ = the side.

For arcane mathematical reasons, we are not supposed to leave a radical in the denominator, but we can multiply top and bottom by $\sqrt{2}$ to get $\dfrac{3\sqrt{2}}{2}$.

- In the right triangle below, is x equal to $4\sqrt{3}$?

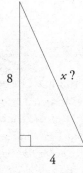

No. Even though it is one of ACT's favorites, you have to be careful not to see a 30-60-90 where none exists. In the triangle above, the short side is half of the *medium* side, not half of the hypotenuse. This is some sort of right triangle all right, but it is not a 30-60-90. The hypotenuse, in case you're curious, is really $4\sqrt{5}$.

Area

The **area** of a triangle can be found using the following formula:

$$\text{area} = \frac{\text{base} \times \text{height}}{2}$$

Height is measured as the perpendicular distance from the base of the triangle to its highest point.

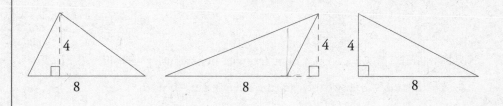

In all three of the above triangles, the area is:

$$\frac{8 \times 4}{2} = 16$$

Don't Get Snared

- Sometimes the height of a triangle can be *outside* the triangle itself, as we just saw in the second example.
- In a right triangle, the height of the triangle can also be one of the sides of the triangle, as we just saw in the third example. However, be careful when finding the area of a *non-right* triangle. Simply because you know two sides of the triangle does not mean that you have the height of the triangle.

Similar Triangles

Two triangles are called similar if their angles have the same degree measures. This means their sides will be in proportion. For example, the two triangles below are similar.

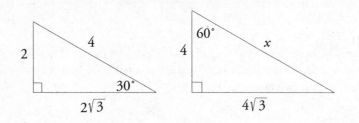

Because the sides of the two triangles are in the same proportion, you can find the missing side, *x*, by setting up a proportion equation.

$$\begin{array}{ccc} & \text{small triangle} & \text{big triangle} \\ \dfrac{\text{short leg}}{\text{hypotenuse}} & \dfrac{2}{4} & = & \dfrac{4}{x} \\ & x = 8 \end{array}$$

$$\frac{4}{2} = \frac{x}{4}$$

$$x = 8$$

ACT TRIANGLE PROBLEMS

In this chapter, we've pretty much given you all the basic triangle information you'll need to do the triangle problems on the ACT. The trick is that you'll have to use a lot of this information all at once. Let's have a look at a typical ACT triangle problem and see how to use the basic approach.

3. In the figure below, square *ABCD* is attached to △*ADE* as shown. If △*EAD* is equal to 30° and $\overline{AE}$ is equal to $4\sqrt{3}$, then what is the area of square *ABCD* ?

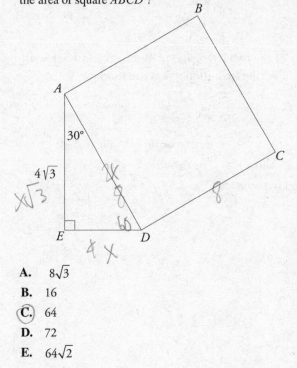

A. $8\sqrt{3}$
B. 16
C. 64
D. 72
E. $64\sqrt{2}$

Here's How to Crack It

Start with Step 1: Know the question. Underline "what is the area of square *ABCD*?" Move to Step 2 and look at the answers. We don't have any values for areas of other shapes within the figure, so there is nothing to Ballpark. But note the presence of $\sqrt{2}$ and $\sqrt{3}$ in the answers: they're an additional clue, if you haven't absorbed the info given, that either 30-60-90 and/or 45-45-90 triangles are in play.

The triangle in the figure is in fact a 30-60-90. Now move to Step 3: Break the problem into bite-sized pieces. Because angle *A* is the short angle, the side opposite that angle is equal to 4 and the hypotenuse is equal to 8. Now move on to Step 3a: mark your figure with these values. Now move to Step 3b: Write down any formulas you need. The area for a square is s^2. Because that hypotenuse is also the side of the square, the area of the square must be 8 times 8, or 64. This is choice (C). If you forgot the ratio of the sides of a 30-60-90 triangle, go back and review it. You'll need it.

POE Pointers

If you didn't remember the ratio of the sides of a 30-60-90 triangle, could you have eliminated some answers using POE? Of course. Let's see if we can use the diagram to eliminate some answer choices.

The diagram tells us that $\overline{AE}$ has length $4\sqrt{3}$. Remember the important approximations we gave you earlier in the chapter? A good approximation for $\sqrt{3}$ is 1.7. So $4\sqrt{3}$ = approximately 6.8. We can now use this to estimate the sides of square $ABCD$. Just using your eyes, would you say that $\overline{AD}$ is longer or shorter than $\overline{AE}$? Of course it's a bit longer; it's the hypotenuse of $\triangle ADE$. You decide and write down what you think it might be. To find the area of the square, simply square whatever value you decided the side equaled. This is your answer.

Now all you have to do is see which of the answer choices still makes sense. Could the answer be choice (A)? $8\sqrt{3}$ equals roughly 13.6. Is this close to your answer? No way. Could the answer be choice (B), which is 16? Still much too small. Could the answer be choice (C), which is 64? Quite possibly. Could the answer be 72? It might be. Could the correct answer be $64\sqrt{2}$? An approximation of radical 2 = 1.4, so $64\sqrt{2}$ equals 89.6. This seems rather large. Thus, on this problem, by using POE we could eliminate choices (A), (B), and (E).

FOUR-SIDED FIGURES

The interior angles of any four-sided figure (also known as a quadrilateral) add up to 360°. The most common four-sided figures on the ACT are the rectangle and the square, with the parallelogram and the trapezoid coming in a far distant third and fourth.

Your Friend the Triangle
Because a quadrilateral is really just two triangles, its interior angles must measure twice those of a triangle: 2(180) = 360.

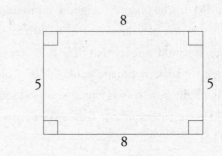

A **rectangle** is a four-sided figure whose four interior angles are each equal to 90°. The area of a rectangle is *base* × *height*. Therefore, the area of the rectangle above is 8 (*base*) × 5 (*height*) = 40. The perimeter of a rectangle is the sum of all four of its sides. The perimeter of the rectangle above is 8 + 8 + 5 + 5 = 26.

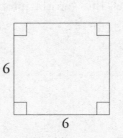

A **square** is a rectangle whose four sides are all equal in length. You can think of the area of a square, therefore, as **side squared**. The area of the above square is 6 (*base*) × 6 (*height*) = 36. The perimeter is 24, or 4*s*.

A **parallelogram** is a four-sided figure made up of two sets of parallel lines. We said earlier that when parallel lines are crossed by a third line, eight angles are formed but that in reality there are only two—the big one and the little one. In a parallelogram, 16 angles are formed, but there are still, in reality, only two.

The area of a parallelogram is also *base × height*, but because of the shape of the figure, the height of a parallelogram is not necessarily equal to one of its sides. Height is measured by a perpendicular line drawn from the base to the top of the figure. The area of the parallelogram above is $9 \times 5 = 45$.

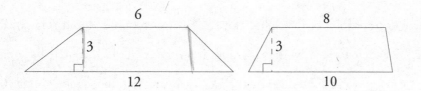

A **trapezoid** is a four-sided figure in which two sides are parallel. Both of the figures above are trapezoids. The area of a trapezoid is the *average of the two parallel sides × the height*, or $\frac{1}{2}$ (*base* 1 + *base* 2)(*height*), but on ACT problems involving trapezoids, there is almost always some easy way to find the area without knowing the formula (for example, by dividing the trapezoid into two triangles and a rectangle). In both trapezoids above, the area is 27.

$avg\ 2// \times h$

OR

$\frac{1}{2}(b_1 + b_2)h$

Geometry Hint
If there isn't a figure, always draw your own.

Doh, I'm in a Square!
To help you remember the area of a four-sided figure (a square, a rectangle, or a parallelogram), imagine that Bart and Homer Simpson are stuck inside of it. To get its area, just multiply **B**art times **H**omer, or (*b*)(*h*), or the base times the height.

CIRCLES

The distance from the center of a circle to any point on the circle is called the **radius**. The distance from one point on a circle through the center of the circle to another point on the circle is called the **diameter**. The diameter is always equal to twice the radius. In the circle on the left below, *AB* is called a **chord**. *CD* is called a **tangent** to the circle.

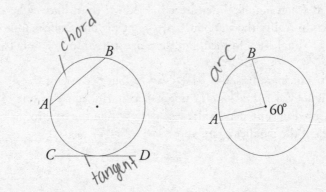

The curved portion of the right-hand circle between points *A* and *B* is called an **arc**. The angle formed by drawing lines from the center of the circle to points *A* and *B* is said to be **subtended** by the arc. There are 360° in a circle, so that if the angle we just mentioned equaled 60°, it would take up $\frac{60}{360}$ or $\frac{1}{6}$ of the degrees in the entire circle. It would also take up $\frac{1}{6}$ of the area of the circle and $\frac{1}{6}$ of the outer perimeter of the circle, called the **circumference**.

> The formula for the **area** of a circle is πr^2.
>
> The formula for the **circumference** is $2\pi r$.

In the circle below, if the radius is 4, then the area is 16π, and the circumference is 8π.

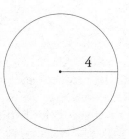

The key to circle problems on the ACT is to look for the word or phrase that tells you what to do. If you see the word *circumference*, immediately write down the formula for circumference, and plug in any numbers the problem has given you. By solving for whatever quantity is still unknown, you have probably already answered the problem. Another tip is to find the radius. The radius is the key to many circle problems.

---

1. If the area of a circle is 16 meters, what is its radius in meters?

    A. $\dfrac{8}{\pi}$

    B. 12π

    C. $\dfrac{4\sqrt{\pi}}{\pi}$

    D. $\dfrac{16}{\pi}$

    E. $144\pi^2$

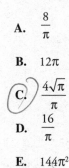

Here's How to Crack It

Step 1: Know the question. We need to solve for the radius. Step 2: Let the answers help. We don't have a figure, so there's nothing to Ballpark. But no figure? Step 3a: Draw your own.

Step 3b: Write down any formulas you need and fill in the information you have. Set the formula for area of a circle equal to $\pi r^2 = 16$. The problem is asking for the radius, so you have to solve for r. If you divide both sides by π, you get

$$r^2 = \frac{16}{\pi}$$

$$r = \sqrt{\frac{16}{\pi}}$$

$$= \frac{4}{\sqrt{\pi}}$$

$$= \frac{4\sqrt{\pi}}{\pi}$$

The correct answer is choice (C).

2. In the figure below, the circle with center O is inscribed inside square $ABCD$ as shown. If a side of the square measures 8 units, what is the area of the shaded region?

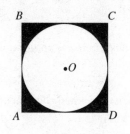

F. $8 - 16\pi$

G. 8π

H. 16π

J. $64 - 16\pi$

K. 64π

Here's How to Crack It

Begin with Step 1 and underline "what is the area of the shaded region?" Step 2 brings us to the answers, and we see all of the answers have π in them. There is no obvious choice to Ballpark just yet, so move to Step 3. Break the problem into bite-sized pieces, but don't get hung up on "inscribed." Yes, that's an important term to know, but since we have the figure, it's irrelevant. Move to Step 3a and 3b: Mark the side of the square "8" and write down the formulas for the area of a circle and square: πr^2 and s^2.

Is there a formula for the shape made by the shaded region? Nope. We just need the basic formulas for the basic shapes. $8^2 = 64$, so we at least know the shaded region is less than 64, the area of the square. But what's the link between the square and the circle? The side of the square equals the diameter. So if the diameter is 8, then the radius must be 4. Use that in the area formula, and $4^2\pi = 16\pi$. Subtract the area of the circle from the area of the square, and we get choice (J).

FUN FACTS ABOUT FIGURES

Read and review the following facts you need to know about plane geometry.

Angle Facts

- There are 90° in a right angle.
- When two straight lines intersect, angles opposite each other are equal.
- There are 180° in a straight line.
- Two lines are perpendicular when they meet at a 90° angle.
- The sign for perpendicular is ⊥ .
- Bisect means to cut exactly in half.
- There are 180° in a triangle.
- There are 360° in any four-sided figure.

Triangle Facts

In any triangle

- The longest side is opposite the largest angle.
- The shortest side is opposite the smallest angle.
- All angles add up to 180°.
- Area = $\frac{1}{2}$ (base × height) = $\frac{1}{2}bh$
- The height is the perpendicular distance from the base to the opposite vertex.
- Perimeter is the sum of the sides.
- The third side of any triangle is always less than the sum and greater than the difference of the other two sides.

In an isosceles triangle

- Two sides are equal.
- The two angles opposite the equal sides are also equal.

In an equilateral triangle

- All three sides are equal.
- All angles are each equal to 60°.

Four-Sided Figure Facts

In a quadrilateral
- All four angles add up to 360°.

In a parallelogram
- Opposite sides are parallel and equal.
- Opposite angles are equal.
- Adjacent angles are supplementary (add up to 180°).
- Area = base × height = bh
- The height is the perpendicular distance from the base to the opposite side.

In a rhombus
- Opposite sides are parallel.
- Opposite angles are equal.
- Adjacent angles are supplementary (add up to 180°).
- All 4 sides are equal.
- Area = base × height = bh
- The height is the perpendicular distance from the base to the opposite side.
- The diagonals are perpendicular.

In a rectangle
- Rectangles are special parallelograms; thus, any fact about parallelograms also applies to rectangles.
- All 4 angles are each equal to 90°.
- Area = length × width = lw
- Perimeter = 2(length) + 2(width) = $2l + 2w$
- The diagonals are equal.

In a square
- Squares are special rectangles; thus, any fact about rectangles also applies to squares.
- All 4 sides are equal.
- Area = (side)^2 = s^2
- Perimeter = 4(side) = $4s$
- The diagonals are perpendicular.

Circle Facts

Circle
- There are 360° in a circle.

Radius (r)
- The distance from the center to any point on the edge of the circle.
- All radii in a circle are equal.

Diameter (d)
- The distance of a line that connects two points on the edge of the circle, passing through the center.
- The longest line in a circle.
- Equals twice the radius.

Chord
- Any line segment connecting two points on the edge of a circle.
- The longest chord is called the diameter.

Circumference (C)
- The distance around the outside of the circle.
- $C = 2\pi r = \pi d$

Arc
- Any part of the circumference.
- The length of an arc is proportional to the size of the interior angle.

Area
- The amount of space within the boundaries of the circle.
- $A = \pi r^2$

Sector
- Any part of the area formed by two radii and the outside of the circle.
- The area of a sector is proportional to the size of the interior angle.

Line Facts

Line
- A line has no width and extends infinitely in both directions.
- Any line measures 180°.
- A line that contains points A and B is called $\overleftrightarrow{AB}$ (line AB).
- If a figure on the ACT looks like a straight line, and that line looks like it contains a point, it does.

Ray
- A ray extends infinitely in one direction but has an endpoint.
- The degree measure of a ray is 180°.
- A ray with endpoint A that goes through point B is called $\overrightarrow{AB}$. Pay attention to the arrow above the points and the order they are given; those will determine the direction the ray is pointing!

Line Segment
- A line segment is a part of a line and has two endpoints.
- The degree measure of a line segment is 180°.
- A line segment, which has endpoints of A and B, is written as $\overline{AB}$.

Tangents
- Tangent means intersecting at one point. For example, a line tangent to a circle intersects exactly one point on the circumference of the circle. Two circles that touch at just one point are also tangent.
- A tangent line to a circle is always perpendicular to the radius drawn to that point of intersection.
- If $\overline{AB}$ intersects a circle at point T, then you would say, "$\overline{AB}$ is tangent to the circle at point T."

PLANE GEOMETRY FORMULAS

Here's a list of all the plane geometry formulas that could show up on the ACT. Memorize the formulas for perimeter/circumference, area, and volume for basic shapes. ACT usually provides the more advanced formulas if they are needed.

Circles

- Area: $A = \pi r^2$
- Circumference: $C = 2\pi r = \pi d$

Triangles

- Area: $A = \dfrac{1}{2}bh$

- Perimeter: P = sum of the sides

- Pythagorean theorem: $a^2 + b^2 = c^2$

SOHCAHTOA

- $\sin(\theta) = \dfrac{\text{opposite}}{\text{adjacent}}$

- $\cos(\theta) = \dfrac{\text{opposite}}{\text{adjacent}}$

- $\tan(\theta) = \dfrac{\text{opposite}}{\text{adjacent}}$

- $\csc(\theta) = \dfrac{1}{\sin}$

- $\sec(\theta) = \dfrac{1}{\cos}$

- $\cot(\theta) = \dfrac{1}{\tan}$

Quadrilaterals

Parallelograms

- Area: $A = bh$
- Perimeter: P = sum of the sides

Rhombus

- Area: $A = bh$
- Perimeter: P = sum of the sides

Trapezoids

- Area: $A = \dfrac{1}{2} h \left(b_1 + b_2 \right)$
- Perimeter: P = sum of the sides

Rectangles

- Area: $A = lw$
- Perimeter: $P = 2(l + w)$

Squares

- Area: $A = s^2$
- Perimeter: $P = 4s$

Polygons

- Sum of angles in an n-sided polygon: $\left(n - 2 \right) 180°$
- Angle measure of each angle in a regular n-sided polygon:

  $$\dfrac{\left(n - 2 \right) 180°}{n}$$

3-D Figures

- Surface area of a rectangular solid: $S = 2 \left(lw + lh + wh \right)$
- Surface area of a cube: $S = 6s^2$
- Surface area of a right circular cylinder: $S = 2\pi r^2 + 2\pi rh$
- Surface area of a sphere: $S = 4\pi r^2$
- Volume of a cube: $V = s^3$
- Volume of a rectangular solid: $V = lwh$
- Volume of a right circular cylinder: $V = \pi r^2 h$
- Volume of a sphere: $V = \dfrac{4\pi r^3}{3}$

GLOSSARY

Arc:	Any part of the circumference
Bisect:	To cut in half
Chord:	Any line segment connecting two points on the edge of a circle
Circumscribed:	Surrounded by a circle as small as possible
Collinear:	Lying on the same line
Congruent:	Equal in size
Diagonal (of a polygon):	A line segment connecting opposite vertices
Equilateral triangle:	All sides are equal and each angle measures 60°
Inscribed (angle in a circle):	An angle in a circle with its vertex on the circumference
Isosceles triangle:	A triangle with two equal sides
Parallel:	Two distinct lines that do not intersect
Perpendicular:	At a 90° angle
Plane:	A flat surface extending in all directions
Polygon:	A closed figure with two or more sides
Quadrilateral:	A four-sided figure
Regular polygon:	A figure with all equal sides and angles
Sector:	Any part of the area formed by two radii and the outside of the circle
Similar:	Equal angles and proportional sides
Surface area:	The sum of areas of each face of a figure
Tangent:	Intersecting at one point
Vertex/Vertices:	A corner point. For angles, it's where two rays meet. For figures, it's where two adjacent sides meet.

Geometry Drill

For the answers to this drill, please go to Chapter 24.

1. In $\triangle ABC$ below, $\angle A = \angle B$, and $\angle C$ is twice the measure of $\angle B$. What is the measure, in degrees, of $\angle A$?

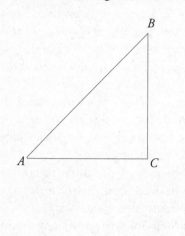

A. 30
B. 45
C. 50
D. 75
E. 90

2. In the figure below, $l_1 \parallel l_2$. Which of the labeled angles must be equal to each other?

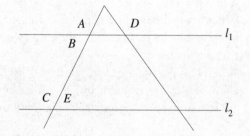

F. A and C
G. D and E
H. A and B
J. D and B
K. C and B

3. In the figure below, right triangles ABC and ACD are drawn as shown. If $\overline{AB} = 20$, $\overline{BC} = 15$, and $\overline{AD} = 7$, then $\overline{CD} = ?$

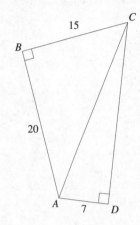

A. 21
B. 22
C. 23
D. 24
E. 25

4. If the area of circle A is 16π, then what is the circumference of circle B if its radius is $\dfrac{1}{2}$ that of circle A ?

F. 2π
G. 4π
H. 6π
J. 8π
K. 16π

5. In the figure below, $\overline{MO}$ is perpendicular to $\overline{LN}$, $\overline{LO}$ is equal to 4, $\overline{MO}$ is equal to $\overline{ON}$, and $\overline{LM}$ is equal to 6. What is $\overline{MN}$?

A. $2\sqrt{10}$
B. $3\sqrt{5}$
C. $4\sqrt{5}$
D. $3\sqrt{10}$
E. $6\sqrt{4}$

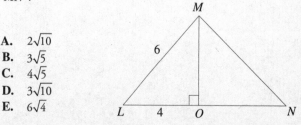

Summary

o Use the basic approach.
- **Step 1**: Know the question. Read the whole problem before calculating anything, and underline the actual question.
- **Step 2:** Let the answers help. Look for clues on how to solve and ways to use Process of Elimination (POE). Ballparking works well on geometry questions on area and angles.
- **Step 3:** Break the problem into bite-sized pieces. When you read the problem a second time, calculate at each step necessary and watch out for tricky phrasing. On geometry, this means
    o **Step 3a:** Write all the information given in the problem on the figure. If there is no figure, draw your own.
    o **Step 3b:** Write down any formulas you need and fill in any information you have.

o There are several things to know about angles and lines.
- A line is a 180° angle.
- When two lines intersect, four angles are formed, but in reality there are only two distinct measures.
- When two parallel lines are cut by a third line, eight angles are formed, but in reality there are still only two (a large one and a small one).

o There are several things to know about triangles.
- A triangle has three sides and three angles; the sum of the angles equals 180°.
- An isosceles triangle has two equal sides and two equal angles opposite those sides.
- An equilateral triangle has three equal sides and three equal angles; each angle equals 60°.
- A right triangle has one 90° angle. In a right triangle problem you can use the Pythagorean theorem to find the lengths of sides.
- Some common right triangles are 3-4-5, 6-8-10, 5-12-13, and 7-24-25.

- ACT test writers also like the isosceles right triangle, in which the sides are always in the ratio $s:s:s\sqrt{2}$, and the 30-60-90 triangle, in which the sides are always in the ratio $s:s\sqrt{3}:2s$.
- Similar triangles have the same angle measurements and sides that are in the same proportion.

- The area of a triangle is equal to $\dfrac{(base \times height)}{2}$, with height measured perpendicular to the base.

○ Four-sided objects are called quadrilaterals and have four angles, which add up to 360°. There are several important things to remember.
  - The area of a rectangle, a square, or a parallelogram can be found using the formula *base × height = area,* with height measured perpendicular to the base.
  - The perimeter of any object is the sum of the lengths of its sides.
  - The area of a trapezoid is equal to the average of the two bases times the height.

○ For any circle problem, you need to know four basic things.
  - Radius
  - Diameter
  - Area (πr^2)
  - Circumference (πd or $2\pi r$)

○ Don't forget that you can plug in on geometry questions that have variables in the answer choices.

Chapter 13
Word Problems

Now that you've refreshed some of the essential geometry concepts, we will see how to integrate those concepts with your test-taking strategy. In addition, we'll see some other Word Problem strategies that will help you to complete problems quickly and accurately.

PLUGGING IN: NOT JUST ALGEBRA

Remember what the main requirements are for a Plugging In problem. You need variables in the answer choices or question: that's it. It doesn't say anywhere that the problem needs to be a pure algebra problem. What is a pure algebra problem anyway? Don't forget: Part of what makes this test so hard is that ACT piles concept on top of concept in its problems. In other words, geometry problems often *are* algebra problems.

WORD PROBLEMS VS. PLUG-AND-CHUG QUESTIONS

We prefer a simple definition of a word problem: It has to tell a story. But as we discussed in Chapter 12, plug-and-chug geometry questions can have so much information in them that they feel like word problems. So treat them like word problems, and let's refresh the basic approach we discussed in Chapter 12.

Step 1: Know the Question

Know the question. Read the whole problem before calculating anything, and underline the actual question.

Step 2: Let the Answers Help

Let the answers help. Look for clues on how to solve and ways to use POE.

Step 3: Break the Problem into Bite-Sized Pieces

Break the problem into bite-sized pieces. When you read the problem a second time, calculate at each step necessary and watch out for tricky phrasing.

For geometry questions, Step 3 has two specific additions:

> **Step 3a:** Write all the information given in the problem on the figure. If there is no figure, draw your own.
>
> **Step 3b:** Write down any formulas you need and fill in any information you have.

Let's see a short, straightforward example:

———————————————◯———————————————

1. A circle with center O has a radius r. What is the area of a circle with a radius three times larger?

A. $3\pi r$
B. $9\pi r$
C. $3\pi r^2$
D. $6\pi r^2$
E. $9\pi r^2$

Here's How to Crack It

Step 1: **Know the question.** We need to find the area of this new larger circle, not the larger radius.

Step 2: **Let the answers help.** First of all, we're looking for the area, which means something will have to be squared, so we can eliminate choices (A) and (B), which can't be right. Now, notice that each of these answer choices has a variable in it. If you're thinking Plugging In, you're thinking right.

Step 3: **Break the problem into bite-sized pieces.** Let's pick an easy value for r, like $r = 2$.

Step 3a: **Write all the information given in the problem on the figure.** There's no figure here, so draw 2 circles.

Step 3b: **Write down any formulas you need and fill in any information you have.** The formula for the area of a circle that we'll need is $A = \pi r^2$.

If the original radius is 2, then the larger radius, which is three times larger, must be 6. Therefore, the area of the larger circle must be $A = \pi(6)^2 = 36\pi$. We've got a target answer, so let's try it in the answer choices. Remember, we've already eliminated choices (A) and (B).

A. ~~$3\pi r$~~
B. ~~$9\pi r$~~
C. $3\pi(2)^2 = 12\pi$ X
D. $6\pi(2)^2 = 24\pi$ X
E. $9\pi(2)^2 = 36\pi$ ✔

Choice (E) is the correct answer. Have another look at those answer choices and think of all the ways you could make mistakes on this problem. Plugging In saves the day again by minimizing the possibility for algebra errors.

———————————————◯———————————————

ARITHMETIC

When it comes to writing word problems, ACT test writers can draw on both algebra and geometry, as we've seen. But lots of word problems, and even some plug-and-chugs, will test a variety of arithmetic concepts. The rest of this chapter will review those topics.

PERCENTAGES, PROBABILITIES, AND RATIOS: DIDN'T WE JUST DO THIS?

Percentages, probabilities, and ratios can get mighty complex in your math classes at school. Do you want the good news or the bad news? Well, the bad news is that ratios, percentages, and probabilities will all appear on the ACT Math test, but the good news is that they're all testing the same basic concept: parts to wholes.

Let's say you're taking batting practice. You are thrown 100 pitches and you hit 20 of them. Ignoring the fact that you're probably not ready for the MLB, let's put this into some math language. Once we get the basics down, we'll try some more advanced problems.

First, what percent of the pitches did you hit? Well, that's easy on this one because we're dealing with 100. But you can always find percentages with this simple part-to-whole formula:

$$\frac{part}{whole} \times 100\%$$

Once we put the numbers in, we'll get this: $\frac{20}{100} \times 100\% = 0.2 \times 100\% = 20\%$. If you hit 20 of the 100 pitches, you hit 20% of them.

Next, what is the probability that you were to hit any given pitch? Remember, this is just a matter of parts to wholes, so we can find this probability as follows: $\frac{part}{whole} = \frac{hits}{pitches} = \frac{20}{100} = 0.2$. In other words, there's a 0.2, or $\frac{1}{5}$, probability you hit any given pitch during batting practice.

Ratios are a little different. Usually these will ask for the relationship of some part to some other part. If we're still using our batting practice statistics, we might want to know something like, What's the ratio of the pitches you hit to the pitches you missed?

Even though we're not dealing with the whole this time, we'll find the ratio the same way, but instead of $\frac{part}{whole}$, we'll use $\frac{part}{whole} = \frac{hits}{misses} = \frac{20}{80} = \frac{1}{4}$. The ratio of hits to misses is $\frac{1}{4}$, or 1 to 4, or 1:4.

If it feels like we just did the same thing three times, it was supposed to. As we've seen a few times already, just because things have different names doesn't mean that they are unrelated. Let's try some problems.

Percentages

1. At a restaurant, diners enjoy an "early bird" discount of 10% off their bills. If a diner orders a meal regularly priced at $18 and leaves a tip of 15% of the discounted meal (no tax), how much does he pay in total?

   A. $13.50
   B. $16.20
   C. $18.63
   D. $18.90
   E. $20.70

Here's How to Crack It
Step 1: **Know the question.** We want the price of the discounted meal plus tip.

Step 2: **Let the answers help.** We are reducing a number by 10%, then increasing it by 15%, so it's not likely that the final number will be much less or much greater than $18. Let's eliminate choices (A) and (E).

Step 3: **Break the problem into bite-sized pieces.**

First, we'll need to figure out what the discounted price of the meal is. There are a number of ways to do this, but if you find this $\frac{part}{whole}$ method useful, you could find the discount this way:

$$10\% = discount$$

$$\frac{10}{100} = \frac{discount}{\$18}$$

$$discount = \$1.80$$

The price of the discounted meal, then, is $18 − $1.80 = $16.20. Let's find the tip the same way.

$$15\% = tip$$

$$\frac{15}{100} = \frac{tip}{\$16.20}$$

$$tip = \$2.43$$

The price of the discounted meal plus tip, therefore, is $16.20 + $2.43 = $18.63. The correct answer is choice (C).

Another Way to Deal with Percents

A percentage is a fraction in which the denominator equals 100. In literal terms, the word *percent* means "divided by 100," so any time you see a percentage in an ACT question, you can punch it into your calculator quite easily. If a question asks for 40 percent of something, for instance, you can express the percentage as a fraction: $\frac{40}{100}$. Any time you are looking for a percent, you can use your calculator to find the decimal equivalent and multiply the result by 100. If four out of five dentists recommend a particular brand of toothpaste, you can quickly determine the percent of doctors who recommend it by typing $\frac{4}{5} \times 100$ and hitting the ENTER key. The resulting "80" just needs a percent sign tacked onto it. To properly translate all percent questions, it is helpful to have a decoding table for the various terms you'll come across.

English	Math Equivalent
percent	/100
of	multiplication (×)
what	variable (y, z)
is, are, were	=
what percent	$\frac{y}{100}$

Percentage Shortcuts

In the last problem, we could have saved a little time if we had realized that $\frac{1}{5} = 20$ percent. Therefore, $\frac{4}{5}$ would be 4×20 percent or 80 percent. Below are some fractions and decimals whose percent equivalents you should know.

Another fast way to do percents is to move the decimal place. To find 10 percent of any number, move the decimal point of that number over one place to the left.

$$10\% \text{ of } 500 = 50$$

$$10\% \text{ of } 50 = 5$$

$$10\% \text{ of } 5 = .5$$

To find 1 percent of a number, move the decimal point of that number over two places to the left.

$$1\% \text{ of } 500 = 5$$

$$1\% \text{ of } 50 = .5$$

$$1\% \text{ of } 5 = .05$$

You can use a combination of these last two techniques to find even very complicated percentages by breaking them down into easy-to-find chunks.

- 20% of 500: 10% of 500 = 50, so 20% is twice 50, or 100.
- 30% of 70: 10% of 70 = 7, so 30% is three times 7, or 21.
- 32% of 400: 10% of 400 = 40, so 30% is three times 40, or 120.
- 1% of 400 = 4, so 2% is two times 4, or 8.

Therefore, 32 percent of 400 = 120 + 8 = 128.

> ### The Big Four: Fraction/Percent Equivalents You Should Know
>
> $$\frac{1}{5} = .2 = 20\%$$
>
> $$\frac{1}{4} = .25 = 25\%$$
>
> $$\frac{1}{3} = .\overline{33} = 33\frac{1}{3}\%$$
>
> $$\frac{1}{2} = .5 = 50\%$$

Let's have a look at another ACT percentage problem.

————————————◯————————————

2. When 15% of 40 is added to 5% of 260, the resulting number is:

   F. 19
   G. 40
   H. 95
   J. 180
   K. 260

Here's How to Crack It

Let's try this one using the decoding table. Although this isn't really a word problem, that doesn't mean we shouldn't be careful and break it into bite-sized pieces.

First, 15% of 40. Remember, % translates ÷100 and "of" translates to multiplication. Therefore, we can rewrite 15% of 40 as $\frac{15}{100} \times 40$. Put this expression in your calculator to find that $\frac{15}{100} \times 40 = 6$.

Now, 5% of 260. Use the same translations to find $\frac{5}{100} \times 260 = 13$. We've done the tough part, so let's substitute what we've found back into the problem: *When 6 is added to 13, the resulting number is*: Now that's a problem we can handle! 6 + 13 = 19, choice (F).

————————————◯————————————

Probability

3. Herbie's practice bag contains 4 blue racquetballs, one red racquetball, and 6 green racquetballs. If he chooses a ball at random, which of the following is closest to the probability that the ball will NOT be green?

   A. 0.09
   B. 0.27
   C. 0.36
   D. 0.45
   E. 0.54

Here's How to Crack It

Step 1: **Know the question.** Make sure you read carefully! We want the probability that the chosen ball will NOT be green.

Step 2: **Let the answers help.** Green balls account for slightly more than half the number of balls in the bag, so the likelihood that the ball will NOT be green should be slightly less than half. That eliminates choices (A), (B), and (E). Not bad!

Step 3: **Break the problem into bite-sized pieces.** This is a pretty straightforward $\frac{part}{whole}$ problem: $\frac{part}{whole} = \frac{NOT\ green}{all} = \frac{5}{11}$. The only slight difficulty is that the answers are not listed as fractions, but it's nothing a calculator can't help. Find $5 \div 11 = 0.45$, choice (D).

Ratios

4. If the ratio of $2x$ to $5y$ is $\dfrac{1}{20}$, what is the ratio of x to y ?

F. $\dfrac{1}{40}$

G. $\dfrac{1}{20}$

H. $\dfrac{1}{10}$

J. $\dfrac{1}{8}$

K. $\dfrac{1}{4}$

Here's How to Crack It

The difficulty of this problem is all in the setup. Just remember that you're comparing parts to wholes, and you'll be fine:

$$\frac{2x}{5y} = \frac{1}{20}$$

To isolate $\dfrac{x}{y}$ on the left side of this equation, let's multiply both sides of the equation by $\dfrac{5}{2}$.

$$\frac{5}{2} \times \frac{2x}{5y} = \frac{1}{20} \times \frac{5}{2}$$

$$\frac{x}{y} = \frac{5}{40}$$

$\dfrac{5}{40}$ reduces to $\dfrac{1}{8}$. The answer is choice (J).

If you got stuck on this one, look at those answer choices: You could've used PITA!

Let's see how ACT might test ratios in a word problem.

---

5. If 3.7 inches of rain fall on Vancouver during the first 4 days of November, and the rain continues to fall at this pace for the rest of the month, approximately how many feet of rain will fall during December? (Note: The month of December has 31 days.)

    A.   2.4
    B.   3.7
    C.   9.5
    D.   28.7
    E.   114.7

Here's How to Crack It

Step 1: **Know the question.** It's in the last line: *how many feet of rain will fall in December?* But be careful: The value given in the problem is in inches. We're going to have to do some converting!

Step 2: **Let the answers help.** Since we know the problem is asking how many *feet* of rain will fall, and the problem tells us that 3.7 *inches* of rain will fall in 4 days, we can do some ballparking. The number of inches will increase, but it will be reduced again when we convert it into feet. Choice (E) is definitely too big, and choice (D) probably is, too.

Step 3: **Break the problem into bite-sized pieces.** There are going to be two main parts to this problem: First, we want to figure out how much rain will fall in 31 days, then we want to convert it to feet. We can do this by using ratios.

The ratio given in the problem is 3.7 inches every four days, or in math terms, $\frac{3.7 \text{ in}}{4 \text{ days}}$. The ratio will remain the same no matter how many days there are, so let's use this ratio to find how many inches of rain will fall in December.

$$\frac{3.7 \text{ in}}{4 \text{ days}} = \frac{? \text{ in}}{31 \text{ days}}$$

We can rearrange the terms to find

$$? \text{ in} = \frac{(3.7 \text{ in})(31 \text{ days})}{4 \text{ days}} = 28.675 \text{ in}$$

But we can't stop here! Remember, the problem is asking for a value in feet. (It's a good thing we did some early POE, isn't it?)

We'll use the same process, and this time we already know the ratio of inches to feet: $\dfrac{12 \text{ in}}{1 \text{ ft}}$. As we did above, let's use this ratio to find our answer:

$$\frac{12 \text{ in}}{1 \text{ ft}} = \frac{28.675 \text{ in}}{? \text{ ft}}$$

Rearrange the equation to find

$$? \text{ ft} = \frac{28.675 \text{ in}(1 \text{ ft})}{12 \text{ in}} \approx 2.4 \text{ ft, choice (A).}$$

AVERAGES

There are only three parts to any average question. Fortunately for you, the ACT must give you two of these parts, which are all you need to find the third. The average pie is an easy way to keep track of the information you get from questions dealing with averages. If you have the total, you can always divide by either the average or the number of things in the set (whichever you are given) to find the missing piece of the pie. Similarly, if you have the number of things and the average, you can multiply the two together to arrive at the total (the sum of all the items in the set).

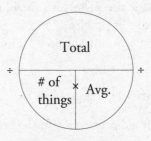

> ### Playing the Averages
> **Arithmetic mean**—just a fancy way of saying "average."
>
> **Median**—the one in the middle, like the median strip on the highway.
>
> **Mode**—you're looking for the element that appears most. Get it? MOde, MOst.

For example, if you want to find the average of 9, 12, and 6 using the average pie, you know you have 3 items with a total of 27. Dividing the total, 27, by the number of things, 3, will yield the average, 9. Your pie looks like this:

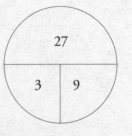

Although you probably could have done that without the average pie, more difficult average questions involve multiple calculations and lend themselves particularly well to using the pie. Let's take a look at one:

---

3. Over 9 games, a baseball team had an average of 8 runs per game. If the average number of runs for the first 7 games was 6 runs per game, and the same number of runs was scored in each of the last 2 games, how many runs did the team score during the last game?

   A. 5
   B. 15
   C. 26
   D. 30
   E. 46

The Missing Number
The ACT loves to leave out totals on average problems. You aren't done until you've found it.

Here's How to Crack It

Step 1: **Know the question.** *How many runs did the team score during the last game?*

Step 2: **Let the answers help.** Eliminate choice (A). Even though the average for the first 7 is higher than all 9, the runs scored in the last two games can't be that few. Similarly, choice (E) is probably too big. If you don't trust your sense of numbers and you're not comfortable Ballparking here, however, leave both. It's a complicated question on a more advanced topic.

Step 3: **Break the problem into bite-sized pieces.** Let's use bite-size pieces to put the information from the first line of this problem into our trusty average pie.

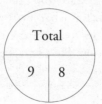

What is the sum of everything for these 9 games? 9×8, or 72.

Now let's put the information from the second line into the average equation.

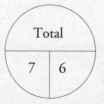

What is the sum of everything for these 7 games? 7 × 6, or 42.

If all 9 games added up to 72, and 7 of these games added up to 42, then the remaining 2 games added up to 72 – 42, or 30. In case you are feeling smug about getting this far, the ACT writers made 30 the answer for choice (D).

But of course you know that they only want the runs they scored in the last game. Because the same number of runs was scored in each of the last two games, the answer is $\frac{30}{2}$ or 15, choice (B).

The Weighted Average

ACT writers have a particular fondness for "weighted average" problems. First, let's look at a regular unweighted average question.

> If Sally received a grade of 90 on a test last week and a grade of 100 on a test this week, what is her average for the two tests?

Piece of cake, right? The answer is 95. You added the scores and divided by 2. Now let's turn the same question into a weighted average question.

> If Sally's average for the entire year last year was 90, and her average for the entire year this year was 100, is her average for the two years combined equal to 95 ?

The answer is "not necessarily." If Sally took the same number of courses in both years, then yes, her average is 95. But what if last year she took 6 courses while this year she took only 2 courses? Can you compare the two years equally? ACT likes to test your answer to this question. Here's an example.

1. The starting team of a baseball club has 9 members who have an average of 12 home runs apiece for the season. The second-string team for the baseball club has 7 members who have an average of 8 home runs apiece for the season. What is the average number of home runs for the starting team and the second-string team combined?

   A. 7.5
   B. 8
   C. 10
   D. 10.25
   E. 14.2

Here's How to Crack It

The ACT test writers want to see whether you spot this as a weighted average problem. If you thought the first-string team was exactly equivalent to the second-string team, then you merely had to take the average of the two averages, 12 and 8, to get 10. In weighted average problems, the ACT test writers always include the average of the two averages among the answer choices, and it is always wrong. 10 is choice (C). Cross off choice (C).

The two teams are not equivalent because there are different numbers of players on each team. To get the true average, we'll have to find the total number of home runs and divide by the total number of players. How do we do this? By going to the trusty average formula as usual. The first line of the problem says that the 9 members on the first team have an average of 12 runs apiece.

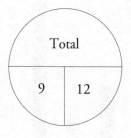

So the sum of everything is 9 × 12, or 108.

The second sentence says that the 7 members of the second team have an average of 8 runs each.

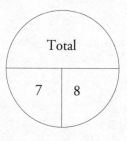

So the total is 7 × 8, or 56.

Now we can find the true average. Add all the runs scored by the first team to all the runs scored by the second team: 108 + 56 = 164. This is the true total. We divide it by the total number of players (9 + 7 = 16).

The answer is 10.25, or choice (D).

CHARTS AND GRAPHS

Since calculators were added to the arsenal you're allowed to bring with you when you take the ACT, more and more of the test has been composed of questions on which calculators are of little or no use, such as questions based on charts and graphs. On this type of question, your math skills aren't really being tested at all; what ACT is interested in is your ability to read a simple graph (not unlike on the Science Reasoning test, which we'll get to later in Part V). All of the questions we have seen in this format have been very direct. If you can read a simple graph, you can always get them right. What's most important on questions like these is paying attention to the labels on the information. Let's take a look at a graph.

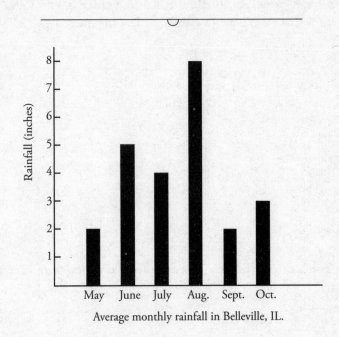

Average monthly rainfall in Belleville, IL.

3. Between which two months was the change in total rainfall the greatest?

   A. May and June
   B. June and July
   C. July and August
   D. August and September
   E. September and October

Here's How to Crack It

The ACT test writers want to see if you can decipher the information presented in the graph. Before you read the question then, you need to take a look at the graph. What is measured here? It says on the bottom: Average monthly rainfall in Belleville, IL. You should look at the values along the left side and bottom of the graph as well. When you do, you'll see that the rain is measured in inches (left-hand side), and the measurements were made each month (bottom).

Now for the question. To determine which two months had the greatest change, we need to compare the change between each pair of months, discarding the smaller ones until we have only one left. The difference from May to June is about 3, and that's larger than June to July and September to October, so choices (B) and (E) are out. July to August is larger still, though, so choice (A) is out, leaving only choices (C) and (D). It should be pretty apparent that the August to September change is larger than the July to August change, though, so the correct answer must be choice (D).

Although most questions involving graphs on the Math test are this simple, you may see slightly more complicated variations. Here's another question based on the same bar graph.

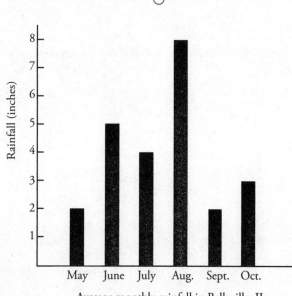

Average monthly rainfall in Belleville, IL.

24. Based on the information presented in the graph above, what is the approximate average monthly rainfall in Belleville, IL, for the period given?

    F.   2
    G.   3
    H.   4
    J.   5
    K.   8

Here's How to Crack It

As with the last question, the first thing you want to do is examine the graph and figure out what information is being given to you and how it is being presented. Because you already did that for this graph, we'll skip that step on this one.

This question combines graph reading with average calculation, so the next thing you'll have to do is estimate the rainfall for each month. Because the question uses the word *approximate*, you don't have to worry too much about making super-exact measurements of the heights of the bar graphs. Eyeballing it and rounding to the closest value given on the left-hand side will be good enough to get you the right answer. Do that now before you read the next sentence.

To us, it looks like about 2 inches fell in May and September, and around 3 fell in October. July saw about 4, June roughly 5, and August about 8. Your estimates should be the same as ours. If they're not, go back now and figure out why not. You probably need to be a little more careful in your estimating. Use another piece of paper as a guide if necessary (you can use your answer sheet in this manner when taking the real ACT).

Now it's just a matter of calculating the average. Find the total first.

$$2 + 2 + 3 + 4 + 5 + 8 = 24$$

There are 6 months, so divide the total by 6 to find the average.

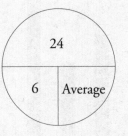

So the answer is 4, or choice (H).

―――――――――――○―――――――――――

COMBINATIONS: CAN YOU SLOT ME IN?

Combination problems ask you how many different ways a number of things could be chosen or combined. The rules for combination problems on the ACT are straightforward.

> 1. Figure out the number of slots you need to fill.
> 2. Fill in those slots.
> 3. Find the product.

Seem confusing? It's not. Let's look at an example. This is what most combination problems on the ACT will look like:

---

6. At the school cafeteria, students can choose from 3 different salads, 5 different main dishes, and 2 different desserts. If Isabel chooses one salad, one main dish, and one dessert for lunch, how many different lunches could she choose?

    F. 10
    G. 15
    H. 25
    J. 30
    K. 50

Here's How to Crack It

We've got three slots to fill here, one for each item: salad, main dish, dessert. And the number of possibilities for each is pretty clear. Set up the slots and take the product:

$$\underline{\ 3\ } \times \underline{\ 5\ } \times \underline{\ 2\ } = 30$$
$$\text{Salad}\quad \text{Main}\quad \text{Dessert}$$

The correct answer here is choice (J).

On a more difficult problem, you may run into a combination with more restricted elements. Just be sure to read the problem carefully before attempting it. If the question makes your head spin, leave it and return to it later, or pick your Letter of the Day and move on. For good measure, though, here's what one of those tougher ones might look like.

---

7. At the school cafeteria, 2 boys and 4 girls are forming a lunch line. If the boys must stand in the first and last places in line, how many different lines can be formed?

    A.   2
    B.   6
    C.   48
    D. 360
    E. 720

Here's How to Crack It

These restrictions might make this problem seem daunting, but this is where the slot method is really helpful. We have six spots in line to fill, so draw six slots:

$$\underline{\quad}\quad\underline{\quad}\quad\underline{\quad}\quad\underline{\quad}\quad\underline{\quad}\quad\underline{\quad}$$

It even looks like the line the boys and girls are standing in! Do the restricted spots first. The problem tells us that the two boys *must stand in the first and last places in line*. This means that either of the boys could stand in first place, and then the other boy will stand in last. This means that we have two options for the first place, but only one for the last.

$$\underline{\;2\;}\quad\underline{\quad}\quad\underline{\quad}\quad\underline{\quad}\quad\underline{\quad}\quad\underline{\;1\;}$$

Now do the same with the unrestricted parts. Any of the four girls could stand in the second spot.

$$\underline{\;2\;}\quad\underline{\;4\;}\quad\underline{\quad}\quad\underline{\quad}\quad\underline{\quad}\quad\underline{\;1\;}$$

Now, since one of the girls is standing in the second spot, there are only three left to stand in the third spot, and so on, and so on.

$$\underline{\;2\;}\quad\underline{\;4\;}\quad\underline{\;3\;}\quad\underline{\;2\;}\quad\underline{\;1\;}\quad\underline{\;1\;}$$

Now, as ever, just take the product, to find that the correct answer is choice (C), 48.

$$\underline{\;2\;}\times\underline{\;4\;}\times\underline{\;3\;}\times\underline{\;2\;}\times\underline{\;1\;}\times\underline{\;1\;}=48$$

Let's try one more that tests a few things.

8. Elias has to select one shirt, one pair of pants, and one pair
    of shoes. If he selects at random from his 8 shirts, 4 pairs of
    pants, and 3 pairs of shoes, and all his shirts, pants, and shoes
    are different colors, what is the likelihood that he will select
    his red shirt, black pants, and brown shoes?

    F. $\dfrac{1}{3}$

    G. $\dfrac{1}{4}$

    H. $\dfrac{1}{15}$

    J. $\dfrac{1}{32}$

    K. $\dfrac{1}{96}$

Here's How to Crack It

Step 1: **Know the question.** The problem is asking what the probability is that he
will select this one group of clothes from all possible combinations of clothes.

Step 2: **Let the answers help.** The answers offer the important reminder that we're
looking for a probability. We know that it will be only one arrangement out of a reasonably large number of them, so we should at least get rid of choices (F) and (G).

Step 3: **Break the problem into bite-sized pieces.** First, we should find the total
number of possible combinations. Then, we can deal with the probability.

We have three slots to fill here, and we want to find the product of the three:

$$\underset{\text{Shirts}}{8} \times \underset{\text{Pants}}{4} \times \underset{\text{Shoes}}{3} = 96 \text{ arrangements}$$

Of the 96 possible arrangements, an ensemble of red shirt, black pants, and
brown shoes is only one. Therefore, we can go to our $\dfrac{part}{whole}$ ratio to find

$$\dfrac{part}{whole} = \dfrac{\text{red, black, brown}}{\text{ALL arrangements}} = \dfrac{1}{96}, \text{ choice (K)}.$$

Word Problems Drill

For the answers to this drill, please go to Chapter 24.

1. The ratio of boys to girls at the Milwood School is 4 to 5. If there are a total of 27 children at the school, how many boys attend the Milwood School?

   A.   4
   B.   9
   C.   12
   D.   14
   E.   17

2. Linda computed the average of her six biology test scores by mistakenly adding the totals of five scores and dividing by five, giving her an average score of 88. When Linda realized her error, she recalculated and included the sixth test score of 82. What is the average of Linda's six biology tests?

   F.   82
   G.   85
   H.   86
   J.   87
   K.   88

3. In the process of milling grain, 3% of the original is lost because of spillage, and another 5% of the original is lost because of mildew. If the mill starts out with 490 tons of grain, how much (in tons) remains to be sold after milling?

   A.   425
   B.   426
   C.   420.5
   D.   440
   E.   450.8

4. A rectangular box has a base measuring a by a meters and height of b meters. Which of the following represents the surface area of the box?

   F. $6ab$
   G. $a^2 b$
   H. $a^2 + 2ab$
   J. $2a(a + 2b)$
   K. $2(a^2 + b^2)$

5. In the word HAWKS, how many ways is it possible to rearrange the letters if none repeat and the letter W must go last?

   A.   5
   B.   15
   C.   24
   D.   120
   E.   650

Summary

o Plugging In works on all kinds of problems, not just Algebra. Always look for opportunities to simplify the math by Plugging In!

o Percentages and Probabilities are all based on a relationship of PART to WHOLE. Ratios are based on a relationship of PART to PART. Probabilities can be found by taking the part (the number of things that meet some given criteria) divided by the whole (all possibilities, including those that don't meet the criteria).

o Percentages can typically be found by multiplying $\frac{part}{whole} \times 100\%$.

  • When dealing with percentages, remember to convert Math into English with the handy chart.

English	Math Equivalent
percent	/100
of	multiplication (×)
what	variable (y, z)
is, are, were	=
what percent	$\frac{y}{100}$

  • Ratios are typically a relationship of one *part* to some other *part*.

o On Combination problems
  1. Figure out the number of slots you need to fill.
  2. Fill in those slots.
  3. Find the product.

o On Average problems, use the average pie.
  1. Divide the total by the number of things to find the average.
  2. Divide the total by the average to find the number of things.
  3. Multiply the number of things by the average to find the total.

Chapter 14
Graphing
and Coordinate
Geometry

We've covered most of what you'll need to get a great score on the ACT Math test. This chapter will give a brief overview of Coordinate Geometry. While it's not tested as heavily as Plane Geometry, Coordinate Geometry offers many fast plug-and-chug opportunities. Though we will be discussing the basic rules and formulas you need, we will always have an eye on how we can crack some of these problems more strategically as well.

COORDINATE GEOMETRY

As we saw in the first Math chapter, coordinate geometry will account for about 9 questions in any given exam. While ACT makes a big deal about how separate this is from plane geometry, really the major difference between the two is that you need more graph paper to do coordinate geometry. We'll cover the basics of graphing and its related functions, but don't forget, you know a lot of this stuff from the earlier geometry chapter already!

Graphing Inequalities

Here's a simple inequality:

$$3x + 5 > 11$$

As you know from reading the algebra chapter of this book, you solve an inequality the same way that you solve an equality. By subtracting 5 from both sides and then dividing both sides by 3, you get the expression

$$x > 2$$

This can be represented on a number line as shown below.

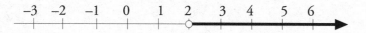

The open circle at 2 indicates that x can include every number greater than 2, but not 2 itself or anything less than 2.

If we had wanted to graph $x \geq 2$, the circle would have to be filled in, indicating that our graph includes 2 as well.

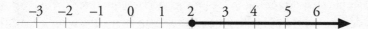

An ACT graphing problem might look like this.

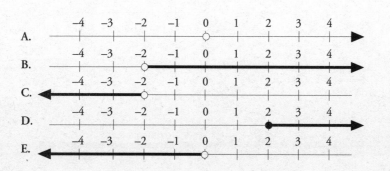

An Open Circle
On the number line, a hollow circle means that point is *not* included in the graph.

A Solid Dot
On the number line, a solid dot means that point is included in the graph.

1. Which of the following represents the range of solutions for inequality $-5x - 7 < x + 5$?

Here's How to Crack It

The ACT test writers want you first to simplify the inequality and then figure out which of the answer choices represents a graph of the solution set of the inequality. To simplify, isolate x on one side of the inequality.

$$\begin{array}{r} -5x - 7 < x + 5 \\ -x \qquad -x \quad\;\; \\ \hline -6x - 7 < \quad 5 \\ +7 \quad +7 \\ \hline -6x \quad < \quad 12 \end{array}$$

Flip Flop
Remember that when you multiply or divide an inequality by a negative, the sign flips.

Now divide both sides by −6. Remember that when you multiply or divide an inequality by a negative, the sign flips over.

$$\frac{-6x}{-6} < \frac{12}{-6}$$
$$x > -2$$

Which of the choices answers the question? If you selected choice (B), you're right.

Graphing in Two Dimensions

More complicated graphing questions concern equations with two variables, usually designated x and y. These equations can be graphed on a Cartesian grid, which looks like this.

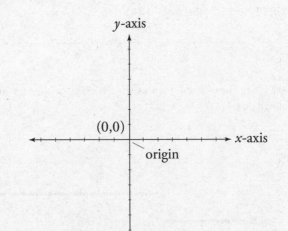

Every point (*x,y*) has a place on this grid. For example, the point *A* (3,4) can be found by counting over on the *x*-axis 3 places to the right of (0,0)—known as the **origin**—and then counting on the *y*-axis 4 places up from the origin, as shown below. Point *B* (5,–2) can be found by counting 5 places to the right on the *x*-axis and then down 2 places on the *y*-axis. Point *C* (–4,–1) can be found by counting 4 places to the left of the origin on the *x*-axis and then 1 place down on the *y*-axis.

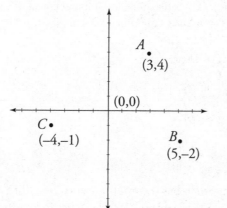

The grid is divided into four quadrants, which go counterclockwise.

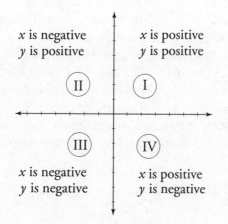

- In the first quadrant, *x* and *y* are both positive.
- In the second quadrant, *x* is negative but *y* is positive.
- In the third quadrant, *x* and *y* are both negative.
- In the fourth quadrant, *x* is positive but *y* is negative.

Note: This is when your graphing calculator (if you have one) will really get a chance to shine. Practice doing all the ACT coordinate geometry questions on your calculator now and you'll blow them away when you actually take the test.

Graphic Guesstimation

A few questions on the ACT might involve actual graphing, but it is more likely that you will be able to make use of graphing to *estimate* the answers to questions that the ACT test writers think are more complicated.

---

1. Point *B* (4,3) is the midpoint of line segment *AC*. If point *A* has coordinates (0,1), then what are the coordinates of point *C* ?

    A. (−4,−1)
    B. (4, 1)
    C. (4, 4)
    D. (8, 5)
    E. (8, 9)

Here's How to Crack It

You may or may not remember the midpoint formula: The ACT test writers expect you to use it to solve this problem. We'll go over it in a moment, along with the other formulas you'll need to solve coordinate geometry questions. However, it is worth noting that by drawing a rough graph of this problem, you can get the correct answer without the formula.

On your TI-83, you can plot independent points to see what the graph should look like. To do this, hit STAT and select option [1: Edit]. Enter the *x*- and *y*-coordinate points in the first two columns; use [L1] for your *x*-coordinates and [L2] for the *y*-coordinates. After you enter the endpoints of the line, hit 2nd Y= to access the STAT PLOT menu. Select option [1: Plot1]. Change the [OFF] status to ON and hit GRAPH. You should now see the two points you entered. Now you can ballpark the answers based on where they are in the coordinate plane. Keep in mind that you can also plot all the points in the answers as well. Just be sure you keep track of all the *x*- and *y*-values. If you don't have a graphing calculator, use the grid we've provided on the next page.

B is supposed to be the midpoint of a line segment AC. Draw a line through the two points you've just plotted and extend it upward until B is the midpoint of the line segment. It should look like this:

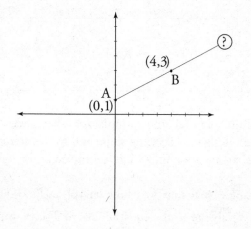

The place where you stopped drawing is the approximate location of point C. Now let's look at the answer choices to see if any of them are in the ballpark.

A.   (−4,−1): These coordinates are in the wrong quadrant.
B.   (4, 1): This point is way below where it should be.
C.   (4, 4): This point does not extend enough to the right.
D.   (8, 5): Definitely in the ballpark. Hold on to this answer choice.
E.   (8, 9): Possible, although the y-coordinate seems a little high.

Which answer choice do you want to pick? If you said choice (D), you are right.

THE IMPORTANT COORDINATE GEOMETRY FORMULAS

By memorizing a few formulas, you will be able to answer virtually all of the coordinate geometry questions on this test. Remember, too, that in coordinate geometry you almost *always* have a fallback—just graph it out.

And always keep your graphing calculator handy on these types of problems. Graphing calculators are great for solving line equations and giving you graphs you can use to ballpark. Be sure you know how to solve and graph an equation for a line on your calculator before you take the ACT.

The following formulas are listed in order of importance:

The Slope-Intercept Formula

$$y = mx + b$$

To find the *x*-intercept
Set *y* equal to zero and solve for *x*.

By putting (x,y) equations into the formula above, you can find two pieces of information that ACT likes to test: the **slope** and the **y-intercept**. Most graphing calculators will put an equation into *y*-intercept form at the touch of a button.

The **slope** is a number that tells you how sharply a line is inclining, and it is equivalent to the variable **m** in the equation above. For example, in the equation $y = 3x + 4$, the number 3 (think of it as $\frac{3}{1}$) tells us that from any point on the line, we can find another point on the line by going up 3 and over to the right 1.

In the equation $y = -\frac{4}{5}x - 7$, the slope of $-\frac{4}{5}$ tells us that from any point on the line, we can find another point on the line by going up 4 and over 5 to the left.

The **y-intercept**, equivalent to the variable **b** in the equation above, is the point at which the line intercepts the *y*-axis. For example, in the equation $y = 3x + 4$, the line will strike the *y*-axis at a point 4 above the origin. In the equation $y = 2x - 7$, the line will strike the *y*-axis at a point 7 below the origin. A typical ACT $y = mx + b$ question might give you an equation in another form and ask you to find either the slope or the *y*-intercept. Simply put the equation into the form we've just shown you.

2. What is the slope of the line based on the equation
$5x - y = 7x + 6$?

    F.   –2
    G.   0
    H.   2
    J.   6
    K.   –6

Here's How to Crack It

Isolate y on the left side of the equation. You can have your graphing calculator do this for you, or you can do it by hand by subtracting $5x$ from both sides.

$$
\begin{array}{r}
5x - y = 7x + 6 \\
\underline{-5x \qquad -5x \quad} \\
-y = 2x + 6
\end{array}
$$

We aren't quite done. The format we want is $y = mx + b$, not $-y = mx + b$. Let's multiply both sides by –1.

$$(-1)(-y) = (2x + 6)(-1)$$
$$y = -2x - 6$$

The slope of this line is –2, so the answer is choice (A).

The Slope Formula

You can find the slope of a line, even if all you have are two points on that line, by using the slope formula.

The Slippery Slope
A line going from bottom left to upper right has a positive slope. A line going from top left to bottom right has a negative slope.

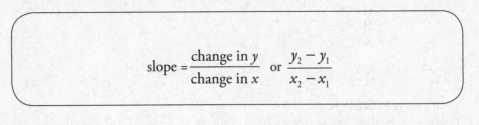

$$\text{slope} = \frac{\text{change in } y}{\text{change in } x} \quad \text{or} \quad \frac{y_2 - y_1}{x_2 - x_1}$$

Parallel Tracks

If two lines have the same slope, those lines are *parallel* to one another.

If two lines have opposite reciprocal slopes, those lines are *perpendicular* to one another.

So how about if #1 on this page asked for the slope of a line parallel to the one given in the problem? How about perpendicular?

A *parallel* line would have a slope of $-\frac{1}{8}$.

A *perpendicular* line would have a slope of 8.

3. What is the slope of the straight line passing through the points (−2,5) and (6,4) ?

   A. $-\dfrac{1}{16}$

   B. $-\dfrac{1}{8}$

   C. $\dfrac{1}{5}$

   D. $\dfrac{2}{9}$

   E. $\dfrac{4}{9}$

Here's How to Crack It

Find the change in y and put it over the change in x. The change in y is the first y-coordinate minus the second y-coordinate. (It doesn't matter which point is first and which is second.) The change in x is the first x minus the second x.

$$\frac{y_2 - y_1}{x_2 - x_1} = \frac{5 - 4}{-2 - 6} = \frac{1}{-8}$$

The correct answer is choice (B).

If you take a look at the formula for finding slope, you'll see that the part on top ("change in *y*") is how much the line is rising (or falling, if the line points down and has a negative slope). That change in position on the *y*-axis is called the *rise*. The part on the bottom ("change in *x*") is how far along the *x*-axis you move and called the *run*. So the slope of a line is sometimes referred to as "rise over run."

In the question we just did, then, the rise was 1 and the run was –8, giving us the slope $-\frac{1}{8}$. Same answer, different terminology.

Midpoint Formula

If you have the two endpoints of a line segment, you can find the midpoint of the segment by using the midpoint formula.

$$\left(x[m], y[m]\right) = \left(\frac{x_1 + x_2}{2}, \frac{y_1 + y_2}{2}\right)$$

It looks much more intimidating than it really is.

To find the midpoint of a line, just take the *average* of the two *x*-coordinates and the *average* of the two *y*-coordinates. For example, the midpoint of the line segment formed by the coordinates (3,4) and (9,2) is just

$$\frac{(3+9)}{2} = 6 \text{ and } \frac{(4+2)}{2} = 3$$
$$\text{or } (6,3)$$

Remember the first midpoint problem we did? Here it is again.

1. Point *B* (4,3) is the midpoint of line segment *AC*. If point *A* has coordinates (0,1), then what are the coordinates of point *C* ?

   A. (–4,–1)
   B. (4, 1)
   C. (4, 4)
   D. (8, 5)
   E. (8, 9)

> **The Shortest Distance Between Two Points Is…a Calculator?**
> If you want to draw a line between two points on your TI-83, you can use the Line function. To access this, you'll want to press [2nd] [PRGM] to access the [DRAW] menu. From there, select option [2: Line]. The format of the line function is Line (X1, Y1, X2, Y2); for example, if you wanted to view the line that passes through the points (–2,5) and (6,4), you would enter Line (–2,5,6,4). Hit [ENTER] to see your line.

Here's How to Crack It

You'll remember that it was perfectly possible to solve this problem just by drawing a quick graph of what it ought to look like. However, to find the correct answer using the midpoint formula, we first have to realize that, in this case, we already *have* the midpoint. We are asked to find one of the endpoints.

The midpoint is (4,3). This represents the average of the two endpoints. The endpoint we know about is (0,1). Let's do the x-coordinate first. The average of the x-coordinates of the two endpoints equals the x-coordinate of the midpoint. So $\frac{(0+?)}{2} = 4$. What is the missing x-coordinate? 8. Now let's do the y-coordinate. $\frac{(1+?)}{2} = 3$. What is the missing y-coordinate? 5. The answer is choice (D).

———————○———————

If you had trouble following that last explanation, just remember that you already understood this problem (and got the answer) using graphing. Never be intimidated by formulas on the ACT. There is usually another way to do the problem.

The Distance Formula

We hate the distance formula. We keep forgetting it, and even when we remember it, we feel like fools for using it because there are much easier ways to find the distance between two points. We aren't even going to tell you what the distance formula is. If you need to know the distance between two points, you can always think of that distance as being the hypotenuse of a right triangle. Here's an example.

———————○———————

4. What is the distance between points A (2,2) and B (5,6) ?

    F. 3
    G. 4
    H. 5
    J. 6
    K. 7

Here's How to Crack It

Let's make a quick graph of what this ought to look like.

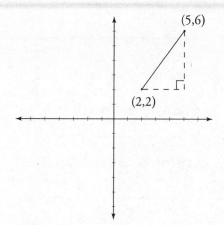

If we extend lines from the two points to form a right triangle under the line segment *AB*, we can use the Pythagorean theorem to get the distance between the two points. What is the length of the base of the triangle? It's 3. What is the length of the height of the triangle? It's 4. So what is the length of the hypotenuse? It's 5. Of course, as usual, it is one of the triples of which ACT is so fond. The answer is choice (C). You could also have popped the points into your calculator and had it calculate the distance for you.

Here's the distance formula if you must know (or know how to program into your calculator):
$$d = \sqrt{(x_2 - x_1)^2 + (y_2 - y_1)^2}$$
Isn't the triangle method so much easier?

Circles, Ellipses, and Parabolas, Oh My!

You should probably have a *vague* idea of what the equations for these figures look like; just remember that there are very few questions concerning these figures, and when they do come up, you can almost always figure them out by graphing.

The standard equation for a circle is shown below.

$$(x - h)^2 + (y - k)^2 = r^2$$

(h,k) = center of the circle

r = radius

The standard equation for an ellipse (just a squat-looking circle) is shown on the next page.

We include the ellipse formula because it has shown up on previous exams, but if you can't remember it, don't worry. It only shows up once in a blue moon, and you never need to reproduce it from memory.

$$\frac{(x-h)^2}{a^2} + \frac{(y-k)^2}{b^2} = 1$$

(h,k) = center of the ellipse

$2a$ = horizontal axis (width)

$2b$ = vertical axis (height)

The standard equation for a parabola (just a U-shaped line) is shown below.

$$y = x^2$$

5. If the equation $x^2 = 1 - y^2$ were graphed in the standard (x,y) coordinate plane, the graph would represent which of the following geometric figures?

   A. Square
   B. Straight line
   C. Circle
   D. Triangle
   E. Parabola

Graphing Circles on Your Calculator

To draw a circle on your TI-83, you first need to alter the Zoom settings. Press ZOOM and select option [5: ZSquare]. Next, hit 2nd PRGM to access the [DRAW] menu. Select option [9: Circle]. All you need to do is enter the coordinates of the circle's center and the value of its radius. If, for instance, you were trying to graph a circle with a center of (2,3) and a radius of 5, your screen would say the following: Circle (2,3,5). Hit ENTER to see the resulting graph. You can draw as many circles as you like, but to clear the graph you need to press 2nd [DRAW] and select option [1: ClrDraw].

Here's How to Crack It

If you're familiar with what the equations of the various elements in the answer choices are supposed to look like, you may be able to figure out the problem without graphing at all. (However, that's why you bought a graphing calculator in the first place....) Let's consider what we know about the equations of geometric figures. If an equation has only x and y, we know that the graph of the equation is a straight line. (Think back to the $y = mx + b$ problems we did earlier.) However, in this equation, both x and y are squared, so we can rule out choice (B). There is no equation for a square, so we can rule out choice (A). Similarly, there's no equation for a triangle, so choice (D) is out. If only one of the variables were squared, this might be a parabola, but in this problem both are squared, which means we can eliminate choice (E). We are left with choice (C).

Estimating Note

Of course, we could also just plug some numbers into the equation and plot them out on a homemade (x,y) axis in the scratchwork column of the test booklet. Let's try this on the grid below.

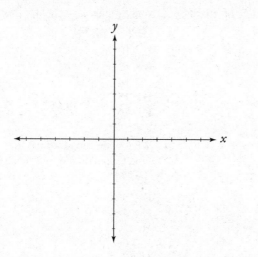

The easiest way to start is to let one of the variables equal 0. If $x = 0$, then y must equal 1. So one point of this equation is $(0,1)$. If we let $y = 0$, then x must equal 1. So another point of this equation is $(1,0)$. Plot out some other points of the equation. How about $(-1,0)$ and $(0,-1)$? What kind of geometric figure does it appear that we have? If you said a circle, you are correct.

Graphing and Coordinate Geometry Drill

For the answers to this drill, please go to Chapter 24.

1. Which of the following represents the solution of the inequality $-3x - 6 > 9$?

   A.

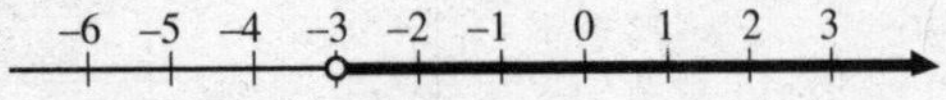

   B.

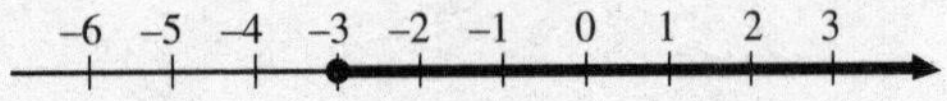

   C.

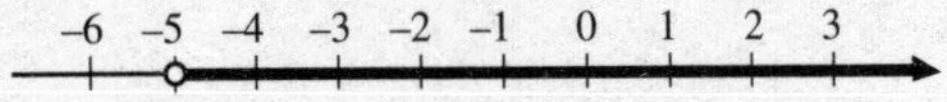

   D.

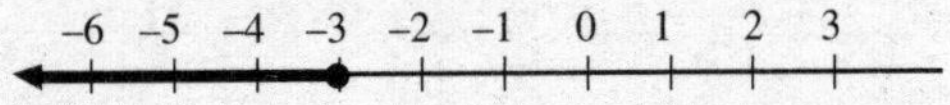

   E.

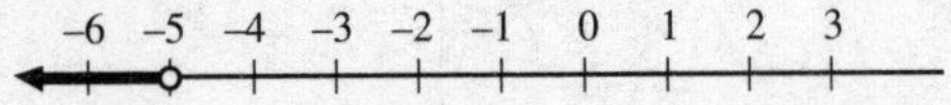

2. What is the midpoint of the line segment whose endpoints are represented on the coordinate axis by the points (3,5) and (−4,3) ?

   F. (−2, −5)

   G. $(-\frac{1}{2}, 4)$

   H. (1, 8)

   J. $(4, -\frac{1}{2})$

   K. (3, 3)

3. What is the slope of the line represented by the equation $10x + 2x = y + 6$?

   A. 10
   B. 12
   C. 14
   D. 15
   E. 16

4. What is the length of the line segment whose endpoints are represented on the coordinate axis by the points (−2,−1) and (1,3) ?

   F. 3
   G. 4
   H. 5
   J. 6
   K. 7

5. What is the slope of the line that contains the points (6,4) and (13,5) ?

   A. $-\frac{1}{8}$

   B. $-\frac{1}{9}$

   C. $\frac{1}{7}$

   D. 1

   E. 7

6. Which of the following gives the center point and radius of circle O, represented by the equation $(x - 3)^2 + (y + 2)^2 = 9$?

	Center	Radius
F.	(−3, 2)	3
G.	(−3, 2)	9
H.	(2, 3)	9
J.	(3,−2)	3
K.	(3,−2)	9

Summary

- Coordinate geometry tests many of the same concepts you've seen elsewhere on the Math test.

- If you are stuck on a coordinate geometry, sketch a graph and draw in a few points.

- Many coordinate geometry questions can be solved by putting them into the format $y + mx = b$, where m is the slope of the line and b is the y-intercept.

- Review the midpoint equation.

$$\left(x[m], y[m]\right) = \frac{x_1 + x_2}{2}, \frac{y_1 + y_2}{2}$$

- You can avoid using the confusing distance formula by drawing a right triangle and using the Pythagorean theorem.

- Every once in a while, ACT asks a question based on the equations of circles, ellipses, and parabolas. If you need a very high score, it might help to memorize these equations, but remember, these questions can frequently be done by using graphing to estimate the correct answer.

Chapter 15
Trigonometry

We've covered most of what you'll need to get a great score on the ACT Math test. This chapter will give a brief overview of one of the more advanced topics covered on the exam: Trigonometry. Though we will be discussing the identities and rules you need, we will always have an eye on how we can crack some of these problems more strategically as well.

A NOTE ON ACT MATH "DIFFICULTY"

As we noted in the first Math chapter in this book, "difficulty" is kind of a weird thing on the ACT. Is a problem difficult because it tests an unfamiliar concept? Or is it difficult because it tests a very familiar concept in a long word problem? We've seen that Plugging In and PITA can make some of the toughest problems pretty easy, so this part of the exam is more about POOD than ever. In this chapter, we will review trigonometry. Trigonometry is one of the more advanced topics on the ACT, and ACT wants to make you think it and the other advanced topics are very difficult. Some of these questions *are* difficult, tapping some of the most advanced topics of algebra II. But as you will see with trigonometry, most if not all of these questions can be answered correctly with a smart approach. We will review the relevant concepts, but we will also keep an eye on how to use the strategies from earlier chapters.

TRIGONOMETRY

It's easy to get freaked out by the trigonometry on the ACT. But remember there are only four questions on any given exam that deal with trig. What this means is that if you haven't learned trig before, it's not worth your time to try to do it now. If you are familiar with trig, on the other hand, here are a few topics that might come up. And don't worry, in four questions, there's no way all of these topics can come up!

Finally, as ever, remember that you don't get bonus points for doing anything the "real" way on the ACT. Always be on the lookout to use some of the great new techniques you've learned in this book.

SOHCAHTOA

There are four trig questions on any given ACT Math test, and typically two of them will ask about very basic trig concepts, covered by the acronym SOHCAHTOA. If you've had trig before, you probably know this acronym like the back of your hand. If not, here's what it means:

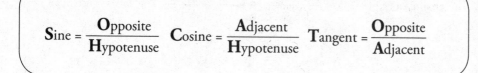

$$\textbf{S}\text{ine} = \frac{\textbf{O}\text{pposite}}{\textbf{H}\text{ypotenuse}} \quad \textbf{C}\text{osine} = \frac{\textbf{A}\text{djacent}}{\textbf{H}\text{ypotenuse}} \quad \textbf{T}\text{angent} = \frac{\textbf{O}\text{pposite}}{\textbf{A}\text{djacent}}$$

Sine is **O**pposite over **H**ypotenuse. Cosine is **A**djacent over **H**ypotenuse. Tangent is **O**pposite over **A**djacent. So in the triangle below, the sine of angle θ [*theta*, a Greek letter] would be $\frac{4}{5}$. The cosine of angle θ would be $\frac{3}{5}$. The tangent of angle θ would be $\frac{4}{3}$.

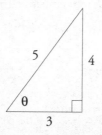

Sine, cosine, and tangent are often abbreviated as sin, cos, and tan, respectively.

The easier trig questions on this test involve the relationships between the sides of a right triangle. In the right triangle below, the angle *x* can be expressed in terms of the ratios of different sides of the triangle.

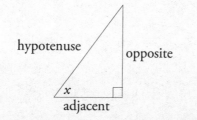

The **sine** of angle $x = \dfrac{\text{length of side opposite angle } x}{\text{length of hypotenuse}}$

The **cosine** of angle $x = \dfrac{\text{length of side adjacent angle } x}{\text{length of hypotenuse}}$

The **tangent** of angle $x = \dfrac{\text{length of side opposite angle } x}{\text{length of side adjacent angle } x}$

YOU'RE ALMOST DONE

There are three more relationships to memorize. They involve the reciprocals of the previous three.

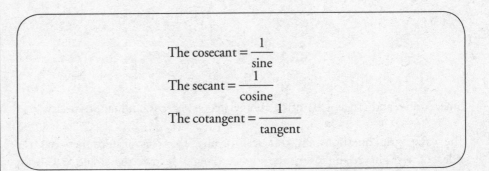

$$\text{The cosecant} = \frac{1}{\text{sine}}$$
$$\text{The secant} = \frac{1}{\text{cosine}}$$
$$\text{The cotangent} = \frac{1}{\text{tangent}}$$

Let's try a few problems.

31. What is sin θ, if tan $\theta = \dfrac{4}{3}$?

    A. $\dfrac{3}{4}$

    B. $\dfrac{4}{5}$

    C. $\dfrac{5}{4}$

    D. $\dfrac{5}{3}$

    E. $\dfrac{7}{3}$

> **Helpful Trig Identities**
>
> $$\sin^2 \theta + \cos^2 \theta = 1$$
>
> $$\frac{\sin \theta}{\cos \theta} = \tan \theta$$

Here's How to Crack It

It helps to sketch out the right triangle and fill in the information we know.

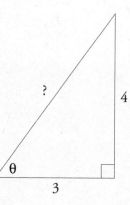

What kind of right triangle is this? That's right—a 3-4-5. Now, we need to know

the sine of angle θ: opposite over hypotenuse, or $\dfrac{4}{5}$, which is choice (B).

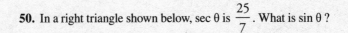

43. For all θ, $\dfrac{\cos \theta}{\sin^2 \theta + \cos^2 \theta} = ?$

   A. $\sin \theta$
   B. $\csc \theta$
   C. $\cot \theta$
   D. $\cos \theta$
   E. $\tan \theta$

Here's How to Crack It

$\sin^2 \theta + \cos^2 \theta$ always equals 1. $\dfrac{\cos \theta}{1} = \cos \theta$. The answer is choice (D).

50. In a right triangle shown below, $\sec \theta$ is $\dfrac{25}{7}$. What is $\sin \theta$?

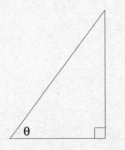

   F. $\dfrac{3}{25}$

   G. $\dfrac{5}{25}$

   H. $\dfrac{7}{25}$

   J. $\dfrac{24}{25}$

   K. $\dfrac{25}{7}$

Here's How to Crack It

The secant of any angle is the reciprocal of the cosine, which is just another way of saying that the cosine of angle θ is $\frac{7}{25}$.

Secant $\theta = \frac{1}{\cos\theta}$ so $\frac{1}{\cos\theta} = \frac{25}{7}$, which means that $\cos\theta = \frac{7}{25}$. Are you done? No! Cross off (H) because you know it's not the answer.

Cosine means adjacent over hypotenuse. Let's sketch it.

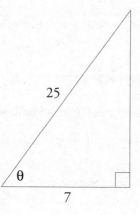

As you can see, we now have two sides of a right triangle. Can we find the third side? If you said this was one of the triples we told you about before, you are absolutely correct, although you also could have derived this by using the Pythagorean theorem. The third side must be 24. The question asks for sin θ. Sine = opposite over hypotenuse, or $\frac{24}{25}$, which is choice (J).

ADVANCED TRIGONOMETRY

When graphing a trig function, such as sine, there are two important **coefficients**, A and B: A{sin (Bθ)}.

The two coefficients A and B govern the **amplitude** of the graph (how tall it is) and the **period** of the graph (how long it takes to get through a complete cycle), respectively. If there are no coefficients, then that means A = 1 and B = 1 and the graph is the same as what you'd get when you graph it on your calculator.

- Increases in A increase the amplitude of the graph. It's a direct relationship.

That means if A = 2, then the amplitude is doubled. If A = $\frac{1}{2}$, then the amplitude is cut in half.

- Increases in B decrease the period of the graph. It's an inverse relationship.

That means if B = 2, then the period is cut in half, which is to say the graph completes a full cycle faster than usual. If B = $\frac{1}{2}$, then the period is doubled.

You can add to or subtract from the function as a whole, and also to or from the variable, but neither of those actions changes the shape of the graph, only its position and starting place.

Here's the graph of sin x. What are the amplitude and period?

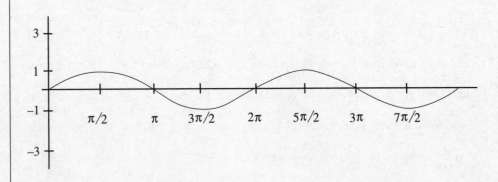

The simple function sin θ goes from −1 to 1 on the y-axis, so the amplitude is 1, while its period is 2π, which means that every 2π on the graph (as you go from side to side) it completes a full cycle. That's what you see in the graph above.

The graph below is also a sine function, but it's been changed. What is the function graphed here?

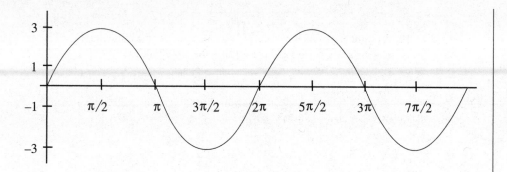

You have three things to check when looking at this graph: Is it sin or cos, is the period changed, and is the amplitude changed?

- This is a sin graph because it has a value of 0 at 0. Cos has a value of 1 at 0.
- It makes a complete cycle in 2π, so the period isn't changed. In other words, B = 1.
- The amplitude is triple what it normally is, so A = 3. The function graphed, therefore, is 3 sin θ.

How about here?

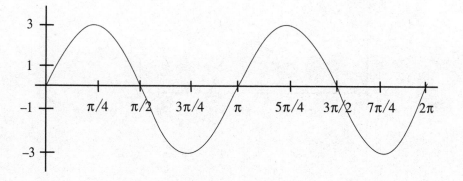

Once again, there are three things to check.

- This is a sin graph because it has a value of 0 at 0. Cos has a value of 1 at 0.
- It makes a complete cycle in π, so the period has changed—it's half of what it usually is. B has an inverse effect, which means B = 2.
- The amplitude is triple what it normally is, so A = 3. The function graphed, therefore, is 3 sin 2θ.

Let's try some practice questions.

49. As compared with the graph of $y = \cos x$, which of the following has the same period and three times the amplitude?

    A. $y = \cos 3x$

    B. $y = \cos \dfrac{1}{2}(x + 3)$

    C. $y = 3 \cos \dfrac{1}{2}x$

    D. $y = 1 + 3 \cos x$

    E. $y = 3 + \cos x$

Here's How to Crack It

Recall that the coefficient on the outside of the function changes the amplitude, and the one on the inside changes the period. Because the question states that the period isn't changed, you can eliminate choices (A), (B), and (C). The amplitude is three times greater, you're told; because there's a direct relationship between choice (A) and amplitude, you want to have a 3 multiplying the outside of the function. That leaves only choice (D) as a possibility.

52. Which of the following equations describes the equation graphed below?

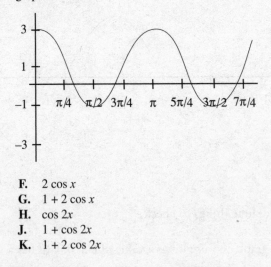

    F. $2 \cos x$
    G. $1 + 2 \cos x$
    H. $\cos 2x$
    J. $1 + \cos 2x$
    K. $1 + 2 \cos 2x$

Here's How to Crack It

At first it looks like this graph has an amplitude of 3, but if you look closer, you'll see that though the top value is 3, the bottom value is –1, which means that the whole graph has been shifted up. Because choices (F) and (H) don't add anything to the function (which is how you move a graph up and down), they're out. The period of this graph is half of what it usually is, so $B = 2$, which eliminates choice (G). Because the amplitude is changed also, you can eliminate choice (J). The answer is choice (K).

Trigonometry Drill

For the answers to this drill, please go to Chapter 24.

1. In $\triangle ABC$ below, the tan θ equals

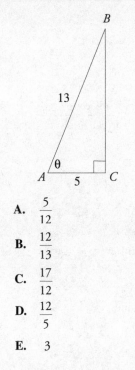

   A. $\dfrac{5}{12}$

   B. $\dfrac{12}{13}$

   C. $\dfrac{17}{12}$

   D. $\dfrac{12}{5}$

   E. 3

2. If the cotangent of an angle θ is 1, then the tangent of angle θ is

   F. −1
   G. 0
   H. 1
   J. 2
   K. 3

3. If $x + \sin^2 θ + \cos^2 θ = 4$, then x = ?

   A. 1
   B. 2
   C. 3
   D. 4
   E. 5

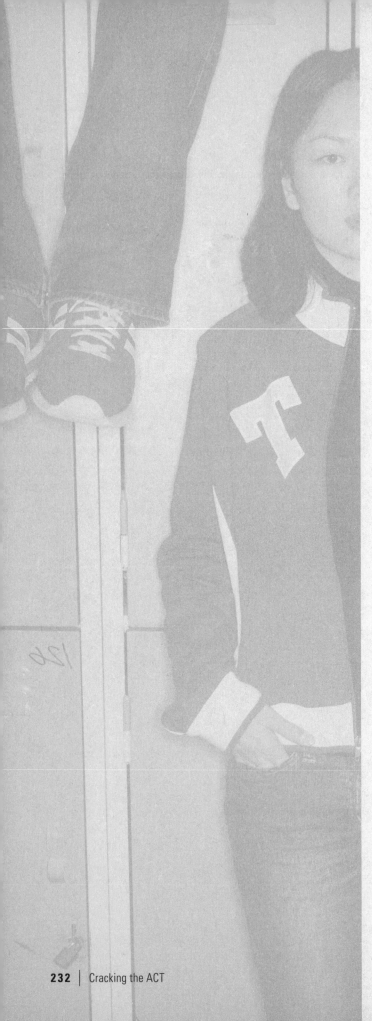

Summary

○ If you haven't had trigonometry in school, use your Letter of the Day on these trig problems. There are only 4!

○ Remember SOHCAHTOA!

$$\text{sine} = \frac{\text{opposite}}{\text{hypotenuse}}\text{ ; }\text{cosine} = \frac{\text{adjacent}}{\text{hypotenuse}}\text{ ;}$$

$$\text{tangent} = \frac{\text{opposite}}{\text{adjacent}}$$

○ For inverse functions, remember

$$\csc\theta = \frac{1}{\text{sine}} \qquad \sec\theta = \frac{1}{\text{cosine}}$$

$$\tan\theta = \frac{1}{\text{tangent}}$$

○ Remember the special trig identities.

$$\sin^2\theta + \cos^2\theta = 1$$

$$\frac{\sin\theta}{\cos\theta} = \tan\theta$$

○ For more advanced trig problems, remember A{*sin* (Bθ)}, where *A* represents the amplitude and *B* represents the period of the function. These are usually the easiest to see on the graph.

Part IV
How To
Crack the ACT
Reading Test

Chapter 16
Introduction to the
ACT Reading Test

The ACT Reading test always comes third, after the Math test and before the Science test. Reading is a unique challenge on a timed standardized test: There are no rules and formulas to review, and the reading skills you've developed throughout your school career do not necessarily work as well on the ACT.

To maximize your score on the ACT Reading test, you need to develop reading skills specific to this test and learn how to use your time effectively.

We'll teach you how to work the passages in a personal order of difficulty that makes best use of the time allotted. We'll also teach you how to employ a strategic and efficient approach that will earn you your highest possible score.

WHAT'S ON THE READING TEST

On the Reading test, you have 35 minutes to work though 4 passages and a total of 40 questions. The category, or genre, of the passages always appears in the same order: Prose Fiction, Social Science, Humanities, and Natural Science. The passages are roughly the same length, 800–850 words, and each is followed by 10 questions.

The passages feature authors and topics that the ACT writers judge typical of the type of reading required in first-year college courses. And your goal, according to ACT, is to read the passages and answer questions that prove you understood both what was "directly stated" as well as what were the "implied meanings."

That's a pretty simple summary of the Reading test, but what is simple on paper can be more challenging in practice. In other words, the description from ACT doesn't really match the experience of trying to read 3,400 words and prove "your understanding" 40 times with a nub of a #2 pencil in your sweaty grip as you face a glaring proctor and a ticking clock.

Your reading comprehension skills and the challenge of the ACT format are intertwined. In Chapter 17, we'll teach you a Basic Approach that draws upon your skills to crack the Reading test. But first, let's pull both apart for further examination.

Passage Content

Within the 4 categories, ACT selects excerpts from books and articles to create one long passage or two shorter passages. For each test, they choose 4 new passages, but the topics are always chosen from the same content areas of study.

Prose Fiction

The passages can be excerpts from novels or short stories, or even short stories in their entirety. While there are occasionally uses of historical fiction, most passages are contemporary, emphasize diversity, and often center on family relationships.

Social Science

Topics are drawn from the fields of anthropology, archaeology, biography, business, economics, education, geography, history, political science, psychology, and sociology.

Humanities

These passages are non-fiction, but they are usually memoirs or personal essays that can read much like fiction. Topics include architecture, art, dance, ethics, film, language, literary criticism, music, philosophy, radio, television, and theater.

Natural Science

Content areas include anatomy, astronomy, biology, botany, chemistry, ecology, geology, medicine, meteorology, microbiology, natural history, physiology, physics, technology, and zoology.

Reading Skills

For school, most of your reading is done with no time limits, at least theoretically. You have assignments of chapters, essays, and articles that you read, reread, highlight, and notate out of class. You may even make flash cards. In class, group discussions and even lectures from the teacher help you grasp the significance, meaning, and context of what you have read. You may need to "show your understanding" in a quiz, test, in-class essay, or paper, but you have had time to work with the text to develop a thorough understanding.

Outside of school, serious readers take time to process what they've read and form an opinion. As a college student, you'll be asked not only to read but also to think about what you've read and offer an opinion. Any professor will tell you that understanding takes thought, and thought usually takes time, more than 35 minutes.

When you take the ACT, you don't have the luxury of time. You can't read thoroughly, much less reread, highlight, notate, or make flashcards. There's certainly no group discussion to help elicit the meaning of each passage. So the first step in raising your score is to *stop treating the Reading test as a school assignment.* You need to read differently on the ACT, but you also need to know that a thorough, thoughtful grasp of the meaning isn't needed to answer the questions correctly.

In Chapters 17 and 18, we'll teach you how to read the passages and apply the Basic Approach to answer the questions correctly. But the next step in raising your scores is to apply your own personal order of difficulty to the order of the passages.

HOW TO CRACKING THE READING TEST

Order the Passages

You shouldn't work the passages in the order ACT offers *just because they're in that order.* Always choose your own order, working first the passages that are easiest for you and leaving for last the most difficult. What if natural science is the easiest for you? If you did the four passages in the order ACT offers, you could easily run out of time before even getting to the natural science, or find yourself with so little time that you manage to answer correctly only half the number of questions you would have otherwise sailed through.

Now, Later, Never

When time is your enemy, as it is on the ACT, find and work Now the passages that are easiest for you. Leave for Later, or perhaps even Never, the passages that are the most difficult for you.

Every time you take an ACT, for practice and for real, pick your own order. In practice, you will likely build up a track record to determine your Personal Order of Difficulty (POOD). However, each ACT features all new passages, and certain characteristics may vary enough to affect the difficulty of a passage. Pay attention to the particulars of each test and be willing to adapt your order for that day's test.

Under the Pacing section of this chapter, we'll help you decide if you should mark any passages as Never.

- **Your POOD:** categories and topics you like best
- **Paragraphs:** smaller and many are better than big and few
- **Questions:** the more line references, the better
- **Answers:** short are better than long

Let's discuss what each of these mean.

Your Personal Order of Difficulty (POOD)

The best way to determine which categories you work the best is through repeated practice tests followed by self-analysis. Regardless of where it is in your order, do you consistently do the best on social science? Do you usually prefer the prose fiction and humanities over the social science and natural science?

Before you've developed your POOD, identify your own likes and dislikes. For example, do you rarely read fiction outside of school? If so, then the prose fiction is unlikely to be a smart choice to do first. On the following pages, we've supplied brief excerpts of each category to give you an idea of what each is like.

Prose Fiction   On the fiction passages, facts typically matter less than do the setting, the atmosphere, and the relationships between characters. The plot and dialogue may even be secondary to the characters' thoughts and emotions, not all of which will be directly stated.

> Allen's grandmother was readying herself to leave. She was, in fact, putting the final touches on her makeup which, as always, looked to Allen as though someone had thrown it on her face with a shovel. As Mrs. Mandale placed her newly purchased bracelet
> 5 over her wrist, a look of troubled ambivalence came over her. "Perhaps this bracelet isn't right for me," she said. "I won't wear it."
>
> Waiting now for 30 minutes, Allen tried to be tolerant. "It is right for you," he said. "It matches your personality. Wear it." The bracelet was a remarkable illustration of poor taste. Its col-
> 10 ors were vulgar and the structure lacked any sign of thoughtful design. The truth is, it did match his grandmother's personality. All that she did and enjoyed was tasteless and induced in Allen a quiet hopelessness.

The questions are more likely to involve identifying the implied meanings than what was directly stated.

1. Allen most likely encouraged his grandmother to wear her bracelet because he:
   - **A.** found it colorful and approved of its appearance.
   - **B.** found its appearance pathetic and wished his grandmother to look pretty.
   - **C.** was impatient with his grandmother for spending time worrying about the bracelet.
   - **D.** felt the bracelet matched his grandmother's bright personality.

If you like to read fiction for school assignments or for pleasure, you may find the prose fiction one of the easier passages. If you don't like to read fiction, you may find them unclear and confusing. Do the prose fiction later, or perhaps never.

For the record, the answer is choice (C). Allen has been waiting and is trying "to be tolerant."

Social Science Social science passages should remind you of the papers you write for school. The organization will flow logically with clear topic sentences and well-chosen transitions to develop the main idea. The author may have a point of view on the subject or may simply deliver informative facts in a neutral tone.

Religion is so fundamental a part of human existence that one might easily forget to ask how it started. Yet it had to start somewhere and there had to be a time when human beings or their apelike ancestors did not entertain notions of the super-
5 natural. Hence the historian should want to probe the origins of religious belief.

It is doubtful that morality played a part in the beginnings of religious belief. Rather, religion is traceable to a far more fundamental human and animal characteristic. Storms, floods,
10 famine, and other adversities inspired *fear* in the hearts of primitive peoples as well they should have. Curiously, humankind early took the position that it might somehow subject such catastrophes to its control. Specifically, it believed it might control them by obedience and submission and by conforming its behavior to
15 their mandates. Worship, ritual, sacrifice of life, and property became means through which early peoples sought to cajole the powers and avoid the blights and miseries the peoples dreaded. As Petronius, in Lucretius's tradition remarked, "It was fear that first made the gods."

11. According to the passage, natural disasters contributed to the development of religion by:

   A. motivating human beings to acquire some command over their environment.

   B. making human beings distinguish themselves from animals.

   C. causing human beings to sacrifice their lives and goods.

   D. providing a need for ritual and tradition.

12. The author believes that the origins of religion:

   F. are extremely easy to ascertain and understand.

   G. should not be questioned by historians because religion is fundamental to civilized life.

   H. are directly tied to apelike subhuman species.

   J. should be the subject of serious historical inquiry.

The correct answer to 11 is choice (A) and the answer to 12 is choice (J).

Subscores

On your score report, ACT groups your performance on prose fiction and humanities under an Arts/ Literature subscore, and your performance on social science and natural science under a Social Studies/Science subscore. The subscores don't connect mathematically to the Reading score or the composite, but the groupings may help you think about your own order.

Humanities   Humanities passages are non-fiction, but because they are memoirs or personal essays, they can feel similar to the fiction passages. The narrative may use a more organic development instead of a linear one, and the tone will be more personal and perhaps more emotional than the more objective tones found in social and natural science.

> I grew up thinking I hated tomatoes. I used to describe the raw fruit as tasting like curdled water and preferred tomato sauce from a can. But it was not by accident that the tomato rapidly insinuated itself into the world's cuisines after 1492: it grows like
> 5 a weed, and wherever this weed took root, locals fell in love with it. To grow a bad tomato takes careful planning. Unfortunately, careful planning is exactly what the North American food industry has provided. It has carefully crafted tomatoes that can be hauled long distances and still look great, and the only casualty is taste.
> 10 And it has done so for so long now that most of us have forgotten, or never learned, what tomatoes are supposed to taste like.

24. In the passage, the phrase "careful planning" (line 7) refers to the method of tomato cultivation that has:

    F. allowed the plant to grow like a weed.
    G. valued appearance and durability over taste.
    H. failed to make the fruit taste less like curdled water.
    J. made the narrator change his opinion of tomatoes.

The answer to 24 is choice (G).

Natural Science   Natural science passages feature a lot of details and sometimes very technical descriptions. Similar to the social science passage, the natural science passage features a linear organization with clear topic sentences and transitions to develop the main idea. The author may or may not have an opinion on the topic.

> It is further noteworthy that the terrestrial vertebrate's most significant muscles of movement are no longer located lateral to the vertebral column as they are in the fish but rather in ventral and dorsal relation to it. This trend in terrestrial evolution
> 5 is highly significant and means that the terrestrial vertebrate's principal movements are fore and back, not side to side. The trend is well documented in the whale, an aquatic animal whose ancestors are terrestrial quadrupeds. The whale, in other words, has "returned" to the sea secondarily after an ancestral stage on
> 10 the land. Unlike the fish, and in accordance with its ancestry, it propels itself by moving the tail up and down, not side to side. In a sense, the whale moves itself by bending up and down at the waist. Indeed, that very analogy is recalled by the mythical mermaid figure who seems to represent a humanlike line returned
> 15 to the water secondarily like the whale.

The questions usually track the text pretty closely and require you to make few inferences.

> **31.** Which of the following best represents a general trend associated with mammalian evolution?
>
>   **A.** Enhancement of bodily movement from right to left and left to right
>   **B.** Minimization of muscle groups oriented lateral to the vertebral column
>   **C.** The development of propulsive fins from paired limbs
>   **D.** Secondary return to the sea

The answer to 31 is choice (B).

Order the Passages, Redux

As you take practice Reading tests, develop a consistent order that works for you, but always be willing to mix it up when you start each test, practice or real. The passages all run roughly the same number of words (800–850), and each features 10 questions followed by 4 answer choices. But the chosen topics, revealed in the blurb, and the way the passages, questions, and answers look can provide valuable clues that should make you reconsider that day's order.

Need Even More Practice?
The Princeton Review's *English and Reading Workout* has 4 more full-length Reading tests.

Paragraphs

Which passage would you rather work, one with 8–10 medium-sized paragraphs or one with three huge paragraphs? The overall length is the same, but the size and number of the paragraphs influences how easily you can navigate the passage and retrieve answers as you work the questions.

Some fiction passages can feature too many paragraphs, with each paragraph an individual line of dialogue. Too many paragraphs can make it just as difficult to locate the right part of the passage to find answers.

Ideally, a passage should feature 8–10 paragraphs, with each paragraph made up of 5–15 lines.

Questions

The questions on the Reading test don't follow a chronological order of the passage, and not every question comes with a line reference. Line references (and paragraph references) are maps, pointing to the precise part of the passage to find the answer. You waste no time getting lost, hunting through the passage to find where to read. Therefore, a passage with only 1–2 line or paragraph reference questions will be more challenging than one that features 4, 5, 6, or more (8 is the most we've ever seen).

Answers

Compare the two "questions" and their answer choices below.

13. Blah blah blah blah:

    A. are caused primarily by humanity's overriding concern with acceptance and peace.

    B. are due in part to a faulty understanding of history.

    C. should make historians question the role of the individual in human affairs.

    D. should provoke historical inquiry into humanity's willingness to tolerate adversity.

14. Blah blah blah blah:

    F. more traditional.

    G. more formal.

    H. less rigid.

    J. less informative.

Which do you think is the easier question? #14, of course! Long answers usually answer harder questions, and short answers usually answer easier questions. A passage with lots of questions with short answers is a good sign.

Use Your Eye, Not Your Brain

Look at the passages to evaluate the paragraphs, line references, and answer choices. Don't thoughtfully ponder and consider each element, and don't read through the questions. Quickly check the blurb to see if you recognize the subject or author.

Use your eye to scan the paragraphs, look for numbers amidst the questions, and the length of answer choices. If you see lots of warning signs on what is typically your first passage, leave it for Later. If you see great paragraphs, line references, and lots of short answers on the passage you typically do third, consider bumping it up to second, maybe first. This should take no more than 1–2 seconds.

The Blurb

The blurb at the top of the passage will provide the title, author, copyright date, and publisher. The title may not make the subject clear, but it's always worth checking to see if it will, or if you recognize the author.

Exercise: Pick Your Order

Put these passages in your own order: 1st, 2nd, 3rd, and 4th. We listed the number of paragraphs and questions with line references and short answers for the purpose of the exercise. This is not a hint that you need to be overly precise on a real test. You're looking for warning signs, a quick visual task.

Exercise I

Prose Fiction: _____

Unknown author and title, a ton of dialogue, over 20 paragraphs, many of them only one line, 2 line/paragraph references, and lots of long answers.

Social Science: _____

The title sounds technical, 6 paragraphs, 3 line/paragraph references, and 4 questions with short answers.

Humanities: _____

The title sounds deep, 9 paragraphs, 6 line/paragraph references, and 1 question with short answers.

Natural Science: _____

The title sounds kind of cool, 9 paragraphs, 4 line/paragraph references, and 4 questions with short answers.

Exercise II

Prose Fiction: _____

Familiar author, 7 paragraphs, 8 line/paragraph references, and 4 questions with short answers.

Social Science: _____

The title sounds sort of interesting, 6 paragraphs, 2 line/paragraph references, and 2 questions with short answers.

Humanities: _____

The title sounds sort of interesting, 11 paragraphs, 5 line/paragraph references, and 4 questions with short answers.

Natural Science: _____

The title sounds kind of dull, 9 paragraphs, 4 line/paragraph references, and 6 questions with short answers.

Order the Questions

In Chapter 17, we'll teach you the Basic Approach of how to attack the passage and the questions, and in that lesson we'll go into more depth about how you order the questions.

The only order you need to know now is the one to avoid: ACT's. The questions aren't in chronological order, nor are they in any order of difficulty from easiest to hardest. You shouldn't work the questions in the order given *just because ACT numbered them in order.*

Now Questions

Work the questions in an order that makes sense for you.

> Do Now questions that are easy to answer or easy to *find* the answer.

Easy to Answer   A question that is easy to answer often simply asks what the passage says, or as ACT puts it, what is directly stated. ACT in fact calls these "Referring questions," requiring the use of your "referral skills" (ACT's words, not ours) to find the right part of the passage. Referring questions don't require much reasoning; the answer will be waiting in black and white, and the correct answer will be barely paraphrased, if at all. Most answers are also relatively short: That's why you look for plenty of questions with short answers in picking your order of passages.

Easy to *Find* the Answer   A question with a line or a paragraph reference comes with a map, showing you where in the passage to find the answer. Some of these questions may be tough to answer, but as long as they come with line or paragraph references, they direct you where to read. Questions that come with a great lead word can also make finding the answer easy. Lead words are the nouns, phrases, and sometimes verbs that are specific to the passage. They're not the boilerplate language like "main idea" or "the passage characterizes."
Look at the following questions. All the lead words have been underlined.

11. Jeremy Bentham probably would have said that lawyers:

12. The author states that common law differs from civil law in that:

13. According to the passage, the integrative movement produced:

31. The main purpose of the passage is to:

35. Which of the following statements most accurately summarizes how the passage characterizes edema and hypoproteinemia?

> Lead words are words and phrases that can be found in the passage.
>
> Great lead words are proper nouns, unusual words, and dates.

Your eye can spot great lead words in the passage just by looking and without reading. They leap off the page. In Chapter 17, we'll teach you how to use lead words as part of the Basic Approach.

Later Questions

Later questions are both difficult to answer and difficult to find the answer, like Question 31 in the last set of examples. Most questions that are difficult to answer require reasoning skills to "show your understanding of statements with implied meaning."

Reasoning Questions   Reasoning questions require more thought than do Referring questions, so they do not qualify as "easy to answer." However, they are Later only if they don't come with a line or paragraph reference, which makes the answer easy to find.

In the description of the Reading test, ACT lists the various tasks that reasoning skills must be applied to.

- Determine main ideas
- Locate and interpret significant details
- Understand sequences of events
- Make comparisons
- Comprehend cause-effect relationships
- Determine the meaning of context-dependent words, phrases, and statements
- Draw generalizations
- Analyze the author's or narrator's voice and method

Any insight into the test writers' purpose and intent always benefits your preparation. However, you don't need to name the specific task when you come across it in a question. During the actual exam, identify questions as Now or Later, and don't forget that questions with a line or paragraph references are Now, regardless of the task assigned in the question.

Pace Yourself

It would be logical to assume that you must pace yourself to spend 8 minutes and 45 seconds on each passage. But to earn your best possible Reading score, you have to invest your time where it will do the most good and where its absence would create the most damage. To raise your score, you have to identify a pacing strategy that works for you.

> Focus on the number of questions that you need to answer correctly in order to earn your goal score.

Let's say you used 35 minutes to do all 4 passages, but because you had to hurry, you missed 2–3 questions per passage for a total of 10 wrong answers and, therefore, a raw score of 30. According to the score grid on page 24, 30 raw points would give you a scaled score of 25.

Letter of the Day (LOTD)
Just because you don't work on a passage doesn't mean you don't bubble in answers. Never leave any bubbles blank on the ACT. Bubble in your Letter of the Day for all the questions on your Never passages.

Let's say instead you used 35 minutes to do just 3 passages. With the extra time spent on your 3 best passages, you missed only 2 questions. And for that Never passage, you used your LOTD, choosing your favorite combination of answer choices to bubble in a nice straight line on the answer sheet. You picked up 2 correct answers, making your raw score 30, and your scaled score 25.

Which pacing strategy is better? Neither and both. Pacing strategies for Reading are just as personal as picking the order of the passages. You have to practice and find a pace that works for you. Some students are better off doing fewer passages, using the extra time per passage to answer most if not all questions correctly. Others find that even with all the time in the world, they'd never get all the questions right on one passage. They find the points they need across more passages, finding all the Now questions and guessing on the Never questions. Which type are you? That's what timed practice tests will help you discover.

One Sample Pacing Strategy

This is only one way to use the 35 minutes. This is a strategy for anyone working all 4 passages.

- First Passage: *11 minutes*
- Second Passage: *10 minutes*
- Third Passage: *8 minutes*
- Fourth Passage: *6 minutes*

Goal Score

Use the score grid on page 24 to find your goal score and determine how many raw points you need. This is the number of questions you need to answer correctly, whether by working them or lucky LOTD. A correct answer is a correct answer, no matter how you earn it.

Just as there is no one pacing strategy for all students, there is no one pace for all passages. In practice, try varying the amount of time you spend on each passage. Some students do best by dividing the 35 minutes equally over all the passages they do. Other students do best by spending more time on the first one or two passages and less on the remaining passages. Experiment in practice until you find a pacing strategy that works for you.

Be Flexible

Flexibility is key to your ACT success, particularly on the Reading test. Picking the order of the passages rests on your willingness to flip your order when you see that day's test. The passages, after all, are new on each test you see, and you have to look at what you've been given and adapt.

Similarly, you have to be flexible in your pacing. Focus on the number of raw points you need, and don't drown in one particular passage or get stuck on one tough question. Get out of a passage on which you've already spent too much time. Force yourself to guess on the question you've been rereading for minutes, use LOTD on any questions still left, and move on.

We're not saying this is easy. In fact, changing your own instinctual behavior is the hardest part of cracking the Reading test. Everyone has made the mistake of ignoring that voice that's screaming inside your head to move on, and we've all answered back, "But I know I'm almost there and if I take just a little more time, I know l can get it."

You may in fact get that question. But that one right answer likely cost you 2–3 others. And even worse, you had probably already narrowed it down to two answer choices. You were down to a fifty-fifty chance of getting it right, and instead you wasted more time to prove the one right answer.

In Chapters 17 and 18, we'll show you how to use that time more effectively to begin with and what to do when you're down to two. But both skills depend on the Process of Elimination, POE.

POE

POE is a powerful tool on a multiple-choice, standardized test. On the Reading test, you may find several Now questions easy to answer and be able to spot the right answer right away among the four choices. There will be plenty of tough Reasoning questions, however, whose answers aren't obvious, either in your own words or among the four choices. You can easily fall into the trap of rereading and rereading to figure out the answer. Wrong answers, however, can be more obvious to identify. After all, they are there to hide the right answer. In fact, if you can cross off all the wrong ones, the right answer will be waiting there for you. Even if you cross off only one or two, the right answer frequently becomes more obvious.

We'll spend more time with POE in the following chapters. For now, just remember that we started this lesson with a reminder that the first step in raising your ACT Reading score is to stop treating this test as if it's a reading assignment for school. You don't get extra points for knowing the answer before you look at the answer choices. You get a point for a correct answer, and you need to get to as many questions as possible in order to answer them. Use POE to escape the death spiral questions that will hold you back.

Process of Elimination
Each time you eliminate a wrong answer, you increase your chance of choosing the correct answer.

Summary

- There are always 4 passages and 40 questions on the Reading test.

- The passages are always in the same order: Prose Fiction, Social Science, Humanities, Natural Science.

- Each passage has 10 questions.

- The passages are all roughly the same length, between 800–850 words.

- Follow your POOD to pick your own order of the passages.

- Look for passages to do Now whose categories and topics you like best or find easier.

- Look for passages with 8–10 paragraphs of 5–15 lines.

- Look for passages with lots of line references.

- Look for passages with lots of questions with short answers.

- Pace yourself. Find the number of questions you need to answer correctly in order to reach your goal score.

- Be Flexible. Be ready to adapt your order, leave a tough passage, or guess on a tough question.

- Use Process of Elimination to cross off wrong answers and save time.

Chapter 17
The 4-Step Basic Approach

To earn your highest possible score on the Reading test, you need an efficient and strategic approach to working the passages. In this chapter, we'll teach you how to work the passages, questions, and answers.

HOW TO CRACK THE READING TEST

The most efficient way to boost your Reading score is to pick your order of the passages and apply our 4-Step Basic Approach to the passages. Use the Basic Approach to enhance your reading skills and train them for specific use on the ACT.

The 4-Step Basic Approach

Step 1: **Preview**. Check the blurb and map the questions.
Step 2: **Work the Passage**. Spend 2–3 minutes reading the passage.
Step 3: **Work the Questions**. Use your POOD to find Now, Later, and Never Questions.
Step 4: **Work the Answers**. Use POE.

Before we train you on each step in cracking the test the right way, let's talk about the temptations to attack the passages in the wrong way.

This Isn't School

In the Introduction, we discussed the reading skills you've spent your whole school career developing. You have been rewarded for your ability to develop a thorough, thoughtful grasp of the meaning and significance of the text. But in school, you have the benefit of time, not to mention the aid of your teachers' lectures, class discussions, and various tools to help you not only understand but also remember what you've read. You have none of those tools on the Reading test, but you walk into it with the instinct to approach the Reading test as if you do.

Where does that leave you on the ACT Reading test? You spend several minutes reading the passage, trying to understand the details and follow the author's main point. You furiously underline what you think may be important points that will be tested later in the questions. And when you hit a particularly confusing chunk of detailed text, what do you do? You read it again. And again. You worry you can't move on until you have solved this one detail. All the while, time is slipping by....

Now, onto the questions. Your first mistake is to do them in order. But as we told you in the Introduction, they are not in order of difficulty, nor chronologically. You confront main-idea questions before specific questions. You try to answer the questions all from memory. After all, you've spent so much time reading the passage, you don't have the time to go back to find or even confirm an answer. And when you do occasionally go back to read a specific part of the passage, you still don't see the answer. So you read the chunk of the passage again and again.

If you approach the Reading test this way, you will likely not earn the points you need to hit your goal score.

The Passage

You don't earn points from reading the passage. You earn points from answering the questions correctly. And you have no idea what the questions will ask. You're searching desperately through the passage, looking for conclusions and main points. You stumble on the details, rereading several times to master them. But how do you even know what details are important if you haven't seen the questions?

The Questions

When you answer the questions from memory, you will either face answer choices that all seem right, or you will fall right into ACT's trap, choosing an answer choice that sounds right with some familiar words, but which in reality doesn't match what the passage said.

The test writers at ACT know everyone is inclined to attack the Reading test this way. They write deceptive answer choices that will tempt you because that's what wrong answers have to do. If the right answer were surrounded by three ridiculous, obviously wrong answers, everyone would get a 36. Wrong answers have to sound temptingly right, and the easiest way to do that is to use noticeable terms out of the passage. You gratefully latch onto them the way a drowning person clutches a life preserver.

Pot Holes

If you're out driving and you hit a pot hole, do you back up and drive over it again? Rereading text you didn't understand is the literary equivalent of driving over and over the same pot hole.

THE 4-STEP BASIC APPROACH

The best way to beat the ACT system is to use a different one. The 4-Step Basic Approach will help you direct the bulk of your time to where you earn points, on the questions and answers. When you read the passage, you'll read knowing exactly what you're looking for.

Step 1: Preview

The first step involves two parts. First, check the blurb at the beginning of the passage to see if it offers any additional information. 99% of the time, all it will offer will be the title, author, copyright date, and publisher. There is even no guarantee that the title will convey the topic. But occasionally, the blurb will define an unfamiliar term, place a setting, or identify a character.

> **Passage III**
>
> **HUMANITIES:** This passage is adapted from the article "The Sculpture Revolution" by Michael Michalski (©1998 Geer Publishing).

True to form, this offers only the basic information.

The real value in Step 1 comes in the work you do with the questions.

Map the Questions

Take no more than 30 seconds to map the questions. Underline the lead words. Star any line or paragraph reference.

Second Time Around
You'll check the blurb twice. Once when you're confirming your order and now as part of Step 1.

Lead Words
We introduced lead words in the Introduction. These are the specific words and phrases that you will find in the passage. They are not the boilerplate language of reading test questions like "main idea" or "author's purpose." They are usually nouns, phrases, or verbs.

Map the following questions that accompany the humanities passage. Even if a question has a line/paragraph reference, underline any lead words in the question.

21. The author expresses the idea that:

22. The information in lines 69–74 suggests that Quentin Bell believes that historians and critics:

23. Which of the following most accurately summarizes how the passage characterizes subjectivism's effect on Rodin??

24. According to the passage, academicism and mannerism:

25. Information in the fourth paragraph (lines 31–38) makes clear that the author believes that:

26. According to the passage, Renoir differs from Daleur in that:

27. According to the passage, Cézanne's work is characterized by:

28. Based on information in the sixth paragraph (lines 45–52), the author implies that:

29. In line 59, when the author uses the phrase "modern" he most nearly means sculpture that:

30. Which of the following statements would the author most likely agree with?

Your mapped questions should look like this:

21. The author expresses the idea that:

☆ 22. The information in lines 69–74 suggests that <u>Quentin Bell</u> believes that <u>historians</u> and <u>critics</u>:

23. Which of the following most accurately summarizes how the passage characterizes <u>subjectivism's effect</u> on <u>Rodin</u>?

24. According to the passage, <u>academicism</u> and <u>mannerism</u>:

☆ 25. Information in the fourth paragraph (lines 31–38) makes clear that the author believes that:

26. According to the passage, <u>Renoir differs from Daleur</u> in that:

27. According to the passage, <u>Cézanne's work</u> is characterized by:

☆ 28. Based on information in the sixth paragraph (lines 45–52) the author implies that:

☆ 29. In line 59, when the author uses the phrase "<u>modern</u>" he most nearly means <u>sculpture</u> that:

30. Which of the following statements would the author most likely agree with?

Two Birds, One Stone

Mapping the questions provides two key benefits. First, you've just identified with stars four questions with easy-to-find answers. With all those great lead words, you have two more questions whose answers will be easy to find. Second, you have the main idea of the passage *before* you've read it. When you read the passage knowing what to look for, you *read actively*.

Look again at all the words you've underlined. They tell you what the passage will be about: modern sculpture, Renoir, Daleur, Cézanne, Rodin, and a bunch of "-isms" that you could safely guess concern art. There is also someone named Quentin Bell, historians, critics, and art. You're ready to move onto Step 2.

Read Actively

Reading actively means knowing in advance what you're going to read. You have the important details to look for, and you won't waste time on details that never appear in a question. Reading passively means walking into a dark cave, wandering in the dark trying to see what dangers or treasures await. Reading actively means walking into the cave with a flashlight and a map, looking for what you know is in there.

Step 2: Work the Passage

Your next step is to work the passage. Spend no more than 2–3 minutes. Look for and underline the lead words, underlining each time any appear more than once.

You're not reading to understand every word and detail. You'll read smaller selections in depth when you work the questions. If you can't finish in three minutes, don't worry about it. We'll discuss time management strategies later in the chapter.

Don't Back Up Over the Pot Hole

If you read something you don't understand, do not reread it. Just keep going and worry about it later only if you have to.

Passage III

HUMANITIES: This passage is adapted from the article "The Sculpture Revolution" by Michael Michalski (©1998 Geer Publishing).

If we were to start fresh in the study of sculpture or any art, we might observe that the record is largely filled by works of relatively few great contributors. Next to the influences of these great geniuses, time periods themselves
5 are of little significance. The study of art and art history are properly directed to the achievements of outstanding individual artists, not the particular decades or centuries in which any may have worked.

Nonetheless, when we study art in historical perspective
10 we select a convenient frame of reference through which diverse styles and talents are to be compared. Hence we write of "movements" and attempt to understand each artist in terms of the one to which he "belongs." Movements have limited use, but we should not talk of realism, impressionism,
15 cubism, or surrealism as though they genuinely had lives of their own to which the artist was answerable. We regard the movement as the governing force and the artist as its servant. Yet it is well to remember that the movements do not necessarily present themselves in orderly chronological series and
20 the individual artist frequently weaves her way into one and out of another over the course of a single career.

Great artists are not normally confined by the "movements" that others may name for them. Rather, they transcend the conventional structure working now in one style, then in
25 another, and later in a third. Picasso's work, for example, echoes many of the artistic movements, and other artists too, moving from one style through another. Indeed, artists are people, and any may decide to alter her style for no more complex a reason than that which makes most people want
30 to "try something new" once in a while.

In studying modern sculpture one is tempted to begin a history with Auguste Rodin (1840–1917), who was a contemporary of Paul Cézanne (1839–1906). Yet the two artists did not, in artistic terms, belong to the same period. Their
35 strategies and objectives differed. Although Rodin was surely a great artist, he did not do for sculpture what Cézanne did for painting. In fact, although Cézanne was a painter, he had a more lasting effect on sculpture than did Rodin.

Cézanne's work constitutes a reaction against impres-
40 sionism and the confusion he thought it created. He searched persistently for the "motif." Cézanne strived for clarity of form and was able to convert his personal perceptions into concrete, recognizable substance. He is justly considered to have offered the first glimmer of a new art—a new classicism.

45 Rodin was surely a great artist, but he was not an innovator as was Cézanne; prevailing tides of subjectivism came over him. Rodin's mission was to reinvest sculpture with the integrity it lost when Michelangelo died. Rodin succeeded in this mission. His first true work, *The Age of Bronze* (1877),
50 marked the beginning of the end of academicism, mannerism, and decadence that had prevailed since Michelangelo's last sculpture, the *Rondanini Pietà*.

Yet it is largely Cézanne, not Rodin, who was artistic ancestor to Picasso, Gonzalez, Brancusi, Archipenko, Lipchitz,
55 and Laurens, and they are unquestionably the first lights in the "new art" of sculpture. This "new art," of course, is the sculpture we call "modern." It is modern because it breaks with tradition and draws little on that which preceded it.

When I speak of "modern" sculpture, I do not refer to
60 every sculptor nor even to every highly talented sculptor of our age. I do not exclude, necessarily, the sculptors of an earlier time. Modern sculpture, as far as I am concerned, is any that consciously casts tradition aside and seeks forms more suitable to the senses and values of its time. Renoir and
65 Daumier are, in this light, modern sculptors notwithstanding the earlier time at which they worked. Daleur and Carpeaux are not modern, although they belong chronologically to the recent era.

Professor Quentin Bell argues that historians and critics
70 name as "modern" those sculptors in whom they happen to be interested and that the term when abused in that way has no historical or artistic significance. That, I think, is not right. The problem is that Professor Bell thinks "modern" means "now," when in fact it means "new."

Your passage should look like this. If you couldn't find all the lead words to underline, don't worry. You'll do those questions Later. But did you notice that there is nothing underlined in the second and third paragraphs? If you hadn't mapped the questions first, you would have likely wasted a lot of time on details that ACT doesn't seem to care about.

Passage III

HUMANITIES: This passage is adapted from the article "The Sculpture Revolution" by Michael Michalski (©1998 Geer Publishing).

If we were to start fresh in the study of sculpture or any art, we might observe that the record is largely filled by works of relatively few great contributors. Next to the influences of these great geniuses, time periods themselves
5 are of little significance. The study of art and art history are properly directed to the achievements of outstanding individual artists, not the particular decades or centuries in which any may have worked.

Nonetheless, when we study art in historical perspective
10 we select a convenient frame of reference through which diverse styles and talents are to be compared. Hence we write of "movements" and attempt to understand each artist in terms of the one to which he "belongs." Movements have limited use, but we should not talk of realism, impressionism,
15 cubism, or surrealism as though they genuinely had lives of their own to which the artist was answerable. We regard the movement as the governing force and the artist as its servant. Yet it is well to remember that the movements do not necessarily present themselves in orderly chronological series and
20 the individual artist frequently weaves her way into one and out of another over the course of a single career.

Great artists are not normally confined by the "movements" that others may name for them. Rather, they transcend the conventional structure working now in one style, then in
25 another, and later in a third. Picasso's work, for example, echoes many of the artistic movements, and other artists too, moving from one style through another. Indeed, artists are people, and any may decide to alter her style for no more complex a reason than that which makes most people want
30 to "try something new" once in a while.

In studying modern sculpture one is tempted to begin a history with Auguste Rodin (1840–1917), who was a contemporary of Paul Cézanne (1839–1906). Yet the two artists did not, in artistic terms, belong to the same period. Their
35 strategies and objectives differed. Although Rodin was surely a great artist, he did not do for sculpture what Cézanne did for painting. In fact, although Cézanne was a painter, he had a more lasting effect on sculpture than did Rodin.

Cézanne's work constitutes a reaction against impres-
40 sionism and the confusion he thought it created. He searched persistently for the "motif." Cézanne strived for clarity of form and was able to convert his personal perceptions into concrete, recognizable substance. He is justly considered to have offered the first glimmer of a new art—a new classicism.

45 Rodin was surely a great artist, but he was not an innovator as was Cézanne; prevailing tides of subjectivism came over him. Rodin's mission was to reinvest sculpture with the integrity it lost when Michelangelo died. Rodin succeeded in this mission. His first true work, *The Age of Bronze* (1877),
50 marked the beginning of the end of academicism, mannerism, and decadence that had prevailed since Michelangelo's last sculpture, the *Rondanini Pietà*.

Yet it is largely Cézanne, not Rodin, who was artistic ancestor to Picasso, Gonzalez, Brancusi, Archipenko, Lipchitz,
55 and Laurens, and they are unquestionably the first lights in the "new art" of sculpture. This "new art," of course, is the sculpture we call "modern." It is modern because it breaks with tradition and draws little on that which preceded it.

When I speak of "modern" sculpture, I do not refer to
60 every sculptor nor even to every highly talented sculptor of our age. I do not exclude, necessarily, the sculptors of an earlier time. Modern sculpture, as far as I am concerned, is any that consciously casts tradition aside and seeks forms more suitable to the senses and values of its time. Renoir and
65 Daumier are, in this light, modern sculptors notwithstanding the earlier time at which they worked. Daleur and Carpeaux are not modern, although they belong chronologically to the recent era.

Professor Quentin Bell argues that historians and critics
70 name as "modern" those sculptors in whom they happen to be interested and that the term when abused in that way has no historical or artistic significance. That, I think, is not right. The problem is that Professor Bell thinks "modern" means "now," when in fact it means "new."

Step 3: Work the Questions

As we told you in the Introduction, you can't do the questions in the order ACT gives you. #21 has no stars or lead words and poses what seems to be a Reasoning question. Thus, it's neither easy to answer, nor is the answer easy to find. #22 is a great question to start with, however. It has a star, and it's a Referral question, asking directly what is stated in the passage.

☆ **22.** The information in lines 69–74 suggests that <u>Quentin Bell</u> believes that <u>historians</u> and <u>critics</u>:

Here's How to Crack It

Make sure you understand what the question is asking. Now read what you need out of the passage to find the answer. The line reference points you to line 69, but you'll find your answer within a window of 5–10 lines of the line references. Read the last paragraph to see what Quentin Bell thinks about historians and critics.

Work the Questions

1. Pick your order of questions. Do Now questions that are easy to answer, easy to find the answer, or best of all, both.
2. Read the question to understand what it's asking.
3. Read what you need in the passage to find your answer. In general, read a window of 5–10 lines.

Step 4: Work the Answers

Do you see the importance of making sure you understand the question? We care here what Quentin Bell thinks about historians and critics, not what the author thinks of them. But the question is a Referral question, asking what is directly stated. Lines 69–72 offers Bell's opinion. Now find the match in the answers.

> ## Work the Answers
> - If you can clearly identify the answer in the passage, look for its match among the answers.
> - If you aren't sure if an answer is right or wrong, leave it. You'll either find one better or three worse.
> - Cross off any choice that talks about something not found in your window.
> - If you're down to two, choose key words in the answer choices. See if you can locate them back in the passage and determine if the answer choice matches what the passage says.

Here's How to Crack It

      F. have no appreciation for the value of modern art.

Bell is critical of historians and critics, and value could refer to significance in the passage. This seems possible, so keep it.

      G. abuse art and its history.

The passage states that the term is abused, not art and its history. This is a trap, and it's wrong. Cross it off.

      H. should evaluate works of art on the basis of their merit without regard to the artist's fame.

There was nothing in the window about "fame." Cross it off.

      J. attach the phrase "modern art" to those sculptors that intrigue them.

Attach the phrase is a good match for *name* as '*modern*' and *sculptors that intrigue them* is a good match for *in whom they happen to be interested*. This answer is better than choice (F), and it is correct.

Steps 3 and 4: Repeat

Look for all the Now questions and repeat Steps 3 and 4. Make sure you understand what the question is asking. Read what you need to find your answer, usually a window of 5–10 lines. Work the answers, using POE until you find your answer.

Referral Questions

Referral questions are easy to answer because they ask what was directly stated in the passage. Read the question carefully to identify what it's asking. The passage directly states something about what? Once you find your window to read, read to find the answer. The correct answers to Referral questions are barely paraphrased and will match the text very closely.

> ### How to Spot Referral Questions
> - Questions that begin with *According to the passage*
> - Questions that ask what the passage or author states
> - Questions with short answers

If the answer to a Referral question is also easy to find, they are great Now questions. Look for Referral questions with line references or great lead words.

---

26. According to the passage, <u>Renoir differs from Daleur</u> in that:

    F. Daleur had no inspiration and Renoir was tremendously inspired.

    G. Renoir's work was highly innovative and Daleur's was not.

    H. Daleur was a sculptor and Renoir was not.

    J. Renoir revered tradition and Daleur did not.

       When I speak of "<u>modern</u>" <u>sculpture</u>, I do not refer to
60 every sculptor nor even to every highly talented sculptor of our
age. I do not exclude, necessarily, the sculptors of an earlier
time. <u>Modern sculpture</u>, as far as I am concerned, is any that
consciously casts tradition aside and seeks forms more suitable
to the senses and values of its time. <u>Renoir</u> and Daumier are,
65 in this light, modern sculptors notwithstanding the earlier time
at which they worked. <u>Daleur</u> and Carpeaux are not modern,
although they belong chronologically to the recent era.

Here's How to Crack It

Renoir and *Daleur* are great lead words, easy for your eye to spot in the eighth paragraph. On the real test, you'll have the passage on the left and all your mapped questions on the right page. For convenience's sake and to avoid flipping back to the passage, we're printing the window to read with the question.

Lines 64–66 state that *Renoir was a modern sculptor* and *Daleur* is not. But that same sentence mentions four artists *in this light*. What light? Any time you see *this*, *that*, or *such* in front of a noun, back up to read the first mention of that topic. *This light* is the author's definition of modern, given on lines 62–64.

Now work the answers. Cross off answers that don't state Renoir is modern and Daleur is not. *Innovative* in choice (G) is a good match for modern and is the correct answer. *Inspiration* in choice (F) doesn't match modern. Choice (H) is disproven by the passage. Choice (J) tempts with *tradition* but compare it to the text, and the author states modern sculptures *consciously casts tradition aside*.

Try another Referral question with great lead words.

---

27. According to the passage, Cézanne's work is characterized by:

   A. a return to subjectivism.
   B. a pointless search for form.
   C. excessively personal expressions.
   D. rejection of the impressionistic philosophy.

> Cézanne's work constitutes a reaction against impres-
> 40 sionism and the confusion he thought it created. He searched
> persistently for the "motif." Cézanne strived for clarity of form
> and was able to convert his personal perceptions into concrete,
> recognizable substance. He is justly considered to have offered
> the first glimmer of a new art—a new classicism.

Here's How to Crack It

Cézanne appears first in the fourth paragraph, but the question is about *Cézanne's work*, which is in the fifth paragraph. Choice (D) matches *reaction against impressionism* and is the correct answer.

Reasoning Questions

Reasoning questions require you to read between the lines. Instead of being directly stated, the correct answer is implied or suggested. In other words, look for the larger point that the author is making.

Reasoning questions aren't as easy to answer as Referral questions, but they're not *that* much harder. If they come with a line or paragraph reference or a great lead word, they should be done Now.

How to Spot Reasoning Questions

- Questions that use *infer*, *means*, *suggests*, or *implies*
- Questions that ask about the purpose or function of part of all of the passage
- Questions that ask what the author or a person written about in the passage would agree or disagree with
- Questions that ask you to characterize or describe all or parts of the passage
- Questions with long answers

☆ **25.** Information in the fourth paragraph (lines 31–38) makes clear that the author believes that:

    A.   Rodin was more innovative than Cézanne.
    B.   Cézanne was more innovative than Rodin.
    C.   Modern art is more important than classical art.
    D.   Cézanne tried to emulate impressionism.

       In studying <u>modern sculpture</u> one is tempted to begin a history with Auguste <u>Rodin</u> (1840–1917), who was a contemporary of Paul <u>Cézanne</u> (1839–1906). Yet the two artists did not, in artistic terms, belong to the same period. Their
35 strategies and objectives differed. Although <u>Rodin</u> was surely a great artist, he did not do for sculpture what <u>Cézanne</u> did for painting. In fact, although <u>Cézanne</u> was a painter, he had a more lasting effect on sculpture than did <u>Rodin</u>.

Here's How to Crack It

The question doesn't provide specific clues what to look for and instead asks what the author's point is in the fourth paragraph. The author is comparing the artists Cézanne and Rodin. The concluding sentence states that *Cézanne . . . had a more lasting effect on sculpture than did Rodin*. Choice (A) says the opposite. The paragraph does not mention either *classical art* or *impressionism* so Choices (C) and (D) can be eliminated. Choice (B) is a good paraphrase of the author's point and is the correct answer.

———————————○———————————

Work Now the Reasoning questions with line or paragraph references or great lead words. Use POE heavily as you work the answers.

———————————○———————————

☆ **28.** Based on information in the sixth paragraph (lines 45–52) the author implies that:

    F. mannerism reflects a lack of integrity.

    G. Rodin disliked the work of Michelangelo.

    H. Rodin embraced the notion of decadence.

    J. Rodin's work represented a shift in style different from the works of artists who preceded him.

45   <u>Rodin</u> was surely a great artist, but he was not an innovator as was <u>Cézanne</u>; prevailing tides of <u>subjectivism</u> came over him. <u>Rodin</u>'s mission was to reinvest sculpture with the integrity it lost when Michelangelo died. <u>Rodin</u> succeeded in this mission. His first true work, *The Age of Bronze* (1877), marked the be-
50   ginning of the end of <u>academicism</u>, <u>mannerism</u>, and decadence that had prevailed since Michelangelo's last sculpture, the *Rondanini Pietà*.

Here's How to Crack It

Use POE. Choices (F) and (H) use terms from the paragraph but garbles them. Rodin wanted to restore elements of sculpture that had changed since the death of Michelangelo, which means he respected Michelangelo's work, so choice (G) is not supported. The last sentence states that Rodin's work *marked the beginning of the end* and therefore represented something new, as the correct answer (J) states.

———————————○———————————

☆ **29.** In line 59, when the author uses the phrase "modern" he most nearly means sculpture that:

- **A.** postdates the *Rondanini Pietà*.
- **B.** is not significantly tied to work that comes before it.
- **C.** shows no artistic merit.
- **D.** genuinely interests contemporary critics.

When I speak of "modern" sculpture, I do not refer to every
60 sculptor nor even to every highly talented sculptor of our age. I do not exclude, necessarily, the sculptors of an earlier time. Modern sculpture, as far as I am concerned, is any that consciously casts tradition aside and seeks forms more suitable to the senses and values of its time. Renoir and Daumier are, in this light, modern
65 sculptors notwithstanding the earlier time at which they worked. Daleur and Carpeaux are not modern, although they belong chronologically to the recent era.

Here's How to Crack It

Use POE. The *Rondanini Pietà* is in the wrong window, so eliminate choice (A). Choice (B) is a good paraphrase of the art that *consciously casts tradition aside and seeks forms more suitable to the sense and values of its time*, and it is the correct answer. Choice (C) can't be proven by the passage; the author doesn't state that they have no worth at all. Choice (D) tempts with *contemporary* as a possible match for *modern* or *its time*, but *critics* are not in this window.

Later Questions

Once you have worked all the questions with line or paragraph references and great lead words, move to the Later questions. The answers to questions without a line or paragraph reference or any great lead words can be difficult to find, which is why you should do them Later. But the later you do them, the easier they become. You've either found them or you've narrowed down where to look. From the windows you've read closely to answer all the Now questions, you may have located lead words you missed when you worked the passage. And if you haven't, then they must be in the few paragraphs you haven't read since you worked the passage.

24. According to the passage, <u>academicism</u> and <u>mannerism</u>:

    F. were readily visible in *The Age of Bronze*.
    G. were partially manifest in the *Rondanini Pietà*.
    H. were styles that Rodin believed lacked integrity.
    J. were styles that Rodin wanted to restore into fashion.

45   <u>Rodin</u> was surely a great artist, but he was not an innovator
as was <u>Cézanne</u>; prevailing tides of <u>subjectivism</u> came over him.
<u>Rodin</u>'s mission was to reinvest sculpture with the integrity it
lost when Michelangelo died. <u>Rodin</u> succeeded in this mission.
His first true work, *The Age of Bronze* (1877), marked the be-
50   ginning of the end of <u>academicism</u>, <u>mannerism</u>, and decadence
that had prevailed since Michelangelo's last sculpture, the
Rondanini Pietà.

Here's How to Crack It

According to the passage means that this is a Referral question and should be easy
to answer. The challenge, however, is finding the lead words. But you read this paragraph when you answered 28. Not only would you find *academicism* and *mannerism*
if you missed them when you worked the passage, but you also know the paragraph
well from working question 28. Use POE to eliminate choices that don't match your
correct answer from 28. Choices (F), (G), and (J) all contradict both the passage and
your previous answer. Choice (H) matches, and it is the correct answer.

Now move onto question 23. Because you worked it Later, the answer is easy to find.

23. Which of the following most accurately summarizes how the
passage characterizes <u>subjectivism's effect</u> on <u>Rodin</u>?

    A. It ended his affiliation with mannerism.
    B. It caused him to lose his artistic integrity.
    C. It limited his ability to innovate.
    D. It caused him to become decadent.

Here's How to Crack It

You know this paragraph well by now, but *subjectivism* didn't play a major role in
the points made for questions 28 and 24. Use POE and eliminate choices (G) and
(J) because they don't match what you've learned about Rodin. You know Rodin
didn't like *mannerism*, but check the part of the window that discusses specifically
subjectivism. Lines 45–47 give *subjectivism* as the explanation of why Rodin *was
not an innovator*. That matches choice (H) perfectly.

Last

Questions 24 and 23 showed how your work on each question builds your understanding of the passage, making the Later questions easier to do than if you hadn't waited. The questions, after all, refer back to the same passage, so the answers should agree with each other. Some questions may ask about a relatively minor detail in the passage, but most should ask about important details, the ones that help the author make the main point.

Use what you've learned about the passage to answer last the questions that ask about the entire passage.

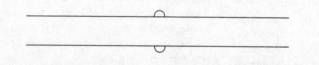

21. The author expresses the idea that:
   A. art should never be studied in terms of movements.
   B. art can be labeled as modern when it introduces a style that is different from those found in works that came earlier.
   C. lesser artists do not usually vary their styles.
   D. great artists are always nonconformists.

Here's How to Crack It

Question 29 helps the most with this question, but several questions echoed the theme of art making a break from the past. The correct answer is choice (B).

30. Which of the following statements would the author most likely agree with?
   F. Cézanne had greater influence on modern sculpture than did Rodin.
   G. Rodin made no significant contribution to modern sculpture.
   H. Daumier should not be considered a modern sculptor.
   J. Carpeaux should be considered a modern sculptor.

Here's How to Crack It

Questions 23, 24, 25, 26, 27, and 28 all help eliminate wrong answers and support choice (A) as the correct answer.

THE 4-STEP BASIC APPROACH

Try a passage on your own. Give yourself up to 12 minutes, but don't worry if you go a little over. Use this passage to help you master the Basic Approach, and worry less about your speed. Later in the chapter and in the next, we'll discuss other strategies to help with time. The answers are given on the page following the passage.

The Basic Approach
1. Preview.
2. Work the Passage.
3. Work the Questions.
4. Work the Answers.

Passage IV

NATURAL SCIENCE: This passage is adapted from the article "The Century's Progress in Chemistry" by Henry Smith Williams (© 1904 by Henry Smith Williams).

Small beginnings can have great endings—sometimes. As a case in point, note what came of the small, original effort of a self-trained, back country Quaker youth named John Dalton. Toward the close of the eighteenth century, he became interested
5 in the weather, which led him to construct a crude water gauge to test the amount of rainfall. But this was only the beginning. The simple rain gauge pointed the way to the most important generalization of the nineteenth century in the field of science with which, to the casual observer, it may seem to have no alli-
10 ance whatever. The wonderful story of the atoms, on which the whole gigantic structure of modern chemistry is founded, was the logical outgrowth of those early studies in meteorology

The way it happened was this: From studying rainfall, Dalton turned naturally to the complementary process of evaporation. He
15 soon came to believe that vapor exists in the atmosphere as an independent gas. But since two bodies cannot occupy the same space at the same time, this implies that the various atmospheric gases are really composed of discrete particles. These ultimate particles are so small that we cannot see them—cannot, indeed,
20 more than vaguely imagine them—yet each particle of vapor, for example, is just as much a portion of water as if it were a drop out of the ocean. But water is a compound substance, for it may be separated, as Cavendish has shown, into the two elementary substances hydrogen and oxygen. Hence the atom
25 of water must be composed of two lesser atoms joined together. Imagine an atom of hydrogen and one of oxygen. Unite them, and we have an atom of water; sever them, the atoms of hydrogen and of oxygen remain hydrogen and oxygen and nothing else. Differently mixed together or united, atoms produce different
30 gross substance, but the elementary atoms never change their chemical nature—their distinct personality.

Around 1803, Dalton first gained a full grasp of the conception of the chemical atom. At once he saw that the hypothesis if true, furnished a marvelous key to secrets of matter hitherto
35 insoluble—questions relation to the relative proportions of the atoms themselves. It is known, for example, that a certain bulk of hydrogen gas unites with a certain bulk of oxygen gas to form water. If it is true that this combination consists essentially of the same union of atoms one with another (each single atom of
40 hydrogen united to a single atom of oxygen), then the relative weights of the original masses of hydrogen and of oxygen must be also the relative weights of each of their respective atoms. If one pound of hydrogen unites with five and one-half pounds of oxygen (as, according to Dalton's experiments, it did), then
45 the weight of the oxygen atom must be five and one-half times that of the hydrogen atom. Other compounds may be plainly tested in the same way. Dalton made numerous tests before he published his theory. He found that hydrogen enters into compounds in smaller proportions than does any other element

50 known to him, and so, for convenience, determined to take the weight of the hydrogen atom as unity. The atomic weight of oxygen then becomes (as given in Dalton's first table of 1803) 5:5: that of water (hydrogen plus oxygen) being of course 6.5. The atomic weights of about a score of substances are given
55 in Dalton's first paper, which was read before the Literary and philosophical Society of Manchester, October 21, 1803.

During the same years, the rising authority of French chemical world, Joseph Louis Gay-Lussac, was conducting experiments with gases. In 1809, the next year after the publication of the
60 first volume of Dalton's New System of Chemical Philosophy, Gay-Lussac published the results of his observations, and among other things brought out the remarkable fact that gases, under the same conditions as to temperature and pressure, combine always in definite numerical proportions as to volume. Exactly
65 two volumes of hydrogen, for example, combine with one volume of oxygen to form water.

The true explanation of Gay-Lussac's law of combination by volumes was thought out almost immediately by an Italian servant, Amadeo Avogadro, and expressed in terms of
70 the atomic theory. The fact must be, said Avogadro, that under similar physical conditions every form of gas contains exactly the same number of ultimate particles in a given volume. Each of these ultimate physical particles may be composed of two or more atoms (as in the case of water vapor), but such a compound
75 atom conducts itself as if it were a simple and indivisible atom, as regards the amount of space that separates it from its fellows under given conditions of pressure and temperature. The compound atom, composed of two or more elementary atoms, Avogadro proposed to distinguish, for purposes of convenience
80 by the name molecule.

The other and even more noted advocate of the atomic theory was Johan Jakob Berzelius. This great Swedish chemist at once set to work to put the atomic theory to such tests of the utmost skill, and for years he devoted himself to the determination of
85 the combining weights, "equivalents" or "proportions," of the different elements. These determinations, in so far as they were accurately made, were simple expressions of empirical facts, independent of any theory; but gradually it became more and more plain that these facts all harmonized with the atomic theory
90 of Dalton. So by common consent the proportionate combining weights of the elements came to be known as atomic weights—the name Dalton had given them from the first. Berzelius proposed to improve upon Dalton's method of notation by using the initial of the Latin name of the element represented—O for oxygen,
95 H for hydrogen, and so on—a numerical coefficient to follow the letter as an indication of the number of atoms present in any given compound. This simple system soon gained general acceptance, and with slight modification it is still universally employed. Every student is now aware that H_2O is the chemical
100 way of expressing the union of two atoms of hydrogen with one of oxygen to form a molecule of water.

1. In the first paragraph, the author discusses Dalton's instrument for measuring rainfall in order to show that:

   A. meteorology is more important than chemistry.
   B. water is an important chemical compound found in many complex substances.
   C. some scientific discoveries arise unexpectedly from simple observations.
   D. many scientists in the eighteenth century had little or no formal training in the scientific method.

2. The scientist who credited with the modern chemical notation in which water is expressed as H_2O is:

   F. Berzelius.
   G. Dalton.
   H. Avogadro
   J. Gay-Lussac.

3. The author's attitude toward the work of Dalton is best characterized as one of:

   A. scholarly detachment.
   B. restrained criticism.
   C. admiring interest.
   D. scientific indifference.

4. The passage states that Gay-Lussac was:

   F. English.
   G. French.
   H. Swedish.
   J. Italian.

5. The author credits Avogadro with:

   A. discovering the law that explains the observations of Gay-Lussac.
   B. measuring the atomic weight of oxygen.
   C. showing that some substances were combinations of more basic elements
   D. ealizing that hydrogen was the lightest atom.

6. In the final paragraph, the author states that Berzelius:

   F. disproved Dalton's version of the atomic theory and replaced it with his own.
   G. was an important influence on the work of Avogadro and Gay-Lussac.
   H. found more evidence that supported Dalton's work.
   J. was the first to show that water can be divided into oxygen and hydrogen.

7. The passage states that Dalton believed that the weight of an atom of oxygen is:

   A. about twice the weight of an atom of hydrogen.
   B. between five and six times the weight of an atom of hydrogen.
   C. between six and seven times the weight of an atom of hydrogen.
   D. slightly more than the weight of a molecule of water.

8. As described in the passage, the works of Gay-Lussac concerned the:

   F. weight of gases.
   G. volumes of gases.
   H. transformation of liquids into gas.
   J. number of electrons in an atom.

9. Which of the following assumptions made by Dalton led to a flaw in his atomic theory?

   A. All atoms have the same volume.
   B. All atoms have the same weight.
   C. Two atoms can occupy the same space at the same time.
   D. Atoms combine only in pairs.

10. The passage associates the origin of the word *molecule* with:

   F. Dalton.
   G. Avogadro.
   H. Cavendish.
   J. Gay-Lussac.

Score and Analyze Your Performance

The correct answers are (C), (F), (C), (G), (A), (H), (B), (G), (D), and (G). How did you do? Were you able to finish in 12 minutes or less? If you struggled with time, identify what step took up the most time. Identify any questions that slowed you down. Did you make good choices of Now and Later questions? Did you use *enough* time? If you finished in less than 12 minutes but missed several questions, next time plan to slow down to give yourself enough time to evaluate the answers carefully. In Chapter 18, we'll work on skills to help you work the questions and answers with more speed and greater accuracy. But first, we'll finish this chapter with strategies to help you increase your speed working the passage.

BEAT THE CLOCK

When you struggle with time, there are several places within the Basic Approach that are eating up the minutes.

> Pacing the Basic Approach
> If you spend 10–11 minutes on your first passage, use your time wisely.
>
> Step 1: Preview. *30–60 seconds*
> Step 2: Work the Passage. *3 minutes*
> Steps 3 and 4: Work the Questions and Answers. *7 minutes.*

Step 1: Preview

To move at the fastest speed when you preview, you can't read the questions. Let your eye *look* for lead words and numbers. Don't let your brain *read*.

Time yourself to see if you can preview the following blurb and questions in less than a minute.

Passage IV

NATURAL SCIENCE: This passage is adapted from the article "What Giotto Saw" by James Herndon (©2001 by Galaxy Press).

31. The author characterizes the comparison of the work of Sagdeev to that of Peale as:

32. The main point of the last paragraph (lines 43–48) Zdenek Sekanina...

33. In terms of their role in studying the rotational period, the 1920 photographs are described the author as:

34. Lines 17–19 mainly emphasize what quality?

35. According to the passage, the nuclear surface of Halley's comet is believed to be:

36. As described in the passage, Giotto's camera was specifically programmed to:

37. As used in the passage, the word *resolution* (line 11) means:

38. The passage indicates that H. Use Keler:

39. Lines 25–28 are best summarized as describing a problem that:

40. According to the passage, the volume of Halley's comet is:

Step 2

Step 2: Work the Passage

This step should take no more than 3 minutes, and you should not be trying to read the passage thoroughly. Your only goal is to find as many of your lead words as you can and underline them.

Skimming, Scanning, and Reading

If we told you to skim the passage, would you know that means? If you do, great. If you don't, don't worry. *Skimming* is something many readers feel they're supposed to do on a timed test, but they don't know what it means and therefore can't do it.

Reading needs your brain on full power. You're reading words, and your brain is processing what they mean and drawing conclusions. Reading is watching the road, searching for directional signs, and glancing at the scenery, all for the purpose of trying to figure out where the road is leading.

Skimming means reading only a few words. When you work the passage, your brain can try to process key parts that build to the main idea, but you don't necessarily need to identify the main idea just yet. Working the questions and answers tells you the main idea and all the important details. Skimming is reading only the directional signs and ignoring the scenery.

Scanning needs very little of your brain. Use your eyes. Look, don't think, and don't try to process for understanding. Scanning is looking for Volkswagen Beetles in a game of Slug Bug.

When you're working the passage, you can skim or scan, but you shouldn't be reading. Read windows of text when you work the questions.

If you feel you can't turn your brain off when you work the passage, or you even skim and scan too slowly, then focus only on the first sentence of each paragraph. You may find fewer lead words, but you will give yourself more time to spend on working the questions and answers and can find the lead words then.

Time yourself to work the following passage, focusing only on the first sentence of each paragraph. We've actually made it impossible to do otherwise. Look for the lead words you underlined in Step 1 and underline any that you see.

Such relatively reliable insights as we have into the nature of Halley's comet's nucleus derive largely from the work done by the Giotto imaging team. Blah blah blah blah blah blah blah blah. Blah blah. Blah blah blah blah blah blah blah blah blah.
5 Blah blah blah. Blah blah blah blah blah blah blah blah blah. Blah blah blah blah blah blah blah blah blah. Blah blah blah blah blah blah blah blah blah.

Discernibility of detail varies at different points in the photograph. Blah blah blah blah blah blah blah blah. Blah blah. Blah
10 blah blah blah blah blah blah blah blah. Blah blah blah. Blah blah blah blah blah blah blah blah blah. Blah blah blah blah blah blah blah blah blah. Blah blah blah blah blah blah blah blah blah. Blah blah blah blah blah blah blah blah. Blah blah blah blah blah blah blah blah blah. Blah blah blah blah blah blah blah blah blah.

15 The Giotto photographs have allowed investigators to conclude that the surface of the nucleus is rough. Blah blah blah blah blah blah blah blah. Blah blah. Blah blah blah blah blah blah blah blah blah. Blah blah blah. Blah blah blah blah blah blah blah blah blah. Blah blah blah blah blah blah blah blah blah.
20 Blah blah blah blah blah blah blah blah blah. Blah blah blah blah blah blah blah blah blah.

On the other hand, the Giotto photographs reveal virtually nothing on the interior of the comet's nucleus or its rotational period. Blah blah blah blah blah blah blah blah. Blah blah. Blah
25 blah blah blah blah blah blah blah blah. Blah blah blah. Blah blah blah blah blah blah blah blah blah. Blah blah blah blah blah blah blah blah. Blah blah blah blah blah blah blah blah blah. Blah blah blah blah blah blah blah blah blah.

Moreover, the comet's overall dimensions were already
30 known to an approximation, and on this basis Rickman took the volume as 500–550 cubic centimeters. Blah blah blah blah blah blah blah blah. Blah blah. Blah blah blah blah blah blah blah blah blah. Blah blah blah. Blah blah blah blah blah blah blah blah blah. Blah blah blah blah blah blah blah blah. Blah
35 blah blah blah blah blah blah blah.

Using an analogous technique, R.Z. Sagdeev and colleagues arrived at a value of 0.2 to 1.5 grams per cubic centimeter. Blah blah blah blah blah blah blah blah. Blah blah. Blah blah blah blah blah blah blah blah blah. Blah blah. Blah blah blah blah blah
40 blah blah blah blah. Blah blah blah blah blah blah blah blah blah. Blah blah blah blah blah blah blah blah. Blah blah blah blah blah blah blah blah.

Finally, Zdenek Sekanina and Stephen M. Larson studied the rotational period by first processing images of 1920 photographs
45 in an attempt to improve the image of spiral dust features. Blah blah blah blah blah blah blah blah. Blah blah. Blah blah blah blah blah blah blah blah blah. Blah blah blah. Blah blah blah blah blah blah blah blah blah. Blah blah blah blah blah blah blah blah blah.

Let's see what you learned in less than three minutes.

Now Questions

You should have several Now questions.

- Questions 32, 34, 37, and 39 all have line references.
- Questions 31, 33, 35, 36, 38, and 40 all have lead words, great lead words in some.
- The lead words in 31 can be found in the first sentence of the sixth paragraph.
- The lead words in 33 can be found in the first sentence of the last paragraph.
- The lead words in 35 and 36 can be found in the first sentence of the first paragraph.
- The lead words in 40 can be found in the first sentence of the fifth paragraph.
- Nine of the ten questions have been located, and the great lead word in 38 should be easy to find easy to find when you're given the whole passage and not a lot of "blahs."

> ### The Pencil Trick
> When you have to look harder for a lead word, use your pencil to sweep each and every line from beginning to end. This will keep your brain from reading and let your eye look for the word.

The Passage

You also have a great outline of the passage. The topic sentences have drawn a map of the passage organization, and the transition words tell you how the paragraphs connect.

- What is the first paragraph about? The nucleus of Halley's Comet and the Giotto camera.
- The second paragraph? The details that the photographs show.
- The third? What scientists have learned from the photographs.
- How does the fourth paragraph relate to the third? *On the other hand* tells you that it is different from the third.
- How does the fifth paragraph relate to the fourth? *Moreover* tells you that they are similar.
- What is the sixth paragraph about? It's still on *volume*, which came up in the fifth paragraph.
- What is the last paragraph? It's the conclusion, which the transition word *Finally* makes clear.

Topic Sentences and Transition Words

Think of your own papers that you write for school. What does a good topic sentence do? It provides at worst an introduction to the paragraph and at best a summary of the paragraph's main idea. What follows will be the details that clarify or prove the main idea. And do you care about the details at Step 2? No, you'll focus on the details if and when there is a question on them.

Transition words are like great road signs. They show you the route, direct you to a detour, and get you back on the path of the main idea. When you *skim*, you're focusing on topic sentences and transition words.

In the next chapter, we'll cover more strategies for working the questions and answers. But now it's time to try another passage.

Look for Transition Words
Here are 15 transition words and/or phrases.

- *Despite*
- *However*
- *In spite of*
- *Nonetheless*
- *On the other hand*
- *But*
- *Rather*
- *Yet*
- *Ironically*
- *Notwithstanding*
- *Unfortunately*
- *On the contrary*
- *Therefore*
- *Hence*
- *Consequently*

Reading Drill 1

Use the Basic Approach on the following passage. Time yourself to complete in 8–10 minutes. Check your answers in Chapter 24.

Passage II

SOCIAL SCIENCE: This passage is adapted from the book *How to Watch Television* by Neil Postman (© 1992 by Penguin Books).

"Now…this" is commonly used on the radio and television newscasts to indicate that what one has just heard or seen has no relevance to what one is about to hear or see, or possibly to anything one is ever likely to hear or see. The phrase is a means of
5 acknowledging the fact that the world as mapped by the speeded-up electronic media has no order or meaning and it is not to be taken seriously. There is no murder so brutal, no earthquakes so devastating, no political blunder so costly—for that matter, no ball score so tantalizing or weather report so threatening—that
10 it cannot be erased from our minds by a newscaster saying, "Now…this." The newscaster means that you have thought long enough on the previous matter (approximately 45 seconds), that you must not be morbidly preoccupied with it (let us say, for 90 seconds), and that you must now give your attention to another
15 fragment of news or a commercial.

Television did not invent the "Now…this" worldview. As I have tried to show, it is the offspring of the intercourse between telegraphy and photography. But it is through television that it has been nurtured and brought to a perverse maturity. For on
20 television, nearly every half hour is a discrete event, separated in content, context, and emotional texture from what precedes and follows it. In part because television sell its time in seconds and minutes, in part because television must use images rather than words, in part because its audience can move freely to and
25 from the television set, programs are structured so that almost each eight-minute segment may stand as a complete event in itself. Viewers are rarely required to carry over any thought or feeling from one parcel of time to another.

Of course, in television's presentation of the "new of the
30 day," we may see the "Now…this" mode of discourse in its boldest and most embarrassing form. For there, we are presented not only with fragmented news but news without context, without consequences, without value, and therefore without essential seriousness; that is to say, news as pure entertainment.

35 Consider for example, how you would proceed if you were given the opportunity to produce a television news show for any station concerned to attract the largest possible audience. You would, first, choose a cast of players, each of whom has a face that is both "likeable" and "credible." Those who apply would
40 in fact, submit to you their eight-by-ten glossies, from which you would eliminate those whose countenances are not suitable for nightly display. This means that you will exclude women who are not beautiful or who are over the age of 50, men who are bald, all people who are overweight or whose noses are too
45 long or whose eyes are too close together. You will try, in other words, to assemble a cast of talking hairdos. At the very least, you will want those whose faces would not be unwelcome on a magazine cover.

Christine Craft has just such a face, and so she applied for
50 co-anchor position on KMBC-TV in Kansas City. According to a lawyer who represented her in a sexism suit she later brought against the station, the management of KMBC-TV "loved Christine's look." She was accordingly hired in January 1981. She was fired in August 1981 because research indicated that her
55 appearance "hampered viewer acceptance." What exactly does "hampered viewer acceptance" mean? And what does it have to do with the news? Hampered viewer acceptance means the same thing for television news as it does for any television show: Viewers do not like looking at the performer. It also means that
60 viewers do not believe the performer, that she lacks credibility. In the case of a theatrical performance, we have a sense of what that implies: The actor does not persuade the audience that he or she is the character being portrayed. But what does lack of credibility imply in the case of a news show? What character
65 is a co-anchor playing? And how do we decide that the performance lacks verisimilitude? Does the audience believe that the newscaster is lying, that what is reported did not in fact happen? That something important is being concealed?

Is it frightening to think that this may be so, that the per-
70 ception of the truth of a report rests heavily on the acceptability of the newscaster? In the ancient world, there was tradition of banishing or killing the bearer of bad tidings. Does the television news show restore, in a curious form, this tradition?

---

1. The author of this passage can most reasonably be described as:

   A. a detective who tries to find evidence proving that a television network is not guilty of misleading the public.
   B. a television executive who discusses important factors for a successful news program.
   C. a critic who warns his readers about the effects that television has had on the reporting of news.
   D. a journalism teacher who wishes to show his students how to write interesting television news stories.

2. As it is used in line 5, the word *mapped* most nearly means:

   F. obscured.
   G. explored.
   H. destroyed.
   J. defined.

3. It can reasonably be inferred that the author would most likely agree with which of the following statements?

   A. News stories are more interesting when they are presented on live television than when they are recorded.
   B. The short amount of time given to news stories on television reduces the value of the facts reported.
   C. Television has done a good job of bringing families together by creating programs that the entire family can watch.
   D. Television news reports should also write news stories for magazines and newspapers.

4. In the fifth paragraph (lines 49–68) the author offers details about Christine Craft in order to:

   F. illustrate the importance of the appearance of the newscaster on television.
   G. show that television gets its nature from both telegraphy and photography.
   H. support a claim about sexism in America.
   J. present the story of a friend and her experiences in television journalism.

5. It can reasonably be inferred that the author believes that:

   A. well-trained actors are better than newscasters at delivering news on television.
   B. television is not well suited to a serious presentation of the news.
   C. newspapers will likely disappear in a few years if people continue to get their news from television.
   D. the presentation of the news has a not fundamentally changed since ancient times.

6. According to the passage, television has become a medium whose main goal is:

   F. to report the facts in an unbiased manner.
   G. to help television reporters become famous.
   H. to inform the public of important news productions.
   J. to entertain viewers.

7. The author's reference to "talking hairdos" (line 46) is a reference to:

   A. people whose faces are pleasing to viewers.
   B. the advertising of hair-care products on television.
   C. animated cartoon characters.
   D. the amount of money spent make television personalities look good.

8. According to the author, the phrase "Now…this" indicates that the nest topic:

   F. will be more important than the previous topic.
   G. will receive less time than the previous topic.
   H. will have no connection to the previous topic.
   J. will begin a new eight-minute segment of news.

9. According to passage, television viewers' perceptions of whether a story is true of false depends largely on the:

   A. appearance of the person reporting the news.
   B. reputation of the television network.
   C. references cited during the news story.
   D. commentary provided by those being interviewed.

10. Which of the following is NOT cited as having an impacted on the presentation of television news?

    F. Airtime is a very valuable commodity for television station.
    G. People are not expected to remain attentive to the television for more than a short period of time.
    H. Television relies on images than on words to transmit its message.
    J. Television sets are relatively expensive, and not everyone can afford them.

Summary

- o Use the 4-Step Basic Approach.
- o Step 1: Preview. Check the blurb and map the questions. Star line and paragraph references and underline lead words.
- o Step 2: Work the Passage. Finish in 2–3 minutes. Look for and underline lead words. One option is to focus only the first sentence of each paragraph.
- o Step 3: Work the Questions. Do Now questions that are easy to answer or whose answers are easy to find. Read what you need in a window of 5–10 lines to find your answer. Save for Later questions that are both hard to find and hard to answer.
- o Step 4: Work the Answers. Use POE to find your answer, particularly on Reasoning questions.
- o Skim and scan when you work the passage.
- o Read windows of text when you work the questions.
- o Look for topic sentences and transition words.

Chapter 18
Advanced Reading Skills

In this lesson, we'll help you hone your skills to crack specific question types and the most challenging of difficult text. We'll also build on your mastery of the 4-Step Basic Approach by teaching you advanced POE (Process of Elimination) strategies.

LATER QUESTIONS

On the Reading test, some questions appear in unique formats that make them stand out among the Referral and Reasoning questions. These questions still require you to show your understanding of what is directly stated or what is implied. However, it's useful to have specific strategies to crack these.

Negatives

The test writers can throw a curveball at you when they ask a question in the negative using EXCEPT, LEAST, or NOT to twist the task. These questions are inherently tricky. What's right is wrong, and the right answer is the one that's wrong. Clear as a bell, isn't?

No wonder it's so easy for your brain to trip all over itself. You may even start off trying to find the one choice that is false. But you somehow lose sight of the trap, and when you come across one of the answers in the passage, you think, "Eureka! This answer is true. I found it right here." Of course it's "right" in the passage: Two other answer choices are somewhere in the passage as well. It's the choice that isn't in the passage that is the "right" answer.

Here's a better approach. Let's take a look at a question after it has been previewed in Step 1.

> The 4-Step Basic Approach
> Step 1: **Preview.** Check the blurb and map the questions. Underline lead words and star line or paragraph references.
> Step 2: **Work the Passage.** Spend 2–3 minutes reading the passage.
> Step 3: **Work the Questions.** Use your POOD to find Now, Later, and Never Questions.
> Step 4: **Work the Answers.** Use POE.

33. The passage mentions <u>transportation of bees by river</u> in all of the following <u>countries</u> EXCEPT:

   A. Scotland
   B. France
   C. Poland
   D. Egypt

When you map the questions, underline *transportation of bees by river* and *countries* but don't underline or mark *EXCEPT*. Wait until you work the question to deal with the trick.

This is a Referral question. If the negative weren't there, it would be easy to answer. What country transports bees by river? But it wouldn't be easy to find the answer, since there is no line or paragraph reference, and none of these lead words qualify as great.

Occasionally, an EXCEPT question will come with a line or paragraph reference to help narrow down your search, but most times they don't. The answers can be scattered throughout the passage or grouped together in one paragraph.

That's why you should always do a negative question Later. By the time you get to it, you should be able to identify where in the passage you'll find at least some of the answers, or you will have narrowed down where to look.

When you do work this question, mark the EXCEPT so your eye can help your brain. You could double underline it. You can circle it and jot down two double exclamation points. You can cross it out altogether and write "True/False," or "T/F." Do whatever you need to keep yourself focused on the goal: Identify the one answer that is not like the others.

33. The passage mentions <u>transportation of bees by river</u> in all of the following <u>countries</u> <u>EXCEPT</u>:

    A. Scotland
    B. France
    C. Poland
    D. Egypt

For question 33, the answers happen to be grouped into the same paragraph, something you would have found easier to spot by using the great lead words in the answers. Always let the answers help in an EXCEPT question.

Now use POE. Locate the countries in the window of text, and read to find out which use rivers. When you find one, cross it off in the answers.

> In Scotland, after the best of the Lowland bloom is past,
> the bees are carried in carts to the Highlands, and set free on the
> heather hills. In France, too, and in Poland, they are carried from
> pasture to pasture among orchards and fields in the same way, and
> 5 along the rivers in barges to collect the honey of the delightful
> vegetation of the banks. In Egypt they are taken far up the Nile,
> and floated slowly home again, gathering the honey-harvest of
> the various fields on the way, timing their movements in accord
> with the seasons. Were similar methods pursued in California
> 10 the productive season would last nearly all the year.

The correct answer is choice (A). All four countries are listed, but only Scotland doesn't involve *rivers*.

Answer Choice Lead Words

In any type of question, lead words may be found in the answers instead of the question.

Negative questions can be more complicated when the question type itself is Reasoning instead of Referral.

Particularly difficult are questions that ask what is NOT answered by the passage. These essentially require four times the amount of work, since you have to look for four answers instead of just one. Sometimes, the question is asked but not answered, and in others, the topic may not arise at all, both of which can frustrate you and make you waste a lot of time, scouring the passage over and over. That's why Negative questions can be good candidates for Never. If you do work a negative question, always use POE. Cross off the ones that you know are true. If you're stuck between two, or even among three, don't waste that much more time before forcing yourself to guess and move on.

These next two questions would both be the last questions you do, and you would have gained a good grasp of the passage, even the details, by reading small windows as you worked the rest of the questions.

For the purposes of this exercise, don't worry about time. Read the excerpt of the passage and use POE.

36. Which of the following questions is NOT answered by information given in the passage?

   F. How many bee ranches might be successfully established in the Sierra Mountains?
   G. What types of flowers attract bees?
   H. Where did the honeybees in the Sierra Mountains come from?
   J. How much honey is produced by bee-trees in the Sierra Mountains?

38. Which of the following statements is LEAST supported by the passage?

   F. The Sierra Mountains have the appropriate requirements to support bee ranching activities.
   G. Bees flourish in the Sierra Mountains in part because the area is not hospitable to traditional cattle ranching.
   H. The presence of bees in the Sierra Mountains prevents sheep from grazing in certain areas.
   J. Bee-ranching is an economically viable and environmentally sound enterprise.

The Sierra region is the largest of the three main divisions of the bee-lands of the State, and the most regularly varied in its subdivisions, owing to its gradual rise from the level of the Central Plain to the alpine summits. Up through the forest region, to a height of about 9,000 feet above sea-level, there are ragged patches of manzanita and five or six species of ceanothus, called deer-brush or California lilac. These are the most important of all the honey-bearing bushes of the Sierra.

From swarms that escaped their owners in the lowlands, the honey-bee is now generally distributed throughout the whole length of the Sierra, up to an elevation of 8,000 feet above sea-level. At this height they flourish without care, though the snow every winter is deep. Even higher than this, several bee-trees have been cut which contained over 200 pounds of honey. . . . Wild bees and butterflies have been seen feeding at a height of 13,000 feet above the sea.

The destructive action of sheep has not been so general on the mountain pastures as on those of the great plain. Fortunately, neither sheep nor cattle care to feed on the manzanita, spiraea, or adenostoma; these fine honey-bushes are too stiff and tall, or grow in places too rough and inaccessible, to be trodden under foot. Also the canyon walls and gorges, which form so considerable a part of the area of the range, while inaccessible to domestic sheep, are well fringed with honey-shrubs and contain thousands of lovely bee-gardens, lying hidden in narrow side-canyons and recesses fenced with avalanche taluses, and on the top of flat, projecting headlands, where only bees would think to look for them.

The plow has not yet invaded the forest region to any appreciable extent, nor has it accomplished much in the foot-hills. Thousands of bee-ranches might be established along the margin of the plain and up to a height of 4,000 feet, wherever water could be obtained. The climate at this elevation admits of the making of permanent homes, and by moving the hives to higher pastures as the lower pass out of bloom, the annual yield of honey would be nearly doubled. The foot-hill pastures, as we have seen, fail about the end of May; those of the chaparral belt and lower forests are in full bloom in June, those of the upper and alpine region in July, August, and September.

Of all the upper flower fields of the Sierra, Shasta is the most honeyful, and may yet surpass in fame the celebrated honey hills of Hybla and hearthy Hymettus. In this flowery wilderness the bees rove and revel, rejoicing in the bounty of the sun, clambering eagerly through bramble and hucklebloom, ringing the myriad bells of the manzanita, now humming aloft among polleny willows and firs, now down on the ashy ground among gilias and buttercups, and anon plunging deep into snowy banks of cherry and buckthorn...

Here's How to Crack Them

Work both questions 36 and 38 as your last questions. For 36, double underline, circle, or cross off the NOT when you work it. As you find the answers to the answer choices—that is, the answers to the questions in the answer choices—cross off that choice. Choice (F) is answered in lines 31–33. Choice (G) is answered in lines 7–8 and again in 18–22. Choice (H) is answered in line 31–33. Choice (J) is never answered, and it is therefore the correct answer.

Question 38 is less specific and less dependent on detail than is question 36. Remember, the answers to your questions should all agree with each other, at least in terms of reinforcing the main points. Double underline, circle, or cross of the LEAST, and use POE any answer that doesn't reinforce the theme in the rest of the questions. Choice (C) is not supported by the passage, and is therefore the correct answer. Choices (A) and (D) describe positive benefits of bees to the Sierra Mountains, and they would likely be the easiest choices to eliminate right away. Choice (B) is supported by lines 18–28.

Vocabulary in Context

In some Referral questions, you'll have to determine the meaning of a word or phrase as it's used in context. The level of the vocabulary can vary, but most of these questions use relatively common words, but their meaning in the passage can be figurative more than literal.

> ### Don't Know the Word?
> If the Vocabulary in Context question tests a more difficult word that you're unfamiliar with, you can still try to read the context to see if you can come up with your own word that fits the meaning and then use POE among the answers. But if you can't eliminate three choices, guess from what's left and move on. Similarly, if you are pressed for time and need to get to the next passage, mark this a Never. Choose your LOTD and move on.

You don't need to read a full window of 5–10 lines for Vocabulary in Context questions, but you do need to read at least the full sentence to determine the meaning in its context. Cross off the phrase and try to substitute your own word. Then move to the answers and use POE to eliminate choices that don't match your word. The correct answer has to be the literal definition of the meaning. Don't choose a word that could be used figuratively to convey the meaning.

Let's try an example.

The plow has not yet invaded the forest region to any ap-
30 preciable extent, nor has it accomplished much in the foot-hills.
    Thousands of bee-ranches might be established along the margin
    of the plain and up to a height of 4000 feet, wherever water could
    be obtained. The climate at this elevation admits of the making
    of permanent homes, and by moving the hives to higher pastures
35 as the lower pass out of bloom, the annual yield of honey would
    be nearly doubled. The foot-hill pastures, as we have seen, fail
    about the end of May; those of the chaparral belt and lower forests
    are in full bloom in June, those of the upper and alpine region in
    July, August, and September.

37. As it is used in lines 33–36, the phrase *admits of* most nearly
    means:

    A. makes possible.
    B. grants permission.
    C. confesses guilt.
    D. leaves out.

Here's How to Crack It

Admits is a common word, but it has different definitions depending on the context. The phrase *admits of* may be a less common phrase, but if you cross it out and read the sentence, you may come up with a word like "allows." Choice (A) works the same way "allows" does, and it's the correct choice. Choice (B) is close, but *grants* is a good example of a word that could be used figuratively to mean "allows." It doesn't literally mean "allows." And *permission* doesn't work for the literal meaning at all. A climate can't literally *permit* anything. Choice (C) is tempting if you don't use the context of the sentence, since *confessing guilt* is a correct definition of *admits* in another context.

Roman Numerals

Roman numeral questions show up on the Reading test very rarely. They can be used in a Referral question or in a Reference question. They may come with line references or great lead words, or they may not. Use those factors to determine when to work the question, but in general, Roman numeral questions are good choices for Later when you know the passage better.

When you do work a Roman numeral question, be efficient. Choose the easiest of the Roman numerals to look up in passage. Once you know yes or no, go to the answer choices and use POE. Look up only the Roman numerals that are still in the running among the answers.

Let's try an example.

They consider the lilies and roll into them, and, like lilies, they toil not for they are impelled by sun-power, as water-wheels by water-power; and when the one has plenty of high-pressure water, the other plenty of sunshine, they hum and quiver alike.
5 Sauntering in the Shasta bee-lands in the sun-days of summer, one may readily infer the time of day from the comparative energy of bee-movements alone—drowsy and moderate in the cool of the morning, increasing in energy with the ascending sun, and, at high noon, thrilling and quivering in wild ecstasy, then gradually
10 declining again to the stillness of night.

39. The passage describes the movement of the bees during the day as which of the following?

    I. Drowsy and moderate
    II. Thrilling and quivering
    III. Cool and still

  A. I only
  B. III only
  C. II and III only
  D. I and II only

Here's How to Crack It

Work efficiently. Use the lead words in the Roman numerals to find them in the passage, beginning with I. *Drowsy* and *moderate* are used in lines 5–10 to describe the bees in the morning. Eliminate all choices without I, which leaves you with just II to review: I and III are not both in any choice. *Thrilling* and *quivering* are used in line 9 to describe the bees at high noon. Choice (D) is correct.

CRITICAL READING

Your use of the 4-Step Basic Approach and your personal order of difficulty (POOD) of both passages and questions should by now make you feel more confident on the Reading test. But you also may still be struggling with time and feel that you just can't work fast enough to get to enough questions.

In Chapter 17, we discussed ways to use your time better when you preview and work the passage. But you may also be wasting time when you work the questions, reading and rereading the window of text, trying to figure out what it's saying. You may have eliminated two answers but when you're still not sure what the correct answer is, what do you do? You read the window yet again, desperate to figure out the meaning and answer the question in your own words.

We've all been there. Part of what makes standardized tests so evil is how they encourage us to listen to our worst instincts. You can't treat the Reading test as you would a school assignment, and you can't fall prey to your own panicked responses. You have to develop both strategies and skills specific to *this* test.

Critical Thinking

The key to better reading skills is to *think* better, which means to think critically. Getting lost in even a small window of text that makes no sense is like getting lost on unfamiliar roads. You don't stare down at the yellow line. You look around, looking for landmarks and road signs, trying to figure out where you are and where the road is going.

When you're lost in a tough section of text, use topic sentences and transitions as your landmarks and road signs. Don't try to understand every single word. Use the topic sentences to identify what the main point of the paragraph is. Look for transitions to see if points are on the same or different sides from each other.

Topic Sentences and Main Points

Think of how you write papers for school. A good topic sentence makes clear the main subject of the paragraph, and it may even provide the author's main point on the subject. The rest of the paragraph will be details or examples that explain that point, and it may also include a more explicit conclusion of the main point. If you don't understand the details, read the main point to know what they mean. Examples and details usually come right before or right after the main point. If you don't understand the details, read the sentence before or after to see if it gives you the main point. If you don't understand the main point, read the sentence before or after to see if the details explain it for you.

Let's see how this works. Read the following topic sentence.

> Studies of American middle and high school students have shown that there is considerable uncertainty among students about what behaviors count as cheating.

What's going to come next in the paragraph? It could be examples of the behaviors. It could be an explanation of why students are uncertain. It could even be a statement of a different study that contradicts this one. You would be safe anticipating any of those outcomes, but the anticipation is the key. Don't sit back and wait to see where the road is going. Lean forward and look for the fork in the road or the detour sign telling you to turn around. In other words, look for transitions.

Transitions

The first word or phrase after the topic sentence can tell you what direction you're heading.

Let's look at some choices for our cheating sentence.

If the next words were *In particular*, what does that tell you is coming next? Examples of the behavior.

If the next word were *However*, what does that tell you is coming next? A contradiction to this study.

Transitions play a key role in critical thinking. Look for transitions to announce additional points, contradictory points, cause and effect relationships, examples, or conclusions. Here are just a few common transitions.

Additional Points	Cause and Effect Relationships
And	Because
Also	Since
As well	So
In addition	
Furthermore	
Moreover	Examples
	For example
	In particular
Contradictory Points	Such as
Although	
But	
Even though	Conclusions
However	Consequently
Nevertheless	In other words
On the other hand	That is
Rather	Therefore
Yet	Thus

Modifiers

Nouns and verbs reliably give you the facts in a statement, but they don't necessarily provide the author's point. Look at the two adverbs in the prior sentence and see how they helped shape the point. *Reliably* means you can infer that nouns and verbs *almost always* give facts. *Necessarily* modifies the verb phrase *don't provide*. Without it, you could infer that nouns and verbs never give you the point. Adjectives and adverbs are just as useful as transitions, conveying the author's opinion on what would otherwise be a statement of fact.

Consider this sentence.

> Surprisingly, students do not consider sharing notes to be cheating.

The point of this sentence is that *sharing notes* is a form of *cheating*, and the author believes students should know this. If you removed *surprisingly* from the sentence, it's just a factual statement of what students think. On the Reading test, most Reasoning questions involve the author's opinion or main point, or as ACT puts it, "the implied meaning."

Try another.

> Students offered a refreshingly candid explanation for their behavior.

Refreshingly means that the author judged the admission unexpected but welcome. *Candid* means the students were honest and open.

Translation

When you're struggling to make sense of a window of confusing text, look for transitions and modifiers to help you determine the main point. You may be in the thick of a body paragraph with the topic sentence in the rearview mirror. Instead of focusing on every single word, use the transitions and modifiers to get the general direction of points and the connections between them.

Let's look at a tough window and see how this works.

> The strikingly tolerant attitudes demonstrated by the students toward cheating cannot be explained by mere immorality and laziness, but may rather point to a sobering conclusion that high-stakes tests have created a ruthless atmosphere in which
> 5 students are desperate to succeed at any cost.

Here's How to Crack It

Focus on the transitions and modifiers. *Strikingly* tells you that the author finds the students' tolerance of cheating noteworthy and unusual. The key verb phrase *cannot be explained* directs you away from what <u>is not</u> the cause and the transitions *but* and *rather* direct you to what <u>is</u> the cause. Even if you didn't understand all the vocabulary words, the transitions act as huge road signs identifying the most important part of the sentence. Students don't cheat because of *immorality* and *laziness* but because *high-stakes tests* have made things *ruthless* and *desperate*. Even just knowing which sentence, or which part of the sentence, to focus on will help, along with POE, to find the right answer.

ADVANCED POE SKILLS

When you're stuck on a confusing window of text, the best use of your time is spent working the answers. Reread your window, even to spot transitions and modifiers, in conjunction with working the answers.

In an ideal situation, you read a question, read the window of text looking for your answer, answer the question in your own words, and then work through the answer choices looking for the best match, using POE to get rid of those that don't.

But situations are seldom ideal on the Reading test. When you don't quite understand the window and therefore have no clue about the answer, go straight to working the answers.

The Art of Wrong Answers

If you worked for ACT, you'd have to sit in a cubicle all day writing test questions. The easy part of the job is writing the correct answer. You may even know that before you write the question. The harder part is coming up with three wrong answers. If you didn't write great wrong answers, everyone would get a 36. So you have to come up with temptingly wrong answers.

Let's take a look at some ways to make wrong answers.

Read the following question, correct answer, and text. We don't care about the right answer in this exercise, so you can read it before you read the window.

13. The main point of the fifth paragraph (lines 40–48) is that:

    A.   cultural norms affect how students judge cheating behaviors.

40   The authors of one such study contend that differences between German students and the other students in the study regarding what constitutes cheating can be explained by differences in social norms. In particular, German students viewed passive cheating more as "helping others" or "cooperation" rather than
45   as unethical or immoral behavior. Costa Rican students also were more liberal than Americans in their views of passive cheating, also due to a cultural tendency toward cooperation rather than competition.

Our goal here is to examine *why* the three wrong answers are wrong.

    B.   German students consider passive cheating to be unethical and immoral.

Look carefully at line 45. Choice (B) took tempting words out of the passage and garbled them. The passage disproves this answer.

    C.   American students have a less liberal view of passive cheating than do Costa Rican students.

Since lines 45–48 say Costa Rican students are *more liberal than Americans*, choice (C) is true. But it's not the correct answer because it's not the main point of the paragraph.

    D.   Russian students do not consider passive cheating to be unethical.

Russian students are not mentioned in this window and have instead been taken from a different window.

Answers can be wrong because they don't match what the passage says, because they answer the wrong question, or because they're not even found in the right window. But no matter how tempting or obvious wrong answers are, they are all easier to understand than 5–10 lines of text, simply because they're shorter. So when you're stuck on tough questions on tough windows, work backwards with the answers.

Work Backwards

Instead of rereading the window to try to determine the meaning, read the answer choices for their meaning. Then see if you can match each back into the passage.

> Read to understand the meaning of the answer choices instead of rereading the window.
>
> - Look for lead words or phrases in the answer choices.
> - Determine if the words match those found in the window.
> - Use POE to cross off choices that don't match the window.

Let's see how this works. Read the following question and window.

> The dictionary defines cheating as unfairly gaining advantage in a given situation by deliberately violating established rules. Cheating behaviors may include plagiarism, copying exam answers, using crib notes, obtaining test questions beforehand (all
> 5 active behaviors), as well as allowing others to copy from you, taking advantage of teacher scoring errors, and failing to report cheating (more passive behaviors). The definition of cheating is not under debate, but the way that students define their behavior, in relation to this definition, and how morally acceptable they
> 10 deem such behavior, is. In other words, there is a large variance regarding which behaviors students consider to be cheating.

13. It can reasonably by inferred that the author provides the dictionary definition of cheating (lines 1–2) in order to:

Take the answer choices one at a time. In each choice, we've put in bold a lead word or phrase in the answer. Can you match these words, or a paraphrased meaning of them, in the window of text?

A. argue that passive behaviors **are more morally acceptable** than active behaviors.

Morally acceptable appears in line 9, but the phrase isn't used to compare *passive* and *active behaviors*. Tempting, but wrong.

B. illustrate what behaviors will get students **expelled or suspended**.

Expelled and *suspended*, or any paraphrases of those words, don't appear anywhere in the window, so choice (B) can't be the right answer.

C. prove that students **deliberately violate established rules**.

Deliberately violating established rules appears in line 2, but it's used as part of the definition of cheating, not as proof of students' conduct. We've eliminated three answers, so choice (D) must be right. But always check all four answers to be sure the one you choose is better than the three you've eliminated.

D. show that students may not consider their own **behavior to be cheating**.

Students' *own behavior* is in the last sentence, and choice (D) matches well the point of that sentence.

Try another example. Choose your own words or phrases out of each answer to work backwards with. Does the passage match the answer?

Patterns of individual cheating behavior in different societies typically reflect their respective normative climates. Students recognize certain activities as cheating and may be able to pro-
60 vide justifications for their unethical behavior in some way. Yet cheating, when identified as such, is overall felt to be wrong. However, an eye-opening study of Russian university students' cheating behaviors by Yulia Poltorak reveals a different type of normative climate that is a unique part of the Communist legacy.
65 According to this study, cheating behavior in Soviet Russia was not only very widespread, but also widely accepted as an appropriate response to social conditions.

12. It can reasonably by inferred by information in the seventh paragraph (lines 57–67) that:

F. Cheating in Soviet Russia was widely rejected as an acceptable response.

G. The cold climate in Russian classrooms motivated students to cheat.

H. The normative climate that produced cheating in Soviet Russia may be explained by the role of the Communist legacy.

J. Students in Soviet Russia failed to provide justifications for their unethical behavior.

Here's How to Crack It

In choice (F), you could choose *widely rejected* and try to place it in line 66. The passage disproves this, stating that cheating is *widely accepted*, so cross off choice (F). Choice (G) misuses the word *climate*, but it also discusses *classrooms*, which are nowhere to be found in the passage. Eliminate it. Choice (H) offers *Communist legacy*, an easy lead word phrase to locate in the passage. Choice (H) could match lines 62–64, so keep it. Choice (J) offers *justifications for their unethical behavior*, words right out of the passage. But the passage doesn't state that Russian students *failed to provide* them. The correct answer is choice (H).

Reading Drill 2

Use the 4-Step Basic Approach on the following passage, and apply your advanced reading skills. Time yourself to complete in 8–10 minutes. Check your answers in Chapter 24.

Passage I

PROSE FICTION: This passage is taken from *The Heart Is a Lonely Hunter,* by Carson McCullers (© 1940 and 1967 by Carson McCullers).

The sun woke Mick early, although she had stayed out late the night before. It was too hot even to drink coffee for breakfast, so she had ice water with syrup in it and cold biscuits. She messed around the kitchen for a while and then went out
5 on the front porch to read the funnies. She had thought maybe Mister Singer would be reading the paper on the porch like he did most Sunday mornings. But Mister Singer was not there, and later on her dad said he came in the night before and had company in his room. She waited for Mister Singer a long
10 time. All the other boarders came down except him. Finally she went back into the kitchen and took Ralph out of his high chair and put a clean dress on him and wiped off his face. Then when Bubber got home from Sunday School she was ready to take the kids out. She let Bubber ride in the wagon with Ralph
15 because he was barefooted and the hot sidewalk burned his feet. She pulled the wagon for about eight blocks until they came to the big, new house that was being built. The ladder was still propped against the edge of the roof, and she screwed up nerve and began to climb.

20 "You mind Ralph," she called back to Bubber. "Mind the gnats don't sit on his eyelids."

Five minutes later Mick stood up and held herself very straight. She spread out her arms like wings. This was the place where everyone wanted to stand. The very top. But if you lost
25 your grip and rolled off the edge it would kill you. All around were the roofs of other houses and the green top of trees. On the other side of town were the church steeples and the smokestacks from the mills. The sky was bright blue and hot as fire. The sun made everything on the ground either dizzy white or black.

30 She wanted to sing. All the songs she knew pushed up toward her throat, but there was no sound. One big boy who had got to the highest part of the roof last week let out a yell and then started hollering out a speech he had learned in High School—"Friends, Romans, Countrymen, Lend me your ears!"
35 There was something about getting to the very top that gave you a wild feeling and made you want to yell or sing or raise up your arms and fly.

She felt the soles of her tennis shoes slipping, and eased herself down so that she straddled the peak of the roof. The house

40 was almost finished. It would be one of the largest buildings in the neighborhood—two stories, with very high ceilings and the steepest roof of any house she had ever seen. But soon the work would be all finished. The carpenters would leave and the kids would have to find another place to play.

45 She was by herself. No one was around and it was quiet and she could think for a while. She took from the pocket of her shorts the package of cigarettes she had bought the night before. She breathed in the smoke slowly. The cigarettes gave her a drunk feeling so that her head seemed heavy and loose
50 on her shoulders, but she had to finish it.

M.K.—That was what she would have written on everything when she was seventeen years old and very famous. She would ride back home in a red-and-white Packard automobile with her initials on the doors. She would have M.K. written in red
55 on her handkerchiefs and underclothes. Maybe she would be a great inventor. She would invent tiny little radios the size of a green pea that people would carry around and stick in their ears. Also flying machines people could fasten on their backs like knapsacks and go zipping all over the world. After that she
60 would be the first one to make a large tunnel through the world to China, and people would go down in big balloons. Those were the first things she would invent. They were already planned.

When Mick had finished half of the cigarette she smashed it dead and flipped the butt down slant on the roof. The she
65 leaned forward so that her head rested on her arms and began to hum to herself.

1. As it is used in line 18, the phrased *screwed up* most nearly means:

   A. lost.
   B. made a mistake.
   C. examined.
   D. gathered.

2. If the passage describes a typical Sunday, Mick then spends part of her Sundays:

   F. learning grammar from Mister Singer.
   G. cooking breakfast for her family.
   H. going to Sunday School.
   J. caring for her younger brothers.

3. Mick believes that the other children in the neighborhood:

   A. did not want to play with her.
   B. also liked to climb the roof.
   C. thought that Mick was crazy for climbing the rooftop.
   D. had more housework then she did.

4. The name of Mick's father is:

   F. Ralph.
   G. Bubber.
   H. Mister Singer.
   J. not mentioned in the passage.

5. It can be reasonably inferred that one of the reasons that Mick enjoyed being on the roof was that:

   A. she could enjoy some time alone.
   B. her friends did not believe that she could do it and she liked proving them wrong.
   C. she felt very athletic while climbing.
   D. she knew that she was the only one who could climb that high.

6. It is suggested that no sound came out of Mick's throat (line 31) because she:

   F. did not think she had a good singing voice.
   G. could not express all that she was feeling.
   H. was afraid of heights.
   J. did not want to scare her brothers by yelling too loudly.

7. It can be inferred from the passage that Mister Singer is:

   A. Mick's father.
   B. a boarder at Mick's house.
   C. a schoolteacher.
   D. a journalist.

8. All the following are included in the list of things Mick would like to invent EXCEPT:

   F. a miniature radio.
   G. a small flying machine.
   H. a big balloon.
   J. a tunnel through the earth.

9. The house that Mick climbs onto is:

   A. three stories tall.
   B. on a hill.
   C. unfinished.
   D. owned by a celebrity.

10. According to the passage, it can be reasonably inferred that Mick spent a great deal of time wishing:

    F. to be famous.
    G. to have children.
    H. to get good grades in school.
    J. to spend more time with her mother.

Summary

- Work special question types Later. They require more work than a typical question, and they will become easier to do the later you do them.
- Double underline, circle, or cross out negative words EXCEPT, LEAST, or NOT. Use POE to cross off answers that are found in the passage.
- For Vocabulary in Context questions, read the entire sentence. Cross off the word or phrase and come up with your own word. Use POE to eliminate answers that don't match your word.
- Work Roman numeral questions efficiently, using POE.
- Don't waste time on special question types if you can't eliminate three answers. Guess from the choices that are remaining and move on.
- Use topic sentences, transitions, and modifiers to help translate confusing windows of text.
- Work backwards with answer choices. Try to match the answer to the passage instead of the passage to the answer.

Part V
How to Crack the ACT Science Test

Chapter 19
Introduction to the ACT Science Test

The ACT Science test always comes fourth, after the Reading test and before the optional Writing test. Fatigue can negatively affect even the founding president of the I Heart Science Club. Even if the Science test were first, many students would find it the most intimidating and feel that they need to crack open their freshman bio textbooks. But this is not a test of science facts: It is instead a test of how well you look up and synthesize information from tables, graphs, illustrations, and passages.

To maximize your score on the Science test, you need to work the passages in a personal order of difficulty. We'll teach you how to order the passages, and we'll teach you how to employ a strategic and efficient approach that will earn you your highest possible score.

WHAT'S ON THE SCIENCE TEST

Remember when you had to study for that tough biology exam, memorizing dozens of facts about things like meiosis, mitosis, and mitochondria? When you sat down to take the test, you either knew the answers or you didn't. Well, that's not the case on the ACT Science test. Even though the word *science* appears in the title, this test doesn't look much like the tests you've taken in your high school science classes. Like the English and Reading tests, the Science test is passage based, but most of the passages present the really important content in figures rather than in text.

The Format
You have 35 minutes for 7 passages and 40 questions.

On the Science test, you have 35 minutes to spend on 7 passages and a total of 40 questions. There are 3 types of passages, but unlike in the Reading test, the order of the passages will vary every time. We'll go into more detail about the 3 types of passages later in this chapter.

What Do You Need to Know?

For the topics of the passages, ACT pulls content from biology, chemistry, physics, and the Earth/space sciences, such as astronomy, geology, and meteorology. While you won't be quizzed on specific facts, background familiarity with the topics certainly helps. If the passage is on genetics, you'll undoubtedly do better if you've recently finished that unit in school and know it cold. But the information you need in order to answer the questions is offered in the passage itself, most frequently presented in a table, graph, or illustration of some kind. The ACT Science test is an open-book test, and you do not need advanced knowledge of any science topic.

You may not need an encyclopedic knowledge of science facts. You *do* need good scientific reasoning skills, a personalized pacing strategy, and a smart, effective approach to working the passages. You also need to be flexible, ready to adapt your strategy or abandon a question you've already spent way too much time on: Guess, and move on. Of all the tests on the ACT, Science is the most time-sensitive. Even the biggest science geeks find themselves barely finishing.

Outside Knowledge

Most of the questions can be answered from the information presented in the passages or figures, but be prepared for 3 to 4 questions that require outside knowledge. The outside-knowledge questions are nothing to stress over, however. There is no way to predict what the outside-knowledge questions will be on the next ACT, so there is nothing you can do to prepare; you cannot, and *should not*, try to review everything you've never learned or already forgotten. Besides, the outside-knowledge questions tend to ask about fairly basic facts, commonly addressed in intro-level high school science courses.

For example, you may need to know that a honey badger is a mammal, or you may need to identify a chemical formula as bleach, or you may need to know where acid falls on the pH scale. In any case, remember that for the overwhelming number of questions, everything that you need to answer them is right there in front of you. Use the basic approach we'll teach you in Chapter 21, and you'll do just fine.

On ACT.org, ACT identifies the skills you need for this test: "interpretation, analysis, evaluation, reasoning, and problem solving." We can boil this down to a more concise list.

You need to be able to

- look up data and trends
- make predictions
- synthesize information

But before you learn how to work the passages, you need to learn how to order them. To understand the reasoning behind the method, it's helpful to know the 3 categories of passages.

The Passages

All of the passages fall within 3 categories. The order of the passages will vary on each test, but the distribution of types of passages is always the same. To pick your order, it's less important what the passage is called than what it looks like. But it is important to know that there are 3 categories of passages and to know their similarities and differences. ACT has very formal-sounding names for the categories, so we made up our own.

Charts and Graphs (aka Data Representation)

3 Passages, 5 Questions Each These passages will *always* come with figures: it's their purpose in life. You'll see one or more charts, tables, graphs, or illustrations. Charts and Graphs passages are intended to test your ability to understand and interpret the information that's presented. There are 3 Charts and Graphs passages per test, and each one has 5 questions, for a total of 15 questions.

Experiments (aka Research Summaries)

3 Passages, 6 Questions Each These passages will *usually* come with figures. They're intended to describe several experiments, and they include more text than do the Charts and Graphs passages. But the results of the experiments are frequently presented in tables or in graphs, and you may have trouble distinguishing the Experiments passages from Charts and Graphs passages. That doesn't matter, however, because in Chapter 21 we'll teach you the basic approach that applies to both types of passages. You'll never need to identify one over the other when you're taking the test. For the record, however, Experiments passages come with more questions. There are 3 Experiments passages per test with 6 questions per passage, for a total of 18 questions.

Fighting Scientists (aka Conflicting Viewpoints)

1 Passage, 7 Questions This passage *sometimes* comes with figures. Even when there are figures, however, the passage is fundamentally different from the Charts and Graphs passages and the Experiments passages. That means it also requires a different way to crack it, and we'll teach you how to do just that in Chapter 22. The Fighting Scientists passage involves much more reading than you'll need to do for the other 2 types. In fact, most of the Fighting Scientists passages will feel more like the passages on the Reading test, and you'll be able to use some of the skills you learned to crack the Reading test as you compare, contrast, and synthesize the different viewpoints.

When it comes to the topics, ACT may use arguments already resolved by the scientific community as well as more cutting-edge issues that are still contested. In either case, remind yourself again that the Science test is an open-book test, providing you the information you need to answer almost all the questions.

HOW TO CRACK THE SCIENCE TEST

Order the Passages

As always on the ACT, time is your enemy. With only 35 minutes to review 7 passages and answer 40 questions, you can't afford to spend too much time on the most difficult only to run out of time for the easiest. ACT doesn't present the passages in order of difficulty, but on every exam, some are easier than others while some are truly tough. What would happen if on your ACT, the most difficult came first and the easiest last? If you did them in order, you could likely run out of time without a chance to correctly answer all the questions on the easiest passage.

That's why you can't do the passages in the order ACT picks—unless that happens to match your Personal Order of Difficulty (POOD). If time is going to run out, you want it to run out on the hardest passage, not the easiest.

Now, Later, Never

We're using the term "easier" only because we're grading the passages on a curve. "Easy" is a loaded term.

Therefore, it's more useful to think of the passages as those you'd do *Now*, those you'd do *Later*, and those you'd *Never* do.

Now Passages

Your goal with all the passages is to crack the main point. You don't necessarily need to know the topic but you do need to spot the conclusions the content offers: trends, patterns, and relationships. You will spot the main point faster when those conclusions are presented in figures rather than in text. The easier the figures are to "read," the faster you'll crack the main point.

As we explained earlier, this is not a test of science knowledge. Instead, it's a test of your scientific reasoning skills. That means spotting the trends and patterns of variables and the relationships between figures and viewpoints.

The best passages to do Now have the most obvious patterns as well as a few other common characteristics.

Look for

1. **Small graphs and tables:** A good Now passage can have only tables, only graphs, or both. Tables should be no more than 3–4 rows and columns, and graphs should have no more than 3–4 lines or curves.
2. **Easy-to-spot consistent trends:** Look for graphs with all lines/curves heading in the same direction: all up, all down, or all flat.
3. **Numbers in the figures:** To show a consistent trend, the figure has to feature numbers, not words or symbols.
4. **Short answers:** Look for as many questions as possible with short answers, specifically answers with numbers and short relationship words like *increase* or *decrease*.

In Chapter 20 we'll show in greater detail how trends and patterns deliver the main point.

Patterns
Look for trends *within* a figure. Look for relationships *between* figures and viewpoints.

Personal Order of Difficulty (POOD)

There is one additional important characteristic you need to look for: topics you know. Even if the figures are really ugly and confusing, if a passage is on a topic you just finished in school and know cold, you'll get the main point of the passage quickly, and that's the goal of choosing a Now passage.

Pace Yourself

Unless you're shooting for a 27 or higher on the Science test, you're better off choosing at least one passage as Never. Take 35 minutes, and do fewer passages. You'll give yourself more time and increase your accuracy. As you steadily increase your scoring goals in practice, target the number of questions you need to reach your goal. The more aggressively you can move through the passages finding all the Now *questions* you can answer—no matter how difficult the passage may be— the better you'll score.

Goal Score

Use the pacing strategies and score grid on page 25 to find your goal score for each practice test and, eventually, the ACT.

Be Flexible

As we've mentioned before, to earn your best score on the ACT, you have to be flexible, and nowhere is this more true than on the Science test. The Science test

Letter of the Day (LOTD)
Just because you don't work on a passage doesn't mean you don't bubble in answers. Never leave any bubbles blank on the ACT. Bubble in your Letter of the Day for all the questions on your Never passages.

shows the greatest change in level of difficulty from one administration to the next. There is no way to predict how difficult the Science test will be, nor what the particular topics will be. Certainly, if you know more about the topic, you'll find even an ugly-looking passage more understandable. But that doesn't mean you're relying on luck. The Princeton Review's basic approach works regardless of what the topics are. The goal is to practice using the basic approach so that the particulars of the passage are irrelevant.

Hard Test = Generous Curve

Don't be scared of a hard Science test on any particular administration. Each test is curved against only the students who took that particular exam. If the Science test is hard, *everyone* will struggle with the hardest questions, and the curve will be more generous.

However, you have to fight your own instincts, or at least retrain them into those of a great test taker. Always be prepared to adapt your order based on what you see, both in practice and on a real test. If you choose a passage that looked good and then find yourself struggling, leave it and find another. Ignore the voice in your head that says, "Well, I've put so much time into this incredibly hard passage already, all that time would be a waste if I didn't finish the passage." Nothing could be further from the truth. You're throwing away perfectly good time if you stick with a passage that you're just not grasping.

You have to be just as strict with a tough question. When you're stumped, your first instinct may be to go back and read the passage or stare at the figure *again*, waiting for a flash of inspirational genius to suddenly make everything clear. Instead, focus on using POE to get rid of answers that can't be right. Even if you can cross off only one answer, guess from what's left and move on. If you stick with one tough question too long, you may be robbing yourself of 2–3 questions.

1 Point Earned, 3 Points Lost

Easy questions earn the same number of points as difficult questions. Don't waste time struggling with a hard question when you can move on and answer easy questions. You can always come back to the question if you have time.

POE

Each time you eliminate a wrong answer, you increase your chance of choosing the correct answer.

Process of Elimination (POE)

Just as in the other tests, POE is a powerful tool on the Science test. Particularly on tougher questions, use POE to eliminate wrong answers that are clearly contradicted by what you're looking at.

Let's see how POE works on the Science test.

1. An epidemiologist claims that a patient infected with chicken pox faces the greatest risk of mortality for any of the diseases studied. Do the results of Experiment 1 support her claim?

    A. Yes; the percentage of fatal chicken pox infections is greater than the percentage of fatal rabies infections.
    B. Yes; the percentage of fatal chicken pox infections is less than the percentage of fatal rabies infections.
    C. No; the percentage of fatal chicken pox infections is greater than the percentage of fatal rabies infections.
    D. No; the percentage of fatal chicken pox infections is less than the percentage of fatal rabies infections.

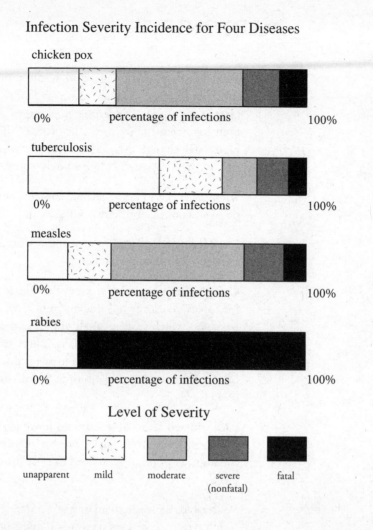

Infection Severity Incidence for Four Diseases

chicken pox

0%   percentage of infections   100%

tuberculosis

0%   percentage of infections   100%

measles

0%   percentage of infections   100%

rabies

0%   percentage of infections   100%

Level of Severity

unapparent   mild   moderate   severe   fatal
                                  (nonfatal)

Here's How to Crack It

Don't waste time staring at the figure trying to look up the answer. Look at how descriptive the answer choices are: POE will be much faster. Ignore the "Yes" and "No," and focus on the reasons given. Do they accurately describe the figure? Choices (A) and (C) are disproven by the figure, so cross them off. The reason given in choices (B) and (D) is the opposite of the reason given in the other two, so both are proven by the figure. If you had no clue what *mortality* meant, you'd have a fifty-fifty chance of getting this right. If you do, you have to consider the claim and reason that chicken pox is less fatal than rabies and therefore poses less of a risk of mortality, i.e., death. The correct answer is choice (D).

Maybe you read the question, and a quick glance at the figure was all you needed to know the answer was "No." Great, cross off choices (A) and (B), and then compare what's different between choices (B) and (D). The point is to save time by looking at the answers and then the figure rather than staring at the figure and then the answers. The harder the figure, the more important POE is to your success.

Summary

o There are always 7 passages and 40 questions on the Science test. There are always 3 Charts and Graphs passages, 3 Experiments passages, and 1 Fighting Scientists passage. The order of the passages will change every time, but the distribution of the 3 types will always be the same.

o You don't need to know science content, but you do need good scientific reasoning skills.

o Look for trends within figures and relationships between figures and viewpoints.

o Order your passages. Use your POOD to look for topics you know a lot about. Look for Now passages, which feature small graphs and tables, easy-to-spot consistent trends, numbers instead of words or symbols, and short answers made up of numbers or short relationship words like *increase* or *lower*.

o Pace yourself. Slow down and do fewer passages, but work up to your goal score by focusing on the number of points you need to earn your goal score.

o Be flexible. Be ready to adapt your order, leave a tough passage, or guess on a tough question.

o Use Process of Elimination to cross off wrong answers and save time.

Chapter 20
Scientific Reasoning Skills

You don't need to know science facts for the ACT. For the most part, the Science test is an open-book test, with the 7 passages offering the content you need to answer nearly all the questions. According to ACT, you do need scientific reasoning skills. But all this really means is that you need some common sense. Science may seem intimidating, but it's based on a lot more common sense than you may think.

YOU KNOW MORE THAN YOU THINK

It's easy to feel very intimidated by the content and even the figures on the Science test. But all of science is built on common sense. The key to building good scientific reasoning skills is to realize you *already have* those skills. You use common sense every day to figure things out, to solve problems, to make conclusions. A scientist does the same. When you solve a problem, you think critically, and that's the basis of scientific reasoning.

How to Solve a Problem

Let's try an experiment. Say you put on a wool sweater and go out to dinner one night. At the restaurant you order some delectable shrimp for dinner, and then a beautiful bowl of strawberries for dessert.

The next morning, you wake up covered in red, itchy hives. What caused them? Do you jump to the conclusion it was the sweater? What about the shrimp? A lot of people have allergies to shellfish. But so, too, do a lot of people have allergies to strawberries. How are you supposed to know which one caused your hives? How do you know any of these options are the only possible culprits?

Assumption = Guess
An assumption is nothing more than a guess, and a lazy one at that, if you are willing to believe the riddle has been solved. A guess doesn't cut it in the scientific world: only proof does.

You don't. That's the first rule of scientific reasoning: Make no assumptions. You can't assume it was the sweater, the shrimp, or the strawberries. But you have to prove it was one and only one of these, if any. So how do you set about finding out which one?

You design an experiment. You first need to narrow the list of suspects down to the sweater, shrimp, and strawberries. Begin with a baseline. You need to see what happens on a day with none of the possible causes in play to compare to the days with them. Wear a cotton T-shirt and eat cauliflower and cantaloupe. Do you still have hives? Then the three suspects have all been vindicated. But if your hives have cleared up, you've confirmed your first hypothesis that it was indeed the sweater, the shrimp, or the strawberries.

Hypothesis
A hypothesis is a theory. An assumption is a guess with no proof. A hypothesis is more advanced than that. It's a theory that tries to explain what happened, but it requires proof.

Now you have to figure out which one of the three caused your hives. We need a day with one, and one only, of the possibilities, or *variables*, in play. That's the second rule of scientific reasoning: Change one variable at a time. On one day wear the sweater, but skip the shrimp and strawberries. On another lose the sweater and eat the shrimp but not the strawberries. On yet another replace the shrimp with the strawberries. On each day check for hives. The itchy red bumps *depend* on whatever *independent* variable is causing them.

Independent and Dependent Variables
The independent variable affects or creates the dependent variable. Does *x* create or affect *y*? Some examples of independent variables include time, temperature, and depth. Dependent variables are the events possibly created or affected by an independent variable, and they can be whatever the scientist is studying. Some examples of dependent variables include volume, solubility, and pressure.

That's all well and good. But what about everything else in your life? Notice we said you couldn't wear the sweater on the days you ate the shrimp and strawberries. But other than the sweater, *you have to wear the exact same clothes on the day you eat shrimp and on the day you eat strawberries.* It's not just what you wear. Everything else in your life has to be exactly the same. If on the day you wore the sweater, you worked out at the gym, but on the day you ate shrimp, you lay on your sofa all day watching television, how much would you know? Not much. Certainly not much of anything with proof, and proof is what it's all about in science. The third rule of scientific reasoning is that you have to keep all the other variables in the experiment the same as you vary one and only one independent variable. In the hives experiment, this means that in order to conclusively prove the cause, you have to keep everything else the same on each day that you change one and only one independent variable. Do the same things. Wear the same clothes (except the sweater). Eat the same things (except the shrimp and strawberries).

Watch it on your DVD

And that's it. If you follow these three rules, you'll know what causes your hives.

Trends

In our first example, we looked at a dependent variable, hives, that were present only when an independent variable was present. You've undoubtedly faced other situations in which different amounts of a variable seem to have an effect on another variable. The more you study, the better your grades. The more pints of ice cream you eat, the more pounds you gain. The more miles you run, the more pounds you lose.

Let's look at another situation. You sleep only 5 hours a night, staying up late and getting up early to study, but you're consistently scoring in the high 70s on your daily math quizzes no matter how many hours you study. Suppose you had a hypothesis that if you slept more, your scores would improve. How would you design an experiment to test this? You already have a baseline of 5 hours and consistent scores in the high 70s. So beginning with the first night, you sleep longer and then see how you score the next day. The next night,

The Three Rules of Scientific Reasoning
1. **Make no assumptions.** You need a standard of comparison to measure against your results. How does your dependent variable react without the presence of any of your independent variables?
2. **Change one variable at a time.** Vary each independent variable to see its effect on your dependent variable.
3. **Keep all other variables the same.** Your other independent variables *and everything else* have to be the same as you vary one and only one independent variable.

you sleep even longer, and check your quiz score the next day. Can you do anything else differently? No, you have to keep all the other variables in your life the same. Each day you eat the same things and study the same number of hours. You even track quiz scores in the same unit to eliminate any possibility that there is any other reason why your quiz scores improve.

To be organized, you record all your data in a simple table.

Table 1	
Hours of sleep	Quiz scores
5	78
6	83
7	88
8	93

Direct Proportion
As *x* increases,
y increases.
As *x* decreases,
y decreases.

As the number of hours of sleep increases, your quiz score increases. In this experiment the number of hours of sleep is the independent variable, and the quiz score is the dependent variable. You've established that your quiz score is ***directly*** proportional to the number of hours you sleep.

Let's look at another experiment. Suppose your hypothesis this time is that the more cups of coffee you drink, the fewer hours you sleep. How would you design the experiment? Same rules as always. First, you need a baseline. You need to get all the caffeine out of your system and cut your consumption down to 0 cups each day. You establish a consistent routine of the same diet, exercise, studying, sports practice, and so on. Then, without changing any of those variables, you begin drinking coffee again—same size cup each day—increasing the number of cups and measuring the number of hours you sleep the following night.

Once again, you record your findings in a table.

Table 2	
Cups of coffee	Hours of sleep
0	8
1	7
2	6
3	5

Inverse Proportion
As *x* increases,
y decreases.
As *x* decreases,
y increases.

As the cups of coffee increase, the hours of sleep decrease. This time, the number of hours of sleep is the dependent variable, and the number of cups of coffee is the independent variable. You've established that the amount you sleep is ***inversely*** proportional to the amount of coffee you drink.

Many passages on the Science test feature passages whose main point is either a direct or inverse trend of the variables. In Chapter 19, we outlined characteristics of Now passages, for example, small tables and graphs with easy-to-spot consistent trends. When you look at the two tables above, the trend is pretty obvious from just a quick glance. You've already cracked the main point, and you will find all the questions that much easier to tackle as a result.

Graphs

Tables and graphs both show the trends of variables. Graphs are more visual, making the trends easier to spot.

If you graphed your data from Table 1, what would it look like?

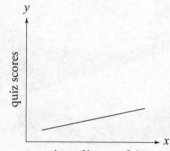

Remember that in math, the horizontal axis is always x: It's the independent variable. The vertical axis is always y: It's the dependent variable. Science follows the same rules. This graph shows you that as x increases, y increases. They have a direct relationship.

Let's stick with using math to understand the graphs on the Science test better. Think about slope. It's the change in y over the change in x. In this graph, the slope is positive. Direct relationships are positive slopes.

$$\text{Slope} = \frac{rise}{run}$$

$$\frac{y_2 - y_1}{x_2 - x_1}$$

Let's graph Table 2.

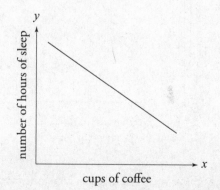

This graph shows you that as x increases, y decreases. They have an inverse relationship, and the slope is negative. Inverse relationships are negative slopes.

Positive and Negative Slope

Using your math skills in coordinate geometry is a great way to see how much graphs tell you. We already pointed out that direct relationships have positive slopes, as shown by the graph of Table 1, and inverse relationships have negative slopes, as shown by the graph of Table 2. But the size of the slope tells you even more.

Let's take a look at another real-life example. You're sweltering in the middle of a heat wave, so it's time to fill your above-ground pool.

You pull out your hose to start filling the pool. The water fills at a constant rate of 1 gallon per hour, and it takes several hours to fill it.

As the number of hours increases (independent variable), the volume of the water, in gallons, increases (dependent variable). The following graph shows the direct relationship.

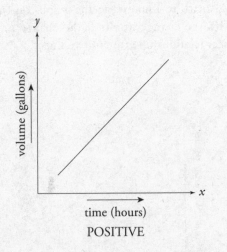

time (hours)
POSITIVE

The slope is positive 1 because the pool fills at a constant rate of 1 gallon per hour.

After a few days of enjoying your pool, the forecasts warn of an impending hurricane. For safety's sake, you have to drain the pool. You unplug the drain, and the water begins to flow out at the same 1 gallon per hour rate. The following graph shows the inverse relationship.

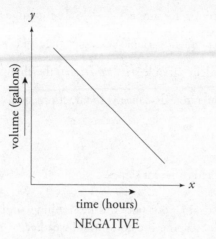

time (hours)
NEGATIVE

The slope is negative 1 because the pool drains at a constant rate of 1 gallon per hour.

It's very useful to spot a positive or negative slope on a graph in a Science passage. As we mentioned before, you've cracked the main point of the passage when you spot the relationship between the variables. But positive and negative linear graphs are not the only ones you'll see, and you'll also see different types of positive graphs and different types of negative graphs.

Let's dive back into the pool.

Flat Lines

At the last minute, the path of the hurricane heads out to sea and avoids landfall. In fact, your pool hasn't even finished draining when the storm changes direction. Now a new heat wave has descended, and you need to refill the pool. You turn your hose on and savor how great that water is going to feel at the end of a long, hot day. Unfortunately for you, you forget to replug the drain. Because you decide to spend the day in an air-conditioned movie theater, you don't even realize the pool isn't filling. Well, it is filling, but it is also draining at the exact same rate. Thus, the volume doesn't change.

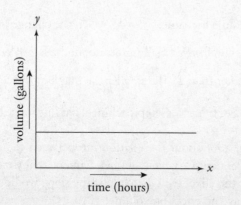

time (hours)

The slope of this line is 0 because the volume doesn't change. As time passes, the number of hours keeps increasing, but the change in time has no effect on the volume.

Think about the formula for slope: $\frac{y_2 - y_1}{x_2 - x_1}$. The change in y is divided by the change in x. The independent variable (x) can change all it wants—as time marches on—but if the dependent variable stays **constant,** the change between y values is 0. When 0 is in the numerator, that means the fraction equals 0.

Flat Line = **Zero Slope**
When there is no change in y, the slope is a flat line. The dependent variable is constant.

Shallow Lines

Different rates will yield different slopes.

Once you replug the drain, your pool finishes refilling, and you spend several days floating in your pool, escaping the hot, humid weather.

Water, however, has a nasty habit of evaporating. But the rate of evaporation is far slower than the rate at which the pool empties when the drain is unplugged. Still, if you don't use the hose to refill the pool, the volume of water will decrease over a number of days. Let's take a look at what that graph would look like.

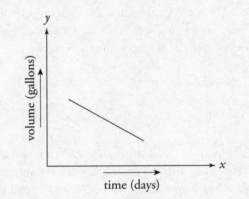

The slope is negative because as time increases, the volume decreases. Time and volume have an inverse relationship. But the effect that time has on volume is relatively small compared to the effects of an open drain.

Bring back the formula for slope: $\frac{y_2 - y_1}{x_2 - x_1}$. When the change in y is small compared to the change in x, you have a small numerator and a large denominator. Thus, you have a fraction smaller than 1. The smaller the fraction, the closer to parallel to the x-axis the line will be. In fact, it's approaching a flat line, or a slope of 0.

Shallow Line = **Small Slope**
When the independent variable has little effect on the dependent variable, the slope will be shallow.

The slope tells you a lot about the relationship between the independent variable (time) and the dependent variable (volume), namely, that time has a very small effect on volume. If the effect were much less, the slope would be 0, which is to say that time would have no effect on volume.

Steep Lines

Back to the pool! You refill the pool to its full volume, but you decide it's time to rake around the pool with a deadly sharp rake. You swing a little wildly too close to the nylon pool and slice a huge gash in the side. Water starts gushing out, at a much faster rate than it empties when the drain is unplugged. Take a look at what the graph of your small accident looks like.

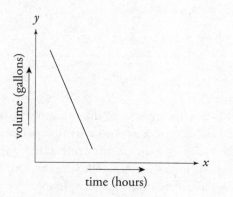

The slope is negative because as time increases, the volume of the water decreases. Time and volume have an inverse relationship. But compared to the rate of decrease when the drain is unplugged, the volume is decreasing at a faster rate. Compared to the rate of decrease from evaporation, the volume is decreasing at a much faster rate.

If you think about this with the formula of slope in mind, the change in y is very large and the change in x very small. Therefore, the numerator is larger than the denominator, leaving a fraction greater than 1. The bigger the fraction, the closer to parallel to the y-axis the line will be. But the line will never be vertical. After all, time can't stand still, so there will always be a change in x. You know from your math review that the denominator can't be zero, so slope can't work if there is no change in x. Even if you had super powers to freeze time, the volume would freeze as well. So there is no way to have a change in y but no change in x.

Curves

In Science passages, not all graphs will feature straight lines. Just as in real life, not all situations are linear.

The heat wave passes, and summer turns to fall. But you're not ready to give up the pool, even as the days turn crisp. You decide to install a heat pump to make it a heated pool. You turn the pump on, and it gradually heats the chilly water to a perfect 78°F. However, the heat pump malfunctions, and the temperature continues to rise, faster and faster, until soon it's over 100°F.

Luckily for you, you witnessed all this safely from outside the pool. But let's take a look at what the graph would look like.

Steep Line = Big Slope
When the independent variable has to change by only a small amount to have a huge effect on the dependent variable, the slope will be steep.

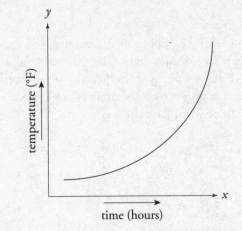

time (hours)

Curves = Exponential Change

When the dependent variable changes by a different amount every time the independent variable changes, the result will be a curved line.

The curve is obviously not linear, so slope doesn't apply. As the independent variable (time) increases, the dependent variable (temperature) increases, so the relationship between the variables is direct. But temperature increases *exponentially* faster, not in a constant, linear pattern. The amount that y changes with each change in x is different at different points on the graph.

Now let's think of this in math terms. What does the graph of $y = x^2$ look like? It's a parabola. Cut the parabola off at the origin and look only at the right half, and it will look just like the graph above.

TRENDS ON THE SCIENCE TEST

The key to cracking the Science test is to look for trends and patterns. Figures with consistent trends point to a Now passage because the figure has provided the main point of the passage, i.e., the relationship between the variables.

In the next chapter, we'll teach you a basic approach to cracking each passage, including passages that *don't* feature small tables and graphs with consistent trends. But we hope that this chapter has convinced you to look for passages featuring figures with consistent trends to do Now. You'll find even the hardest questions are easier to tackle when the figure tells you everything you need to know.

Look at each of the following figures. What are the relationships between the variables?

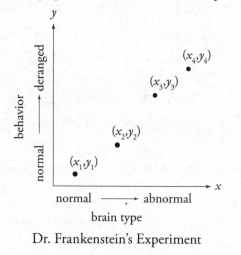

Dr. Frankenstein's Experiment

As the positive slope of the ordered pairs shows, it's a direct, linear relationship. The more abnormal the brain, the more deranged the behavior.

Try another.

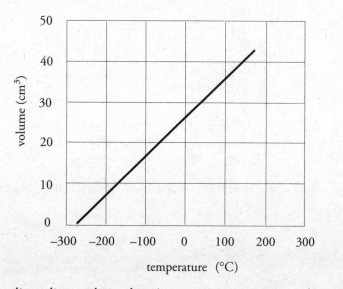

This, too, is a direct, linear relationship. As temperature increases, volume increases.

What about the next one?

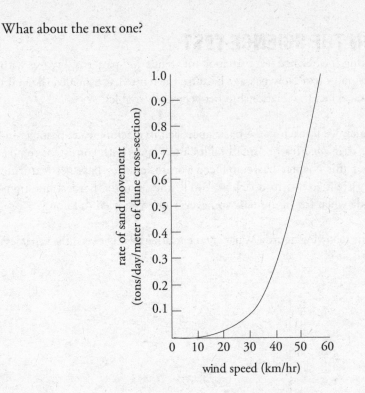

When the wind speed is 40 km/hr, what is the rate of sand movement? It's 0.3. When the wind speed is 50 km/hr, the rate of sand movement increases to 0.6, double the last reading even though the wind speed increased by only 10 km/hr. The relationship is direct, but the curve shows you it's an exponential relationship, not a linear one.

Try the next one.

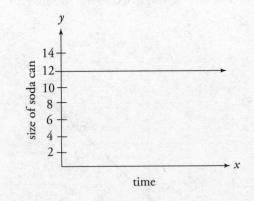

Does time actually affect the size of a soda can? Of course not. As a result, we get a flat line.

Try one more.

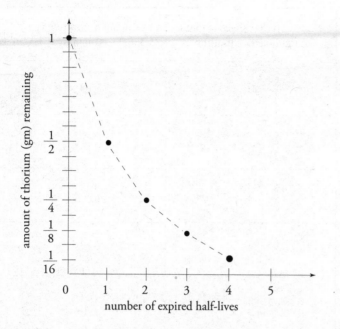

As the number of expired half-lives increases, the amount of thorium remaining decreases, so the two have an inverse relationship. But because the curve is headed downward, it's a negative relationship.

Do you need to know what "expired half-lives" and "thorium" are? No, you don't need to (but it's always helpful when you're familiar with the content). To answer the questions for this passage, everything you need to know comes from the relationships between the variables. The main point of the passage is just a summary of these relationships.

Tables

When we began this chapter, we showed you tables before switching to graphs. Everything we've discussed about graphs applies to tables. A table with consistent trends is just as helpful as a graph with consistent trends. The only difference is that tables are not as visual as graphs, so it's up to you to make them visual.

Look at the table below.

Number of half-lives expired for radioactive thorium	Amount of thorium (gm) remaining
0	1
1	$\frac{1}{2}$
2	$\frac{1}{4}$
3	$\frac{1}{8}$
4	$\frac{1}{16}$

This is the same information we saw in a graph. What direction is the number of half-lives headed? It's headed up. Draw an arrow to reflect the trend. What direction is the amount of thorium headed? It's headed down. Draw an arrow to reflect the trend. Your table should now look like this:

Number of half-lives expired for radioactive thorium	Amount of thorium (gm) remaining
0	1
1	$\frac{1}{2}$
2	$\frac{1}{4}$
3	$\frac{1}{8}$
4	$\frac{1}{16}$

↑   ↓

You've just gotten a preview of the next chapter. Marking the trends in a figure is the first step in the basic approach to cracking Science passages.

Inconsistent Trends and No Relationships

Wouldn't it be great if you saw only tables and graphs with consistent trends on the ACT? Yes, it would, but there will be uglier figures as well. Now that you know how powerful consistent trends are, you can actually use that knowledge even when there is no consistency. The absence of consistency tells its own story.

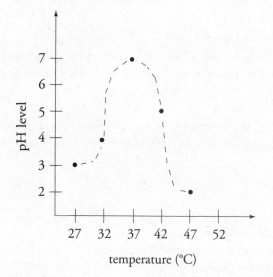

As temperature increases, what does pH do? It barely increases at first, then makes a sharp jump before an equally sharp fall to a point that is lower than what it began. You may have immediately identified this as a **bell curve**. Is a bell curve consistent?

A bell curve is certainly not as consistent as a straight line or even a curve that moves in a positive or negative direction. There is some consistency, however. It increases, then decreases. The problem is that we can't make a prediction of what it will do next. That's the real beauty of consistent lines and curves: We can predict what will happen off the figure. But with a bell curve, we can't determine whether it will repeat its trend or if it will steadily decrease.

What about the next graph? What story does it tell?

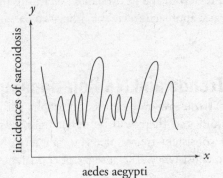

There is no relationship at all between aedes aegypti and sarcoidosis. The incidence of sarcoidosis is *independent* of the aedes aegypti, not *dependent*. And unlike the relationship in a flat line, the incidence of sarcoidosis is not constant. Instead, it fluctuates wildly.

That's a good deal of information from a confusing figure with two strange variables. But would you want to do the passage with this figure Now or Later? Definitely Later.

Multiple Variables

In many Experiments passages, you'll see multiple tables and graphs. Take a look at the following tables (Tables 3 and 4).

Table 3	
Length (m)	Resistance (Ω)
0.9	7.5
1.8	15.0
3.6	30.0

Table 3

Table 4	
Cross-sectional area (mm²)	Resistance (Ω)
0.8	35.0
1.6	18.0
3.2	7.5

Table 4

First, mark the trends within each figure. In Table 3, as length increases, resistance increases. Length is the independent variable, resistance is the dependent variable, and the two have a direct relationship. In Table 4, as cross-sectional area increases, resistance decreases, and the two have an inverse relationship. What's the relationship between the figures? Look at the variable they have in common: resistance.

In Experiments passages—as well as in scientific studies in real life—it's common to test different independent variables to measure their effect on the same dependent variable. But recall our second and third rules of scientific reasoning skills:

2. **Change one variable at a time.** Vary each independent variable to see its effect on your dependent variable.

3. **Keep all other variables the same.** Your other independent variables *and everything else* has to be the same as you vary one and only one independent variable.

When length is varied, can cross-sectional area vary at the same time? No, it has to stay the same, that is, constant. And when cross-sectional area is varied, length has to stay constant.

On the Science test, you are likely to see a question that tests your ability to spot the constants.

———————————○———————————

1. Based on the results shown in Table 3 and Table 4 above, the cross-sectional area used in the first experiment (resulting in Table 3), was most likely:

   A. 0.8 mm^2.
   B. 1.6 mm^2.
   C. 3.2 mm^2.
   D. 4.8 mm^2.

Here's How to Crack It

Find the link between the two tables by looking at the variable they have in common, resistance. Look for a value of resistance that is the same in both tables. In Table 3, resistance is 7.5 Ω when length is 0.9 m. In Table 4, resistance is 7.5 Ω when cross-sectional area is 3.2 mm^2. Thus, we know that as length was varied, cross-sectional area was held constant at 3.2 mm^2, and as cross-sectional area was varied, length was held constant at 0.9 m. The correct answer is choice (C).

———————————○———————————

Graphs can also have multiple variables. Take a look at the following graph.

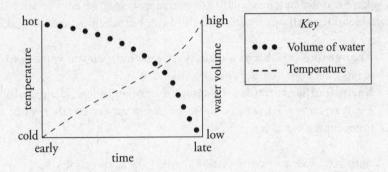

When there are multiple variables on a graph, you always need to be careful to look at the correct line and the correct axis. As time increases, temperature increases. As time increases, water volume decreases. Does that mean temperature and water volume have a relationship? Not directly, they don't. What's the variable they have in common? Time.

Try another question.

───────────────────○───────────────────

2. According to the figure above what was the temperature when water volume was at its highest?

    F. High
    G. Hot
    H. Low
    J. Cold

Here's How to Crack It

Find the link between the two axes by looking at the variable they have in common, time. Be sure to look at the correct curve on the correct axis. Water volume is the bubbled line, and when it's at its highest, the time on the *x*-axis is early. When time is early, look at the dashed line for the temperature. When it's early, the temperature is cold.

The correct answer is choice (J).

───────────────────○───────────────────

In the next lesson, we'll teach you how to use your scientific reasoning skills on ACT Science passages, which will feature plenty of tables and graphs with various trends and relationships.

Summary

- Scientific reasoning is based on common sense.

- The three rules of scientific reasoning skills are
  1. Make no assumptions.
  2. Change one variable at a time.
  3. Keep all other variables the same.

- A hypothesis is a theory that needs proof to become a conclusion.

- An independent variable creates or causes an effect on a dependent variable.

- In a direct relationship, as x increases, y increases.

- Direct linear relationships on a graph have positive slopes.

- In an inverse relationship, as x increases, y decreases.

- Inverse linear relationships on a graph have negative slopes.

- A flat line means the dependent variable is constant, and the independent variable has no effect.

- A steep slope means the independent variable has a drastic effect on the dependent variable.

- A shallow slope means the independent variable has a slight effect on the dependent variable.

- When the dependent variable changes by different amounts every time the independent variable changes, the result is a curved line.

Chapter 21
The Basic Approach

To earn your highest possible score on the Science test, you need an efficient and strategic approach to working the passages. In this chapter, we'll teach you how to apply your scientific reasoning skills to assess quickly the content of the passage and figures and make your way methodically through the questions.

Fighting Scientists
The Fighting Scientists passage is fundamentally different from the Charts and Graphs passages and Experiments passages, and requires a different approach. In Chapter 22, we teach you the approach for Fighting Scientists.

HOW TO CRACK THE SCIENCE TEST

The most efficient way to boost your Science score is to pick your order of the passages and apply our 3-Step Basic Approach to the Charts and Graphs passages and Experiments passages. Follow our smart, effective strategy to earn as many points as you can.

Step 1: Work the Figures

Take 10–30 seconds to review the figures. In the last chapter, we taught you how to look for and identify trends, patterns, and relationships. Your goal in Step 1 is to quickly identify the main point of the passage and the relationships between the variables that convey the main point. Consistent trends are the fastest to assess, but all trends and patterns tell a story. In Chapter 19, we gave you a way to spot the Now passages, which are chiefly characterized by consistent trends.

Now Passages
1. **Small tables and graphs:** No more than 3–4 curves on a graph, no more than 3–4 rows and columns on a table.
2. **Easy-to-spot consistent trends:** All lines headed in same direction, numbers in a table in easy-to-spot order.
3. **Numbers, not words or symbols:** Avoid tables and graphs with words or symbols.
4. **Short answers:** Numbers, or trend words like *increase* and *decrease* or *higher* and *lower*.

Graphs

Graphs visually represent the relationship between the variables. When you work a graph, identify the relationship, and take note of the variables and their units.

Look at the graph on the next page.

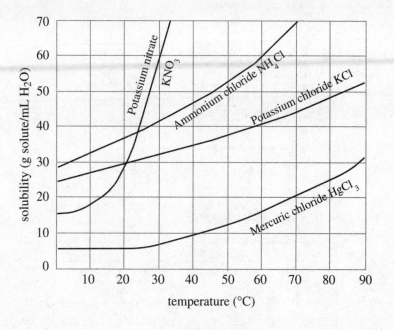

Figure 1

1. Look at the direction of the curves: They are all headed up.
2. Take note of the variables and their units. Temperature, in °C, is on the x-axis; solubility, in g solute/100 mL H_2O is on the y-axis.
3. Identify the relationship. A positive slope means it's a direct relationship. As temperature increases, solubility increases.

Tables

For tables, you need to make the trends visual. Take a look at the table below.

Table 1	
Length (m)	Resistance (Ω)
0.9	7.5
1.8	15.0
3.6	30.0

1. What is length doing? It's increasing. Mark it with an arrow.
2. What is resistance doing? It's increasing. Mark it with an arrow.
3. What are the units of the variables? m and Ω.
4. Identify the relationship. Both variables move in the same direction, so it's a direct relationship.

Here's what your table should look like.

Table 1	
Length (m)	Resistance (Ω)
0.9	7.5
1.8	15.0
3.6	30.0

↑ ↑

Try another table from the same passage.

Table 2	
Cross-sectional area (mm²)	Resistance (Ω)
0.8	30.0
1.6	15.0
3.2	7.5

1. What is the cross-sectional area doing? It's increasing. Mark it with an arrow.
2. What is resistance doing? It's decreasing. Mark it with an arrow.
3. What are the units of the variables? mm² and Ω.
4. Identify the relationship. As the cross-sectional area increases, resistance decreases. It's an inverse relationship.

Here's what your table should look like.

Table 2	
Cross-sectional area (mm²)	Resistance (Ω)
0.8	30.0
1.6	15.0
3.2	7.5

↑ ↓

Last, identify the relationship between the tables. Each table has the variable **resistance** in common.

Step 2: Work the Questions
Once you've marked the figures, go straight to the questions.

Now, Later, Never

There is no set order of difficulty of the questions. Follow your Personal Order of Difficulty (POOD): If a question is fairly straightforward, do it Now. Most of the questions you consider straightforward will likely ask you to identify a trend, look up a value, or make a prediction. Now questions will have values or trend words like *increase* or *lower* in the answers. If a question strikes you as confusing or time-consuming, come back to it Later. Occasionally, you'll judge a question tough enough you may Never want to do it. Select your Letter of the Day (LOTD), and move on to the next passage. In Step 3, we'll address how smart use of Process of Elimination (POE) may eliminate the need for any Never questions on a Now passage. But for now, let's look at a sample Now question.

Acronyms Rule!
You've seen our favorite Princeton Review acronyms before and you'll see them again: POOD, LOTD, POE.

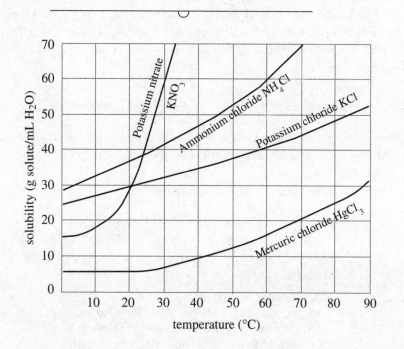

1. Based on the figure, as temperature increases, the solubility of HgCl$_3$:

   A. increases.
   B. decreases.
   C. increases, then decreases.
   D. decreases, then increases.

Here's How to Crack It

This question is asking you to identify a trend. You already cracked this question in Step 1, when you worked the figures and identified the trends. All the curves are headed up, so as temperature increases, the solubility of HgCl$_3$ increases. The correct answer is choice (A).

Try another.

***

2. According to Figure 1, KNO$_3$ and KCl have the same solubility at what temperature?

   F. Between 0° and 10°
   G. Between 10° and 20°
   H. Between 20° and 30°
   J. Between 30° and 40°

Here's How to Crack It

This question is asking you to look up a value in the figure. Find where KNO$_3$ and KCl have the same solubility. They have the same solubility when the lines intersect, at a solubility of 30 g/100 mL H$_2$O. Draw a line down to the *x*-axis to see what the temperature is when solubility is 30; it's just over 20°, so the correct answer is choice (H).

***

Many questions on Science passages will entail nothing more than looking up a trend or value in a figure. Both of these are great Now questions.

Let's try one more question from the same passage.

***

3. Based on the figure, at 100°C the solubility of HgCl$_3$ would most likely be:

   A. less than 5 g/100 mL H$_2$O.
   B. between 10 g/100 mL H$_2$O and 20 g/100 mL H$_2$O.
   C. between 20 g/100 mL H$_2$O and 30 g/100 mL H$_2$O.
   D. greater than 30 g/100 mL H$_2$O.

Here's How to Crack It

If a question cites a specific value, first check to see if that value is in the figure. If it's not, the question is asking you to make a prediction. Because the trend is consistent, you can predict what the curve will do. At 90°C, the solubility of HgCl$_3$ is already over 30 g/100 mL H$_2$O. Thus at 100°C, the solubility will be greater than 30 g/100 mL H$_2$O. The correct answer is choice (D).

***

Read If and Only When You Need To

On most of the questions, particularly on Now passages, you will be able to answer the questions by the figures. Whether it's a Charts and Graphs passage or Experiments passage, waste no time reading any of the introduction, or in the case of the Experiments passages, the descriptions of each experiment/study. If you can't answer a question from the figures, read.

Let's take a look at some questions from an Experiments passage. We've already marked the tables from this passage.

Passage III

The *resistance* of a material that obeys Ohm's Law can be calculated by setting up a potential difference at the ends of a wire made of that material and then measuring the current in the wire; the resistance is the ratio of potential difference to current. Because resistance is dependent on length and cross-sectional area, scientists created a standard measure, *resistivity*, which is the measure of how strongly a material opposes the flow of current. In the experiments below, scientists examined the factors affecting resistance in an Ohmic material that they invented.

Experiment 1

In their first experiment, scientists examined the relationship between the length of a wire and its resistance. The resistivity of the wires used in this experiment was 27.5 ρ and the cross-sectional area of the wires was 3.2 mm^2.

Table 1	
Length (m)	Resistance (Ω)
0.9	7.5
1.8	15.0
3.6	30.0

↑   ↑

Experiment 2

In their second experiment, scientists examined the relationship between the cross-sectional area of a wire and its resistance. The resistivity of the wires used in this experiment was 27.5 ρ and the length of the wires was 0.9 m. The results are shown in Table 2.

Table 2	
Cross-sectional area (mm^2)	Resistance (Ω)
0.8	30.0
1.6	15.0
3.2	7.5

↑   ↓

Opposites
Whenever there is only
one pair of answers
that are exact opposites,
the correct answer is
frequently one of the two
opposites.

4. *Conductivity* measures a material's ability to conduct an electric current, and is defined as the reciprocal of a material's ability to oppose the flow of electric current. If the scientists wanted to increase the conductivity of the material they invented, they would:

    F.   increase the length.
    G.   decrease the cross-sectional area.
    H.   increase the resistivity.
    J.   decrease the resistivity.

When to Read
Read if and only when you can't answer a question from the figures. If a question introduces a new term that you can't identify as one of the variables on the figures, look for information about that term in the introduction and/or experiments.

Here's How to Crack It
The question defines a new term, **conductivity,** and asks how the scientists would increase the conductivity of their specific material. As part of the definition, the question states that conductivity is the reciprocal of a material's ability to oppose the flow of current. The tables do not feature an obvious variable for this quality, so you have to read the introduction and studies.

In the introduction, the term **resistivity** is defined as a material's ability to oppose the flow of electric current. The question adds the information that conductivity is the reciprocal of resistivity. Therefore, to increase the conductivity, the scientists would decrease the resistivity. The correct answer is choice (J). Notice that choices (H) and (J) are exact opposites. Whenever there is only one pair of exact opposites, the correct answer is frequently one of the pair.

Step 3: Work the Answers
On more difficult questions, POE will be much faster and more effective than scouring the text or figures to find an answer. If the answers are wordy—that is, anything but a simple value or trend word like *increase* or *lower*—use POE. Read each answer choice, and eliminate any that are contradicted by the figures.

Let's try a question from a different passage.

The term *solubility* refers to the amount of a substance (solute) that will dissolve in a given amount of a liquid substance (solvent). The solubility of solids in water varies with temperature. The graph below displays the water solubility curves for four crystalline solids.

6. A solution is *saturated* when the concentration of a solute is equal to the solubility at that temperature. If a saturated solution of potassium chloride (KCl) at 10°C were heated to 80°C, would the solution remain saturated?

   F. Yes, because solubility decreases with increasing temperature.
   G. Yes, because concentration decreases with increasing temperature.
   H. No, because solubility is unaffected by increasing temperature.
   J. No, because concentration is unaffected by increasing temperature.

Here's How to Crack It

The question defines a new term, saturated, identifies KCl as saturated at a given temperature, and asks if KCl will remain saturated at a new temperature. If you're familiar with the topic of saturation, you may already know whether it's yes or no. If so, cross off the two answers you know to be wrong and examine the reasons given in the two remaining answers.

But if you didn't understand the new information and can't process what will happen at a new temperature, use POE on all four answers. Ignore the yes/no, and focus on the reasons given in each answer.

Choice (F) says that solubility will decrease with increasing temperature, but the figure disproves this. No matter what the new information in the question is, this cannot be the correct answer. Cross it off. Choice (G) brings in a new variable, concentration. Quickly check the introduction to see if concentration is defined. It's not, so you have to leave choice (G). You can't eliminate an answer about a variable that you know nothing about. You can eliminate choice (H), however, because the figure disproves the reason. Choice (J) revolves around concentration, so you have to keep that as well.

At worst, you have a fifty-fifty chance of getting this question right if you guessed from here and moved on. We can offer one extra tip to help sway you in your guess. Avoid an answer that provides either a value or describes a trend of an unknown variable if you have no proof of how that new variable will behave. Thus, between choices (G) and (J), the smart money is on (J), and it is the correct answer. Concentration is the number of grams of the substance per unit volume, and the concentration will not change with temperature.

POE and Pacing

POE is so powerful on Science, you should be able to eliminate at least one, sometimes two, wrong answers, and therefore have few Never questions, particularly on a Now passage.

Depending on your pacing, you may try to reason between the remaining answers. Don't spend more than another minute. Even if you get the question right, spending too much time on one question will likely cost 2–3 questions later on.

THE 3-STEP BASIC APPROACH AND LATER PASSAGES

The 3-Step Basic Approach works on all passages with figures, not just the Now passages featuring consistent trends in tables and graphs.

Take a look using the 3-Step Basic Approach at a Later passage in the following section.

Step 1: Work the Figures

Some ACT passages will feature an illustration, a diagram, or tables and graphs with no consistent trends. Take 10–15 seconds to review the figure. When there are no consistent trends, a figure doesn't reveal the main point as readily. You'll learn the main point as you work the questions and answers. Spend the limited time devoted to Step 1 looking for any patterns or terms.

Try this figure.

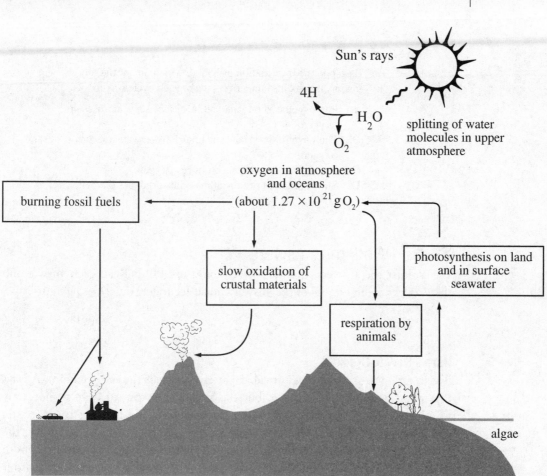

The terms **oxygen**, **fossil fuels**, **oxidation**, **respiration**, and **photosynthesis** all appear.

Step 2: Work the Questions

Even on Later passages, several questions will ask you to look something up in the figure. The more confusing the figure, however, the more likely you are to waste valuable time trying to figure everything out from staring at the figure, waiting for a flash of inspiration to hit. As we mentioned before, spend 10–15 seconds looking for any patterns or terms. Your time is better spent moving to Steps 2 and 3. Working the questions and answers will help you crack the main point of the passage.

Try a question.

13. Based on the information provided, which one of the following statements concerning the oxygen cycle is true?

    A. Photosynthesis on land and in surface seawater uses up oxygen.
    B. Photosynthesis on land and in surface seawater produces oxygen.
    C. Respiration by animals produces oxygen.
    D. Slow oxidation of crustal materials produces oxygen.

Step 3: Work the Answers

The wordier the answers, the more you should use POE. Read each answer and then review the figure: Does the answer choice accurately describe the figure?

Here's How to Crack It

Pay attention to arrows. They provide a pattern that tells the story. Choice (A) says that photosynthesis uses oxygen, but the arrows lead toward oxygen, not away. Eliminate choice (A). Choice (B) is the exact opposite and matches the direction of the arrows. Keep it. Whenever there is only one pair of exact opposites, the correct answer is frequently one of the two opposites. Choices (C) and (D) both describe producing oxygen, but the arrows move away from oxygen, not toward it. Both descriptions are contradicted by the arrows. The correct answer is choice (B).

Basic Approach Drill 1

Use the Basic Approach on the passage below. For the answers to this drill, please go to Chapter 24.

The kinetic molecular theory provides new insights into the movement of molecules in liquids. It states that molecules are in constant motion and collide with one another. When the temperature of a liquid increases, there will be an increase in the movement of molecules and in the average kinetic energy. The figure below depicts the distribution of the kinetic energy of two volumetrically identical samples of water at different temperatures (T).

Water has attractive intermolecular forces that keep the molecules together. When enough heat is added to water, it will weaken these forces and allow some molecules to evaporate and escape the liquid as a gas. The activation energy (Ea) is the minimum energy necessary for molecules to escape the liquid and undergo a phase change.

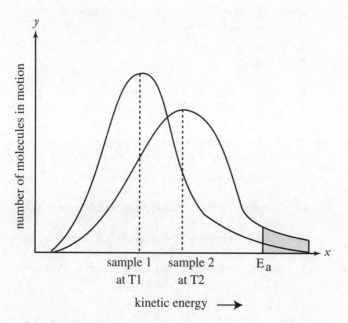

Distribution of Kinetic Energy for Two Samples of Water

1. Which of the following statements best describes the changes observed in the graph?

   A. At T1, Sample 1 has a lower kinetic energy than does Sample 2.
   B. At T2, Sample 1 has a lower kinetic energy than does Sample 2.
   C. An increase in temperature leads to a decrease in kinetic energy.
   D. Water never undergoes a phase change.

2. Assume that water undergoes a phase change to a gas. Which of the following statements would be true?

   F. The attractive intermolecular forces of the escaping molecules are weak.
   G. The average kinetic energy of the water remains the same.
   H. The rate of movement of the gas molecules decreases.
   J. The gas will undergo no further phase changes.

3. Suppose a third sample of water is heated to a higher temperature than Sample 2. It is then found that a greater number of molecules escaped the liquid in Sample 3 than in Sample 2. Would these results be consistent with the results depicted in Figure 1 ?

   A. Yes, an increase in temperature leads to a decrease in the number of escaping molecules in the liquid.
   B. Yes, as the temperature increases, it leads to more molecules escaping the liquid.
   C. No, the temperature reading of Sample 2 would be five times as high as that of the third sample.
   D. No, the average kinetic energy of the water will decrease.

4. It can be inferred from the passage that when a substance undergoes a phase change from a liquid to a gas it will:

   F. evaporate.
   G. condense.
   H. disintegrate.
   J. remain the same.

5. Given the samples at T1 and T2, and the kinetic energies measured and shown in Figure 1, which temperature produces the highest single kinetic energy measurement?

   A. Both T1 and T2
   B. T2
   C. T1
   D. Neither T1 nor T2

Basic Approach Drill 2

Use the Basic Approach on the passage below. For the answers to this drill, please go to Chapter 24.

Amphibians are unique organisms that undergo drastic physical changes during the transformation from an immature organism into an adult form. This process, called metamorphosis, begins with the determination of cells at the tadpole stage. A study was conducted using tadpoles to determine the influence of thyroxine (a hormone) on metamorphosis.

As shown in the graph below, tadpoles were placed in solutions containing various concentrations of thyroxine. Increased levels of thyroxine correlated with increased rates of tail reabsorption and the appearance of adult characteristics such as lungs and hind legs.

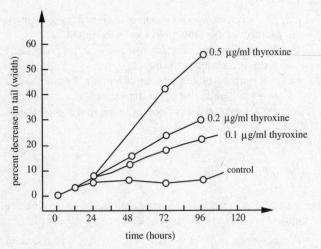

Decrease in tail width in relation to varying levels of thyroxine solutions

Figure 1

1. Suppose that a tadpole was immersed in a 0.3 μg/ml solution for 72 hours. What would be the expected approximate decrease in tail width?

   A. 22%
   B. 30%
   C. 41%
   D. 50%

2. Which of the following generalizations about tadpoles is supported by the results of the study?

   F. They will not undergo metamorphosis if they are not given thyroxine.
   G. Metamorphosis in a normal tadpole takes at least five days.
   H. The most rapid disappearance of the tail is associated with the immersion of tadpoles in the most dilute thyroxine solution.
   J. Temperature plays a major role in metamorphosis.

3. After four days, the tadpoles are checked for development. In all samples other than the control, which of the following concentrations of thyroxine would the tadpoles be likely to show the LEAST development?

   A. 0.5 μg/ml
   B. 0.2 μg/ml
   C. 0.1 μg/ml
   D. All of the tadpoles would show the same development.

4. Based on the information in the passage, which of the following would be a correct order of the stages of tadpole development?

   F. Tadpole → adult → reabsorption of tail → cell determination
   G. Tadpole → cell determination → reabsorption of tail → adult
   H. Tadpole → reabsorption of tail → cell determination → adult
   J. Cell determination → tadpole → adult → reabsorption of tail

5. According to Figure 1, immersing the tadpoles in solutions containing various concentrations of thyroxine does not begin to affect the rate of tadpole metamorphosis until when?

   A. No time at all; the thyroxine affects the rate of metamorphosis immediately.
   B. 0–12 hours after immersion
   C. 12–24 hours after immersion
   D. 24–36 hours after immersion

Basic Approach Drill 3

Use the Basic Approach on the passage below. For the answers to this drill, please go to Chapter 24.

Each element is arranged in the periodic table according to its atomic number, which represents the number of protons in the nucleus. In every neutrally charged atom, the number of electrons equals the number of protons. The table below lists some of the properties of row 2 elements in the periodic table. *Electronegativity* is a measure of the relative strength with which the atoms attract outer electrons. Within a row of the periodic table, the electronegativity tends to increase with increasing atomic number, due to the tighter bonding between protons and electrons. The highest value for electronegativity is 4.0.

Element	Atomic number	Atomic radius	Electro–negativity	Characteristic
Li	3	1.52	1.0	metal
Be	4	1.13	1.5	metal
B	5	0.88	2.0	non-metal
C	6	0.77	2.5	non-metal
N	7	0.70	3.0	non-metal
O	8	0.66	3.5	non-metal
F	9	0.64	4.0	non-metal

1. Which of the following graphs best represents the relationship between atomic number and atomic radius for row 2 elements?

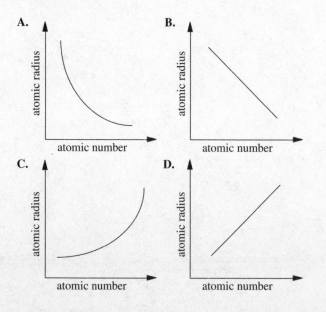

2. What conclusion could be appropriately drawn from the data regarding electronegativity in Table 1 ?

F. An element with high electronegativity has an even atomic number.

G. An element with high electronegativity will be a metal.

H. An element with high electronegativity will have little tendency to attract outer electrons.

J. An element with high electronegativity will be a non-metal.

3. What generalization can one make concerning the relationship between two properties of elements?

A. As the atomic radius decreases, the electronegativity decreases.

B. As the atomic radius decreases, the electronegativity increases.

C. All metals have higher electronegativity values than non-metals.

D. The atomic radius of F is larger than that of N.

4. Which of the following is true regarding the comparative electronegativity of fluorine (F) and lithium (Li)?

F. The electronegativity of F is greater than Li because F has fewer electrons in its outer shell.

G. The electronegativity of F is greater than Li because F electrons are more tightly bound.

H. The electronegativity of Li is greater than F because Li has a greater metallic character.

J. The electronegativity of F is greater than Li because Li has a greater metallic character.

5. Generally speaking, ionization energy follows the same trends as does electronegativity. Elements with a high electronegativity also have a high ionization energy. Which of the following is a correct order of elements with INCREASING ionization energies?

A. Li, N, F

B. F, N, Li

C. B, N, Be

D. Be, O, Li

Summary

o   All Charts and Graphs passages and most Experiments passages come with figures.

o   Use the 3-Step Basic Approach on passages with figures.

> **Step 1. Work the Figures.** Look at the trends and patterns in the figure to identify the relationship between the variables. Mark trends in tables with arrows.
>
> **Step 2. Work the Questions.** Do Now the straightforward questions that involve looking up a trend or value on the figure, or making a prediction of what a variable will do. Read if and only when you can't answer a question from the figures. Do Later any question that strikes you as more difficult or time consuming.
>
> **Step 3. Work the Answers.** For tougher questions, POE should help you eliminate at least one wrong answer if not 3.

o   Pace yourself. If you've eliminated at least one wrong answer, guess and move on to the next passage.

Chapter 22
Fighting Scientists

The third type of passage on the Science test is called "Fighting Scientists." There will be only 1 of these passages and it will be accompanied by 7 questions. Two, three, or possibly more conflicting views on a scientific phenomenon will be presented. Make a plan of the order in which you will read the scientists, and work one theory at a time before tackling the questions that require comparing and contrasting all the theories.

Think of it as a debate. Each debater proposes a hypothesis and then supports that hypothesis with facts, opinions, and assumptions. The ACT test writers want you to evaluate and compare the arguments made by each debater, but they don't care who wins the debate. We don't care either, but we do want you to answer correctly seven questions about the debate. In order to do that, you must understand each viewpoint and how it agrees and disagrees with the others. Some questions will ask about just one theory, but most of the questions will ask you to compare and contrast two or more. That's a lot to keep track of. Wouldn't it be easier to navigate this passage if you had a plan?

FOLLOW A PLAN

The Fighting Scientists passage has a lot in common with the Reading test, and you might recognize some of the same strategies we taught you to employ for Reading. Remember when we asked you how you would fare if your boss assigned you the task of checking out an empty building? How well do you do when you don't know what you're looking for? Not very well. How well would you fare if you dived right into a passage on the Reading test if you didn't know what you're looking for? Right. So how can you succeed on the Fighting Scientists passage if you don't know what you're looking for?

Step 1: Preview

Your first task is to map the order in which you will read the scientists. Just as on the Reading test, you should look at the questions first. In the Fighting Scientists section, the questions help you determine which hypothesis to read and which questions to answer first.

Let's try this with the questions on the next page. Read each question and mark it with a "1" if it asks about Hypothesis 1, a "2" if it asks about Hypothesis 2, and a "1 & 2" if it asks about both hypotheses.

1. Hypotheses 1 and 2 agree that the dinosaurs:

2. The basis of Hypothesis 1 is that a meteorite striking Earth was the primary cause of the dinosaurs' demise. Which of the following discoveries would best support this case?

3. Suppose a geologist discovered that the fossilized bones of dinosaurs contained traces of radioactive iridium. How would this evidence influence the two hypotheses?

4. The authors of the two hypotheses would disagree over whether the extinction of the dinosaurs was:

5. If current climatic changes turn out to be as dramatic as those described by the author of Hypothesis 2, which of the following would he say is most likely to occur?

6. Studies have shown that climatic conditions are interdependent. As conditions become less favorable for life in one locale, they improve in another. If fossil evidence were found which showed that this happened at the K-T boundary, how would it affect Hypothesis 2 ?

7. Both Hypothesis 1 and 2 would be supported by evidence showing that:

You should have a "1 & 2" next to questions 1, 3, 4, and 7. Question 2 should have a "1" next to it, and questions 5 and 6 should have a "2" next to them. What does this tell us? We should read Hypothesis 2 first.

Step 2: One Side at a Time

In order to compare and contrast multiple hypotheses, you need to understand each viewpoint and how it agrees and disagrees with the others. Reading and working the questions for one scientist at a time will give you the firm grasp of each theory you need.

Once the questions have provided a map, read the introduction to identify the disagreement.

Approximately 65 million years ago (at the boundary between the Cretaceous and Tertiary periods, known as the K-T boundary), the dinosaurs became extinct.

Here are two of the hypotheses that have been presented to explain their disappearance.

What will the hypotheses debate? They will debate what caused the extinction of the dinosaurs.

Next, read Hypothesis 2. You don't need to comprehend everything in the passage or remember every point of fact or argumentation, and until you read the other hypothesis, you have no basis for comparison. You do need to grasp the argument each is making, so as you read Hypothesis 2, find and underline the scientist's main point.

Hypothesis 2

This event at the K-T boundary was neither sudden nor isolated. It was a consequence of minor shifts in the earth's weather that spanned the K-T boundary. Furthermore, its effect was not as sweeping as some have suggested. While the majority of dinosaurs disappeared, some were able to adapt to the changing world. We see their descendants every day—the birds.

Alterations in the earth's *jet stream* (a steady, powerful wind that blows from west to east, circling the globe) shifted rains away from the great shallow seas that extended across much of what is now North America. As these late-Cretaceous seas began to dry up, a chain reaction of extinctions was set into motion. First affected was plant life. Next, animals that fed on plants began dying off. Ultimately, the lack of prey caused the demise of the dinosaurs. It was the mobility of the winged dinosaurs that saved them, allowing them to move to more favorable locations as conditions in their ancestral homes deteriorated.

What Are They Fighting About?

Some of the scientific theories you'll read about in a Fighting Scientists passage were settled a long time ago. In reading a passage arguing that Earth is the center of the universe, you may think, "Wait, Earth is NOT the center of the solar system—why in the world are they arguing about this?" For the ACT, the arguments presented are what count. Even though an argument may have been disproved a long time ago, it's still possible to evaluate it scientifically, and that's all you're being asked to do on this test.

What is the main point of Hypothesis 2?

According to Hypothesis 2, the extinction of dinosaurs was caused by a chain reaction prompted by changes in the weather.

Your Underlined Version Should Look Like This

Hypothesis 2

<u>This event at the K-T boundary was neither sudden nor isolated. It was a consequence of minor shifts in the earth's weather that spanned the K-T boundary.</u> Furthermore, its effect was not as sweeping as some have suggested. While the majority of dinosaurs disappeared, some were able to adapt to the changing world. We see their descendants every day—the birds.

Alterations in the earth's *jet stream* (a steady, powerful wind that blows from west to east, circling the globe) shifted rains away from the great shallow seas that extended across much of what is now North America. As these late-Cretaceous seas began to dry up, a chain reaction of extinctions was set into motion. First affected was plant life. Next, animals that fed on plants began dying off. Ultimately, the lack of prey caused the demise of the dinosaurs. It was the mobility of the winged dinosaurs that saved them, allowing them to move to more favorable locations as conditions in their ancestral homes deteriorated.

Did you notice that we didn't underline the details of the theory in the second paragraph? It's not that they are unimportant, but until we dive into the questions, we don't know what to pay attention to other than the main point. As we work the questions for Hypothesis 2, we'll gain a deeper understanding of the details of the theory.

Without further ado, let's go to the questions about Hypothesis 2.

5. If current climatic changes turn out to be as dramatic as those described by the author of Hypothesis 2, which of the following would he say is most likely to occur?

A. A rapid extinction of most of Earth's life, beginning with sea dwellers such as krill (a microscopic crustacean) and progressing through the food chain.

B. A gradual and complete extinction of Earth's life forms that moves through the food chain from the bottom up.

C. An extinction of most life forms on Earth that is gradual and simultaneous, affecting predators as well as prey at roughly the same rates.

D. A progressive extinction that begins with vegetation and eventually reaches to the top of the food chain, affecting most dramatically those life forms least suited to relocation.

Here's How to Crack It

The main point of Hypothesis 2 is that changes in the weather prompted a chain reaction of extinctions through the food chain until the dinosaurs were affected. We need to look for an answer that would predict a similar result from today's climatic changes. Use POE as you make your way through the answer choices.

Choice (A) is tempting because it mentions a progression "through the food chain," but the word "rapid" contradicts the first sentence of Hypothesis 2: "The event at the K-T boundary was neither sudden nor isolated." Choice (B) looks good, until we go back to the passage to confirm it and see that some dinosaurs survived, those that evolved into birds. Because of the word "complete," we have to eliminate it. Choice (C) is out because of the word "simultaneous," which we know from evaluating choice (A) is contradicted by the passage. The answer must be choice (D), and it paraphrases nicely what we underlined as the main point.

6. Studies have shown that climatic conditions are interdependent. As conditions become less favorable for life in one locale, they improve in another. If fossil evidence were found which showed that this happened at the K-T boundary, how would it affect Hypothesis 2 ?

    F. It would strengthen the hypothesis by supporting one of the argument's assumptions.

    G. It would weaken the hypothesis, because the area of improving climatic conditions should have provided a means for the survival of the dinosaurs well into the Tertiary period.

    H. It would weaken the hypothesis by introducing additional evidence that the author could not have anticipated.

    J. It would have no bearing on the hypothesis because the mobility of the winged dinosaurs would render such shifts irrelevant.

Here's How to Crack It

We've learned a lot about Hypothesis 2. We read it and underlined the main point, and then evaluated some of the nuances of the argument to eliminate wrong answers for question number 5. When you consider the import of this new fossil evidence, you should draw upon the deeper understanding you've gained. The correct answer to question 5 reminded us that those *least* suited to relocation are more impacted by the changes in weather. The author stated explicitly that some dinosaurs survived and evolved into birds. Those two facts together allow us to realize this new evidence would make Hypothesis 2 more credible. Eliminate choices (G), (H), and (J), and select choice (F) as the correct answer.

Step 3: The Other Side

Now it's time to read Hypothesis 1, but we know more than we did before reading Hypothesis 2 and thus should read more proactively. When you read the second theory, you should look for and underline the following:

- the main idea

- how this hypothesis disagrees from the first

- how this hypothesis agrees with the first

Differentiate Between Theories
Questions on the Fighting Scientists passages often ask about the areas of agreement as well as disagreement between the scientists' theories. Make sure you know what both the similarities and differences are.

Hypothesis 1

For many years, scientists have speculated about the cause of the extinction of the dinosaurs. Fossil records confirm that dinosaurs as well as other life forms were suddenly wiped out. The natural cause of extinction is the inability of an organism to adapt to environmental changes, yet the extinction of all life forms is unlikely. Chemical analysis of clay found from this era attributes the sweeping extinction of dinosaurs to the collision of a huge meteorite with Earth. These fossil records confirm the presence of a high concentration of iridium, a rare heavy metal that is abundant in meteorites. It is believed that a meteorite hit the earth and created a huge crater, which threw up a dust cloud that blocked the sun for several months. This event led first to the destruction of much plant life and eventually all other life forms that consumed plants and/or herbivores, including the dinosaurs.

Write, Write, Write
Underlining and taking notes in the margins helps you keep track of the differences between the scientists.

What is the main point? Hypothesis 1 believes a meteorite struck Earth and wiped out the dinosaurs.

How do the two hypotheses differ? Hypothesis 2 believes the extinction was gradual; Hypothesis 1 believes it was sudden.

How do they agree? Both hypotheses mention the food chain.

If you didn't come up with those points, look at the underlined portions of the passage below.

Hypothesis 1

For many years, scientists have speculated about the cause of the extinction of the dinosaurs. <u>Fossil records confirm that dinosaurs as well as other life forms were suddenly wiped out.</u> The natural cause of extinction is the inability of an organism to adapt to environmental changes, yet the extinction of all life forms is unlikely. <u>Chemical analysis of clay found from this era attributes the sweeping extinction of dinosaurs to the collision of a huge meteorite with Earth.</u> These fossil records confirm the presence of a high concentration of iridium, a rare heavy metal that is abundant in meteorites. It is believed that a meteorite hit the earth and created a huge crater, which threw up a dust cloud that blocked the sun for several months. <u>This event led first to the destruction of much plant life and eventually all other life forms that consumed plants and/or herbivores, including the dinosaurs.</u>

Fighting Scientists
In a Fighting Scientists passage, you're given two or more opinions about a scientific phenomenon. Your job is to identify the differences between or among the viewpoints and the information the scientists use to support their points of view.

Now let's do the one question on Hypothesis 1 before we tackle the questions on both.

—————————○—————————

2. The basis of Hypothesis 1 is that a meteorite striking Earth was the primary cause of the dinosaurs' demise. Which of the following discoveries would best support this case?

   F. The existence of radioactive substances in the soil.
   G. The presence of other rare metals common to meteorites in the clay beds of the ocean from that period.
   H. Fossil records of land-dwelling reptiles that roamed Earth for an additional 10 million years.
   J. Evidence of dramatic changes in sea levels 65 million years ago.

Here's How to Crack It

What type of evidence would support Hypothesis 1? Any evidence that shows that dinosaurs were wiped out as a result of the impact of a meteorite. Would the presence of radioactive substances in the soil support Hypothesis 1? It could support the passage only if the radioactive elements were from meteorites (like iridium). Choice (F) did not specify that. Would the fact that some land-dwelling reptiles survived past this period support Hypothesis 1? No, so choice (H) is out. We can also get rid of choice (J) because it supports Hypothesis 2. What about choice (G)? What if other rare metals that are known to be found in meteorites were discovered? Would this support Hypothesis 1? Yes. The correct answer is choice (G).

—————————○—————————

Step 4: Compare and Contrast

We are now armed with a clear understanding of each hypothesis's main point, how the two differ, and how they agree.

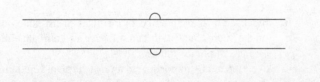

1. Hypothesis 1 and 2 agree that the dinosaurs:

 I. vanished because of a meteorite impact with the earth.

 II. became extinct due to disruptions in their food chain.

 III. became extinct due to some external force other than predation

 A. I only
 B. I and II only
 C. II and III only
 D. III only

Here's How to Crack It

We've already identified the area in which the two agree: the impact on the food chain. We can also eliminate choices that support only one of the theories. Statement 1 supports only Hypothesis 1, so it's out. Eliminate all answer choices with Statement 1 and we're left with choices (C) and (D) only. Because Statement II is in both answer choices, we know it must be correct. Of course, we'd identified the food chain as a point of agreement. Now let's check Statement III. Do both hypotheses state that dinosaurs became extinct because of some external force? Yes, so the correct answer is choice (C).

3. Suppose a geologist discovered that the fossilized bones of dinosaurs contained traces of radioactive iridium. How would this evidence influence the two hypotheses?

 A. It would support both hypotheses.
 B. It would support Hypothesis 2 and weaken Hypothesis 1.
 C. It would support Hypothesis 1 and weaken Hypothesis 2.
 D. It would not support Hypothesis 1 or Hypothesis 2.

Here's How to Crack It

Which of the hypotheses would be supported if a geologist found fossil bones that contained traces of radioactive iridium? Hypothesis 1 of course! The passage states that radioactive iridium is abundant in meteorites. If dinosaurs were exposed to the dust of meteorites, their bones would contain this metal. Hypothesis 2 didn't mention anything about iridium, so choice (C) is the correct answer.

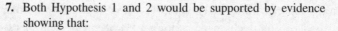

4. The authors of the two hypotheses would disagree over whether the extinction of the dinosaurs was:

    F. a natural process.
    G. rapid.
    H. the result of a disruption on the food chain of the late-Cretaceous period.
    J. preventable.

Here's How to Crack It

The two hypotheses disagreed about the cause of the extinction, but they also disagreed on the pace. Hypothesis 1 believed it was sudden, whereas Hypothesis 2 believed it was gradual. Thus, choice (G) is the correct answer. Be careful with choice (H), because that's an issue on which both *agree*.

7. Both Hypothesis 1 and 2 would be supported by evidence showing that:

    A. pterodactyls (winged dinosaurs) survived well into the Tertiary period, adapted to changes in the earth's environment, and eventually evolved into a non-dinosaur life form.
    B. blockage of the sun's rays by particles measurable only on the microscopic scale can still have a significant effect on rates of photosynthesis.
    C. even apparently minor degradation of the plant population in a given ecosystem can have far-reaching effects on the animal population within that ecosystem.
    D. iridium is extremely likely to remain trapped in an ocean's bed when that ocean dries up.

Here's How to Crack It

On what point do the hypotheses agree? Look for an answer choice that provides evidence about the food chain. Eliminate any answer choice that supports only one hypothesis. Choice (A) is out because Hypothesis 1 never mentioned relocation or winged dinosaurs. Choice (B) looks good because it mentions photosynthesis, so keep it. Choice (C) looks much better because it explicitly mentions the effects of plants on animals. Choice (D) is incorrect because Hypothesis 2 never mentioned iridium and Hypothesis 1 never mentioned the ocean drying up. The test writers are trying to distract you with a switch, but you won't fall for it when you take the passages one at a time and learn each thoroughly before working the questions on both. The correct answer is choice (C).

Fighting Scientists Drill 1

How did the continents take on their current shape? Two differing views are presented below. For the answers to this drill, please go to Chapter 24.

Scientist 1

According to a theory based on plate tectonics, the land surface of Earth once comprised a single continent, termed *Pangaea,* which was surrounded by a single vast ocean. Pangaea broke apart because the surfaces of Earth floated on massive plates above the deeper mantle of the ocean's basin. Horizontal movement of the plates began to split up the land about 137 million years ago during the Jurassic period. The continents and the ocean basins moved along convection currents in the mantle, resulting in a continuous degeneration of Earth's physical features. The movement of these rigid plates produced zones of tectonic activity along their margins such as earthquakes, volcanoes, and mountain formations. Fossil records as well as geological evidence show similarities between widely displaced continents. For instance, the coastlines of South America and Africa contain similar rock formations and appear to fit together like a jigsaw puzzle.

Scientist 2

The continents and the ocean basins of Earth are permanent, fixed features of the planet. The hypothesis of plate tectonics is flawed because there is insufficient evidence to support it. The force of gravity is stronger than any known tangential force that can act on Earth's crust. The layers of crust that support the continents and ocean basins are strong enough to preserve Earth's physical features and are too strong to permit horizontal drift. Tectonic activity has always been present, but the hypothesis of plate tectonics explains such activity only in one late period of ancient history. In addition, it is not clear what kind of force could allow the continents, composed largely of granite, to move through areas of dense, iron-rich rock that comprise the ocean basins. Any geological evidence that supports such a theory may be because of the existence of similar conditions on different continents.

1. Which of the following statements is the most inconsistent with the beliefs of Scientist 1 ?

   A. Continents were once part of a large land mass.
   B. Continents split up and drifted apart.
   C. Ocean basins have not changed for millions of years.
   D. Geological evidence shows similarities between widely displaced continents.

2. Scientist 1 studied the fossils along the coast of South America and Africa and found identical fernlike plants on rocks of the same age. What claim could Scientist 2 make to refute the findings of Scientist 1 ?

   F. The dating and comparison of plant fossils is an exact science.
   G. The soil and climate conditions along the two coasts must have been very similar at the time the fossils were created.
   H. The ferns were extremely large.
   J. Ferns will only thrive in their original habitat.

3. A new zone of tectonic activity has been discovered in the large land mass of Eurasia. This zone shows geological evidence of having been active for several thousand years. Which scientist is supported by this finding and why?

   A. Scientist 1, because it proves that tectonic activity occurs on the planet.
   B. Scientist 1, because it shows that Pangaea and Eurasia are the same land mass.
   C. Scientist 2, because it proves that tectonic activity occurs in land masses and not solely in the ocean basin and along coastlines.
   D. Scientist 2, because it shows that the continents are made out of granite.

4. Both Scientist 1 and Scientist 2 are experts in plate tectonics. To what discipline of science do these scientists belong?

   F. Physics
   G. Geology
   H. Biology
   J. Chemistry

5. Which of the following claims would be supported by both scientists?

   I. Tectonic activity has always been a factor in the geology of land masses.
   II. The continents and the ocean basins are fixed features of the planet.
   III. Continental drift occurred in the Jurassic period.

   A. I only
   B. II only
   C. I and II only
   D. II and III only

Fighting Scientists Drill 2

How did life on Earth originate? Two differing views are presented. For the answers to this drill, please go to Chapter 24.

Hypothesis 1

In 1953, a graduate student attempted to recreate the conditions of primeval Earth in a sealed glass apparatus that he filled with methane, ammonia, hydrogen, and water. Sparks were released into the glass to simulate lightning, and heat was applied to the water. The result was the formation of organic compounds, known as amino acids, which are the building blocks of proteins. Since that time, others have shown how DNA may have been synthesized under various conditions as well. RNA, which is DNA's partner in the translation of genetic information into protein products, has been found to have the ability to reproduce itself under certain conditions. Thus, the origins of life are to be found in the "primordial soup" of the ancient earth that provided conditions for the simplest forms of organic matter to form and develop increasingly sophisticated means of organization. With the ability of compounds to make copies of themselves comes the opportunity for evolution by the mechanisms of heredity and mutation.

Hypothesis 2

Previous assumptions about the makeup of the "primordial soup" are inaccurate. It is not at all clear that methane and ammonia were present on the primeval earth or that conditions were as favorable as in the graduate student's experiment. The ability of RNA to reproduce itself is also limited to particular conditions that the primeval earth is unlikely to have provided. There is a possibility that, given enough time, random events could alone have resulted in the development of entire single-celled organisms, but some have likened that possibility to the chance that a tornado whirling through a junkyard could result in the formation of a 747 jetliner. During much of the time when the "primordial soup" was to have existed, Earth was a regular target of meteors that kept oceans boiling and the atmosphere inhospitable to organic development. Clearly much more research is needed before this theory can be widely accepted.

1. Which of the following statements about the conditions on primeval Earth could be used to support Hypothesis 2 ?

    A. Atmospheric conditions were too unstable to support the gases essential to the theories of the "primordial soup."
    B. Organic molecules were able to thrive under primeval Earth conditions.
    C. The origin of life began in the "primordial soup."
    D. The atmosphere contained methane, ammonia, hydrogen, and water.

2. To accept Hypothesis 1, one must assume that:

    F. Earth was bombarded by meteors during that time period.
    G. the conditions in the glass were analogous to the conditions on primeval Earth.
    H. proteins are the building blocks of amino acids.
    J. Earth lacked hydrogen in the atmosphere.

3. Which of the following shows how, according to Hypothesis 1, the building blocks of life were formed?

    A. Methane + Ammonia + Hydrogen + Water → Primordial Soup → Amino Acids
    B. Meteors → Primordial Soup → Amino Acids
    C. Amino Acids → Primordial Soup → DNA → Methane + Ammonia + Hydrogen + Water
    D. Primordial Soup → proteins → Amino Acids

Fighting Scientists Drill 3

Will Earth experience another ice age? Two differing views are presented. For the answers to this drill, please go to Chapter 24.

Hypothesis 1

Scientists have long speculated whether glaciation will ever take place again. Given that glaciation is an unusual event, it is highly unlikely that such a phenomenon will ever repeat itself. Glaciation usually takes place under periods of extremely cool temperatures. However, it appears that the temperature on Earth has been milder and more stable than at any other period. In fact, it would take a 5°C drop in the average surface temperature in order for glaciation to occur. In addition, there would have to be a significant increase in precipitation.

Hypothesis 2

Although Earth has not experienced glaciation in a long time, the event, no matter how rare, can occur if the right conditions are met. Two factors that are critical to the growth of glaciers are precipitation and temperature. There are a number of areas, specifically land masses in the polar regions, that are currently cold enough to produce glaciers but do not have sufficient snowfall to develop glacier systems. However, if enough events occur simultaneously, they could bring on an ice age. For instance, if there is an increase in the level of snowfall in the winter in these polar regions, this could eventually lead to glaciation. On the other hand, the level of pollution in the atmosphere is also sufficient to gradually cool Earth. Under these conditions, it is quite clear that glaciation is only a matter of the right combination of events at the right time.

1. Which of the following discoveries would most clearly favor Hypothesis 2 ?

   A. Canada has more snowfall this year than any other year.
   B. When snow falls, it sticks to the ground.
   C. The more pollution in the air, the more the temperature drops.
   D. Earth's bodies of waters are becoming more polluted.

2. Which of the following statements is the strongest argument a supporter of Hypothesis 2 would use to counter Hypothesis 1 ?

   F. The temperature around polar regions fluctuates.
   G. The precipitation rate has been increasing in the Swiss Alps.
   H. Just because ideal conditions are rare does not mean they will not occur in the future.
   J. The temperature in the North Pole has gone up 2°C.

3. If Hypothesis 2 is correct and glaciation can take place in the future, what regions would be most affected?

   I.   Heavily polluted regions
   II. Polar regions
   III. Humid regions

   A. I only
   B. II only
   C. I and II only
   D. II and III only

4. According to Hypothesis 2, what conditions could cause glaciation?

   F. Low levels of pollution leading to high precipitation.
   G. High levels of pollution leading to a blanketing effect that blocks out the sun and decreases the temperature dramatically.
   H. A lack of snowfall and low temperatures.
   J. A 5°C drop in the average surface temperature.

Summary

o   There is one Fighting Scientists passage on the Science test. In this passage, two, three, or more scientists present their differing views on a scientific subject.

o   Don't pick a side. The ACT test writers want you to evaluate and compare the arguments presented, not decide which one is correct. Even if you know something about the topic, answer the questions using only what is presented in the passage.

o   First, use the questions to make a map of the order in which you will read the theories and answer questions on each, one at a time.

o   Leave the questions on more than one theory for last.

o   Don't forget to guess your Letter of the Day if there are questions that you don't know how to do.

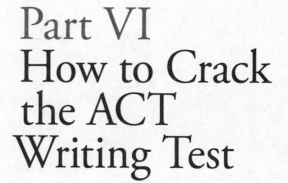

Part VI
How to Crack the ACT Writing Test

Chapter 23
The Essay

The ACT includes an optional Essay section. Some schools are requesting an essay while others are not. We recommend that you take the essay when you take the ACT because you can't take the essay on its own later if you find that you need it; you'd have to take the whole ACT over again. The essay follows a predictable format, so preparation and practice help a lot.

THE KIND-OF OPTIONAL ESSAY

The ACT includes an "optional" essay component, but if you've already started to skip this section, stop for a moment. Although most students would not voluntarily choose to spend an extra half hour on a Saturday morning writing an essay for a standardized test, we **do** recommend that you write the essay. Why? There are two reasons.

- First, some schools require that you take the essay portion. You wouldn't want to have to take the entire test over again if you discover that your dream school wants an essay and you had decided not to write one.
- Second, writing the essay can make your college application look more attractive. Your essay score will appear on every score report you send to colleges, regardless of whether or not the school requires an essay. Every school to which you apply will see that you took the initiative to write the essay, which is a good thing.

Plus, it's not that difficult to get a good score on the essay, especially if you follow the guidelines in this chapter. An impressive score is an impressive score, optional or not.

OK, OK, I'LL WRITE THE ESSAY…
WHAT DO I HAVE TO DO?

The ACT essay will provide you with a prompt "relevant" to high school students—basically it's a topic on which the ACT test writers believe almost any typical high school student will have some opinion. Here's an example of a sample prompt.

The Children's Internet Protection Act (CIPA) requires all school libraries receiving certain federal funds to install and use blocking software to prevent students from viewing material considered "harmful to minors." However, some studies conclude that blocking software in schools damages educational opportunities for students, both by blocking access to Web pages that are directly related to the state-mandated curriculums and by restricting broader inquiries of both students and teachers. In your view, should the schools block access to certain Internet websites?

In your essay, take a position on this question. You may write about either one of the two points of view given, or you may present a different point of view on this question. Use specific reasons and examples to support your position.

Your job is to write an essay in which you take some sort of position on the prompt and develop your position through the use of appropriate supporting examples. You've probably written an essay like this in your high school English class. The only difference is that on the ACT you have a mere 30 minutes to read the prompt, brainstorm some examples, organize the essay, write it, and proofread it. You may be thinking that there's no way that you can write a great essay in such a short amount of time on a topic you've never seen before, and that is indeed true. But that's okay, because the ACT essay graders don't expect a perfect essay; they don't want to penalize you for minor spelling and grammar mistakes. Instead, graders will focus on the major components of your essay.

WHAT THE GRADERS ARE GRADING

If you think you have a tough job writing an essay in only 30 minutes, have some sympathy for the graders. They have to grade each essay in a matter of minutes. Imagine how you would feel if you spent an entire day grading thousands of essays on the same topic. By essay number 50 or so, you probably wouldn't care much if a student used "except" instead of "accept."

ACT Graders vs. English Teachers

The graders who grade for ACT aren't like your English teachers. They don't have the time to focus on the little details of each essay, and frankly, they don't care about your grade the way your English teacher does. So, don't sweat the small stuff. Focus on the big picture for the ACT: good thesis, organization, strong examples, and neatness.

ACT graders focus on the big picture. Your essay will be read by two graders, each of whom will assign it a score from 1 to 6 (for a total essay score from 2 to 12) based on how closely it adheres to the standards below. The essays are graded **holistically**, meaning the graders don't keep track of all the good things and bad things in an essay on a checklist or score sheet. Each reader simply reads the entire essay, and based on his or her overall impressions of the essay assigns it a grade.

According to the ACT guidelines, essay graders will base your score on your ability to do the following:

1. Take a position on the prompt   To score well on the ACT essay, you need a clear thesis statement. Essay graders will look for one when determining your score.

2. Maintain focus on topic   Once you come up with a thesis, stick to it. Avoid digressions in your essay—or even worse, changing or countering your thesis halfway through the paper.

3. Support your ideas   Good essays support their thesis statements with supporting examples. There is no magic number of examples. However, you do need to show that you understand the issue in the prompt, that you have a position on that issue, that you have a reason for that position, and that you can support that reason with evidence. You have to address the other side of the issue, but you don't want to argue it as strongly as your own side. Address the other issues and then point out why your examples are better.

4. Organize your ideas   This is one of the most important criteria. You must write an organized essay, meaning it needs to contain an introduction, body paragraphs, and a conclusion.

5. Use language clearly and effectively   The graders will look at stylistic issues, but those issues are not as important as the issues above. As a rule of thumb, graders will take issue with your grammar and language only if it detracts from their ability to identify the previous criteria.

HOW TO GET A GOOD SCORE

The way to get a good score on the essay is to make the graders' job easy: Show that you have a thesis, a clear essay structure, and some relevant examples. By following the guidelines presented here, you'll be able to write a clear, effective essay in the limited time available. Let's look at each step in the process. Be sure to practice each step individually, and then try to put all the steps together.

Step 1

Step 1: Work with the Prompt
Our first task is to read the prompt. Here's the one we saw earlier.

The Children's Internet Protection Act (CIPA) requires all school libraries receiving certain federal funds to install and use blocking software to prevent students from viewing material considered "harmful to minors." However, some studies conclude that blocking software in schools damages educational opportunities for students, both by blocking access to Web pages that are directly related to the state-mandated curriculums and by restricting broader inquiries of both students and teachers. In your view, should the schools block access to certain Internet websites?

In your essay, take a position on this question. You may write about either one of the two points of view given, or you may present a different point of view on this question. Use specific reasons and examples to support your position.

After reading the prompt, you must decide what side of the argument you will defend. Even if you don't have a strong opinion either way, you still must pick a side. Although it is possible to write an essay that examines both sides of the issue at length, it is difficult to do that on the ACT because of the time limit. It's much easier to pick one side and defend it.

Key Words and Phrases

When reading the prompt, underline the key words and phrases. What are some of the key words in the prompt on the previous pages?

_____

_____

Some of the key words we see in the prompt are "school libraries," "blocking software," "prevent students," "harmful to minors," "damages educational opportunities," and "Internet websites." By identifying key words before you start to write, you can focus your essay and find the most pertinent examples.

On your test booklet, jot down something like this:

Pro   Con

Decide which side you wish to defend—there is no right or wrong answer, so just pick the side that you think will be easier to support. Next, brainstorm two or three reasons why you chose the side you did. Fill them in under the appropriate heading.

Pro   **Con**

_____   _____

_____   _____

_____   _____

_____   _____

At this point, you should have something that looks like this:

3 Pro	Con
• Internet contains many offensive/objectionable sites	_____
• Dangerous spyware and adware can harm computers	_____
• School computers should be used only for school work	_____
	_____

Of course, your reasons or examples may differ. The actual examples that you come up with do not matter, as long as they are related to the prompt. Now that you have your examples, you're halfway done. But before you move on, you need to think of an example or two for the other side of the argument. To get a top score on the essay, you have to consider both sides of the issue. So let's brainstorm an example or two for the opposing side.

Now you should have something like this:

3 Pro	3 Con
• Internet contains many offensive/objectionable sites	• Restricting access is a form of censorship
• Dangerous spyware and adware can harm computers	• Students are deprived of opportunities to learn about certain topics
• School computers should be used only for school work	

If you're having trouble coming up with appropriate examples, the prompt usually contains some good ideas.

Step 2: Structure Your Essay

Good ACT essays have a clear, logical structure. Your essay must contain an introductory paragraph, body paragraphs, and a conclusion. Although what you write in each paragraph of any given type will change, the structure of each paragraph should be fairly consistent.

Let's look at an introductory paragraph first.

Introductions

Your introductory paragraph should accomplish two major things.

1. Frame the discussion   You must tell the reader exactly what the topic of the essay will be. Introduce the topic by restating or, better yet, paraphrasing the prompt.

2. State your thesis   Establish which side of the issue you are on and why. Use the lines below to write your introduction, and then compare it with the sample paragraph that follows.

_____

_____

_____

_____

_____

_____

_____

_____

Here's our sample.

The Internet has brought many changes to our world. Computers are used in businesses, homes, and of course, schools. However, with increased use of computers comes increased dangers. A new law, the Children's Internet Protection Act, requires schools to use blocking programs to restrict students' Internet access. Although some parents, students, and teachers believe that this law is a bad one, the dangers from the Internet make it clear that schools should block student access to certain Internet sites.

Notice that this introduction accomplishes the two basic goals mentioned previously. It paraphrases the prompt—expanding on it a bit by discussing the impact of the Internet and computers on everyday life—and introduces the question of whether schools should block student access to certain sites. Then the paragraph clearly states the author's position; in this case, the author agrees that schools should block student access.

That is all that is required in an introductory paragraph. Don't try to do too much with the first paragraph. Many writers make the mistake of trying to explain why they chose a particular side, but you should save that for the body paragraphs.

Body Paragraphs, Part I: Supporting Your Position

Body paragraphs are where you will give the reasons or support for your position. A good body paragraph will contain three major things.

1. A good transition/topic sentence   Transition sentences contribute to the flow and organization of the essay. Using transitions will help the grader follow your argument. Topic sentences show the grader that you are focused on your thesis.

2. A relevant example   Each body paragraph should discuss one and only one example. Otherwise, the paragraph becomes muddled and hard to follow. If you are using only one example, however, you'll want to break it up into logical paragraphs.

3. An explanation of how the example supports your position   It's not enough simply to throw a couple of examples into your essay and expect the grader to know what to make of them. Your job as a writer is to show the grader why the examples you chose support your position. Let's try to write a body paragraph. Using the lines below and one of the examples you've chosen (or one of ours) from the Pro/Con list, write a body paragraph. Then compare it with the sample paragraph that follows.

_____

_____

_____

_____

_____

Here's our sample.

One convincing reason that schools should block access to certain Internet sites is that the Internet contains many offensive or objectionable sites. For example, there are sites on the Internet that contain racist and sexist jokes and content. Other sites might display material that is inappropriate for children. Because there is no censorship, there is no telling what sites a student can visit. This sort of material has no place in a school. If students see violent or offensive sites, they might be influenced. They could insult or hurt other students. For this reason, it is a good idea for schools to block access to certain sites.

Let's examine this body paragraph. The paragraph starts with a good topic sentence. The first sentence repeats the thesis, making it easy for the reader to follow the argument. Next, the author brings in an example—the presence of objectionable sites on the Internet. The following sentences expand on the example, presenting different sites that are inappropriate for a school setting. Finally, and most important, the last sentences tell the grader why the example supports the point—objectionable sites could lead students to insult or harm other students. Also, the last sentence again mentions the thesis. This helps the essay stay focused and makes the argument more forceful.

Practice writing body paragraphs for your remaining examples. For each one, try to start with a transition or topic sentence that restates the thesis. Then present your example. Finally, state how your example supports your position. Try to end your body paragraph by restating the thesis again.

Writing to Your Grader
We're not talking about writing personal letters here. Rather, we're referring to modifying your writing style to make it fit what the grader wants to see. You do this all the time. When you get a new English teacher, you figure out how that teacher wants you to write your essays, and you tweak your style a little to meet expectations. You should do the same thing for the ACT graders. Figure out what they want to see and write that type of essay. It will help you get a better score.

Body Paragraphs, Part II: Attacking the Other Position

To get a good score on the ACT, you'll also have to write another type of body paragraph—one that discusses the "con," or opposite, side of the argument. This paragraph is similar to the supporting paragraph in structure. The only difference is that you will now attack the example and state why it is not an important consideration. Take a look at our sample paragraph first, and then try to write your own body paragraphs using one of the examples from the other side of the example.

Some people believe that it is wrong for schools to restrict access to certain Internet sites. These people think that restricting access is the same thing as censorship. However, this argument is incorrect. The school is not trying to control what students think or write. It is only trying to control what sorts of things a student can or cannot do at a school computer. This is well within the rights of the school. After all, schools can impose dress codes and dictate what classes students can take. It doesn't make sense to say that a school can determine what books a student reads or what clothes he or she wears, but cannot restrict access to certain Internet sites. Thus, this argument is not convincing.

The purpose of this paragraph is to look at the opposing side of the argument and then show the grader why the opposing side is wrong. The topic sentence clearly states the opposing position, and the next sentence gives a reason that some might consider the opposing side valid. The most important part of this paragraph comes in the third sentence. You must clearly indicate to the grader that you do not agree with this side. If you don't, your essay might seem to support both sides of the issue. Next, attack the opposing side by showing that the reason stated is inadequate, insufficient, or just plain wrong.

If you're having trouble attacking the other position, try one of the three techniques below.

1. The example is true, but...   State the example, and then look for ways in which it could still be true but not relevant to the argument.

Example: Although it is true that restricting Internet access is a form of censorship, this is not relevant to the argument. The issue is whether students should be allowed to view the content at school.

2. The example is true, but not as important as...   In this case, acknowledge that the example is relevant, but not as important as some other factor. A good way to attack a position is to compare the con example with the pro example and then state why the pro example is a more important consideration.

Example: It may be true that restricting Internet access is a form of censorship, but there is a more important consideration in this argument. Isn't it more important to keep the students safe than to worry about censorship?

3. The example is flawed because...   Try to attack the actual example.

Example: Some people believe that restricting access to the Internet is a form of censorship. But this is flawed because the school isn't dictating what a student can think or write. It is only stating that students cannot view this material at school.

Now try it on your own. Use the lines here to write a body paragraph attacking one side of the argument.

_____

_____

_____

_____

_____

_____

_____

After you've written your body paragraphs, it's time to wrap things up.

Conclusions

Conclusions have only one purpose. Without looking below, try to guess what that purpose is.

1. A conclusion should restate the thesis

If you said the conclusion should conclude the essay, give yourself a prize. The conclusion should restate the thesis and sum up the essay. Go ahead and use the lines provided to write a conclusion paragraph. Then compare your conclusion with the sample one.

_____

_____

_____

_____

_____

_____

_____

_____

Here's our sample.

As this essay has shown, it is important and necessary for schools to block student access to certain Internet sites. The Internet has many potential dangers for a student, from objectionable sites to harmful computer viruses and bugs. A school that doesn't restrict access to the Internet puts itself at risk for far more serious issues.

This conclusion gets the job done. The first sentence restates the thesis and the next sentence repeats some of the major arguments of the essay. The final sentence of the conclusion is a good place to get a little sentimental or philosophical. It's the last thing the grader will see, so it's a nice touch.

Putting It All Together

The trick now is to string all of these individual paragraphs into a focused and coherent essay that addresses both sides of the issue, yet still clearly supports only one perspective. At first this seems like a daunting task, but if you practice using the outline below, you'll master it in no time.

Your essay should conform to the following outline:

I.   Introduction paragraph
    A.   Paraphrase the prompt
    B.   State your thesis
II. Con body paragraph
    A.   Topic sentence
    B.   Con example
III. Pro body paragraph
    A.   Topic sentence
    B.   Pro example
IV. Pro body paragraph II
    A.   Topic sentence
    B.   Pro example II
V.   Conclusion
    A.   Restate thesis

Here's what the essay looks like in its entirety.

The Internet has brought many changes to our world. Computers are used in businesses, homes, and, of course, schools. However, with increased use of computers comes increased dangers. A new law, the Children's Internet Protection Act, requires schools to use blocking programs to restrict students' Internet access. Although some parents, students, and teachers believe that this law is a bad one, the dangers from the Internet make it clear that schools should block student access to certain Internet sites.

Some people believe that it is wrong for schools to restrict access to certain Internet sites. These people think that restricting access is the same thing as censorship. However, this argument is incorrect. The school is not trying to control what students think or write. It is only trying to control what sort of things a student can or cannot do at a school computer. This is well within the rights of the school. After all, schools can impose dress codes and dictate what classes students can take. It doesn't make sense to say that a school can determine what books a student reads or what clothes he or she wears, but cannot restrict access to certain Internet sites. Thus, this argument is not convincing.

One convincing reason that schools should block access to certain Internet sites is that the Internet contains many offensive or objectionable sites. For example, there are sites on the Internet that contain racist and sexist jokes and content. Other sites might display material that is inappropriate for children. Because there is no censorship, there is no telling what sites a student can visit. This sort of material has no place in a school. If students see violent or offensive sites, they might be influenced. They could insult or hurt other students. For this reason, it is a good idea for schools to block access to certain sites.

Another good reason to restrict student access to the Internet is the presence of dangerous computer viruses, spyware, and other harmful computer programs. These programs can infect a computer via the Internet and affect the hardware of the system and all the computers that are attached to it. A student who visits certain restricted sites puts the entire computer network at risk. One infected computer can wipe out or ruin all the other computers in the school. Thus, it would be a very wise move for schools to restrict access to certain dangerous Internet sites.

As this essay has shown, it is important and necessary for schools to block student access to certain Internet sites. Although some people think restricting sites is censorship, the Internet has many potential dangers for a student, from objectionable sites to harmful computer viruses and bugs. A school that doesn't restrict access to the Internet puts itself at risk for far more serious issues.

Now it's your turn. Using the following prompt, write an essay. Don't time yourself; just focus on structuring your essay according to the guidelines.

In recent years, many schools have adopted a "Great Books"–based curriculum. These schools require students to study certain designated classic books of Western civilization, arguing that familiarity with these "Great Books" is essential to education. However, opponents of this curriculum argue that forcing teachers and students to use only the "Great Books," most of which are written by white, European authors, results in a biased view on the world. In your opinion, should schools adopt a "Great Books"–based curriculum?

In an essay, take a position on this question. You may write on either one of the views presented, or on a different point of view relevant to the question. Use examples and reasons to support your position.

_____

_____

_____

_____

_____

_____

_____

_____

_____

_____

_____

_____

Step 3: Proofread

After you finish your essay, spend one or two minutes proofreading your essay if you have time. You don't have to catch every single grammatical and spelling mistake, but try to make sure there are no glaring errors. You can also edit as you go, but a quick review at the very end never hurts.

If you do find an error, erase it completely or cross it out with a single line and then neatly write the correction above it. Although you won't be graded on neatness, it is important. A neatly written essay makes for a happy grader, and a happy grader is a good thing.

OTHER THINGS TO KEEP IN MIND

Here are some other factors to consider when writing your essay. These factors are not nearly as crucial as the ones discussed earlier, but they can help boost your essay grade.

1. Length   ACT graders tend to reward longer essays. Try to write at least five paragraphs spanning one and a half to two pages. If your writing tends to be small, you may want to practice writing larger, especially because it will also make your essay a bit neater and easier to read. If your handwriting is large, make sure you write an extra page to compensate.

2. Sentence structure   Varying your sentence structure helps to improve the rhythm of your essay. If you write a really long sentence with lots of modifiers and dependent clauses, it sometimes helps to follow it with a shorter, more direct sentence. It really works. Don't try to be too fancy, though. The longer the sentence is, the more opportunity there is to confuse the reader or to make a grammatical mistake.

3. Diction   Diction refers to word choice. You certainly want to sprinkle some nice vocabulary words throughout your paper. But make sure to use and spell them correctly. If you're uncertain about the meaning or spelling of a word, it's best just to pick a different word. Using a big word incorrectly makes a worse impression than using a smaller word correctly.

4. Neatness   Make sure you indent each new paragraph. Align your essay using the lines on the paper. Don't go over the lines or write down the side of the page. Avoid messy cross-outs. Although the grader should not take these kinds of things into consideration when determining your grade, a neat, legible essay will be easier to read. Your grader will read hundreds, if not thousands of essays. A neat essay will make the grader happier.

PRACTICE ESSAY PROMPTS

Here are four sample essay prompts on which to practice. After you finish each essay, read it over—or better yet, have someone else read it—and use the Essay Checklist on page 382 to see how well your essay conforms to the ACT's grading standards. When you practice writing essays, it's best to limit your time to 30 minutes to experience how short the allotted time really is.

Practice Prompt #1

New laws are being proposed that would require schools to accommodate students who wish to transfer to a different school if the school falls below a certain level on statewide standardized tests. Supporters of this law believe that it is a student's right to transfer to a new school if his or her current school is not fulfilling its duties. Opponents argue that this law is impractical—what would happen if all the students requested transfers?—and unfairly weights test scores without considering other factors at a school. In your opinion, should students be allowed to transfer if schools score below a certain level on standardized tests?

In an essay, take a position on this question. You may write on either one of the views presented or on a different point of view relevant to the question. Use examples and reasons to support your position.

Colleges reward professors, who have significant research and teaching experience, with tenure. Once tenured, a professor holds his or her job without review and with little danger of being fired or replaced. Some people believe that high school teachers should be tenured as a reward for dedicated service. These people argue that tenure will attract highly qualified candidates to the profession and also allow teachers to do their jobs without fear of losing them. Opponents of this plan believe that tenure only leads to poor teaching. Without any fear of losing their jobs, teachers will not care as much about their students. In your opinion, should high school teachers receive tenure?

In an essay, take a position on this question. You may write on either one of the views presented, or on a different point of view relevant to the question. Use examples and reasons to support your position.

Practice Prompt #3

Many communities are considering adopting curfews for high school students. Some educators and parents favor curfews because they believe they will encourage students to focus more on their homework and make them more responsible. Others feel curfews are up to families, not the community, and that students today need freedom to work and participate in social activities in order to mature properly. Do you think that communities should impose curfews on high school students?

In an essay, take a position on this question. You may write on either one of the views presented or on a different point of view relevant to the question. Use examples and reasons to support your position.

Practice Prompt #4

In response to articles examining sensitive topics such as dating and partying, many schools are considering censoring their newspapers. Some schools believe that these topics are inappropriate for student-run papers, while others believe that, as long as what is printed is true, student papers should have the same freedoms as regular newspapers do. What is your opinion on this topic?

In an essay, take a position on this question. You may write on either one of the views presented or on a different point of view relevant to the question. Use examples and reasons to support your position.

Summary:
An Essay Checklist

Now look at your essays and see if you applied the strategies presented in this chapter.

- o The Introduction
  Did you
  - start with a topic sentence that paraphrases or restates the prompt?
  - clearly state your position on the issue?

- o Body Paragraph 1
  Did you
  - start with a transition/topic sentence that discusses the opposing side of the argument?
  - give an example of a reason that one might agree with the opposing side of the argument?
  - clearly state that the opposing side of the argument is wrong or flawed?
  - show what is wrong with the opposing side's example or position?

- o Body Paragraphs 2 and 3
  Did you
  - start with a transition/topic sentence that discusses your position on the prompt?
  - give one example or reason to support your position?
  - show the grader how your example supports your position?
  - end the paragraph by restating your thesis?

- o Conclusion
  Did you
  - restate your position on the issue?
  - end with a flourish?

- o Overall
  Did you
  - write neatly?
  - avoid multiple spelling and grammar mistakes?
  - try to vary your sentence structure?
  - use a few impressive-sounding words?

Part VII
Drill
Answers and
Explanations

Chapter 24
Drill Answers and
Explanations

Complete Drill (Chapter 6)

1. B   Draw a vertical line in between *flowers* and *blooms*. The ideas on both sides are incomplete, which eliminates choice (C). Among the answers that remain, the comma after *blooms* is needed because the list of the houses' features is coming to a close. You need the comma before the *and* immediately after the underlined portion ends. Eliminate choice (D). *Flowers* and *blooms* make a list of two things in the gardens, but as one feature buried in a list of items separated by commas, the use of *and* instead of a comma makes the groupings clear.

2. H   Draw a vertical line in between *inhabitants* and *the*. Both ideas are complete, so they need Stop punctuation. Only choice (H) works.

3. C   Draw a vertical line in between *fiord* and *Where*. The idea to the right of the vertical line is incomplete, which eliminates all Stop punctuation. Only choice (C) works.

4. G   The entire sentence is incomplete. Delete the conjunction *since* to fix. In choice (J) the extra commas are unnecessary.

5. B   Draw a vertical line after *time* and after *and*, since comma + FANBOYS is stop punctuation. The idea before the line is complete, but the idea after the line is incomplete. Eliminate choices (A), (C), and (D).

6. G   With the presence of the semicolon in choice (J), you could use the vertical line test, but it's better to consider the double dashes in choice (G) first. A pair of dashes sets off unnecessary info, just like a pair of commas. The information is unnecessary and choice (G) is the correct answer.

7. C   Use a comma after an introductory idea. Both choices (C) and (D) have a comma between the incomplete and complete ideas, but you don't need a comma after *on*. Eliminate choice (D).

8. J   Commas and conjunctions are changing among the answers. Read to the end of the sentence: there are two complete ideas, separated by a comma. Change the first idea to incomplete by adding a conjunction. Only choice (J) uses a conjunction.

9. D   Draw a vertical line. The idea to the left of the vertical line is complete, but the idea to the right is incomplete. Eliminate choices (A) and (B). The colon makes the meaning clearer than the comma.

10. H   This is a list of three things, and each needs a comma after it, including one before the *and*. There is an extra comma in choice (G) that separates the adjective *freshwater* from its noun, *shale*.

Consistent, Clear, Concise Drill (Chapter 7)

1. B   Always choose the object pronoun after a preposition. Choice (C) adds the verb *were*, creating an error.

2. H   Choose the most concise choice: it makes the meaning clear.

3. D   Be consistent with the rest of the paragraph. The narrator is expressing his own thoughts.

4. G   The rest of the paragraph is written in the past tense, but the past perfect—the use of *had* with the past participle—is necessary when something happened before another event in the past.

5. D   The presence of the helping verb *would* works only with *believe* if the events are in the present or *have believed* if the events are in the past. *Of* is not a verb, and ACT is trying to trap your ear into thinking it's the same as *have*.

6. F   Choose the correct transition word to link the two ideas. The two ideas agree so only choice (F) makes sense.

7. C   Use the context to determine that the narrator is discussing his own grades.

8. H   Choose the correct form for *throw* and then choose the correct pronoun. *Myself* is correct here because the subject and object are the same. You could also eliminate choice (G) because there is no clear original for *it*.

9. B   Use POE carefully with apostrophes. The lab belongs to the professor, a singular noun, so all choices are incorrect except for choice (B).

Rhetorical Skills Drill (Chapter 8)

1. B   Cross off LEAST, and use POE. *Fame*, *stardom*, and *greatness* can all work the same way as *prominence* in the context of the sentence. *Projection* does not mean the same thing and is the correct answer.

2. J   Try out each answer choice. *Live television* is the intended meaning.

3. A   Evaluate the reasons given in the answers. The reason given in choice (A) could be true, but you have to read through the third paragraph to be able to judge. This makes this a good question to do later. In fact, the proposed clause does provide necessary context for the information given in the second and third sentences of the second paragraph.

4. G   Identify the purpose in the question. The correct choice must convey extreme skill. *Honing their craft* does just that, while all of the other choices contain no specific mention of skill.

5. D   Use POE. Sentences 2 and 3 should go back to back, with sentence 3 providing a list of the *young talents* mentioned in sentence 2. Eliminate choices (B) and (C), and compare the difference between choices (A) and (D). Sentence 1 should precede sentence 4, so choice (D) is correct.

6. F   Identify the purpose in the question. The correct choice must introduce the paragraph. Finish reading the paragraph and then return to the question. Since the topic involves problems with the live broadcast, choice (F) is the best introduction.

7. C   To crack this type of strategy question, use POE and consider which choice correctly describes the sentence to be deleted. Choice (C) is the best description.

8. F   Identify the purpose in the question and connect to the best reason among the answers. Choices (G), (H), and (J) offer reasons that do not support the purpose well, nor describe the content of the essay accurately.

9. D   If you didn't see the warning at the beginning of the passage, you may have found the flow of the essay jarring. Even if you didn't, always use POE with order of paragraph questions. Look for topic and concluding sentences to make the flow of ideas consistent. The topic sentence of paragraph 2 makes a good transition after the discussion of accidents in paragraph 4.

PART III: MATH

Fundamentals Drill (Chapter 10)

1. C   You'll need to find the prime factorization of 54, so use a factor tree. In using this tree, you'll find the prime factorization of $54 = 6 \times 9 = (2 \times 3) \times (3 \times 3) = 2 \times 3^3$. The *distinct* prime factors of 54, therefore, are 2 and 3. The product of these two numbers is 6, choice (C). If you chose (E), you may have missed the word *distinct*! Read carefully!

2. G   Take this problem in bite-size pieces. If x is the least odd prime number, x must be 3. If y is the least positive integer multiple of 10, y must be 10. The difference between these two numbers is therefore $10 - 3 = 7$ or choice (G). If you selected choice (K), be careful, you may have thought that 20 was the first integer multiple of 10, but the first multiple of any number is that number itself!

3. D   Remember MADSPM, and don't forget Order of Operations, or PEMDAS. Do the parentheses first, and remember, when you raise an exponent to a *power*, you *multiply* those exponents: $(x^{-1}y^{-3})^{-2}(x^4y^7)^3 = (x^2y^6)(x^{12}y^{21})$. Now, combine like terms, and remember, when you multiply numbers with exponents, you add those exponents to one another: $(x^2y^6)(x^{12}y^{21}) = x^{14}y^{27}$, choice (D).

4. H   Although this problem involves an imaginary number, you can still use a traditional FOIL method to find the answer. You are asked to square the expression, so do so, and remember to multiply the First, Outer, Inner, and Last terms: $(i + 4)(i + 4) = i^2 + 8i + 16$. None of the answer choices look quite like this, but remember, $i^2 = -1$, so substitute this term: $i^2 + 8i + 16 = -1 + 8i + 16 = 8i + 15$, or choice (H).

5. C   The prime numbers between 10 and 20 are as follows: 11, 13, 17, 19. You want the *least* sum of three *distinct* numbers, so the only possible answer is $11 + 13 + 17 = 41$, or choice (C). If you chose (B), you may have missed the word *distinct*.

Algebra Drill (Chapter 11)

1. **C** This might look like a traditional plug-and-chug problem, but the problem is asking for a specific value, and the answer choices are all real numbers. A great indication that you can PITA! This time, the problem is asking for the *largest*, so start with choice (E). Does the equation work if $x = 5$? $5^2 - 4(5) + 3 = 25 - 20 + 3 \neq 0$. Eliminate choice (E). Try choice (D), $4^2 - 4(4) + 3 = 16 - 16 + 3 \neq 0$. Try choice (C), $3^2 - 4(3) + 3 = 9 - 12 + 3 = 0$. It works, and because you're using PITA, you can stop once you've found a correct answer. If you selected choice (A), be careful, this is the *smallest* value of x that solves the equation!

2. **G** There are variables in the answer choices, so let's Plug In. Let's say $x = 2$ and plug this in to the equation: $\dfrac{(2)^2 + 6(2) - 27}{(2+9)} = \dfrac{4 + 12 - 27}{11} = \dfrac{-11}{11} = -1$, which means your target answer is -1. Try $x = 2$ in the answer choices to see which one gives this target answer. Only choice (G) works.

3. **A** This problem is very confusingly worded, so let's make sure we use PITA to keep all the work manageable. We'll start with choice (C) and work out from there, so our number is 11. "2 less than 3 times" 11 is $3(11) - 2 = 31$. "4 more than the product of 5 and 3" is $4 + (5 \times 3) = 19$. The problem tells us these numbers should be the same, and they're not here, so eliminate choice (C), and eliminate choices (D) and (E), because we know we need something smaller than 31. Try choice (B), 10. "2 less than 3 times" 10 is $3(10) - 2 = 28$, still too big. You can actually stop here, because there's only one answer choice left, but let's check it just to be on the safe side. Try choice (A), 7. "2 less than 3 times" 7 is $3(7) - 2 = 19$. Bingo! Choice (A) is the correct answer.

4. **G** There are no variables in this problem, but it deals with fractions of a "certain number," which means that this is a Hidden Plug-In. Let's plug something in for the number of books: it's usually a good idea to do some common multiple of the denominators, so let's say there are 30 books. $\dfrac{2}{5}$ of the books are distributed in the morning, which means $\dfrac{2}{5} \times 30 = 12$ books are distributed in the morning, leaving 18 books. $\dfrac{1}{3}$ of the remaining books are distributed in the afternoon, which means $\dfrac{1}{3} \times 18 = 6$ books are distributed in the afternoon, leaving 12 books. We're looking for the fraction of remaining books, so find $\dfrac{12}{30} = \dfrac{6}{15} = \dfrac{2}{5}$, choice (G).

5. **B** We need to find out what happens as b increases, and there's no easier way to do that than to try it out. Let's start with $b = 2$. If $b = 2$, $a = \dfrac{3}{2}$. We want to see what happens when b increases, so let's try $b = 3$. If $b = 3$, $a = \dfrac{3}{3} = 1$. We can see, then, even from these two numbers, that as b increases, a decreases, and we can eliminate choices (A), (D), and (E). Now, the remaining question is whether a gets closer to 1 or if it continues to get closer to 0. Try $b = 4$. If $b = 4$, $a = \dfrac{3}{4}$. It has continued decreasing past 1, so eliminate choice (C). Only (B) works.

Geometry Drill (Chapter 12)

1. **B** Although this is a geometry problem, it is asking for a specific value and giving a list of numerical answer choices as possibilities. This means you can use PITA. Start with choice (C). If $\angle A = 50$, then $\angle B = 50$, and because it is twice as large as $\angle B$, $\angle C = 100$. The sum of the three angles will then be $50 + 50 + 100 = 200$, which is too big, so you can eliminate choices (C), (D), and (E). Try choice (B). If $\angle A = 45$, then $\angle B = 45$, and because it is twice as large as $\angle B$, $\angle C = 90$. The sum of the three angles will then be $45 + 45 + 90 = 180$, which is exactly what you need, so the best answer is choice (B).

2. **F** When two parallel lines are intersected by a third line, it creates two kinds of angles: BIG angles and small angles. All the BIG angles are equal and all the small angles are equal. Because $\angle D$ is on a separate line, you don't know anything about it, so it can't possibly be correct, eliminating choices (G) and (J). The BIG angles, therefore, are A and C. The small angles are B and E. Only choice (F) matches like angles, so it is the only possible correct answer.

3. **D** Deal with the two right triangles separately. We already have the two legs of $\triangle ABC$, so use the Pythagorean theorem ($a^2 + b^2 = c^2$) to find the hypotenuse. In this case, $AB^2 + BC^2 = AC^2$, so $(20)^2 + (15)^2 = AC^2$, and $AC = 25$. Notice this is a special right triangle: it's a 3:4:5 with a multiplier of 5! Now that we have AC, we have two sides of the other right triangle and can find the third. This, too, is a special right triangle with sides 7:24:25, and since we have sides 7 and 25, the remaining side must be 24, or choice (D). If you don't spot these special right triangles, you can always use the Pythagorean theorem.

4. **G** If you have one piece of information about a circle, you find everything else you need. The area of circle A is 16π and because $A = \pi r^2$, the radius of circle A must be 4. If the radius of circle B is half that of circle A, then the radius of circle B must be 2. Then find the circumference of circle B, with $C = 2\pi r = 2\pi(2) = 4\pi$, or choice (G).

5. **A** Separate the triangles and take this problem in bite-size pieces. You know two sides of the left triangle, so find the third with the Pythagorean theorem: $LO^2 + MO^2 = LM^2$. Substitute the values you know, $(4)^2 + MO^2 = (6)^2$, and $MO = 2\sqrt{5}$. Then because we know MO is equal to ON, ON must also be equal to $2\sqrt{5}$. You can either use the Pythagorean theorem to find the third side, or note that this is a 45:45:90 triangle, which means its sides must be in a ratio of $x : x : x\sqrt{2}$, and the third side therefore must be $2\sqrt{5} \times \sqrt{2} = 2\sqrt{10}$, or choice (A).

Word Problems Drill (Chapter 13)

1. **C** The question is asking for a specific number and offering a list of numerical answer choices as options. Use PITA! Start with choice (C). If there are 12 boys in the class, then there must be $27 - 12 = 15$ girls. The ratio of boys to girls is therefore 12:15, which, when divided by 3, reduces to 4:5, exactly what you need! Choice (C) is the answer.

2. J   Use an average pie to help Linda fix her mistake. She initially worked with only 5 items to get an average of 88. Multiply this average and this number of items to find the sum total of these five tests: 88 × 5 = 440. Now, add the sixth score to the total to find a new total of 522. Divide this number by the correct number of things, 6, to find an average of 87, choice (J). You're welcome, Linda.

3. E   Read this problem carefully. Because both percentages are taken "of the original," add them together to find that 8% of the original amount is lost. Use the percentage translation to find how much is lost: *8% of 490 tons is how much?* In math terms, $\frac{8}{100} \times 490 = 39.2$ tons lost. The question asks for how much remains, so subtract 490 – 39.2 = 450.8 tons, or choice (E).

4. J   There's no figure in this problem, so draw one! This problem has variables in the answer choices, which is a dead giveaway that you can Plug In. Let's say $a = 2$ and $b = 3$. To find the surface area, simply find the area of all the surfaces, remember that there will be six in all. The surfaces will have areas of 4, 4, 6, 6, 6, and 6. Add them together to find 4 + 4 + 6 + 6 + 6 + 6 = 32, your target answer. Go to the answer choices to find the one that matches this answer when $a = 2$ and $b = 3$. Choice (F) gives 36. Choice (G) gives 24. Choice (H) gives 16. Choice (J) gives 32. Choice (K) gives 26. Only choice (J) works!

5. C   This problem is asking for arrangements, so start by creating the number of slots you will need:

_____ _____ _____ _____ _____

There is a restriction on the last in that only one letter, W, can go there, so fill this one in first:

_____ _____ _____ _____ ___1___

Then, fill the rest in as normal, remembering that W is already taken, so there are only four letters left:

___4___ ___3___ ___2___ ___1___ ___1___

Now that you've got the slots filled in, go ahead and multiply the numbers to find the number of possible arrangements:

___4___ × ___3___ × ___2___ × ___1___ × ___1___ = 24 possible arrangements, or choice (C).

Graphing and Coordinate Geometry Drill (Chapter 14)

1. E   First, use POE to eliminate some answer choices. Since this is only a > sign, we can eliminate choices (B) and (D) right off the bat. Now, let's use Plugging In to narrow down the rest. First, let's try $x = -2$ $-3(-2) - 6 > 9$. This equation doesn't work, because 0 is NOT greater than 9, so eliminate any answer choices that include -2, leaving only choice (E).

2. G   Use the midpoint formula with the two given points. The midpoint formula is $\left(\dfrac{x_1 + x_2}{2}, \dfrac{y_1 + y_2}{2} \right)$, so plug the points into the equation to find $\left(\dfrac{3 + (-4)}{2}, \dfrac{5 + 3}{2} \right)$, resulting in a midpoint of $\left(-\dfrac{1}{2}, 4 \right)$, or choice (G).

3. B   In order to find the slope, put this equation into slope-intercept form, or $y = mx + b$. Combine the x-terms and subtract 6 from each side to find $12x - 6 = y$, in which the m term must be 12, or choice (B).

4. H   Plot your points on a graph and use them to draw a right triangle. The triangle will rise 4 units and run 3 units, meaning the legs of the triangle will be 3 and 4. You can then use the Pythagorean theorem to find the third side, or if you notice this is a 3:4:5 Pythagorean triple, the third side of the triangle must be 5, or choice (H).

5. C   Use the slope formula, $\dfrac{rise}{run}$ or $\dfrac{y_2 - y_1}{x_2 - x_1}$ with the given points to find that the slope is equivalent to $\dfrac{5 - 4}{13 - 6} = \dfrac{1}{7}$, or choice (C). If you selected choice (E), you may have switched the x- and y-terms!

6. J   The circle formula is $(x - h)^2 + (y - k)^2 = r^2$ in which (h, k) is the center of the circle and r is its radius. Since $r^2 = 9$, the radius of the circle must be 3, eliminating choices (G), (H), and (K). Then look at the first part of the equation, the $(x - 3)$ matches up without any manipulation with the $(x - h)$ part of the equation, so h must equal 3, eliminating choice (F). Only (J) is left, and we don't even need to solve for k!

Trigonometry Drill (Chapter 15)

1. D   Use SOHCAHTOA to find that $\tan \theta = \dfrac{opp}{adj}$. Your first impulse here may be to solve for the unknown side, but take a close look at where the θ is. Its adjacent side is 5, meaning the tangent of that angle must have a denominator of 5. Only choice (D) has it, so it's the only answer that can work. If you *do* solve for the unknown side, remember your Pythagorean triples: this is a 5:12:13 triangle, so the unknown side must be 12.

2. H $\cot \theta$ is defined as $\dfrac{1}{\tan \theta}$. Therefore, because $\tan \theta = 1$, substitute to find $\cot \theta = \dfrac{1}{\tan \theta} = \dfrac{1}{1} = 1$. Only choice (H) works!

3. C   Remember the special trig identity which states $\sin^2 \theta + \cos^2 \theta = 1$. Substitute this into the equation, $x + \sin^2 \theta + \cos^2 \theta = 4$ to find that $x + 1 = 4$ so x must be equal to 3. Choice (C) is the best answer.

PART IV: READING

Reading Drill 1 (Chapter 17)

1. C   This is another great example of how POE works on the ACT. From the first paragraph we know that the author thinks television has a negative effect on news reporting. This will allow us to eliminate choices (B) and (D): Choice (A) states that he is defending news stations, which also can't be right. This leaves us with choice (C) as the best answer.

2. J   Let's look at how this word is used in context. The sentence in question states *the world as mapped by the speeded-up electronic media has no order or meaning and is not to be taken seriously.* What word could we put in the place of *mapped*? Something like *described* or *presented*. The choice that comes closest to this idea is (J).

3. B   Let's try to eliminate what we know is wrong and work our way to the best answer. The question of live television as opposed to recorded television isn't addressed in the passage, so we can eliminate choice (A). The passage also does not discuss how television brings families together, so we can also eliminate choice (C). Although the author might believe that television reporters should also write articles, he doesn't actually say that anywhere in this passage, so choice (D) can also be crossed off. There is evidence to support choice (B) in lines 29–34, so the best bet is choice (B).

4. F   The point of the paragraph immediately preceding these lines is that television reporters are chosen based on how they look. Then Christine Craft is cited as an example of someone who was fired because people did not like how she looked. This makes choice (F) the best answer.

5. B   The author doesn't talk about the future of newspapers, so choice (C) can be eliminated. Because the passage argues that television has significantly changed the nature of news, choice (D) isn't likely either. Choice (A) might be something the author thinks, but he doesn't discuss actors in these paragraphs. We can find support for choice (B) in the third paragraph, where he states that *on television we are presented not only with fragmented news but news without context…*and, therefore, without essential seriousness.

6. J   The author doesn't really discuss the unbiased reporting of facts or informing the public about new products. For this reason we can eliminate choices (F) and (H). Although choice (G) might be tempting, nowhere does it actually state that the point of television is to make individuals popular. At the end of the third paragraph, however, the author says that television news has become *pure entertainment*. This makes choice (J) the best answer.

7. A   Let's look back to the passage where the author mentions "talking hairdos" and reread just these lines. There the author says that television executives will *exclude women who are not beautiful or who are over the age of 50, men who are bald, all people who are overweight or whose noses are too long…*(lines 42–45) and this best supports choice (A).

8. H Let's look back to the beginning of the passage. It says "Now…this" *is commonly used on radio and television newscast to indicate that what one has just heard or seen has no relevance to what one is about to hear or see.* Choice (H) sounds closest to this.

9. A At the beginning of the last paragraph, the author claims that the *perception of the truth of a report rests heavily on the acceptability of the newscaster.* This best supports choice (A).

10. J In the second paragraph, the author states that *television sells its time in seconds and minutes, that it must use images rather than words,* and that *viewers are rarely required to carry over any thought or feeling from one parcel of time to another.* Therefore, choices (F), (G), and (H) are cited: the one that is not is (J).

Reading Drill 2 (Chapter 18)

1. D Let's look at how these words are used in context. On the last line of the first paragraph, Mick is wondering whether to climb the ladder, and the passage says that she *screwed up nerve and began to climb.* What word could we put in place of the words *screwed up*? Something like *found* or *gathered.* The choice that comes closest to this idea is (D).

2. J In the first paragraph, Mick does not find Mr. Singer, so choice (F) can be eliminated. She doesn't make breakfast for her family, so choice (G) can also be crossed off. Although the passage says that Bubber does go to Sunday School, it doesn't say that Mick does, so choice (H) won't be right either. The paragraph does, however, describe how she cares for her younger brothers; this makes (J) the best choice.

3. B In the third sentence of the third paragraph, Mick is on top of the roof and thinks to herself this is *where everybody wanted to stand.* This supports choice (B).

4. J In the first paragraph, we find that Mick cares for Ralph and Bubber, so they aren't her father. The first paragraph also states that her father tells Mick that Mr. Singer came in late the night before. Therefore, we can eliminate choices (F), (G), and (H), which leaves us with (J) as the answer.

5. A According to the fourth paragraph, other children also climbed the roof, so we can eliminate choice (D). Although choices (B) and (C) might be true, there isn't really any evidence in the paragraph to support them. Choice (A) has some support because the sixth paragraph tells us that Mick was finally somewhere *by herself. No one was around and it was quiet and she could think for a while.* This makes (A) the best answer.

6. G   This is a good example of using POE to solve a problem. There is nothing in line 31 that tells us that Mick felt she had a poor singing voice or that she did not want to scare her brothers, so we can eliminate choices (F) and (J). While there is some reason from the first paragraph to believe that she was slightly afraid of climbing the ladder, we need to find an answer that has support in this particular line, which doesn't mention fear of heights. Therefore, we should avoid choice (H) as well. Even if it's not entirely clear what choice (G) is saying, we should pick it because we're sure that the others aren't correct.

7. B   The first paragraph tells us that Mick *waited for Mister Singer a long time. All the other boarders came down….* This is evidence that Mr. Singer is a boarder in Mick's house.

8. H   In the next-to-last paragraph of this passage, Micks dreams of inventing a tiny radio, a flying machine, and a tunnel through the earth. The passage mentions big balloons but doesn't state that Mick intends to invent them. This makes (H) the best choice.

9. C   Toward the end of the first paragraph, it states that the house was being built, and the fifth paragraph says *soon the work would all be finished*. This tells us that the house is unfinished, so the answer is choice (C).

10. F   The passage doesn't mention getting good grades in school or wanting to spend more time with parents, so choices (H) and (J) can be eliminated. Moreover, while Mick does care for her younger brothers, the passage doesn't actually state that she wants to have children of her own. This makes choice (G) not very promising either. In the seventh paragraph, Mick spends time thinking about what she would do when she was very famous. This makes (F) the most reasonable choice.

PART V: SCIENCE

Basic Approach Drill 1 (Chapter 21)

1. B   As you were reading the question, did you notice that choices (A) and (B) were the same except that the words "T1" and "T2" were switched? The answer choices are opposites, and one of them will probably be correct. Let's try choices (A) and (B) first. At T1, Sample 1 has a greater number of molecules in motion. The introduction clarifies that this corresponds to an increase in kinetic energy. The graph contradicts choice (A), so the answer appears to be choice (B). Now let's check the other two choices. Does an increase in temperature lead to a decrease in kinetic energy? No. The passage states that an increase in temperature leads to an increase in kinetic energy. So we can eliminate choice (C). Now let's look at choice (D). Is it true that water never undergoes a phase change? No; in fact, the text accompanying the graph says just the opposite. So we can eliminate choice (D). Also, remember to be cautious of extreme language such as "never." The correct answer is choice (B).

2. F   The question refers to the second paragraph, which mentions phase changes. What happens during a phase change? Two things happen: (1) Increased kinetic energy weakens the attractive intermolecular forces in the water, and (2) Some molecules escape the liquid as a gas. Now that we have reviewed this information, it's pretty easy to eliminate choices (G) and (H). Now let's look at choice (J). Did we read anything in the passage that told us about other phase changes? No. This answer is beyond the realm of the passage and can be eliminated. So the correct answer is choice (F), and again we've reached it by using POE.

3. B   The ACT test writers want to see if you can predict what will happen if you raise the temperature of water higher than that of Sample 2. What answer choices should you eliminate? Decide whether the correct answer should begin with a yes or a no. How do we do that? Just check the graph with the results for Samples 1 and 2. When you increase the temperature, will the sample have more or less kinetic energy? It will have more. That means we can rule out choice (D). We can eliminate choice (C) because the temperature reading of Sample 2 is lower than the third sample. Now compare choices (A) with (B) to see which one is correct. Does an increase in temperature lead to greater or fewer numbers of molecules escaping the liquid? Greater. Thus, the correct answer is choice (B).

4. F   The passage states that when a substance goes from the liquid to the gas phase, it will evaporate. When a substance has reached the temperature at which it undergoes the phase change, it will evaporate. That's how molecules will escape. Therefore, the answer is choice (F).

5. C   When you look at the figure, which line goes the highest? Which has the highest kinetic energy at any one point? Well, the curve for T1 goes higher than the curve for T2. T2 has the highest average kinetic energy, but that's not what this question asks us to find. Therefore, choices (A) and (B) can be eliminated. Choice (D) is a nonsensical answer choice. Choice (C) is the best answer.

Basic Approach Drill 2 (Chapter 21)

1. B   Do we see a solution of thyroxine that is 0.3 µg/ml? No. The ACT test writers want you to "guesstimate" where 0.3 µg/ml would fall on the table. This value would have to lie somewhere between 0.2 µg/ml and 0.5 µg/ml. The question requires that you make a guess within the values given. What do we call this skill? Interpolation! Now if we move across the x-axis to the value of 72 hours, and we move up to the range of values between 0.2 µg/ml and 0.5 µg/ml, we see that the y-values range from about 23 percent to 37 percent. The only one that falls in that range is choice (B)—30 percent.

2. G   Notice that they want to know what is true for tadpoles in general. Let's start with choice (F). This is a ridiculous answer choice. We know that all normal tadpoles undergo metamorphosis. If you're not sure, take a look at the graph. The control group in the graph represents normal tadpoles. They do have some decrease in tail width, although not a lot, in 120 hours or 5 days. (Notice that you needed to know that 5 days is the same as 120 hours.) Thus, choice (F) is incorrect. You can also rule out choice (H) because the figure clearly shows that high concentrations of thyroxine solutions lead to the greatest decrease in tail width. The passage doesn't mention anything about temperature, thus choice (J) is out. The correct answer is choice (G). We see that the control sample shows some reduction in tail size in 120 hours, so it must take longer for the process to be complete.

3. C   You must realize that as the tadpole develops, the tail is reabsorbed—or it shrinks. The graph compares percent decrease in tail width to hours. At 96 hours (4 days), the tadpoles showing the lowest percent decrease in tail width would be the least developed. Therefore, the answer must be choice (C), the tadpoles in 0.1 µg/ml.

4. G   Thyroxine affects the metamorphosis of the tadpole by influencing the process of cell determination from tadpole cells into mature adult cells. You don't have to understand this process—just realize that it occurs between tadpole and adult stages. Begin with choices (F), (G), and (H), because you need a tadpole to start the process. Using POE, the correct answer can be only choice (G).

5. C   Take a look at the figure provided. When do the lines start to differentiate from one another (showing different rates of tail reabsorption)? We can see that by 24 hours, the tadpoles placed in the various thyroxine solutions have each had a larger percent of their tails reabsorbed than the tadpoles in the control group. Choice (D) can be eliminated. Now look between 0 and 24 hours. At 0 hours and at 12 hours, the percent decrease in tail width is the same for all the tadpoles. Therefore, the change in metamorphosis rate must occur between 12 and 24 hours, so choice (C) is correct.

Basic Approach Drill 3 (Chapter 21)

1. A   Finally, a question about drawing a graph! This question was easy because you only needed to look at the x- and y-axes. The atomic number of the elements was the independent variable, and the atomic radius was the dependent variable. What happens to the atomic radius as you increase the atomic number? It gets smaller. That means we can eliminate choices (C) and (D). Now we have to decide if it's a linear relationship or an exponential one. Just check the numbers. Notice that the numbers decrease by a smaller amount each time—so it's a curve, not a straight line. Thus, the correct answer is choice (A).

2. J   You should look at relationships between electronegativity and one of the other properties of elements. Let's start with choices (G) and (J). Why? They are opposites (the switch again), so they can't both be true. If an element has a high electronegativity, is it a metal or a non-metal? It's a non-metal, so eliminate choice (G). Now we can check the other answer choices. Must an element with a high electronegativity have an even or an odd atomic number? Let's check. If you look at the two highest electronegative elements, O and F, one is even and one is odd. So choice (F) is not true. As for choice (H), we know that elements with high electronegativity pull their outer electrons (the passage defines electronegativity as a measure of that strength). Therefore, we can eliminate choice (H). The correct answer is choice (J).

3. B   This question asks you to make a generalization about trends in the chart, with regard to the bigger picture. Let's take a moment to think about the answer choices. If we want to make generalizations about elements, would an answer that refers to specific elements be the correct one? Probably not. So we can probably eliminate choice (D). But let's look at choice (D) more closely to be sure. Is the atomic radius of F larger than that of N? No. Do all metals have high electronegativity values? No. Now notice that choices (A) and (B) state opposite trends. Use the chart to determine which is correct. As the atomic radius decreases, electronegativity increases. Thus, the correct is choice (B).

4. G   The first part is easy. Look at the chart to tell you which has a greater electronegativity, Li or F. F, of course! So we can get rid of choice (J). Now why is the electronegativity of F greater than that of Li? We have to choose between choices (F) and (G). Can you determine which one of these is correct by using the information in the chart? No. Go back to the introduction and skim for information about electronegativity. The passage says specifically that within a row of the periodic table, the electronegativity tends to increase with increasing atomic number, due to the tighter bonding between protons and electrons. It's not the number that's important, but rather how tightly bound they are. F has a higher atomic number than Li and more electrons than Li, so, F's electrons are more tightly bound than Li's. Therefore, the best answer is choice (G).

5. A   You must take new information given in the question and apply it to the chart given in the passage. Fortunately, this is very easy. Be careful; the question asks for increasing order of ionization energies. Because it follows the same trend as electronegativity, just find the answer that lists elements with increasing electronegativities. The answer can only be choice (A).

Fighting Scientists Drill 1 (Chapter 22)

1. **C** What are the beliefs of Scientist 1? His main point is that Pangaea (one continent) existed 137 million years ago. Now let's start by looking at each of the answer choices. Were the continents once part of one large land mass? Yes. We read that in the passage. What about choice (B)? Did the continents break up and drift apart? Definitely. Does the statement that the ocean basins remained fixed agree with the theory? No. If so, how would the continents drift apart? So choice (C) is inconsistent. Choice (D) is not inconsistent with the theory of Scientist 1. So the correct answer is choice (C).

2. **G** Scientist 2 needs to show how what Scientist 1 said fits with Scientist 2's hypothesis. It will also probably be something which disagrees with Scientist 1's argument. Choice (F) states that the techniques used to date and compare fossils are accurate. This is an argument Scientist 1 makes but that Scientist 2 doesn't mention. Cross it out. Choice (G) says that the soil and climate conditions were once the same—a nice paraphrase of what Scientist 2 says at the end of the argument. Keep choice (G) for now. Choice (H) supports Scientist 1 because extremely large ferns would have a hard time floating thousands of miles across the ocean. You can eliminate choice (J) because it doesn't support either scientist. Scientist 2 would infer that these ferns grew well in both places; choice (G) has to be right.

3. **C** Either scientist could use this information to support his theory if he could come up with a valid reason. Choice (A) says that Scientist 1 is supported because the finding shows tectonic activity. But we already knew about that and besides, that's a point on which the scientists agree. So eliminate choice (A). Choice (D) also gives us information that was already stated in Scientist 2's statement, so this choice is weak. Choice (B) is ridiculous because neither scientist believes that Pangaea exists today, so cross it out. At this point, choice (C) is looking pretty good. Scientist 2 could soundly reason that tectonic activity in a solid land mass demonstrates that this geological phenomenon does not lead to continental drift. The best answer is choice (C).

4. **G** The passage tells us about the formation of land masses, tectonic plates, and other geological evidence—namely, fossils. You must be able to add this together and determine that the scientists know something about geology. So only choice (G) can be correct.

5. **A** You must know what each scientist supports. Let's go through the choices one by one. Statement I is supported by both scientists because both believe that tectonic activity exists and changes geological formations. (Scientist 1 thinks it's more important than does Scientist 2, but that doesn't matter here.) So Statement I is correct and we're down to choices (A) and (C). Let's keep checking. Only Scientist 2 supports Statement II and only Scientist 1 supports Statement III. Therefore, choice (A) must be the correct answer.

Fighting Scientists Drill 2 (Chapter 22)

1. A   To do this, we must understand the argument. What's the main point of Hypothesis 2? The debater believes that the chance of RNA reproducing as the graduate student described is extremely small. Look for an answer choice that supports this argument. Choice (A) states that conditions in the atmosphere were too unstable to support the necessary gases. Does this statement support Hypothesis 2? Yes. How? Because it weakens Hypothesis 1. So choice (A) is correct. Choices (B), (C), and (D) are wrong because they support Hypothesis 1.

2. G   What does Scientist 1 believe? That the experiment shows how the first organic compounds were made. Is choice (F) an assumption in this argument? No. It refers to Hypothesis 2. What about choice (G)? Yes. The scientist assumed that the experiment mimicked the conditions of primeval Earth. So choice (G) is correct. Choice (H) states that proteins are the building blocks of amino acids. That's wrong; as stated in Hypothesis 1, amino acids are the building blocks of proteins. So get rid of choice (H). Choice (J) is incorrect because Earth had to have hydrogen in order to form organic compounds.

3. A   What does Hypothesis 1 say about amino acids? The passage tells us that amino acids are the building blocks of life, so let's start with the answer choices that list amino acids last. We can quickly eliminate choice (C). We can also eliminate choice (B) because the meteor theory was part of Hypothesis 2, not Hypothesis 1. And we're down to choices (A) and (D). We can also find in the passage that amino acids are the building blocks of proteins, so amino acids should be before proteins in the list. So by POE and understanding the passage, we arrive at the correct answer, choice (A).

Fighting Scientists Drill 3 (Chapter 22)

1. C   We are looking for an answer that supports Hypothesis 2. Hypothesis 2 states that an increase in precipitation or an increase in pollution would lead to a significant drop in temperature. Choice (A) states that there is more snow in Canada this year, but we don't know if that's enough snow for glaciation. So we can eliminate it. Let's look at choice (B). If snow didn't stick to the ground, would there be an ice age? Choice (B) is silly; eliminate it. What about choice (C)? If there is a drop in temperature for every increase in the pollution rate, could that lead to glaciation? Yes. Let's look at choice (D). If the water became more polluted, would that necessarily lead to the next ice age? We're not sure. The passage states that pollution in the air, not necessarily in the water, leads to a decrease in temperature. So the correct answer is choice (C).

2. H   For this question we're looking for an answer that could disprove Hypothesis 1. What is the main point of Hypothesis 1? The debater says that it is highly unlikely that Earth will experience another ice age. Why? Because he believes that the necessary conditions will not be met in the future. What is the best way to disprove this point? Just indicate that the conditions could change in the future and then the chance for glaciation could increase. Which choice states that? Choice (H). Now let's look at choice (F). A fluctuation in temperature would not necessarily mean that the temperature was low enough for glaciation to occur. We therefore can eliminate this choice. Even if there was more snowfall in the Swiss Alps, we are not given an indication of how long it lasted. So you can get rid of choice (G). Now, if the temperature went up 5°C in the North Pole, it would be warmer, not colder, so choice (J) is out. So the correct answer is choice (H).

3. C   Let's start with Statement II, because it appears in the most answer choices. Based on the passage, would glaciation take place in polar regions? The passage tells us that polar regions would be one of the first locations in which glaciation would take place. Now that you can eliminate answer choices that don't include Statement II, you can eliminate choice (A). What about heavily polluted regions? Yes. The passage refers to the other possible cause of a temperature drop—pollution. We can eliminate choices (B) and (D) because they don't include Statement II. Therefore, choice (C) must be correct.

4. G   According to Hypothesis 2, there are two conditions that are critical to glaciation: temperature and precipitation. Choice (F) is incorrect because pollution doesn't cause precipitation. Choice (G) sounds good because it states that pollution leads to a major drop in temperature (it has one of the conditions). What about choice (H)? You can eliminate choice (H) because glaciation needs both low temperatures and high precipitation. Choice (J) supports Hypothesis 1, not Hypothesis 2, so we can eliminate it. The best answer is choice (G).

Part VIII
The Princeton Review ACT Practice Exam 1

Chapter 25
Practice Exam 1

ENGLISH TEST

45 Minutes—75 Questions

DIRECTIONS: In the five passages that follow, certain words and phrases are underlined and numbered. In the right-hand column, you will find alternatives for the underlined part. In most cases, you are to choose the one that best expresses the idea, makes the statement appropriate for standard written English, or is worded most consistently with the style and tone of the passage as a whole. If you think the original version is best, choose "NO CHANGE." In some cases, you will find in the right-hand column a question about the underlined part. You are to choose the best answer to the question.

You will also find questions about a section of the passage, or about the passage as a whole. These questions do not refer to an underlined portion of the passage, but rather are identified by a number or numbers in a box.

For each question, choose the alternative you consider best and fill in the corresponding oval on your answer document. Read each passage through once before you begin to answer the questions that accompany it. For many of the questions, you must read several sentences beyond the question to determine the answer. Be sure that you have read far enough ahead each time you choose an alternative.

PASSAGE I

I Am Iron Man

[1] The term "Iron Man" has many connotations, including references to a song, a comic book icon, even a movie. [2] Yet only one definition of the term truly lives up to its name: the Ironman Triathlon held annually in Hawaii a picturesque setting for a challenging race. [3] This grueling race demands amazing physical prowess and the ability to swim, bike, and run a marathon, all in less than 12 hours with no break. [4] Very few individuals are up to the task. ☐2

1. **A.** NO CHANGE
   B. Hawaii,
   C. Hawaii, being
   D. Hawaii, it is

2. If the writer were to delete Sentence 4, the essay would primarily lose details that:
   F. emphasize how difficult the race truly is.
   G. mourn how few athletes are able to visit Hawaii in order to compete in the race.
   H. highlight that most athletes prefer the run to the swimming or biking components of the race.
   J. suggest that women are not truly competitive in the race.

Otherwise, Gordon Haller is a notable exception. Growing up in the 1950s, Haller developed an interest in many sports categorized as endurance athletics, and welcomed their grueling physical demands. As he pursued a degree in physics he drove a

3. **A.** NO CHANGE
   B. As a result,
   C. In addition,
   D. However,

4. **F.** NO CHANGE
   G. athletics and welcomed their
   H. athletics, and welcomed there,
   J. athletics and, welcomed there

GO ON TO THE NEXT PAGE.

taxi to pay the bills, but competitive training <u>proved</u> his passion.
₅
So when he heard about the race in 1978, the first year it was

held, he immediately signed up.

The race <u>somewhat</u> originated in an amusing way. The
₆
members of two popular sports clubs, the Mid-Pacific Road

<u>Runners of Honolulu, and the Waikiki Swim Club</u> of Oahu, had
₇
a long-standing and good-natured debate going over who made

better athletes: runners or swimmers. However, some local

bikers thought both clubs were wrong, <u>while claiming</u> that they,
₈
in fact, deserved the title. Wanting to settle the dispute once and

for all, <u>when</u> they decided to combine three separate races
₉

<u>already held annually on the island</u> into one massive test of
₁₀
endurance. Thus, the Waikiki Roughwater Swim of 2.4 miles,

the Around-Oahu Bike race of 112 miles, and the Honolulu

Marathon of 26.2 miles were all combined to form the Ironman

Triathlon.

Haller was one of only fifteen competitors to show up that

February morning to start the race. He quickly scanned the few

pages of rules and instructions, <u>and while reading those pages</u> on
₁₁
the last page he discovered a sentence that would become the

race's famous slogan: "Swim 2.4 miles! Bike 112 miles! Run

26.2 miles! Brag for the rest of your life!" Haller took that to

5. A. NO CHANGE
   B. verified
   C justified
   D. certified

6. The best placement for the underlined word would be:
   F. where it is now.
   G. before the word *in*.
   H. before the word *amusing* (changing *an* to *a*).
   J. before the word *way*.

7. A. NO CHANGE
   B. Runners, of Honolulu, and the Waikiki Swim Club
   C. Runners of Honolulu and the Waikiki Swim Club
   D. Runners, of Honolulu, and the Waikiki Swim Club,

8. F. NO CHANGE
   G. and while claiming
   H. they claimed
   J. claiming

9. A. NO CHANGE
   B. and
   C. where
   D. DELETE the underlined portion.

10. The best placement for the underlined phrase would be:
    F. where it is now.
    G. before the word *Wanting* (revising the capitalization accordingly).
    H. before the word *once*.
    J. after the word *endurance* (ending the sentence with a period).

11. A. NO CHANGE
    B. and
    C. and while perusing those pages
    D. and in those sheets of paper

GO ON TO THE NEXT PAGE.

heart, and at the end of the day, he <u>had became</u> the first Ironman
                                          12

champion in history. [13]

    In the approximately thirty years since that very first race, the Ironman has become a tradition in Hawaii and now boasts approximately 1,500 entrants every year. <u>The competitors who</u>
                                                                          14
complete the race don't have to be the first across the finish line to claim success: just finishing is a victory unto itself.

12. **F.** NO CHANGE
    G. become
    H. became
    J. becamed

13. Which of the following true statements, if added here, would most effectively and specifically emphasize Haller's achievement as described in this essay?

    A. Twelve other people also finished the race that day.
    B. There were points in the race when Haller thought he couldn't possibly finish.
    C. No women raced this year, but that was soon to change.
    D. Haller's amazing physical strength had enabled him to do what no one else in the past had accomplished.

14. Which of the following alternatives to the underlined portion would be LEAST acceptable?

    F. The individuals
    G. That
    H. The athletes
    J. The people

> Question 15 asks about the preceding passage as a whole.

15. If the writer were to delete the final paragraph of this essay, the essay would primarily lose information that:

    A. discusses the level of interest the race attracts in the present day.
    B. describes the way the current race is different from the race that Haller ran in 1978.
    C. describes how the victors respond when they cross the finish line.
    D. explains why 1,500 people would be willing to compete in such a difficult race.

GO ON TO THE NEXT PAGE.

New Beginnings

[1]

As a junior in high school, I am very concerned about college. I'm trying to do everything right: <u>when I keep my</u>
₁₆
grades up, participate in a few extracurricular activities, prepare for standardized tests, even perform community service. I spend most days thinking about the <u>future hoping</u> that I'm on the right
₁₇
path, I do my best at everything I can.

[2]

[1] I'm interested in a career in <u>nursing,</u> I decided to try to
₁₈
secure a spot as a volunteer at the local hospital. [2] I accepted

his offer immediately, thinking to myself that here <u>lies</u> all the
₁₉
opportunities I could ever want! [3] It would be the best of both worlds: helping people while gaining valuable on-the-job experience! [4] So I put on a nice <u>pair of slacks, a blouse, and</u>
₂₀
some comfortable shoes—don't all nurses wear comfortable shoes?—and went to visit the business office. [5] Fortunately, the hospital director was quite willing to let me help out, and he said I could start that summer as soon as I finished my finals. ⬚₂₁

[3]

The director gave me a brief tour of various departments as he told me about the primary focus of each, <u>an expert himself</u>
₂₂
<u>in every facet of hospital administration</u>, until we stopped right
₂₂
in front of the maternity ward. "This is where you're going to work," he said, ushering me through the brown double doors.

16. **F.** NO CHANGE
G. I keep
H. I am keeping
J. I have kept

17. **A.** NO CHANGE
B. future, hoping
C. future. Hoping
D. future praying

18. **F.** NO CHANGE
G. nursing, therefore,
H. nursing, so
J. nursing, but

19. **A.** NO CHANGE
B. lays
C. lay
D. lie

20. **F.** NO CHANGE
G. pair, of slacks, a blouse,
H. pair, of slacks, a blouse
J. pair of slacks a blouse

21. For the sake of the logic and coherence of this paragraph, Sentence 2 should be placed:

A. where it is now.
B. after Sentence 3.
C. after Sentence 4.
D. after Sentence 5.

22. **F.** NO CHANGE
G. expert, himself in every facet of hospital administration,
H. expert, himself, in every facet of hospital administration
J. expert himself in every facet of hospital administration

GO ON TO THE NEXT PAGE.

Walking into the ward, my ears were immediately overwhelmed.
23
Women yelled and newborns wailed. Nurses rushed around to
23
adjust medical instruments that screamed for attention. I felt

suspicious in the center of so much action and wondered if I had
24
been too hasty in seeking out such a difficult service project.

[4]

Apparently my fear must have shown clearly on my

face as I looked around because the director said, "Don't worry.
25
You'll get used to the pace up here. You are going to help in the

nursery." With that, we walked down the busy hallway past
26
the numerous delivery rooms and into the most peaceful room
26
I've ever seen. The pastel colors provided a quiet backdrop to the

humming of machines and soft coos of sleeping infants. A

whispering nurse, the one in charge of the nursery, welcomed
27
me, thanked me for volunteering, and asked me to start folding

some baby blankets and placing it in the appropriate drawer. The
28
director gave me a questioning look, which I returned with a

quiet nod. ⬚29 I got right to work.

23. **A.** NO CHANGE
    B. my ears immediately felt overwhelmed, women
    C. I was overwhelmed by the sounds. Women
    D. hearing and overwhelmed. Women

24. Which choice would be most consistent with the figurative description provided elsewhere in this paragraph?
    F. NO CHANGE
    G. besieged
    H. weak
    J. defenseless

25. Which of the following alternatives to the underlined portion would be LEAST acceptable?
    A. face while
    B. face when
    C. face at the same time that
    D. face since

26. Given that all the choices are true, which one provides the most vivid description of the hospital hallway?
    F. NO CHANGE
    G. down a hallway filled with bright blue and pink balloons, beautiful flowers, and jubilant fathers
    H. past a nurses' station and a handful of expectant fathers
    J. under the yellowing ceiling of the dated hospital

27. **A.** NO CHANGE
    B. nurse the one in charge of the nursery,
    C. nurse the one in charge of the nursery
    D. nurse, the one in charge of the nursery

28. **F.** NO CHANGE
    G. place them
    H. placed them
    J. placing these

29. If the writer were to delete the phrase "which I returned with a quiet nod" from the preceding sentence and end the sentence with a period, the sentence would primarily lose:
    A. a detail that expresses the narrator's ease while in the nursery.
    B. a specific description of the narrator's anger toward the director.
    C. information that indicates the narrator will quit the hospital as soon as the director leaves.
    D. nothing at all, because this information had already been provided earlier in the passage.

GO ON TO THE NEXT PAGE.

Question 30 asks about the preceding passage as a whole.

30. Upon reviewing the essay and realizing that some key information has been left out, the writer composes the following sentence incorporating that information:

> Soon enough, I showed up for my first day at the hospital.

This sentence would most logically be placed before the first sentence in Paragraph:

F. 1.
G. 2.
H. 3.
J. 4.

PASSAGE III

Give a Snake a Break

Throughout much of history, snakes have had a reputation for being more deadly then they actually are. Negative associations abound: a "snake in the grass" is a seemingly innocent person intent on causing harm. 32 A "snake charmer" uses flattery to distract you from his shady intent. Nearly every reference to a snake that is popular in modern society bears this negative connotation. Despite this perception, the snake, with its ugly, slimy appearance, is one of the most unjustly maligned creatures on the planet.

31. A. NO CHANGE
B. a reputation for being more deadly than
C. a reputation as the most deadly than
D. the deadliest reputation then

32. Given that all the following statements are true, which one provides the most relevant information at this point in the essay?
F. "Snake oil" refers to fake medicine that promises impossible results.
G. Most snakes are passive creatures that will never cause you injury.
H. Snakes are carnivorous reptiles that can be found on every continent except Antarctica.
J. Pet snakes have becomes increasingly common over the last decade.

33. A. NO CHANGE
B. reference that is popular about a snake
C. famous reference they have about a snake
D. popular reference to a snake

34. F. NO CHANGE
G. who's
H. sporting it's
J. with its'

GO ON TO THE NEXT PAGE.

Snakes are only rarely dangerous to humans. Their fangs, so
<u>   </u>
                                                          35
intimidating when the snakes are hissing, are designed not to

attack people but to hold small prey; small rodents, birds, insects,
<u>   </u>
                               36
etc. Only exceptionally large snakes, like pythons or anacondas,

pose a real threat. Most of the time, the typical snake you

encounter in your backyard is more afraid of you than you are of

it and will gladly avoid any contact with you.

Poisonous snakes—such as rattlesnakes, vipers, and

cobras—are most frightening to people, but <u>they attack if they</u>
                                                              37
<u>are only provoked.</u> While certainly venomous, these snakes pose
       37
a threat mainly to smaller animals. Of the 5 million snake bites

that occur each year to humans around the world, only about

2.5 percent prove fatal. ☐38 Prompt treatment with one of the

available antivenoms <u>do much</u> to ensure the victim's survival.
                         39
Although you may get an infection at the wound site, you can be

effectively treated, <u>seeing as</u> you are still shaken from the
                        40
encounter, you will survive.

Why put up with snakes at all? Even if they don't normally

kill humans, most people still <u>considering them a nuisance and</u>
                                                     41
<u>avoiding</u> them like the plague. Individuals who dislike snakes for
   41
this reason do not appreciate the great service snakes do for

humanity. The typical diet of a snake includes small rodents like

rats, mice, gophers, and prairie dogs, as well as lizards, birds,

fish, and insects. We may not like <u>snakes, if they</u> were
                                        42
mysteriously wiped out of existence, however, we would be

virtually overrun with other vermin that would spread disease and

filth.

---

35. **A.** NO CHANGE
  B. fangs being
  C. fangs, so they are
  D. fangs, they are

36. **F.** NO CHANGE
  G. prey,
  H. prey:
  J. prey

37. **A.** NO CHANGE
  B. they will provoke and attack them.
  C. they will attack humans only if provoked.
  D. if provoked, they will attack them.

38. The writer is considering deleting the preceding sentence from this paragraph. If the writer made this deletion, the paragraph would primarily lose:
  F. scientific proof that snakes are too dangerous to coexist with humans.
  G. an example of the various locations where most fatalities take place.
  H. a specific statistic to support a previous claim.
  J. excessive detail that distracts the reader from the broader message of the passage.

39. **A.** NO CHANGE
  B. can do much
  C. are able to do much
  D. have much ability

40. **F.** NO CHANGE
  G. but because
  H. and even if
  J. however

41. **A.** NO CHANGE
  B. consider them a nuisance and avoid
  C. considering them a nuisance and avoid
  D. considered them a nuisance to avoid

42. **F.** NO CHANGE
  G. snake's if they
  H. snakes, they
  J. snakes; if they

GO ON TO THE NEXT PAGE.

So, next time you hear about someone putting down snakes, stand up for our legless friends. These snakes in the grass help us more than we might think.
₄₃

43. The writer wants to provide a sentence here that will tie the conclusion of the essay to its beginning. Which choice does that best?

    A. NO CHANGE
    B. Snakes make excellent pets.
    C. Let's reduce the incidence of snake bites around the world.
    D. Wouldn't you rather see a snake in your yard than a rat?

Questions 44 and 45 ask about the preceding passage as a whole.

---

44. The writer is considering deleting the last sentence of the first paragraph of the essay. If the writer were to make this deletion, the essay would primarily lose a statement that:

    F. adds a bit of sarcasm to a rather humorous introduction.
    G. identifies the overall point of the entire passage.
    H. summarizes the list of examples previously provided by the author.
    J. provides a list of animals more useful than the snake.

45. Suppose the writer's goal had been to write an essay focusing on the various ways in which humans were threatened by snakes. Would this essay fulfill that goal?

    A. Yes, because the author gives specific statistical evidence that proves snake bites happen around the world.
    B. Yes, because the essay focuses on many of the negative stereotypes associated with snakes.
    C. No, because the essay primarily focuses on the fact that snakes are not harmful to humans.
    D. No, because the essay points out that snakes feed primarily on rodents and other small animals.

PASSAGE IV

Zora Neale Hurston, Independent Woman

Zora Neale Hurston proves to be a study in contrasts: a black writer reaching a white audience, a woman struggling in a man's profession, an independent thinker living in a conformist era. Now, almost 50 years since her death, her hard work and
₄₆
fabulous novels still have much to teach the modern audience.

46. Which of the following alternatives to the underlined portion would be LEAST acceptable?

    F. Presently,
    G. Currently,
    H. Instantly,
    J. At the present,

She overcame the challenges she faced and demonstrated that
₄₇
perseverance makes anything possible.

47. Which of the following alternatives to the underlined portion would be LEAST acceptable?

    A. faced, and in so doing,
    B. faced and, thus,
    C. faced that
    D. faced, an action that

GO ON TO THE NEXT PAGE.

Hurston ascribed much of her deeply individualistic
personality to the experience of growing up in Eatonville,

Florida. The town was unique in that it was particularly hot in
the summer, but mild at other times of the year. Hurston always
said growing up in a community totally separate from the larger

white society allowed her a freedom that independence not
available to everyone in the south.

[1] Hurston began her undergraduate studies at Howard
University, but her obvious intelligence and talent soon earned
her a scholarship to Barnard College in New York City. [2]

Moving north in the 1920s thrust her into the midst of the
Harlem Renaissance, a black cultural movement that spawned

exceptional achievements in literature, books, poems, and plays,
art, and music. [3] Interacting with the likes of Langston
Hughes, W.E.B. DuBois, Billie Holiday, and Duke Ellington,

Hurston developed her skills as a writer and published numerous

short stories and poems. 55 [4] The most influential work that
came to define her career grew out of her attempt to capture the
black experience. [5] That novel, called *Their Eyes Were
Watching God*, traced three generations of a family living in

48. **F.** NO CHANGE
    G. personally individualistic
    H. freely independent
    J. truly egotistical

49. Given that all the choices are true, which one most effectively
    identifies why Eatonville has a history unlike any other city
    in the United States?

    A. NO CHANGE
    B. a fairly representative small town, founded in the mid-
    nineteenth century.
    C. the first all-black town to be incorporated in the country.
    D. not yet in existence at the start of the Civil War.

50. **F.** NO CHANGE
    G. and was
    H. it featured
    J. and

51. **A.** NO CHANGE
    B. intelligence, and talent
    C. intelligence, and talent,
    D. intelligence and talent,

52. **F.** NO CHANGE
    G. 1920s, thrust
    H. 1920s, thrust,
    J. 1920s; thrust

53. **A.** NO CHANGE
    B. literature, written records of stories once transmitted orally,
    C. literature, which includes all forms of written expression,
    D. literature,

54. **F.** NO CHANGE
    G. developed up
    H. develops up
    J. develops

55. At this point, the writer is considering adding the following
    true statement:

    > Billie Holiday's music evokes such feeling and melan-
    > choly that it's no wonder she became so popular.

    Should the writer add this sentence here?

    A. Yes, because it provides an interesting detail about one of
    the other Harlem Renaissance artists.
    B. Yes, because music was an important influence on Hur-
    ston's work.
    C. No, because it doesn't clearly identify which of Billie
    Holiday's songs were popular.
    D. No, because it distracts the reader from the main point of
    this paragraph.

GO ON TO THE NEXT PAGE.

Eatonville. [6] Her interesting representation of the southern
_____
56
dialect caused her Harlem Renaissance contemporaries to belittle

the work for what they saw as its propagation of inaccurate

stereotypes. [7] Hurston, however, remained true to it, convinced
_____
57
that the accuracy of her representation would ultimately prevail over

the political pressures her peers sought to inflict upon her. ⬚58

History has shown that Hurston was right. However, modern
_____
59
critics admire her authentic and skillful representation of the

language as well as her realistic portrayal of daily life in the

early twentieth century. She is universally applauded, as one of
_____
60
the best writers of her era, ranked with Toni Morrison, Maya
_____
60
Angelou, and Alice Walker as one of the most important African-

American writers of all time.

PASSAGE V

Jimmy Carter, Humanitarian

[1]

Everyone has heard of Jimmy Carter. As president of the

United States from 1977 to 1981. He oversaw a particularly
_____
61
turbulent time in American history. Americans taken hostage in

the Middle East, serious inflation woes, major gasoline shortages

around the country, and a tenuous relationship with a potential

56. Which choice would most clearly indicate that the dialect referenced in the passage was a realistic representation of the actual way language was spoken in Eatonville?

   F. NO CHANGE
   G. unusual
   H. authentic
   J. fascinating

57. A. NO CHANGE
   B. her project,
   C. that thing,
   D. which,

58. The writer has decided to divide this paragraph into two. The best place to add the new paragraph break would be at the beginning of Sentence:

   F. 4, because it would indicate that Hurston's writing was most strongly influenced by Langston Hughes.
   G. 4, because it would signal the essay's shift in focus to one of Hurston's novels.
   H. 5, because all the remaining sentences in the paragraph provide a detailed summary of the plot of Hurston's novel.
   J. 5, because it would indicate that the essay is now going to focus on social conditions in Eatonville.

59. A. NO CHANGE
   B. Modern
   C. Thus, modern
   D. In addition, modern

60. F. NO CHANGE
   G. applauded as one of the best writers of her era and
   H. applauded as one of the best writers of her era
   J. applauded, as one of the best writers of her era, she is

61. A. NO CHANGE
   B. 1981 but he
   C. 1981, and he
   D. 1981, he

GO ON TO THE NEXT PAGE.

enemy—the Soviet Union—are hardly the stuff of pleasant
memories.
62

[2]

Yet even though Carter held Americas most, powerful office,
63

he will probably be remembered more for the work he has done
64

since he left the White House. His record on humanitarian issues

around the world sets him apart as a caring, dedicated person

who wants to see the underprivileged, those of low economic
65

or social status, benefit from the great wealth, power, and
65

generosity of this country.

[3]

One of the major issues Carter has focused on throughout his

career is peace in the Middle East. He questioned a national
66

energy policy designed to reduce American dependence long

before it was popular to do so on foreign oil and brokered a
67

peace treaty between Israel and Egypt. Likewise, he was among

the first to insist publicly on basic human rights for everyone

around the world, founding a non-profit organization, The Carter
68

Center, to work toward that end. In his opinion, this includes

extending modern health care to developing nations in order to

contain disease and improve quality of life around the world, in
69

many different countries.
69

62. F. NO CHANGE
G. enemy the Soviet Union—
H. enemy the Soviet Union
J. enemy—the Soviet Union

63. A. NO CHANGE
B. held America's most,
C. held America's most
D. held Americas, most

64. F. NO CHANGE
G. himself
H. him
J. itself

65. A. NO CHANGE
B. underprivileged, who may not have many resources,
C. underprivileged
D. underprivileged, who have less than others in society,

66. F. NO CHANGE
G. promoted
H. purchased
J. rejected

67. The best placement for the underlined portion would be:
A. where it is now.
B. after the word *designed*.
C. after the word *dependence*.
D. after the word *was*.

68. Which of the following alternatives to the underlined portion would NOT be acceptable?
F. world, and he found
G. world, and he founded
H. world, so he founded
J. world and founded

69. A. NO CHANGE
B. world.
C. world, both east and west of the United States.
D. world, including countries on every continent except Antarctica.

GO ON TO THE NEXT PAGE.

[4]

[1] Carter works actively to improve the standard of living at home here in the United States as well. [2] He and his wife Roslyn are enthusiastic supporters of Habitat for Humanity. [3] This volunteer-based organization devotes itself to building affordable but quality housing for those who otherwise might not be able to buy a home. [4] However, Carter does not focus abroad all his efforts. [5] Community workers come together on their own free time to construct, paint, and landscape simple homes, working side-by-side with the families that will occupy the residences. ▣ 72

[5]

For all these reasons, Carter deserves respect for dedicating his career to public service. Everyone can agree for his impressive philanthropy and acknowledge his obvious devotion to all of humanity.

70. F.   NO CHANGE
    G.   at home, not just abroad,
    H.   at home, within the area over which he was president,
    J.   at home,

71. A.   NO CHANGE
    B.   focus all his efforts abroad.
    C.   focus all abroad his efforts.
    D.   focus all his abroad efforts.

72. For the sake of the logic and coherence of this paragraph, Sentence 4 should be placed:
    F.   where it is now.
    G.   before Sentence 1.
    H.   after Sentence 2.
    J.   after Sentence 5.

73. A.   NO CHANGE
    B.   agree to
    C.   agree by
    D.   agree with

74. Which choice would best help this sentence to summarize key points made in the essay?
    F.   NO CHANGE
    G.   he should have been president for a second term.
    H.   he has the right to express his opinions as much as any other American.
    J.   he clearly didn't want the hostages to be harmed.

Question 75 asks about the preceding passage as a whole.

75. Upon reviewing notes for this essay, the writer comes across the following true statement:

    Habitat does more than build houses: it builds communities.

    If the writer were to use this sentence, the most logical place to add it would be at the end of Paragraph:

    A.   1
    B.   2
    C.   3
    D.   4

END OF TEST 1
STOP! DO NOT TURN THE PAGE UNTIL TOLD TO DO SO.

MATHEMATICS TEST
60 Minutes—60 Questions

DIRECTIONS: Solve each problem, choose the correct answer, and then darken the corresponding oval on your answer sheet.

Do not linger over problems that take too much time. Solve as many as you can; then return to the others in the time you have left for this test.

You are permitted to use a calculator on this test. You may use your calculator for any problems you choose, but some of the problems may best be done without using a calculator.

Note: Unless otherwise stated, all of the following should be assumed:

1. Illustrative figures are NOT necessarily drawn to scale.
2. Geometric figures lie in a plane.
3. The word *line* indicates a straight line.
4. The word *average* indicates arithmetic mean.

---

1. On a level field, a telephone pole 24 feet tall casts a shadow 6 feet long, and at the same time of day, another nearby telephone pole casts a shadow 18 feet long. How many feet tall is the second telephone pole?

   A.   6
   B.   12
   C.   24
   D.   36
   E.   72

2. The membership fees for WebFilms consist of a monthly charge of $14 and a one-time new-member fee of $16. Sherwood made a credit card payment of $100 to pay his WebFilms fees for a certain number of months, including the new-member fee. How many months of membership did Sherwood include in his credit card payment?

   F.   4
   G.   6
   H.   7
   J.   12
   K.   14

3. If $y = -6$, what is the value of $\dfrac{y^2 - 4}{y - 2}$?

   A.   −8
   B.   −4
   C.   4
   D.   9
   E.   28

DO YOUR FIGURING HERE.

GO ON TO THE NEXT PAGE.

4. A school offered its students an optional field trip. If 15 or fewer students went on the field trip, the charge for each student would be $11.50. If more than 15 students chose to go on the field trip, the charge for each student would be $10.25. 18 students opted to go on the tour, but each pre-paid $11.50. The students agreed to put the extra amount toward dinner on the trip. How much total money will be put toward dinner on the trip?

- **F.** $12.50
- **G.** $14.75
- **H.** $21.75
- **J.** $22.50
- **K.** $33.00

DO YOUR FIGURING HERE.

5. A 16-piece orchestra wants to choose one of its members to speak at performances. They decide that this member CANNOT be one of the 4 soloists in the group. What is the probability that Itzhak, who is NOT a soloist, will be chosen as the speaker?

- **A.** 0
- **B.** $\dfrac{1}{16}$
- **C.** $\dfrac{1}{12}$
- **D.** $\dfrac{1}{4}$
- **E.** $\dfrac{1}{3}$

6. What is the perimeter, in feet, of a rectangle with width 8 feet and length 17 feet?

- **F.** 25
- **G.** 34
- **H.** 50
- **J.** 136
- **K.** 272

7. Passes to the Renaissance Faire cost $9 when purchased online and $12 when purchased in person. The group sponsoring the fair would like to make at least $4,000 from sales of passes. If 240 passes were sold online, what is the minimum number of tickets that must be sold in person in order for the group to meet its goal?

- **A.** 153
- **B.** 154
- **C.** 290
- **D.** 334
- **E.** 445

GO ON TO THE NEXT PAGE.

8. For what value of q is the equation $\dfrac{9}{q} = \dfrac{6}{10}$ true?

   F. 3
   G. 5
   H. 13
   J. 15
   K. 19

9. If $-9(y - 13) = 16$, then $y = ?$

   A. $-\dfrac{133}{9}$

   B. $-\dfrac{29}{9}$

   C. $-\dfrac{16}{9}$

   D. $-\dfrac{1}{3}$

   E. $\dfrac{101}{9}$

10. In the figure below, F, G, H, and J are collinear. $\overline{FG}$, $\overline{GK}$, and $\overline{HK}$ are line segments of equivalent length, and the measure of $\angle JHK$ is 120°. What is the degree measure of $\angle GFK$?

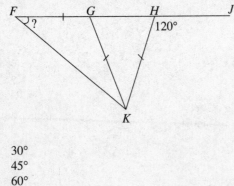

   F. 30°
   G. 45°
   H. 60°
   J. 120°
   K. 150°

11. If $f(x) = 7x^2 - 9x + 4$, then $f(-3) = ?$

   A. −32
   B. −2
   C. 32
   D. 40
   E. 94

GO ON TO THE NEXT PAGE.

12. What is the least common multiple of 25, 16, and 40 ?

    F.   27

    G.   32

    H.   320

    J.   400

    K. 16,000

DO YOUR FIGURING HERE.

13. While working on a problem on his calculator, Tex had meant to multiply a number by 3, but he accidentally divided the number by 3. Which of the following calculations could Tex then do to the result on the screen in order to obtain the result he originally wanted?

    A. Multiply by 3

    B. Multiply by 9

    C. Divide by 3

    D. Divide by 9

    E. Add the original number

14. The 8-sided figure below is divided into 12 congruent isosceles right triangles. The total area of the 12 triangles is 96 square centimeters. What is the perimeter, in centimeters, of the figure?

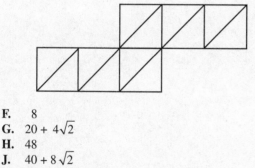

    F.   8

    G. $20 + 4\sqrt{2}$

    H. 48

    J. $40 + 8\sqrt{2}$

    K. 56

15. In $\triangle XYZ$, $\angle Y$ is a right angle and $\angle Z$ measures less than 52°. Which of the following phrases best describes the measure of $\angle X$?

    A. Greater than 38°

    B. Equal to 38°

    C. Equal to 45°

    D. Equal to 142°

    E. Less than 38°

GO ON TO THE NEXT PAGE.

16. Among the following arithmetic operations, which could the emoticon ☺ represent given that the equation $(8 ☺ 2)^3 - (4 ☺ 1)^2 = 48$ is true?

    I. Subtraction
    II. Multiplication
    III. Division

    F. I only
    G. III only
    H. II and III only
    J. I and III only
    K. I, II, and III

17. Which of the following equations represents the linear relation shown in the standard (x,y) coordinate plane below?

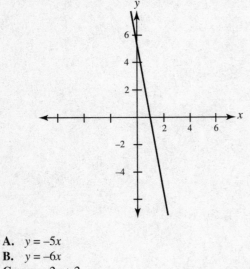

    A. $y = -5x$
    B. $y = -6x$
    C. $y = -2x + 2$
    D. $y = -5x + 6$
    E. $y = -2x + 6$

18. An integer, x, is subtracted from 6. That difference is then multiplied by 3. This product is 15 more than half the original integer. Which of the following equations represents this relationship?

    F. $3(6 - x) = \dfrac{x}{2} + 15$

    G. $3(6 - x) + 15 = \dfrac{x}{2}$

    H. $3(6 - x) = 15 - \dfrac{x}{2}$

    J. $x - 6 \times 3 = \dfrac{15}{2}$

    K. $6 + 3 = \dfrac{x}{2} + 15$

GO ON TO THE NEXT PAGE.

19. The employees of two factories, X and Y, are comparing their respective production records. Factory X has already produced 18,000 units and can produce 120 units per day. Factory Y has produced only 14,500 units but can produce 155 units per day. If *d* represents the number of days (that is, days during which each factory is producing its maximum number of units), which of the following equations could be solved to determine the number of days until X's total production equals Y's total production?

A. $18{,}000 + 120d = 14{,}500 + 155d$
B. $18{,}000 + 155d = 14{,}500 + 120d$
C. $(18{,}000 + 120)d = (14{,}500 + 155)d$
D. $(120 + 155)d = 18{,}000 - 14{,}500$
E. $(120 + 155)d = 18{,}000 + 14{,}500$

DO YOUR FIGURING HERE.

20. A ramp used to access the side entrance to the DPC Candy Store, which is located 7 meters above the ground, covers 24 meters along the level ground from the edge of the building. How many meters long is the ramp?

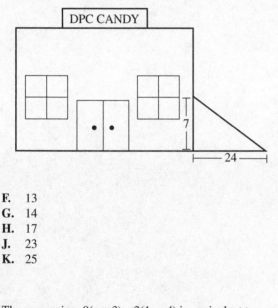

F. 13
G. 14
H. 17
J. 23
K. 25

21. The expression $9(y + 3) - 2(4y - 4)$ is equivalent to:

A. $y - 1$
B. $y + 15$
C. $y + 18$
D. $y + 23$
E. $y + 35$

22. If $a + 3b = 27$ and $a - 3b = 9$, then $b = ?$

F. 3
G. 9
H. 14
J. 18
K. 36

GO ON TO THE NEXT PAGE.

23. When $(2x + 4)^2$ is written in the format $ax^2 + bx + c$, where a, b, and c are integers, what is the value of $a + b - c$?

A. −20
B. 4
C. 20
D. 32
E. 36

DO YOUR FIGURING HERE.

24. What is the area, in square meters, of the figure below?

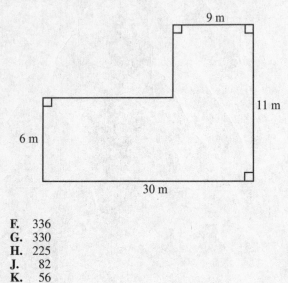

9 m

11 m

6 m

30 m

F. 336
G. 330
H. 225
J. 82
K. 56

25. The table below gives the values of two functions, g and h, for various values of x. One of the functions expresses a relationship that can be expressed by the formula $a + bx$, where a and b are real number coefficients. What is the value of that function for $x = 0$?

x	$g(x)$	$h(x)$
−3	4	
−2	2	3
−1	1	6
0		
1	1	
2		15
3		18

A. 0
B. 0.5
C. 1
D. 2
E. 9

GO ON TO THE NEXT PAGE.

26. What is the slope of the line represented by the equation $10y - 16x = 13$?

F. -16

G. $\dfrac{13}{10}$

H. $\dfrac{8}{5}$

J. 10

K. 16

27. What is the sum of the 2 solutions of the equation $x^2 + 5x - 24 = 0$?

A. -24
B. -8
C. -5
D. 0
E. 5

28. Two similar triangles have perimeters in the ratio 5:6. The sides of the larger triangle measure 12 in, 7 in, and 5 in. What is the perimeter, in inches, of the smaller triangle?

F. 18
G. 20
H. 22
J. 24
K. 32

29. In early November in Winnipeg, Manitoba, the temperatures for each of nine consecutive days were $-9°C$, $3°C$, $-7°C$, $2°C$, $5°C$, $1°C$, $0°C$, $-8°C$, and $-7°C$. What was the median of the temperatures for these nine days in early November?

A. $-7°C$
B. $0°C$
C. $1.5°C$
D. $3°C$
E. $5°C$

GO ON TO THE NEXT PAGE.

30. When asked the price, in dollars, of his fancy calculator, Albert responded, "If you take the square root of the price, then add $\frac{3}{8}$ the price, the result is 66." What is the price, in dollars, of Albert's calculator?

F. 169
G. 144
H. 121
J. 13
K. 12

31. The kinetic energy, KE, of an object travelling at v velocity can be modeled by the equation $KE = \frac{1}{2}mv^2$, where m is the mass of the object. If an object is moving at a velocity of 9, and it has a kinetic energy of 120, about how great is the object's mass?

A. Between 0 and 1
B. Between 1 and 2
C. Between 2 and 3
D. 6
E. 13

32. Let x, y, and z be distinct positive integers. What is the fourth term of the geometric sequence below?

$$2xz, 2x^2yz, 2x^3y^2z, \ldots$$

F. $2x^2yz$
G. $2x^4y^3z$
H. $2x^3yz^2$
J. $4x^3y^2z$
K. $4x^4y^3z^2$

GO ON TO THE NEXT PAGE.

DO YOUR FIGURING HERE.

Use the following information to answer questions 33–35.

A recent survey of book critics asked 30 critics how many stars out of a possible 5 they gave to a recent novel from a popular author. The 30 critics' responses are summarized by the histogram below.

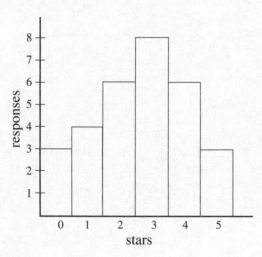

33. What fraction of the critics gave the book a one-star review?

    A. $\dfrac{1}{2}$

    B. $\dfrac{3}{8}$

    C. $\dfrac{17}{50}$

    D. $\dfrac{3}{10}$

    E. $\dfrac{2}{15}$

34. The group that took the survey wants to show the data in a circle graph (pie chart). What should be the measure of the central angle of the portion for one-star reviews?

    F. 15°
    G. 24°
    H. 30°
    J. 48°
    K. 60°

GO ON TO THE NEXT PAGE.

35. To the nearest hundredth, what is the average star review for the 30 reviews?

- **A.** 2.00
- **B.** 2.33
- **C.** 2.50
- **D.** 2.63
- **E.** 3.00

---

36. For all $x > 8$, $\dfrac{(x^2+7x+12)(x-2)}{(x^2+2x-8)(x+3)} = ?$

- **F.** $\dfrac{-3(x-2)}{(x+3)}$

- **G.** $\dfrac{-2(x-2)}{(x+3)}$

- **H.** $\dfrac{(x-2)}{(x+2)}$

- **J.** $\dfrac{11}{4}$

- **K.** 1

37. A rock band, The Young Sohcahtoans, is trying to design a t-shirt logo. The measurements they have chosen are represented on the figure below. The angle to the right of the logo "TYS" has a degree measure of 35°, and the side of the figure has a measure of 10 in. Which of the following expressions gives the measure, in inches, of the diagonal top side of the figure?

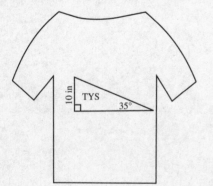

- **A.** $10 \tan 35°$

- **B.** $10 \cos 35°$

- **C.** $10 \sin 35°$

- **D.** $\dfrac{10}{\sin 35°}$

- **E.** $\dfrac{10}{\cos 35°}$

GO ON TO THE NEXT PAGE.

DO YOUR FIGURING HERE.

38. The endpoints of the diameter of a circle O are A and C. In the standard (x,y) coordinate plane, A is at $(4,3)$ and C is at $(-9,-2)$. What is the y-coordinate of the center of the circle?

F. -5

G. $-\dfrac{5}{2}$

H. $\dfrac{1}{2}$

J. 1

K. 2

39. On a sonar map in the standard (x,y) coordinate plane, the Yellow Submarine and the Sandwich Submarine are located at the points $(-7,4)$ and $(-2,6)$, respectively. Each unit on the map represents an actual distance of 5 nautical miles. Which of the following is closest to the distance, in nautical miles, between the two submarines?

A. 5
B. 19
C. 27
D. 30
E. 67

40. All of the following statements about rational and/or irrational numbers must be true EXCEPT:

F. the sum of any two rational numbers is rational.
G. the product of any two rational numbers is rational.
H. the sum of any two irrational numbers is irrational.
J. the product of a rational and an irrational number may be rational or irrational.
K. the product of any two irrational numbers is irrational.

41. For the imaginary number i, which of the following is a possible value of i^n if n is an integer less than 5 ?

A. 0
B. -1
C. -2
D. -3
E. -4

GO ON TO THE NEXT PAGE.

42. The table below gives the values of $f(x)$ for selected values of x in the function $f(x) = (x + 4)^2 - 1$, where x and y are both real numbers.

x	$f(x)$
−7	8
−5	0
−3	0
−1	8
0	15
1	24

For the equation above, which of the following values of x gives the greatest value of $f(x)$?

F. −4
G. −5
H. −6
J. −7
K. −8

43. The volume of the right circular cylinder shown below is 64π cubic inches. If its height is 4 in., what is its radius in inches?

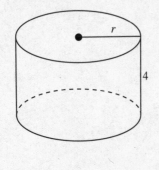

A. 2
B. 4
C. 8
D. 10
E. 16

GO ON TO THE NEXT PAGE.

DO YOUR FIGURING HERE.

44. Line segments $\overline{GH}$, $\overline{JK}$, and $\overline{LM}$ are parallel and intersect line segments $\overline{FL}$ and $\overline{FM}$ as shown in the figure below. The ratio of the perimeter of $\triangle FJK$ to the perimeter of $\triangle FLM$ is 3:5, and the ratio of $\overline{FH}$ to $\overline{FM}$ is 1:5. What is the ratio of $\overline{GJ}$ to $\overline{FG}$?

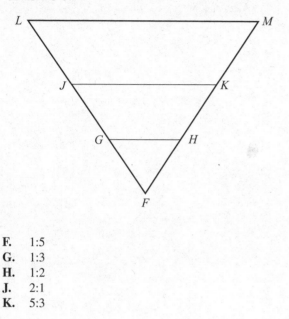

F. 1:5
G. 1:3
H. 1:2
J. 2:1
K. 5:3

45. Avi is trying to draw a map of his most recent bike ride. He chose to place Market Street on the x-axis and Broad Street on the y-axis. He rode 60 m at an angle of 60° relative to Market Street, then rode 100 m at an angle of 45° relative to Market Street, and finally rode 35 m directly north on Broad Street. How many meters north of Market Street did Avi ride?

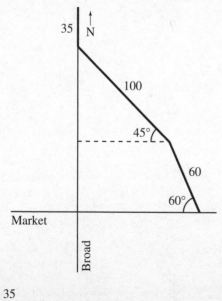

A. 35
B. 115
C. 195
D. $50\sqrt{2} + 30\sqrt{3}$
E. $35 + 50\sqrt{2} + 30\sqrt{3}$

GO ON TO THE NEXT PAGE.

46. In the standard (x,y) coordinate plane, what is the area of the circle $(x - 3)^2 + (y + 2)^2 = 25$?

    F. 5π
    G. 10π
    H. 25π
    J. 125π
    K. 225π

47. In the standard (x,y) coordinate plane below, the base of a right triangle lies along the x-axis and is bisected by the y-axis. The vertex of the angle opposite the base is on the graph of the parabolic function $f(x) = 2x^2 - 4$. Let b represent any value of x such that $-\sqrt{2} < x < 0$. Which of the following is an expression in terms of b for the area, in square coordinate units, of any such right triangle?

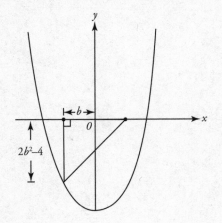

    A. $4b^4 - 16b^2 + 16$
    B. $4b^3 - 8b$
    C. $2b^3 - 4b$
    D. $2b^2 + b - 4$
    E. $b^2 - 4b + 4$

48. Which of the following expressions must be an even integer if x is an integer?

    F. $x + 5$

    G. $\dfrac{x}{4}$

    H. x^4

    J. $4x$

    K. 5^x

49. Which of the following ranges of consecutive integers contains the value of the expression $\log_9(9^{\frac{7}{3}})$?

    A. 0 and 1
    B. 1 and 2
    C. 2 and 3
    D. 5 and 6
    E. 7 and 8

GO ON TO THE NEXT PAGE.

Use the following information to answer questions 50–52.

The employees at Belinda's Paint Store are having a competition to see who can create the most new accounts over a period from January to June in a certain year. Data is missing because one of the employees began to erase it from the white board, thinking that the competition was over. The numbers in the chart below have been confirmed with the assistant manager's personal records.

Employee	Jan.	Feb.	Mar.	Apr.	May	June
			Month			
Don	64					
Maura	31	25		27	29	24
Cameron	23	19	22	17	20	22
Belinda	78	92	83	86		90

50. Which of the following is closest to the percent decrease in Cameron's new accounts from January to February?

F. 4.0%
G. 17.4%
H. 19.4%
J. 20.0%
K. 21.1%

51. At the beginning of the year, Maura wanted to average 30 new accounts per month for the first four months of the year. How many new accounts did she need to create in March in order to reach this goal?

A. 25
B. 27
C. 29
D. 31
E. 37

52. Additional records are uncovered that show that Don's sales decreased 5% each month from January to May because his responsibilities in the store mounted and he could not seek out new accounts as frequently. Which of the following is closest to the number of new accounts Don created in May?

F. 44
G. 52
H. 56
J. 72
K. 84

GO ON TO THE NEXT PAGE.

53. The amplitude of the trigonometric function shown below is defined as the average of the absolute values of the maximum value of $f(x)$ and the minimum value of $f(x)$. The trigonometric function graphed below can be described by the equation $f(x) = a \sin(bx + c)$, where a, b, and c are real numbers. Which of the following values describes the amplitude of this function?

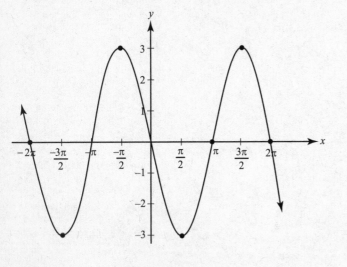

A. 1
B. 2
C. 3
D. π
E. 2π

54. A group of die-hard baseball fans has purchased a house that gives them a direct view of home plate, although their view of the rest of the field is largely impeded by the outfield wall. The house is 30 meters tall, and their angle of vision from the top of the building to home plate has a tangent of $\frac{7}{6}$. What is the horizontal distance, in meters, from home plate to the closest wall of the fans' house?

DO YOUR FIGURING HERE.

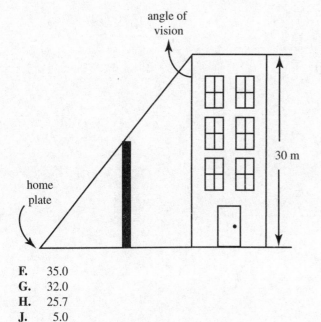

F.   35.0
G.   32.0
H.   25.7
J.   5.0
K.   4.3

55. Given the equation $|y^2 - 11| - 2 = 0$, which of the following is a solution but NOT a rational number?

A. $11\sqrt{13}$

B. $4\sqrt{13}$

C. $2\sqrt{13}$

D. $\sqrt{13}$

E.   3

GO ON TO THE NEXT PAGE.

56. Below is the graph that a specialty automobile manufacturer uses to plot the speed tests done on his new cars. The speed is recorded in units of $\frac{m}{s}$ and is conducted for a period of 9 seconds. A certain order of 3 of the following 6 actions describes the results of the speed test depicted in the graph below. Which order is it?

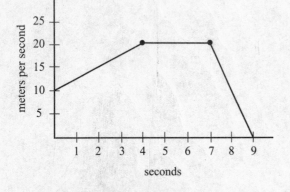

    I. Constant speed for 1 second
    II. Constant speed for 3 seconds
    III. Speed increase for 4 seconds
    IV. Speed increase for 9 seconds
    V. Speed decrease for 2 seconds
    VI. Speed decrease for 7 seconds

F. IV, II, VI
G. III, II, V
H. I, III, V
J. III, I, VI
K. V, I, II

57. As shown in the figure below, a compass has marks for every 10° and "North" and "South" are the endpoints of a line segment. If the point of the needle of this compass travels 42 mm as it moves in a clockwise direction from "East" to "North," how long is the needle to the nearest tenth of a millimeter?

A. 6.7
B. 8.9
C. 13.4
D. 14.0
E. 17.8

GO ON TO THE NEXT PAGE.

58. For θ, an angle whose measure is between 270° and 360°, $\cos\theta = \dfrac{5}{13}$. Which of the following equals tan θ ?

F. $-\dfrac{5}{12}$

G. $-\dfrac{5}{13}$

H. $\dfrac{5}{13}$

J. $\dfrac{5}{12}$

K. $\dfrac{12}{13}$

59. Consider all positive integer values a and b such that the product $ab = 8$. For how many values does there exist a positive integer c that satisfies both $2^a = c$ and $c^b = 256$?

A. Infinitely many
B. 6
C. 4
D. 2
E. 0

60. A sphere is inscribed in a cube with a diagonal of $3\sqrt{3}$ ft. In feet, what is the diameter of the sphere?

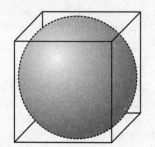

F. $3\sqrt{2}$

G. 2

H. $2\sqrt{2}$

J. 3

K. $3\sqrt{3}$

END OF TEST 2

STOP! DO NOT TURN THE PAGE UNTIL TOLD TO DO SO.

DO NOT RETURN TO A PREVIOUS TEST.

READING TEST

35 Minutes—40 Questions

DIRECTIONS: There are four passages in this test. Each passage is followed by several questions. After reading a passage, choose the best answer to each question and fill in the corresponding oval on your answer document. You may refer to the passages as often as necessary.

Passage I

PROSE FICTION: This passage is adapted from the novel *A Well-Worn Jacket* by Antonia Duke (© 2008 by Antonia Duke).

Monique was enjoying this afternoon more than she had anticipated. Often, the tryouts for the spring musical tested the limits of her patience and nerves, with one hopeful girl after the next taking turns strutting onto the tarnished wooden stage,
5 delivering a competent but uninspired version of some Rodgers & Hammerstein number, and then being politely excused by Mrs. Dominguez as the next name on the list was called.

However, this was to be Monique's third straight year in the musical, and the confidence that her seniority afforded her
10 around the more nervous newcomers allowed her to bask in the radiance of her own poise.

She had already sung her audition song an hour ago, commencing the day's ceremonies. This year, Monique used "God Bless the Child," a choice she found to be quite sophisticated
15 since Billie Holiday's version of it was familiar mostly to adults, and even then, mostly to adults of the previous generation. More importantly, it required a reserved performance, which Monique felt showcased her maturity, especially because most of the other auditioners chose songs that would show their enthusiasm, even
20 if it meant their technical mastery would not be on full display.

Normally, the first audition slot was dreaded by most. Mrs. Dominguez would ask if anyone wanted to volunteer to "get it over with," but no one would make a sound. Then, she would call the first name off her list and the room would drop into an
25 uncomfortably solemn silence as the first student walked nervously up to the stage. Monique often imagined during those moments that she was witness to a death-row inmate taking his inexorable march toward a quick curtain.

But not this year. Monique had decided to make a show
30 of her own self-confidence by volunteering to go first. Such a defiantly fearless act, she had figured, would probably instill even more fear into her competition because they would realize that Monique had something they clearly lacked. Mrs. Dominguez had seemed neither surprised nor charmed by Monique's
35 decision to go first. Although she was annoyed by Monique's escalating arrogance, she also acknowledged that Monique was one of the more talented actors and was probably correct in assuming herself a shoo-in.

At this late stage of the afternoon, Monique felt like a mon-
40 arch, sitting in the back of the auditorium with her royal court of friends and admirers. They took care to sit far enough away from Mrs. Dominguez that they would not be caught in the act of belittling the other students' auditions.

To Monique, the endless parade of aspirants who sang their
45 hearts out for three minutes each were like jesters performing for her amusement. As Mrs. Dominguez read Esperanza Solito's name off her list, Monique and her entourage prepared themselves for a special treat.

Esperanza was one of the most awkward students at Thorn-
50 ton High. Her caramel-colored face was usually hidden behind thick tortoise shell glasses. Her wavy black hair exploded off her scalp like a snapshot of an atom bomb. She wore clothing that looked like it had spent years in a musty attic. Understanding her debased position on the social totem pole, Esperanza scur-
55 ried through the high school's hallways with her eyes looking narrowly at the back of the person walking in front of her, trying to disappear within the herd lest she be recognized by any malicious onlookers as easy prey.

Esperanza had been sitting alone in the front row, paying little
60 attention to the other auditions, working on geometry homework until her name was called. Shuffling her feet toward the center of the stage, Esperanza did not look up until she was there, and even then looked only at Mrs. Dominguez.

"Whenever you're ready," Mrs. Dominguez said politely,
65 sensing the potential for this audition to devolve into a painful target of ridicule.

As Esperanza began the opening notes to "The Star Spangled Banner," Monique and her friends looked at each other in total disbelief. Clearly, they thought, Esperanza had no theater
70 pedigree, or she would never stoop to singing such a trite, formulaic song. Standing perfectly still, Esperanza moved methodically through the tune with little flair or emotion. However, the

GO ON TO THE NEXT PAGE.

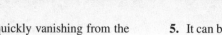

expectant smiles of mockery were quickly vanishing from the faces of all who listened.

75   Anticipating a tentative, mousy voice that would befit such a quirky presence as Esperanza's, the audience instead heard an unusually smooth, rich tone with full command of the multiple registers that the national anthem's melody requires. At the climactic "rocket's red glare," Esperanza's voice filled the room with
80 a calm resonance that forced one's heart to lift within one's chest as though some reluctant patriotism was determined to find its way out. The final phrase of the song, so often soaked in vibrato by melodramatic singers, was gently performed, with a touch that felt like a mother tucking in her baby to sleep.

85   Although Monique was loath to admit it and Esperanza was reluctant to want it, Esperanza had just set herself apart from the herd.

1. It can reasonably be inferred from the passage that Monique believed the song she chose for her audition:

   A. would be the most inspiring Rodgers & Hammerstein number she could choose.
   B. was the most sophisticated song in Billie Holiday's repertoire.
   C. would likely be more recognizable to Monique's parents than to her friends.
   D. would allow Monique to more effectively showcase her enthusiasm.

2. The passage initially portrays Monique and her friends as:

   F. concerned and nervous.
   G. confused and surprised.
   H. friendly and inclusive.
   J. aloof and disparaging.

3. According to the narrator, what did Esperanza do prior to singing "The Star Spangled Banner"?

   A. Looked only at Mrs. Dominguez
   B. Walked confidently up to the stage
   C. Watched the other auditions carefully
   D. Finished her geometry homework

4. The main purpose of the statement in line 29 is to:

   F. inform the reader that students' fears of going first were largely a thing of the past.
   G. present reasons for why this year's audition was the strangest yet.
   H. suggest that Monique's imagination no longer involved the same imagery.
   J. offer a contrast created by Monique's choice of audition slot.

5. It can be reasonably inferred from the passage that Esperanza Solito:

   A. was teased more than anyone else at her school.
   B. was not sitting near Monique and her friends during the auditions.
   C. had her audition immediately after Monique's audition.
   D. had previously explained her stage fright to Mrs. Dominguez.

6. According to the passage, Monique figured that volunteering to perform "God Bless the Child" as the first audition of the day would:

   F. bolster her confidence in her performance.
   G. make the other auditioners feel they could not compete with her.
   H. guarantee her a part in the play.
   J. impress and charm Mrs. Dominguez.

7. According to the passage, when Esperanza Solito got to the climax of "The Star Spangled Banner," she:

   A. raised her voice to emphasize the lines.
   B. demonstrated her patriotism.
   C. had a sudden bout of nerves.
   D. could be heard throughout the auditorium.

8. The passage states that Mrs. Dominguez suspected Esperanza's audition could be:

   F. vulnerable to ridicule.
   G. one of the most awkward.
   H. a special treat.
   J. neither surprising nor charming.

9. Which of the following details is used in the passage to describe how Monique and her friends responded to hearing Esperanza's audition?

   A. Their decision to sit comfortably behind Mrs. Dominguez
   B. Their preconceived notions about Esperanza's voice
   C. Their fading facial expressions of mockery
   D. Their fondness for patriotic songs

10. The passage most strongly suggests that Esperanza's choice of audition material was:

   F. good for a mousy voice.
   G. often partly sung with vibrato.
   H. an impressive, original choice.
   J. something Monique's friends had anticipated.

GO ON TO THE NEXT PAGE.

Passage II

SOCIAL SCIENCE: This passage is adapted from the article "Information Stupor-highway" by Cal Jergenson (© 2005 by Cal Jergenson).

Think about a remote control. Something so simple in function is seemingly capable of invisible magic to most of us. Only those with an engineering and electronics background probably have any real idea of *why* a remote control works. The rest of us
5 just assume it *should*. And the longer a given technology exists, the more we take it for granted.

Consider for a moment a split screen showing modern remote control users versus the first remote control users: the original users would be cautiously aiming the remote directly at
10 the television, reading the names of the buttons to find the right one, and deliberately pressing the button with a force that adds nothing to the effectiveness of the device. The modern users would be reclined on a sofa, pointing the remote any which way, and instinctively feeling for the button they desired, intuiting its
15 size, shape, and position on the remote.

Humans are known for being handy with tools, so it is no surprise that we get so comfortable with our technology. However, as we become increasingly comfortable with how to *use* new technologies, we become less aware of how they *work*.
20 Most people who use modern technology know nothing of its underlying science. They have spent neither mental nor financial resources on its development. And yet, rather than be humbled by its ingenuity, we consumers often become unfairly demanding of what our technology should do for us.

25 Many of the landmark inventions of the twentieth century followed predictable trajectories: initial versions of each technology (television, video games, computers, portable phones, etc.) succeeded in wowing the general public. Then, these wondrous novelties quickly became commonplace. Soon, the focus of
30 consumer attitudes toward these inventions changed from awed gratitude to discriminating preference.

Televisions needed to be bigger and have a higher resolution. Video games needed to be more realistic. Computers needed to be more powerful yet smaller in size. Cell phones needed to be
35 smaller yet capable of performing other tasks such as taking pictures, accessing the Internet, and even playing movies.

For children of the last twenty years born into this modern life, these technological marvels seem like elements of the periodic table: a given ingredient that is simply part of the universe.
40 Younger generations don't even try to conceive of life without modern conveniences. They do not appreciate the unprecedented technology that is in their possession; rather, they complain about the ways in which it fails to live up to ideal expectations.

"The videos that my phone can record are too pixelated."
45 "My digital video recorder at home doesn't allow me to program it from my computer at work." "It's taking too long for this interactive map to display on my portable GPS." "My robotic vacuum cleaner never manages to get the crumbs out of the cracks between the tiles."

50 If it sounds as though we're never satisfied, we aren't. Of course, our fussy complaints do actually motivate engineers to continually refine their products. After all, at the root of our toolmaking instinct is the notion that "there must be a better way." Thus, the shortcomings of any current version of technology are
55 pinned on the limitations of its designers, and the expectation is that someone, somewhere is working on how to make the existing product even better.

The most dangerous extension of this mindset is its effect on our outlook on solving global climate problems. The firmly
60 substantiated problem of global warming threatens to quickly render the planet Earth inhospitable to most humans.

The solution? If you ask most people, you will hear that the solution resides in creating more efficient versions of our current technologies and devising alternative forms of energy
65 than those that burn fossil fuels.

Blindly confident that the creativity of human problemsolvers can wriggle us out of any dilemma, most people feel guiltless in continuing to live their lives with the assumption that someone else is working on these problems.

70 Unfortunately, having no real scientific perspective on the problems to be solved or the complexity of global weather patterns, most people are unduly optimistic about humanity's ability to think its way out of this problem. In a culture completely spoiled by the idea that technology can achieve whatever
75 goal it is tasked to perform, the idea that a global climate crisis may be beyond the reach of a clever technological solution is unthinkable.

Hence, the idea that we, as a culture, may need to reexamine our lifestyles and consumer habits is too alien to take seriously.
80 In contemporary society, the leaders who are most able to communicate the state of the world do not dare suggest to the public the unpopular ideas that "times will be rough," "sacrifices must be made," or "we may have to take some steps backwards."

As a result, the human race will continue defiantly with the
85 status quo and, ultimately, blame technology when problems arise. At that point, we'll all be searching for the "rewind" button on the remote control.

GO ON TO THE NEXT PAGE.

11. The passage states that original users of remote controls likely did all of the following EXCEPT:
   A. use more strength pressing the button than is necessary.
   B. aim the remote directly at the television.
   C. feel instinctively for the desired button.
   D. read the names of the buttons carefully.

12. In the passage, the author answers all of the following questions EXCEPT:
   F. How do most people think the global climate crisis should be solved?
   G. What was the most significant invention of the twentieth century?
   H. What idea underlies humanity's tool-making instinct?
   J. How do consumer attitudes about new technology change?

13. The descriptions offered by the author in the second paragraph (lines 7–15) are used to illustrate the concept that:
   A. consumer behavior toward new forms of technology changes over time.
   B. modern humans do not pay enough attention to instructions.
   C. the first consumers of new technology used new devices with ease and comfort.
   D. remote controls have become far more effective over the years.

14. The principal tone of the passage can best be described as:
   F. nostalgic.
   G. critical.
   H. sympathetic.
   J. frightened.

15. As it is used in line 79, the word *alien* most nearly means:
   A. extraterrestrial.
   B. repetitive.
   C. unusual.
   D. hilarious.

16. The author uses the statement "these technological marvels seem like elements of the periodic table" (lines 38–39) most nearly to mean that:
   F. children learn technology while they learn chemistry.
   G. consumers regard many technological inventions as unremarkable.
   H. space exploration gives us most of our technology.
   J. consumers complain when modern conveniences break down.

17. The phrase *the status quo* (line 85) most likely refers to:
   A. reexamining the scope and complexity of technology.
   B. making sacrifices to combat the global climate crisis.
   C. blaming technology for the problems we encounter.
   D. our current pattern of lifestyles and consumer habits.

18. One form of consumer behavior the author describes is a discriminating preference for:
   F. less realistic video games.
   G. needing to understand technology.
   H. more powerful computers.
   J. wanting to make sacrifices.

19. Among the following quotations from the passage, the one that best summarizes what the author sees as a potential danger is:
   A. "the shortcomings of any current version of technology" (line 54).
   B. "devising alternative forms of energy" (line 64).
   C. "the complexity of global weather patterns" (lines 71–72).
   D. "our outlook on solving global climate problems" (line 59).

20. The last paragraph differs from the first paragraph in that in the last paragraph the author:
   F. makes a prediction rather than making an observation.
   G. refutes a scientific theory.
   H. quotes experts to support his opinions.
   J. uses the word "we" instead of "I."

GO ON TO THE NEXT PAGE.

Passage III

HUMANITIES: The following passage is adapted from the article "Conquering Jazz" by Patrick Tyrrell (© 2006 by Patrick Tyrrell).

From the time I started playing instruments, I have been intrigued and slightly mystified by the world of jazz. I'm not talking about adventurous, atonal, confusing jazz that normal music listeners have a hard time following. I'm talking about the lively,
5 accessible, beautiful jazz that came of age in the swinging 1920s and 1930s: the simultaneously hip and regal symphonic swing of Duke Ellington and Count Basie; the carnival of contrapuntal melodies that inexplicably harmonize with each other in New Orleans' jazz; the buoyant, atmosphere-touching saxophone solos
10 of Charlie Parker and the young John Coltrane.

The one thing I had always heard about jazz but could never accept was that jazz was an improvised form of music. How could this be?

The trademark of beautiful jazz is the complexity of the
15 music. All the instrumentalists are capable of dizzying arrays of notes and rhythms. The soloists find seemingly impossible transitions from one phrase to the next that are so perfect one would think they had spent weeks trying to devise *just* the right route to conduct safe passage. To think they spontaneously craft
20 these ideas seems preposterous.

My first nervous jabs into the world of jazz came during college. I was in a rock band, but my fellow guitarist and bandmate, Victor, also played in a jazz ensemble. At our practices, I would sometimes show off a new chord I had just "invented" only to
25 have him calmly and confidently name it, "Oh, you mean C-sharp diminished?" Often, in between our band's simplistic rock songs, I would look over and see him playing chord shapes on his guitar I had never seen before. Were we playing the same instrument?

Of course, rock music, as well as most early classical mu-
30 sic, operates within a much simpler harmonic world than does jazz. There are 12 tones in Western music: A-flat, A, B-flat, B, C, D-flat, D, E-flat, E, F, G-flat, and G. There are major chords, which sound happy, and minor chords, which sound sad. Essentially, rock music requires only that you learn the major and
35 minor chord for each of the 12 tones. If you do, you can play 99 percent of all the popular radio songs from the 1950s onward.

Jazz uses the same twelve tones as do rock and classical, but it employs a much more robust variety of chords. Major sevenths, augmented fifths, flat ninths, and diminished chords all add to
40 the depth and detail of the music. These often bizarre-sounding chords toss in subtle hints of chaos and imbalance, adding a worldly imperfection to otherwise standard chord values. Jazz starts sounding better the older you get, just as candy starts tasting too sweet and a bit of bitterness makes for a more appealing flavor.

45 For the most part, Victor's elliptical personality prevented him from ever giving me straightforward explanations when I asked him to divulge the "magician's secrets" of jazz. But I did learn that jazz is only *partly* improvised. The musicians aren't inventing the structure of songs spontaneously, just the specific
50 details and embellishments. A sheet of jazz music doesn't look like a sheet of classical music. There aren't notes all over the page dictating the "ideas." There are just chord names spaced out over time, dictating the "topic of conversation."

There's a legendary book in the jazz world known as "The
55 Real Book." It's a collection of a few hundred classic songs. Open it up in any room full of jazz musicians, and they could play in synchrony for a week. For years, I wanted my own copy, but I had always been too afraid to buy it, afraid that I wouldn't know how to use the book once I had it. Then, at age 30, more
60 than a decade since Victor and I had gone our separate ways, I bought myself a copy. I resolved to learn how to play all the chords on guitar and piano. For the next few months, I quietly plucked away at these strange, new combinations. F-sharp minor-7 flat-5? Each chord was a cryptic message I had to decode and
65 then understand. It felt like being dropped off alone in a country where I didn't speak the language.

But I made progress. Chords that initially took me twenty seconds to figure out started to take only a few. My left hand was becoming comfortable in its role of supplying my right hand
70 with a steady bass line. Meanwhile, to my amazement, my right hand began to improvise melodies that sounded undeniably *jazzy*.

It seemed like the hard work of figuring out the exotic jazz chords had sent new melodic understanding straight to my hand, bypassing my brain entirely. I felt like a witness to performances
75 by detached hands; I couldn't believe that I was the one creating these sounds. I'm sure this feeling will not last, but for now I'm enjoying the rare and miraculous feeling of improvising music that I still consider beyond my abilities.

21. Which chord, if any, does the author eventually conclude is the most confusing jazz chord to play?

   A. The passage does not indicate any such chord.
   B. C-sharp diminished
   C. Major sevenths
   D. F-sharp minor-7 flat-5

GO ON TO THE NEXT PAGE.

22. As it is used in line 47, "magician's secrets" most nearly means:

    F. information on how to play jazz.
    G. forbidden bits of knowledge.
    H. instances of harmless trickery.
    J. the true nature of a private person.

23. As portrayed by the author, Victor responds to the author's *invented* chord with what is best described as:

    A. amazement.
    B. jealousy.
    C. confusion.
    D. nonchalance.

24. The author states that "The Real Book" was something he explored for a few:

    F. years.
    G. months.
    H. weeks.
    J. days.

25. The details in lines 40–44 primarily serve to suggest the:

    A. aspects of jazz's complexity that more mature listeners enjoy.
    B. lack of depth and detail found in rock and classical music.
    C. confusion and awkwardness of standard jazz chord values.
    D. unpleasantly bitter taste of candy that develops with age.

26. In the context of the passage, the author's statement in lines 68–71 most nearly means that:

    F. he was so overworked that his hands could still move, but his thoughts were turned off.
    G. he had accidentally trained his hands to resist being controlled by his brain.
    H. it was easier to decode the exotic jazz chords by pointing at them with his hands.
    J. his hand was capable of playing music that his mind was incapable of fully comprehending.

27. The author implies that F-sharp minor-7 flat-5 is an example of a chord that he:

    A. had little trouble decoding now that he had "The Real Book."
    B. had previously only seen during his travels abroad.
    C. knew how to play on guitar but not on a piano.
    D. initially found confusing and struggled to understand.

28. The passage supports which one of the following conclusions about Victor?

    F. He played music with the author until the author turned 30 years old.
    G. He gave his copy of "The Real Book" to the author as a gift.
    H. He was at one time a member of multiple musical groups.
    J. He invented a chord and named it C-sharp diminished.

29. The passage is best described as being told from the point of view of someone who is:

    A. reviewing the chain of events that led to his career in jazz.
    B. discussing reasons why jazz is less complicated than it seems.
    C. relating his impressions of jazz music and his attempts to play it.
    D. highlighting an important friendship that he had in college.

30. Assessing his early and later experiences with "The Real Book," the author most strongly implies that it was:

    F. pleasantly strange to begin with but annoyingly familiar by the end.
    G. initially difficult to decipher, but ultimately manageable following diligent practice.
    H. almost impossible to understand because its pages didn't look like sheets of classical music.
    J. very useful as a learning tool, but not useful for more profound study.

GO ON TO THE NEXT PAGE.

Passage IV

NATURAL SCIENCE: This passage is adapted from the article "Fair-Weather Warning" by Julia Mittlebury (© 2007 by Julia Mittlebury).

Could the sun be causing epidemics? Take cholera, for example, an often fatal disease caused by the bacterium *Vibrio cholerae* (*V. cholerae*). Every so often, coastal areas suffer massive outbreaks of cholera due to infected food or water. Where
5 do these outbreaks come from?

The bacterium that causes cholera is found in areas that contain the copepod, a certain type of crustacean. The copepod depends on zooplankton for nourishment, and these zooplankton in turn depend on phytoplankton for their nourishment. Phyto-
10 plankton use photosynthesis to feed on sunlight. Although one might need to go to the bottom of the food chain, the evidence shows that an increase in sunlight might mean an increase in the potential for cholera.

Interested in this correlation, Rita Calwell and her fellow
15 researchers at the University of Maryland are studying ways to use satellite measurements of sea temperatures, sea height, and chlorophyll concentrations in order to predict when conditions favoring a cholera outbreak are more likely. As sea temperatures rise, photosynthetic organisms such as phytoplankton become
20 more abundant. As sea levels rise, the phytoplankton, zooplankton, copepods, and, by extension, the cholera bacterium are all brought closer to the shore. This increases the likelihood of food and water contamination.

By monitoring the cholera food chain in reverse, Calwell and
25 her colleagues believe they can predict the emergence of cholera 4 to 6 weeks in advance. Calwell's model predicted the rate of infection during one recent cholera outbreak in Bangladesh with 95 percent accuracy. Unfortunately, because this field of study is so new and its insights are so speculative, local public health
30 officials have not yet begun to base any preventative measures on these satellite-based forecasts.

Just up the road from Calwell and the University of Maryland, Kenneth Linthicum is leading similar efforts at the NASA Goddard Space Flight Centre in Greenbelt, Maryland. He has
35 designed a model to analyze the spread of Rift Valley fever, a mosquito-spread virus that killed about 100,000 animals and 90,000 people back in December 1997.

Scientists observed that prior to the outbreak, the equatorial region of the Indian Ocean saw a half-degree increase in surface
40 temperature. Although half of a degree sounds like only a slight difference, the temperature of an ocean does not change easily. Warmer ocean water in this region corresponds with strong and prolonged rains, increased cloud cover, and warmer air over equatorial parts of Africa. These characteristics favor the pro-
45 liferation of mosquitoes and help keep them alive long enough for the virus to become easily transmittable.

In September 2007, Linthicum and his team became alerted to similar environmental changes. Over the next few months, they warned local health officials in Kenya, Somalia, and Tanzania that
50 conditions were ripe for a mosquito-based outbreak. As a result, only 300 lives were lost, an almost miraculous improvement from the devastation of the 1997 outbreak. While it is impossible to know if this outbreak would have been as far-reaching as that of 1997, it seems likely that the advance warning succeeded in
55 saving thousands, if not tens of thousands, of lives.

Similarly, a study by David Rogers at Oxford University has helped to predict outbreaks of sleeping sickness, a parasitic disease caused by West African tsetse flies. Here, Rogers first calibrated regional levels of photosynthesis to the size of a vein
60 in the wings of the flies. The vein size is a good measure of how numerous and robust the tsetse fly population is. Today, by reading the photosynthetic levels from satellite data, even researchers outside of West Africa can predict potential epidemics in the region.

65 This type of research is encouraging to many in the disease prevention field, because traditional methods involve slow, costly research. The newfound ability to cull massive amounts of meteorological data from satellites and to run that data through computer models has been much more efficient.

70 The goal of these models is to study the relationships between disease data and climate data. However, to do so requires decades', if not centuries', worth of high quality data to identify correlating factors with accuracy. Currently, the climatic data is much more reliable than the disease data. Nevertheless, excite-
75 ment about the potential usefulness of satellite-based predictions is persuading health agencies to compile and integrate their disease data more efficiently to give easier access to those trying to discover climate-disease links.

It may still take a good deal of time and energy before this
80 technology is ready for practical application. Critics claim that the number of variables underlying the spread of disease are too numerous and varied for a climate-based approach ever to be reliable. Fluctuations in the immunity of local populations, human and animal migrations, and the resistance to drugs used
85 to commonly treat certain diseases could confuse climate-based models. Advocates respond, though, that these non-climatic factors can similarly be incorporated into their research as long as the relevant data is collected, and the resulting models will have even better accuracy.

GO ON TO THE NEXT PAGE.

31. According to Calwell, scientists may be able to predict cholera outbreaks more than a month in advance by:

   A. noticing increased activity in a known food chain.
   B. using accurate climatic models derived from weather in Bangladesh.
   C. measuring the decline of zooplankton with falling sea temperatures.
   D finding connections between chlorophyll levels and diseased marine life.

32. According to the passage, levels of sunlight can influence cholera because:

   F. phytoplankton feed on sunlight and contaminate the water.
   G. the *V. cholerae* bacterium increases its photosynthetic rate.
   H. sunlight promotes the growth of organisms upon which copepods depend.
   J. many epidemics are caused by direct, prolonged exposure to sunlight.

33. According to the passage, the use of satellite data has aided the attempts of Oxford University researchers to predict outbreaks of sleeping sickness by providing information about:

   A. the number of West African parasites.
   B. which areas globally have the most photosynthesis.
   C. the health and number of tsetse flies.
   D. which flies have the biggest veins.

34. The passage states that Linthicum is conducting similar efforts to Calwell's in that Linthicum:

   F. studies the climatic triggers of cholera.
   G. works at the University of Maryland.
   H. managed to save thousands of lives in 2007.
   J. uses satellite data to build predictive models.

35. According to the passage, the use of satellite data to predict potential epidemics is encouraging because:

   A. computer number-crunching is quicker and less expensive than traditional research methods.
   B. it allows scientists to control the photosynthetic levels in West Africa.
   C. satellites do not make the same mathematical errors that human forecasters often do.
   D. there is already a large supply of long-term disease data available from satellites.

36. As it is used in line 44, the word *favor* most nearly means:

   F. errand.
   G. task.
   H. promote.
   J. request.

37. It can reasonably be inferred that the phrase *similar environmental changes* (line 48) refers to:

   A. the beginning of the rainy season in Kenya.
   B. the amount of bacteria circulating in the jet stream.
   C. the proliferation of mosquitoes throughout central Africa.
   D. warmer ocean water influencing rain and cloud cover.

38. The passage states that climatic satellite data has helped to do all of the following EXCEPT:

   F. measure sea height.
   G. predict tsetse fly populations.
   H. forecast disease outbreaks.
   J. raise the ocean temperature.

39. The phrase *confuse climate-based models* (line 85–86) refers directly to the fact that:

   A. current models do not account for non-climate related factors.
   B. drug resistance sometimes results in disorientation.
   C. epidemics sometimes vanish more quickly than they arise.
   D. researchers are not used to non-climate data.

40. It can reasonably be inferred from the passage that the information about the use of satellite-based data is presented primarily to:

   F. demonstrate the various kinds of data that must be collected.
   G. analyze the data's potential use in disease-prevention.
   H. illustrate how few scientists do on-the-ground research.
   J. show how West African tsetse fly populations have been predicted.

END OF TEST 3

STOP! DO NOT TURN THE PAGE UNTIL TOLD TO DO SO.

DO NOT RETURN TO A PREVIOUS TEST.

SCIENCE TEST

35 Minutes–40 Questions

Directions: There are seven passages in this test. Each passage is followed by several questions. After reading a passage, choose the best answer to each question and fill in the corresponding oval on your answer document. You may refer to the passages as often as necessary.

You are NOT permitted to use a calculator on this test.

Passage I

Two ways to measure the quality of soil are *bulk density* and the *soil organic matter test*, SOM (a measure of the active organic content). High quality soil provides structure to plants and moves water and nutrients, so plants grow in larger quantities, leading to higher crop yields at harvest.

Bulk density is measured as the dry weight of a sample of soil divided by the volume of the sample. A bulk density measure above 1.33 g/cm³ negatively affects soil quality. Figure 1 shows the bulk density levels for 5 different years at Fields A and B.

Table 1 shows how soil quality varies with SOM. Table 2 shows the average SOM at the end of each of the 5 years.

Table 1	
SOM	Soil quality rating
<0.25	poor
0.25 to 0.50	fair
0.51 to 0.75	good
>0.75	excellent

Table 2	
Field	Average SOM
A	0.89
B	0.28

Figure 2 shows the total crop yield at each field at the end of the 5 years.

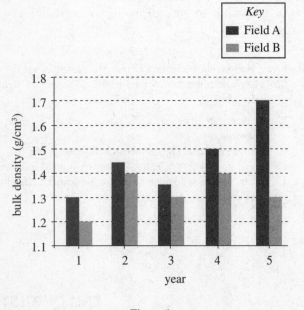

Figure 1

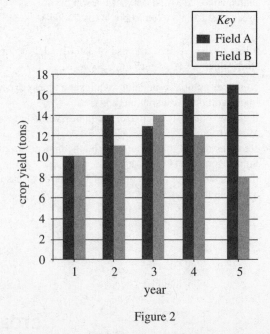

Figure 2

GO ON TO THE NEXT PAGE.

1. Which set of data best supports the claim that Field A has *lower* soil quality than Field B ?

   A. Figure 1
   B. Figure 2
   C. Table 1
   D. Table 2

2. If 8 tons or fewer in crop yields were considered a failed harvest, in which year and in which field would there have been a failed harvest?

   F. Field A in Year 1
   G. Field A in Year 3
   H. Field B in Year 4
   J. Field B in Year 5

3. Suppose a new crop rotation for Field B included legumes and other deep-rooted and high-residue crops. The SOM of this field will most likely change in which of the following ways? The SOM will:

   A. decrease, because soil quality is likely to increase.
   B. decrease, because soil quality is likely to decrease.
   C. increase, because soil quality is likely to increase.
   D. increase, because soil quality is likely to decrease.

4. Based on Figures 1 and 2, consider the average bulk density and the average crop yields for Fields A and B over the study period. Which site had the lower average crop yield, and which site had the higher average bulk density?

	Lower crop yield	Higher bulk density
F.	Field A	Field A
G.	Field B	Field B
H.	Field A	Field B
J.	Field B	Field A

5. As soil quality improves, the number of earthworms increases. Students hypothesized that more earthworms would be found in Field B. Are the data presented in Table 2 consistent with this hypothesis?

   A. Yes; based on SOM, Field B had a soil quality rating of fair and Field A had a soil quality rating of poor.
   B. Yes; based on SOM, Field B had a soil quality rating of excellent and Field A had a soil quality rating of fair.
   C. No; based on SOM, Field B had a soil quality rating of poor and Field A had a soil quality rating of fair.
   D. No; based on SOM, Field B had a soil quality rating of fair and Field A had a soil quality rating of excellent.

GO ON TO THE NEXT PAGE.

Passage II

Ferric oxide (Fe_2O_3) is more commonly known as rust. This is produced in a reaction between iron, a common metal, and water, H_2O.

$$2Fe + 3 H_2O \longrightarrow Fe_2O_3 + 3H_2$$

Table 1 shows the amount of Fe_2O_3 produced over time from 15 g Fe submerged in different liquids: 100 mL distilled water, a salt solution made from dissolving 20 g of salt in 100 mL of distilled water, and a sugar solution made from dissolving 20 g of sugar in 100 mL of distilled water.

Table 1				
Solution	g Fe_2O_3 produced			
	Day 2	Day 4	Day 6	Day 8
Distilled water	0.34	0.40	0.59	0.72
Salt solution	0.56	0.81	1.23	1.84
Sugar solution	0.00	0.05	0.11	0.19

The distilled water trial was repeated four times, but for each trial, a total volume of 100 mL of water was buffered to different pH levels.

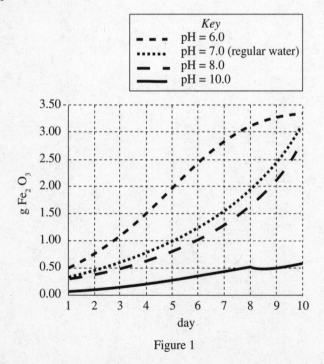

Key
- - - pH = 6.0
...... pH = 7.0 (regular water)
– – pH = 8.0
—— pH = 10.0

Figure 1

6. Based on Table 1, if the amount of Fe_2O_3 produced on Day 9 had been measured for the salt solution, it would most likely have been:

F. less than 0.56 g.
G. between 0.59 g and 0.72 g.
H. between 1.23 g and 1.84 g.
J. greater than 1.84 g.

7. In the experiments shown in Table 1 and Figure 1, by measuring the rate at which Fe_2O_3 was formed every day, the experimenters could also measure the rate at which:

A. H_2O was produced.
B. H_2 was produced.
C. Fe was produced.
D. FeO was produced.

8. Consider the amount of Fe_2O_3 produced by the salt solution on Day 2. Based on Table 1 and Figure 1, the water buffered to pH = 10.0 produced approximately the same amount of Fe_2O_3 on which of the following days?

F. Day 1
G. Day 3
H. Day 6
J. Day 10

9. According to Table 1, what was the amount of Fe_2O_3 produced by the sugar solution from the time the amount was measured on Day 6 until the time the amount was measured on Day 8 ?
A. 0.08 g
B. 0.11 g
C. 0.19 g
D. 0.30 g

GO ON TO THE NEXT PAGE.

10. Based on Table 1, which graph best shows how the amount of
Fe_2O_3 produced by the sugar solution changes over time?

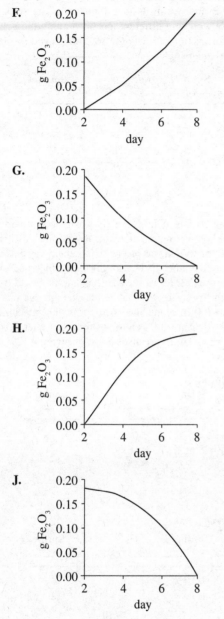

F.

G.

H.

J.

Passage III

Some physics students conducted experiments to study forces and springs. They used several identical springs attached to the bottom of a level platform, shown below in Figure 1.

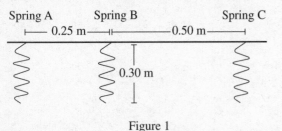

Figure 1

The length of each spring was 0.30 m when there were no weights attached. The springs had identical spring constants. When weights were attached, the length of the springs increased as the force of the weights stretched the springs downward. The length the springs stretched was proportional to the force of the weight.

Experiment 1

The students attached different weights to two springs at once. When the springs stopped oscillating and came to a rest, the students measured their length. In Trial 1, a 10.0 N weight was attached to Spring A and Spring B, which were attached 0.25 m apart on the board. In Trial 2, a 15.0 N weight was attached to Spring A and Spring B. In Trial 3, a 20.0 N weight was attached to Spring A and Spring B. The effects of the weights on Springs A and B for the three trials are shown below in Figure 2.

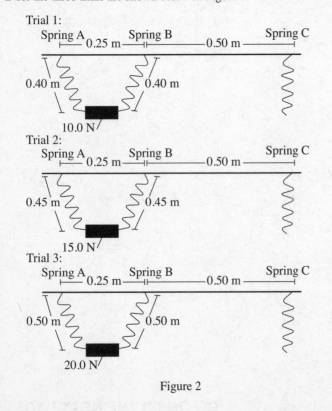

Figure 2

Experiment 2

The students attached a 0.25 m board with a high friction surface to Spring B and Spring C (see Figure 3). The students then placed a 5.0 N weight at different locations along the board. Because of the high friction surface, the weights stayed in place when the board was at an angle.

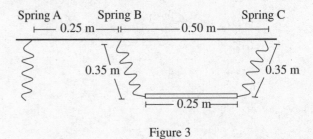

Figure 3

In each of these 3 trials, a 5.0 N weight was placed at various distances along the board from the attachment with Spring B (see Figure 4). In Trial 4, the weight was placed so its center was 0.075 m along the board from the attachment with Spring B. In Trial 5, the weight was placed so its center was 0.125 m along the board from the attachment with Spring B. In Trial 6, the weight was placed so its center was 0.200 m along the board from the attachment with Spring B. The effects of the weight position on the lengths of Springs B and C for the 3 trials are also shown in Figure 4.

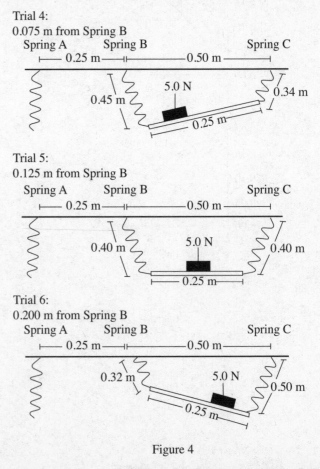

Figure 4

GO ON TO THE NEXT PAGE.

11. In a new study, suppose the students had placed a 10.0 N weight on Spring A only. Which of the following drawings most likely represents the results of this experiment?

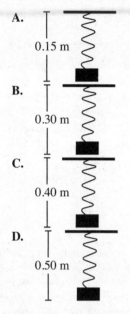

A. 0.15 m

B. 0.30 m

C. 0.40 m

D. 0.50 m

12. In Experiment 2, as the distance between the 5.0 N weight and the attachment of the board to Spring B increased, the force exerted on Spring B:

F. increased only.
G. decreased only.
H. increased, then decreased.
J. decreased, then increased.

13. Which of the following statements is most likely the reason that the students used identical springs in Trials 1–3 ?

A. To ensure that the springs stretched similarly when a weight was attached.
B. To ensure that the springs did not share the weight evenly.
C. To compensate for the effects of oscillation on the results of the experiment.
D. To compensate for the weight of the board exerted on each of the springs.

14. Based on the results of Trials 1 and 5, the weight of the board used in Experiment 2 was:

F. 0 N.
G. 2.5 N.
H. 5.0 N.
J. 10.0 N.

15. In which of the following trials in Experiment 2, if any, was the force exerted by the weight and the board equally distributed between Springs B and C ?

A. Trial 4
B. Trial 5
C. Trial 6
D. None of the trials

16. Assume that when a spring is stretched from its normal length, it stores the energy to return to its normal state as potential energy. Assume also that the greater the force of the weight stretching the spring, the more the spring will stretch. Was the potential energy stored by Spring C higher in Trial 5 or Trial 6 ?

F. In Trial 5, because the force of the weight on Spring C was greater in Trial 5.
G. In Trial 5, because the force of the weight on Spring C was less in Trial 5.
H. In Trial 6, because the force of the weight on Spring C was greater in Trial 6.
J. In Trial 6, because the force of the weight on Spring C was less in Trial 6.

GO ON TO THE NEXT PAGE.

Passage IV

Sodium chloride, or salt, is used to de-ice roads and sidewalks during the winter because it lowers the freezing point of water. Water with sodium chloride freezes at a lower temperature than water alone, so putting sodium chloride on icy sidewalks and roads can cause the ice to melt. Sodium chloride is highly effective as a de-icer and is given a *de-icer proof* of 100. Distilled water is ineffective as a de-icer and is given a de-icer proof of 0.

Different proportions of sodium chloride and distilled water were combined to create mixtures with de-icer proofs between 0 and 100.

Table 1		
De-icer proof	Volume of distilled water	Volume of sodium chloride
100	0 mL	50 mL
80	10 mL	40 mL
60	20 mL	30 mL
40	30 mL	20 mL
20	40 mL	10 mL
0	50 mL	0 mL

Experiment 1

A 125-g cube of ice, frozen from distilled water, was submerged in 500-mL of each de-icing mixture listed in Table 1. After 300 seconds, the portion of the cube that had not been melted was removed and weighed. The de-icing rate was calculated by determining the weight of ice melted per second. By doing this, it was possible to determine de-icer proof for a solution based on the rate at which ice was melted.

Experiment 2

The addition of magnesium chloride to a de-icer changes its de-icer proof. Different amounts of magnesium chloride were added to 500-mL samples of sodium chloride. Each de-icing mixture was tested under the same conditions as Experiment 1 and the measured de-icing rate was used to calculate the de-icer proof. The results are shown in Figure 1.

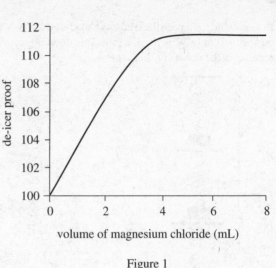

Figure 1

Experiment 3

The *temperature rating* (TR) is the minimum de-icer proof of a de-icing solution for a de-icer to have any effect on ice. 125-g cubes of ice were submerged in 500-mL samples of De-icers A and B and the samples were then placed in freezers at different temperatures. Table 2 shows the de-icer proof determined for each de-icer at each freezer temperature and the known TR for that temperature.

Table 2			
Freezer temperature	TR	Proof of:	
		De-icer A	De-icer B
−10°C	24.1	90.3	70.1
−25°C	36.9	78.9	64.9
−50°C	49.7	68.8	59.7
−75°C	52.3	56.6	51.7

17. Suppose a trial had been performed in Experiment 3 with a freezer temperature of −30°C. At this temperature, which of the following sets of proofs would most likely have been determined for De-icer A and De-icer B ?

	De-icer A	De-icer B
A.	68.8	59.7
B.	70.1	70.5
C.	75.5	61.8
D.	78.9	64.9

GO ON TO THE NEXT PAGE.

18. Based on Table 1, if 1 mL distilled water were added to 4 mL sodium chloride, the proof of this mixture would be:

    F. 4.
    G. 8.
    H. 40.
    J. 80.

19. Based on Experiment 3, as temperature decreases, the minimum proof for a de-icer to be effective:

    A. increases only.
    B. decreases only.
    C. increases, then decreases.
    D. decreases, then increases.

20. Which of the following expressions is equal to the proof for each de-icer mixture listed in Table 1 ?

    F. $\dfrac{\text{volume of sodium chloride}}{\text{volume of water}} \times 100$

    G. $\dfrac{\text{volume of water}}{\text{volume of sodium chloride}} \times 100$

    H. $\dfrac{\text{volume of sodium chloride}}{(\text{volume of water} + \text{volume of sodium chloride})} \times 100$

    J. $\dfrac{\text{volume of water}}{(\text{volume of water} + \text{volume of sodium chloride})} \times 100$

21. Based on Table 1 and Experiment 2, if 6 mL magnesium chloride were added to a mixture of 10 mL distilled water and 40 mL sodium chloride, the proof of the resulting de-icer would most likely be:

    A. less than 60.
    B. between 60 and 80.
    C. between 80 and 112.
    D. greater than 112.

22. Which of the 2 de-icers from Experiment 3 would be better to use to melt ice if the temperature were between –10°C and –75°C ?

    F. De-icer A, because its proof was lower than the TR at each temperature tested.
    G. De-icer A, because its proof was higher than the TR at each temperature tested.
    H. De-icer B, because its proof was lower than the TR at each temperature tested.
    J. De-icer B, because its proof was higher than the TR at each temperature tested.

GO ON TO THE NEXT PAGE.

Passage V

Comets originate from regions of our solar system that are very far from the sun. The comets are formed from debris thrown from objects in the solar system: they have a nucleus of ice surrounded by dust and frozen gases. When comets are pulled into the earth's atmosphere by gravitational forces and become visible, they are called *meteors*. Meteors become visible about 50 to 85 km above the surface of Earth as air friction causes them to glow. Most meteors vaporize completely before they come within 50 km of the surface of Earth.

The Small Comet debate centers on whether dark spots and streaks seen in images of the Earth's atmosphere are due to random technological noise or a constant rain of comets composed of ice. Recently, images were taken by two instruments, UVA and VIS, which are located in a satellite orbiting in Earth's magnetosphere. UVA and VIS take pictures of the aurora borealis phenomenon, which occurs in the magnetosphere. The UVA and VIS technologies provide images of energy, which cannot be seen by the human eye.

The pictures taken by VIS and UVA both show dark spots and streaks. Scientists debate whether these spots and streaks are due to a natural incident, such as small comets entering the atmosphere, or random technological noise. The layers of Earth's atmosphere are shown in Figure 1.

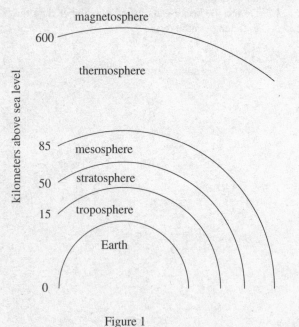

Figure 1

Two scientists debate whether there is a constant rain of comets burning up in Earth's magnetosphere.

Scientist 1

Small comets are pulled into Earth's atmosphere by gravitational effects and burn up in the magnetosphere. They are about 20 to 30 feet in diameter and burn up in the magnetosphere because they are much smaller than the comets that become meteors. Comets with larger radii will burn up in portions of the atmosphere much closer to Earth. About 30,000 small comets enter the Earth's magnetosphere every day. The dark spots and streaks on UVA and VIS images occur when the small comets begin to boil in the magnetosphere, releasing krypton and argon and creating gaseous H_2O, which interacts with hydroxyl, OH^-, radicals. Images taken by these instruments at different points in time show the same frequency of dark spots and streaks and give conclusive evidence in favor of the Small Comet theory. If the spots and streaks were due to random technological noise, then the frequency of their appearance would fluctuate.

Scientist 2

The dark spots and streaks in the UVA and VIS images are due to technological noise, not small comets. If the Small Comet Theory were true, and 20 small comets bombarded Earth's atmosphere per minute, there would be a visible bright object at least twice every five minutes. This is because, as objects enter the Earth's mesosphere, they burn up, creating large clouds of ice particles. As the ice particles vaporize, they have a brightness in the sky approximately equal to that of Venus. Because comets rarely enter Earth's atmosphere, such bright flashes are rare occurrences, far less than two times every five minutes, so the Small Comet theory cannot be correct. Further, since comets originate from regions of space beyond the orbit of the farthest planet, they contain argon and krypton. If the Small Comet theory were true and Earth were bombarded by 30,000 comets per day, there would be 500 times as much krypton in the atmosphere as there actually is.

23. According to Scientist 2, which of the following planets in our solar system is most likely the closest to the region of space where comets originate?

    A. Jupiter
    B. Venus
    C. Neptune
    D. Saturn

GO ON TO THE NEXT PAGE.

24. Based on Scientist 1's viewpoint, a comet that burns up in the thermosphere would have a diameter of:

    F. 5–10 ft.
    G. 10–20 ft.
    H. 20–30 ft.
    J. greater than 30 ft.

25. Which of the following generalizations about small comets is most consistent with Scientist 1's viewpoint?

    A. No small comet ever becomes a meteor.
    B. Some small comets become meteors.
    C. Small comets become meteors twice every five minutes.
    D. All small comets become meteors.

26. During the *Perseids*, an annual meteor shower, more than 1 object burning up in the atmosphere is visible per minute. According to the information provided, Scientist 2 would classify the Perseids as:

    F. typical comet frequency in the magnetosphere.
    G. unusual comet frequency in the magnetosphere.
    H. typical meteor frequency in the mesosphere.
    J. unusual meteor frequency in the mesosphere.

27. Given the information about Earth's atmosphere and Scientist 1's viewpoint, which of the following altitudes would most likely NOT be an altitude at which small comets burn up?

    A. 750 km
    B. 700 km
    C. 650 km
    D. 550 km

28. Suppose a study of the dark holes and streaks in the UVA and VIS images revealed krypton levels in the atmosphere 500 times greater than normal levels. How would the findings of this study most likely affect the scientists' viewpoints, if at all?

    F. It would strengthen Scientist 1's viewpoint only.
    G. It would strengthen Scientist 2's viewpoint only.
    H. It would weaken both Scientists' viewpoints.
    J. It would have no effect on either Scientist's viewpoint.

29. Scientist 1 would most likely suggest enhanced imaging technology that can take pictures of objects in the atmosphere be used to look at what region of the atmosphere to search for small comets?

    A. The region between 15 km above sea level and 50 km above sea level.
    B. The region between 50 km above sea level and 85 km above sea level.
    C. The region between 85 km above sea level and 600 km above sea level.
    D. The region between above 600 km above sea level.

GO ON TO THE NEXT PAGE.

Passage VI

A cotton fiber is composed of one very long cell with two cell walls. During a 2-week period of cell life called elongation, cotton fibers grow 3 to 6 cm. The level of hydrogen peroxide in cotton fiber cells during elongation is very high. Scientists wanted to study whether the level of hydrogen peroxide affected the length of the cotton fiber.

The amount of hydrogen peroxide is controlled by an enzyme called *superoxide dismutase* (SOD). This enzyme turns superoxide into hydrogen peroxide. Four identical lines of cotton fiber plants were created. Each line was able to express only one of three types of superoxide dismutase. The gene for SOD1 was incorporated into L1, the gene for SOD2 was incorporated into L2, and the gene for SOD3 was incorporated into L3.

Experiment

Five cotton plants of each line were grown in nutrient solution until cotton fibers completed the elongation period. The average length of cotton fibers and the average concentration of hydrogen peroxide were determined. This information is shown in Table 1.

Table 1

| Line | At the end of elongation period: | | |
	Average elongation period length (days)	Average amount of hydrogen peroxide (µmol/mg)	Average cotton fiber length (cm)
L1	8	2.1	3.6
L2	4	0.2	1.4
L3	20	5.6	5.9
L4	12	2.3	4.5

Next, because the scientists had determined the average elongation period, they measured the amount of hydrogen peroxide and the length of the cotton fibers halfway through their elongation period. This information is shown in Table 2.

Table 2

| Line | At the midpoint of elongation period: | | |
	Day of elongation period	Average amount of hydrogen peroxide (µmol/mg)	Average cotton fiber length (cm)
L1	4	4.1	2.7
L2	2	5.3	1.0
L3	10	12.4	2.0
L4	6	8.7	3.2

Finally, the scientists measured the amount of hydrogen peroxide and the length of cotton fibers on the first day of the elongation period. This information is shown in Table 3.

Table 3

| Line | On the first day of elongation period: | | |
	Day of elongation period	Average amount of hydrogen peroxide (µmol/mg)	Average cotton fiber length (cm)
L1	1	1.2	0.2
L2	1	6.0	0.5
L3	1	5.7	0.1
L4	1	1.9	0.2

30. For L2, as the elongation period moved from the first day to the end, the amount of hydrogen peroxide:
    F. increased only
    G. decreased only
    H. increased, then decreased
    J. decreased, then increased

31. Which of the following is a dependent variable in the experiment?
    A. The point in time during the elongation period
    B. The type of superoxide dismutase the plant could express
    C. The length of the cotton fiber
    D. The type of cotton plant

32. A cotton fiber is one very long cell with two cell walls. A cotton fiber is a special kind of what type of cell?
    F. Prokaryotic
    G. Animal
    H. Plant
    J. Bacterial

33. One plant had an average cotton fiber length of 0.5 cm, and the average amount of hydrogen peroxide in its fibers was 5.9 µmol/mg. Which of the following most likely describes this plant?
    A. It was from L1 and at the end of its elongation period.
    B. It was from L1 and at the midpoint of its elongation period.
    C. It was from L2 and at the beginning of its elongation period.
    D. It was from L2 and at the end of its elongation period.

GO ON TO THE NEXT PAGE.

34. The scientists used one of the four lines of cotton plants as a control. Which line was most likely the control?

   F. L1
   G. L2
   H. L3
   J. L4

35. Suppose the data for all the plants were plotted on a graph with the time of the elongation period on the x-axis and the average length of the cotton fiber on the y-axis. Suppose also that the best-fit line for these data was determined. Which of the following would most likely characterize the slope of this line?

   A. The line would have a positive slope.
   B. The line would have a negative slope.
   C. The line would have a slope equal to zero.
   D. The line would have no slope, because the line would be vertical.

GO ON TO THE NEXT PAGE.

Passage VII

Convection is a heat transfer process caused by moving liquid or gas currents from a hot region to a cold region. As a liquid or gas cools, it gets more dense. An example of a convection process is a cup of hot coffee: the liquid toward the top is cooled by the air, so it becomes more dense and sinks to the bottom of the cup; the hotter liquid toward the bottom of the cup is less dense, so it rises toward the top. See Figure 1, below.

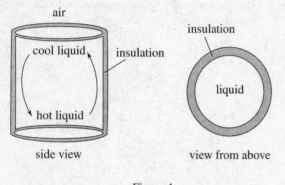

side view   view from above

Figure 1

The temperature of the liquid at the hot end of the insulated system is higher than the temperature at the cool end of the system. The difference (ΔT) between the hot liquid at the bottom and the cold liquid at the top changes depending on the starting temperature of the system. Table 1 gives ΔT for 500 mL of water in an insulated container with a height of 6.0 cm and a cross-sectional area of 4.0 cm² when the container is heated to different temperatures.

Table 1	
Heated temperature (°C)	ΔT (°C)
80	1
100	4
120	10
140	19

Figure 2 shows how ΔT changes with cross-sectional area for 500 mL of 100°C water in a container with a height of 6.0 cm. Figure 3 shows how ΔT changes with height for 500 mL 100°C water in a container with a cross-sectional area of 4.0 cm².

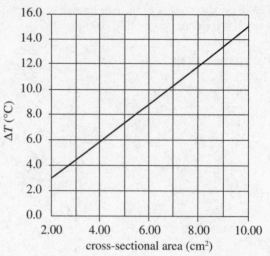

Figure 2

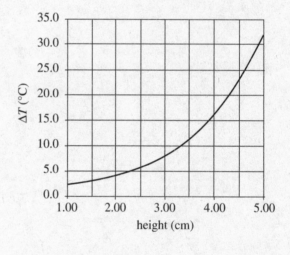

Figure 3

36. System 1 and System 2 are two convection systems. Based on Figure 2, if System 1 were the same height as System 2, but had two times the cross-sectional area and the systems were heated to the same temperature, the ratio of ΔT for System 1 to ΔT for System 2 would be:

F. 1:1
G. 1:2
H. 2:1
J. 3:1

GO ON TO THE NEXT PAGE.

37. For the systems described in the passage, if the containers were metal containers rather than insulated containers, heat would be transferred from the water to the container by which of the following heat transfer processes?

   I.   Convection
   II. Conduction
   III. Radiation

   A. I only
   B. II only
   C. I and III only
   D. I and II only

38. Which of the following systems, if all were heated to the same temperature, would have the greatest ΔT?

   F.

   G.

   H.

   J.

39. Based on the information in Table 1, if an insulated container of 500 mL of water with a height of 6.0 cm and a cross-sectional area of 4.0 cm^2 were heated to 120°C, which of the following pairs could represent the temperatures of the liquid at the top and bottom ends of the container?

	Bottom end	Top/Exposed to air end
A.	140°C	120°C
B.	140°C	110°C
C.	115°C	115°C
D.	120°C	110°C

40. The data in the passage supports the hypothesis that ΔT increases as which of the following increases?

   F. Amount of insulation
   G. Volume of liquid
   H. Radius of the container
   J. Air temperature

END OF TEST 4

STOP! DO NOT RETURN TO ANY OTHER TEST.

DIRECTIONS

This is a test of your writing skills. You will have thirty (30) minutes to write an essay. Before you begin planning and writing your essay, read the writing prompt carefully to understand exactly what you are being asked to do. Your essay will be evaluated on the evidence it provides of your ability to express judgments by taking a position on the issue in the writing prompt; to maintain a focus on the topic throughout your essay; to develop a position by using logical reasoning and by supporting your ideas; to organize ideas in a logical way; and to use language clearly and effectively according to the conventions of standard written English.

You may use the unlined pages in this test booklet to plan your essay. These pages will not be scored. *You must write your essay on the lined pages in the answer folder.* Your writing on those lined pages will be scored. You may not need all the lined pages, but to ensure you have enough room to finish, do NOT skip lines. You may write corrections or additions neatly between the lines of your essay, but do NOT write in the margins of the lined pages. *Illegible essays cannot be scored, so you must write (or print) clearly.*

If you finish before time is called, you may review your work. Lay your pencil down immediately when time is called.

DO NOT OPEN THIS BOOK UNTIL YOU ARE TOLD TO DO SO.

ACT Assessment Writing Test Prompt

Most schools have established honor codes or other rules to prevent students from cheating on exams and other school assignments. Many students admit to cheating, arguing that the practice has become so common—and is so rarely penalized—that it is the only way to survive in today's competitive academic world. Educators, however, feel that such behaviors only hurt the students, and that cheating in school is just the first step to more academic dishonesty, professional misconduct, and unethical business practices in the future. In your view, should high schools become more tolerant of cheating?

In your essay, take a position on this question. You may write about either one of the two points of view given or you may present a different point of view on this question. Use specific reasons and examples to support your position.

ACT Diagnostic Test Form

Use a No. 2 pencil only. Be sure each mark is dark and completely fills the intended oval. Completely erase any errors or stray marks.

1. YOUR NAME: _____
(Print)　　　　Last　　　　　　　　First　　　　　　　M.I.

SIGNATURE: _____　**DATE:** _____ / _____ / _____

HOME ADDRESS: _____
(Print)　　　　　　　Number and Street

_____
City　　　　　　　State　　　　Zip

E-MAIL: _____

PHONE NO.: _____
(Print)

SCHOOL: _____

CLASS OF: _____

IMPORTANT: Please fill in these boxes exactly as shown on the back cover of your tests book.

2. TEST FORM

_____

3. TEST CODE

⓪	⓪	⓪	⓪
①	①	①	①
②	②	②	②
③	③	③	③
④	④	④	④
⑤	⑤	⑤	⑤
⑥	⑥	⑥	⑥
⑦	⑦	⑦	⑦
⑧	⑧	⑧	⑧
⑨	⑨	⑨	⑨

4. PHONE NUMBER

⓪	⓪	⓪	⓪	⓪	⓪	⓪
①	①	①	①	①	①	①
②	②	②	②	②	②	②
③	③	③	③	③	③	③
④	④	④	④	④	④	④
⑤	⑤	⑤	⑤	⑤	⑤	⑤
⑥	⑥	⑥	⑥	⑥	⑥	⑥
⑦	⑦	⑦	⑦	⑦	⑦	⑦
⑧	⑧	⑧	⑧	⑧	⑧	⑧
⑨	⑨	⑨	⑨	⑨	⑨	⑨

5. YOUR NAME

First 4 letters of last name				FIRST INIT	MID INIT
Ⓐ	Ⓐ	Ⓐ	Ⓐ	Ⓐ	Ⓐ
Ⓑ	Ⓑ	Ⓑ	Ⓑ	Ⓑ	Ⓑ
Ⓒ	Ⓒ	Ⓒ	Ⓒ	Ⓒ	Ⓒ
Ⓓ	Ⓓ	Ⓓ	Ⓓ	Ⓓ	Ⓓ
Ⓔ	Ⓔ	Ⓔ	Ⓔ	Ⓔ	Ⓔ
Ⓕ	Ⓕ	Ⓕ	Ⓕ	Ⓕ	Ⓕ
Ⓖ	Ⓖ	Ⓖ	Ⓖ	Ⓖ	Ⓖ
Ⓗ	Ⓗ	Ⓗ	Ⓗ	Ⓗ	Ⓗ
Ⓘ	Ⓘ	Ⓘ	Ⓘ	Ⓘ	Ⓘ
Ⓙ	Ⓙ	Ⓙ	Ⓙ	Ⓙ	Ⓙ
Ⓚ	Ⓚ	Ⓚ	Ⓚ	Ⓚ	Ⓚ
Ⓛ	Ⓛ	Ⓛ	Ⓛ	Ⓛ	Ⓛ
Ⓜ	Ⓜ	Ⓜ	Ⓜ	Ⓜ	Ⓜ
Ⓝ	Ⓝ	Ⓝ	Ⓝ	Ⓝ	Ⓝ
Ⓞ	Ⓞ	Ⓞ	Ⓞ	Ⓞ	Ⓞ
Ⓟ	Ⓟ	Ⓟ	Ⓟ	Ⓟ	Ⓟ
Ⓠ	Ⓠ	Ⓠ	Ⓠ	Ⓠ	Ⓠ
Ⓡ	Ⓡ	Ⓡ	Ⓡ	Ⓡ	Ⓡ
Ⓢ	Ⓢ	Ⓢ	Ⓢ	Ⓢ	Ⓢ
Ⓣ	Ⓣ	Ⓣ	Ⓣ	Ⓣ	Ⓣ
Ⓤ	Ⓤ	Ⓤ	Ⓤ	Ⓤ	Ⓤ
Ⓥ	Ⓥ	Ⓥ	Ⓥ	Ⓥ	Ⓥ
Ⓦ	Ⓦ	Ⓦ	Ⓦ	Ⓦ	Ⓦ
Ⓧ	Ⓧ	Ⓧ	Ⓧ	Ⓧ	Ⓧ
Ⓨ	Ⓨ	Ⓨ	Ⓨ	Ⓨ	Ⓨ
Ⓩ	Ⓩ	Ⓩ	Ⓩ	Ⓩ	Ⓩ

6. DATE OF BIRTH

MONTH		DAY		YEAR	
◯ JAN					
◯ FEB					
◯ MAR		⓪	⓪	⓪	⓪
◯ APR		①	①	①	①
◯ MAY		②	②	②	②
◯ JUN		③	③	③	③
◯ JUL			④	④	④
◯ AUG			⑤	⑤	⑤
◯ SEP			⑥	⑥	⑥
◯ OCT			⑦	⑦	⑦
◯ NOV			⑧	⑧	⑧
◯ DEC			⑨	⑨	⑨

7. SEX

◯ MALE
◯ FEMALE

8. OTHER

1	Ⓐ Ⓑ Ⓒ Ⓓ Ⓔ
2	Ⓐ Ⓑ Ⓒ Ⓓ Ⓔ
3	Ⓐ Ⓑ Ⓒ Ⓓ Ⓔ

OpScan iNSIGHT™ forms by Pearson NCS EM-255315-1:654321　　Printed in U.S.A.

THIS PAGE INTENTIONALLY LEFT BLANK

The Princeton Review
Diagnostic ACT Form

Completely darken bubbles with a No. 2 pencil. If you make a mistake, be sure to erase mark completely. Erase all stray marks.

ENGLISH

1 Ⓐ Ⓑ Ⓒ Ⓓ	21 Ⓐ Ⓑ Ⓒ Ⓓ	41 Ⓐ Ⓑ Ⓒ Ⓓ	61 Ⓐ Ⓑ Ⓒ Ⓓ
2 Ⓕ Ⓖ Ⓗ Ⓙ	22 Ⓕ Ⓖ Ⓗ Ⓙ	42 Ⓕ Ⓖ Ⓗ Ⓙ	62 Ⓕ Ⓖ Ⓗ Ⓙ
3 Ⓐ Ⓑ Ⓒ Ⓓ	23 Ⓐ Ⓑ Ⓒ Ⓓ	43 Ⓐ Ⓑ Ⓒ Ⓓ	63 Ⓐ Ⓑ Ⓒ Ⓓ
4 Ⓕ Ⓖ Ⓗ Ⓙ	24 Ⓕ Ⓖ Ⓗ Ⓙ	44 Ⓕ Ⓖ Ⓗ Ⓙ	64 Ⓕ Ⓖ Ⓗ Ⓙ
5 Ⓐ Ⓑ Ⓒ Ⓓ	25 Ⓐ Ⓑ Ⓒ Ⓓ	45 Ⓐ Ⓑ Ⓒ Ⓓ	65 Ⓐ Ⓑ Ⓒ Ⓓ
6 Ⓕ Ⓖ Ⓗ Ⓙ	26 Ⓕ Ⓖ Ⓗ Ⓙ	46 Ⓕ Ⓖ Ⓗ Ⓙ	66 Ⓕ Ⓖ Ⓗ Ⓙ
7 Ⓐ Ⓑ Ⓒ Ⓓ	27 Ⓐ Ⓑ Ⓒ Ⓓ	47 Ⓐ Ⓑ Ⓒ Ⓓ	67 Ⓐ Ⓑ Ⓒ Ⓓ
8 Ⓕ Ⓖ Ⓗ Ⓙ	28 Ⓕ Ⓖ Ⓗ Ⓙ	48 Ⓕ Ⓖ Ⓗ Ⓙ	68 Ⓕ Ⓖ Ⓗ Ⓙ
9 Ⓐ Ⓑ Ⓒ Ⓓ	29 Ⓐ Ⓑ Ⓒ Ⓓ	49 Ⓐ Ⓑ Ⓒ Ⓓ	69 Ⓐ Ⓑ Ⓒ Ⓓ
10 Ⓕ Ⓖ Ⓗ Ⓙ	30 Ⓕ Ⓖ Ⓗ Ⓙ	50 Ⓕ Ⓖ Ⓗ Ⓙ	70 Ⓕ Ⓖ Ⓗ Ⓙ
11 Ⓐ Ⓑ Ⓒ Ⓓ	31 Ⓐ Ⓑ Ⓒ Ⓓ	51 Ⓐ Ⓑ Ⓒ Ⓓ	71 Ⓐ Ⓑ Ⓒ Ⓓ
12 Ⓕ Ⓖ Ⓗ Ⓙ	32 Ⓕ Ⓖ Ⓗ Ⓙ	52 Ⓕ Ⓖ Ⓗ Ⓙ	72 Ⓕ Ⓖ Ⓗ Ⓙ
13 Ⓐ Ⓑ Ⓒ Ⓓ	33 Ⓐ Ⓑ Ⓒ Ⓓ	53 Ⓐ Ⓑ Ⓒ Ⓓ	73 Ⓐ Ⓑ Ⓒ Ⓓ
14 Ⓕ Ⓖ Ⓗ Ⓙ	34 Ⓕ Ⓖ Ⓗ Ⓙ	54 Ⓕ Ⓖ Ⓗ Ⓙ	74 Ⓕ Ⓖ Ⓗ Ⓙ
15 Ⓐ Ⓑ Ⓒ Ⓓ	35 Ⓐ Ⓑ Ⓒ Ⓓ	55 Ⓐ Ⓑ Ⓒ Ⓓ	75 Ⓐ Ⓑ Ⓒ Ⓓ
16 Ⓕ Ⓖ Ⓗ Ⓙ	36 Ⓕ Ⓖ Ⓗ Ⓙ	56 Ⓕ Ⓖ Ⓗ Ⓙ	
17 Ⓐ Ⓑ Ⓒ Ⓓ	37 Ⓐ Ⓑ Ⓒ Ⓓ	57 Ⓐ Ⓑ Ⓒ Ⓓ	
18 Ⓕ Ⓖ Ⓗ Ⓙ	38 Ⓕ Ⓖ Ⓗ Ⓙ	58 Ⓕ Ⓖ Ⓗ Ⓙ	
19 Ⓐ Ⓑ Ⓒ Ⓓ	39 Ⓐ Ⓑ Ⓒ Ⓓ	59 Ⓐ Ⓑ Ⓒ Ⓓ	
20 Ⓕ Ⓖ Ⓗ Ⓙ	40 Ⓕ Ⓖ Ⓗ Ⓙ	60 Ⓕ Ⓖ Ⓗ Ⓙ	

MATHEMATICS

1 Ⓐ Ⓑ Ⓒ Ⓓ Ⓔ	16 Ⓕ Ⓖ Ⓗ Ⓙ Ⓚ	31 Ⓐ Ⓑ Ⓒ Ⓓ Ⓔ	46 Ⓕ Ⓖ Ⓗ Ⓙ Ⓚ
2 Ⓕ Ⓖ Ⓗ Ⓙ Ⓚ	17 Ⓐ Ⓑ Ⓒ Ⓓ Ⓔ	32 Ⓕ Ⓖ Ⓗ Ⓙ Ⓚ	47 Ⓐ Ⓑ Ⓒ Ⓓ Ⓔ
3 Ⓐ Ⓑ Ⓒ Ⓓ Ⓔ	18 Ⓕ Ⓖ Ⓗ Ⓙ Ⓚ	33 Ⓐ Ⓑ Ⓒ Ⓓ Ⓔ	48 Ⓕ Ⓖ Ⓗ Ⓙ Ⓚ
4 Ⓕ Ⓖ Ⓗ Ⓙ Ⓚ	19 Ⓐ Ⓑ Ⓒ Ⓓ Ⓔ	34 Ⓕ Ⓖ Ⓗ Ⓙ Ⓚ	49 Ⓐ Ⓑ Ⓒ Ⓓ Ⓔ
5 Ⓐ Ⓑ Ⓒ Ⓓ Ⓔ	20 Ⓕ Ⓖ Ⓗ Ⓙ Ⓚ	35 Ⓐ Ⓑ Ⓒ Ⓓ Ⓔ	50 Ⓕ Ⓖ Ⓗ Ⓙ Ⓚ
6 Ⓕ Ⓖ Ⓗ Ⓙ Ⓚ	21 Ⓐ Ⓑ Ⓒ Ⓓ Ⓔ	36 Ⓕ Ⓖ Ⓗ Ⓙ Ⓚ	51 Ⓐ Ⓑ Ⓒ Ⓓ Ⓔ
7 Ⓐ Ⓑ Ⓒ Ⓓ Ⓔ	22 Ⓕ Ⓖ Ⓗ Ⓙ Ⓚ	37 Ⓐ Ⓑ Ⓒ Ⓓ Ⓔ	52 Ⓕ Ⓖ Ⓗ Ⓙ Ⓚ
8 Ⓕ Ⓖ Ⓗ Ⓙ Ⓚ	23 Ⓐ Ⓑ Ⓒ Ⓓ Ⓔ	38 Ⓕ Ⓖ Ⓗ Ⓙ Ⓚ	53 Ⓐ Ⓑ Ⓒ Ⓓ Ⓔ
9 Ⓐ Ⓑ Ⓒ Ⓓ Ⓔ	24 Ⓕ Ⓖ Ⓗ Ⓙ Ⓚ	39 Ⓐ Ⓑ Ⓒ Ⓓ Ⓔ	54 Ⓕ Ⓖ Ⓗ Ⓙ Ⓚ
10 Ⓕ Ⓖ Ⓗ Ⓙ Ⓚ	25 Ⓐ Ⓑ Ⓒ Ⓓ Ⓔ	40 Ⓕ Ⓖ Ⓗ Ⓙ Ⓚ	55 Ⓐ Ⓑ Ⓒ Ⓓ Ⓔ
11 Ⓐ Ⓑ Ⓒ Ⓓ Ⓔ	26 Ⓕ Ⓖ Ⓗ Ⓙ Ⓚ	41 Ⓐ Ⓑ Ⓒ Ⓓ Ⓔ	56 Ⓕ Ⓖ Ⓗ Ⓙ Ⓚ
12 Ⓕ Ⓖ Ⓗ Ⓙ Ⓚ	27 Ⓐ Ⓑ Ⓒ Ⓓ Ⓔ	42 Ⓕ Ⓖ Ⓗ Ⓙ Ⓚ	57 Ⓐ Ⓑ Ⓒ Ⓓ Ⓔ
13 Ⓐ Ⓑ Ⓒ Ⓓ Ⓔ	28 Ⓕ Ⓖ Ⓗ Ⓙ Ⓚ	43 Ⓐ Ⓑ Ⓒ Ⓓ Ⓔ	58 Ⓕ Ⓖ Ⓗ Ⓙ Ⓚ
14 Ⓕ Ⓖ Ⓗ Ⓙ Ⓚ	29 Ⓐ Ⓑ Ⓒ Ⓓ Ⓔ	44 Ⓕ Ⓖ Ⓗ Ⓙ Ⓚ	59 Ⓐ Ⓑ Ⓒ Ⓓ Ⓔ
15 Ⓐ Ⓑ Ⓒ Ⓓ Ⓔ	30 Ⓕ Ⓖ Ⓗ Ⓙ Ⓚ	45 Ⓐ Ⓑ Ⓒ Ⓓ Ⓔ	60 Ⓕ Ⓖ Ⓗ Ⓙ Ⓚ

The Princeton Review
Diagnostic ACT Form

Completely darken bubbles with a No. 2 pencil. If you make a mistake, be sure to erase mark completely. Erase all stray marks.

READING

1 Ⓐ Ⓑ Ⓒ Ⓓ	11 Ⓐ Ⓑ Ⓒ Ⓓ	21 Ⓐ Ⓑ Ⓒ Ⓓ	31 Ⓐ Ⓑ Ⓒ Ⓓ
2 Ⓕ Ⓖ Ⓗ Ⓙ	12 Ⓕ Ⓖ Ⓗ Ⓙ	22 Ⓕ Ⓖ Ⓗ Ⓙ	32 Ⓕ Ⓖ Ⓗ Ⓙ
3 Ⓐ Ⓑ Ⓒ Ⓓ	13 Ⓐ Ⓑ Ⓒ Ⓓ	23 Ⓐ Ⓑ Ⓒ Ⓓ	33 Ⓐ Ⓑ Ⓒ Ⓓ
4 Ⓕ Ⓖ Ⓗ Ⓙ	14 Ⓕ Ⓖ Ⓗ Ⓙ	24 Ⓕ Ⓖ Ⓗ Ⓙ	34 Ⓕ Ⓖ Ⓗ Ⓙ
5 Ⓐ Ⓑ Ⓒ Ⓓ	15 Ⓐ Ⓑ Ⓒ Ⓓ	25 Ⓐ Ⓑ Ⓒ Ⓓ	35 Ⓐ Ⓑ Ⓒ Ⓓ
6 Ⓕ Ⓖ Ⓗ Ⓙ	16 Ⓕ Ⓖ Ⓗ Ⓙ	26 Ⓕ Ⓖ Ⓗ Ⓙ	36 Ⓕ Ⓖ Ⓗ Ⓙ
7 Ⓐ Ⓑ Ⓒ Ⓓ	17 Ⓐ Ⓑ Ⓒ Ⓓ	27 Ⓐ Ⓑ Ⓒ Ⓓ	37 Ⓐ Ⓑ Ⓒ Ⓓ
8 Ⓕ Ⓖ Ⓗ Ⓙ	18 Ⓕ Ⓖ Ⓗ Ⓙ	28 Ⓕ Ⓖ Ⓗ Ⓙ	38 Ⓕ Ⓖ Ⓗ Ⓙ
9 Ⓐ Ⓑ Ⓒ Ⓓ	19 Ⓐ Ⓑ Ⓒ Ⓓ	29 Ⓐ Ⓑ Ⓒ Ⓓ	39 Ⓐ Ⓑ Ⓒ Ⓓ
10 Ⓕ Ⓖ Ⓗ Ⓙ	20 Ⓕ Ⓖ Ⓗ Ⓙ	30 Ⓕ Ⓖ Ⓗ Ⓙ	40 Ⓕ Ⓖ Ⓗ Ⓙ

SCIENCE REASONING

1 Ⓐ Ⓑ Ⓒ Ⓓ	11 Ⓐ Ⓑ Ⓒ Ⓓ	21 Ⓐ Ⓑ Ⓒ Ⓓ	31 Ⓐ Ⓑ Ⓒ Ⓓ
2 Ⓕ Ⓖ Ⓗ Ⓙ	12 Ⓕ Ⓖ Ⓗ Ⓙ	22 Ⓕ Ⓖ Ⓗ Ⓙ	32 Ⓕ Ⓖ Ⓗ Ⓙ
3 Ⓐ Ⓑ Ⓒ Ⓓ	13 Ⓐ Ⓑ Ⓒ Ⓓ	23 Ⓐ Ⓑ Ⓒ Ⓓ	33 Ⓐ Ⓑ Ⓒ Ⓓ
4 Ⓕ Ⓖ Ⓗ Ⓙ	14 Ⓕ Ⓖ Ⓗ Ⓙ	24 Ⓕ Ⓖ Ⓗ Ⓙ	34 Ⓕ Ⓖ Ⓗ Ⓙ
5 Ⓐ Ⓑ Ⓒ Ⓓ	15 Ⓐ Ⓑ Ⓒ Ⓓ	25 Ⓐ Ⓑ Ⓒ Ⓓ	35 Ⓐ Ⓑ Ⓒ Ⓓ
6 Ⓕ Ⓖ Ⓗ Ⓙ	16 Ⓕ Ⓖ Ⓗ Ⓙ	26 Ⓕ Ⓖ Ⓗ Ⓙ	36 Ⓕ Ⓖ Ⓗ Ⓙ
7 Ⓐ Ⓑ Ⓒ Ⓓ	17 Ⓐ Ⓑ Ⓒ Ⓓ	27 Ⓐ Ⓑ Ⓒ Ⓓ	37 Ⓐ Ⓑ Ⓒ Ⓓ
8 Ⓕ Ⓖ Ⓗ Ⓙ	18 Ⓕ Ⓖ Ⓗ Ⓙ	28 Ⓕ Ⓖ Ⓗ Ⓙ	38 Ⓕ Ⓖ Ⓗ Ⓙ
9 Ⓐ Ⓑ Ⓒ Ⓓ	19 Ⓐ Ⓑ Ⓒ Ⓓ	29 Ⓐ Ⓑ Ⓒ Ⓓ	39 Ⓐ Ⓑ Ⓒ Ⓓ
10 Ⓕ Ⓖ Ⓗ Ⓙ	20 Ⓕ Ⓖ Ⓗ Ⓙ	30 Ⓕ Ⓖ Ⓗ Ⓙ	40 Ⓕ Ⓖ Ⓗ Ⓙ

I hereby certify that I have truthfully identified myself on this form. I accept the consequences of falsifying my identity.

_____

Your signature

_____

Today's date

The Princeton Review
Diagnostic ACT Form

ESSAY

Begin your essay on this side. If necessary, continue on the opposite side.

The Princeton Review
Diagnostic ACT Form

Continued from previous page.

PLEASE PRINT
YOUR INITIALS

First   Middle   Last

Chapter 26
Practice Exam 1:
Answers
and Explanations

English		Math		Reading		Science	
1. B	40. H	1. E	40. K	1. C	40. G	1. A	40. H
2. F	41. B	2. G	41. B	2. J		2. J	
3. D	42. J	3. B	42. K	3. A		3. C	
4. G	43. A	4. J	43. B	4. J		4. J	
5. A	44. G	5. C	44. J	5. B		5. D	
6. H	45. C	6. H	45. E	6. G		6. J	
7. C	46. H	7. B	46. H	7. D		7. B	
8. J	47. C	8. J	47. C	8. F		8. J	
9. D	48. F	9. E	48. J	9. C		9. A	
10. F	49. C	10. F	49. C	10. G		10. F	
11. B	50. J	11. E	50. G	11. C		11. D	
12. H	51. A	12. J	51. E	12. G		12. G	
13. D	52. F	13. B	52. G	13. A		13. A	
14. G	53. D	14.K	53. C	14. G		14. H	
15. A	54. F	15. A	54. F	15. C		15. B	
16. G	55. D	16. G	55. D	16. G		16.H	
17. C	56. H	17. D	56. G	17. D		17. C	
18. H	57. B	18. F	57. B	18. H		18. J	
19. D	58. G	19. A	58. F	19. D		19. A	
20. F	59. B	20. K	59. C	20. F		20. H	
21. D	60. G	21. E	60. J	21. A		21. C	
22. F	61. D	22. F		22. F		22. G	
23. C	62. F	23. B		23. D		23. C	
24. G	63. C	24. H		24. G		24. J	
25. D	64. F	25. E		25. A		25. A	
26. G	65. C	26. H		26. J		26. J	
27. A	66. G	27. C		27. D		27. D	
28. G	67. C	28. G		28. H		28. F	
29. A	68. F	29. B		29. C		29. D	
30. H	69. B	30. G		30. G		30. G	
31. B	70. J	31. C		31. A		31. C	
32. F	71. B	32. G		32. H		32. H	
33. D	72. G	33. E		33. C		33. C	
34. F	73. D	34. J		34. J		34. J	
35. A	74. F	35. D		35. A		35. A	
36. H	75. D	36. K		36. H		36. H	
37. C		37. D		37. D		37. B	
38. H		38. H		38. J		38. F	
39. B		39. C		39. A		39. D	

ENGLISH TEST

1. **B** This sentence needs a comma after the complete idea and before the incomplete one. This brief pause clarifies that the incomplete idea is modifying Hawaii. Choices (C) and (D) introduce additional words that are unnecessary or create an error.

2. **F** In Sentence 4, the writer provides additional support for how difficult the race is. If deleted, the passage would lose this emphasis, as choice (F) describes. Choices (G), (H), and (J) all introduce extraneous details that have not been provided by the passage.

3. **D** This sentence requires a contrast to the previous paragraph. Only choice (D) provides that with *however*.

4. **G** As written, this sentence incorrectly places a comma after the word *athletics*, which is not needed since an incomplete idea follows. This eliminates choices (F) and (H). Choice (J) is not correct because it places a comma after the word *and*, and uses the incorrect pronoun *there* to refer to sports' *physical demands*, which requires the possessive.

5. **A** This sentence is correct as written, because *proved* as it is used means *became*. All the other options are synonyms of a different definition of *proved* and thus change the intended meaning of the sentence.

6. **H** The word *somewhat* is referring to the *amusing way* in which the race started. Therefore, *somewhat* needs to be before the word *amusing* to correctly modify it, choice (H).

7. **C** This sentence is providing the names of two sports clubs and the island on which they functioned. There is no need to separate anything here with a comma because it is a list of only two items, so that eliminates choices (A), (B), and (D). Only choice (C) correctly removes the commas.

8. **J** *Claiming* describes the bikers and does not require a conjunction, eliminating choices (F) and (G). Choice (H) would create a comma splice.

9. **D** The phrase before the comma is incomplete, and the word *when* introduces a second incomplete idea, leaving the sentence without any complete ideas. Therefore, the only possible answer is to delete the underlined portion, or choice (D).

10. **F** The underlined phrase refers to the three separate races that were eventually combined into the single race of the Triathlon. Therefore, it should remain where it is now, choice (F).

11. **B** As written, the underlined section is redundant because it references the pages he is reading, although they were just mentioned a few words before. This redundancy can be eliminated by selecting choice (B).

12. **H** You can never join the helping verb *had* with the simple past tense *became*. This eliminates choice (F). Choice (G) is the present tense of the verb, and choice (J) is the incorrect form of the past tense, so both of those can be eliminated as well. Only choice (H) provides the correct form of the simple past tense.

13. D   Only choice (D) points out Haller's great achievement of winning the first Ironman. Choices (A) and (C) detract from his achievement by focusing on other competitors, and choice (B) discusses a moment of doubt Haller has.

14. G   Choices (F), (H), and (J) all provide specific, plural phrases that could represent the competitors to whom the sentence is referring. Choice (G) is a singular, ambiguous *that* that cannot refer to the competitors.

15. A   The final paragraph discusses how many compete in the race today, as well as how popular the race has become since its inception. This most closely aligns with choice (A).

16. G   The underlined portion is incorrect as written because the *when* makes the second part of the sentence incomplete. Therefore, choice (F) can be eliminated. Whenever there is a list, all the elements of that list must be parallel. None of the other items in the sentence as written end in *-ing*, so that eliminates choice (H). Nor are any of them in the past tense, which eliminates choice (J). Only choice (G) matches the others, and thus must be the correct answer.

17. C   As written, this sentence contains two complete ideas with no punctuation in between, which eliminates choice (A). Simply adding a comma does not fix the problem, so choice (B) cannot be correct. Changing *hoping* to *praying* does not help either, so choice (D) cannot be correct. Only choice (C), which separates the sentence into two by introducing a period, offers a viable solution.

18. H   A conjunction is needed to join the two halves of the sentence together, eliminating choices (F) and (G) (note: *therefore* is an adverb, not a conjunction). *But* is not the right conjunction to use because the two clauses do not disagree with each other. That eliminates choice (J). The only answer left is choice (H).

19. D   The subject of this sentence, *all the opportunities*, comes after the verb. However, the verb still must agree with it. Since the subject is plural, choices (A) and (B) are inappropriate because those are singular forms of the verb. Choice (C) is incorrect because the verb *lay* refers to placing an item down, like a book on the table, which is inappropriate in this context. The only acceptable answer is choice (D).

20. F   In a list, there should be a comma after every item, including the one before the *and*. The first item in this list is *a nice pair of slacks*, so the first comma is needed after that expression but nowhere inside of it. This eliminates all the answers except choice (F).

21. D   Sentence 2 refers to the narrator's acceptance of the volunteer position. This must logically follow the sentence that contains the director's offer of the position, Sentence 5.

22. F   The phrase *an expert himself in every facet of hospital administration* is an additional descriptive detail that is not essential to the sentence. Therefore, it should have a comma on both sides of it. The correct answer is choice (F).

23.   C   The phrase preceding the comma at the beginning of this sentence must refer to the first noun following the phrase. As written, that noun is *my ears*, which cannot be correct because ears do not walk anywhere. Only choice (C) corrects the misplaced modifier by making *I* the subject.

24.   G   In an earlier sentence in this paragraph, the narrator describes herself as *overwhelmed* by all the noise in the hospital. Therefore, as the sounds continue, she becomes more overwhelmed, or *besieged*, as in choice (G).

25.   D   The underlined section of the sentence refers to how the narrator's face revealed her fear at the same time that she looked around the ward. Choice (D) changes this meaning, so it is therefore the LEAST acceptable option.

26.   G   This question calls for a vivid description of the hallway. Only choice (G) provides this, by giving specific details about all the family members and colorful decorations. Choice (F) just describes the hallway as busy, which is not particularly vivid. Choices (H) and (J) don't specifically refer to the hallway at all.

27.   A   The phrase *the one in charge of the nursery* provides an extra detail that is not essential to the meaning of the sentence. As such, it needs to be set off by commas on both sides. Only choice (A) gives us this option.

28.   G   The pronoun *it* should be referring to the blankets. However, *it* is singular, so choice (F) can be eliminated. *Them* is the appropriate pronoun to use, so choice (J) can be eliminated as well. Finally, *placing* doesn't match *start* as it needs to. Therefore, choice (H) can be eliminated and choice (G) must be the answer.

29.   A   The final paragraph expresses the narrator's comfort in the nursery, especially as compared to the maternity ward. Therefore, when she gives the hospital director a nod, she is acknowledging the fact that she enjoys the new atmosphere. This most closely aligns with choice (A). At no point in the passage does the narrator express anger or the intention to quit, so choices (B) and (C) cannot be correct. Finally, nowhere else in the passage is the narrator nodding, so choice (D) can be eliminated as well.

30.   H   This new information acts as an introduction to the narrator's first day working at the hospital. This most logically should be inserted at the beginning of Paragraph 3, in which the actual activities of her first day are described.

31.   B   In this sentence, the author is making a comparison between the reputation snakes have and the reputation they deserve. Such a comparison will always be separated by the word *than*, which eliminates choices (A) and (D). Choice (C) can be eliminated because it changes the meaning of the sentence to imply that snakes have the deadliest reputation, which was not stated.

32.   F   At this point in the essay, the author is identifying numerous negative associations related to the snake. Only choice (F) adds to this list. Choices (G), (H), and (J) do not contain anything particularly negative in their portrayals of the snake.

33. **D** As written, the phrase *that is popular* refers to *a snake*, which is incorrect. The phrase should refer to the *reference*. The only choice which provides this concisely is choice (D).

34. **F** Choice (G) contains the word *who's*, which is the contraction for *who is* and is inappropriate in this sentence. Choice (H) contains the word *it's*, a contraction for *it is* and likewise inappropriate. Choice (J) contains the word *its'*, which is never correct. The only remaining answer is choice (F).

35. **A** This sentence is correct as written. The phrase following *fangs* is an unnecessary descriptive piece added to the sentence, which should be set off with commas. It is not necessary to introduce any additional words, because that would make the sentence a run-on.

36. **H** The word *prey* is followed by a list of the items that fall into this category. A colon is needed before such a list, which makes choice (H) correct.

37. **C** As written, the phrase *they are provoked* is ambiguous. Does it refer to the snakes or the people? Only choice (C) clarifies this ambiguity in a concise way.

38. **H** The statistic quoted acts as support for the preceding sentence, arguing that snakes normally do not pose much threat to humans. Therefore, choice (H) is the correct response.

39. **B** The underlined phrase needs a verb consistent with the singular subject of *Prompt treatment*. Only choice (B) is consistent and concise.

40. **H** As underlined, the transition in this sentence is neither parallel nor logical, because the second half of the sentence is a separate idea that does not follow from the first. Only choice (H) provides a parallel transition.

41. **B** As written, this sentence is not a complete thought. It needs verbs, and without helping verbs like *was* or *is*, the words *considering* and *avoiding* can't stand alone. Choices (A) and (C) don't fix the problem. Choice (D) incorrectly changes the sentence to past tense, as well as combines two clauses. Only choice (B) gives two present tense verbs, "consider" and "avoid," to fix the fragment in the original sentence.

42. **J** As written, this sentence has complete ideas joined incorrectly. Two complete thoughts cannot be joined by a comma, which eliminates choices (F) and (H). Nor can two complete thoughts have no punctuation between them, so choice (G) must also be incorrect. Only choice (J) correctly uses a semicolon between the two thoughts.

43. **A** The opening paragraph referred to all the common derogatory phrases associated with snakes. Therefore, since choice (A) refers to the *snake in the grass* referenced in that paragraph, it would achieve the writer's aim of referencing the opening paragraph. All the other choices refer to items mentioned elsewhere in the passage, not in the first paragraph.

44.   G   The final sentence of the first paragraph refers to the snake as *unjustly maligned* despite its *ugly, slimy appearance*. The essay goes on to describe some of the misconceptions people have about snakes. Therefore, this sentence sets up the main idea of the passage as a whole, as choice (G) suggests.

45.   C   Choice (C) is correct because the author takes a positive view of snakes: they do not hurt humans to the degree commonly believed, and they help society by keeping the population of undesirable rodents and other pests in check.

46.   H   The underlined portion needs a word to indicate the present day. All the choices do this except choice (H), which changes the meaning.

47.   C   Choice (C) changes the meaning to indicate that the challenges showed anything was possible, whereas the original meaning of the sentence indicates that Hurston's perseverance is what made anything possible. Therefore, choice (C) is not acceptable.

48.   F   The underlined portion is correct as is, because it is the only choice that accurately reflects Hurston as an individualistic person, in keeping with the description of her provided in the previous paragraph. All the other choices change the meaning of the phrase in ways not supported by the passage.

49.   C   This question calls for something historical in nature that makes Eatonville unique. Only choice (C) provides this. Choice (A) doesn't make the town unique, as many cities share a similar climate. Likewise, choices (B) and (D) discuss the town's founding but do not indicate that the town is different from any other community founded in the same era.

50.   J   This sentence needs a simple conjunction to join the two items listed, *freedom* and *independence*. For this reason, choice (J) is the answer. Choice (F) makes no sense in the context of the sentence because what follows *that* is not a separate clause. Choice (G) incorrectly introduces an unnecessary verb. Choice (H) makes the sentence two complete ideas linked incorrectly.

51.   A   The underlined portion is correct as written, choice (A). This list of two items is essential to the meaning of the sentence, so it should not be set off with commas. Only information that could be removed without altering the meaning requires commas.

52.   F   This sentence is correct as written. Choices (G) and (H) introduce a comma into the sentence that incorrectly separates the subject from the verb. Choice (J) incorrectly introduces a semicolon, which can only be used to connect two complete thoughts.

53.   D   The correct choice is (D), because it correctly eliminates the redundancy in the underlined passage. The term *literature* means *books, poems, and plays*, so there is no need to repeat it, as choice (A) does. The same applies to choices (B) and (C), so they are likewise incorrect.

54.   F   This sentence needs a verb in the past tense. This eliminates choices (H) and (J). Choice (G) cannot be correct, because *developed* does not require a preposition to follow it. Therefore, the correct answer must be choice (F).

55. **D** This additional information relating to Billie Holiday is not relevant at this point in a passage dedicated to Hurston. It provides interesting but superfluous detail, which most closely aligns with choice (D).

56. **H** This question wants a word that indicates the novel accurately reflects the actual dialect spoken. Choice (H) does this, because if something is authentic, it is true to the original. Choices (F), (G), and (J) positively comment on the dialect, but tell us nothing about how accurate it is.

57. **B** As written, the underlined *it* is ambiguous. The sentence needs to clearly identify what *it* is referring to. This eliminates both choices (A) and (C). Choice (D) cannot work, because *which* does not refer to Hurston's work. Therefore, choice (B) must be correct.

58. **G** Sentence 4 identifies one of Hurston's novels, and the following sentences provide additional information about the plot of that novel and the critical reception it received. Choice (G) most closely aligns with this summary. Choice (F) is incorrect because nothing in the remaining sentences indicates one specific influence. Choice (H) is incorrect because only one of the subsequent sentences provides a plot detail. Finally, choice (J) is incorrect because the remaining sentences focus on the novel, not Eatonville specifically.

59. **B** As written, the underlined portion is incorrect because the transition it uses indicates the sentence disagrees with the one that came before it. Therefore, choice (A) can be eliminated. However, choices (C) and (D) are incorrect as well, because there is no direct cause and effect relationship between the two sentences. Choice (B) is the best choice because no transition is necessary at all.

60. **G** The phrase *as one of the best writers of her era* is essential to the meaning of the sentence, which means it cannot be set off by commas. It does, however, need an *and* after it to join the two halves of the sentence together. Thus, choice (G) must be correct.

61. **D** As written, this sentence is incomplete and cannot be ended with a period. This eliminates choice (A). There is also no need to introduce a conjunction, because that does not fix the problem. Therefore, the correct answer must be choice (D).

62. **F** The phrase *Soviet Union* is extra information that is not essential to the meaning of the sentence. As such, it should have a dash on both sides of it, which only choice (F) provides.

63. **C** The word *Americas* is being used as a possessive, because it owns the *powerful office* that follows. Therefore, it should have an apostrophe before the *s*. This eliminates choices (A) and (D). The phrase *most powerful* is modifying the word *office* and does not need a comma. Therefore, choice (C) must be correct.

64. **F** The underlined portion is correct as written. A pronoun in the subject case is needed here, because it is the subject of the verb in the idea that follows.

65.	C	The phrase *underprivileged* indicates that these individuals are not as fortunate as others in a given society. As such, it would be redundant to specify this again. Only choice (C) eliminates this redundancy.

66.	G	This sentence indicates that Carter supported a national energy policy. Only choice (G) aligns with this information.

67.	C	The phrase *on foreign oil* refers to what America depended upon. Therefore, it should be as close as possible to the word *dependence*, or choice (C).

68.	F	All the answer choices refer to the creation of the Carter Center. However, choice (F) changes the meaning to imply that Carter discovered the Center, rather than started it.

69.	B	The phrase *around the world* already refers to many different countries, so it would be redundant to specify those countries. Therefore, the correct answer is choice (B).

70.	J	The first words in this phrase, *at home*, indicate that Carter works within the United States. There is no need to identify this again, making the sentence redundant. Therefore, the correct answer is choice (J).

71.	B	As written, the placement of *abroad* incorrectly modifies the verb *focus*, which changes the intended meaning of the sentence. The word *abroad* refers to where Carter expends his efforts, or choice (B).

72.	G	Sentence 4 functions as a transition between the previous paragraph and this paragraph. As such it should come first, as choice (G) suggests.

73.	D	The correct preposition needs to be *with* in order to maintain the intended meaning of the sentence: someone concurring with Carter. Choices (A) and (C) use prepositions that never work with *agree*. Choice (B) changes the meaning to taking on an obligation.

74.	F	This essay intends to identify some of the positive humanitarian goals Carter has sought to achieve in his career. Choice (F) most closely aligns with this goal. Choices (G) and (J) focus on his politics while ignoring his humanitarian interests, so they can be eliminated. Choice (H) comments on a right as an American, which has nothing to do with the rest of the passage.

75.	D	The new sentence references Habitat for Humanity, which was discussed in Paragraph 4. Therefore, it would most logically be added to the end of that paragraph, or choice (D).

MATHEMATICS TEST

1. **E** Set up a proportion with the information you have and the information you are looking for:

$$\frac{\text{height}}{\text{length of shadow}} = \frac{24 \text{ ft}}{6 \text{ ft}} = \frac{x \text{ ft}}{18 \text{ ft}}$$

Do the cross-multiplication to find that $x = 72$ feet, choice (E).

2. **G** Remember that Sherwood's $100 payment covers both his one-time new-member fee and a few months of a membership. Since the new-member fee is $16, this means that Sherwood put $100 − $16 = $84 toward his monthly fees. Since each month costs $14, Sherwood paid for $84 ÷ $14 = 6 months of membership.

3. **B** Although this looks like a problem in which you'll need to factor, you actually can just substitute the y value: $\dfrac{y^2 - 4}{y - 2} = \dfrac{(-6)^2 - 4}{(-6) - 2} = \dfrac{(36) - 4}{-8} = \dfrac{32}{-8} = -4.$

4. **J** Because the group ended up with more than 15 students, they overpaid. Figure out the total amount they should have paid and subtract it from the amount that they did pay: (18)($11.50) − (18)($10.25) = $22.50.

5. **C** When you are finding a probability, you need to figure out a basic part/whole relationship. In this case, there are 16 members in the orchestra, but only 12 of them are eligible to become speakers, so the "whole" (the denominator) must be 12. If you selected choice (B), you forgot to omit the 4 soloists. The likelihood that Itzhak would be chosen for this person is therefore $\dfrac{1}{12}$, because he represents one possibility out of the twelve eligible for the speaker position.

6. **H** In order to find the perimeter of a rectangle, remember that there are four sides. In this case the four sides add up as follows: 8 ft + 8 ft + 17 ft + 17 ft = 50 ft. If you selected choice (F), you may have only added two sides of the rectangle, and if you selected choice (J), be careful—this is the area!

7. **B** Work slowly through this problem. The group has sold 240 passes online at $9 each. This means that they have already made (240)($9) = $2,160. In order to reach their goal, they will need $4,000 − $2,160 = $1,840. Since the question asks how many in-person tickets they will need to sell, you can approximate how many tickets will get them $1,840 by dividing: $1,840 ÷ $12 = 153.333. Since there is no such thing as 0.333 tickets, you have to round up to get 154 tickets, choice (B).

8. **J** Do basic cross-multiplication here. $\dfrac{9}{q} = \dfrac{6}{10}$ becomes (9)(10) = 6q, so $q = \dfrac{(9)(10)}{6} = \dfrac{90}{6} = 15.$

9. **E** Make sure you keep all your negative signs straight and distribute properly. The original equation is −9(y − 13) = 16. First, distribute the (−9) to find (−9y + 117) = 16. Subtract the 117 from both sides to find (−9y) = −101. Divide each side by the (−9) to find $y = 11.2 = \dfrac{101}{9}.$

10. F Because Points *F, G, H*, and *J* are collinear, you can figure out $\angle GHK$ by subtracting $180° - \angle JHK = 180° - 120° = 60°$. Segments $\overline{GK}$ and $\overline{HK}$ are equivalent, so angles $\angle GHK$ and $\angle HGK$ are congruent, and $\angle HGK = 60°$. Again because they are collinear, $\angle HGK + \angle FGK = 180°$, so $\angle FGK = 120°$. Isolate this triangle to find $\angle GFK$. Because of the two congruent sides, $\angle GFK \cong \angle GKF$, so $\angle FGK + \angle GFK + \angle GKF = \angle FGK + 2(\angle GFK) = 120° + 2(\angle GFK) = 180°$, and $\angle GFK = 30°$.

11. E To find the answer, substitute (-3) for x throughout the equation $f(x) = 7x^2 - 9x + 4$. Once you've done this, you will find the following: $7(-3)^2 - 9(-3) + 4 = 7(9) + 27 + 4 = 63 + 27 + 4 = 94$. If you chose any of the other answers, you may not have distributed the negative properly.

12. J Use the answer choices and work backwards. Find the smallest number that divides evenly by 16, 25, and 40. This is 400: $400 ÷ 16 = 25$; $400 ÷ 25 = 16$; and $400 ÷ 40 = 10$. If you selected choice (K), be careful—this is a common multiple of all three numbers, but it is not the *least* common multiple.

13. B In order to cancel the original mistake, Tex will need to multiply by 3. Then to get the number he wants, he will need to multiply by another 3. In total, he will be multiplying by 9, as in choice (B).

14. K There are 12 triangles, and the area of the whole figure is 96 cm², so each of the triangles has an area of 8 cm². Because each of the triangles is right isosceles, the base and height of each triangle are equivalent, so to find the length of each of these, use the area formula: $A = \frac{1}{2} = bh = \frac{1}{2}b^2$. Solve for b: $b = \sqrt{2A}$. The area of each triangle is 8, so you can find the base: $b = \sqrt{2A} = \sqrt{2(8)} = \sqrt{16} = 4$. You don't need to find the hypotenuse of the triangle, because this problem asks for the perimeter of the figure, so count up the sides (there are 14) to find that the perimeter is 56 cm.

15. A The sum of the measures of all angles in a triangle is 180°. $\angle Y$ is described as a right angle, which means its measure is 90°. The other two angles, therefore, will have to add up to 90° to complete the 180° in the triangle. If $\angle Z$ measures less than 52°, then $\angle X$ must be *greater* than $90° - 52° = 38°$. It cannot be *equal* to this value [as in choice (B)], because $\angle Z$ is described as *less than* 52°.

16. G Try the different operations listed. You will find that the only operation that makes the statement true is division. Replace all the emoticons with division signs: $(8 ÷ 2)^3 - (4 ÷ 1)^2 = (4)^3 - (4)^2 = 64 - 16 = 48$.

17. D First, identify a point on the graph. The easiest place to start is with the intercepts. The *x*-intercept is unclear, but the *y*-intercept passes through (0,6), eliminating choices (A), (B), and (C). Between the latter two choices, you can solve for the *x*-intercept, to find that in choice (D), $x = \frac{6}{5}$ and in choice (E), $x = 3$. Although the exact *x*-intercept is unclear on the graph, it is definitely less than 2, so you can eliminate choice (E).

18.   F   Translate the English in this problem into the math of the answer choices. The problem reads, "An integer, x, is subtracted from 6. That difference is then multiplied by 3." This translates into the following: $(6 - x) \cdot 3$ or $3(6 - x)$. The second part of the problem reads, "This product is 15 more than half the original integer." Therefore $3(6 - x)$ will equal "15 more than half the original integer": $15 + \frac{1}{2}x$ or $\frac{1}{2}x + 15$. Therefore, $3(6 - x) = \frac{1}{2}x + 15$.

19.   A   Find the total production of each company after d days. Factory X starts with 18,000 units and can produce 120 units per day, so its production after d days will be $18{,}000 + 120d$. Factory Y starts with only 14,500 units, but it can produce 155 units per day, so its production after d days will be $14{,}500 + 155d$. Since you are looking for the number of days after which the total production of each factory will be equal, set the two equations equal to one another: $18{,}000 + 120d = 14{,}500 + 155d$. That's all there is to it—you don't have to solve this!

20.   K   Use the Pythagorean theorem to find the length of the hypotenuse: $a^2 + b^2 = c^2$, where c is the hypotenuse. $c = \sqrt{a^2 = b^2} = \sqrt{7^2 + 24^2} = \sqrt{50{,}625} = 25$. Note that this is 7:24:25, a Pythagorean triple. If you remember a few of the basic triples, you can save yourself a lot of figuring.

21.   E   Make sure you are distributing properly: $9(y + 3) - 2(4y - 4) = 9y + 27 - 8y + 8 = y + 35$.

22.   F   Set up a system of equations to find a:

$a + 3b = 27$

$\underline{a - 3b = 9}$

$2a = 36$

If $2a = 36$, then $a = 18$. Use this value to find the value of b:

$18 - 3b = 9$

$3b = 18 - 9$

$3b = 9$

$b = 3$

23.   B   Make sure you FOIL the equation properly: $(2x + 4)^2 = 4x^2 + 8x + 8x + 16 = 4x^2 + 16x + 16$. In this case $a = 4$, $b = 16$, and $c = 16$, so $a + b - c = 4 + 16 - 16 = 4$. If you selected choice (C), you may have forgotten to FOIL. If you selected choice (E), you may done $a + b + c$ rather than $a + b - c$.

24.   H   Split the figure into two rectangles and find the area of each. See the figure below:

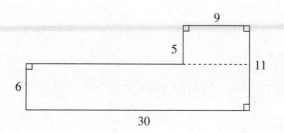

The smaller rectangle has sides of length 9 and 5, so its area by the formula $A = lw$ is 45. The larger rectangle has sides 30 and 6, so by the same formula, its area is 180. Add the two areas together to get $180 + 45 = 225$. If you selected choice (J), be careful—this is the perimeter.

25.   E   Look carefully at the values for each function. If a function can be graphed as $ax + b$, it is a linear function, and it will increase at constant increments. Function g decreases then increases in value. In fact, note the symmetry—this is a parabolic function, and can be graphed according to $ax^2 + bx + c$. Note that all the values in h increase by 3, so this is the function you want to work with. Since $h(-1) = 6$, $h(0)$ must equal 9.

26.   H   Put the equation into the slope-intercept form, $y = mx + b$. The m in this equation is the slope of the line. From the equation given, $10y - 16x = 13$, isolate the y term to get $10y = 16x + 13$, and divide through by 10 to get $y = \dfrac{16}{10}x + \dfrac{13}{10}$. Reduce to $y = \dfrac{8}{5}x + \dfrac{13}{10}$. The m term in this equation is $\dfrac{8}{5}$.

27.   C   First, simplify the expression: $x^2 + 5x - 24 = (x + 8)(x + 3)$. Now that you have the two expressions, find the solutions by setting each quantity equal to 0. If $x + 8 = 0$, then $x = -8$. If $x - 3 = 0$, then $x = 3$. Now find the sum of the solutions: $-8 + 3 = -5$. If you selected choice (E), you may have simplified correctly but found the roots incorrectly. If you selected choice (A), you found the product, not the sum.

28.   G   The perimeter of the larger triangle is 12 in. + 7 in. + 5 in. = 24 in. Since you know the ratio of the perimeters, you do not have to find each side of the smaller triangle; you can set up the following ratio:

$$\frac{5}{6} = \frac{x}{24}$$

$$\frac{5(24)}{6} = x$$

$$x = 20 \text{ in}$$

29. B To find the median of a list of numbers, those numbers must be listed in order. Make sure you rearrange the numbers given before you find the median. If you didn't rearrange the numbers, you may have picked (E). When you rearrange the numbers in this list, they are in this order: –9°C, –8°C, –7°C, –7°C, 0°C, 1°C, 2°C, 3°C, 5°C. 0°C is the median. If you selected choice (A), be careful—this is the mode.

30. G You can set up an equation to find the price of the calculator. If we call the price of the calculator x, then the equation will look like this: $\sqrt{x} + \left(\dfrac{3}{8}\right)x = 66$. A simpler tactic is to try out the answer choices to see which works in this equation. You will find this to be 144: $\sqrt{144} + \left(\dfrac{3}{8}\right)144 = 66$.

31. C You need to solve for m in the equation given. The equation as written is $KE = \dfrac{1}{2}mv^2$. Once you've solved for m, the equation should look like this: $m = \dfrac{2KE}{v^2}$. Once you have this equation, substitute the values from the problem: $m = \dfrac{2KE}{v^2} - \dfrac{2(120)}{9^2} = \dfrac{240}{81} \approx 2.97$, between 2 and 3. If you selected choice (B), you may have forgotten to apply the $\dfrac{1}{2}$.

32. G A "geometric sequence" is one in which all subsequent numbers have a fixed ratio to one another. In order to figure out this ratio, look at how the numbers change. The first term $2xz$ is multiplied by xy to become the second term $2x^2yz$. This second term is multiplied again by xy to become $2x^3y^2z$. Multiply this term by xy to find the answer: $2x^4y^3z$. Note, Process of Elimination may be more effective here. Throughout the sequence given, neither 2 nor the z has changed, so you can eliminate choices (H), (J), and (K). The exponents have increased, not decreased, so you can eliminate choice (F).

33. E Use the histogram. Four critics gave the book a one-star review. There are thirty total critics, so the relationship you need is $\dfrac{4}{30} = \dfrac{2}{15}$.

34. J There are 360° in a circle, and, as the histogram shows, one-star reviews make up $\dfrac{2}{15}$ of all the reviews. As a result, the one-star reviews will make up $\dfrac{2}{15}$ of the whole circle: $\dfrac{2}{15} \times 360° = 48°$.

35. D Make sure you count every review. There are thirty of them, and the sum of the thirty reviews is 79. To find the average, divide $\dfrac{79}{80}$ to get 2.63, rounded to the nearest hundredth.

36. **K** Simplify the expression by factoring.

$$\frac{(x^2+7x+12)(x-2)}{(x^2+2x-8)(x+3)} = \frac{(x+3)(x+4)(x-2)}{(x+4)(x-2)(x+3)} = \frac{(x+4)(x-2)(x+3)}{(x+4)(x-2)(x+3)} = 1$$

37. **D** The logo in the t-shirt is a right triangle. You are given the 35° angle, so you need to determine which side you have and which side you need to find relative to this angle. On the figure, you have the 10-inch side, which is *opposite* this angle. You're looking for the top diagonal side of the triangle, which in this case is the *hypotenuse* of the triangle. Sine is the function that requires *opposite* and *hypotenuse* by the following formula: $\sin\theta = \frac{opp}{hyp}$. By this equation, $hyp = \frac{opp}{\sin\theta}$ and the top side = $\frac{10}{\sin 35°}$.

38. **H** The center of the circle will be the midpoint of the diameter. Use the midpoint formula to find the midpoint of the points (4,3) and (–9,–2): $\left(\frac{x_1+x_2}{2}, \frac{y_1+y_2}{2}\right)$. Insert the points to find $\left(\frac{4+(-9)}{2}, \frac{3+(-2)}{2}\right)$. If you selected choice (J), be careful—you may have forgotten to divide by 2, and if you selected choice (G), you mixed up the *x*- and *y*-coordinates.

39. **C** Use the distance formula to find the distance between the two points (–7,4) and (–2,6): $d = \sqrt{(x_2-x_1)^2+(y_2-y_1)^2} = \sqrt{(-7-(-2))^2+(4-6)^2} = \sqrt{(-5)^2+(-2)^2} = \sqrt{29}$

This value is approximately 5.385, but if you selected choice (A), you didn't complete the problem. Every unit on the map is equal to 5 nautical miles, and the problem is asking for the value in nautical miles. Multiply 5.385 by 5 nautical miles to find 26.92 nautical miles, which is closest to choice (C).

40. **K** On a "must be" question, the relationships must be true in all cases. If there is one case in which a relationship is not true, that answer choice is incorrect. Because this is an EXCEPT question, the incorrect relationship will be the correct answer. Choice (K) is often true, but not always. If you multiply $\sqrt{2}$, an irrational number, by itself, you get a rational number: 4.

41. **B** Because *i* is defined as the square root of negative one ($\sqrt{-1}$), its range of possibility when raised to certain powers is limited. $i = \sqrt{-1}$, $i^2 = -1$, $i^3 = -\sqrt{-1}$, $i^4 = 1$. If you continue the pattern, you will find that these are the only possible values for *i* raised to any power (including negative powers). Choice (B) is the only answer choice that lists one of these values.

42. **K** Note the symmetry in the chart. The equation given shows that this graph is a parabola, but even if you haven't made that deduction, the values in the chart show a general trend in the data. When *x* is –3 and –5, *y* = 0; when *x* is –1 and –7, *y* = 8. According to this data, you can infer that values less than –7 and greater than –1 will be greater than 8. Therefore, –8 will have a greater value than the others listed in the answer choices. If you have trouble reading the chart, you can always try out the values in the equation and see which gives you the greatest *f*(*x*).

43. **B** The formula for the volume of a right circular cylinder is $V = \pi r^2 h$. This question asks for the radius and gives V and h, so solve the equation for r: $r = \sqrt{\dfrac{V}{\pi h}}$. Substitute the values that you know to find r: $r = \sqrt{\dfrac{64\pi}{\pi(4)}} = \sqrt{16} = 4$. If you selected choice (E), you may have forgotten to take the square root of the radius. If you selected choice (C), you may have forgotten to include the height in your calculation.

44. **J** First, consider the relationships that you know. The ratio of the perimeter of $\triangle FJK$ to $\triangle FLM$ is 3:5, and the ratio of $\overline{FH}$ to $\overline{FM}$ is 1:5. Because all triangles share $\angle F$ and the lines are parallel, the three triangles are similar, which means all their sides—and therefore the perimeters—are proportional. From the proportions given, you can determine that the ratio of $\triangle FGH$ to $\triangle FJK$ to $\triangle FLM$ is 1:3:5; therefore, the ratio of $\overline{FG}$ to $\overline{FJ}$ to $\overline{FL}$ is also 1:3:5. Based on this ratio, you can substitute values for each of the segments to figure out the ratio of $\overline{GJ}$ to $\overline{FG}$. You can say that $\overline{FG} = 1$, $\overline{FJ} = 3$, and $\overline{FL} = 5$. This enables you to calculate $\overline{GJ} = \overline{FJ} - \overline{FG} = 3 - 1 = 2$. The ratio of $\overline{GJ}$ to $\overline{FG}$ is therefore 2:1. If you selected choice (H), make sure you read the question carefully—you may have switched the segments.

45. **E** You need to find the distance along the y-axis that Avi traveled in total. Isolate each part of Avi's ride. Note that each of these legs can be made into the hypotenuse of a right triangle. The first part of the ride creates a special 30-60-90 triangle, and the second part of the trip creates a special 45-45-90 triangle. See the figures below:

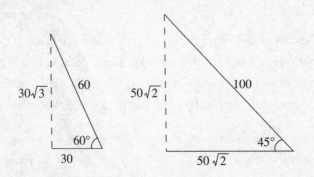

Therefore, the vertical height of the first part of the ride is $30\sqrt{3}$, and the vertical height of the second part of the ride is $50\sqrt{2}$. Don't forget to add the 35 m he rode along Broad St. at the end, to get a full vertical distance of $35 + 50\sqrt{2} + 30\sqrt{3}$. Choice (C) is the amount of the actual ride— read carefully; you just want the distance he traveled along the y-axis.

46. **H** The formula for a circle to which this problem is referring is $(x - h)^2 + (y - k)^2 = r^2$. In other words, the 25 in the equation $(x - 3)^2 + (y + 2)^2 = 25$ is the r^2. If $r^2 = 25$, then $r = 5$. With the radius, you can find the area of the circle with the basic formula $A = \pi r^2$. In this problem, since $r = 5$, the area will be $A = \pi(5)^2 = 25\pi$.

47. C   Nearly everything you need is written on the figure. The only real piece of information you need from the text of the problem is that the y-axis bisects the base of the triangle. This tells you that the base of this triangle is $2b$. The height, according to the figure, is $2b^2 - 4$. With the base and height, you have all you need to find the area of the triangle with the standard formula $A = \frac{1}{2}bh$. Substitute the expressions to find $A = \frac{1}{2}(2b)(2b^2 - 4) = (b)(2b^2 - 4) = 2b^3 - 4b$. If you selected choice (B), you may have forgotten to divide by two.

48. J   Because of the words "must be," the expression given must produce an even number in every instance. If you can find one instance in which an expression produces an odd number, you can eliminate that expression and answer choice. Since x can be any integer, there are many combinations you can try. In Choice (F), x could be 4, in which case $x + 5 = 4 + 5 = 9$, which is not even. In choice (G), x could be 1, which would make $\frac{x}{4} = \frac{1}{4}$, which is not even (nor is it an integer). If $x = 1$, choice (H) gives $x^4 = 1$, which is not even, and in choice (K), 5 raised to any integer power will always be odd. Only choice (J) generates an even number with every integer. This is because the product of an even number multiplied by either an even or an odd number will always be even.

49. C   First, bring the exponent to the front of the expression: $\log_9(9^{\frac{7}{3}}) = \frac{7}{3}\log_9 9$. Once you're done, you can simplify the log portion of the expression. By the rules of logarithms, $\log_9 9$ can be rewritten as either $9^x = 9$ or $\frac{\log_9}{\log_9}$. As both expressions show, $\log_9 9 = 1$, which means you're left with $\frac{7}{3}$, between 2 and 3.

50. G   In order to find the percent change, use the formula: % change $= \frac{difference}{original} \times 100\%$. In this case, Cameron's sales decreased from 23 to 19. In other words, he started at 23 (the original number), and he decreased to 19 (a difference of 4). Therefore, % change $= \frac{4}{23} \times 100 \approx 17.4\%$. If you selected choice (K), you may have calculated the increase from 19 to 23 rather than the decrease from 23 to 19.

51. E   Maura wanted an average of 30 new accounts over the course of 4 months. This means that over the course of these four months, she had to create a total of 120 new accounts. Write this in an equation: Total = Jan. + Feb. + Mar. + Apr. Substitute what you know. 120 = 31 + 25 + Mar. + 27. The total accounts needed in March will therefore be 120 − 31 − 25 − 27 = 37.

52. G   Don had 64 sales in January, and this value decreased by 5% each month. Do the calculations as follows, and don't round until you're done! February accounts = (64) − (0.05)(64) = 60.8. March accounts = (60.8) − (0.05)(60.8) = 57.76. April accounts = (57.76) − (0.05)(57.76) = 54.872. May accounts = (54.872) − (54.872)(0.05) = 52.1284 ≈ 52 accounts.

53.   C   You can disregard the long equation of the function given in the problem. All you need to answer this question is the graph. As the problem says, the amplitude of this function is the "average of the absolute values" of the minimum and maximum values of $f(x)$. Pull this information from the graph. The graph goes up to $y = 3$ and down to $y = -3$. Take the average of the absolute values of these: $\frac{|3| + |3|}{2} = 3$. If you selected choice (E), be careful—this is the period.

54.   F   Start with the tangent relationship. The problem says that the tangent of the angle of vision is $\frac{7}{6}$. From SOHCAHTOA, you know that the tangent relationship is defined as $\tan\theta = \frac{opp}{adj}$, or, in terms of this problem, the tangent of the angle of vision is $\frac{\text{horizontal distance}}{\text{height of the building}}$. Set up a proportion: $\frac{7}{6} = \frac{\text{horizontal distance}}{\text{height of the building}}$. Fill in what you know: $\frac{7}{6} = \frac{\text{horizontal distance}}{30}$. Cross multiply to find that the horizontal distance from home plate to the building is 35 m. If you selected choice (H), you may have found the opposite relationship.

55.   D   If you selected choice (E), be careful—3 is a solution to this equation, but it is rational. This question asks for a solution that is NOT rational. To find the solutions, solve the equation for y. First, isolate the absolute value expression $|y^2 - 11| = 2$. Remember as you're solving this equation that you will have to create two different equations as you're removing the absolute value sign: $y^2 - 11 = 2$ and $y^2 - 11 = -2$. Solve each of these equations to find that $y^2 = 13$ and $y^2 = 9$, and therefore $y = \pm 3$ and $y = \pm\sqrt{13}$. The irrational solutions are $\pm\sqrt{13}$.

56.   G   A positive slope indicates a speed increase; a 0 slope indicates a constant speed; a negative slope indicates a speed decrease. The speed increases for 4 seconds, remains constant for 3 seconds, then decreases to 0 over 2 seconds. This is best described by choice (G). Note, if you're not sure how to read the graph, recall that the problem says the entire test takes 9 seconds. Therefore, whether speeds are increasing or decreasing, the times during which they do so will have to add to 9 seconds.

57.   B   Because the compass is a circle, it has a degree measure of 360°. "East" starts at 90° from "North," so the point of the needle will need to travel 270° to get back to "North" in a clockwise direction. In other words, the point of the needle will have to travel across $\frac{3}{4}$ of the circle as it goes from "East" to "North" in a clockwise direction. The problem states that the point of the needle travels 42 mm, so if you apply the ratio to this problem, you can say that 42 mm is $\frac{3}{4}$ of the circumference of the circle. Use this to find the full circumference: $42 = \frac{3}{4}C$ and $C = 56$ mm. Use this value to find the length of the needle, which is just the radius of this circle: $C = 2\pi r$. Solve the equation for r to find its value: $r = \frac{C}{2\pi} = \frac{56 \text{ mm}}{2\pi} \approx 8.9$.

58.   F   From 270° to 360°, the cosine function has a range of values from 0 to 1. In other words, it is always positive. Sine, by contrast, has a range of values from –1 to 0—it's always negative. Because the problem is asking for a tangent value from 270° to 360°, you know it must be negative because $\tan\theta = \dfrac{\sin\theta}{\cos\theta}$. Therefore, you can eliminate choices (H), (J), and (K). Then, because $\cos\theta = \dfrac{12}{13}$, the adjacent side, opposite side, and hypotenuse relative to the angle θ form the Pythagorean triple 5:12:13, respectively. $\tan\theta = \dfrac{opp}{adj}$, and within the range from 270° to 360°, tangent is negative, so $\tan\theta = \dfrac{-5}{12}$.

59.   C   Since you need a and b such that $ab = 8$, your four possible pairs are $a = 1$, $b = 8$; $a = 2$, $b = 4$; $a = 4$, $b = 2$; $a = 8$, $b = 1$. Keep your work organized as you figure:

a	b	2^a	c	c^b
1	8	2	2	256
2	4	4	4	256
4	2	16	16	256
8	1	256	256	256

As this small chart demonstrates, there are four values of c that work in both expressions. If you selected choice (D), you may have forgotten that both $a = 1$, $b = 8$ and $a = 8$, $b = 1$ are distinct and valid pairs.

60.   J   The formula for the length of the diagonal of a rectangular prism is $a^2 + b^2 + c^2 = d^2$ where a, b, and c represent the edges of the rectangular prism and d represents its diagonal. In the case of a cube, $a = b = c$, so the equation can be rewritten as follows: $3a^2 = d^2$. In this problem, $d = 3\sqrt{3}$, so $3a^2 = (3\sqrt{3})^2$. Therefore, $3a^2 = (9)(3)$ and $a = 3$. Therefore, the length of the edge of this cube is 3. Look at the figure—you can see from the figure that the length of the diameter of the sphere is equivalent to the length from one side of the figure to another, an edge. The diameter of the sphere is equivalent to an edge of the cube, so the diameter is 3, choice (J).

READING TEST

1. **C** Choice (C) is correct because the third paragraph states that "God Bless the Child" was *familiar mostly to adults*. Because of this, it is more likely that the song would be familiar to Monique's parents, who must be adults, than it would be to her friends, who are presumably high school students and not yet adults. Choice (A) is incorrect because the passage never identifies "God Bless the Child" as a Rodgers & Hammerstein number. Choice (B) is incorrect because the passage does not support the extreme claim that "God Bless the Child" is the *most* sophisticated Billie Holiday song. Choice (D) is incorrect because Monique's song choice is presented as a contrast to the overly enthusiastic choices of her peers.

2. **J** Choice (J) is correct because the passage initially describes Monique and her friends as *aloof*, because they isolate themselves in the auditorium and Monique acts like a monarch with a royal court, and *disparaging*, because they are anxious to belittle the other students during their auditions. Choice (F) is incorrect because, although the passage describes that most students are nervous about going first, this does not describe how Monique and her friends are presented. Choice (G) is incorrect because, although Monique and her friends react to Esperanza's song choice with *disbelief*, that is not how they are initially portrayed in the passage. Choice (H) is incorrect because Monique and her friends are portrayed as being unfriendly and excluding.

3. **A** Choice (A) is correct because the passage states that Esperanza did not look up until she got to center stage and then *looked only at Mrs. Dominguez*. Choice (B) is incorrect because the passage says she shuffled her feet on her walk to the stage, which is not a confident stride. Choice (C) is incorrect because the passage states she was *paying little attention to the other auditions*. Choice (D) is incorrect because the passage only states that she was *working* on her geometry homework, not that she finished it.

4. **J** The question is asking for the rhetorical effect of the statement *But not this year*. The previous paragraph establishes that students generally dread the first audition slot and relates the tense manner in which Monique used to view the first slot. The paragraph that follows this phrase explains that Monique had decided to embrace the first slot as a means of surprising her peers. Choice (J) is correct because it identifies the statement in question as a contrast between the status quo and Monique's surprising decision. Choice (F) is incorrect because the passage provides no evidence that most students have resolved their fears of going first, only that Monique has. Choice (G) is incorrect because the passage never establishes the extreme claim that this year's audition was the *strangest yet*. Choice (H) is incorrect because the passage does not go on to describe any different imagery Monique associates with the uncomfortable first slot but rather to say she is no longer uncomfortable with it at all.

5. **B** The passage describes in the sixth paragraph that Monique and her friends are *sitting at the back of the auditorium*. In the ninth paragraph the passage states that *Esperanza had been sitting alone in the first row*. Together, these facts justify choice (B). Choice (A) is incorrect because it makes the extreme claim that Esperanza is the *most* teased student, for which there is no evidence in the passage. Choice (C) is incorrect because the passage does not say that Monique and Esperanza auditioned consecutively, and the seventh paragraph implies that there was *an endless parade* of students who auditioned in between them. Choice (D) is incorrect because, although Mrs. Dominguez was sensitive to possible ridicule meeting Esperanza's audition, there is no evidence of a conversation taking place beforehand.

6. **G** Choice (G) is correct because the passage states that Monique figured going first would *instill fear into her competition because they would realize that Monique had something they clearly lacked*. Choice (F) is incorrect because, although going first is evidence of Monique's self-confidence, the passage does not say Monique chose to go first to increase her self-confidence. Choices (H) and (J) are incorrect because Monique's stated motivation for going first is to intimidate her rivals, not to increase her chances of getting a part or to gain any favor with Mrs. Dominguez.

7. **D** The passage states that at the *climactic* moment of "rockets' red glare," *Esperanza's voice filled the room with a calm resonance*. This makes choice (D) correct. Choice (A) is incorrect because it is not supported in the passage. Choice (B) is incorrect because while the passage states that her version of the song caused the people in the room to feel *some reluctant patriotism*, it does not suggest that Esperanza was patriotic herself. Choice (C) is incorrect because the passage contradicts it by saying that Esperanza was *calm*.

8. **F** When Mrs. Dominguez tells Esperanza she can begin to audition, the passage states that Mrs. Dominguez was *sensing the potential for the audition to devolve into a painful target of ridicule*. This makes choice (F) correct. Choice (G) is incorrect because this is how Esperanza is described in relation to Thornton High. Choice (H) is incorrect because this is what is anticipated by Monique and her friends. Choice (J) is incorrect because this relates to how Mrs. Dominguez viewed Monique's decision to audition first.

9. **C** Choice (C) is correct because the passage states that, once Esperanza was moving *methodically through the tune, the expectant smiles of mockery were quickly vanishing from the faces of all who listened*. Choice (A) is incorrect because the decision of where to sit was based on wanting to make comments about all the auditions and came before Esperanza's audition. Choice (B) is incorrect because their preconceived notions are described prior to Esperanza's audition, not as a reaction to the audition. Choice (D) is incorrect because the passage states that Monique and her friends were critical of Esperanza's song choice and even the resulting patriotism they felt is described as *reluctant*.

10. **G** Esperanza sings "The Star Spangled Banner" for her audition. The twelfth paragraph explains that *the final phrase of the song* is *often soaked in vibrato*. This makes choice (G) correct. Choice (F) is incorrect because the passage states that Monique and her friends anticipated a "mousy" voice from Esperanza, but says nothing about "The Star Spangled Banner" being well suited to that type of voice. Choice (H) is incorrect because, although Esperanza's performance is ultimately impressive, the passage says that the song is *trite* and *formulaic*. Choice (J) is incorrect because when Esperanza begins singing her song, *Monique and her friends looked at each other in total disbelief*.

11. **C** The third paragraph asks the reader to consider a contrast between an original user of a remote and a modern user. Choices (A), (B), and (D) are details provided to describe the original user. Choice (C) is a detail provided to describe the modern user. Hence, choice (C) is correct.

12. **G** Choice (G) is correct because the author lists several important inventions of the twentieth century but does not identify any of them as the *most significant*. Choice (F) is incorrect because the author states that most people think the solution is new clean energy technology. Choice (H) is incorrect because the author attributes the root of tool-making to the mindset of *There's got to be a better way*. Choice (J) is incorrect because the author describes how consumers go from *awed gratitude to discriminating preference*.

13. **A** The point that an example is used to illustrate is often found right before the example. In this case, the end of the first paragraph states that *the longer a given technology exists, the more we take it for granted*. The comparison between different users of remote controls is designed to illustrate this idea. Choice (A) best summarizes this concept and so is correct. Choice (B) is incorrect because the author never stresses a need to read instructions. Choice (C) is incorrect because modern users are described as using remote controls with ease and comfort. Choice (D) is incorrect because, while likely true, there is no support in the passage for the idea that remote controls have become *far more effective* than they were.

14. **G** The passage focuses on the technology around us that often goes unappreciated, ultimately warning us that our unrealistic faith in technology may lead us into global climate trouble. Words and phrases like *spoiled*, *unduly optimistic*, and *unfairly demanding* indicate the author's attitude that most modern humans are somewhat in the wrong. Choice (G) is the safest match for this tone, which makes it the correct answer. Choice (F) is incorrect, because although the passage does look backward in time at certain spots, it is primarily focused on how the present is rather than a wish to return to the past. Choice (H) is incorrect because the author seems to be calling attention to the *dangerous extension of our mindset*, rather than sympathizing with it. Choice (J) is incorrect because the majority of the passage does not indicate the author's fear. The various references to shock and awe for new technology indicate amazement but not fright. The possible doomsday scenario toward the end of the passage does sound scary, but it functions only to demonstrate that modern humans have some problematic attitudes toward technology.

15. C   The context for this sentence explains that, because we are spoiled by technology, we typically believe it can fix any problem. The notion that we might need to fix ourselves is unthinkable. Choice (C) is the correct answer because it best expresses that the suggestion that we need to change our own habits would be *unlike* our normal assumptions about technology. Choice (A) is incorrect because *extraterrestrial* literally means "not from earth," and the context does not suggest the idea is *that* exotic. Choice (B) is incorrect because the passage indicates this idea is seldom heard within our culture, so the notion that it is a repetitive idea is not supported. Choice (D) is incorrect because, although we do not take the idea in question seriously, it is because we are not accustomed to hearing the idea, not because the idea itself is funny.

16. G   The point of this paragraph is that children born into a society that already possesses impressive technology do not tend to appreciate how impressive it is that this technology is human-made. They accept it as a given, much as one accepts the elements of the periodic table as the given substances found in the universe. Choice (G) is correct because it best expresses this idea. Choice (F) is incorrect because the passage does not suggest that children are literally learning about technology side-by-side as they learn about the periodic table. Choice (H) is incorrect because the reference to the *universe* does not provide any support for such an extreme claim as *most technology* comes from space exploration. Choice (J) is incorrect because it confuses the point of this paragraph, which is that children tend *not* to be impressed by the technology around them.

17. D   The penultimate paragraph discusses how people in our culture assume that technology will solve our problems and do not want to hear about needing to change or reassess our lifestyles. Because leaders are too afraid to tell the public otherwise, the final paragraph says that we will continue as we have been. Hence, choice (D) is correct. Choice (A) is incorrect because it misses the correct meaning of the phrase, and *scope* and *complexity* were discussed in relation to assessing the global climate problem, not technology. Choice (B) is incorrect because this describes specifically what the passage explains we will *not* be doing. Making sacrifices would mean *changing* the status quo. Choice (C) is incorrect because the passage is saying that if we ever find ourselves in a disastrous situation as a result of maintaining our current lifestyles and habits, *then* we would blame technology. This would be a result of following the status quo but not the idea to which the phrase itself refers.

18. H   *Discriminating preference* is used at the end of the seventh paragraph to foreshadow the ever-evolving demands of consumers for new technology. The eighth paragraph lists some of them. The passage states that *computers needed to become more powerful*. This makes choice (H) correct. Choice (F) is incorrect because the fifth paragraph contradicts that idea. Choice (G) is incorrect because the passage repeatedly suggests that most users of technology are happily oblivious to *how* it works. Choice (J) is incorrect because the second to last paragraph portrays this idea as something the public does not want to hear.

19.   D   The first half of the passage discusses the modern mindset toward technology. Then it says that the *most dangerous extension of this mindset* is how it relates to our ability to solve global climate problems. The second half of the passage explains why our attitude toward technology may worsen the situation. Choice (D) is correct because it precisely identifies the reason the author finds our overconfidence in technology to be potentially dangerous. Choice (A) is incorrect because this phrase refers to the flaws we consumers find with existing technology that we hope will be fixed. This is not directly relevant to the global warming problem with which the author associates the most danger. Choices (B) and (C) are incorrect because they refer to things that indirectly relate to the author's central concern. However, the author does not consider *devising new forms of energy* or *the complexity of global weather* to be dangerous in and of themselves.

20.   F   The passage ends with a severe prediction that humanity may ruin its habitat, all the while blaming technology for failing to rescue it. This makes choice (F) correct. Choice (G) is incorrect because the last paragraph does not contain any refutation of a theory. Choice (H) is incorrect because the last paragraph does not include an expert opinion. Choice (J) is incorrect because both paragraphs use "we."

21.   A   Choice (A) is correct because, although the author discusses having great difficulty and confusion in learning jazz chords, he does not ever identify one that is *most* confusing. Choices (B), (C), and (D) are incorrect because none of the chords are ever identified as the *most* confusing chords.

22.   F   In the context of the passage as a whole, the author discusses Victor as a source of knowledge about jazz. The author states he did not get *straightforward explanations* from Victor but that he *did learn* some things. Choice (F) is correct because, given the context of the passage, it refers to the most likely subject matter the author would be trying to get from Victor. Choice (G) is incorrect because the idea that knowledge about jazz would be *forbidden* is too strong. There is no evidence that the author was being purposefully excluded from learning about jazz. Choice (H) is incorrect because there is no context to support the idea that the author was asking about literal magic tricks. Choice (J) is incorrect because there is no context to support the idea that the author was trying to learn more about Victor as a person, nor does the passage ever describe Victor as *private*.

23.   D   Upon seeing the author's *invented* chord, Victor *calmly* informs the author of the chord's proper name. Choice (D) is correct because *nonchalance* indicates a relaxed, unimpressed manner, which is how Victor responds. Choice (A) is incorrect because Victor would not be amazed by a chord for which he already knows the technical name. Choice (B) is incorrect because Victor would not be jealous that the author could play a chord that was already familiar to Victor. Choice (C) is incorrect because Victor does not show confusion; he shows immediate recognition of what chord the author is playing.

24.   G   In the eighth paragraph, the author states that *for the next few months, I quietly plucked away* at the music found in "The Real Book." Hence, choice (G) is correct and choices (F), (H), and (J) are incorrect.

25. A   The passage describes the more complex chord types of jazz and describes the effects of using them as introducing *subtle hints of chaos and imbalance*, *adding a worldly imperfection*, and becoming more enjoyable as one's age starts making things like candy taste too sweet and "imperfections" like bitterness make *for a more appealing flavor*. Choice (A) provides the best summary for these ideas. Choice (B) is incorrect because the description of jazz's complexity is not intended to be a critical comment about fundamental flaws in rock and classical music. Just because jazz's unique chords add *detail and depth to the music*, that doesn't mean the author thinks that other styles of music necessarily lack detail and depth. Choice (C) is incorrect because the passage does not specify anything about the confusion and awkwardness of *standard jazz chord values*; it describes what elements jazz chords add to *standard chord values*. Choice (D) is incorrect because the context explains that candy starts tasting unpleasantly *sweet* the older one gets.

26. J   The end of the passage describes the author beginning to develop an ability to play jazz, but his newfound ability is still mentally surprising. Choice (J) summarizes this context best and is therefore correct. Choice (F) is incorrect because the passage does not support the idea that the author was *overworked*. Choice (G) is incorrect because, although the author is surprised by what his hands can do musically, there is no context to support that the author is actually losing the ability to *control* his hands. Choice (H) is incorrect because there is no information to support the idea that the author *pointing* at chords was part of his learning process.

27. D   Choice (D) is correct because the eighth paragraph describes the author's initial attempts to work through the *strange, new combinations* he found in "The Real Book." He mentions F-sharp minor-7 flat-5 while speaking of chords that he *had to decode and then understand*. Choice (A) is incorrect because the context of this paragraph suggests that the author did indeed have some trouble with these unfamiliar chords. Choice (B) is incorrect because the remark about not knowing the language of a foreign country has no literal relation to this specific chord or the author's previous travels (about which we know nothing). Choice (C) is incorrect because the passage provides no evidence that the author knew how to play this chord on guitar.

28. H   The fifth paragraph identifies Victor as a member of the author's rock band as well as a member of a jazz ensemble. This makes choice (H) correct. Choice (F) is incorrect because the passage states that at age 30, it had been *over a decade* since the author and Victor had gone their separate ways. Choice (G) is incorrect because the passage states that the author bought his own copy of "The Real Book." Choice (J) is incorrect because the passage does not say that Victor invented this chord, rather that he told the author the name of the chord the author presumed to have invented.

29. C   The passage begins with the author's love for jazz. It transitions into his own experiences learning how to play jazz and culminates with his early successes in doing so. Choice (C) is correct because it encompasses the various points of focus throughout the passage. Choice (A) is incorrect because the passage only occasionally refers to a chain of events and never establishes that the author has a jazz career. Choice (B) is incorrect because the author does not try to show that jazz is uncomplicated; he describes the hard work he put into learning its complexity. Choice (D) is incorrect

because the central focus of the passage is the author's learning of jazz. Although the author's friendship with Victor relates to jazz, it is not the central focus of the author's discussion.

30.   G   In the last few paragraphs, the author describes the process by which he struggled to learn jazz. He begins by seeing jazz as *a cryptic message to decode* but later describes himself as *becoming comfortable* and possessing a *new melodic understanding*. These details make choice (G) correct. Choice (F) is incorrect because the author never says that the book becomes *annoyingly familiar* by the end. Choice (H) is incorrect because the author identifies a difference between jazz sheet music and classical sheet music, but this detail does not enter his discussion of his experiences with "The Real Book." Choice (J) is incorrect because the author has not suggested that he has moved on to other learning tools or more profound study.

31.   A   The third and fourth paragraphs discuss Calwell's work. Paragraph 4 explains that *by monitoring the cholera food chain in reverse*, Calwell is able to make predictions. This makes choice (A) correct. Choice (B) is incorrect because, while climatic models were used to predict an outbreak in Bangladesh, these models were derived from Oceanic data, not land-based measurements. Choice (C) is incorrect because, in addition to being too narrow a description of Calwell's method, the decline of zooplankton and falling sea temperatures would each suggest a reduced risk of a potential cholera outbreak. Choice (D) is incorrect because, while the passage states that cholera is found in areas that contain copepod, the passage never suggests that this marine life is diseased.

32.   H   The first few paragraphs explain the food chain that allows the cholera bacterium to grow. The bacterium grows around copepods, which feed on zooplankton, which feed on phytoplankton, which feed on sunlight. Hence, sunlight influences cholera by influencing the food chain on which the cholera bacterium depends. This makes choice (H) correct. Choice (F) is incorrect because the passage never says that phytoplankton *contaminate* the water. Choice (G) is incorrect because the passage does not state that *V. cholerae* uses photosynthesis at all. Choice (J) is incorrect because there is no support for this broad generalization about sunlight causing many epidemics. The first sentence of the passage is a rhetorical question, and the way in which the passage describes sunlight facilitating outbreaks has nothing to do with *direct, prolonged exposure*.

33.   C   The eighth paragraph explains that researchers at Oxford *calibrated regional levels of photosynthesis to the size of a vein in the wings of the flies*. The vein size measures *how numerous and robust the tsetse fly population is*. Therefore, the satellite data that measures photosynthesis is used to tell researchers how big the veins of tsetse flies are and hence how strong and prevalent their population is. This makes choice (C) correct. Choice (A) is incorrect because the passage does not say that the satellite data can be used to determine the total number of *parasites* in West Africa. Choice (B) is incorrect because measuring photosynthesis is done to gauge the size of tsetse fly populations in West Africa, not to find the global area with the *most* photosynthesis. Choice (D) is incorrect because the point of the data is not to find the flies with the biggest veins but to estimate the size of veins in tsetse flies.

34. J The passage as a whole is presenting ways in which satellite data is being used to predict disease outbreaks, and both Calwell and Linthicum are offered as examples of those efforts. Hence, choice (J) is correct. Choice (F) is incorrect because Linthicum is studying Rift Valley fever, not cholera. Choice (G) is incorrect because Linthicum works at NASA in Greenbelt, Maryland. Choice (H) is incorrect because this does not indicate a similarity between Linthicum and Calwell since the passage never indicates that Calwell may have saved thousands of lives.

35. A The ninth paragraph states that satellite data is more efficient than the traditional method of doing research for the reasons discussed in choice (A). Thus, choice (A) is correct. Choice (B) is incorrect because the passage does not indicate that scientists can *control* photosynthetic levels, just that they can measure them. Choice (C) is incorrect because the passage does not discuss the types of *mathematical errors* that human forecasters make. Choice (D) is incorrect because the tenth paragraph contradicts this idea by indicating there is not a lot of reliable disease data available.

36. H The context of this word discusses conditions that would encourage or help mosquito populations to grow. *Promote* means to encourage or help, so choice (H) is correct. Choices (F) and (G) are incorrect because the weather is not performing an *errand* or a *task* for the mosquitoes. Similarly, choice (J) is incorrect because weather conditions would not *request* the growth of mosquito populations. The three incorrect answer choices relate more to the sense of *doing someone a favor* than to how the word is used in this context.

37. D The sixth paragraph explains the weather conditions that facilitate the growth and spread of mosquito populations, which include increased rain, more clouds, and warmer air. The environmental changes Linthicum is studying are those that would precede a growth in mosquito populations. Hence, choice (D) is correct. Choice (A) is incorrect because the beginning of the rainy season in Kenya is not identified as the precursor to mosquito population growth. Choice (B) is incorrect because the passage never mentions bacteria in the jet stream. Choice (C) is incorrect because the environmental changes Linthicum is monitoring are those that precede mosquito population growth, not the population growth itself.

38. J While it is true that satellite data has *measured* increases in ocean temperature, the passage never suggests or states that satellite data has actually *helped to* raise the ocean temperature. For this reason, choice (J) is correct. Choice (F) is incorrect because it is mentioned in the Calwell research. Choice (G) is incorrect because it is mentioned as part of the Oxford study. Choice (H) is incorrect because it is mentioned several times throughout the passage and represents the main point of the passage.

39. A The context for this phrase is that fluctuations in certain variables would make climate-based models inaccurate predictors. The variables are labeled as *non-climatic factors* in the following sentence. This makes choice (A) the correct answer. Choice (B) is incorrect because there is no discussion of the effects of drug resistance. Choice (C) is incorrect because it does not address the source of confusion, which is a failure to incorporate certain variables into the model. Choice (D) is incorrect because it implies—without any textual evidence—that researchers are unfamiliar with non-climate data, although the passage suggests only that they are not currently using it in their models.

40.	G	With the examples of Calwell, Linthicum, and Rogers, the author presents researchers who are using satellite-based data to predict disease outbreaks. The passage ends by assessing the value of these efforts. This makes choice (G) the correct answer. Choice (F) is incorrect because the passage does not itemize which satellite data *must* be collected, nor is the type of data the primary focus. Choice (H) is incorrect because the author does not stress that a small number of scientists do research by traditional methods. Choice (J) is incorrect because it is too narrow a purpose for an author who also discussed applications relating to predicting cholera and Rift Valley fever.

SCIENCE TEST

1.	A	Higher bulk density means lower soil quality. Figure 1 shows that Field A consistently has a higher bulk density, so choice (A) is the correct answer. Table 1 does not contain any information about Field A or B, eliminating choice (C). Figure 2 and Table 2 show that the crop yields and average soil organic matter (SOM) for Field A are higher, which goes against what the question looks to prove, eliminating choices (B) and (D).

2.	J	Figure 2 shows that Field B had a harvest of approximately 8 tons in Year 5. Of the values given in the figure, this is the only one that has a harvest less than or equal to 8 tons, thus making it a failed harvest.

3.	C	Table 1 shows that as the SOM increases, the soil quality increases. Eliminate choices (A) and (D) because both show an inverse, rather than a direct, relationship. With the new information provided in the question, you can infer that legumes and *deep-rooted and high-residue crops* will increase the amount of organic matter in the soil, and thus lead to an increase in the SOM rating. Only choice (C) provides this relationship.

4.	J	Figure 1 shows that Field A had a higher bulk density every year; therefore, regardless of the actual values, it can be assumed that the average bulk density was higher for Field A. Figure 2 shows that Field B had the lower crop yield in every year but Year 3. Therefore, it can be assumed that Field B has a lower average crop yield than Field A. The only choice that is correct for both parts of the question is choice (J).

5.	D	Use Table 1 to judge the average SOM for Field A and Field B given in Table 2. Field A's average SOM of 0.89 rates as excellent and Field B's average SOM of 0.28 rates as fair. This means the hypothesis is not consistent with the data presented, so the correct answer is choice (D).

6.	J	Based on Table 1, the salt solution increased the amount of rust every day. On Day 8, the sample had 1.84 g of rust, so on Day 9 the amount of rust would likely be higher than 1.84 g, choice (J).

7.	B	The formula shows that when rust is produced, H_2 is also produced, so choice (B) is the only possible correct answer.

8.   J   Table 1 shows that the salt solution produced 0.56 g Fe_2O_3 on Day 2. Figure 1 shows that the water buffered to pH = 10.0 had less than 0.50 g Fe_2O_3 until Day 8, so the only correct answer is choice (J).

9.   A   Table 1 shows that the sugar solution produced 0.11 g Fe_2O_3 by Day 6 and 0.19 g by Day 8. The amount produced from Day 6 to Day 8, then, would have been 0.19 − 0.11 = 0.08 g.

10.   F   Table 1 shows that the sugar solution had 0.00 g Fe_2O_3 on Day 2 and shows a steady increase. Choices (G) and (J) show the amount of Fe_2O_3 produced decreasing as time passes, so they cannot be correct. Choice (H) shows a big increase in Fe_2O_3 between Day 2 and Day 6, then a small increase between Day 6 and Day 8. Table 1 shows that the biggest increase in Fe_2O_3 was between Day 6 and Day 8, 0.08 g, so choice (H) cannot be correct. Only choice (F) shows 0.00 g on Day 1 and steady increases in g Fe_2O_3 produced, so this must be the correct answer.

11.   D   Based on Experiment 1, shown in Figure 2, you can see that a 10.0 N weight shared between two springs caused Spring A to stretch to 0.40 m, so a 10.0 N weight on Spring A alone must cause it to stretch further. Choice (D) is the best answer.

12.   G   Based on Experiment 2, shown in Figure 4, you can see that as the weight moved farther from Spring B, Spring B stretched less as the force on Spring B decreased. Choice (G) is the correct answer.

13.   A   Because the students were attaching weights to two springs at once in Trials 1–3, it was important to use identical springs so that the effects on each spring would be the same. If they had used different springs, there would be no way of determining the relationship between the length of the spring and the weight. Choice (A) best describes this reason. Choice (B) does not make much sense, for the same reasons, so it should be eliminated. Choice (D) must be eliminated because it discusses the weight of the board, which is not used in Trials 1–3. Choice (C) discusses oscillation, which is only mentioned in the passage to state that the students waited until oscillation ceased before measuring. Once you are left with choices (A) and (C), choice (A) is clearly the better answer.

14.   H   Experiment 2, Trial 5 shows the 5.0 N weight at exactly the midpoint of the board, and the springs stretched to 0.40 m. Experiment 1, Trial 1 has springs stretched to 0.40 m and a weight of 10.0 N. So the board in Experiment 3 must weigh 10.0 N − 5.0 N = 5.0 N, choice (H).

15.   B   Experiment 2, Trial 5 is the only trial in Experiment 2 in which the springs are stretched the same amount, choice (B).

16.   H   If potential energy is highest when the springs are stretched the most, then the correct answer must be the trial wherein the spring was stretched the most, so you can eliminate choices (F) and (G) right away. Now, you need to find the answer that gives the correct reason for this phenomenon. Spring C was stretched the most because the force of the weight was greater, choice (H).

17. C Based on Table 2, you know that the proofs for both de-icers decrease as temperature decreases, so you know that the proof at –30°C for each de-icer must be *less than* the proof at –25°C and *greater than* the proof at –50°C. Knowing this, you can eliminate choice (A) right away because the proofs are the same as the proofs at –50°C. You can eliminate choice (D) because the proofs are the same as the proofs at –25°C. Choice (B) shows the proof for De-icer B greater than the proof for De-icer A, but Table 2 shows that De-icer A always has a greater proof than De-icer B, so choice (B) cannot be correct. This leaves the correct answer, choice (C).

18. J You can see from Table 1 that when 10 mL of distilled water is added to 40 mL of sodium chloride, the de-icer proof is 80. The de-icer proof changes based on the relative proportions of distilled water and sodium chloride. Choices (F) and (G) can be eliminated because proofs that small must be from de-icers that have almost all water. Because the proportion of water to sodium chloride is the same as in the problem, choice (J) is the correct answer.

19. A The passage tells you that TR is the minimum proof for a de-icer to be effective at a particular temperature. Table 2 shows that as temperature decreases, TR increases only, so choice (A) is the correct answer.

20. H Based on Table 1, you can see that when the amount of sodium chloride is 0, the de-icer proof is 0, so you can eliminate choice (J). You can also eliminate choices (F) and (G), because Table 1 shows de-icer proof values when the volume of distilled water or sodium chloride is 0, but those formulas involve division by 0, which isn't possible. This leaves you with choice (H), which a quick check of de-icer proof of 0 and 100 will show you is correct.

21. C Table 1 shows you that a mixture of 10 mL of distilled water and 40 mL of sodium chloride produces a de-icer proof of 80. Figure 1 shows you that adding magnesium chloride increases the proof of a 100 proof de-icer, but that no matter how much magnesium chloride is added the proof never goes above 112. Based on this, you can eliminate choices (A) and (B) because they indicate that the proof would decrease and choice (D) because it indicates that the proof would exceed 112. The correct answer is choice (C).

22. G The passage tells you that TR is the minimum proof for a de-icer to be effective, so the better de-icer will be one that has a proof higher than the TR for each temperature, so you should eliminate choices (F) and (H). Based on Table 2, you can see that only De-icer A had a proof higher than the TR for each temperature, so choice (G) is the correct answer.

23. C Scientist 2 says that small comets originate from regions of the solar system beyond the farthest planet's (Neptune's) orbit, choice (C).

24. J Scientist 1 says that small comets have a diameter of 20–30 ft and burn up in the magnetosphere. Since larger comets burn up in the parts of the atmosphere closer to the earth, a comet that burns up in the thermosphere must have a diameter of greater than 30 ft, choice (J).

25.　A　Scientist 1 states that small comets are too small to be meteors. Scientist 1 also states that small comets burn up in the magnetosphere, but the passage says that meteors burn up between 50 and 85 km above Earth's surface, in the mesosphere. The correct choice, therefore is that no small comet ever becomes a meteor, choice (A).

26.　J　The passage states that visible objects burning up in the atmosphere are called meteors, so you should eliminate choices that do not call the objects meteors, choices (F) and (G). Second, Scientist 2 tells you that meteors are seen "far less" often than twice every five minutes, so to see bright objects every minute is not typical, eliminating choice (H). This leaves the correct answer, choice (J).

27.　D　Scientist 1 says that all small comets burn up in the magnetosphere. Figure 1 shows the magnetosphere is above 600 km, so the answer is choice (D). The other values given in the answer choices represent altitudes in or above the magnetosphere.

28.　F　Scientist 1's viewpoint is that the dark spots are not mere noise; a change in the atmospheric conditions around these spots would support that viewpoint. Scientist 1 also states that the comets release krypton as they burn up, so the discovery of krypton around the spots confirms Scientist 1's viewpoint, choice (F). The other choices can be eliminated because none state that Scientist 1's viewpoint was strengthened.

29.　D　Scientist 1 states that small comets all burn up in the magnetosphere. According to this hypothesis, only enhanced imaging technology that could take pictures of the magnetosphere would be useful for seeing small comets. Therefore, only enhanced imaging technology that could record data above 600 km above sea level would be effective, choice (D).

30.　G　In Tables 1, 2, and 3, the amount of hydrogen peroxide decreases consistently from the first day (Table 3) to the end of the elongation period (Table 1), choice (G).

31.　C　The dependent variable of the experiment is a variable that the experimenter is not intentionally manipulating or changing (which is the independent variable) or controlling (control groups or variables); it's the variable that the experimenter is trying to understand or predict. In this experiment, the experimenter manipulated the type of plant, the type of superoxide dismutase, and the point in time that measurements were taken. The length of the cotton fiber was neither intentionally changed nor controlled (represented as L1, L2, and L3). The introduction indicates that the *scientists wanted to study whether the level of hydrogen peroxide affected the length of the cotton fiber*. Choice (C) is the correct answer.

32.　H　Only plant cells have cell walls, so the correct answer is choice (H). Choice (F), *prokaryotic*, refers to unicellular life forms without a membrane-bound nucleus; cotton plants are not unicellular, so choice (F) cannot be correct. *Animal cells*, choice (G), do not have cell walls, so this choice can be eliminated. *Bacteria*, choice (J), are also unicellular and cotton plants are not bacteria, so choice (J) cannot be correct. In addition, you could use "cotton" as the clue; because of the answer choices, *plant* is the best approximation of what cotton is.

33.   C   Take the information given, length of cotton fiber and amount of hydrogen peroxide, and find the most similar line and point in time. The correct answer is choice (C), L2 at the beginning of its elongation period.

34.   J   The only cotton plant line which did not have its genetic structure altered was L4, so this was the control.

35.   A   The x-axis will move in a positive direction, so determine how the average lengths change. For all the data, the lengths increase with increasing elongation periods. Thus, you can conclude that the line will have a positive slope, choice (A).

36.   H   Figure 2 shows that there is a linear relationship between cross-sectional area and ΔT. You can also see that as cross-sectional area increases, ΔT increases. If System 1 has a larger cross-sectional area than System 2, it must have a larger ΔT, so you can eliminate choices (F) and (G). The question tells you that System 1 has twice the cross-sectional area of System 2, so choice (H) is the correct answer. A quick check of Figure 2 confirms this: when cross-sectional area is 4 cm^2, ΔT is 6°C and when cross-sectional area is 8 cm^2, ΔT is 12°C.

37.   B   Based on the definition given in the passage, convection would not transfer heat from the water to the metal containers. This eliminates all choices except for choice (B).

38.   F   Figure 2 shows that ΔT increases with cross-sectional area. Figure 3 shows that ΔT increases with height. In particular, Figures 2 and 3 show that height affects ΔT more than cross-sectional area, although choice (H) has the greatest cross-sectional area, choices (F) and (G) have much greater height. Since choice (G) has a smaller height, the system with the greater ΔT is choice (F). Choice (F) is the best answer because it has larger values for both than any other choice.

39.   D   Table 1 shows that for water in the setup described, ΔT should be 10°C. Find the differences in temperature in the answer choices given. Choice (A) has a difference of 20°C. Choice (B) has a difference of 30°C. Choice (C) has a difference of 0°C. Only choice (D) has the appropriate ΔT of 10°C.

40.   H   The passage gives relationships between ΔT and only three variables: cross-sectional area, length, and starting temperature. None of these are possible choices, but radius is linked to cross-sectional area. As radius increases, area increases. Figure 2 shows that as cross-sectional area increases, ΔT increases, so the correct answer is choice (H). Insulation, amount of liquid, and air temperature are not discussed as being related to ΔT in the passage.

WRITING TEST

To grade your essay, see the Essay Checklist on the following page. The following is an example of a top-scoring essay for the prompt given in this test. Note that it's not perfect, but it still follows an organized outline and has a strong introductory paragraph, a concluding paragraph, and transitions throughout.

Today's high school student is presented with many opportunities to cheat. The Internet is a ready source of resources for the unscrupulous, even including papers already written on just about any topic imaginable. But the problem of cheating reaches farther than just homework assignments—students today also have chances to cheat during exams in school, as teachers cannot possibly monitor the behavior of every student in a classroom simultaneously. Because the pressure to get great grades and get into a good college is so high, the pressure to cheat is very high. Nevertheless, it is critically important that schools do not give up in the fight against cheating because cheating is unfair to the students who play by the rules, because the consequences of being caught only increase later in life, and because one of the purposes of school is to teach students values.

Contrary to popular belief, not every student cheats. In all likelihood, the percentage of students cheating regularly is much lower than 50 percent. But the damage these students do to the students who don't cheat is very real and very severe. Colleges are choosing students based on their GPA and their class rank (in part—there are obviously other factors). When students cheat, they get higher grades that they don't deserve. As these cheaters move up the class rank, they are pushing down students who deserve to be higher, hurting those students' college opportunities. Cheaters will often say "Who cares if I cheat—it doesn't hurt anyone else's grades." Maybe not, but the damage done is even worse—it's hurting other people's futures.

Because it's hard for teachers in high school to keep an eye on every student, cheaters believe that they won't get caught, and for a while they are probably going to be right. Cheaters learn tricks that work well in the high school environment. The problem is, though, that they will keep on cheating through life and eventually will get caught. Colleges and businesses take this sort of behavior much more seriously, and so the cost of being caught cheating becomes much higher. If the cheater gets caught in high school and learns not to continue this behavior in the future, it will be embarrassing, but the real cost will be much easier for him or her to bear. So, schools should work hard to catch cheating during high school and should treat it seriously.

Finally, schools have a responsibility to set an example to their students. Part of the school's job, whether students like it or not, is to teach them the values of right and wrong. If schools are perceived by the student body to be giving up in the face of cheating, that not only sends us the message that this sort of devious behavior is acceptable (which we know is not true), it also ruins the reputation of the administration in our eyes. We will no longer take the school seriously on any matter, which will have a long-term damaging effect on the school community.

Clearly, cheating is wrong. There is no disagreement on this point, even from those who cheat. Just as clearly, schools have to do their very best to prevent cheating from occurring. Of all the reasons given, the first is the most important: These people are stealing college opportunities from their classmates.

WRITING TEST

Essay Checklist

1. The Introduction
   Did you
   o   start with a topic sentence that paraphrases or restates the prompt?
   o   clearly state your position on the issue?

2. Body Paragraph 1
   Did you
   o   start with a transition/topic sentence that discusses the opposing side of the argument?
   o   give an example of a reason that one might agree with the opposing side of the argument?
   o   clearly state that the opposing side of the argument is wrong or flawed?
   o   show what is wrong with the opposing side's example or position?

3. Body Paragraphs 2 and 3
   Did you
   o   start with a transition/topic sentence that discusses your position on the prompt?
   o   give one example or reason to support your position?
   o   show the grader how your example supports your position?
   o   end the paragraph by restating your thesis?

4. Conclusion
   Did you
   o   restate your position on the issue?
   o   end with a flourish?

5. Overall
   Did you
   o   write neatly?
   o   avoid multiple spelling and grammar mistakes?
   o   try to vary your sentence structure?
   o   use a few impressive-sounding words?

SCORING YOUR PRACTICE EXAM

Step A

Count the number of correct answers for each section and record the number in the space provided for your raw score on the Score Conversion Worksheet below.

Step B

Using the Score Conversion Chart on the next page, convert your raw scores on each section to scaled scores. Then compute your composite ACT score by averaging the four subject scores. Add them up and divide by four. Don't worry about the essay score; it is not included in your composite score.

Score Conversion Worksheet		
Section	Raw Score	Scaled Score
1	_____/75	_____
2	_____/60	_____
3	_____/40	_____
4	_____/40	_____

SCORE CONVERSION CHART

Scaled Score	Raw Scores			
	Test 1 Engish	Test 2 Math	Test 3 Reading	Test 4 Science
36	75	59–60	40	39–40
35	72–74	57–58	—	38
34	71	56	39	37
33	70	54–55	38	—
32	69	53	37	36
31	68	51–52	—	35
30	66–67	50	36	34
29	65	49	35	33
28	64	47–48	34	32
27	62–63	45–46	33	31
26	60–61	42–44	32	29–30
25	58–59	40–41	31	27–28
24	56–57	38–39	30	26
23	53–55	35–37	29	24–25
22	51–52	33–34	27–28	22–23
21	47–50	32	26	20–21
20	44–46	30–31	24–25	18–19
19	41–43	28–29	22–23	17
18	39–40	26–27	21	15–16
17	37–38	22–25	19–20	14
16	34–36	18–21	17–18	13
15	31–33	14–17	15–16	12
14	29–30	10–13	13–14	11
13	27–28	08–09	11–12	10
12	25–26	07	09–10	09
11	23–24	05–06	08	08
10	20–22	04	06–07	07
09	17–19	—	—	05–06
08	15–16	03	05	04
07	12–14	—	04	—
06	10–11	02	03	03
05	07–09	—	—	02
04	06	01	02	—
03	04–05	—	—	01
02	02–03	—	01	—
01	00–01	00	00	00

Part IX
The Princeton Review ACT Practice Exam 2

Chapter 27
Practice Exam 2

ENGLISH TEST

45 Minutes—75 Questions

DIRECTIONS: In the five passages that follow, certain words and phrases are underlined and numbered. In the right-hand column, you will find alternatives for each underlined part. In most cases, you are to choose the one that best expresses the idea, makes the statement appropriate for standard written English, or is worded most consistently with the style and tone of the passage as a whole. If you think the original version is best, choose "NO CHANGE." In some cases, you will find in the right-hand column a question about the underlined part of the passage. You are to choose the best answer to the question.

You will also find questions about a section of the passage or the passage as a whole. These questions do not refer to an underlined portion of the passage, but rather are identified by a number or numbers in a box.

For each question, choose the alternative you consider best and blacken the corresponding oval on your answer document. Read each passage through once before you begin to answer the questions that accompany it. For many of the questions, you must read several sentences beyond the question to determine the answer. Be sure that you have read far enough ahead each time you choose an alternative.

PASSAGE I

Crocheting Makes a Good Hobby

Crocheting is the art of making fabric by twisting yarn or thread with a hook. Although many associate it by older women,
[1]

crocheting can be a fun hobby for people of both genders and all
[2]

ages. Once you start crocheting, you won't be able to put down the hook; you'll have a hobby for life. [3]

1. **A.** NO CHANGE
   B. to
   C. by
   D. with

2. **F.** NO CHANGE
   G. for people of both genders, masculine and feminine,
   H. for male and female people of both genders
   J. for people of both genders, both males and females,

3. At this point, the author is considering adding the following true statement:

   > Irish nuns helped save lives with crocheting when they used it as a way to make a living during the Great Irish Potato Famine of 1846.

   Should the writer add this sentence here?

   A. Yes, because it is essential to know when crocheting became internationally prominent and how it did so.
   B. Yes, because the reference to the Great Irish Potato Famine demonstrates that the author is conscious of historical events.
   C. No, because the reference to the Great Irish Potato Famine is not relevant to the main topic of this essay.
   D. No, because many people who left Ireland in 1846 brought crocheting with them to the United States and Australia.

GO ON TO THE NEXT PAGE.

Time-honored and easily taught to all, crocheting is an easy
                        ___
                         4
hobby to pick up. Instructional books are readily available, and

once you've learned a few basic stitches. Picking up the more
                                  _____
                                     5
advanced ones is a snap. Once you learn how to crochet, you can

purchase store-bought books that detail crocheting patterns that
_____
                          6
tell you exactly how to make the projects that interest you. Even

if you want to try several projects, the supplies required for

it's completion are minimal; all you need are a crochet hook,
__
 7
yarn, and a pair of scissors. You don't need to worry about

making a big investment, either; fifteen dollars will buy you no

fewer than three starter kits!
_____
         8

[1] As you grow more proficient, you can expand your

supplies by purchasing hooks of different types to vary the
                                        _____
                                          9
size of your stitches. [2] Crochet hooks are available in all

sizes, ranging, from very small to very large, with everything in
_____
       10
between. [3] Some are so big that you need to use two strands of

yarn. [4] Other hooks are very tiny, so small that you must use

thread. [5] These hooks are suitable for making smaller, more

delicate things such as lace doilies, tablecloths, and bedspreads.

[6] These hooks make big stitches, so you can finish a project

with them very quickly. [7] It is best to start with hooks that are

medium in size; these are the easiest to manipulate and require

only one strand of yarn. ▭11

4. F. NO CHANGE
   G. teaches
   H. taughted
   J. teached

5. A. NO CHANGE
   B. stitches; picking
   C. stitches, picking
   D. stitches since picking

6. F. NO CHANGE
   G. buy books and other pamphlets at craft and book stores
       detailing certain specific patterns
   H. buy pattern books
   J. acquire store-bought pattern books

7. A. NO CHANGE
   B. its
   C. its'
   D. their

8. F. NO CHANGE
   G. fewer then
   H. less than
   J. less then

9. A. NO CHANGE
   B. types;
   C. types:
   D. types,

10. F. NO CHANGE
   G. sizes, ranging
   H. sizes; ranging
   J. sizes ranging,

11. For the sake of the logic and coherence of this paragraph,
    Sentence 6 should be placed:

   A. where it is now.
   B. after Sentence 1.
   C. after Sentence 3.
   D. after Sentence 7.

GO ON TO THE NEXT PAGE.

Because it seems like there are a million hooks to keep
_____ 12
track of, crocheting makes a good hobby because it requires only
_____ 12
time and patience, not attention or tremendous investment. You

can crochet while watching television, listening to music, or

visiting with other people. It is fun and relaxing and allows you

to express your creative side in an easy way. Also, you
_____ 13
have finished a project, you have a cherished keepsake. Whether

you have made an afghan to keep you warm on cold winter
_____ 14
nights or a lace tablecloth to add a touch of elegance to your

dining room, your creation is sure to be cherished for a long time

to come.

12. Given that all the choices are true, which one provides the most effective transition from the preceding paragraph to this one?
   F. NO CHANGE
   G. Because it can take a long time to finish a project,
   H. With such a simple and inexpensive set of materials,
   J. No longer a field dominated primarily by older women,

13. A. NO CHANGE
   B. Also, finally you
   C. Also, despite the fact you
   D. Also, once you

14. F. NO CHANGE
   G. at
   H. of
   J. within

Question 15 asks about the preceding passage as a whole.

15. Suppose the writer's goal had been to write an essay that demonstrates the commercial potential of crocheting. Would this essay successfully accomplish that goal?

   A. Yes, because it gives examples of end products of crocheting and shows the different kinds of materials needed to produce a wide range of products.
   B. Yes, because it discusses the supplies necessary to create crocheted products, and it shows the usefulness of many of them during the cold winter months.
   C. No, because it does not mention the market value of crocheted products or how one might go about selling them.
   D. No, because it describes other industries and hobbies that would be more commercially successful.

PASSAGE II

Seurat's Masterpiece

[1] How can I describe the wonder I felt the first time I saw

my favorite painting, Georges Seurat's *A Sunday on La Grande

Jatte*? [2] I had admired the work for years in art books, but I

never thought I saw the actual painting, which was housed in
_____ 16
Chicago, many miles from where I lived. [3] I finally got my

16. F. NO CHANGE
   G. would see
   H. had seen
   J. was seeing

GO ON TO THE NEXT PAGE.

chance to when I met someone else who loved the painting as
₁₇
much as I did. [4] We both had three days off at the same time,

so we decided to make a road trip to Chicago so we could see

the painting in all it's grandeur. [5] We packed our bags,
₁₈

jumped in the car, and headed on our way toward Chicago. | 20 |
<u>jumped in the car, and headed on our way toward Chicago.</u>
₁₉

[1] The first thing that struck me as we entered the room

where the painting was <u>displayed; was</u> the size of the painting.
₂₁
[2] A common size for canvases is 24 by 36 inches. [3] It was

enormous! [4] It covered a large part of an even larger wall. [5]

The painting's size amazed me since it was painted with dots, a

technique called pointillism. [6] To create a painting of such

magnitude using this technique seemed an almost impossible

task. [7] Seurat had done it, though, and had made it look easy! | 23 |
₂₂

17. A. NO CHANGE
  B. at the moment
  C. just to
  D. DELETE the underlined portion.

18. F. NO CHANGE
  G. our
  H. its
  J. its'

19. A. NO CHANGE
  B. jumped in the car, and had headed
  C. jumped in the car, and head
  D. had jumped in the car, and headed

20. Upon reviewing this paragraph and noticing that some information has been left out, the writer composes the following
  sentence, incorporating the information:

  > Her name was Lisa; she lived in my dorm, and a mutual
  > friend had introduced us to each other, knowing how
  > much both of us loved art.

  For the sake of the logic of this paragraph, this sentence should
  be placed after Sentence:

  F. 2.
  G. 3.
  H. 4.
  J. 5.

21. A. NO CHANGE
  B. displayed:
  C. displayed,
  D. displayed

22. F. NO CHANGE
  G. task and difficult to complete.
  H. task, difficult to complete.
  J. task, overwhelming in its difficulty.

23. Which of the following sentences is LEAST relevant to the
  development of this paragraph and therefore could be deleted?

  A. Sentence 2
  B. Sentence 4
  C. Sentence 5
  D. Sentence 6

GO ON TO THE NEXT PAGE.

Even more impressive, however, was the beauty of the
$\overline{\text{24}}$
painting. Viewed from a distance, the colors looked muted,

capturing the idyllic mood of a summer day in the park.

When I approached the painting, though, its colors exploded into
$\overline{\text{25}}$
myriad hues, illustrating the artist's skill in combining colors to

create a mood. Even the parts of the painting that appeared white

from a distance were vibrantly multicolored when viewed up

close. ⬚26 The effect was incredible;

he sat and stared at the painting in wonder for a good portion of
$\overline{\text{27}}$

the afternoon. ⬚28

My friend and I saw many other sights, on our trip to
$\overline{\text{29}}$
Chicago, but the best part by far was being able to see our favorite

work of art. The image is forever imprinted in my mind

24. Given that all of the choices are accurate, which provides the most effective and logical transition from the preceding paragraph to this one?

F. NO CHANGE
G. One thing that struck me was
H. Many art critics have written about
J. The debate rages on over

25. Which of the following alternatives to the underlined portion would NOT be acceptable?

A. As I approached the painting, though,
B. However, as I approached the painting,
C. I approached the painting, though,
D. However, when I approached the painting,

26. If the writer were to delete the phrase "from a distance" from the preceding sentence, the paragraph would primarily lose:

F. an essential point explaining the author's love of the painting.
G. the first part of the contrast in this sentence, which the author uses to describe viewing the painting.
H. a further indication of the length of the road trip taken by the author and her friend.
J. nothing, because the information provided by this phrase is stated more clearly elsewhere in the paragraph.

27. A. NO CHANGE
    B. one
    C. they
    D. we

28. At this point, the writer is considering adding the following true statement:

> The Art Institute of Chicago contains many other famous paintings, among them Edvard Munch's *The Scream* and Grant Wood's *American Gothic*.

Should the writer make this addition here?

F. Yes, because it gives additional details essential to understanding the collection at the museum.
G. Yes, because it demonstrates a contrast between the author's favorite painting and those in this sentence.
H. No, because it provides information that is not relevant at this point in the paragraph and essay.
J. No, because it is contradicted by other information presented in this essay.

29. A. NO CHANGE
    B. sights, which
    C. sights;
    D. sights

GO ON TO THE NEXT PAGE.

at the museum gift shop, even when I'm not looking at the
<u>30</u>
<u>souvenir print I bought</u>.
30

30. The best placement for the underlined portion would be:

   F. where it is now.

   G. after the word *image*.

   H. after the word *looking*.

   J. after the word *bought* (ending the sentence with a period).

PASSAGE III

The Language of Cats

    Many people believe that language is the domain of human beings. However, cats have <u>developed an intricate language</u> not
31
for each other, but for the human beings who

<u>have adopted them as pets</u>.
32

31. **A.** NO CHANGE

   B. developed, an intricate language

   C. developed an intricate language,

   D. developed; an intricate language

32. Which choice would most clearly and effectively express the ownership relationship between humans and cats?

   F. NO CHANGE

   G. like to have cats around.

   H. often have dogs as well.

   J. are naturally inclined to like cats.

    When communicating with each other, <u>cats' "talk" is a
33
complex system of nonverbal signals</u>. In particular, their tails,
33

33. **A.** NO CHANGE

   B. a complicated system of nonverbal signals is used by cats to "talk."

   C. cats "talk" with a complex system of nonverbal signals.

   D. "talking" is done by them with a system of complex nonverbal signals.

rather than any kind of "speech," <u>provide</u> cats' chief means of
34
expression. They also use physical contact to express their
feelings. With other cats, cats will use their voices only to
express pain. |35|

34. **F.** NO CHANGE

   G. having provided

   H. has provided

   J. were provided by

35. If the preceding sentence were deleted, the essay would primarily lose:

   A. a redundant point made elsewhere in the essay.

   B. another description of the ways in which cats communicate nonverbally.

   C. an exception to the general trend described in this paragraph.

   D. a brief summary of the information contained in the essay up to this point.

<u>Next, incredibly, all</u> of that changes when a human walks
36
into the room. Cats use a wide range of vocal expressions when
they communicate with a person, from affectionate meows to

36. **F.** NO CHANGE

   G. (Do NOT begin new paragraph) Incredibly,

   H. (Begin new paragraph) Next incredibly,

   J. (Begin new paragraph) Incredibly,

GO ON TO THE NEXT PAGE.

menacing hisses. Since <u>cats verbal expressions</u> are not used to
    37

communicate with other cats, it is <u>logical and reasonable</u>
                                          38
to conclude that cats developed this "language" expressly to
communicate with their human owners.

This fact is demonstrated more <u>clear since</u> observing
                                     39
households that have only one cat. An only cat is usually very
vocal, since the only creature around with whom the cat can
communicate is its owner. Cats with other feline companions,
though, are much quieter. If they want to have a conversation, they
need only go to their fellow cats and communicate in their natural
way. 40

Since cats learned to meow for the sole purpose of
communicating with human beings, owners should take the time
to learn what their different meows mean. If an owner
<u>knows, to</u> name just a few examples, which meow means the cat is
     41
hungry, which means the cat wants to be petted, and which means
the cat wants to have a little "conversation," the bond between cat
and owner will grow deeper. 42 Certainly, after a time, owners
will see that communicating with their pets, not just cats, is every
bit as important to forging good relationships

<u>as to communicate</u> with other humans. Once, as an owner,
     43
you know that the cat is not just

37. **A.** NO CHANGE
    B. cat's verbal expressions
    C. cats' verbal expressions
    D. cats verbal expressions,

38. **F.** NO CHANGE
    G. logical and well-reasoned
    H. logical to a startling degree
    J. logical

39. **A.** NO CHANGE
    B. clear when
    C. clearly since
    D. clearly when

40. At this point, the writer is considering adding the following true statement:

    > On the other hand, the natural way for most birds to communicate is vocally, by way of the "bird song."

    Should the writer add this sentence here?

    F. Yes, because it shows that cats are truly unique in communicating nonverbally.
    G. Yes, because it adds a relevant and enlightening detail about another animal.
    H. No, because it basically repeats information given earlier in the essay.
    J. No, because it does not contribute to the development of this paragraph and the essay as a whole.

41. **A.** NO CHANGE
    B. knows, to,
    C. knows to,
    D. knows to

42. If the writer wanted to emphasize that cats communicate vocally with their owners to express a large number of different emotions in addition to those listed in the previous sentence, which of the following true statements should be added at this point?

    F. Many animals communicate hunger similarly to cats.
    G. Cats will tell their owners when they feel pain, sadness, irritation, or love.
    H. Cats communicate these emotions differently to other cats.
    J. Humans have the easiest time communicating with other mammals.

43. **A.** NO CHANGE
    B. as being communicative
    C. as communicating
    D. through communicating

GO ON TO THE NEXT PAGE.

making senseless noises without any rhyme or reason but is
$\overline{}$
44
making an attempt to communicate, you can make an effort to
communicate back. After all, your cat isn't meowing just for the
sake of making noise; however, cats are less communicative than
$\overline{}$
45
many other animals.
$\overline{}$
45

44. F. NO CHANGE
 G. making senseless noises
 H. senselessly making noises with no thought involved
 J. making senseless noises, having no idea what they mean,

45. Which choice would best summarize the main point the essay makes about cats' communication with their human owners?

 A. NO CHANGE
 B. rather, there's a good chance your cat is trying to tell you something.
 C. instead, your cat is probably trying to communicate with other cats by meowing.
 D. on the other hand, it is better to have more than one cat so they can undergo a natural development.

PASSAGE IV

Visiting Mackinac Island

  Visiting Mackinac (pronounced "Mackinaw") Island is like
taking a step back to the past in time. Victorian
$\overline{}$
46

houses' and a fort dating back to the War of 1812 surround the
$\overline{}$
47
historic downtown, where horses and buggies still pull
passengers down the road.

  The only way to get to Mackinac Island is by boat or private
$\overline{}$
48
plane, and you may not bring your car. Automobiles are

outlawed on the little, isolated, Michigan, island, so visitors can
$\overline{}$
49

see the sights only by horse, carriage, or by riding a bicycle, or
$\overline{}$
50
on foot. Luckily, the island is small enough that cars are not

necessary, Mackinac measures only a mile and a half in
$\overline{}$
51
diameter.

46. F. NO CHANGE
 G. moving in a past-related direction
 H. going back to the past, not the future,
 J. stepping back

47. A. NO CHANGE
 B. house's
 C. houses
 D. houses,

48. F. NO CHANGE
 G. your sweet self over to
 H. yourself on down to
 J. over to

49. A. NO CHANGE
 B. isolated Michigan island
 C. isolated Michigan island,
 D. isolated, Michigan, island

50. F. NO CHANGE
 G. by bicycle,
 H. riding on a bicycle,
 J. bicycle,

51. A. NO CHANGE
 B. necessary, furthermore, Mackinac
 C. necessary. Mackinac
 D. necessary Mackinac

GO ON TO THE NEXT PAGE.

There are many things to see while visiting Mackinac Island. The majestic Grand Hotel is a popular tourist spot, as are the governor's mansion and Arch Rock, a towering limestone arch formed naturally by water erosion. [52] Fort Mackinac, where they still set off cannons every hour, is also a popular place to visit. Visible from parts of the island are Mackinac Bridge—the longest suspension bridge ever built—and a picturesque old lighthouse.

Shopping is also a favorite pastime on Mackinac Island. The island's biggest industry is tourism, [53] For the island's many

tourists, the most popular item of sale on Mackinac Island is
                                       ―――
                                        54

fudge. The downtown streets are lined with fudge shops, where
                                                         ―――――
                                                           55
tourists can watch fudge of all different flavors being made before lining up to buy some for themselves. These fudge shops

are so numerous and abundant that the local residents have even
       ―――――――――――――――――
              56

developed a special nickname for these tourists: I call the
                                                 ―――――――
                                                    57
tourists "fudgies."

Apart from sightseeing and shopping, Mackinac Island is a great place to just sit back and relax. In the summer, a gentle lake breeze floats through the air, when it creates a beautiful,
                                        ――――――――――――――――――
                                              58
temperate climate. It is peaceful to sit in the city park and watch the ferries and private boats float into the harbor. The privacy of

52. If the writer were to delete the phrase "formed naturally by water erosion" (placing a period after the word *arch*), this sentence would primarily lose:

F. a detail describing the unique formation of the Arch Rock.
G. factual information concerning the geological formations of the tourist attractions on Mackinac Island.
H. a contrast to the governor's mansion, which was constructed by human hands.
J. nothing; this information is detailed elsewhere in this paragraph.

53. Given that all the following are true, which one, if added here at the end of this sentence, would provide the most effective transition to the topic discussed in the sentence that follows?

A. so there are many souvenir stores, T-shirt shops, and candy and ice cream parlors.
B. so Mackinac Island has not been negatively affected by outsourcing.
C. which is a big change from the island's eighteenth-century use in the fur trade.
D. but it's not a tourist attraction like many others with theme parks and chain restaurants.

54. F. NO CHANGE
G. for selling
H. for sale
J. of selling

55. Which of the following alternatives to the underlined portion would NOT be acceptable?

A. which
B. so
C. and
D. in which

56. F. NO CHANGE
G. abundantly numerous
H. numerous
J. of an abundance truly numerous

57. A. NO CHANGE
B. one calls
C. it calls
D. they call

58. F. NO CHANGE
G. creating
H. once it creates
J. as if it had created

GO ON TO THE NEXT PAGE.

the island's environs certainly <u>don't give</u> it the hustle-bustle
₅₉
quality of a city, but the relaxing atmosphere makes Mackinac
Island the perfect place to visit to get away from the hectic pace
of everyday life.

59. A. NO CHANGE
 B. isn't giving
 C. hasn't given
 D. doesn't give

Question 60 asks about the preceding passage
as a whole.

---

60. Suppose the writer had intended to write an essay on the difficulty the residents of Mackinac Island have had prohibiting automobile traffic from the historic island. Would this essay have successfully fulfilled that goal?

 F. Yes, because the automobile has become such an essential part of American tourist travel that the residents are clearly threatened.

 G. Yes, because this essay discusses the fact that automobiles are outlawed and goes on to detail many of the reasons this was possible.

 H. No, because the essay focuses instead on other aspects of Mackinac Island, mentioning automobiles in only one part of the passage.

 J. No, because this essay describes the ways the residents of Mackinac Island have sought to bring automobiles back to the island, not to outlaw them.

PASSAGE V

Fun with Karaoke

[1]

[1] Karaoke is one of the most popular forms of entertainment in the world. [2] What defies understanding, though, is why so many ordinary people insist on getting up on stage in public, humiliating themselves in front of both their <u>friends; and peers.</u> [3] Whether practiced at home, in a
₆₁
restaurant, or at a party, karaoke is a form of entertainment

that <u>provides</u> people with a great time and a positive feeling. [4]
₆₂
It is understandable that people would enjoy singing in the

61. A. NO CHANGE
 B. friends and peers.
 C. friends, and peers.
 D. friends and, peers.

62. Which of the following alternatives to the underlined portion would NOT be acceptable?

 F. that has provided
 G. , providing
 H. , that is, providing
 J. that having provided

GO ON TO THE NEXT PAGE.

privacy of their homes. [5] There are many different ways to respond to this question. 63

[2]

Looking more closely, and you'll see a main reason for karaoke's success is its glitz and glamour. Karaoke provides people with a moment when they are more than just everyday folks—they are stars. Even though their performances may be heard only in dimly lit bars or busy restaurants, but karaoke singers are still performing as if in a true concert with such

concert-hall staples, as microphones, lights, and applause. Even though the singers' voices are not spectacular, the audience

has known that it's all for fun and responds anyway. And in the

end, everyone would like to be a rock star. Karaoke is as close as many people will get to fame and stardom, but this is not the only reason for its enduring popularity.

[3]

There is another, more obvious reason why karaoke is so popular and singing in public is such fun. The average person allows his or her singing to be heard only in the shower or in the car as the radio plays. Karaoke, by contrast, allows the average person the opportunity to share that ordinarily solitary

experience with other people. In lieu of how good or bad their voices are, people can experience the sheer joy of music with

63. For the sake of logic and coherence, Sentence 2 should be placed:

    A. where it is now.
    B. after Sentence 3.
    C. after Sentence 4.
    D. after Sentence 5.

64. **F.** NO CHANGE
    G. Having looked
    H. To look
    J. Look

65. **A.** NO CHANGE
    B. restaurants which
    C. restaurants,
    D. restaurants but

66. **F.** NO CHANGE
    G. staples:
    H. staples
    J. staples;

67. **A.** NO CHANGE
    B. is knowing
    C. knew
    D. knows

68. Given that all the choices are true, which one would most effectively conclude this paragraph while leading into the main focus of the next paragraph?

    F. NO CHANGE
    G. This is why AudioSynTrac and Numark Electronics were so successful in debuting the first sing-along tapes and equipment back in the 1970s.
    H. Japan's lasting influence on karaoke is obvious all the way down to its name—the Japanese word karaoke translates roughly to "empty orchestra."
    J. Singing in front of people is more fun for many people than singing in the shower or in the car.

69. **A.** NO CHANGE
    B. furthermore,
    C. moreover,
    D. as a result,

70. **F.** NO CHANGE
    G. Regardless of
    H. However
    J. Because of

GO ON TO THE NEXT PAGE.

others, whose singing is mostly a private affair as well, through
$\overline{71}$
karaoke.

[4]

The effect karaoke has on people may also provide an explanation for its popularity: it helps bring people who are ordinarily shy out of their shells. [72] Karaoke helps them overcome stage fright, build their self-confidence, and conquer

their fears. The singers may feel nervous or silly if they first take the stage, but when the audience breaks out into applause, the singers are sure to feel rewarded.

[5]

Whatever the reason, karaoke continues to grow in popularity. Last year, karaoke made no less than $7 billion in profit in Japan. Many dismiss it as a fad, but as long as karaoke is fun and leaves people feeling good, it will not disappear.

---

71. **A.** NO CHANGE
    B. who
    C. whom
    D. who's

72. If the writer were to delete the clause "who are ordinarily shy" from the preceding sentence, the essay would primarily lose:
    F. a detail that explains why karaoke is so popular in the international community.
    G. a detail meant to indicate that karaoke is popular among those not normally inclined to sing in public.
    H. information that emphasizes the possible psychological benefits of karaoke for the chronically shy.
    J. an indication that karaoke may be used at some future time to help singers overcome stage fright.

73. **A.** NO CHANGE
    B. when
    C. unless
    D. where

74. **F.** NO CHANGE
    G. lesser than
    H. fewer then
    J. few than

Question 75 asks about the preceding passage as a whole.

---

75. Upon reviewing notes for this essay, the writer comes across some information and composes the following sentence incorporating that information:

    While different regions of the United States prefer different artists, the most popular karaoke requests are invariably for country artists, varying from the modern Carrie Underwood to the classic Johnny Cash.

    For the sake of the logic and coherence of this essay, this sentence should be:

    A. placed at the end of Paragraph 3.
    B. placed at the end of Paragraph 4.
    C. placed at the end of Paragraph 5.
    D. NOT added to the essay at all.

END OF TEST 1

STOP! DO NOT TURN THE PAGE UNTIL TOLD TO DO SO.

MATHEMATICS TEST

60 Minutes—60 Questions

DIRECTIONS: Solve each problem, choose the correct answer, and then darken the corresponding oval on your answer sheet.

Do not linger over problems that take too much time. Solve as many as you can; then return to the others in the time you have left for this test.

You are permitted to use a calculator on this test. You may use your calculator for any problems you choose, but some of the problems may best be done without using a calculator.

Note: Unless otherwise stated, all of the following should be assumed:

1. Illustrative figures are NOT necessarily drawn to scale.
2. Geometric figures lie in a plane.
3. The word *line* indicates a straight line.
4. The word *average* indicates arithmetic mean.

---

1. Point X is located at –15 on the real number line. If point Y is located at –11, what is the midpoint of line segment XY ?

   A. –13
   B. –4
   C. –2
   D. 2
   E. 13

DO YOUR FIGURING HERE.

2. Given triangle CDE (shown below) with a right angle at point E, what is the length of leg DE ?

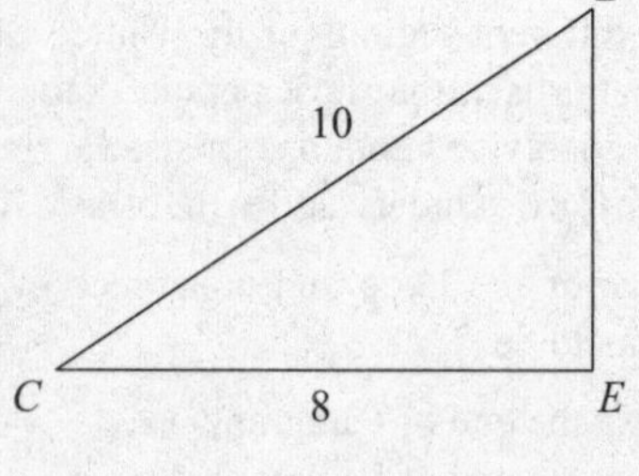

   F. $\sqrt{2}$
   G. 2
   H. 6
   J. $\sqrt{164}$
   K. 16

GO ON TO THE NEXT PAGE.

3. Lucy is studying her ant farm. She needs to approximate the number of ants in the population, and she realizes that the number of ants, N, is close to 50 more than double the volume of the ant farm, V. Which of the formulas below expresses that approximation?

DO YOUR FIGURING HERE.

A. $N \approx \dfrac{1}{2}V + 50$

B. $N \approx \dfrac{1}{2}(V + 50)$

C. $N \approx 2V + 50$

D. $N \approx 2(V + 50)$

E. $N \approx V^2 + 50$

4. Lisa has 5 fiction books and 7 nonfiction books on a table by her front door. As she rushes out the door one day, she takes a book at random. What is the probability that the book she takes is fiction?

F. $\dfrac{1}{5}$

G. $\dfrac{5}{7}$

H. $\dfrac{1}{12}$

J. $\dfrac{5}{12}$

K. $\dfrac{7}{12}$

5. In the spring semester of her math class, Katie's test scores were 108, 81, 79, 99, 85, and 82. What was her average test score in the spring semester?

A. 534
B. 108
C. 89
D. 84
E. 80

GO ON TO THE NEXT PAGE.

6. Given parallel lines *l* and *m*, which of the following choices lists a pair of angles that must be congruent?

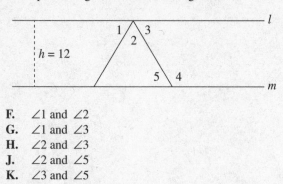

F. ∠1 and ∠2
G. ∠1 and ∠3
H. ∠2 and ∠3
J. ∠2 and ∠5
K. ∠3 and ∠5

7. Gregor works as a political intern and receives a monthly pay-check. He spends 20% of his paycheck on rent and deposits the remainder into a savings account. If his deposit is $3,200, how much does he receive as his monthly pay?

A. $ 4,000
B. $ 5,760
C. $ 7,200
D. $ 8,000
E. $17,000

8. Given parallelogram *ABCD* below and parallelogram *EFGH* (not shown) are similar, which of the following statements must be true about the two shapes?

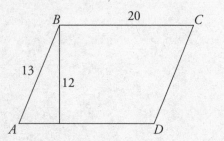

F. Their areas are equal.
G. Their perimeters are equal.
H. Side *AB* is congruent to side *EF*.
J. Diagonal *AC* is congruent to diagonal *EG*.
K. Their corresponding angles are congruent.

9. A size 8 dress that usually sells for $60 is on sale for 30% off. Victoria has a store credit card that entitles her to an additional 10% off the reduced price of any item in the store. Excluding sales tax, what is the price Victoria pays for the dress?

A. $22.20
B. $24.75
C. $34.00
D. $36.00
E. $37.80

GO ON TO THE NEXT PAGE.

DO YOUR FIGURING HERE.

10. Erin and Amy are playing poker. At a certain point in the game, Erin has 3 more chips than Amy. On the next hand, Erin wins 4 chips from Amy. Now how many more chips does Erin have than Amy?

    F.   1
    G.   4
    H.   7
    J.   11
    K.   14

11. If $y = 4$, then $|1 - y| = ?$

    A.   −5
    B.   −3
    C.   3
    D.   4
    E.   5

12. $(3a + 2b)(a - b^2)$ is equivalent to:

    F. $4a + b^2$
    G. $3a^2 - 2b^3$
    H. $3a^2 + 2ab + 2b^3$
    J. $3a^2 - 3ab^2 + a^2 b^2$
    K. $3a^2 - 3ab^2 + 2ab - 2b^3$

13. For all real values of y, $3 - 2(4 - y) = ?$

    A. $-2y - 9$
    B. $-2y + 8$
    C. $-2y - 1$
    D. $2y - 5$
    E. $2y + 11$

14. Which of the following is equivalent to $(y^3)^8$?

    F. y^{11}
    G. y^{24}
    H. $8y^3$
    J. $8y^{11}$
    K. $24y$

15. If the first day of the year is a Monday, what is the 260th day?

    A.   Monday
    B.   Tuesday
    C.   Wednesday
    D.   Thursday
    E.   Friday

GO ON TO THE NEXT PAGE.

16. If a square has an area of 64 square units, what is the area of the largest circle that can be inscribed inside the square?

    F. 4π
    G. 8π
    H. 16π
    J.   64
    K. 64π

DO YOUR FIGURING HERE.

17. What is the product of the solutions of the expression $x^2 - 5x - 14 = 0$?

    A. -14
    B. -2
    C.   0
    D.   5
    E.   7

18. Factoring the polynomial $x^{12} - 9$ reveals a number of factors for the expression. Which of these is NOT one of the possible factors?

    F. $x^6 + 3$
    G. $x^{12} - 9$
    H. $x^3 + \sqrt{3}$
    J. $x^3 - \sqrt{3}$
    K. $x - \sqrt{3}$

19. What is the value of $\dfrac{2x+4}{3x}$ when $x = \dfrac{1}{6}$?

    A. $4\dfrac{1}{3}$

    B. 2

    C. $\dfrac{26}{3}$

    D. 12

    E. 24

20. If you drive 60 miles at 90 miles an hour, how many minutes will the trip take you?

    F. 15
    G. 30
    H. 40
    J. 60
    K. 90

GO ON TO THE NEXT PAGE.

21. The area of a trapezoid is found by multiplying the height by the average of the bases: $A = \frac{1}{2}h(b_1 + b_2)$. Given the side measurements below, what is the area, in square inches, of the trapezoid?

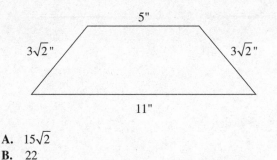

A. $15\sqrt{2}$
B. 22
C. 24
D. $24\sqrt{2}$
E. $30\sqrt{2}$

22. If $x = -\frac{2}{3}$ and $x = \frac{1}{4}$ are the roots of the quadratic equation $ax^2 + bx + c = 0$, then which of the following could represent the two factors of $ax^2 + bx + c$?

F. $(3x + 2)$ and $(4x - 1)$
G. $(3x + 1)$ and $(4x - 2)$
H. $(3x - 1)$ and $(4x + 2)$
J. $(3x - 2)$ and $(4x + 1)$
K. $(3x - 2)$ and $(4x - 1)$

23. In the rhombus below, diagonal $AC = 6$ and diagonal $BD = 8$. What is the length of each of the four sides?

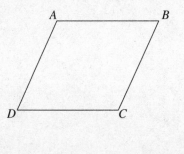

A. $\sqrt{7}$
B. $\sqrt{14}$
C. 5
D. 7
E. 10

DO YOUR FIGURING HERE.

GO ON TO THE NEXT PAGE.

24. A rectangular rug has an area of 80 square feet, and its width is exactly 2 feet shorter than its length. What is the length, in feet, of the rug?

   F. 8
   G. 10
   H. 16
   J. 18
   K. 36

DO YOUR FIGURING HERE.

25. In the Cartesian plane, a line runs through points $(1,-5)$ and $(5,10)$. Which of the following represents the slope of that line?

   A. $\dfrac{4}{15}$

   B. $\dfrac{4}{5}$

   C. 1

   D. $\dfrac{5}{4}$

   E. $\dfrac{15}{4}$

26. The equation of a circle in the standard (x,y) coordinate plane is given by the equation $(x+5)^2 + (y-5)^2 = 5$. What is the center of the circle?

   F. $(-\sqrt{5}, \sqrt{5})$
   G. $(-5, \quad 5)$
   H. $(\sqrt{5}, -\sqrt{5})$
   J. $(\;5, \quad -5)$
   K. $(\;5, \quad 5)$

27. The graph below shows the function $f(x)$ in the coordinate plane. Which of the following choices best describes the *domain* of this function?

(Note: The domain is defined as the set of all values of x for which a function is defined.)

   A. $\{0, 1, 2, 3, 4\}$
   B. $\{0, 1, 2\}$
   C. $\{x: 0 < x < 2\}$
   D. $\{x: 0 < x < 4\}$
   E. All real values of x

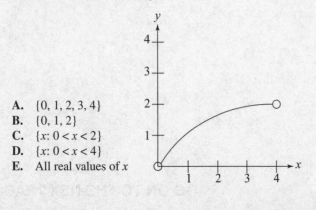

GO ON TO THE NEXT PAGE.

28. Amber decides to graph her office and the nearest coffee shop in the standard (x,y) plane. If her office is at point $(-1,-5)$ and the coffee shop is at point $(3,3)$, what are the coordinates of the point exactly halfway between those of her office and the shop? (You may assume Amber is able to walk a straight line between them.)

- **F.** $(1,-1)$
- **G.** $(1, 4)$
- **H.** $(2,-1)$
- **J.** $(2, 4)$
- **K.** $(2, 0)$

DO YOUR FIGURING HERE.

29. For a chemistry class, Sanjay is doing an experiment that involves periodically heating a container of liquid. The graph below shows the temperature of the liquid at different times during the experiment. What is the average rate of change of temperature (in degrees Celsius per minute) during the times in which Sanjay is applying heat to this container?

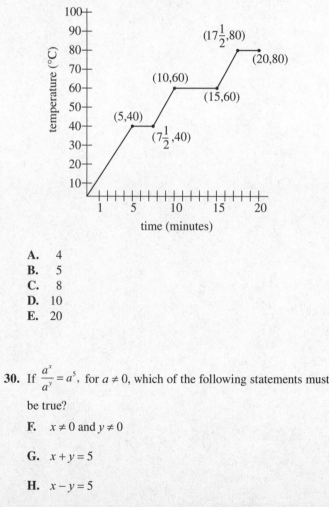

- **A.** 4
- **B.** 5
- **C.** 8
- **D.** 10
- **E.** 20

30. If $\dfrac{a^x}{a^y} = a^5$, for $a \neq 0$, which of the following statements must be true?

- **F.** $x \neq 0$ and $y \neq 0$

- **G.** $x + y = 5$

- **H.** $x - y = 5$

- **J.** $xy = 5$

- **K.** $\dfrac{x}{y} = 5$

GO ON TO THE NEXT PAGE.

31. What is the slope of the line given by the equation $8 = 3y - 5x$?

A. -5

B. $-\dfrac{5}{3}$

C. $-\dfrac{3}{5}$

D. $\dfrac{3}{5}$

E. $\dfrac{5}{3}$

DO YOUR FIGURING HERE.

32. When adding fractions, a useful first step is to find the least common denominator (LCD) of the fractions. What is the LCD for these fractions?

$$\frac{2}{3^2 \cdot 5}, \frac{13}{5^2 \cdot 7 \cdot 11}, \frac{2}{3 \cdot 11^3}$$

F. $3 \cdot 5 \cdot 7 \cdot 11$

G. $3^2 \cdot 5^2 \cdot 7 \cdot 11$

H. $3^2 \cdot 5^2 \cdot 11^3$

J. $3^2 \cdot 5^2 \cdot 7 \cdot 11^3$

K. $3^3 \cdot 5^3 \cdot 7 \cdot 11^4$

33. $\dfrac{1}{4} \cdot \dfrac{2}{5} \cdot \dfrac{3}{6} \cdot \dfrac{4}{7} \cdot \dfrac{5}{8} \cdot \dfrac{6}{9} \cdot \dfrac{7}{10} = ?$

A. $\dfrac{1}{720}$

B. $\dfrac{1}{360}$

C. $\dfrac{1}{120}$

D. $\dfrac{27}{49}$

E. 1

GO ON TO THE NEXT PAGE.

34. Dave is in Pikeston and needs to go to Danville, which is about 110 miles due south of Pikeston. From Danville, he'll head east to Rocketville, about 200 miles from Danville. As he sets out on his trip, a plane takes off from the Pikeston airport and flies directly to Rocketville. Approximately how far, in miles, does the plane fly?

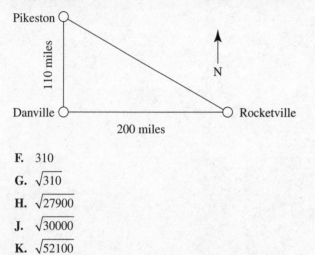

F. 310

G. $\sqrt{310}$

H. $\sqrt{27900}$

J. $\sqrt{30000}$

K. $\sqrt{52100}$

35. The figure below is a pentagon (5-sided figure). Suppose a second pentagon were overlaid on this pentagon. At most, the two figures could have how many points of intersection?

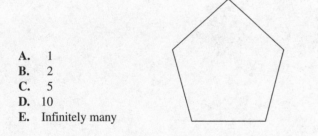

A. 1
B. 2
C. 5
D. 10
E. Infinitely many

36. MicroCorp will hold its annual company picnic next week and will assign 3 planning duties to its employees. One person selected will reserve a venue, another will arrange catering, and a third will plan activities. There are 10 employees eligible to fulfill these duties, and no employee can be assigned more than one duty. How many different ways are there for duties to be assigned to employees?

F. 7^3

G. 9^3

H. 10^3

J. $9 \cdot 8 \cdot 7$

K. $10 \cdot 9 \cdot 8$

GO ON TO THE NEXT PAGE.

37. In the (x,y) coordinate plane below, points P (6,2) and Q (1,4) are two vertices of $\triangle PQR$. If $\angle PQR$ is a right angle, then which of the following could be the coordinates of R ?

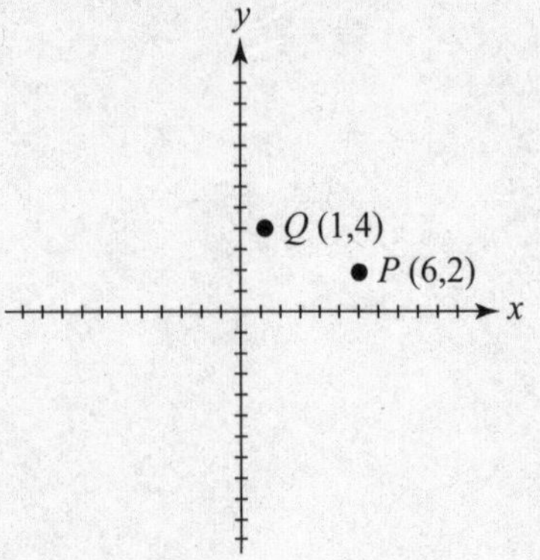

A. (4,−3)
B. (3, 0)
C. (2, 1)
D. (2, 4)
E. (3, 9)

38. If $y = 0.25(100 - y)$, then what is the value of y ?

F. 200
G. 75
H. 25
J. 20
K. 18

39. If $0° \leq x \leq 180°$ and $4\cos^2 x = 1$, then $x =$?

A. 0°
B. 60°
C. 90°
D. 150°
E. 180°

40. Danielle's living room is a rectangle with the dimensions 16 feet by 18 feet. If she partially covers the bare floor with a circular throw rug with a diameter of 12 feet, what is the approximate area of bare floor, in square feet, that remains exposed?

(Note: Assume the rug lies completely flat and does not touch any wall.)

F. 113
G. 144
H. 175
J. 288
K. Cannot be determined without knowing the exact position of the rug

GO ON TO THE NEXT PAGE.

41. In the standard (x,y) coordinate plane, which of the following is the equation of the line perpendicular to the line $y = -2x + 2$ and that passes through the point $(0,-3)$?

A. $y = -2x - 3$

B. $y = -\dfrac{1}{2}x + 2$

C. $y = \dfrac{1}{2}x - 3$

D. $y = \dfrac{1}{2}x + 2$

E. $y = 2x - 3$

42. In the figure given below, what is $\sin \theta$?

F. $\dfrac{1}{2}$

G. $\dfrac{\sqrt{3}}{3}$

H. $\dfrac{\sqrt{3}}{2}$

J. 1

K. $\sqrt{3}$

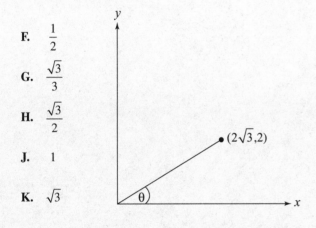

$(2\sqrt{3}, 2)$

θ

43. If $a = 5$ and $b = -\dfrac{1}{4}$, which of the following expressions will be the greatest?

A. $a + b$
B. $a - b$
C. $a \times b$
D. $a \div b$
E. $|a \times b|$

GO ON TO THE NEXT PAGE.

DO YOUR FIGURING HERE.

44. When $\dfrac{x}{3} - 1 = -\dfrac{13}{12}$, which of the following must be true?

F. $-12 < x < -3$

G. $-3 < x < 0$

H. $0 < x < 3$

J. $3 < x < 4$

K. $4 < x$

45. Which choice below is the complete solution set of $|2z - 3| \geq 7$?

A. $z \geq 5$

B. $z \leq -2$ or $z \geq 5$

C. $-5 \leq z \leq 5$

D. $z \leq -6$ or $z \geq 2$

E. $z \leq -5$ or $z \geq 2$

46. Which trigonometric function (where defined) is equivalent to

$\dfrac{\sin^2 x}{\cos x \tan x}$?

F. $\dfrac{\cos x}{\sin^2 x}$

G. $\dfrac{1}{\cos x}$

H. $\sin x$

J. $\dfrac{1}{\sin x}$

K. $\dfrac{1}{\sin^2 x}$

GO ON TO THE NEXT PAGE.

47. When $a \neq b$, the expression $\dfrac{ax - bx}{4a - 4b} < 0$. Which of the following describes the complete set of x values that make this inequality true?

A. $x = -4$ only

B. $x = 4$ only

C. $x = -\dfrac{1}{4}$ only

D. $x < 0$

E. $x > 0$

48. The volume of a cone, which is derived by treating it as a pyramid with infinitely many lateral faces, is given by the formula $V = \dfrac{1}{3}\pi r^2 h$, where r is the radius of the base and h is the height. If the radius is halved and the height is doubled, what will be the ratio of the new volume to the old volume?

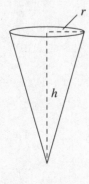

F. 4:1
G. 2:1
H. 1:1
J. 1:2
K. 1:4

GO ON TO THE NEXT PAGE.

49. Al bikes a trail to the top of a hill and back down. He bikes up the hill in m minutes, then returns twice as quickly downhill on the same trail. What is the total time, in hours, that Al spends biking up the hill and back down?

A. $\dfrac{m}{60}$

B. $\dfrac{m}{40}$

C. $\dfrac{m}{30}$

D. $\dfrac{3m}{2}$

E. $2m$

DO YOUR FIGURING HERE.

50. Pippin the guinea pig is running on her wheel when, due to a manufacturing error, the wheel breaks free of its axis. Pippin remains in her wheel, running in a straight line until the wheel has rotated exactly 15 times. If the diameter of the wheel is 10 inches, how many inches has the wheel rolled?

F. 75

G. 150

H. 75π

J. 150π

K. $1,500\pi$

51. A circle is inscribed in a square, as shown below. If x is the distance from the center of the circle to a vertex of the square, then what is the length of the radius of the circle, in terms of x ?

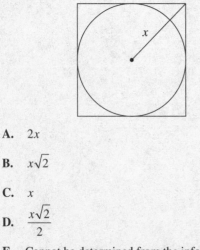

A. $2x$

B. $x\sqrt{2}$

C. x

D. $\dfrac{x\sqrt{2}}{2}$

E. Cannot be determined from the information given

GO ON TO THE NEXT PAGE.

DO YOUR FIGURING HERE.

52. A function is defined for x and y such that
$f_{(x,y)} = -2xy + y + x - 4$. So, for $x = 2$ and $y = 3$,
$f_{(2,3)} = -2 \times 2 \times 3 + 3 + 2 - 4 = -12 + 1 = -11$. If x and y
are to be chosen such that $f_{(x,y)} = f_{(y,x)}$, then which of
the following restrictions must be placed on x and y?

F. $x > 0$ and $y > 0$

G. $x < 0$ and $y < 0$

H. $x = y$

J. $xy < 0$

K. No restrictions are needed.

53. A pipe of radius 4 feet sends water to two smaller pipes of equal
size. If each of the smaller pipes allows exactly half as much
water to flow as the larger pipe, what is the radius of one of
the smaller pipes?

A. 2

B. 2π

C. $2\sqrt{2}$

D. $4\sqrt{2}$

E. $2\pi\sqrt{2}$

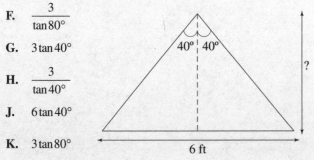

54. The cross-sectional view of a tent is shown below. If the
tent is 6 feet wide at its base, then which of the following
expressions could be used to calculate the height of the tent,
in feet?

F. $\dfrac{3}{\tan 80°}$

G. $3\tan 40°$

H. $\dfrac{3}{\tan 40°}$

J. $6\tan 40°$

K. $3\tan 80°$

40° | 40°

?

6 ft

GO ON TO THE NEXT PAGE.

55. Two girls walk home from school. Starting from school, Susan walks north 2 blocks and then west 8 blocks, while Cindy walks east 3 blocks and then south 1 block. Approximately how many blocks apart are the girls' homes?

A. 7.1
B. 10.4
C. 11.4
D. 12.7
E. 16.0

56. For all integer values of a and b such that $a > 0$ and $b < 0$, which of the following must also be an integer?

F. 3^{a+b}

G. 3^{a-b}

H. 3^{ab}

J. 3^{-a}

K. $3^{\frac{a}{b}}$

57. If x and y are real numbers and $0 < x < y < \dfrac{y}{x}$, which of the following gives the set of all values which $\dfrac{y}{x}$ could have?

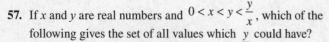

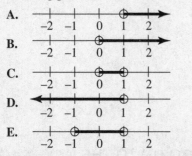

A.
B.
C.
D.
E.

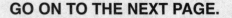

GO ON TO THE NEXT PAGE.

58. A circular running track is being built in a fenced-in athletic field 100 feet wide and 150 feet long. If a border of 10 feet is needed between the outside edge of the track and the fence, what is the radius of the largest track that can be built?

F. 40
G. 45
H. 65
J. 90
K. 110

59. If a sphere is cut by two different planes, dividing it into sections, how many sections is it possible to end up with?

A. 2 only
B. 2 or 4 only
C. 3 only
D. 3 or 4 only
E. 2, 3, or 4 only

60. For all real values of a and b, the equation $|a - b| = 5$ can be interpreted as "the positive difference of a and b is 5." What is the positive difference between the 2 solutions for a ?

F. b

G. $b + 5$

H. $2b$

J. $\sqrt{b^2 - 25}$

K. 10

END OF TEST 2

STOP! DO NOT TURN THE PAGE UNTIL TOLD TO DO SO.

DO NOT RETURN TO A PREVIOUS TEST.

READING TEST
35 Minutes—40 Questions

DIRECTIONS: There are four passages in this test. Each passage is followed by several questions. After reading a passage, choose the best answer to each question and fill in the corresponding oval on your answer document. You may refer to the passages as often as necessary.

Passage I

PROSE FICTION: The following passage is excerpted from the coming-of-age novel *The Year of the Unicorn* by Krista Prouty (©2008 by Krista Prouty).

It was always the same, every Christmas. My sister and I would wake up early, my parents would send us back to bed, and we would instead huddle in my room, discussing which gifts might be waiting for us downstairs. One year it was a bicycle
5 that I wanted, and I can still remember telling my sister exactly what it would look like: pink, with silver streamers and a sparkly silver seat. Eventually we would hear our parents moving around downstairs and we would know that it was almost time. Once the scent of coffee made it to our rooms, we would hurl
10 ourselves downstairs since that signified that our parents were not only awake but caffeinated and ready for gift-giving.

The year that I was nine, and Lily was six, the gift that I had been craving was the Barbie Dream House. Another girl from my school had one and I had been lucky enough to be allowed
15 a glimpse of it after school one day. She was like a princess bestowing largesse; allowing one or two people over after school most days, demonstrating the various clever mechanisms, then sitting quietly, contentedly, while we gazed in wonder for a few minutes. Then, she sent us on our way. I knew that if I could only
20 have a Dream House of my own, my life would be complete. It was a bigger gift than I usually requested but, logically, I felt, that meant I was all the more likely to have my wish granted.

One night I overheard my parents, after they thought Lily and I had gone to bed.

25 "Bill, what are we going to do about Christmas this year?" My mother's voice, quiet and unsettlingly uncertain, came from the kitchen.

"I don't know yet, Mel, but we'll figure something out. We always do, honey."

30 "I know. I just can't help but worry." Whatever my mother said next was drowned out by the running water—she must have been washing up after dinner. I crept back to my bedroom, a little bit troubled by what I had heard but, as is the way of children, soon forgot and went back to Barbie Dream House dreaming.

35 On the Christmas morning in question, Lily and I huddled in my room, waiting for the signal to appear. She wanted a new bike and kept asking me if Santa would get it for her, but all I could think about was my Dream House. Somehow, I had convinced myself that I was certain to get it, that life and the fates
40 could not possibly be cruel enough to deny me this. I could see the wallpaper that was printed on the plastic walls, the darling matching furniture, and the ingenious hand-operated elevator. It would smell like new plastic. I inhaled deeply, imagining myself showing my gift off to friends and foes alike. Instead of
45 new plastic, however, my nostrils quivered to the odor of freshly brewed coffee. It was time.

My eyes still full of the glories I expected, I barreled down the stairs, almost knocking Lily down in my haste. Both of my parents were standing in the kitchen, sipping coffee. I tore past
50 them, even though I knew that they would expect me to stop and wait for them to walk into the living room with me. My longing was simply too exquisite to wait any longer. I burst through the double doors into our living room, words of joy and gratitude ready on my lips, only to find—there was no Dream House. Fran-
55 tically, I began to paw through the boxes under the tree, certain that it had to be there, somewhere, blind to the movement of my parents and sister entering the room behind me, nervous smiles on both my parents' faces. Eventually I was forced to concede that the tree was not somehow harboring a Dream House under
60 its limbs. I looked up at my parents, grief and confusion painted large on my features.

"Hold up a minute, honey. Santa brought you one more gift that wouldn't quite fit under the tree. Bill, go ahead—show her."

As I watched my father head towards a corner where a
65 large blanket was draped over some bulky object, hope flickered back to life a bit. But the size was all wrong, as was the shape. Still smiling anxiously, my father pulled the blanket away from what appeared to be a huge dollhouse. If Barbie's Dream House was sleek and modern, this was awkward and old-fashioned. It
70 had a peaked roof and a patio, with what looked like handmade furniture and wallpaper that looked suspiciously like the paper my parents had hung in Lily's room last fall. Slowly, realization dawned—my father had made it for me.

GO ON TO THE NEXT PAGE.

Looking back, I can only recall the rest of that day hazily,
75 even though the events up until that moment are as clear today
as they were at the time. I remember the feeling of devastation
that I felt, as I realized that the other girls from school would
not, in fact, be blown away by my Christmas gift. I tried to be as
grateful as I could, understanding even then that my father had
80 probably spent countless hours working on the house, but my
disappointment was only too evident. I just couldn't understand
why they had given me this crude approximation instead of my
heart's desire. As an adult, I wish I could go back in time, whis-
per the reason to my younger self, try to be more appreciative
85 of my father's efforts, but that is not the way of the world. I still
have the house, though, and when I have children of my own, I
will tell them the whole story, and I hope they will understand
better than I did.

1. Which of the following statements does NOT describe one of
the narrator's reactions to her Christmas gift?

   A. She is devastated by the realization that the other children
   at school will not be impressed by this gift.
   B. She wishes that her parents had bought her a real Barbie
   Dream House instead of a handmade one.
   C. She despises the house for its old-fashioned appearance
   and lack of modern conveniences, such as an elevator.
   D. She appreciates all the effort her father went to in order to
   give her this gift and tries to convey a sense of gratitude.

2. According to the passage, when the narrator smells coffee on
Christmas morning, it means that:

   F. her parents are ready to proceed with the Christmas festivi-
   ties.
   G. she and her sister should hurry to the kitchen for breakfast.
   H. her father has finally finished preparing her Christmas gift.
   J. it is time to burst into the living room in front of her parents.

3. The narrator would most likely agree with which of the
following statements about owning a Barbie Dream House?

   A. She would become a princess able to bestow largesse on
   other children.
   B. She would, at least for the moment, be content with her
   life.
   C. It would allow her to appreciate her parents' hard work
   and sacrifices.
   D. She would then be able to pass it on to her own children
   someday.

4. What is the main point of the first paragraph?

   F. The smell of coffee still reminds the narrator of the Christ-
   mases of her childhood.
   G. The narrator's family had a specific ritual that was
   followed every Christmas morning.
   H. Most years, the narrator and her sister would hurl themselves into their gifts without warning.
   J. The narrator had once desperately wanted a pink and silver
   bicycle.

5. Which of the following statements most accurately expresses
the narrator's feelings when she first sees the gift that her father
made for her?

   A. She is disappointed that it is not the exact gift that she had
   hoped to receive.
   B. She gratefully acknowledges the long hours her father
   must have put into the gift.
   C. She admires the traditional architecture of the house and
   its attractive wallpaper.
   D. She looks forward to showing her new house off to all of
   the other girls at school.

6. The narrator's father can most accurately be characterized as:

   F. ignorant and cruel.
   G. thoughtful but lazy.
   H. concerned and hard-working.
   J. caring but inaccessible.

7. It can logically be inferred from the passage that the reason
the narrator was not given the official Barbie Dream House
for Christmas is because:

   A. it is too costly a gift for her parents to buy that year.
   B. she had already been given the pink and silver bicycle that
   she wanted.
   C. her father had always wanted to make his daughter a doll-
   house.
   D. her parents do not wish for their daughter to be happy.

8. According to the passage, the reason the narrator hopes to
someday tell the children the story of her dollhouse is that she:

   F. wants them to be able to impress the other children at
   school as she once did.
   G. knows that, by that time, it is likely to be worth a great
   deal of money.
   H. remembers how much she appreciated the gift when it was
   given to her.
   J. hopes that they will be better able to understand the meaning behind the gift than she was.

GO ON TO THE NEXT PAGE.

9. A reasonable conclusion that the narrator draws regarding her dollhouse is that:

A. it is far more beautiful than was the plastic Barbie Dream House that she had initially desired.

B. without an elevator, it is less valuable than it would otherwise have been.

C. it was given to her with the intention that she keep it to pass on to her own children someday.

D. constructing it must have been time-consuming and labor-intensive.

10. The main point of the last paragraph is that:

F. the narrator would have been much happier if she had been given a Barbie Dream House.

G. it is not fair to give one child a long-desired gift and not give the same to another child.

H. the disappointments suffered in childhood affect people well into adulthood.

J. the passage of time can alter the way events from the past are viewed.

Passage II

SOCIAL SCIENCE: This passage is adapted from T. H. Watkins' *The Great Depression* (©1993, Little, Brown and Co.; Blackside Inc.).

One of the most durable and well regarded of all the New Deal's programs came from President Roosevelt himself, who had his own share of inventiveness. If the president cared about the fate of people, he also cared about the fate of trees, having
5 practiced the art of silviculture on his Hyde Park estate with such enthusiasm that on various official forms he was fond of listing his occupation as "tree farmer." It was in early March, 1933, that he proceeded to bring the two concerns together—enlisting young unemployed men in a kind of volunteer "army" to be put to
10 work in the national forests, national parks, and on other federal public lands. When he went to Congress for authorization of the program, he called the new agency the Civilian Corps Reforestation Youth Rehabilitation Movement, but before sinking under the weight of an acronym like CCRYRM, it was soon changed
15 to the Civilian Conservation Corps (known forever after as the CCC). Congress chose not to handle the details itself. It simply authorized the president to create the program and structure it as he saw fit by executive order; it was to last two years. Responsibility was divided up among the Labor Department, which was
20 to screen and select the enrollees, the War Department, which would house and feed them in their nonworking hours, and the Departments of Agriculture and Interior, which would design and supervise projects in regional and national forests, national parks, and other public lands. The men would be paid $30 a
25 month, anywhere from $23 to $25 of it to be sent to their families.

The CCC officially began on April 5, 1933, calling for an enrollment of 250,000 to be housed in 1,468 camps around the country. The cost for the first year was estimated at $500 million. The men had to be US citizens between the ages of seventeen
30 and twenty-seven (later, twenty-four), out of school, out of work, capable of physical labor, over 60 inches but under 78 inches in height, more than 107 pounds in weight, and had to possess no fewer than "three serviceable natural masticating teeth above and below." They would serve terms of no more than nine months
35 so that as many as possible could be accommodated over the course of time.

Among the earliest enrollees were some veterans who had returned to Washington, setting up camp and demanding payment of their bonuses for service during the war. While making
40 it clear that he opposed the payments on economic grounds, FDR provided tents, showers, mess halls, and latrines, and, waiving the age restriction for them, invited the members of this new Bonus Army to join his new agency. What was more, Eleanor Roosevelt dropped by one rainy day for a visit, slogging through
45 ankle-deep mud to meet and talk with the men. "Hoover sent the army," said one veteran of the previous summer's BEF disaster, "Roosevelt sent his wife." When it became clear that no bonus would be forthcoming, about twenty-five hundred of the men took Roosevelt up on his offer and joined the CCC.

50 In the summer of 1934, Roosevelt expanded the size of the CCC to 350,000 and would raise it to 500,000 in 1935. Congress continued to reauthorize it faithfully over the next seven years, and by the time it was closed out in 1942, the CCC had put more than three million young "soil soldiers" to work. In the national
55 forests alone they built 3,470 fire towers, installed 65,100 miles of telephone lines, scraped and graded thousands of fire breaks, roads, and trails, and built 97,000 miles of truck trails and roads, spent 4.1 million man-hours fighting fires, and cut down and hauled out millions of diseased trees and planted more than 1.3
60 billion young trees in the first major reforestation campaign in the country's history. For the National Park Service, they built roads, campgrounds, bridges, and recreation and administration facilities; for the Biological Survey (a predecessor of today's Fish and Wildlife Service), they conducted wildlife surveys
65 and improved wildlife refuge lands; and for the Army Corps of Engineers, they built flood control projects in West Virginia, Vermont, and New York State.

In return, the CCC, at its best, took at least some young men out of the urban tangle of hopelessness where so many resided,
70 introduced them to the intricacies and healing joy of the outdoors, and clothed and fed them better than many had been for years. Moreover, the program taught more than a hundred thousand to read and write, passed out twenty-five thousand eighth-grade diplomas and five thousand high-school diplomas, gave struc-
75 ture and discipline to lives that had experienced little of either, strengthened bodies and minds, and for many provided a dose of self-esteem they had never known.

GO ON TO THE NEXT PAGE.

11. The main idea of the passage is that:

A. the CCC forced unemployed young men to work in the national forests, national parks, and on other federal public lands for no payment or bonus.

B. it was only after President Roosevelt created the CCC that veterans had suitable employment during the Great Depression.

C. research into the history of the New Deal shows that the idea for the CCC came from Congress.

D. among the programs of the New Deal, the CCC employed young men to build public works projects on public lands in return for modest wages, food, clothing, and some education.

12. The main idea of the third paragraph (lines 37–49) is that:

F. President Hoover had dispatched the army to meet with disgruntled veterans, but President Roosevelt sent his wife, Eleanor, to meet with the Bonus Army.

G. when they realized President Roosevelt would not pay the bonus, many veterans abandoned the Bonus Army and accepted his invitation to join the CCC.

H. President Roosevelt supplied shelter and food to the veterans before paying the bonus the veterans demanded.

J. many of the veterans were above the age requirement of the CCC.

13. As it is used in line 7 to describe President Roosevelt, the term *tree farmer* most nearly means that Roosevelt:

A. had supported his family by growing trees before he entered politics.

B. believed in an agrarian economy over urban industrialization.

C. continued his successful business selling trees while in office.

D. had a great interest in trees and knew a good deal about them.

14. According to the passage, which of the following was a project the CCC performed for the National Park Service?

F. Building fire towers

G. Building campground facilities

H. Installing telephone lines

J. Conducting wildlife surveys

15. According to the passage, which of the following statements is true about the CCC?

A. The agency provided enrollees with academic instruction.

B. The agency provided enrollees with urban job training.

C. The agency accepted only men with six teeth.

D. The agency offered courses in nutrition and self-esteem.

16. Information in the fourth paragraph (lines 50–67) makes it clear that the CCC:

F. was voluntary and therefore did not pay members anything.

G. ran for more years and employed more men than was originally intended.

H. employed 4.1 million men.

J. battled fires in West Virginia, Vermont, and New York.

17. The passage most strongly suggests that before the 1930s, the national forests:

A. received no federal support or aid for projects to clear diseased trees.

B. included land reserved for wildlife refuges.

C. had never undergone a major reforestation campaign.

D. experienced more floods than forest fires.

18. According to the passage, when did the CCC change its name?

F. After President Roosevelt received authorization from Congress.

G. After Congress protested that CCRYRM was too difficult to say.

H. In the same year the size expanded to 500,000 men.

J. After the Bonus Army disbanded.

19. The passage states that the same year the CCC was authorized enrollees had to be:

A. over 78 inches in height.

B. in school.

C. between the ages of seventeen and twenty-seven.

D. between the ages of seventeen and twenty-four.

20. According to the passage, CCC programs in national parks and forests were:

F. conducted far from where the members were fed and housed.

G. under the control of the Departments of Agriculture and the Interior.

H. supervised by the Labor Department.

J. minimum-wage jobs.

GO ON TO THE NEXT PAGE.

Passage III

HUMANITIES: This passage is adapted from John Gattuso, ed., *Native America* (©1993, Houghton Mifflin Co.).

Northwest natives are carvers by tradition, but it was the natives of the far north, in what is now British Columbia and Alaska, who first carved totem poles. The history of these fascinating works is surprisingly brief, for it wasn't until the mid-18th
5 century, when European explorers first encountered these remote tribes, that the unique sculptures began to appear. Although the natives were already expert carvers of canoes, tools, longhouses, and furniture, they lacked the iron tools necessary to fell a massive tree in one piece and carve its entire length.

10 With the iron axes they got in trade for their baskets, boxes, and pelts, the coastal tribes of the far north could take advantage of the trees that grew so tall and straight in their wet climate. Initially, the poles were made to stand against the front of a house, with figures facing out and a door cut through the base, so all
15 would enter the house through the pole. In this case, the totem pole functioned as a family crest, recounting genealogies, stories, or legends that in some way identified the owner. Towards the end of the 19th century, the poles stood free on the beach or in the village outside the carvers' homes. Some villages were virtual
20 forests of dozens, sometimes hundreds, of poles.

The family that carved the pole gave a potlatch with feasting, games, and much gift-giving. The guests, in return, raised the pole. These gatherings were costly and required a great deal of preparation and participation. The custom frustrated whites
25 trying to "civilize" the Indians, especially missionaries who solved the problem by knocking the poles down. Employers, too, complained that their Indian workers were unreliable when a pole was being carved or a potlatch planned. Eventually, both the Canadian and United States governments banned potlatches,
30 and pole carving nearly died out. The ban was lifted in the 1950s.

The Tlingit, on the southeastern coast of Alaska, and the Haidas and Tsimshian of western Canada are known for their pole carving. On a tour in 1899, a group of Seattle businessmen visited the Tlingit village of Tongas and, finding no one there, took
35 one of the poles. They erected it in Seattle where, at a towering 50 ft., it became one of the city's most distinctive monuments. In 1938, Tlingit carvers copied the pole after the original was destroyed by fire, and it remains in Pioneer Square today.

Poles serve the important purpose of recording the lore of
40 a clan, much as a book would. The top figure on the pole identifies the owner's clan, and succeeding characters (read from top to bottom) tell their stories. Raven, the trickster, might tell the story of how he fooled the Creator into giving him the sun, or Frog might tell how he wooed a human woman. With slight
45 variations between villages, everyone knew these stories, and

potlatch guests dramatized them at the pole-raising with masks, drumming, and songs. And so the legends were preserved from one generation to the next.

There is a story behind almost every image on the pole. For
50 example, if an animal had the power to transform itself into other beings, the carver would portray it in all its forms. If Raven were sometimes bird, sometimes human, he would be carved with both wings and limbs, or have a human face with a raven's beak. Other images are used to describe the spirits' special abilities.
55 Eyes are frequently used to suggest acuteness or skill. So, for example, if an eye appears in an animal's ear, it might indicate that that animal has a sharp sense of hearing. And human figures in unexpected places, like an ear or nose, might mean that the animal has great powers.

60 Learning to read totem poles is like learning to read a language. They speak of history, mythology, social structure, and spirituality. They serve many purposes and continue to be carved by the descendants of the original carvers.

Today, Haida, Tlingit, Tsimshian, Kwakiutl and other na-
65 tive craftsmen carve, predominantly for the tourist trade, small "souvenir" totem poles in wood and black slate (or argillite). They also carve extraordinarily beautiful masks, effigies, boxes, house posts, and fixtures…

21. Which of the following statements best expresses the main idea of the passage?

   A. Many Native American tribes created totem poles with meaningful symbols, but these poles were less important than the canoes carved before the mid-18th century.
   B. Although the Tlingit village was deserted, the Seattle businessmen who took the totem pole were not right to take it without permission.
   C. The history of totem pole carving dates back to only the mid-18th-century, but these poles have played an important role in Native American culture since that time.
   D. The ban issued by the Canadian and United States governments against potlatches was lifted in the 1950s, but interest in totem-pole carving had diminished by that time.

22. Which of the following questions is NOT answered in the passage?

   F. In terms of geographical region, which were the first groups to carve totem poles?
   G. What is the tallest totem pole in North America?
   H. What is the predominant use of the small totem poles carved today?
   J. What prevented Native American tribes from carving totem poles before the 18th century?

GO ON TO THE NEXT PAGE.

23. The passage suggests that one of the main purposes of totem poles is the way in which they:

    A. demonstrate the artistic skill of the carvers.
    B. function as landmarks in major North American cities.
    C. document the history and mythology of various clans.
    D. complement the festivities of the potlatch.

24. The main function of the sixth paragraph (lines 49–59) is to:

    F. identify the origins of the stories behind every image on a totem pole.
    G. describe and explain some of the images that might appear on a totem pole.
    H. contrast the images on the totem poles of the Northwest natives with those of British Columbia and Alaska.
    J. explain the role of the Raven in Native American mythology.

25. All of the following are used in the passage as illustrations of the role totem poles play in Native American culture EXCEPT the:

    A. function of the top figure on the pole.
    B. descriptions of the Raven and Frog as characters on the pole.
    C. reference to the popularity of totem poles in the tourist industries of many tribes.
    D. placement of the Tlingit totem pole in Seattle's Pioneer Square.

26. The second paragraph (lines 10–20) establishes all of the following about the totem poles carved by the coastal tribes of the far north EXCEPT that they were:

    F. initially used as the entryways of houses.
    G. fashioned from tall, straight trees.
    H. used to identify the owners of the poles.
    J. produced only by clans with family crests.

27. One of the main points of the fifth paragraph (lines 39–48) is that the various characters on a totem pole are meant to represent:

    A. the owner of the totem pole.
    B. the lore of the owner's clan.
    C. Raven, the trickster, fooling the Creator.
    D. Frog wooing a human woman.

28. According to the passage, which of the following places is home to the Tlingit?

    F. Seattle
    G. Western Canada
    H. Pioneer Square
    J. Alaska

29. The author most likely includes the information in lines 60–63 to suggest that:

    A. totem poles are notable for reasons beyond physical beauty.
    B. totem poles have replaced books for Native American tribes.
    C. Native American tribes have no spoken or written language.
    D. the descendants of the original carvers of totem poles carve copies of older poles.

30. Which of the following words best describes the attitude of the employers referred to in the third paragraph (lines 21–30) in reaction to potlatches?

    F. Patient
    G. Accepting
    H. Irritated
    J. Civilized

GO ON TO THE NEXT PAGE.

Passage IV

NATURAL SCIENCE: This passage is adapted from the article "The Pioneer Mission to Venus" by Janet G. Luhmann, James B. Pollack, and Lawrence Colin (©1994, Scientific American).

Venus is sometimes referred to as the Earth's "twin" because it resembles the Earth in size and in distance from the sun. Over its 14 years of operation, the National Aeronautics and Space Administration's *Pioneer Venus* mission revealed that the rela-
5 tion between the two worlds is more analogous to Dr. Jekyll and Mr. Hyde. The surface of Venus bakes under a dense carbon dioxide atmosphere, the overlying clouds consist of noxious sulfuric acid, and the planet's lack of a magnetic field exposes the upper atmosphere to the continuous hail of charged particles
10 from the sun. Our opportunity to explore the hostile Venusian environment came to an abrupt close in October 1992, when the *Pioneer Venus Orbiter* burned up like a meteor in the thick Venusian atmosphere. The craft's demise marked the end of an era for the U.S. space program; in the present climate of fiscal
15 austerity, there is no telling when humans will next get a good look at the earth's nearest planetary neighbor.

The information gleaned by *Pioneer Venus* complements the well-publicized radar images recently sent back by the *Magellan* spacecraft. *Magellan* concentrated on studies of Venus's surface
20 geology and interior structure. *Pioneer Venus*, in comparison, gathered data on the composition and dynamics of the planet's atmosphere and interplanetary surroundings. These findings illustrate how seemingly small differences in physical conditions have sent Venus and the Earth hurtling down very different evo-
25 lutionary paths. Such knowledge will help scientists intelligently evaluate how human activity may be changing the environment on the Earth.

Well before the arrival of *Pioneer Venus*, astronomers had learned that Venus does not live up to its image as Earth's near-
30 twin. Whereas Earth maintains conditions ideal for liquid water and life, Venus's surface temperature of 450 degrees Celsius is hotter than the melting point of lead. Atmospheric pressure at the ground is some 93 times that at sea level on Earth.

Even aside from the heat and the pressure, the air on Venus
35 would be utterly unbreathable to humans. The Earth's atmosphere is about 78 percent nitrogen and 21 percent oxygen. Venus's much thicker atmosphere, in contrast, is composed almost entirely of carbon dioxide. Nitrogen, the next most abundant gas makes up only about 3.5 percent of the gas molecules. Both planets
40 possess about the same amount of gaseous nitrogen, but Venus's atmosphere contains some 30,000 times as much carbon dioxide as does Earth's. In fact, Earth does hold a quantity of carbon dioxide comparable to that in the Venusian atmosphere. On Earth, however, the carbon dioxide is locked away in carbonate
45 rocks, not in gaseous form in the air. The crucial distinction is responsible for many of the drastic environmental differences that exist between the two planets.

The large *Pioneer Venus* atmospheric probe carried a mass spectrometer and gas chromatograph, devices that measured
50 the exact composition of the atmosphere of Venus. One of the most stunning aspects of the Venusian atmosphere is that it is extremely dry. It possesses only a hundred thousandth as much water as Earth has in its oceans. If all of Venus's water could somehow be condensed onto the surface, it would make a global
55 puddle only a couple of centimeters deep.

Unlike the Earth, Venus harbors little if any molecular oxygen in its lower atmosphere. The abundant oxygen in the earth's atmosphere is a by-product of photosynthesis by plants; if not for the activity of living things, Earth's atmosphere also
60 would be oxygen poor. The atmosphere of Venus is far richer than the earth's in sulfur-containing gases, primarily sulfur dioxide. On Earth, rain efficiently removes similar sulfur gases from the atmosphere.

Pioneer Venus revealed other ways in which Venus is more
65 primordial than Earth. Venus's atmosphere contains higher concentrations of inert, or noble, gases—especially neon and isotopes of argon—that have been present since the time the planets were born. This difference suggests that Venus has held on to a far greater fraction of its earliest atmosphere. Much of
70 Earth's primitive atmosphere may have been stripped away and lost into space when our world was struck by a Mars-size body. Many planetary scientists now think the moon formed out of the cloud of debris that resulted from such a gigantic impact.

31. With regard to the possibility of returning to the planet Venus, information presented in the passage makes it clear that the author is:

    A. cheerful and optimistic.
    B. sarcastic and contentious.
    C. doubtful and pragmatic.
    D. uncertain and withdrawn.

32. Which of the following statements most accurately summarizes how the passage characterizes the state of scientific knowledge about Venus before the *Pioneer* mission?

    F. The scientific community was hesitant to return to Venus after an earlier mission had ended in disaster.
    G. Scientists saw Earth and Venus as near polar opposites in atmospheric conditions.
    H. The common belief that Earth and Venus were "twins" had been eroding under the weight of scientific evidence.
    J. Scientists knew little about the planet Venus because they were more interested in other planets.

GO ON TO THE NEXT PAGE.

33. Based on the passage, discoveries made in which two areas of study have caused scientists to re-evaluate their theories about Earth and Venus?

    A. Water content and bedrock composition

    B. Sulfuric gases and photosynthesis

    C. Carbon dioxide and climate change

    D. Atmosphere and surface temperature

34. The main point of the second paragraph (lines 17–27) is to:

    F. account for the failure of the *Magellan* mission and to show the superiority of the *Pioneer* mission.

    G. suggest that information from both the *Magellan* and *Pioneer* missions can bring the scientific community to a deeper understanding of Venus.

    H. show that the *Magellan* had sent back information regarding the physical characteristics while the *Pioneer* had not.

    J. hypothesize that the findings of the *Pioneer* mission will help scientists to approach problems more intelligently.

35. The passage indicates that if humans were to attempt to live on the planet Venus, survival would not be possible because:

    A. of the mistaken belief that Venus and Earth are "twin" planets.

    B. carbon dioxide is locked away in bicarbonate rocks, not in gaseous form.

    C. the atmospheric pressure, heat, and air are not suitable for human life.

    D. all of the water on Venus is condensed onto the surface.

36. According to the passage, some evidence gained before the *Pioneer Venus* mission suggesting that Earth and Venus are not near-twins stated that:

    F. Venus produces no lead on or underneath its surface.

    G. Earth was found to be much farther from the sun than was previously thought.

    H. the atmosphere of Venus contains 78 percent nitrogen and 21 percent oxygen.

    J. the surface temperature of Venus is 450 degrees Celsius and thus unlivable for humans.

37. As it is used in line 56, the word *harbors* most nearly means:

    A. sails.

    B. hides.

    C. holds.

    D. soaks.

38. According to the passage, "primordial" describes planets that:

    F. are oxygen-poor due to a lack of activity by living things.

    G. are not hospitable to humans because they have thick atmospheres and high surface temperatures.

    H. have preserved many of the characteristics present when the planets were formed.

    J. have been struck by large bodies which have altered the planets' atmospheres.

39. It can reasonably be inferred that the "activity of living things" described in line 59 directly refers to organisms on Earth that:

    A. produce oxygen by their own natural processes and influence the contents of Earth's atmosphere.

    B. remove sulfur gases from the atmosphere during heavy rainfall.

    C. lock away carbon dioxide in carbonate rocks and maintain a reserve of the gas.

    D. could easily live in oppressive atmospheres similar to the atmosphere of Venus.

40. According to the passage, the *Pioneer Venus* mission to Venus involved investigating details relating to the planet's:

    F. surface geology and interior structure.

    G. atmosphere as it has been changed by the influence of photosynthesis.

    H. similarities to the planet Earth.

    J. atmospheric contents.

END OF TEST 3

STOP! DO NOT TURN THE PAGE UNTIL TOLD TO DO SO.

DO NOT RETURN TO A PREVIOUS TEST.

SCIENCE TEST

35 Minutes—40 Questions

Directions: There are seven passages in this test. Each passage is followed by several questions. After reading a passage, choose the best answer to each question and fill in the corresponding oval on your answer document. You may refer to the passages as often as necessary.

You are NOT permitted to use a calculator on this test.

Passage I

Metallic *alloys*, solid mixtures of metal, are useful for coin production when they contain a high percentage of zinc. When electric current is applied to zinc in the presence of precious metal solutions of *silver nitrate*, *copper sulfate* or *potassium gold cyanide*, the precious metals *plate* (form a coating) on the zinc surface.

- Silver nitrate, formed when silver dissolves in *nitric acid*, reacts with zinc to form solid silver and *zinc nitrate*.
- Copper sulfate, formed when copper dissolves in *sulfuric acid*, reacts with zinc to form solid copper and *zinc sulfate*.
- Potassium gold cyanide contains reactive gold ions.

A chemist performed experiments on precious metal plating.

Experiment 1

The chemist obtained 4 coin-like samples of a high percentage zinc alloy. All samples were circular, had a radius of 1 cm, and had the same thickness. The mass of each coin was recorded. Each coin was wired via a battery to a strip of either pure silver or copper metal. Coins wired to silver were placed in dilute nitric acid and coins wired to copper were placed in dilute sulfuric acid. Electric current of either 1,000 milliamperes (mA) or 2,000 mA was applied for 30 minutes to each sample. The coins were removed and the increase in mass from precious metal plating was recorded in milligrams. Results of the experiment are shown in Table 1.

| Coin sample | Precious metal solution | | Increased mass from plating (mg) |
	Identity	Electric Current (mA)	
I	silver nitrate	1,000	2.0
II	silver nitrate	2,000	4.0
III	copper sulfate	1,000	1.2
IV	copper sulfate	2,000	2.4

Table 1

Experiment 2

The chemist completely dissolved equal amounts of pure silver in 4 beakers of nitric acid. He then placed equivalent coin-like samples of zinc into the beakers for different lengths of time measured in minutes (min). The coin surfaces developed a silver metal coating without any electric current applied. The concentrations of silver coating on the coin and zinc nitrate in the surrounding solution were determined in parts per billion (ppb) and recorded in Table 2.

Table 2

Coin sample	Time (min)	Silver coating concentration (ppb)	Zinc nitrate concentration (ppb)
V	5	75	30
VI	15	125	55
VII	30	200	75
VIII	60	500	85

1. A comparison of the results for coin samples II and IV supports the hypothesis that zinc is plated more extensively when exposed to:

   A. silver nitrate and a current of 1,000 mA than silver nitrate and a current of 2,000 mA.
   B. copper sulfate and a current of 1,000 mA than copper sulfate and a current of 2,000 mA.
   C. silver nitrate than when exposed to copper sulfate.
   D. copper sulfate than when exposed to silver nitrate.

GO ON TO THE NEXT PAGE.

2. If the chemist were to repeat Experiment 1, but compress each coin sample to a radius of 0.5 cm to decrease the surface area exposed to the surrounding solution, how would the mass of precious metal plated most likely be affected?

   F. The mass of precious metal plated would decrease for all coin samples.
   G. The mass of precious metal plated would decrease for coin samples I and III and increase for coin samples II and IV.
   H. The mass of precious metal plated would remain constant for all coin samples.
   J. The mass of precious metal plated would increase for all coin samples.

3. According to the information in the passage, a zinc alloy coin sample exposed to which of the following conditions would result in the greatest concentration of zinc nitrate?

   A. 10 minutes in a solution with a high initial concentration of silver nitrate
   B. 10 minutes in a solution with a low initial concentration of silver nitrate
   C. 6 minutes in a solution with a high initial concentration of silver nitrate
   D. 6 minutes in a solution with a low initial concentration of silver nitrate

4. In Experiment 1, if the chemist had applied 1,580 mA to a 1 cm radius zinc alloy coin sample in a copper sulfate solution, approximately how much copper would have plated after 30 minutes?

   F. 0.6 mg
   G. 1.1 mg
   H. 1.9 mg
   J. 4.6 mg

5. In Experiment 1, which of the following variables was the same for all 4 zinc alloy coin sample trials?

   A. Change in mass from plating
   B. Electric current applied
   C. Type of precious metal solution used
   D. Initial radius of the sample

6. According to the passage, if a chemist wants to study the effect of plating zinc alloys with silver, the chemist should monitor the concentration of which of the following substances in the surrounding solution?

   F. Potassium gold cyanide
   G. Zinc nitrate
   H. Copper sulfate
   J. Sulfuric acid

GO ON TO THE NEXT PAGE.

Passage II

Organic compounds are molecules that frequently contain carbon (C), hydrogen (H), and oxygen (O) joined together by covalent bonds (symbolized by straight lines in chemical notation). As the number of bonds to oxygen atoms increases in a carbon chain, the overall molecule is increasingly oxidized. For example, aldehydes are more oxidized than alcohols, which are more oxidized than alkanes as shown in Table 1. The melting points of these compounds are listed in Table 2, and their *viscosities* (resistance to flow, or "stickiness,") are listed in Table 3.

Table 1				
Carbons in the chain	Name prefix	Structure		
		alkane (suffix -ane)	alcohol (suffix -anol)	aldehyde (suffix -analdehyde)
4	but-			
5	pent-			
6	hex-			
7	hept-			
8	oct-			

Table 2			
Carbons in the chain	Melting point (K)		
	alkane	alcohol	aldehyde
4	135	183	174
5	143	194	213
6	178	221	217
7	182	239	231
8	216	257	285

Table 3			
Carbons in the chain	Viscosity (cP)		
	alkane	alcohol	aldehyde
4	0.01	3.0	0.4
5	0.24	5.1	0.5
6	0.29	5.4	0.8
7	0.39	5.8	1.0
8	0.54	8.4	1.2

GO ON TO THE NEXT PAGE.

7. Which organic compounds in Table 2 are solids at 215 K ?

A. All alkanes, alcohols, and aldehydes with 5 carbons or fewer.

B. Alcohols and aldehydes with 6 or more carbons and octane.

C. The 4- and 5-carbon alcohols and aldehydes, and all alkanes with 7 or fewer carbons.

D. The 5-carbon pentane and pentanol compounds and the 4-carbon butane, butanol, and butanaldehyde.

8. According to Tables 1 and 3, which organic compound has the highest viscosity?

F. Octanol

G. Octanaldehyde

H. Hexanol

J. Butane

9. According to Table 3, how do the different types of 5-carbon molecules differ with respect to their viscosity?

A. The alkane has a higher viscosity than the aldehyde and the aldehyde has a higher viscosity than the alcohol.

B. The alkane has a higher viscosity than the alcohol and the alcohol has a higher viscosity than the aldehyde.

C. The alcohol has a higher viscosity than the alkane and the alkane has a higher viscosity than the aldehyde.

D. The alcohol has a higher viscosity than the aldehyde and the aldehyde has a higher viscosity than the alkane.

10. For each type of organic compound, what is the relationship between the length of the carbon chain to the melting point and viscosity? As the number of carbons in the chain increases, the melting point:

F. decreases and the viscosity decreases.

G. increases and the viscosity increases.

H. increases but the viscosity decreases.

J. decreases but the viscosity increases.

11. According to Table 2, the difference in melting point between an alkane and an alcohol with the same number of carbons is approximately how much?

A. 25 K

B. 35 K

C. 45 K

D. 65 K

GO ON TO THE NEXT PAGE.

Passage III

A mass suspended by a lightweight thread and swinging back and forth approximates the motion of a *simple gravity pendulum*, a system in which gravity is the only force acting on the mass, causing an acceleration of 9.8 m/sec². The time to complete one cycle of swinging back and forth is the *period* and is inversely related to gravitational acceleration.

Using the same type and length of thread, 2 cubes were suspended, lifted to the same starting angle, and let go. The amount of time required for each pendulum to complete one swinging cycle (1 period) was recorded with a timer capable of reading to the nearest 0.01 sec. The measured times were used to calculate acceleration.

Experiment 1

A cube of lead (11.3 grams) and a cube of tin (7.4 grams) were suspended from a 0.5 m length of thread. Both cubes had the same length. (Note: A cube's volume is proportional to its length cubed; its surface area is proportional to its length squared.) The cubes were set in motion from a fixed starting angle, and the period for each was recorded.

Table 1		
Trial	Measured period (sec)	
	lead cube	tin cube
1	1.48	1.51
2	1.45	1.47
3	1.46	1.42
4	1.49	1.45
5	1.39	1.53

The average periods were 1.46 sec and 1.48 sec for the lead and tin cubes, respectively. The average accelerations were 9.3 m/sec² for lead and 9.1 m/sec² for tin.

Experiment 2

The same procedures used in Experiment 1 were repeated using a thread length of 1.0 m and the same fixed starting angle. Results were recorded in Table 2.

Table 2		
Trial	Measured period (sec)	
	lead cube	tin cube
6	2.10	2.12
7	2.04	2.06
8	2.05	2.07
9	2.12	2.11
10	2.00	2.10

The average periods were 2.06 sec and 2.09 sec for the lead and tin cubes, respectively. The average accelerations were 9.3 m/sec² for lead and 9.0 m/sec² for tin.

Experiment 3

Given the results of the first 2 experiments, the accuracy of the timer was tested. The procedures of Experiment 1 were repeated using only the lead cube. The trials were recorded on digital video at 100 frames per second. The video was then reviewed to obtain precise measurements of the period for each trial and results are shown in Table 3.

Table 3	
Trial	Measured period (sec)
11	1.47
12	1.42
13	1.49
14	1.50
15	1.46

The average period recorded in Table 3 was 1.47 sec.

12. To demonstrate that a pendulum's acceleration is reduced by drag force from air resistance, which additional experiment can be performed in addition to those in the passage?

F. The cubes are suspended by 0.5 m and 1 m springs and set in motion by extending the spring 9.8 cm and letting go in a vacuum chamber with no air pressure.

G. The cubes are suspended by 0.5 m and 1 m threads and set in motion from the same starting angle in a vacuum chamber with no air pressure.

H. The cubes are suspended by 0.5 m and 1 m springs and set in motion by extending the spring 9.8 cm and letting go in a vacuum chamber at 1 atmosphere of pressure.

J. The cubes are suspended by 0.5 m and 1 m threads and set in motion from the same starting angle in a vacuum chamber at 1 atmosphere of pressure.

GO ON TO THE NEXT PAGE.

13. In Experiment 1, could a timer that reads to the nearest second be used to obtain similar results, and why?

    A. No, because the period of both pendulums was between 1 and 2 seconds.

    B. No, because the pendulums would have traveled farther in 1 second than they did in 1 period.

    C. Yes, because the period of both pendulums was approximately 1.5 seconds.

    D. Yes, because the pendulums would not have traveled as far in 1 second as they did in 1 period.

14. The results of the experiments indicate that forces other than gravity are acting on the pendulums because the calculated values of acceleration were:

    F. the same for pendulums of different lengths.

    G. the same for cubes of different mass.

    H. lower than the expected 9.8 m/sec^2 from gravity alone.

    J. greater than the expected 9.8 m/sec^2 from gravity alone.

15. Based on the passage, if a tin cube is suspended from a 2.0 m thread and set in motion multiple times from the same starting angle, the average measured period will most likely be:

    A. less than 1.48 sec.

    B. approximately 1.48 sec.

    C. approximately 2.09 sec.

    D. greater than 2.09 sec.

16. In Experiment 2, if an additional trial were conducted using the lead cube, the cube's measured period would most likely be nearest:

    F. 1.90 sec.

    G. 2.05 sec.

    H. 2.15 sec.

    J. 2.20 sec.

17. Experiments 1 and 2 were conducted using lead and tin cubes most likely to determine whether a pendulum's period was altered by the material attached to the string and the cube's:

    A. length.

    B. surface area.

    C. starting angle.

    D. mass.

GO ON TO THE NEXT PAGE.

Passage IV

Accepted classification systems of life do not include *viruses*. Although viruses possess certain features of cellular organisms, including genetic material that codes for making new viral particles, they cannot *replicate* (make copies of) themselves without first infecting a living cell. Biologists agree that viruses originated from genetic material called *nucleic acid*, but it is difficult to prove any single theory regarding how this occurred. Three hypotheses of viral origin are presented here.

Coevolution Hypothesis

Some biologists argue that viruses evolved alongside other organisms over billions of years. They suggest that simple molecules of *ribonucleic acid* (RNA), a *nucleotide* that forms the genetic code for proteins, joined to form more complex sequences. These RNA sequences developed enzyme-like abilities including the ability to self-replicate and insert themselves into other nucleotide sequences. While some RNA sequences became incorporated into membrane-bound cells, others were packaged inside proteins as the first viral particles that could replicate after infecting cellular organisms (see Figure 1).

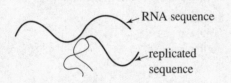

ancestral self-replicating RNA

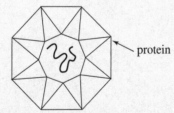

first coevolved viral particle

Figure 1

Cellular Origin Hypothesis

Some biologists claim that nucleotide sequences within *prokaryotic* (non-nucleated) and *eukaryotic* (nucleated) cellular organisms incorporated into a protein coating and escaped from the cell as a viral particle. Initially, DNA or RNA nucleotide sequences gained the code required for other cells to replicate them. Next, these sequences associated with proteins to form an outer *capsid*. Finally, the *virion* (viral particle) became capable of passing through the cell membrane and infecting other cells where it could be replicated. After the initial escape, viruses evolved independently from their initial host and ultimately could infect either prokaryotic or eukaryotic cells.

Regressive Evolution Hypothesis

An alternative explanation of viral origin is that viruses evolved from cellular organisms. Some cellular organisms, particularly certain bacteria, are *obligate intracellular parasites* because they must infect a host cell in order to reproduce. Regressive evolution suggests that some bacterial parasites gradually lost the structures required for survival outside of a cell. The result was a virus particle containing only nucleotides, a capsid (protein coating), and at times an outer membrane or envelope. This would account readily for viruses that contain complex *deoxyribonucleic acid* (DNA) similar to that found in bacteria and other cellular organisms (see Figure 2).

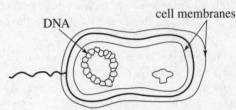

ancestral intracellular parasite bacteria

first regressive evolved virus

Figure 2

18. The development of which of the following is addressed in the passage by the Coevolution Hypothesis, but NOT by the Regressive Evolution Hypothesis?

   F. Self-replication
   G. Capsid
   H. Deoxyribonucleic acid
   J. Cell membrane transit

19. Supporters of all of the theories presented in the passage would agree with the conclusion that the first viruses:

   A. evolved from bacteria.
   B. could self-replicate outside a cell.
   C. were enclosed within a membrane.
   D. contained nucleic acid.

20. The Coevolution Hypothesis does NOT provide an explanation for the earliest virus particles possessing:

   F. protein.
   G. enzyme-like activity.
   H. nucleotides.
   J. DNA.

GO ON TO THE NEXT PAGE.

21. If the Cellular Origin Hypothesis is correct, which of the following conclusions can be made about modern T4 DNA viruses, which infect *Escherichia coli* bacteria, and modern PP7 RNA viruses, which infect *Pseudomonas aeruginosa* bacteria?

A. T4 and PP7 are more closely related to each other than to bacteria genetically.

B. T4 and PP7 are only distantly related genetically through a cellular organism.

C. T4 and PP7 both evolved from prokaryotic organisms.

D. T4 and PP7 both evolved from eukaryotic organisms.

22. The discovery of which of the following living organisms would provide the most support for the Regressive Evolution Hypothesis?

F. Extracellular parasites with DNA resembling a known virus

G. Extracellular parasites with unique RNA nucleotide sequences

H. Intracellular parasites with DNA resembling a known virus

J. Intracellular parasites with unique RNA nucleotide sequences

23. Supporters of all the theories presented would agree with which of the following conclusions about the origin of viruses?

A. Viral capsids contain a protein structure similar to the cell walls of modern bacteria.

B. The first viruses did not originate before the first cellular organisms.

C. RNA viruses are more advanced than DNA viruses.

D. The first virus contained DNA and was surrounded by an envelope similar to a cell membrane.

24. Which of the following questions is raised by the Coevolution Hypothesis, but is NOT answered in the passage?

F. Why were some RNA sequences packaged into protein structures and others incorporated into cell structures?

G. Why did obligate intracellular parasites lose their ability to survive outside of cells?

H. How could two different types of cellular organisms account for the origin of viruses?

J. How did virions develop the ability to pass through the cell membrane out of the cell?

GO ON TO THE NEXT PAGE.

Passage V

Wind causes *topsoil deflation*, a type of erosion that is affected by plant and organic cover as well as water content of the soil. Scientists performed 2 experiments using equal-sized fields containing the same volume of soil. The soil samples were primarily a mixture of sand and silt, but differed in the percentage of clay they contained. Soil X was composed of 5% clay and soil Y was composed of 40% clay. Large fans were used to simulate wind. Topsoil deflation was measured in kilograms per hectare (kg/ha) following 10 hours of wind.

Experiment 1

A mixture of compost and straw was used to represent plant and organic cover. The percentage of soil covered with the mixture was considered to approximate an equivalent percentage of natural vegetative cover. One field remained uncovered, and the other fields were covered with different percentages of compost and straw. The topsoil deflation from each field was recorded in Table 1.

Table 1				
Soil	Topsoil deflation (kg/ha) by percentage of organic cover			
	0%	25%	50%	75%
X	105,000	68,000	46,000	20,000
Y	65,000	42,000	28,500	12,000

Experiment 2

Rainfall was simulated using a sprinkler system. Sprinklers were turned on for either 4 hours or 8 hours for fields of each kind of soil. Two additional fields composed of each type of soil were left unwatered. Afterward, soil samples were taken from all of the fields to determine their water content percentage, which was recorded in Table 2. Wind was applied as in Experiment 1 and topsoil deflation for all fields was recorded in Table 3.

Table 2			
Soil	Water content of soil following various sprinkler times		
	0 hours	4 hours	8 hours
X	10%	13%	16%
Y	10%	14%	22%

Table 3			
Soil	Topsoil deflation (kg/ha) following various sprinkler times		
	0 hours	4 hours	8 hours
X	89,250	66,000	14,000
Y	53,400	40,100	10,300

25. According to the results of Experiments 1 and 2, topsoil deflation will be minimized by:

A. decreased organic cover, increased amount of rainfall, and the use of either Soil X or Y as topsoil.
B. decreased organic cover, decreased amount of rainfall, and the use of Soil Y as topsoil.
C. increased organic cover, increased amount of rainfall, and the use of Soil Y as topsoil.
D. increased organic cover, increased amount of rainfall, and the use of Soil X as topsoil.

26. If Experiment 1 were repeated using a soil containing 10% clay with 0% organic cover, which of the following would be the most likely topsoil deflation amount?

F. 110,200 kg/ha
G. 99,800 kg/ha
H. 70,700 kg/ha
J. 60,200 kg/ha

27. To further investigate the effect of water content on erosion from topsoil deflation, the scientists should repeat Experiment:

A. 1, using a different type of topsoil.
B. 1, using plastic covers over the fields.
C. 2, using no sprinklers.
D. 2, using fields exposed to various amounts of rainfall.

28. What assumption in experimental design is most important to consider when applying the findings of Experiment 1 to a practical situation?

F. The quantity of topsoil deflation is independent of the percentage of clay present in the soil.
G. The presence of straw on the soil does not accurately simulate vegetation and organic cover.
H. Air movement from fans provides an accurate simulation of the wind responsible for topsoil deflation.
J. Compost is more effective than water content in the prevention of topsoil erosion.

GO ON TO THE NEXT PAGE.

29. In Experiment 2, the water content in the two soil types was similar after 4 hours of sprinkling, yet the topsoil deflation was significantly different. Which of the following statements provides the best explanation for these findings?

   A. Topsoil erosion is independent of the water content found in the soil.
   B. Fields are susceptible to topsoil deflation only when water completely evaporates from the topsoil.
   C. Soil with a lower percentage of clay is more prone to erosion from topsoil deflation than one with a higher percentage of clay.
   D. Water is trapped in the topsoil by wind and this increases the rate of topsoil deflation.

30. If Experiment 2 were repeated with soil containing 10% clay, which of the following values would be expected for water content and topsoil deflation in a field following 8 hours of water sprinkling?

   F. water content of 17%; topsoil deflation of 13,400 kg/ha
   G. water content of 21%; topsoil deflation of 9,700 kg/ha
   H. water content of 15%; topsoil deflation of 10,900 kg/ha
   J. water content of 14%; topsoil deflation of 101,000 kg/ha

GO ON TO THE NEXT PAGE.

Passage VI

The oceans of Earth are exposed to various climates and consequently have different physical properties. Deep oceans can be divided into zones based on temperature gradient and penetration of sunlight. Figure 1 shows the zones of a typical deep-water ocean, the depth of the zone boundaries in meters (m), and the overall pressure at those depths in kilopascals (kPa). Figure 2 shows the water temperature in degrees Celsius (°C) in warmer tropical oceans and cooler temperate oceans at varying depths. Sound waves are used to measure water temperature at depth, and readings from two different ocean regions are recorded in Table 1.

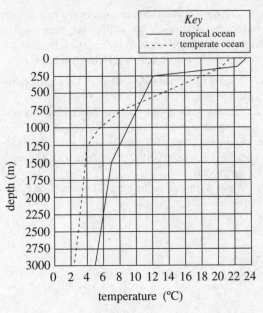

Figure 2

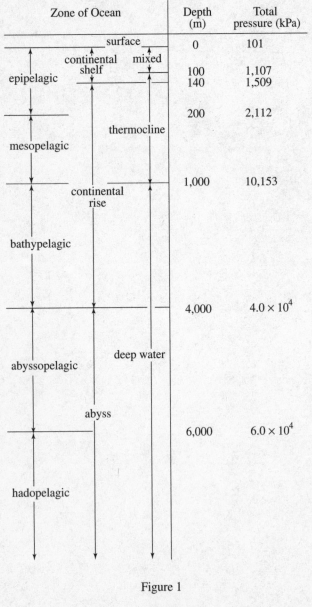

Figure 1

(Note: Figure is NOT drawn to scale)

Table 1			
Total pressure (kPa)	Depth (m)	Ocean temperature (°C)	
		Region 1	Region 2
101	0	24	21
200	9.8	22	20
300	19.8	14	11
400	29.7	11	9
500	39.7	10	8
600	49.6	9	8
700	59.6	7	6
800	69.5	5	3
900	79.5	4	2

GO ON TO THE NEXT PAGE.

31. According to Figure 1, the regions of several ocean zones overlap. Which of the following pairs of ocean zones share part of a common depth range?

- **A.** Bathypelagic and mesopelagic
- **B.** Bathypelagic and epipelagic
- **C.** Epipelagic and thermocline
- **D.** Epipelagic and mesopelagic

32. According to Figure 1, an oceanographic reading taken at a total pressure of 1,200 kPa is most likely from which of the following zones?

- **F.** Abyss
- **G.** Continental rise
- **H.** Mixed
- **J.** Continental shelf

33. According to Figure 2, a sonographic measurement of temperature would be unable to distinguish the difference between tropical and temperate oceans at which of the following depths?

- **A.** 250 m
- **B.** 500 m
- **C.** 625 m
- **D.** 750 m

34. According to Table 1, the relationship between depth and ocean temperature is best described by which of the following statements?

- **F.** The water temperature increased with increasing depth in Region 1 only.
- **G.** The water temperature decreased with increasing depth in Region 1 only.
- **H.** The water temperature increased with increasing depth in Region 2 only.
- **J.** The water temperature decreased with increasing depth in Region 2 only.

35. According to Figure 1 and Table 1, if water temperature measurements were taken at depths greater than 79.5, the total pressure at those depths would most likely:

- **A.** decrease to less than 101 kPa.
- **B.** increase to more than 900 kPa.
- **C.** stay at 900 kPa.
- **D.** increase to 101 kPa.

GO ON TO THE NEXT PAGE.

Passage VII

Although many forms of bacteria are helpful for human health, they can also cause illness and even death from severe infections. *Antibiotics* are a class of medicines used to combat bacterial infections. *Bacteriostatic* activity inhibits bacteria cell division and *bactericidal* activity kills bacterial cells. Both actions eliminate populations of bacteria over time. Several classes of bacteriostatic and bactericidal antibiotics are described in Table 1.

The effectiveness of several antibiotics against a bacterium known to cause common skin infections was tested. Drugs were introduced to the bacterial culture by themselves or in combination with sulfamethoxazole (forming SMX compounds). The effectiveness of these antibiotics at eliminating the responsible bacterium is shown in Figure 1.

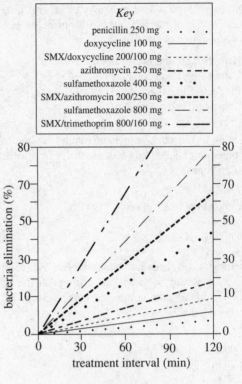

Figure 1

		Table 1		
Class	Example	Active against	Mechanism	Common uses
β-lactams	ampicillin	some gram-positive and gram-negative bacteria	disrupt cell wall synthesis; bactericidal	respiratory and skin infections
Tetracyclines	doxycycline	atypical gram-indeterminate bacteria	disrupt bacterial mRNA synthesis; mostly bacteriostatic	respiratory and genitourinary infections
Macrolides	azithromycin	gram-positive and atypical bacteria	disrupt bacterial protein synthesis; mostly bacteriostatic	atypical and respiratory infections
Aminoglycosides	gentamicin, streptomycin	gram-negative bacteria	disrupt bacterial protein synthesis; bactericidal	severe systemic infections
Quinolones	ofloxacin, gatifloxacin	broad spectrum of bacteria	disrupt bacterial DNA replication; bactericidal	respiratory, genitourinary, and gastrointestinal infections
Antifolates	sulfamethoxazole, trimethoprim	some gram-positive and gram-negative bacteria	disrupt bacterial DNA and RNA synthesis; mostly bacteriostatic	genitourinary and skin infections

GO ON TO THE NEXT PAGE.

36. According to the information in Table 1 and Figure 1, what can be concluded about the use of sulfamethoxazole as an antibiotic for common skin infections?

F. Using sulfamethoxazole 800 mg is ineffective as an antibiotic.
G. Increasing the dosage of sulfamethoxazole decreases its overall effectiveness as an antibiotic.
H. As an antibiotic, the mechanism of action of sulfamethoxazole is unknown.
J. Compounding antibiotics with sulfamethoxazole increases their effectiveness against common skin infections.

37. According to Figure 1, if an investigator administered a sulfamethoxazole dose of 600 mg, 20% of the original bacteria would remain after a treatment interval:

A. greater than 120 min.
B. between 90 and 120 min.
C. between 60 and 90 min.
D. between 30 and 60 min.

38. After treatment of a bacterial culture similar to that in the passage with 250 mg of penicillin for 2 hours, the culture will probably contain:

F. less bacteria overall, but most will have survived.
G. less bacteria overall, and most will have been killed.
H. the same amount of bacteria overall, and most will have survived.
J. the same amount of bacteria overall, and most will have been killed.

39. Is the statement "antibiotics compounded with sulfamethoxazole are more effective against common skin infections than when administered alone" supported by the information shown in Figure 1, and why?

A. No, because penicillin is more effective against a common skin infection bacterium than sulfamethoxazole 400 mg.
B. No, because azithromycin is more effective against a common skin infection bacterium than SMX/azithromycin.
C. Yes, because sulfamethoxazole 800 mg is more effective against a common skin infection bacterium than SMX/azithromycin.
D. Yes, because SMX/doxycycline is more effective against a common skin infection bacterium than doxycycline.

40. According to the passage, the most effective antibiotic against bacteria is one that results in the:

F. lowest percentage of bacterial elimination in the shortest treatment interval.
G. lowest percentage of bacterial elimination in the longest treatment interval.
H. greatest percentage of bacterial elimination in the shortest treatment interval.
J. greatest percentage of bacterial elimination in the longest treatment interval.

END OF TEST 4

STOP! DO NOT RETURN TO ANY OTHER TEST.

DIRECTIONS

This is a test of your writing skills. You will have thirty (30) minutes to write an essay. Before you begin planning and writing your essay, read the writing prompt carefully to understand exactly what you are being asked to do. Your essay will be evaluated on the evidence it provides of your ability to express judgments by taking a position on the issue in the writing prompt; to maintain a focus on the topic throughout your essay; to develop a position by using logical reasoning and by supporting your ideas; to organize ideas in a logical way; and to use language clearly and effectively according to the conventions of standard written English.

You may use the unlined pages in this test booklet to plan your essay. These pages will not be scored. *You must write your essay on the lined pages in the answer folder.* Your writing on those lined pages will be scored. You may not need all the lined pages, but to ensure you have enough room to finish, do NOT skip lines. You may write corrections or additions neatly between the lines of your essay, but do NOT write in the margins of the lined pages. *Illegible essays cannot be scored, so you must write (or print) clearly.*

If you finish before time is called, you may review your work. Lay your pencil down immediately when time is called.

DO NOT OPEN THIS BOOK UNTIL YOU ARE TOLD TO DO SO.

ACT Assessment Writing Test Prompt

Schools in some states have changed their school calendars so that they are now year-round schools. Advocates of year-round schooling argue that the traditional summer break is a waste of students' time that could otherwise be spent learning. Opponents charge that today's students are already overburdened with the stresses of school and need the summer to get a much-needed break. In your view, should the traditional three-month summer vacation from school be maintained?

In your essay, take a position on this question. You may write about either one of the two points of view given, or you may present a different point of view on this question. Use specific reasons and examples to support your position.

ACT Diagnostic Test Form

Use a No. 2 pencil only. Be sure each mark is dark and completely fills the intended oval. Completely erase any errors or stray marks.

1. YOUR NAME: _____
   (Print)   Last   First   M.I.

SIGNATURE: _____   DATE: _____ / _____ / _____

HOME ADDRESS: _____
   (Print)   Number and Street

_____
   City   State   Zip

E-MAIL: _____

IMPORTANT: Please fill in these boxes exactly as shown on the back cover of your tests book.

PHONE NO.: _____
   (Print)

SCHOOL: _____

CLASS OF: _____

2. TEST FORM

_____

3. TEST CODE

⓪	⓪	⓪	⓪
①	①	①	①
②	②	②	②
③	③	③	③
④	④	④	④
⑤	⑤	⑤	⑤
⑥	⑥	⑥	⑥
⑦	⑦	⑦	⑦
⑧	⑧	⑧	⑧
⑨	⑨	⑨	⑨

4. PHONE NUMBER

⓪	⓪	⓪	⓪	⓪	⓪	⓪
①	①	①	①	①	①	①
②	②	②	②	②	②	②
③	③	③	③	③	③	③
④	④	④	④	④	④	④
⑤	⑤	⑤	⑤	⑤	⑤	⑤
⑥	⑥	⑥	⑥	⑥	⑥	⑥
⑦	⑦	⑦	⑦	⑦	⑦	⑦
⑧	⑧	⑧	⑧	⑧	⑧	⑧
⑨	⑨	⑨	⑨	⑨	⑨	⑨

5. YOUR NAME

First 4 letters of last name				FIRST INIT	MID INIT
Ⓐ	Ⓐ	Ⓐ	Ⓐ	Ⓐ	Ⓐ
Ⓑ	Ⓑ	Ⓑ	Ⓑ	Ⓑ	Ⓑ
Ⓒ	Ⓒ	Ⓒ	Ⓒ	Ⓒ	Ⓒ
Ⓓ	Ⓓ	Ⓓ	Ⓓ	Ⓓ	Ⓓ
Ⓔ	Ⓔ	Ⓔ	Ⓔ	Ⓔ	Ⓔ
Ⓕ	Ⓕ	Ⓕ	Ⓕ	Ⓕ	Ⓕ
Ⓖ	Ⓖ	Ⓖ	Ⓖ	Ⓖ	Ⓖ
Ⓗ	Ⓗ	Ⓗ	Ⓗ	Ⓗ	Ⓗ
Ⓘ	Ⓘ	Ⓘ	Ⓘ	Ⓘ	Ⓘ
Ⓙ	Ⓙ	Ⓙ	Ⓙ	Ⓙ	Ⓙ
Ⓚ	Ⓚ	Ⓚ	Ⓚ	Ⓚ	Ⓚ
Ⓛ	Ⓛ	Ⓛ	Ⓛ	Ⓛ	Ⓛ
Ⓜ	Ⓜ	Ⓜ	Ⓜ	Ⓜ	Ⓜ
Ⓝ	Ⓝ	Ⓝ	Ⓝ	Ⓝ	Ⓝ
Ⓞ	Ⓞ	Ⓞ	Ⓞ	Ⓞ	Ⓞ
Ⓟ	Ⓟ	Ⓟ	Ⓟ	Ⓟ	Ⓟ
Ⓠ	Ⓠ	Ⓠ	Ⓠ	Ⓠ	Ⓠ
Ⓡ	Ⓡ	Ⓡ	Ⓡ	Ⓡ	Ⓡ
Ⓢ	Ⓢ	Ⓢ	Ⓢ	Ⓢ	Ⓢ
Ⓣ	Ⓣ	Ⓣ	Ⓣ	Ⓣ	Ⓣ
Ⓤ	Ⓤ	Ⓤ	Ⓤ	Ⓤ	Ⓤ
Ⓥ	Ⓥ	Ⓥ	Ⓥ	Ⓥ	Ⓥ
Ⓦ	Ⓦ	Ⓦ	Ⓦ	Ⓦ	Ⓦ
Ⓧ	Ⓧ	Ⓧ	Ⓧ	Ⓧ	Ⓧ
Ⓨ	Ⓨ	Ⓨ	Ⓨ	Ⓨ	Ⓨ
Ⓩ	Ⓩ	Ⓩ	Ⓩ	Ⓩ	Ⓩ

6. DATE OF BIRTH

MONTH	DAY		YEAR	
◯ JAN				
◯ FEB				
◯ MAR	⓪	⓪	⓪	⓪
◯ APR	①	①	①	①
◯ MAY	②	②	②	②
◯ JUN	③	③	③	③
◯ JUL		④	④	④
◯ AUG		⑤	⑤	⑤
◯ SEP		⑥	⑥	⑥
◯ OCT		⑦	⑦	⑦
◯ NOV		⑧	⑧	⑧
◯ DEC		⑨	⑨	⑨

7. SEX

◯ MALE
◯ FEMALE

8. OTHER

1 Ⓐ Ⓑ Ⓒ Ⓓ Ⓔ
2 Ⓐ Ⓑ Ⓒ Ⓓ Ⓔ
3 Ⓐ Ⓑ Ⓒ Ⓓ Ⓔ

OpScan *i*NSIGHT™ forms by Pearson NCS EM-255315-1:654321   Printed in U.S.A.

THIS PAGE INTENTIONALLY LEFT BLANK

The Princeton Review
Diagnostic ACT Form

Completely darken bubbles with a No. 2 pencil. If you make a mistake, be sure to erase mark completely. Erase all stray marks.

ENGLISH

1 (A) (B) (C) (D)	21 (A) (B) (C) (D)	41 (A) (B) (C) (D)	61 (A) (B) (C) (D)
2 (F) (G) (H) (J)	22 (F) (G) (H) (J)	42 (F) (G) (H) (J)	62 (F) (G) (H) (J)
3 (A) (B) (C) (D)	23 (A) (B) (C) (D)	43 (A) (B) (C) (D)	63 (A) (B) (C) (D)
4 (F) (G) (H) (J)	24 (F) (G) (H) (J)	44 (F) (G) (H) (J)	64 (F) (G) (H) (J)
5 (A) (B) (C) (D)	25 (A) (B) (C) (D)	45 (A) (B) (C) (D)	65 (A) (B) (C) (D)
6 (F) (G) (H) (J)	26 (F) (G) (H) (J)	46 (F) (G) (H) (J)	66 (F) (G) (H) (J)
7 (A) (B) (C) (D)	27 (A) (B) (C) (D)	47 (A) (B) (C) (D)	67 (A) (B) (C) (D)
8 (F) (G) (H) (J)	28 (F) (G) (H) (J)	48 (F) (G) (H) (J)	68 (F) (G) (H) (J)
9 (A) (B) (C) (D)	29 (A) (B) (C) (D)	49 (A) (B) (C) (D)	69 (A) (B) (C) (D)
10 (F) (G) (H) (J)	30 (F) (G) (H) (J)	50 (F) (G) (H) (J)	70 (F) (G) (H) (J)
11 (A) (B) (C) (D)	31 (A) (B) (C) (D)	51 (A) (B) (C) (D)	71 (A) (B) (C) (D)
12 (F) (G) (H) (J)	32 (F) (G) (H) (J)	52 (F) (G) (H) (J)	72 (F) (G) (H) (J)
13 (A) (B) (C) (D)	33 (A) (B) (C) (D)	53 (A) (B) (C) (D)	73 (A) (B) (C) (D)
14 (F) (G) (H) (J)	34 (F) (G) (H) (J)	54 (F) (G) (H) (J)	74 (F) (G) (H) (J)
15 (A) (B) (C) (D)	35 (A) (B) (C) (D)	55 (A) (B) (C) (D)	75 (A) (B) (C) (D)
16 (F) (G) (H) (J)	36 (F) (G) (H) (J)	56 (F) (G) (H) (J)	
17 (A) (B) (C) (D)	37 (A) (B) (C) (D)	57 (A) (B) (C) (D)	
18 (F) (G) (H) (J)	38 (F) (G) (H) (J)	58 (F) (G) (H) (J)	
19 (A) (B) (C) (D)	39 (A) (B) (C) (D)	59 (A) (B) (C) (D)	
20 (F) (G) (H) (J)	40 (F) (G) (H) (J)	60 (F) (G) (H) (J)	

MATHEMATICS

1 (A) (B) (C) (D) (E)	16 (F) (G) (H) (J) (K)	31 (A) (B) (C) (D) (E)	46 (F) (G) (H) (J) (K)
2 (F) (G) (H) (J) (K)	17 (A) (B) (C) (D) (E)	32 (F) (G) (H) (J) (K)	47 (A) (B) (C) (D) (E)
3 (A) (B) (C) (D) (E)	18 (F) (G) (H) (J) (K)	33 (A) (B) (C) (D) (E)	48 (F) (G) (H) (J) (K)
4 (F) (G) (H) (J) (K)	19 (A) (B) (C) (D) (E)	34 (F) (G) (H) (J) (K)	49 (A) (B) (C) (D) (E)
5 (A) (B) (C) (D) (E)	20 (F) (G) (H) (J) (K)	35 (A) (B) (C) (D) (E)	50 (F) (G) (H) (J) (K)
6 (F) (G) (H) (J) (K)	21 (A) (B) (C) (D) (E)	36 (F) (G) (H) (J) (K)	51 (A) (B) (C) (D) (E)
7 (A) (B) (C) (D) (E)	22 (F) (G) (H) (J) (K)	37 (A) (B) (C) (D) (E)	52 (F) (G) (H) (J) (K)
8 (F) (G) (H) (J) (K)	23 (A) (B) (C) (D) (E)	38 (F) (G) (H) (J) (K)	53 (A) (B) (C) (D) (E)
9 (A) (B) (C) (D) (E)	24 (F) (G) (H) (J) (K)	39 (A) (B) (C) (D) (E)	54 (F) (G) (H) (J) (K)
10 (F) (G) (H) (J) (K)	25 (A) (B) (C) (D) (E)	40 (F) (G) (H) (J) (K)	55 (A) (B) (C) (D) (E)
11 (A) (B) (C) (D) (E)	26 (F) (G) (H) (J) (K)	41 (A) (B) (C) (D) (E)	56 (F) (G) (H) (J) (K)
12 (F) (G) (H) (J) (K)	27 (A) (B) (C) (D) (E)	42 (F) (G) (H) (J) (K)	57 (A) (B) (C) (D) (E)
13 (A) (B) (C) (D) (E)	28 (F) (G) (H) (J) (K)	43 (A) (B) (C) (D) (E)	58 (F) (G) (H) (J) (K)
14 (F) (G) (H) (J) (K)	29 (A) (B) (C) (D) (E)	44 (F) (G) (H) (J) (K)	59 (A) (B) (C) (D) (E)
15 (A) (B) (C) (D) (E)	30 (F) (G) (H) (J) (K)	45 (A) (B) (C) (D) (E)	60 (F) (G) (H) (J) (K)

The Princeton Review
Diagnostic ACT Form

Completely darken bubbles with a No. 2 pencil. If you make a mistake, be sure to erase mark completely. Erase all stray marks.

READING

1 Ⓐ Ⓑ Ⓒ Ⓓ	11 Ⓐ Ⓑ Ⓒ Ⓓ	21 Ⓐ Ⓑ Ⓒ Ⓓ	31 Ⓐ Ⓑ Ⓒ Ⓓ
2 Ⓕ Ⓖ Ⓗ Ⓙ	12 Ⓕ Ⓖ Ⓗ Ⓙ	22 Ⓕ Ⓖ Ⓗ Ⓙ	32 Ⓕ Ⓖ Ⓗ Ⓙ
3 Ⓐ Ⓑ Ⓒ Ⓓ	13 Ⓐ Ⓑ Ⓒ Ⓓ	23 Ⓐ Ⓑ Ⓒ Ⓓ	33 Ⓐ Ⓑ Ⓒ Ⓓ
4 Ⓕ Ⓖ Ⓗ Ⓙ	14 Ⓕ Ⓖ Ⓗ Ⓙ	24 Ⓕ Ⓖ Ⓗ Ⓙ	34 Ⓕ Ⓖ Ⓗ Ⓙ
5 Ⓐ Ⓑ Ⓒ Ⓓ	15 Ⓐ Ⓑ Ⓒ Ⓓ	25 Ⓐ Ⓑ Ⓒ Ⓓ	35 Ⓐ Ⓑ Ⓒ Ⓓ
6 Ⓕ Ⓖ Ⓗ Ⓙ	16 Ⓕ Ⓖ Ⓗ Ⓙ	26 Ⓕ Ⓖ Ⓗ Ⓙ	36 Ⓕ Ⓖ Ⓗ Ⓙ
7 Ⓐ Ⓑ Ⓒ Ⓓ	17 Ⓐ Ⓑ Ⓒ Ⓓ	27 Ⓐ Ⓑ Ⓒ Ⓓ	37 Ⓐ Ⓑ Ⓒ Ⓓ
8 Ⓕ Ⓖ Ⓗ Ⓙ	18 Ⓕ Ⓖ Ⓗ Ⓙ	28 Ⓕ Ⓖ Ⓗ Ⓙ	38 Ⓕ Ⓖ Ⓗ Ⓙ
9 Ⓐ Ⓑ Ⓒ Ⓓ	19 Ⓐ Ⓑ Ⓒ Ⓓ	29 Ⓐ Ⓑ Ⓒ Ⓓ	39 Ⓐ Ⓑ Ⓒ Ⓓ
10 Ⓕ Ⓖ Ⓗ Ⓙ	20 Ⓕ Ⓖ Ⓗ Ⓙ	30 Ⓕ Ⓖ Ⓗ Ⓙ	40 Ⓕ Ⓖ Ⓗ Ⓙ

SCIENCE REASONING

1 Ⓐ Ⓑ Ⓒ Ⓓ	11 Ⓐ Ⓑ Ⓒ Ⓓ	21 Ⓐ Ⓑ Ⓒ Ⓓ	31 Ⓐ Ⓑ Ⓒ Ⓓ
2 Ⓕ Ⓖ Ⓗ Ⓙ	12 Ⓕ Ⓖ Ⓗ Ⓙ	22 Ⓕ Ⓖ Ⓗ Ⓙ	32 Ⓕ Ⓖ Ⓗ Ⓙ
3 Ⓐ Ⓑ Ⓒ Ⓓ	13 Ⓐ Ⓑ Ⓒ Ⓓ	23 Ⓐ Ⓑ Ⓒ Ⓓ	33 Ⓐ Ⓑ Ⓒ Ⓓ
4 Ⓕ Ⓖ Ⓗ Ⓙ	14 Ⓕ Ⓖ Ⓗ Ⓙ	24 Ⓕ Ⓖ Ⓗ Ⓙ	34 Ⓕ Ⓖ Ⓗ Ⓙ
5 Ⓐ Ⓑ Ⓒ Ⓓ	15 Ⓐ Ⓑ Ⓒ Ⓓ	25 Ⓐ Ⓑ Ⓒ Ⓓ	35 Ⓐ Ⓑ Ⓒ Ⓓ
6 Ⓕ Ⓖ Ⓗ Ⓙ	16 Ⓕ Ⓖ Ⓗ Ⓙ	26 Ⓕ Ⓖ Ⓗ Ⓙ	36 Ⓕ Ⓖ Ⓗ Ⓙ
7 Ⓐ Ⓑ Ⓒ Ⓓ	17 Ⓐ Ⓑ Ⓒ Ⓓ	27 Ⓐ Ⓑ Ⓒ Ⓓ	37 Ⓐ Ⓑ Ⓒ Ⓓ
8 Ⓕ Ⓖ Ⓗ Ⓙ	18 Ⓕ Ⓖ Ⓗ Ⓙ	28 Ⓕ Ⓖ Ⓗ Ⓙ	38 Ⓕ Ⓖ Ⓗ Ⓙ
9 Ⓐ Ⓑ Ⓒ Ⓓ	19 Ⓐ Ⓑ Ⓒ Ⓓ	29 Ⓐ Ⓑ Ⓒ Ⓓ	39 Ⓐ Ⓑ Ⓒ Ⓓ
10 Ⓕ Ⓖ Ⓗ Ⓙ	20 Ⓕ Ⓖ Ⓗ Ⓙ	30 Ⓕ Ⓖ Ⓗ Ⓙ	40 Ⓕ Ⓖ Ⓗ Ⓙ

I hereby certify that I have truthfully identified myself on this form. I accept the consequences of falsifying my identity.

_____

Your signature

_____

Today's date

The Princeton Review
Diagnostic ACT Form

ESSAY

Begin your essay on this side. If necessary, continue on the opposite side.

Continue on the opposite side if necessary.

The Princeton Review
Diagnostic ACT Form

Continued from previous page.

_____

_____

_____

_____

_____

_____

_____

_____

_____

_____

_____

_____

_____

_____

_____

_____

_____

_____

_____

PLEASE PRINT
YOUR INITIALS

First	Middle	Last

Chapter 28
Practice Exam 2:
Answers
and Explanations

English		Math		Reading		Science	
1. D	40. J	1. A	40. H	1. C	40. J	1. C	40. H
2. F	41. A	2. H	41. C	2. F		2. F	
3. C	42. G	3. C	42. F	3. B		3. A	
4. F	43. C	4. J	43. B	4. G		4. H	
5. C	44. G	5. C	44. G	5. A		5. D	
6. H	45. B	6. K	45. B	6. H		6. G	
7. D	46. J	7. A	46. H	7. A		7. B	
8. F	47. C	8. K	47. D	8. J		8. F	
9. A	48. F	9. E	48. J	9. D		9. D	
10. G	49. C	10. J	49. B	10. J		10. G	
11. C	50. J	11. C	50. J	11. D		11. C	
12. H	51. C	12. K	51. D	12. G		12. G	
13. D	52. F	13. D	52. K	13. D		13. A	
14. F	53. A	14. G	53. C	14. G		14. H	
15. C	54. H	15. A	54. H	15. A		15. D	
16. G	55. A	16. H	55. C	16. G		16. G	
17. D	56. H	17. A	56. G	17. C		17. D	
18. H	57. D	18. K	57. A	18. F		18. F	
19. A	58. G	19. C	58. F	19. C		19. D	
20. G	59. D	20. H	59. D	20. G		20. J	
21. D	60. H	21. C	60. K	21. C		21. B	
22. F	61. B	22. F		22. G		22. H	
23. A	62. J	23. C		23. C		23. B	
24. F	63. C	24. G		24. G		24. F	
25. C	64. J	25. E		25. D		25. C	
26. G	65. C	26. G		26. J		26. G	
27. D	66. H	27. D		27. B		27. D	
28. H	67. D	28. F		28. J		28. H	
29. D	68. F	29. C		29. A		29. C	
30. J	69. A	30. H		30. H		30. F	
31. A	70. G	31. E		31. C		31. C	
32. F	71. A	32. J		32. H		32. J	
33. C	72. G	33. C		33. D		33. C	
34. F	73. B	34. K		34. G		34. G	
35. C	74. F	35. E		35. C		35. B	
36. J	75. D	36. K		36. J		36. J	
37. C		37. E		37. C		37. A	
38. J		38. J		38. H		38. F	
39. D		39. B		39. A		39. D	

ENGLISH TEST

1. **D**   The verb *associate* requires the preposition *with*. None of the other choices are idiomatically correct.

2. **F**   All the proposed substitutions essentially expand upon the word *genders* without adding any new information to the sentence. As a result, you can eliminate choices (G), (H), and (J) because they are all unnecessarily wordy.

3. **C**   You can eliminate choices (A) and (B) right away because the proposed sentence is totally out of context with what you've read so far. Only choice (C) gives the correct reason why you shouldn't include the proposed sentence: the content of the sentence is irrelevant to the passage as a whole.

4. **F**   Eliminate choices (H) and (J) immediately because these will not be correct under any circumstances. Only choice (F) uses the correct form of the past participle.

5. **C**   Choices (A) and (B) contain punctuation that is used to separate independent clauses. Since *once you've learned a few basic stitches* is not an independent clause, neither answer choice can work. Instead, *once you've learned a few basic stitches* operates more as an introductory idea, which must be set off with a comma, as in choice (C).

6. **H**   In this situation, choice (H) is the most concise answer that makes sense in the context. Notice all the other choices contain redundant words and phrases.

7. **D**   This sentence is talking about the *completion of several projects*. Only choice (D) has the appropriate plural pronoun. If you picked choice (B), be careful: pronouns must agree in number.

8. **F**   Since you can count the starter kits (there are three, as the passage says), use *fewer* rather than *less*. With that, you can eliminate choices (H) and (J). Next, you need to use *than*, which is a comparison word, rather than *then*, which is a word used to describe a sequence of events in time. Only choice (F) works in this sentence.

9. **A**   No change is necessary here because no pause is needed after the word *types*. Choices (B) and (C) in particular use punctuation that is much too strong in this context.

10. **G**   Use Process Of Elimination aggressively here. The idiomatic phrase *ranging from* should not be split up with a comma, so eliminate choices (F) and (J). Then eliminate choice (H) because *ranging from very small to very large, with everything in between* is not an independent clause. Only choice (G) works in the context.

11. **C**   This sentence talks about hooks that are *so big that you need to use two strands of yarn*, so it must be moved closer to other sentences that do the same. Only Sentence 3 works, because it talks about large hooks.

12. **H**   Choices (F) and (G) don't make sense in the context. These are actually ideas with a negative slant and would be more appropriate in a sentence that was talking about some negative aspect of crocheting. Choice (J) might have worked better in the first paragraph. In this paragraph, however, choice (H) provides the most effective lead-in.

13.   D   As written, this sentence contains a comma splice in its use of a comma to separate two independent clauses, so eliminate choice (A). Choices (C) and (D) both contain words that turn the first part of the sentence into a dependent clause, but choice (C) suggests a contrast where none exists. Choice (D) is the best answer because it fixes the dependency problem and contains the appropriate transition word.

14.   F   Only choice (F) gives the idiomatically correct preposition. The others change the meaning of the sentence or use incorrect idioms.

15.   C   The essay is clearly in favor of crocheting, but it has not discussed the commercial potential of crocheting at all, so you can eliminate choices (A) and (B). Neither has it talked about the commercial potential of any other hobby, so you can eliminate choice (D).

16.   G   The verbs in this sentence are fairly complex, so use Process of Elimination aggressively. You can eliminate choices (F), (H), and (J) because all would be used in a situation in which the author *had seen* the painting. In the context of this sentence, however, the author is trying to suggest that she never believed that she *would see* the painting, so only choice (G) can work.

17.   D   This sentence may sound correct as written, but be careful. If you're going to use the *chance to* construction, you must complete the infinitive. In other words, in this situation, the sentence would have to read, *I finally got my chance to see the painting.* In this case, the only possible solution is to delete the underlined portion. Note that this is the most concise answer that works. Always give these deletions and omissions special consideration—they can often get some of the tangled logic out of the sentences as written.

18.   H   This sentence refers to the *grandeur* of the *painting*. In other words, you need the possessive pronoun *its* when describing the painting's grandeur. Only choice (H) works.

19.   A   The verbs in this sentence form a kind of list, so make sure all the verbs in the sentence are consistent (or "parallel") with one another. The verbs should read *packed*, *jumped*, and *headed*. Only choice (A) keeps all three verbs consistent with one another.

20.   G   The proposed insertion has the word *her* right at the beginning, which means that you need to find the sentence that contains its antecedent. Notice the clause in Sentence 3, *I met someone else who loved the painting as much as I did.* This *someone else* is the best available antecedent for *her* in the paragraph.

21.   D   There are dependent clauses on either side of this sentence, so you can't use either a colon or a semicolon. Even a comma gives the sentence a pause where none is necessary. Only choice (D) gives the sentence its appropriate flow and does not break up the compound subject and its verb.

22.   F   Notice the word *impossible* directly before the underlined portion. Since this word is not underlined, it can't be changed, thus making choices (G), (H), and (J) redundant.

23.   A   Sentence 1 does talk about the size of the canvas, but Sentence 2 is out of context in this paragraph. This paragraph is about the author's impressions of the painting; the kind of technical detail presented in Sentence 2 is not part of these impressions.

24. **F** Remember that transitions are used to connect the ideas in paragraphs. The previous paragraph is about the author's impression of the painting, particularly relating to the size of the painting. The new paragraph goes on to present the author's impression of another element of the painting, which she finds *even more impressive*, as in choice (F). Choices (G), (H), and (J) might work in a different context, but they don't connect these paragraphs as well as choice (F).

25. **C** Notice that choices (A), (B), (D), and the underlined portion of the original sentence all contain the subordinating conjunctions *as* and *when*. The absence of any of these conjunctions in choice (C) creates a comma splice, and choice (C) is therefore NOT an acceptable substitution.

26. **G** *From a distance* is the first part of the contrast in this sentence, the second part of which is *up close*. If you were to delete the prepositional phrase *from a distance*, this contrast would be unclear.

27. **D** The subjects of these paragraphs have been the author and her friend, so of all the answer choices, only choice (D), which contains the first-person plural pronoun *we*, could work here.

28. **H** This essay has been about the author's love of a single painting, so there is no need to mention other paintings at this point in the essay; eliminate choices (F) and (G). You can also eliminate choice (J) because this information is not contradicted elsewhere in the passage.

29. **D** No pause is necessary between *sights* and *on our trip*, so eliminate all answer choices that suggest this pause with unnecessary punctuation.

30. **J** The only clear placement for the underlined portion is after the word *bought*, completing the phrase *bought at the museum gift shop*. The other answer choices make the sentence unclear.

31. **A** The clause *cats have developed* is not an independent clause, so a semicolon can't be used after it. Eliminate choice (D). In fact, no pause is needed anywhere in this sentence, so any of the choices that introduce unnecessary commas can be deleted. Choice (A) is the only choice that does not contain unnecessary pauses.

32. **F** Make sure you read the question carefully. It's asking for something that expresses the *ownership* relationship between people and cats. Choice (H) can be eliminated because it talks about dogs, and choices (G) and (J) can be eliminated because they don't express the ownership relationship for which the question is asking.

33. **C** In this sentence, the phrase *When communicating with each other* is a misplaced modifier. As written it sounds like the "*talk*" is somehow *communicating with each other*. It is of course the *cats* that are communicating with each other, which means that only choice (C) fixes the misplaced modifier.

34. **F** First, since this question is testing changes in verb tense, identify the subject of the verb. In this case, the subject is the plural noun *tails*, which requires a plural verb. You can eliminate choice (H) immediately, and choice (G) makes the sentence incomplete. Choice (J) changes the meaning of the sentence and uses a wordy passive construction. Given the new mistakes in all the proposed substitutions, the best answer is choice (F), NO CHANGE.

35. C   The paragraph has been discussing the ways that cats communicate nonverbally. The sentence gives an exception to this rule, which only choice (C) adequately describes.

36. J   You'll want to begin a new paragraph here, because the focus of the essay changes with the introduction of the word *human*. Because this sentence is not describing a step in a process, and there's no first idea for which this can be the *next*, you can eliminate choice (H). Only choice (J) works.

37. C   Use context. The previous sentence is describing plural cats, so this sentence should do the same. Only choice (C) gives the correct possessive form of the plural, *cats'*.

38. J   Choices (F) and (G) are redundant. The word *logical* alone gets the point across here. Choice (H) modifies *logical*, but it does so unnecessarily—*to a startling degree* is not specific. Only choice (J) is concise while preserving the meaning of the sentence.

39. D   *Clear* is an adjective, which modifies a noun; *clearly* is an adverb, which can modify a verb, an adjective, or another adverb. The word being modified here is *demonstrated*, which is a verb, so you'll need the adverb *clearly* and can eliminate choices (A) and (B). Choice (C) can't work because the subordinating conjunction *since* is not the appropriate transition between ideas in the sentence. Only choice (D) contains the correct adverb with the proper subordinating conjunction *when*.

40. J   The information given is true and may be interesting, but in the context of this passage, it would be out of context. Remember, this is a passage about cats, so it is not at all likely that a sentence about birds will contribute to the main idea of the passage.

41. A   The structure of this sentence is clumsy, but you can change only what appears in the underlined portion. In this instance, your most important clue is the comma after the word *examples*. This comma suggests that the infinitive phrase *to name only a few examples* is being set off as unnecessary to the meaning of the sentence. The sentence as written is the only choice that does not contain a grammatical error.

42. G   Of all the possibilities listed here, only choice (G) establishes any kind of link between *cats* and *their owners*. Other answer choices talk about *mammals*, but this question asks specifically about *cats*.

43. C   The underlined portion must be parallel with the rest of the sentence. Early in the sentence, the author speaks of *communicating as every bit as important as forging good relationships*. A second *as* will be needed to complete the comparison, and any verb used will need the same conjugation as *forging*. Choices (B) and (C) both meet these criteria, but of the two, choice (C) is more concise.

44. G   Choice (G) is the most concise substitution that maintains the meaning of the sentence. Choices (F), (H), and (J) are redundant because they contain some form of the word *senseless* and other words that mean the same thing.

45.   B   Some of the transition words offered in the answer choices may seem similar, so it is best in this situation to compare what comes after those transition words. Again, you need an answer that expresses the relationship between *cats* and their *owners*. Although the word *human* does not appear in it, choice (B) is the only one of the answer choices that talks about a relationship between cats and humans.

46.   J   Choices (F), (G), and (H) all give redundant constructions. Only choice (J) gives a concise construction and maintains the meaning of the sentence.

47.   C   The *houses* described here are not in possession of anything, so you can eliminate choices (A) and (B). You can also eliminate choice (D) because it introduces an unnecessary pause after the word *houses*.

48.   F   Only choice (F) maintains the meaning of the subject without introducing new, unnecessary information. Choice (J) might look appealing, but choice (F) is still more concise. Think of it this way: to say the same thing, choice (F) takes one word and choice (J) takes two. Go with the most concise choice that works.

49.   C   *Michigan island* is a compound noun in this case, so the adjective *isolated* should not be set off from *Michigan* with a comma. Eliminate choices (A) and (D). Then notice the coordinating conjunction *so* directly after the underlined portion. If a coordinating conjunction is being used to link two independent clauses, it must be preceded by a comma. Only choice (C) works.

50.   J   All items in a list must be parallel. In this sentence, the list should read *by horse, carriage, or bicycle*. Choices (F), (G), and (H) are not within this parallel structure.

51.   C   As written, this sentence creates a comma splice. The clause that ends with the word *necessary* and the clause that begins with the word *Mackinac* are both independent, so of the different possible punctuation marks in the answer choices, only a period can be used to separate them.

52.   F   If the end of this sentence were deleted, the meaning of the sentence would not fundamentally change, but you would lose an interesting detail about Arch Rock, as choice (F) suggests. Choice (G) is misleading in that it suggests the geological descriptions of multiple tourist attractions, while the underlined portion gives the geological description of only one attraction. There is no contrast with the governor's mansion, so eliminate choice (H); the information is not detailed elsewhere in the passage, so eliminate choice (J).

53.   A   The next sentence discusses *fudge*, and only choice (A) contains any mention of stores that might sell this product.

54.   H   This question is testing the idiom *for sale*. The only viable alternative to this would be *on sale*, but that doesn't appear in the answer choices. Choices (F), (G), and (J) all suggest incorrect idioms.

55.   A   Choices (B), (C), and (D) are all grammatically correct while preserving the basic meaning of the sentence. Choice (A), *which*, is neither grammatically correct nor consistent with the meaning of the sentence. Therefore, choice (A) would NOT be an acceptable alternative.

56. H Only choice (H) removes the redundancy problem and maintains the meaning of the sentence.

57. D The pronoun in this portion of the sentence should refer back to the *local residents*. As such, it should be a third-person plural. Only choice (D) has the appropriate pronoun, *they*.

58. G Of all the answer choices, only choice (G) reduces the wordiness of the sentence while clarifying its meaning.

59. D The subject of this sentence is *privacy*, so the verb in the underlined portion must agree with a singular noun. Eliminate choice (A). Choices (B) and (C) change the meaning of the sentence by changing the tense of the auxiliary verbs. Only choice (D) maintains the meaning of the sentence and fixes the verb-conjugation problem.

60. H This passage discusses Mackinac Island as a tourist destination and mentions cars only in the beginning of this essay. If the writer's intention is to show the difficulties residents have with cars, this essay has not succeeded; its subject has been the island itself and its many tourist attractions.

61. B The two nouns *friends* and *peers* are not part of a list or separate ideas. Instead, they are both the objects of the prepositional phrase *in front of*, and they should thus not be separated with any punctuation.

62. J Choice (J) is grammatically incorrect because it makes the sentence unable to stand on its own (i.e., it changes the sentence from an independent to a dependent clause). It is therefore NOT an acceptable alternative to the underlined portion.

63. C Sentence 2 refers to something that *defies understanding*, and the word *though* suggests that something in a previous sentence does not defy understanding. Sentence 4 reads, *It is understandable that people would enjoy singing in the privacy of their homes.* Sentence 2 should follow this sentence because it describes, by way of a contrast, something that is not so understandable.

64. J Notice the other verb in this sentence, *see*. These verbs should be parallel; the basic subjects and verbs of each part of the sentence should read *look and you'll see*. Only choice (J) contains the parallel verb and maintains the meaning of the sentence.

65. C The *Even though* at the beginning of this sentence operates as a subordinating conjunction, thus making everything up to *busy restaurants* part of a single dependent clause. Choices (A) and (C) set this dependent clause off with a comma correctly, but choice (A) has the coordinating conjunction *but*. A coordinating conjunction preceded by a comma can only be used to separate two independent clauses.

66. H The phrase *such staples as* should not be divided with any punctuation. Only choice (H) gives the appropriate absence of punctuation. In order to use a colon, the clause before the colon must be independent. This one is not, so you can eliminate choice (G).

67. D The verb in the underlined portion must be parallel with the other major verb in this sentence, *responds.* Only choice (D) establishes this parallelism. Choices (A) and (C) are in the wrong tense, and choice (B) makes for an awkward construction.

68. F The beginning of the next paragraph speaks of *another, more obvious reason.* The underlined portion, therefore, must contain a reason of some kind. Only choice (F) contains anything close, particularly in the final clause, *this is not the only reason for its enduring popularity.* The other answer choices do not link these two paragraphs, nor do they make sense in the larger context of the passage.

69. A This sentence should be in contrast with the previous sentence, and the sentence as written signals this contrast. The others give adverbs that suggest a comparison rather than a contrast.

70. G This sentence needs something that will suggest that the quality of people's voices doesn't matter. Only choice (G) does this with the word *regardless.* The prepositional phrase *in lieu of* suggests a substitution, but nothing is being substituted here; rather, the poor singing of many of karaoke's participants is being disregarded in consideration of other, more important things.

71. A Choice (D) gives the contraction *who is,* which does not work here, so you can eliminate that immediately. Choices (B) and (C) are not grammatically correct in this situation. The sentence as written contains the appropriate possessive pronoun and should therefore not be changed.

72. G The clause *who are ordinarily shy* is important in its modification of the word *people.* It would be incorrect to say that in general, karaoke brings people out of their shells. The clause is necessary because it clarifies that the sentence is talking about people not normally inclined to perform in public.

73. B The word *first* indicates that the underlined portion will need to have something to do with time. Choice (D) suggests a place, so you can eliminate it. Choices (A) and (C) suggest a cause and effect that is not substantiated in the rest of the sentence. Only choice (B), *when,* gives the appropriate time word.

74. F If you are not sure how to use *less* and *fewer,* look at the second word in each underlined portion. *Then* refers to a sequence of events; *than* is a comparison word. In this sentence, the author is making a comparison, so you need *than.* Eliminate choice (H). Now choice (F) is the only choice that makes the sentence grammatically correct. As a general note, *less* is used with general quantities (e.g., less money) and *fewer* is used with quantities that can be counted (e.g., fewer dollars). This question actually tests an exception to the rule in which both adjectives can work depending on the context; if were you to expand this sentence, it would read *less money than $7 billion* rather than *fewer than 7 billion dollars.*

75. D This passage deals with the international popularity of karaoke. At no point does the passage discuss specific regions. Therefore, the proposed insertion would not be appropriate at any point in the passage.

MATHEMATICS TEST

1. **A** The midpoint of segment XY is the average of X and Y, so add them up and divide by 2: $\dfrac{-15-11}{2} = \dfrac{-26}{2} = -13$.

2. **H** Use the Pythagorean theorem ($a^2 + b^2 = c^2$) to find the length of DE: $8^2 + (DE)^2 = 10^2$, so $64 + (DE)^2 = 100$, $(DE)^2 = 36$, $DE = \sqrt{36} = 6$. Also note that this is a Pythagorean triple with sides of 6, 8, and 10.

3. **C** The phrase *double the volume of the ant farm* means your equation must contain the expression $2V$, so eliminate choices (A), (B), and (E). The second sentence also says that the number of ants *is close to 50 more*, so your expression will have to contain the expression $2V + 50$; choice (C) is correct because it adds 50. Choice (D) is incorrect because, when the 2 is distributed, it becomes $2V + 100$.

4. **J** The probability that Lisa will take a fiction book can be defined as a fraction: the number of fiction books divided by the total number of books. Therefore, the probability of Lisa taking a fiction book is $\dfrac{5}{5+7} = \dfrac{5}{12}$: choice (J). Choice (K) is the probability that she will take a nonfiction book; choice (G) is the ratio of fiction books to nonfiction books.

5. **C** To find the average, add up all the test scores and divide by the number of tests: $\dfrac{108+81+79+99+85+82}{6} = \dfrac{534}{6} = 89$, choice (C). You can eliminate choices (A) and (B) because the average must be less than the highest test score.

6. **K** Angles 3 and 5 are alternate interior angles and therefore congruent. Angles 1 and 3 look congruent only because the triangle appears to be isosceles—the problem does not give any indication that it is, so eliminate choice (G).

7. **A** If p is Gregor's monthly pay, write an equation that represents Gregor's deposit. He spends 20% and deposits the rest, so $p - (0.2)p = 3{,}200$ or $(0.8)p = 3{,}200$. Divide through by the (0.8) to find that $p = 4{,}000$. If you're not sure how to set up the equation, you could also try out the answer choices as possibilities for Gregor's monthly pay to see which gives a deposit value of $3,200.

8. **K** By definition, similar polygons have equal corresponding angles, making choice (K) the correct response. Two similar polygons are really the same figure on different scales: smaller or larger versions of each other. Therefore, their dimensions are not necessarily the same, making choices (F), (G), (H), and (J) incorrect.

9. **E** Work through this word problem one step at a time. $60 × .30 = $18, so the dress is discounted $18. $60 − $18 = $42, the sale price. Now calculate Victoria's second discount: $42 × .10 = $4.20. $42 − $4.20 = $37.80, the price Victoria pays. Choice (D) incorrectly discounts the dress 40%; this is wrong because Victoria gets 10% off the *reduced price*, not the original price.

10. J   Erin begins with x chips, which means (according to the second sentence of the question) Amy has $x - 3$. When Erin wins 4 of Amy's chips, Erin's total increases to $x + 4$ while Amy's drops to $x - 7$. Subtract $(x + 4) - (x - 7) = 11$, the difference in their chip totals.

11. C   Since absolute value must always be greater than or equal to zero, you can eliminate choices (A) and (B). Substitute $y = 4$ into the expression $|1 - y| = |1 - 4| = |-3| = 3$.

12. K   FOIL: multiply the First terms $3a \times a = 3a^2$, the Outer terms $3a \times (-b^2) = (-3ab^2)$, the Inner terms $2b \times a = 2ab$, and the Last terms $2b \times (-b^2) = -2b^3$. Add these terms to get $3a^2 - 3ab^2 + 2ab - 2b^3$, choice (K).

13. D   Simplify the expression: $3 - 2(4 - y) = 3 - 8 + 2y = -5 + 2y$, which is the same as choice (D). Be careful when you multiply two negative values, such as $(-2) \times (-y)$: you should get a positive value.

14. G   When raising a number with an exponent to another power, you multiply the exponents; therefore, $(y^3)^8 = y^{3 \times 8} = y^{24}$.

15. A   Sketch out a little calendar until you see a pattern: Day 1 is Monday, 2 is Tuesday, 3 Wednesday, 4 Thursday, 5 Friday, 6 Saturday, 7 Sunday, 8 Monday, and so on. Notice that Sundays are always multiples of 7. Pick a multiple of 7 close to 260, such as 259. That means Day 259 is a Sunday, so Day 260 is a Monday.

16. H   Draw yourself a figure to see the relationship between the two shapes. Since the formula for area of a square is $A = s^2$ (where s is the side length of the square), you can find that a square with area 64 has side length 8, which would also be the diameter of the circle inscribed in this square, meaning the circle's radius would be 4. The formula for the area of a circle is $A = \pi r^2$, so $A = \pi(4)^2 = 16\pi$.

17. A   Factor $x^2 - 5x - 14 = 0$ to $(x - 7)(x + 2) = 0$; therefore, the solutions (the values of x that make this true) are 7 and -2. Their product: $7 \times -2 = -14$. Also, note than in the standard formula $ax^2 + bx + c$, the product of the solutions will always be $\dfrac{c}{a}$.

18. K   Factor $x^{12} - 9$ to $(x^6 - 3)(x^6 + 3)$; eliminate choices (F) and (G). Factor $(x^6 - 3)$ to $(x^3 - \sqrt{3})(x^3 + \sqrt{3})$; eliminate choices (H) and (J).

19. C   Plug $x = \dfrac{1}{6}$ into the expression: $\dfrac{2x + 4}{3x} = \dfrac{2 \times \frac{1}{6} + 4}{3 \times \frac{1}{6}} = \dfrac{\frac{2}{6} + \frac{24}{6}}{\frac{3}{6}} = \dfrac{\frac{26}{6}}{\frac{3}{6}} = \dfrac{26}{3}$.

20. H   Use the formula Distance = Rate × Time. Substitute the values from the problem: $60 = 90 \times t$. Therefore, $t = \dfrac{60}{90} = \dfrac{2}{3}$ hours. To convert from hours into minutes, multiply 60 minutes by $\dfrac{2}{3}$ hours: $60 \times \dfrac{2}{3} = 40$ minutes.

21. C   Begin by drawing a perpendicular height by drawing vertical lines from the top vertices straight down to the base: these segments are the height of the trapezoid, and your figure should now look like a rectangle and two right triangles. Since the bottom base of the trapezoid is 11" and the top

base is 5", the difference is 6". Assume the two triangles you've created are the same size, which means the base of each is 3" (and the base of your rectangle is 5"). Use the Pythagorean theorem ($a^2 + b^2 = c^2$) to find the height (which we'll call h) of one of the triangles: $h^2 + 3^2 = (3\sqrt{2})^2$, so $h^2 + 9 = 18$, $h^2 = 9$, and $h = 3$. This is also the height of the trapezoid, so plug these values (height and two bases) into the formula in the question: $A = h\left(\dfrac{b_1 + b_2}{2}\right) = 3\left(\dfrac{5+11}{2}\right) = 3\left(\dfrac{16}{2}\right) = 3(8) = 24$. If you hadn't been given the formula for the area of a trapezoid, or if you just find the formula too confusing, notice that the vertical heights split this figure into three familiar shapes: two triangles and a rectangle. You can find the area of each of these smaller pieces and add them together.

22. F By definition, the roots of a quadratic equation are the values for the variable that cause the equation to equal zero. Starting with the first answer choice, set each factor equal to zero and solve for x: $3x + 2 = 0$ yields $x = -\dfrac{2}{3}$, and $4x - 1 = 0$ yields $x = \dfrac{1}{4}$. None of the other answer choices yields both roots given in the problem.

23. C Draw the line segments $\overline{AC}$ and $\overline{BD}$; these are the diagonals. By definition, the diagonals of a rhombus bisect each other; therefore, the two halves of $\overline{AC}$ are 3 each and the two halves of $\overline{BD}$ are 4 each. The diagonals of a rhombus also (by definition) are perpendicular; this means that each of the four triangles inside this rhombus are right triangles. Use the Pythagorean theorem to find the length of the side of the rhombus: $3^2 + 4^2 = s^2$, so $9 + 16 = s^2$, $25 = s^2$, and $5 = s$. Note that these sides create a 3:4:5 Pythagorean triple.

24. G The formula for the area of a rectangle is $A = lw$. Fill in what you know: $80 = l(l - 2) = l^2 - 2l$. Solve the quadratic to find solutions $l = 10$ and $l = -8$. You can't have a negative side, so the length of the rectangle must be 10. Since this is a tough algebraic problem, you can also work backwards from the answer choices. Try choice (H) first: if the length is 16, then the width (2 shorter) is 14. Area of a rectangle formula is $A = lw$, so $A = 16 \times 14 = 224$. That's too big, so eliminate choices (H), (J), and (K). Try choice (G) next: if the length is 10, the width is 8, then the area is $10 \times 8 = 80$.

25. E Don't be intimidated by the Cartesian plane: it's the same (x,y) coordinate plane you're used to. Slope is defined as $\dfrac{rise}{run}$, so use the two points given in the slope formula: $\dfrac{y_2 - y_1}{x_2 - x_1} = \dfrac{10 - (-5)}{5 - 1} = \dfrac{10 + 5}{4} = \dfrac{15}{4}$.

26. G The equation of a circle is $(x - h)^2 + (y - k)^2 = r^2$, where (h,k) is the center of the circle and r is the radius. The first part of the equation tells you that the x-coordinate of the center is -5, since $(x + 5)^2 = (x - [-5])^2$, so $h = -5$. The second part more clearly matches the formula, so it's easier to see that the y-coordinate of the center is 5. Therefore, the center of the circle is $(-5,5)$.

27. D The open circles at $x = 0$ and $x = 4$ mean that $x \neq 0$ and $x \neq 4$; therefore, eliminate choices (A), (B), and (E). The solid line between $x = 0$ and $x = 4$ means that x can be any value between 0 and 4, so eliminate choice (C). Make sure you read the question carefully. If you selected choice (C), you may have mistaken it for the range.

28. F The *point exactly halfway between* is another way to describe the midpoint, so plug the two points into the midpoint formula: $\left(\dfrac{x_1 + x_2}{2}, \dfrac{y_1 + y_2}{2} \right)$. This gives you $\left(\dfrac{-1+3}{2}, \dfrac{-5+3}{2} \right)$, which simplifies to $\left(\dfrac{2}{2}, \dfrac{-2}{2} \right)$, or $(1, -1)$.

29. C To find the *average rate of change*, begin by finding the total change: the liquid begins at $0°$ and eventually reaches $80°$, so the total change is the difference, $80°$. The question asks for the rate of change *during the times in which Sanjay is applying* heat to the container. Sanjay applies heat from minutes 0 to 5, $7\frac{1}{2}$ to 10, and 15 to $17\frac{1}{2}$. Find the difference in each of these pairs of numbers to see that Sanjay applied heat for 5 minutes, then 2.5 minutes, then another 2.5 minutes, or 10 minutes total. Therefore, the average rate of change in degrees per minute is $\dfrac{80°}{10\,\text{min}} = 8$ degrees/min.

30. H When you divide exponentials with the same base, you subtract the exponents, so $\dfrac{a^x}{a^y} = a^{x-y}$; therefore, $a^{x-y} = a^5$ and $x - y = 5$.

31. E The slope of a line in standard form ($Ax + By = C$) is $-\dfrac{A}{B}$; therefore, the slope of $-5x + 3y = 8$ is $-\left(\dfrac{-5}{3} \right) = \dfrac{5}{3}$. Or, if you prefer, rearrange the equation into slope-intercept form ($y = mx + b$). $8 - 3y = 5x$ becomes $3y = 5x + 8$, or $y = \dfrac{5}{3}x + \dfrac{8}{3}$. In slope-intercept form, m is the slope; in this case, $\dfrac{5}{3}$.

32. J The least common denominator (LCD) must be a multiple of the denominator of each of the three given fractions. Take the factors of each denominator (3, 5, 7, 11) to the highest powers they appear: 3^2 (first fraction), 5^2 (second fraction), 7 (second fraction), and 11^3 (third fraction). This results in $3^2 \cdot 5^2 \cdot 7 \cdot 11^3$, choice (J). Choice (K) is the product of all three denominators and is wrong because choice (J) is smaller and still a multiple of all three denominators; in other words, both are common denominators but choice (J) is the "least."

33. C To multiply fractions, you multiply all the numbers on top of the fractions and all the numbers on the bottom of the fractions: $\dfrac{1}{4} \times \dfrac{2}{5} \times \dfrac{3}{6} \times \dfrac{4}{7} \times \dfrac{5}{8} \times \dfrac{6}{9} \times \dfrac{7}{10} = \dfrac{1 \times 2 \times 3 \times 4 \times 5 \times 6 \times 7}{4 \times 5 \times 6 \times 7 \times 8 \times 9 \times 10}$. Now, before you pull out the calculator, you can cancel out numbers that appear on both the top and bottom (4, 5, 6, and 7) because a number divided by itself (such as $\dfrac{4}{4}$) is 1, which doesn't affect the final product. After canceling, you get $\dfrac{1 \times 2 \times 3}{8 \times 9 \times 10} = \dfrac{6}{720}$, which reduces to $\dfrac{1}{120}$.

34. K The figure provided is a right triangle, so use the Pythagorean theorem ($a^2 + b^2 = c^2$) to find the distance asked for. $110^2 + 200^2 = c^2$, so $12{,}100 + 40{,}000 = c^2$, $52{,}100 = c^2$, and $\sqrt{52{,}100} = c$.

35. E The key phrase in this question is *at most*. It's possible that the second pentagon is the same size and is laid directly over the original pentagon. Because all points of one pentagon are the same as the other, select choice (E).

36. K When assigning employees to duties, there are 10 available to reserve a venue (the first duty). That leaves 9 remaining to arrange catering (because no one can be assigned more than one duty) and then 8 to plan activities. Then multiply $10 \times 9 \times 8$ to find how many different ways these duties can be assigned. Note the format of the answer choices—don't do more work than you have to.

37. E The easiest way to work this problem is to sketch it out. Draw $\overline{PQ}$, then draw the line perpendicular to $\overline{PQ}$ at Q; R is somewhere on this line. All of the answer choices have x-values greater than 1 and you can see the line rising to the right of Q $(1,4)$ in your sketch. This means that the y-value of R must be greater than 4, which leaves only choice (E). Alternatively, you could find the slope of $\overline{PQ}$: the slope formula is $\dfrac{y_2 - y_1}{x_2 - x_1}$, so $\dfrac{2-4}{6-1} = \dfrac{-2}{5}$. Since $\angle PQR$ is a right angle, $\overline{PQ} \perp \overline{QR}$. In the coordinate plane, the slopes of perpendicular lines are negative reciprocals, which makes the slope of $\overline{QR}$ $\dfrac{5}{2}$. Then use the points given in each answer choice to see which gives you the correct slope. It's choice (E): $\dfrac{9-4}{3-1} = \dfrac{5}{2}$.

38. J Solve the given equation for y. Start with $y = 0.25(100 - y)$. You can either distribute the 0.25 or divide both sides by the 0.25. In this case, it is easier to divide by 0.25. After doing this your equation becomes: $4y = 100 - y$. Add y to both sides to get $5y = 100$. Divide both sides by 5 to get $y = 20$. If you chose to begin the problem by distributing the 0.25, you should have gotten the same answer.

39. B Since $4\cos^2 x = 1$, $\cos^2 x = 0.25$ and $\cos x = 0.5$. You want to know x, the degree measure whose cosine is 0.5. A scientific/graphing calculator can help you calculate that: the $\cos^{-1}$ key will tell you the degree measure that yields the cosine you give it. $\cos^{-1}(0.5) = 60°$, so choice (B) is correct. If you prefer, you can try each of the answers in your scientific/graphing calculator. When you plug in choice (B), you can find that $\cos 60° = 0.5$, so $\cos^2 60° = 0.25$, and $4\cos^2 60° = 1$. Make sure your calculator is in degree mode!

40. H Sketch the rug over the floor to help you visualize the situation. The area of the exposed floor is the difference between the area of the entire floor and the area of the rug. First, find the area of the entire floor: area of a rectangle formula is $A = lw$, so $A = 16 \times 18 = 288$. Area of a circle formula is $A = \pi r^2$, where r is the radius. The diameter is 12, so $r = 6$. Therefore, $A = \pi \times 6^2 = \pi \times 36$, which is approximately 113. The difference: $288 - 113 = 175$. If you got a negative number when you did the calculation, you may have used the diameter of the circle in the Area of a circle formula rather than the radius.

41.   C   The equation of the given line is in slope-intercept form: $y = mx + b$, where m is the slope and b is the y-intercept. That tells you the slope of this line is -2. Since the slopes of perpendicular lines are negative reciprocals, the slope of the line in the credited answer choice must be $\frac{1}{2}$: eliminate choices (A), (B), and (E). The question says that the line you're looking for passes through the point $(0, -3)$: that makes the y-intercept (by definition) -3, so eliminate choice (D).

42.   F   Draw a vertical line from the point $\left(2\sqrt{3}, 2\right)$ straight down to the x-axis; this creates a right triangle with base $2\sqrt{3}$ and height 2. Use the Pythagorean theorem ($a^2 + b^2 = c^2$) to find the hypotenuse: $(2\sqrt{3})^2 + 2^2 = c^2$, so $4 \times 3 + 4 = c^2$, $12 + 4 = c^2$, $16 = c^2$, so $4 = c$. (A shortcut is to recognize that this is a 30°-60°-90° triangle. Such a triangle has a ratio of side lengths $1 : \sqrt{3} : 2$, which means this triangle's sides are 2, $2\sqrt{3}$, and 4.) Since sine is the ratio of the opposite side to the hypotenuse, $\sin\theta = \frac{2}{4} = \frac{1}{2}$.

43.   B   Substitute $a = 5$ and $b = -\frac{1}{4}$ into the answer choices. Before you actually work each out, you can eliminate choices (C) and (D) because the product and quotient of a positive and a negative number will be negative. Now try choice (A): $5 + \left(-\frac{1}{4}\right) = 4\frac{3}{4}$. (B): $5 - \left(-\frac{1}{4}\right) = 5\frac{1}{4}$. (E): $\left|5 \times \left(-\frac{1}{4}\right)\right| = \left|-\frac{5}{4}\right| = \frac{5}{4}$. Choice (B) is the greatest.

44.   G   Solve for x: add 1 to both sides to get $\frac{x}{3} = -\frac{13}{12} + 1$, or $\frac{x}{3} = -\frac{13}{12} + \frac{12}{12}$. Simplify to $\frac{x}{3} = -\frac{1}{12}$. Multiply both sides by 3 to get $x = -\frac{1}{4}$. Only choice (G) is true.

45.   B   Because the statement includes an absolute value, you'll need to solve it twice: once assuming the expression inside is positive, once assuming it's negative. First, the positive assumption: $2z - 3 \geq 7$, so $2z \geq 10$ and $z \geq 5$. Eliminate choices (C), (D), and (E). Now, assume the expression is negative: you'd multiply a negative number by -1 to make it positive, so $-(2z - 3) \geq 7$. Solve by multiplying both sides by -1 (remember to flip the sign): $2z - 3 \leq -7$, so $2z \leq -4$ and $z \leq -2$. Eliminate choice (A). Alternatively, you could try substituting in values for z. Try $z = 4$: $|2 \times 4 - 3| = |8 - 3| = |5| = 5$. This expression is supposed to be ≥ 7; since it isn't, you can eliminate any answer choices that include $z = 4$, so eliminate choices (C), (D), and (E). Try $z = -3$: $|2 \times (-3) - 3| = |-6 - 3| = |-9| = 9$. This is ≥ 7, so z could be equal to -3; therefore, eliminate choice (A).

46.   H   To simplify this expression, recall the identity $\tan x = \frac{\sin x}{\cos x}$. Now $\frac{\sin^2 x}{\cos x \tan x} = \frac{\sin^2 x}{\cos x \left(\dfrac{\sin x}{\cos x}\right)}$. Simplify: $\dfrac{\sin^2 x}{\cos x \left(\dfrac{\sin x}{\cos x}\right)} = \frac{\sin^2 x}{\sin x} = \sin x$.

47. D Try the values of x given in the answer choices in the expression. Try $x = -4$:

$$\frac{a(-4)-b(-4)}{4a-4b} = \frac{-4a-(-4b)}{4a-4b} = \frac{-4a+4b}{4a-4b} = \frac{-(4a-4b)}{4a-4b}. \quad \text{Since} \quad \frac{4a-4b}{4a-4b}=1, \quad \frac{-(4a-4b)}{4a-4b}$$

simplifies to -1. Since $-1 < 0$, $x = -4$ is valid: eliminate choices (B), (C), and (E). Now try $x = -\frac{1}{4}$:

$$\frac{a\left(-\frac{1}{4}\right)-b\left(-\frac{1}{4}\right)}{4a-4b} = \frac{-\frac{1}{4}a-\left(-\frac{1}{4}b\right)}{4a-4b} = \frac{-\frac{1}{4}a+\frac{1}{4}b}{4a-4b} = \frac{-\frac{1}{4}(a-b)}{4(a-b)} = \frac{-\frac{1}{4}}{4} = -\frac{1}{16}. \text{ This is also less than}$$

0, so eliminate choice (A).

48. J The original volume of the figure is described by the equation $V = \frac{1}{3}\pi r^2 h$. The new cylin-

der has had its radius halved and its height doubled, so the volume of the new cylinder will be

$V = \frac{1}{3}\pi\left(\frac{r}{2}\right)^2(2h) = \left(\frac{1}{3}\right)\pi\left(\frac{r^2}{4}\right)(2h) = \frac{1}{6}\pi r^2 h$. This volume is then one-half of the earlier volume,

and the ratio is 1:2. If you selected choice (H), be careful—you may have forgotten to square the new

radius value.

49. B Al's biking time going up the hill was m minutes, and because he went down the hill twice as fast,

his time going down was $\frac{1}{2}m$. His total time going up and down the hill was therefore $m + \frac{1}{2}m$

or $\frac{3}{2}m$. If you pick choice (D), be careful—you're not done here! The variable m represents the

time in minutes, and the question asks for the time in hours; therefore, you need to divide the total

value by 60: $\dfrac{\left(\frac{3}{2}m\right)}{60} = \dfrac{3}{120}m = \dfrac{m}{40}$.

50. J Since the wheel's diameter is 10, you can find the circumference ($C = \pi d$) of Pippin's wheel:
    $C = \pi d = 10\pi$. This means Pippin's wheel travels 10π inches in one rotation. Since her wheel
    rotated 15 times, multiply $10\pi \times 15 = 150\pi$.

51. D Draw a horizontal line, which is also the radius of the circle, from the center of the circle to the

right side of the square: this creates a 45°-45°-90° triangle. Recall that the ratio of sides in this type

of triangle is $s:s:s\sqrt{2}$. To find the length of the sides, and hence the radius, divide the hypotenuse

(x) by $\sqrt{2}$, giving $\dfrac{x}{\sqrt{2}}$, which, after multiplying by $\dfrac{\sqrt{2}}{\sqrt{2}}$ to rationalize the denominator, becomes

$\dfrac{x\sqrt{2}}{2}$, choice (D). You just found the radius, so choice (E) is wrong.

52. K No restrictions are needed because $f_{(x,y)} = f_{(y,x)}$ in all cases. Follow the same rules as the original function, just switch x and y. Because $-2yx = -2xy$, this is the same result that $f_{(x,y)}$ produced in the question and $f_{(y,x)} = -2yx + x + y - 4$. Therefore, all values of x and y will result in $f_{(x,y)} = f_{(y,x)}$, so choice (K) is correct. If you don't see this relationship immediately, you can use real numbers to test each of the answer choices. The question has already told you that $f_{(2,3)} = -11$, so see if $f_{(3,2)} = -11$ also. According to the original definition, $f_{(3,2)} = -2 \times 3 \times 2 + 2 + 3 - 4 = -12 + 1 = -11$. This means that $x = 2$ and $y = 3$ satisfy the goal $f_{(x,y)} = f_{(y,x)}$; therefore, eliminate choices (G), (H), and (J). Now you need to find out whether both variables must be positive, so try negative values: $x = -2$ and $y = -3$. $f_{(-2,-3)} = -2 \times -2 \times -3 + (-3) + (-2) - 4 = -12 - 3 - 2 - 4 = -21$ and $f_{(-3,-2)} = -2 \times -3 \times -2 + (-2) + (-3) - 4 = -12 - 2 - 3 - 4 = -21$. Since both are equal to -21, x and y don't have to be positive, so eliminate choice (F).

53. C *Each of the smaller pipes can handle exactly half as much water as the large pipe* means that the area of the cross-section of the small pipe is one-half the area of the cross-section of the large pipe. So start by finding the area of the circular cross-section of the large pipe: $A = \pi r^2$, so $A = \pi r^4 = 16\pi$. Therefore, the area of the cross-section of the smaller pipe is one-half that, or 8π. So for the smaller pipe's circular area $8\pi = \pi r^2$, $8 = r^2$, $r = \sqrt{8} = \sqrt{4} \times \sqrt{2} = 2\sqrt{2}$.

54. H The height (which we'll call h) divides this figure into two right triangles, each with base length of 3 feet. Tangent is the ratio of the opposite side to the adjacent side, so $\tan 40° = \dfrac{3}{h}$. Solve for h by multiplying both sides by h: $h(\tan 40°) = 3$, so $h = \dfrac{3}{\tan 40°}$.

55. C Sketch the girls' paths out on the coordinate plane. They start at school $(0,0)$, then Susan walks to $(-8,2)$ and Cindy walks to $(3,-1)$. Use the distance formula $\left(d = \sqrt{(x_1 - x_2)^2 + (y_1 - y_2)^2}\right)$ to find how far apart their homes are: $d = \sqrt{(-8-3)^2 + (2-[-1])^2} = \sqrt{(-11)^2 + 3^2} = \sqrt{121+9} = \sqrt{130} \approx 11.4$.

56. G If a is a positive integer and b is a negative integer, the only answer choice that will never yield a negative exponent (and therefore a fraction) is choice (G). If you're unsure, try substituting values for a and b. Let's say $a = 2$ and $b = -3$. Choice (F) becomes $3^{2-3} = 3^{-1} = \dfrac{1}{3}$; that's not an integer, so you can eliminate choice (F). Likewise, for choice (H), $3^{2(-3)} = 3^{-6} = \dfrac{1}{3^6} = \dfrac{1}{729}$, choice (J), $3^{-2} = \dfrac{1}{3^2} = \dfrac{1}{9}$, and (K), $3^{-\frac{2}{3}} = \dfrac{1}{3^{\frac{2}{3}}} = \dfrac{1}{\sqrt[3]{3^2}} = \dfrac{1}{\sqrt[3]{9}}$. Only choice (G) gives you an integer: $3^{2-(-3)} = 3^{2+3} = 3^5 = 243$.

57. A The question tells you that $0 < \frac{y}{x}$, which means $\frac{y}{x} \neq 0$, so eliminate choices (D) and (E). The only way $\frac{y}{x}$ could be larger than y itself is if $x < 1$ and $y \geq 1$. In other words, y could be 1 in this situation, and since we are told that $\frac{y}{x} > y$, $\frac{y}{x}$ must be greater than 1. This is a tough problem, and if you're not sure how to come up with these relationships, try to find numbers that make the initial relationship true and try them out on the number line. If $x = 0.5$ and $y = 1$, then $\frac{y}{x} = 2$, for example, so you can eliminate choice (C) [and choices (D) and (E), which you've already eliminated]. You'll find that you can't get a number less than 1 for $\frac{y}{x}$.

58. F Sketch out the rectangular 100-ft by 150-ft field described in the question. The 10-ft border within the field creates a new, smaller rectangle, 80 feet by 130 feet. The largest circle that can fit in this rectangle has a diameter of 80 feet, and therefore a radius of 40 feet. If you picked choice (G), be careful—you may have forgotten to subtract 10 feet on both sides of the track.

59. D Imagine cutting an orange: the first slice (one plane) cuts it into two pieces. If you hold those two pieces together and make another slice (the second plane), you cut both of those pieces, thereby creating 4 sections. Eliminate choices (A) and (C). Now, if you repeat this orange-slicing experiment, but your second slice is parallel to the first slice, it cuts a circular slice off only one piece, thereby creating 3 sections, so eliminate choice (B). The only way to keep the orange in two pieces after the first slice is for the second slice to repeat the first exactly. Since the question said the sphere was to be cut by two *different* planes, this cannot happen; therefore, it's impossible to get only 2 pieces, so eliminate choice (E).

60. K "Positive difference" means that when you subtract $a - b$ you can get +5 or −5. (That's also what the absolute value indicates.) Solve for a in both cases: $a - b = 5$, so $a = b + 5$; and $a - b = -5$, so $a = b - 5$. Now subtract these two values: $(b + 5) - (b - 5) = b + 5 - b + 5 = 10$, choice (K). Alternatively, you could substitute a number for b: let's say $b = 2$, so $|a - 2| = 5$. Then solve: $a - 2 = 5$, so $a = 7$; and $a - 2 = -5$, so $a = -3$. The positive difference is $7 - (-3) = 7 + 3 = 10$.

READING TEST

1. C When the narrator first sees her gift, her first response is confusion, followed by devastation that she won't be able to show her gift off to the other girls at school. Eliminate choice (A). She then recognizes that her father put a lot of effort into her gift and tries to be grateful. Eliminate choice (D). She then returns to being confused as to why they made her this house instead of buying her the real Barbie Dream House. Eliminate choice (B). That leaves choice (C), the correct answer. Disappointed and upset as the narrator is, the passage does not state that she hates the house.

2. F   The narrator of the story explains that only when she and her sister could smell coffee were they allowed to go downstairs to start Christmas. Therefore, choice (F) is the best answer. Choice (G) incorrectly refers to breakfast, which is not mentioned in the passage. Choice (H) incorrectly refers to the narrator's father's preparation of a gift instead of general morning readiness. Choice (J) is incorrect because the passage explicitly states that the narrator was expected to wait in the kitchen for her parents; she just burst in ahead of them one year because she was too excited to wait.

3. B   The narrator talks about her dream of owning the Dream House in the second paragraph, when she says "I knew that if I could only have a Dream House of my own, my life would be complete." Therefore, choice (B) is the best answer, as it is a good paraphrase of that statement. Choice (A) incorrectly refers to the other girl who owns the house and is not meant to be taken literally. Choice (C) confuses the actual result, based on her parents' hard work, with the narrator's dream, based on buying a particular toy. Choice (D) refers to the narrator's eventual comment that she will pass her gift on to her children someday, but that refers not to the Dream House but to her father's actual gift.

4. G   The first paragraph describes the family's tradition of waiting until the parents have had a chance to wake up and make coffee before beginning to open the presents. Choice (G) is the best paraphrase of that summary and is the best answer. Choice (F) might be true but it is not mentioned in the passage and is not the best summary of the entire paragraph. Choice (H) states the opposite of what the passage says. Choice (J) is true, but is not the main point of the paragraph.

5. A   When the narrator first sees her handmade doll house, she is confused and upset as she compares her house to her idealized Barbie Dream House. Choice (A) is the best paraphrase of her reaction. Choice (B) is incorrect because although the narrator does eventually try to be grateful, that is not her first response and she is not immediately successful in her attempt. Choice (C) goes against the passage—she compares the old-fashioned style of her house with the modern Barbie house and finds her house lacking. Choice (D) is incorrect because that was her goal before she saw her house, when she believed she would receive the official Barbie Dream House.

6. H   The narrator's father is described in a few different places in the passage. First, he is overheard reassuring Mel, the mother, regarding Christmas. Then, when he is preparing to present his daughter with her gift, he is described as *smiling anxiously*. Finally, the narrator eventually realizes that her father had "spent countless hours working on the house." Therefore, choice (H) is the best characterization of the father in the story.

7. A   In lines 25–30, the narrator overhears her parents discussing Christmas, wondering what they will do. This implies that there is some kind of problem. Her father then proceeds to make a home-made version of the Dream House that his daughter wants, implying that for some reason, he cannot give her the gift she wants but is willing to work very hard to give her something similar. Therefore, choice (A) is the best answer, because it explains what problem might cause him to act in such a manner. Choice (B) is incorrect because it refers to an early comment regarding a previous Christmas, not the one being described. Choice (C) is incorrect because there is no evidence

that the father made the dollhouse because he had always wanted to do so. Choice (D) is incorrect because the fact that the father put so much time and effort into making the dollhouse implies that they do in fact want their daughter to be happy.

8.   J   At the end of the passage, the narrator comments that she still has the dollhouse and that she hopes to someday tell her own children the story of how she got it. Therefore, choice (J) is the best answer, since it refers only to her hopes of passing on the story. Choice (F) incorrectly refers to the narrator's initial hopes of impressing other children with an official Barbie Dream House. Choice (G) focuses on the possible value of the house, which is not discussed in the passage. Choice (H) is incorrect because the narrator did not in fact appreciate the gift initially.

9.   D   The narrator concludes, at the time of the gifting, that although she does not like her dollhouse as much as she would have liked a Barbie Dream House, it must have taken her father a lot of time and effort to build. Therefore, choice (D) is the best answer. Choice (A) is incorrect because she refers to the dollhouse as a crude approximation of what she wanted. Choice (B) is incorrect because the absence of an elevator is not mentioned in the passage. Choice (C) is incorrect because there is no evidence that her eventual decision to pass the house on to her children was anticipated by her or her parents at the time when it was given to her.

10.   J   The last paragraph is told as if the narrator is looking back on her childhood and having trouble remembering the events that followed the previous part of the passage. She reflects that she now more fully understands her parents' actions and wishes she could go back in time and explain things to her younger self. Therefore, the best answer is choice (J). Choice (F) might be true, but the focus of the last paragraph is on the narrator as an adult, not as a child. Choice (G) is incorrect because the passage does not discuss the narrator's sister's gift. Choice (H) is too negative—the narrator is looking back on the events with greater wisdom and understanding, not bitterness.

11.   D   This passage describes the formation and activities of the CCC. No one was "forced" to work in the CCC, so you can eliminate choice (A). The CCC did employ many veterans, but nothing in the passage supports the claim that veterans had suitable employment "only after" the creation of the CCC.

12.   G   While choice (F) is true, it isn't the main idea of the paragraph. Choice (H) is incorrect because the bonuses were never paid. For choice (J), the paragraph says that the age restriction was waived, but at no point does it say how many of these veterans were over the age limit. Only choice (G) gives a reasonable summation of the content of the paragraph.

13.   D   The passage states that Roosevelt "also cared about the fate of trees, having practiced the art of silviculture on his Hyde Park estate with such enthusiasm that on various official forms he was fond of listing his occupation as 'tree farmer.'" Choice (A) makes an assumption that is not supported in the passage; there is nothing to suggest that his interest in silviculture predated his political life. Choices (B) and (C) are not supported in the passage. Only choice (D) is supported by the sentence cited above.

14. **G** Read this question carefully. The lines you need are 61–63: "For the National Park Service, they built roads, campgrounds, bridges, and recreation and administration facilities." This clearly supports choice (G). The other activities in the answer choices are mentioned in the passage, but not as things the CCC did *for the National Park Service*.

15. **A** Starting on line 72, the passage reads, "the program taught more than a hundred thousand to read and write, passed out twenty-five thousand eighth-grade diplomas and five-thousand high-school diplomas." This line most clearly supports choice (A). Choices (B) and (D) contain deceptive language from elsewhere in the passage, but they do not describe the CCC. Choice (C) is a trap because of the placement of the word *only*. As written, choice (C) means that all men the CCC accepted were those with six teeth.

16. **G** Lines 24–25 describe the terms of payment in the CCC, so eliminate choice (F). Line 58 describes the "4.1 million man-hours" spent fighting forest fires; it does NOT say that the CCC employed 4.1 million men, so eliminate choice (H). The states referred to in choice (J) are described in the passage as the sites of "flood control projects," not firefighting projects. Only choice (G) has support in the passage.

17. **C** Lines 60–61 describe the "first major reforestation campaign in the country's history." Although the specific years during which this reforestation campaign took place are unclear, the campaign must have taken place after the establishment of the CCC in 1933. It can therefore be inferred, because this was the "first," that the nation had not undergone a major reforestation campaign before, as choice (C) suggests.

18. **F** Lines 11–16 state the following: "When he went to Congress for authorization of the program, he called the new agency the Civilian Corps Reforestation Youth Rehabilitation Movement, but before sinking under the weight of an acronym like CCRYRM, it was soon changed to the Civilian Conservation Corps (known forever after as the CCC)." These lines describe the change, and only choice (F) is supported by the time of these events. The only other answer that might work chronologically would be choice (G), but nothing in the passage supports the claim that Congress complained about the length of the name.

19. **C** Lines 29–30 state that the "men had to be US citizens between the ages of seventeen and twenty-seven (later twenty-four)." Since the question asks about enrollees when the CCC was founded, you can disregard the "later" age; choice (C) gives the correct age range.

20. **G** Lines 21–24 state that "the Departments of Agriculture and Interior... would design and supervise projects in regional and national forests, national parks, and other public lands." These lines give direct support to choice (G), and show that the others are incorrect or inadequate responses to the question.

21. **C** This passage deals with the importance of the totem pole and the role the totem pole plays in Native American culture. Even with this very general overview of the passage, the only answer that fits is choice (C). The others are too specific or suggest incorrectly that the tone of the passage is negative.

22. **G** The question in choice (F) is answered in lines 2–3. The question in choice (H) is answered in line 65–66. The question in choice (J) is answered in lines 8–9. Only the question posed in choice (G) goes unanswered in the passage. The discussion in the fourth paragraph is distracting, but notice this paragraph does not claim that the pole in Pioneer Square is the largest.

23. **C** Note the opening sentence of the fifth paragraph on line 39: "Poles serve the important purpose of recording the lore of a clan, much as a book would." The other choices describe some minor functions of totem poles, but only the function described in choice (C) is described as "important."

24. **G** This paragraph describes the meanings of some of the symbols used on totem poles. Choice (F) would be fine if it did not contain the word "every." Clearly, a short paragraph cannot describe *every* possible symbol. There are no regional comparisons, so you can eliminate choice (H). Choice (J) is too limited. Think in terms of the larger point of this paragraph; it describes figures other than the Raven. Only choice (G) adequately describes the main idea of the paragraph.

25. **D** Choice (A) is addressed in lines 40–41. Choice (B) is addressed just after this in lines 42–44. Choice (C) is addressed in lines 64–66. Choice (D) may seem like it is addressed in the passage, but read this part of the passage carefully. There is no reference to the importance of this pole in Native American culture; after all, the group that took it, according to line 33, were "Seattle businessmen," not the Tlingit.

26. **J** Choice (F) is addressed in lines 13–15. Choice (G) is addressed in line 12. Choice (H) is addressed in line 17. Choice (J) is not addressed in the passage; the "family crest" is mentioned in line 16, but there is no evidence in the passage that the poles were constructed exclusively by clans who had family crests.

27. **B** As lines 39–41 indicate, one of the main functions of the poles is to identify the lore of a clan. The points referred to in choices (A), (C), and (D) are mentioned, but none could be described as a "main point." Only choice (B) is general enough to be described as a "main point."

28. **J** When the Tlingit are introduced in line 31, they are described as coming from "the southeastern coast of Alaska." Only choice (J) could work. Don't be distracted by the other places mentioned in this paragraph; those places may have some significance for the Tlingit, but could not be described as the "home of the Tlingit."

29. **A** This paragraph is used to conclude some of the ideas in the preceding paragraphs and to suggest the broader importance of totem poles beyond their physical beauty. Choices (B), (C), and (D) all use words from the passage, but they use those words in misleading ways. Only choice (A) can be supported by evidence from the passage.

30. **H** All we know about the employers is that they "complained that their Indian workers were unreliable when a pole was being carved or a potlatch planned" (lines 27–28). Because this is the only reference the author gives to these employers, we can only infer that the employers were "irritated," as choice (H) suggests.

31. C   Lines 14–16 state, "…in the present climate of fiscal austerity, there is no telling when humans will next get a good look at the earth's nearest planetary neighbor." Choice (A) can be eliminated because the author is clearly not cheerful and optimistic. Choice (B) can be eliminated because the author's tone does not suggest sarcasm or condescension. Choice (D) can be eliminated because of the word *withdrawn*. Only choice (C) is supported by the lines quoted above: he is doubtful ("there is no telling") and pragmatic ("in the present climate of fiscal austerity").

32. H   Lines 28–33 discuss the state of scientific knowledge before the arrival of *Pioneer Venus*. The paragraph discusses in detail the differences in surface temperatures and atmospheric pressures. Choice (G) is too strong: the two planets are not "twins," but the passage does not say that they are anything like "polar opposites." The best answer is choice (H), because the paragraph details the objections to the term *twins*.

33. D   This question asks about the same portion of the passage as question 32. Lines 28–33 detail some of the ways in which the "twin" characterization of Earth and Venus was reconsidered. The main evidence in this paragraph relates to surface temperature and atmosphere.

34. G   The paragraph in question concerns the *Magellan* and *Pioneer Venus* missions. Each mission studied different elements of Venus's physical composition, and the information from each can be used in tandem with the other. The missions are contrasted, but neither is cast in a negative light, so you can eliminate choices (F) and (H), and choice (J) is too narrow in that it does not include the findings of the *Magellan*. Only choice (G) adequately summarizes the paragraph.

35. C   Lines 34–35 state, "Even aside from the heat and the pressure, the air of Venus would be utterly unbreathable to humans." It then goes on to discuss the atmospheric conditions in more detail. Choice (C) is the only one of the answer choices that addresses these issues. Choices (B) and (D) describe the physical properties of the planet, but they do not give any indication why human survival would not be possible. Eliminate choice (A) because it is not the mistaken belief that makes survival impossible—the belief is mistaken because survival would be impossible.

36. J   Choice (J) is supported in lines 31–32, which say that Venus's "surface temperature of 450 degrees Celsius is hotter than the melting point of lead." Choice (H) is misleading; these physical properties describe the Earth. Choice (F) can be eliminated because "lead" is introduced as a point of comparison, not as one of the constitutive elements of Venus's surface. Choice (G) can be eliminated because it does not contain any mention of Venus.

37. C   The full sentence in lines 56–57 reads as follows: "Unlike the Earth, Venus harbors little if any molecular oxygen in its lower atmosphere." In other words, Venus contains or holds or has little if any molecular oxygen in its lower atmosphere.

38. H   The word *primordial* appears in line 65. The lines that follow state that Venus is "more primordial" than Earth because it "has held on to a far greater fraction of its earliest atmosphere." Only choice (H) contains the appropriate reference to these early formations.

39. A The full sentence starting on line 57 establishes a clear link between the activity of these plants (i.e., living things) and the composition of the earth's atmosphere. The only answer that even mentions the earth is choice (A), and this choice provides a reasonable paraphrase of the passage.

40. J Choice (J) is the only answer that accurately paraphrases lines 20–22.

SCIENCE TEST

1. C Looking at Table 1 and examining the trials with coin samples II and IV shows that electric current is held constant at 2,000 mA. The current does not change, eliminating choices (A) and (B). The variable that does change is the identity of precious metal solution. For coin sample II exposed to silver nitrate, 4.0 mg of precious metal plates. For coin sample IV exposed to copper sulfate, only 2.4 mg of precious metal plates. Therefore, choice (D) is eliminated and choice (C) is correct.

2. F The precious metal solutions react with zinc to form a coating of pure precious metal on the coin samples. If the available surface area exposed to the solutions decreased, the amount of precious metal coating is expected to decrease. There is no specific evidence in the passage to support the plating amount remaining constant or increasing.

3. A Table 2 shows that increasing the exposure time of a zinc coin to silver nitrate results in higher concentrations of zinc nitrate in the surrounding solution. Therefore, choices (C) and (D) are eliminated. The passage states that *silver nitrate, formed when silver dissolves in nitric acid, reacts with zinc to form solid silver and zinc nitrate.* Therefore, increasing the amount of silver nitrate available to react with zinc is expected to result in higher concentrations of zinc nitrate. This eliminates choice (B) and makes choice (A) the best answer.

4. H The question describes using the same sized sample of zinc and same exposure time as Experiment 1. Table 1 shows that when electric current is increased from 1,000 to 2,000 mA for zinc coins exposed to copper sulfate for 30 minutes, the plated copper increases from 1.2 to 2.4 mg. 1,580 mA is between 1,000 and 2,000 mA, so the amount of plated copper should fall between 1.2 and 2.4 mg.

5. D In the description of Experiment 1, all coin samples were stated to have a radius of 1 cm. Table 1 shows that the change in mass from precious metal plating, electric current applied, and identity of precious metal solution used were not constant for samples I–IV.

6. G The passage states that *silver nitrate, formed when silver dissolves in nitric acid, reacts with zinc to form solid silver and zinc nitrate.* Therefore, when zinc is plated with solid silver, zinc nitrate is also formed as a product. Choices (F), (H), and (J) are not involved in this reaction.

7. B   Melting point is the temperature at which a substance changes from a solid to a liquid. Any compound with a melting point above 215 K will still be a solid at that temperature. For alkanes, according to Table 2, only octane will still be a solid at 215 K. Octane must be in the answer, and on this basis alone, choices (A), (C), and (D) can all be eliminated, leaving only choice (B). The remaining data in choice (B) are supported in Table 2 as well.

8. F   According to Table 3, the 8-carbon alcohol has the highest value for viscosity. Referring to Table 1 for the prefix and suffix of the compound's name, the structure is called octanol.

9. D   Reading across any single row of Table 3 demonstrates that for a fixed number of carbons in the molecule, the alcohol has the highest viscosity. This eliminates choices (A) and (B). Further, for any given row, the alkane has the lowest viscosity, eliminating choice (C).

10. G   Reading down any single column in Table 2 demonstrates that as the number of carbons in the molecule increases, the melting point increases. Therefore, choices (F) and (J) are eliminated. Reading down any single column in Table 3 demonstrates that as the number of carbons in the molecule increases, the viscosity increases as well, eliminating choice (H) and making choice (G) the correct answer.

11. C   Compare the melting points of the alkanes and alcohols in Table 2. For any given number of carbons in the molecule, the melting points between these two types of compounds differ by varying but similar amounts between 41 and 57 K. Of the possible answer choices, choice (C) is the best approximation of the average of these differences.

12. G   When testing the effects of different variables, all variables must be held constant except those being tested. To determine the effects of drag force or air resistance, therefore, all variables except drag force and air resistance must be held constant. Altering the apparatus to use a spring makes this into a completely different experiment, so choices (F) and (H) are eliminated. To negate the effects of air resistance, using a vacuum with no air pressure would be best, making choice (G) the best answer.

13. A   In experiments, more precision is nearly always better. A timer that reads to the nearest second can give only whole number results. Therefore, it would read either "1" or "2" for each trial. This would not greatly alter the results for the tin cube (Trials 1 and 5 would be 2 sec, and Trials 2–4 would be 1 sec for an average of 1.4 sec). However, all of the trials for the lead cube would round down to 1 sec for an average of 1 sec. This is significantly different from the 1.46 sec obtained with the more precise timer, eliminating choices (C) and (D). Choice (B) is eliminated because the period of both pendulums is greater than 1 sec, meaning they would travel a shorter distance in 1 second than they would in the time it takes them to complete a cycle.

14. H   Choices (F) and (G) are true statements, but they do not explain why forces other than gravity must be acting on the pendulums. The passage states that for a *simple gravity pendulum, gravity is the only force acting on the mass causing an acceleration of 9.8 m/sec²*. The times obtained in Experiments 1 and 2 resulted in acceleration calculations less than this, indicating some other force was slowing the pendulum down (air resistance and friction). This eliminates choice (J) and makes choice (H) the best answer.

15. D   Comparing the results of Experiments 1 and 2 presented in Tables 1 and 2, doubling the length of the thread from 0.5 m to 1.0 m increases the observed period. Since the average period observed for the tin cube in Experiment 2 (pendulum length of 1.0 m) was 2.09 sec, doubling the length of the thread once again would be expected to result in an increase in average period observed.

16. G   The text below Table 2 states that the average period for the lead cube in Experiment 2 was 2.06 sec. An additional trial of the same experiment would be expected to give a result closest to this value.

17. D   For both Experiments 1 and 2, comparisons between the lead and tin pendulums held length and starting angle constant, eliminating choices (A), (B), and (C). The mass and density of the lead and tin cubes were different. The main difference noted in the text of the passage is that between the masses of the two objects, so choice (D) provides the best-supported option.

18. F   In the description of the Coevolution Hypothesis, the passage states that *RNA sequences developed enzyme-like abilities including the ability to self-replicate*. Development of capsids was mentioned in the Regressive Evolution Hypothesis, but not in Coevolution, eliminating choice (G). DNA was not mentioned in the Coevolution Hypothesis, eliminating choice (H). Cell membrane transit was mentioned only in the Cellular Origin Hypothesis, eliminating choice (J).

19. D   The first paragraph states that biologists agree that viruses originated from nucleic acid. Choice (A) is eliminated because the Coevolution Hypothesis does not provide an explanation for viruses evolving from bacteria. Choice (B) is eliminated because according to the passage, viruses cannot replicate unless they first infect a cell. Choice (C) is eliminated because only the Regressive Evolution Hypothesis and Coevolution Hypothesis mentions anything about viruses having membranes or envelopes.

20. J   The Coevolution Hypothesis specifically mentions that the first virus particles were RNA nucleotides with enzyme-like activity that incorporated into protein structures. Therefore, choices (F), (G), and (H) are all eliminated. DNA is not mentioned as a component of the earliest virus particles in this hypothesis.

21.   B   The Cellular Origin Hypothesis states that viruses originated from cellular-organism ancestors. They could have come from prokaryotic or eukaryotic organisms, and the type of ancestor cell does not necessarily determine what type of cell they will evolve to infect. Therefore, choices (C) and (D) are eliminated because they cannot necessarily be determined from the information given. Given that both T4 and PP7 infect bacteria, they likely contain genetic material similar to the bacteria they infect. However, given that one is a DNA virus and one is an RNA virus, if they are related at all it is likely through a very distant ancestor virus that escaped a cellular organism long ago. This eliminates choice (A) and makes choice (B) the best answer.

22.   H   Since the Regressive Evolution Hypothesis suggests that viruses originated from obligate intracellular parasites, one would expect that they would share features of these ancestors. The hypothesis specifically states that intracellular parasites evolved into viruses, eliminating choices (F) and (G). Between the remaining choices, finding a parasite with DNA similar to a known virus could suggest that this organism and the known virus evolved from a common ancestor, making choice (H) the best answer.

23.   B   The passage states that viruses cannot replicate unless they first infect a cell. Therefore, the first viruses were unlikely to originate before cells, making choice (B) the best answer. There is nothing in the passage to support that viral capsids are similar to bacterial cell walls, and the word "capsid" does not even appear in the first hypothesis, eliminating choice (A). Choice (C) is eliminated because the differences in RNA and DNA viruses are not elaborated in the passage. Moreover, given that RNA viruses are mentioned in the Coevolution Hypothesis and DNA viruses are mentioned in the hypotheses that relate to more complex cellular organisms, it seems unlikely that RNA viruses would be considered more advanced than DNA viruses. Choice (D) is eliminated because the Coevolution Hypothesis specifically states that the first viruses contained RNA.

24.   F   The incorporation of RNA sequences into protein structures versus cell structures is specifically mentioned in the Coevolution Hypothesis. Choices (G) and (J) relate to the Regressive Evolution Hypothesis and choice (H) relates to the Cellular Origin Hypothesis.

25.   C   Table 1 shows that as organic cover percentage increases, erosion from topsoil deflation decreases, eliminating choices (A) and (B). Choices (C) and (D) both state that increased rainfall will reduce erosion as shown in Table 3. The choice comes down to the type of topsoil. Tables 1 and 3 consistently show that Soil Y resists erosion more than Soil X does, eliminating choice (D).

26.   G   Soil X contains 5% clay and Soil Y contains 40% clay. A soil with 10% clay should have topsoil deflation between the values for X and Y with 0% organic cover in Table 1, eliminating choices (F) and (J). Since 10% clay is most similar to the 5% clay found in Soil X, the topsoil deflation value is expected to be closer to 105,000 kg/ha than to 65,000 kg/ha, eliminating choice (H) and making choice (G) the best answer.

27. D Only Experiment 2 involved a variation in water content, eliminating choices (A) and (B). Between choices (C) and (D), only choice (D) provides a clear manner of comparing soils with different water contents.

28. H Experiment 1 investigates wind erosion of different types of topsoil with varying amounts of organic cover. If the fans did not adequately simulate the effects of real wind, it would be difficult to apply the findings to any practical situation, making choice (H) the best answer. Choice (F) is not an assumption but a variable being tested by the experiment. Choice (G) is the opposite of an assumption made in the experiment, that compost and straw do adequately simulate vegetation and organic cover. Choice (J) is not addressed in Experiment 1 because water content is not varied.

29. C Table 3 demonstrates that regardless of the water content, Soil X with the smaller clay percentage is more prone to topsoil deflation, making choice (C) the correct answer. Table 3 shows that erosion is related to water content for both soils, eliminating choice (A). Further, erosion takes place in the presence of water content, eliminating choice (B). Finally, Table 3 demonstrates that increased water content tends to decrease topsoil deflation, eliminating choice (D).

30. F Soil X contains 5% clay and Soil Y contains 40% clay. A soil with 10% clay should have water content and topsoil deflation in Tables 2 and 3 that are between the values for Soils X and Y after 8 hours of sprinkling. Choices (H) and (J) have water contents that are too low, and choice (G) has an erosion value that is too low. Therefore, only choice (F) can be correct.

31. C According to Figure 1, bathypelagic, mesopelagic, and epipelagic zones are all within mutually exclusive depth ranges. In other words, none of them overlap, so answer choices (A), (B), and (D) are all eliminated and only choice (C) is possible. Depths between 100 and 200 m can be categorized in either the epipelagic or thermocline zone according to Figure 1.

32. J According to Figure 1, when total pressure is 1,200 kPa, the ocean zone can be classified as epipelagic, continental shelf, or thermocline. Therefore, choice (J) is the best answer. Choices (F) and (G) are at higher pressures, and choice (H) is at a lower pressure.

33. C The points on Figure 2 where the two oceans would be indistinguishable for any temperature and depth combination would be where the two lines intersect. The tropical and temperate lines on Figure 2 intersect at two points, at depths of approximately 125 m and 625 m. This makes choice (C) the best answer. All other answer choices give depths where the two lines would yield different values of temperature and would thus be distinguishable from one another.

34. G The general trend for both regions in Table 1 is a decrease in ocean temperature with an increase in depth. This eliminates choices (F) and (H). However, Region 2 had a temperature of 8°C at a depth of both 39.7 m and 49.6 m whereas Region 1 showed a decrease in temperature for every increased depth. Therefore, only Region 1 showed a consistent decrease in ocean temperature with increasing depth.

35.　B　Both Figure 1 and Table 1 demonstrate that as depth increases, total pressure increases. If the pressure at 79.5 m is 900 kPa, it would be expected to increase beyond 900 kPa at greater depth. Only choice (B) is possible. Note that choice (D) is eliminated because it is impossible to increase from 900 to 101 kPa.

36.　J　Looking at Figure 1, since 800 mg of sulfamethoxazole results in greater bacterial elimination than 400 mg over time, choices (F) and (G) are both eliminated. Table 1 provides insight to the mechanism of action of sulfamethoxazole, so choice (H) is also eliminated. According to Figure 1, combining sulfamethoxazole (SMX) with either doxycycline or azithromycin increases overall elimination of a common skin infection bacterium, making choice (J) the best answer.

37.　A　According to Figure 1, it takes 120 minutes for an 800 mg dose of sulfamethoxazole to achieve 80% bacterial elimination and hence 20% original bacterial survival. At the same time, the 400 mg dose only achieves between 40–50% elimination. A 600 mg dose would be expected to give results between these two values at the 120 minute mark. Therefore, only choice (A) is possible because the time required to reach 20% survival would be greater than 120 minutes for a 600 mg dose.

38.　F　According to the passage and the data in Figure 1, penicillin is not very effective against the bacterium studied, but it does eliminate some bacteria, eliminating choices (H) and (J). In the experiment in the passage, less than 10% of the bacteria are eliminated by penicillin after 120 minutes (2 hours), meaning most survived. Therefore, choice (F) is better than choice (G).

39.　D　Figure 1 shows greater bacterial elimination by doxycycline and azithromycin when compounded with sulfamethoxazole (SMX). This eliminates choices (A) and (B). Choice (C) is a true statement. However, even though sulfamethoxazole 800 mg is more effective than SMX/azithromycin according to the figure, this does not answer the question of whether or not azithromycin is more effective when *combined with* sulfamethoxazole. Therefore, choice (D) is the best answer.

40.　H　The passage describes the goal of antibiotics as eliminating bacteria, so choices (F) and (G) are incorrect. From the data in Figure 1, it can be inferred that antibiotics that eliminate a large amount of bacteria in a short amount of time are most effective. This eliminates choice (J) and makes choice (H) the best answer.

WRITING TEST

To grade your essay, see the Essay Checklist on the following page. The following is an example of a top-scoring essay for the prompt given in this test. Note that it's not perfect, but it still follows an organized outline and has a strong introductory paragraph, a concluding paragraph, and transitions throughout.

The traditional academic calendar of school in the fall, winter, and spring, with summers off, was developed to accommodate the needs of an agrarian society. Simply put, children were needed to work in the fields during the summer. There is an argument that spring break existed to allow for help with planting, and fall break to help with the harvests. Although the shape of our nation has changed dramatically since the academic calendar was created, there are still powerful reasons for keeping it in place: School has become much more stressful, and students need the break during summer; colleges have become much more expensive, and students need the chance to earn money in the summer; childhood is something special, and the things which make it special should not be casually stripped from the young simply because we're no longer a nation of farmers.

Contrary to high school in years past, high school is no longer a gentle nine-month trek through classes. High school today is a very difficult academic exercise designed to prepare students for college, not just for getting a job when they graduate. Consequently, the classes have become harder, and the amount of homework and other preparation has increased. Every student has heard his or her parents comment that they never worked so hard when they were in school. The fact is, this is the truth. Students today have to take AP classes (which are really college-level classes in high school) if they are serious about getting into a top college. These classes run all year and end with a very difficult exam in May. The amount of work being demanded from students is so high that during the year many students need help coping with the stress. If summer vacation did not exist and students had to go at this pace all the time, it would be disasterous.

Furthermore, summer is also for more than just recovering from the school year. Most students today have jobs in the summer, which are critically important to their ability to pay for college. Because college has become more expensive, and because financial aid is so hard to get, many high school students work during the summers. The money they earn is usually for their college savings, although some of them even give this money to their families to help support them. If this flow of money were cut off, perhaps some students would not be able to afford college, or their families would suffer.

Also, we should be cautious about altering the academic calendar in high school because summer vacation is one of those things that make being a child special. Every parent has fond memories of their summers playing, and tells those stories to his or her children. Teachers talk about this in classes as well. The truth is, there is a difference between children and adults, and we should not act rashly to take away those things which mark that difference. We should be cautious when considering decisions that will make childhood less like childhood and more like the "real world" inhabited by adults. Although it is hard to explain in a concrete way exactly how this is a damaging thing to do, that difficulty makes it no less damaging. The simple pleasures mean a lot and should be protected, not eliminated in the name of efficiency.

For a wide variety of reasons, from the very concrete to the somewhat abstract, it would be a bad idea to force students to go to school year-round. Although there may be problems like overcrowding, which cause administrators to consider abolishing the academic calendar and going to a year-round calendar, the proper solution is not changing the calendar, the proper solution is spending more money on education. Because students need a break from the rigors of the classroom, a chance to earn much needed money, and a childhood full of memories to pass on to their own kids, the academic calendar should remain the way it is.

WRITING TEST

Essay Checklist

1. The Introduction
   Did you
   - start with a topic sentence that paraphrases or restates the prompt?
   - clearly state your position on the issue?

2. Body Paragraph 1
   Did you
   - start with a transition/topic sentence that discusses the opposing side of the argument?
   - give an example of a reason that one might agree with the opposing side of the argument?
   - clearly state that the opposing side of the argument is wrong or flawed?
   - show what is wrong with the opposing side's example or position?

3. Body Paragraphs 2 and 3
   Did you
   - start with a transition/topic sentence that discusses your position on the prompt?
   - give one example or reason to support your position?
   - show the grader how your example supports your position?
   - end the paragraph by restating your thesis?

4. Conclusion
   Did you
   - restate your position on the issue?
   - end with a flourish?

5. Overall
   Did you
   - write neatly?
   - avoid multiple spelling and grammar mistakes?
   - try to vary your sentence structure?
   - use a few impressive-sounding words?

SCORING YOUR PRACTICE EXAM

Step A

Count the number of correct answers for each section and record the number in the space provided for your raw score on the Score Conversion Worksheet below.

Step B

Using the Score Conversion Chart on the next page, convert your raw scores on each section to scaled scores. Then compute your composite ACT score by averaging the four subject scores. Add them up and divide by four. Don't worry about the essay score; it is not included in your composite score.

Score Conversion Worksheet		
Section	Raw Score	Scaled Score
1	_____ /75	_____
2	_____ /60	_____
3	_____ /40	_____
4	_____ /40	_____

SCORE CONVERSION CHART

Scaled Score	Raw Scores			
	Test 1 Engish	Test 2 Math	Test 3 Reading	Test 4 Science
36	75	60	40	40
35	73–74	59	39	39
34	72	58	38	––
33	71	57	37	38
32	70	54–56	36	37
31	69	52–53	35	36
30	68	50–51	34	––
29	66–67	48–49	33	35
28	65	46–47	32	33–34
27	63–64	44–45	30–31	32
26	61–62	42–43	29	31
25	59–60	40–41	28	29–30
24	57–58	37–39	26–27	28
23	55–56	35–36	25	26–27
22	52–54	33–34	24	24–25
21	49–51	31–32	23	23
20	46–48	29–30	21–22	21–22
19	44–45	26–28	20	19–20
18	41–43	23–25	19	17–18
17	39–40	20–22	18	14–16
16	36–38	17–19	16–17	13
15	33–35	14–16	15	11–12
14	31–32	12–13	14	09–10
13	29–30	10–11	12–13	08
12	27–28	08–09	10–11	06–07
11	25–26	06–07	09	05
10	23–24	05	07–08	––
09	22	04	06	04
08	18–21	––	––	03
07	15–17	03	05	02
06	12–14	02	04	––
05	09–11	––	03	––
04	07	––	––	01
03	05–06	01	02	––
02	03–04	––	01	––
01	00–02	00	00	00

Part X
Paying for College 101

If you're reading this book, you've already made an investment in your education. You may have shelled out some cold hard cash for this book, and you've definitely invested time in reading it. It's probably even safe to say that this is one of the smaller investments you've made in your future so far. You put in the hours and hard work needed to keep up your GPA. You've paid test fees and applications fees, perhaps even travel expenses. You have probably committed time and effort to a host of extracurricular activities to make sure colleges know that you're a well-rounded student.

But after you get in, there's one more issue to think about: How do you pay for college?

More Great Titles from The Princeton Review
Paying for College Without Going Broke,
The Best 378 Colleges

Let's be honest, college is not cheap. The average tuition for a private four-year college is over $33,000 a year. The average tuition of a four-year public school is about $6,695 a year. And the cost is rising. Every year the sticker price of college education bumps up about 6 percent.

Like many of us, your family may not have 33 grand sitting around in a shoebox. With such a hefty price tag, you might be wondering: "Is a college education really worth it? The short answer: Yes! No question about it. According to a 2010 report by the College Board, the median earnings of full-time workers with bachelor's degrees were $55,700 in 2008—$21,900 more than those of workers who finished only high school.

Still, the cost of college is no joke. It's said that a college education ultimately pays for itself; however, some colleges pay better than others. It's best to be prudent when determining the amount of debt that is reasonable for you to take on.

Here's the good news. Even in the wake of the current financial crisis, financial aid is available to almost any student who wants it. There is an estimated $177 billion—that's right, billion!—in financial aid offered to students annually. This comes in the form of federal grants, scholarships, state financed aid, loans, and other programs.

We know that financial aid can seem like an overwhelmingly complex issue, but the introductory information in this chapter should help you grasp what's available and get you started in your search.

How Much Does College Really Cost?

When most people think about the price of a college education, they think of one thing and one thing alone: tuition. It's time to get that notion out of your head. While tuition is a significant portion of the cost of a college education, you need to think of all the other things that factor into the final price tag.

Let's break it down.

- Tuition and fees
- Room and board
- Books and supplies
- Personal expenses
- Travel expenses

Collectively, these things contribute to your total Cost of Attendance (COA) for one year at a college or university.

Understanding the distinction between tuition and COA is crucial because it will help you understand this simple equation:

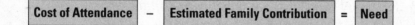

$$\boxed{\text{Cost of Attendance}} - \boxed{\text{Estimated Family Contribution}} = \boxed{\text{Need}}$$

When you begin the financial aid process, you will see this equation again and again. We've already talked about the COA, so let's talk about the Estimated Family Contribution, or EFC. The EFC simply means, "How much you and your family can afford to pay for college." Sounds obvious right?

Here's the catch: What you think you can afford to pay for college, what the government thinks you can afford to pay for college, and what a college or university thinks you can afford to pay for college are, unfortunately, three different things. Keep that in mind as we discuss financing options later on.

The final term in the equation is self-explanatory. Anything that's left after what you and your family have contributed, still needs to be covered. That's where financial aid packages come in.

Check out our Financial Aid Library
PrincetonReview.com/scholarships-financial-aid.aspx

WHAT'S IN A FINANCIAL AID PACKAGE?

A typical financial aid package contains money—from the school, federal government, or state—in various forms: grants, scholarships, work-study programs, and loans.

Let's look at the non-loan options first. Non-loan options include grants, scholarships, and work-study programs. The crucial thing about them is that they involve monetary assistance that you won't be asked to pay back. They are as close as you'll get to "free money."

Grants

Grants are basically gifts. They are funds given to you by the federal government, state agencies, or individual colleges. They are usually need-based, and you are not required to pay them back.

One of the most important grants is the Pell Grant. Pell Grants are provided by the federal government but administered through individual schools. Amounts can change yearly. The maximum Federal Pell Grant award is $5,645 for the 2013–2014 award year (July 1, 2013 to June 30, 2014).

You apply for a Pell Grant by filling out the Free Application for Federal Student Aid (FAFSA). Remember that acronym because you'll be seeing it again. Completing the FAFSA is the first step in applying for any federal aid. The FAFSA can be found online at FAFSA.ed.gov.

There are several other major federal grant programs that hand out grants ranging from $100 to thousands of dollars annually. Some of these grants are given to students entering a specific field of study and others are need-based, but all of them amount to money that you never have to pay back. Check out the FAFSA website for complete information about qualifying and applying for government grants.

The federal government isn't the only source of grant money. State governments and specific schools also offer grants. Use the Internet, your guidance counselor, and your library to see what non-federal grants you might be eligible for.

Scholarships

Like grants, you never have to pay a scholarship back. But the requirements and terms of a scholarship might vary wildly. Most scholarships are merit- or need-based, but they can be based on almost anything. There are scholarships based on academic performance, athletic achievements, musical or artistic talent, religious affiliation, ethnicity, and so on.

Believe It or Not...
The Chick and Sophie Major Memorial Duck Calling Contest, held annually by the Chamber of Commerce of Stuggart, Arkansas, gives out college scholarships to those high school seniors who can master hailing, feeding, comeback, and mating duck calls.

When hunting for scholarships, one great place to start is the United States Department of Labor's "Scholarship Search," available at CareerInfoNet.org/scholarshipsearch. It includes over 5,000 scholarships, fellowships, loans, and other opportunities.

There is one important caveat about taking scholarship money. Some, but not all, schools think of scholarship money as income and will reduce the amount of aid they offer you accordingly. Know your school's policy on scholarship awards.

Federal Work-Study (FWS)

One of the ways Uncle Sam disperses aid money is by subsidizing part-time jobs, usually on campus, for students who need financial aid. Because your school will administer the money, they get to decide what your work-study job will be. Work-study participants are paid by the hour, and federal law requires that they cannot be paid less than the federal minimum wage.

One of the benefits of a work-study program is that you get a paycheck just like you would at a normal job. The money is intended to go toward school expenses, but there are no controls over exactly how you spend it.

Colleges and universities determine how to administer work-study programs on their own campuses.

LOANS

Most likely, your entire COA won't be covered by scholarships, grants, and work-study income. The next step in gathering the necessary funds is securing a loan. Broadly speaking, there are two routes to go: federal loans and private loans. Once upon a time, which route to choose might be open for debate. But these days the choice is clear: *Always* try to secure federal loans first. Almost without exception, federal loans provide unbeatable low fixed-interest rates; they come with generous repayment terms; and, although they have lending limits, these limits are quite generous and will take you a long way toward your goal. We'll talk about the benefits of private loans later, but they really can't measure up to what the government can provide and should be considered a last resort.

Stafford Loans

The Stafford loan is the primary form of federal student loan. Loans can be subsidized or unsubsidized. Students with demonstrated financial need may qualify for subsidized loans. This means that the government pays interest accumulated during the time the student is in school. Students with unsubsidized Stafford loans are responsible for the interest accumulated while in school. You can qualify for a subsidized Stafford loan, an unsubsidized Stafford loan, or a mixture of the two.

Check out the Financial Aid Library
PrincetonReview.com/ scholarships-financial-aid. aspx

The Bottom Line? Not So Fast!
It is possible to appeal the amount of the financial aid package a school awards you. To learn more about how to do that, check out "Appealing Your Award Package" at PrincetonReview.com/ appealing-your-award.aspx

Stafford loans are available to all full-time students and most part-time students. Though the terms of the loan are based on demonstrated financial need, lack of need is not considered grounds for rejection. No payment is expected while the student is attending school. The interest rate on your Stafford loan will depend on when your first disbursement is. The chart below shows the fixed rates set by the government.

First disbursement made on or after	Interest rate on unpaid balance
July 1, 2010 to June 30, 2011	4.5 percent
July 1, 2011 to June 30, 2012	3.4 percent
July 1, 2012 to June 30, 2013	6.8 percent
July 1, 2013 to June 30, 2014	3.9 percent

As with grants, you must start by completing the FAFSA to apply for a Stafford loan.

PLUS Loans

Another important federal loan is the PLUS loan. This loan is designed to help parents and guardians put dependent students through college. Unlike the Stafford loan, the PLUS has no fixed limits or fixed interest rates. The annual limit on a PLUS loan is equal to your COA minus any other financial aid you are already receiving. It may be used on top of a Stafford loan. The interest rates on PLUS loans are variable though often comparable to, or even lower than, the interest rates on Stafford loans. Your PLUS Loan enters repayment once your loan is fully disbursed (paid out).

To become eligible for a PLUS loan, you need only complete a Free Application for Federal Student Aid (FAFSA). There are no other special requirements or forms to fill out.

Perkins Loans

A third and final federal loan you should be aware of is the Perkins loan. Intended to help out students in extreme need, the Perkins loan is a government-subsidized loan that is administered only through college and university financial aid offices. Under the terms of a Perkins loan, you may borrow up to $5,500 a year of undergraduate study, up to $27,500. The Perkins loan has a fixed interest rate of just 5 percent. Payments against the loan don't start until nine months after you graduate. Apply for Perkins loans through your school's financial aid office. More information about Perkins Loans can be found on their website, StudentAid.ed.gov/types/loans/perkins.

Private Lenders

We said it before, and we'll say it again: DO NOT get a private loan until you've exhausted all other options.

That said, there are some benefits to securing a private loan. First off, many students find that non-loan and federal loan options don't end up covering the entire bill. If that's the case, then private lenders might just save the day. Second, loans from private sources generally offer you greater flexibility with how you use the funds. Third, private loans can be taken out at anytime during your academic career. Unlike most non-loan and government-backed financial options, you can turn to private lenders whenever you need them.

All private lenders are not the same! As the old song says, "You better shop around." Every lender is going to offer you a different package of terms. What you need to do is find the package that best fits your needs and plans. Aside from low interest rates, which are crucially important, there are other terms and conditions you will want to look out for.

Low origination fees   Origination fees are fees that lenders charge you for taking out a loan. Usually the fee is simply deducted automatically from your loan checks. Obviously, the lower the origination fee, the better.

Minimal guaranty fees   A guaranty fee is an amount you pay to a third-party who agrees to insure your loan. That way, if the borrower—that is, you—can't pay the loan back, the guarantor steps in and pays the difference. Again, if you can minimize or eliminate this fee, all the better.

Interest rate reductions   Some lenders will reduce your interest rates if you're reliable with your payments. Some will even agree to knock a little off the interest rate if you agree to pay your loans through a direct deposit system. When shopping for the best loan, pay careful attention to factors that might help you curb your interest rates.

Flexible payment plans   One of the great things about most federal loans is the fact that you don't have to start paying them off until you leave school. In order to compete, many private lenders have been forced to adopt similarly flexible payment plans. Before saying yes to a private loan, make sure that it comes with a payment timetable you can live with.

IT'S YOUR CALL

Only you (and your parents or guardians) can make the decision of what is right for you. Before deciding to attend college or selecting a school, you should attempt to secure as much assistance (in the form of financial aid: grants, scholarships, work study) as you can, then weigh your options. Thankfully, there are plenty of excellent financing options out there. With a little effort (and a lot of form-filling!) you'll be able to pay your way through school without breaking the bank.

About the Authors

Geoff Martz attended Dartmouth College and Columbia University before joining The Princeton Review in 1985 as a teacher and writer. His first book for The Princeton Review was *Cracking the GMAT*, published in 1989. He is also the author or coauthor of *Cracking the GED* and *Paying for College Without Going Broke*.

Kim Magloire is a graduate of Princeton University with a master's degree from Columbia University where she is currently completing her doctorate in Epidemiology. She joined The Princeton Review in 1984 as an SAT teacher and has since taught SAT, MCAT, GMAT, LSAT, GRE, and science SAT Subject tests.

Ted Silver is a graduate of Yale University, the Yale University School of Medicine, and the law school at the University of Connecticut. He has been intensely involved in the fields of education and testing since 1976 and has written several books and computer tutorials pertaining to those fields. He became affiliated with The Princeton Review in 1988 as the chief architect of The Princeton Review's MCAT course. Dr. Silver's full-time profession is as Associate Professor of Law at Touro College Jacob D. Fuchsberg Law Center.

BONUS MATERIALS

ACT INSIDER

Admissions and Financial Aid Advice

While *Cracking the ACT* will prepare you for your exam, *ACT Insider* will help you navigate what comes next. The bonus materials included here contain invaluable information about finding your best fit college, wending your way through the financial aid process, figuring out post-college plans, extra drills, and more. We wish you the best of luck on your studies and preparation for college.

Contents

Part 1

25 Tips to Help You Pay Less for College

by Kalman A. Chany, author of
Paying for College Without Going Broke
(Random House/Princeton Review Books)

GETTING FINANCIAL AID

1. Learn how the financial aid process works. The more and the sooner you know about the process, the better you can take steps to maximize your aid eligibility.

2. Apply for financial aid no matter what your circumstances. Some merit-based aid can only be awarded if the applicant has submitted financial aid application forms.

3. Don't wait until you receive an acceptance letter from your top choice school to apply for financial aid. Do it when applying for admission.

4. Complete all the required aid applications. All students seeking aid must submit the FAFSA (Free Application for Federal Student Aid); however, other forms may also be required by individual schools. Check with each college to see what's required and when.

5. Get the best scores you can on the SAT or ACT as they are used not only in decisions for admission but also financial aid. If your scores and other stats exceed the school's admission criteria, you are likely to get a better aid package than a marginal applicant.

6. Apply strategically to colleges. Your chances of getting aid will be better at schools that have generous financial aid budgets.

7. Don't rule out any school as too expensive. A generous aid award from a pricey private school can make it less costly than a public school with a lower sticker price.

8. Take advantage of education tax benefits. A dollar saved on taxes is worth the same as a dollar in scholarship aid. Look into Coverdells, education tax credits, and loan deductions.

SCHOLARSHIPS AND GRANTS

9. Get the best score you can on the PSAT: It is the National Merit Scholarship Qualifying Test and is also used in the selection of students for other scholarships and recognition programs.

10. Check your eligibility for grants and scholarships in your state. Some (but not all) states will allow you to use such funds out of state.

11. Look for scholarships locally. Find out if your employer offers scholarships or tuition assistance plans for employees or family

members. Also look into scholarships from your church, community groups, and high school.

12. Look for outside scholarships realistically: they account for less than five percent of aid awarded. Research them at PrincetonReview.com or other free sites. Steer clear of scholarship search firms that charge fees and "promise" scholarships.

PAYING FOR COLLEGE

13. Invest wisely. Considering a 529 plan? Compare your own state's plan which may have tax benefits with other states' programs. Get info at savingforcollege.com.

14. If you have to borrow, first pursue federal education loans (Perkins, Stafford, PLUS). Avoid private loans at all costs.

15. Never put tuition on a credit card. The debt is more expensive than ever given recent changes to interest rates and other fees some card issuers are now charging.

16. Try not to take money from a retirement account or 401(k) to pay for college. In addition to likely early distribution penalties and additional income taxes, the higher income will reduce your aid eligibility.

PAYING LESS FOR COLLEGE

17. Attend a community college for two years and transfer to a pricier school to complete the degree. Plan ahead: Be sure the college you plan to transfer to will accept the community college credits.

18. Look into "cooperative education" programs. Over 900 colleges allow students to combine college education with a job. It can take longer to complete a degree this way but graduates generally owe less in student loans and have a better chance of getting hired.

19. Take as many Advanced Placement (AP) courses as possible and get high scores on AP exams. Many colleges award course credits for high AP scores. Some students have cut a year off their college tuition this way.

20. Earn college credit via "dual enrollment" programs available at some high schools. These allow students to take college level courses during their senior year.

21. Earn college credits by taking CLEP (College-Level Examination Program) exams. Depending on the college, a qualifying score on any of the thirty-three CLEP exams can earn students three to twelve college credits. (See Princeton Review's *Cracking the CLEP*—5th Edition.)

22. Stick to your college and your major. Changing colleges can result in lost credits. Aid may be limited/not available for transfer students at some schools. Changing majors can mean paying for extra courses to meet requirements.

23. Finish college in three years if possible. Take the maximum number of credits every semester, attend summer sessions, and earn credits via online courses. Some colleges offer three-year programs for high-achieving students.

24. Let Uncle Sam pay for your degree. ROTC (Reserve Officer Training Corps) programs available from United States Armed Forces branches (except the Coast Guard) offer merit-based scholarships up to full tuition via participating colleges in exchange for military service after you graduate.

25. Better yet: Attend a tuition-free college!

Part 2

7 Essential Tips for Writing Your College Essay

Most selective colleges require you to submit an essay or personal statement. It may sound daunting to represent your best self in only a few hundred words, and it will certainly take a substantial amount of work. But it's also a unique opportunity that can make a big difference at decision time. Admissions committees put the most weight on your high school grades and your test scores. However, colleges receive applications from many worthy students and use your essay (along with your letters of recommendation and extracurricular activities) to find out what sets you apart from the other talented candidates.

1. What does set you apart?

Your background, interests and personality combine to make you more than just a GPA and a standardized test score. The best way to tell your story is to write a personal, thoughtful essay about something that has meaning for you. If you're honest and genuine, your unique qualities will shine through.

2. Sound like yourself!

For examples of strong application essays, check out The Princeton Review's book, *College Essays that Made a Difference*.

Admissions counselors have to read an unbelievable number of essays. Many students try to sound smart rather than sounding like themselves. Others write about a subject they don't care about, but that they think will impress admissions brass. Don't write about the same subjects as every other applicant. You don't need to have started a company or discovered a lost Mayan temple. Colleges are simply looking for thoughtful, motivated students who will add something to the freshman class.

3. Write about something that's important to you.

It could be an experience, a person, a book—anything that has had an impact on your life. Don't just recount—reflect! Anyone can write about how they won the big game or the time they spent in Rome. Describe what you learned from the experience and how it changed you.

4. Be consistent and avoid redundancies.

What you write in your application essay or personal statement should not contradict any other part of your application, nor should it repeat it. This isn't the place to list your awards or discuss your grades or test scores. Answer the question being asked. Don't reuse an answer to a similar question from another application.

5. Use humor with caution!

Being funny is a challenge. A student who can make an admissions officer laugh never gets lost in the shuffle. But beware: What you think is funny and what an adult working in a college thinks is funny might be very different. We caution against one-liners, limericks and anything off-color.

6. Start early and write several drafts.

Set the essay aside for a few days and read it again. Put yourself in the shoes of an admissions counselor: Is the essay interesting? Do the ideas flow logically? Does it reveal something about the applicant? Is it written in the applicant's own voice?

7. Ask for feedback!

Have at least one other person edit your essay—a teacher or college counselor is best. And before you send it off, triple check to make sure your essay is free of spelling or grammar errors. We recommend asking a second person to proofread your essay, as spellcheck and grammar software won't pick up every typo. It can be tricky to spot mistakes in your own work, especially after you've spent so much time writing and rewriting.

Part 3

Planning
the Perfect
College Visit

By The Staff of The Princeton Review

WHY SHOULD YOU DO A CAMPUS VISIT?

A campus visit won't tell you everything you need to know about life at your prospective college, but it will give you a richer, more detailed view than you would get from surfing websites, browsing brochures, watching videos, or reading college guides. Every school has its own culture, its own unique way of doing things, something you can't divine from a brochure! And even though you won't learn all there is to know from a brief visit, you'll get a sense of the "big picture" issues that define life on a campus. You'll probably get enough of a sense of those issues to determine whether the school is a good fit for you.

Spend a weekday on campus while classes are in session and you'll get a feel for the rhythm of life there, the attitudes of the students toward their studies, and—if you get the chance to attend a few classes—some idea of the atmosphere in the classrooms. Visit over a weekend and you'll experience the school's social life (or lack thereof). You'll also find students relaxing and taking it easy, making it easier to approach them with any questions you may have about the school.

Let's look at some of the benefits of a campus visit:

You'll get a feel for the type of student who attends the school

For many students, whom they go to school with is just as important as where they go to school and what they study. You may think this is a frivolous concern, but it's not; your fellow students will be your peers, friends, competitors and, in some cases, rivals throughout your tenure at the school. If you're a bad fit with the student body, you could be in for four miserable years (fewer, probably, because most "bad fits" eventually transfer out; regardless, being the "sore thumb" at a school is an unpleasant scenario that you'll probably want to avoid).

There are lots of different issues to consider as you assess a student body. First, note the degree of similarity among students. Do they all look alike, or is the population diverse? Consider not just racial diversity but also economic diversity, religious diversity, and diversity of personality types. Are you more comfortable surrounded by people just like yourself, or do you want a college that will give you the opportunity to encounter people with different backgrounds and perspectives? More specifically, think about:

- *Personality type:* Do you see lots of students in sweats and sneakers? Or are most students decked out in alpaca sweaters, skinny jeans, or pearls? Is the campus an ocean of polo shirts? The way students dress can tell you about more than their economic status; it can also tell you about the group or personality type with which they associate. You'll be surprised at how many students you will immediately identify as jocks, hippies, preps, nerds, etc. You've probably encountered most of these personality types in high school. Which type reigns supreme on campus, if any? Is this a group you're comfortable spending four years among? Keep in mind, of course, that you can't judge a book entirely by its cover. Before you draw any definitive conclusions about students' personalities, talk with some students. You may well find that college students don't fit your assumptions as neatly as do your peers in high school.

- *Intellectualism:* Observe students in class, at the library, and in conversation as they walk across campus. Do you get the sense that students study primarily for the sake of learning? Or is their primary goal to score a high-paying job? If you're the type who wants to stay up all night discussing Plato, you won't likely be happy at a school full of pre-professionals with little interest in pure academics. Conversely, if your only goal is to get great grades in order to get into the best med, law, or b-school, you probably won't be happy at a school with a bunch of philosophizing dreamers.

- *Class/Status:* Is the parking lot filled with new sports cars and SUVs? Or are most of the cars clunkers (if they are, make sure you haven't stumbled onto the faculty parking lot by mistake!)? Do students dress as though they do all their shopping at high-priced, name-brand stores? Do the men and women seem especially fashion-conscious? Are they wearing nice but affordable clothing? Are students flashing a lot of high-priced gadgets or the newest, hottest technology? Ask yourself, "Can I envision myself a part of this community?" For many students, answering this question means having to think about class issues and the social circles they feel the most comfortable navigating.

- *Religion:* Are students religious? Are there frequent and obvious demonstrations of religious belief across campus? Deeply religious students may find the rampant secularism of many college campuses off-putting. Students with a more secular bent will likely have a hard time adjusting to life on deeply religious campuses, particularly those with strict behavioral codes or those where students openly proselytize.

- *Sexuality/Gender Issues:* To what extent do couples display affection on campus? Do you see indicators of an active and accepted gay community (e.g., posters for GLBT events)? Here's another area where it can be important to find a good personal fit. Socially conservative students may be uncomfortable on a campus with a large and active gay community, such as New York University or Smith. Conversely, gay students may be uncomfortable on campuses with profoundly conservative social attitudes.

While it's important for the school's academic program to be the right fit for you, it's just as important for the campus community to be a good fit, too. A college visit, even a brief one, will give you a good sense of who your classmates will be and whether you'll be comfortable among them. Yes, it's true: You really can't know exactly what a school is going to be like until you get there. Even your own opinion of your college experience will change as you grow more accustomed to being on campus. In the meantime, as you're searching, trust your instincts. The real "scoop" lies not so much in the specific information you receive, as the applicability of the information to your interests, needs, and wants.

So know your priorities. Exactly what type of atmosphere are you looking for? Urban or rural? Big or small? Laid-back or focused? Getting a handle on what will make you happy and settled at college is half the battle.

You'll get a feel for the academic atmosphere and whether it's a good fit for you

Academics are the primary reason you're attending college, so you want to know whether you and the school you're considering are a good academic fit. The quality of the school's academic life and the intensity of student-teacher relationships will strongly impact your experience at college. Look for clues about both during your campus visit.

If possible, attend a class or two during your visit (make sure to arrange for this with the Admissions Office well in advance). If asked for your preference, request to sit in on a class that is required for all freshmen so that you'll get a better sense of what your first year will be like—or, alternatively, try to pick a low-level class within the subject you're planning to major in, if you've already decided that. When you're there, keep your eyes and ears open. Are the classes huge or small? Is the teacher a full professor or a graduate student? Is the class format lecture, lab, discussion, or a hybrid of several formats? Are student contributions to the class interesting? Are students furiously scribbling notes? Are they asking questions? Is "Will this be on the test?" the only question any of them asks? Answer these questions and you'll get a pretty good sense of how students approach their studies at the school and whether you'll be comfortable with that approach.

If you can't attend a class, at least take time to walk around campus and to observe the students and faculty. Pay close attention to students as they travel to and from class. Are they in a hurry? Do they look stressed? Or are they walking at a leisurely pace, conversing, and laughing? Do faculty members talk with students as they walk across campus? Do you even see faculty members walking across campus, or are they missing from the picture? If faculty members are conspicuously absent, it could mean that they have numerous commitments off campus (e.g., conferences, serving on corporate boards, or teaching at more than one school) that would leave them less time to devote to undergraduates on campus.

You'll get a feel for extracurricular life

Your college experience will consist of more than studying and hanging out with friends. There will be all sorts of clubs and organizations available for participation, and you may want to join one or more, which why it's important to explore the extracurricular life of a school. What do students do when they're not in class, in the library, or hanging around the dorms with friends? Look for the following:

- *Active clubs and organizations:* All schools have some clubs and organizations, but what those are exactly will vary from school to school. You can find out which clubs are registered on campus by visiting the student activity center, where a list of the school's organizations is usually posted. In addition, most schools list all their clubs and organizations on their websites and many provide separate sites for each group. Look for posters announcing meetings and events to determine which groups are most active.

- *Greek organizations:* Does the school have a Greek scene? How active is it? Is it simply one aspect of campus life or is it the dominant feature? Are lots of students wearing T-shirts and sweatshirts emblazoned with the names of their houses? Are there posters around campus announcing upcoming parties at Greek houses? Ask students—Greeks and independents alike—about the school's fraternity and sorority scene. Their answers will reveal what you can expect from the social scene on campus.

- *The party scene:* The Greek scene and the party scene are synonymous at some schools, but not at all of them. Some schools have no Greek organizations while others place strict restrictions on Greek parties, forcing the party scene elsewhere. At many schools the Greek houses are the locus of parties for underclassmen, while students of drinking age prefer local bars or even smaller parties at their apartments or houses. And some schools have minimal party scenes: military academies, single-sex schools, and religious schools are the most likely candidates, but small schools with large commuter populations or a large in-state population (at some schools, in-state students leave campus for the weekend immediately after their last class of the week) can also be relatively party-free. Whether you're looking for a year-round Mardi Gras, a cloister, or something in between, you should consider the school's party scene when choosing your undergraduate institution. Even if you have no interest in partying—especially if you have no interest in partying, really—the intensity of the party scene will have a big impact on your life at school. During your visit, survey the campus for evidence of an active party scene: dumpsters full of empties, posters advertising huge blowout parties, bleary-eyed students in pajamas straggling across campus in the early afternoon, etc. Better still, schedule a weekend visit so you can experience the party scene firsthand.

- *The arts:* Some schools house well-known museums and frequently host touring theatrical, musical, and dance productions. Others host regular student theatrical and musical productions, galleries displaying student and faculty art, and a steady diet of movies, old and new. Still others have practically no arts scene at all; there's no interest on campus, so it doesn't exist. If your idea of fun is a Truffaut double feature or a night of experimental theater, make sure you find a school that can accommodate you. Scan the bulletin boards for notices about upcoming arts events. Survey the campus map for evidence of student galleries, art and dance studios, concert halls, etc.

- *Athletics:* Most schools have some form of an athletic program, but the degree to which athletics are a major campus focal point varies greatly from school to school. At some schools, football or basketball season is the high point of the school year; students are passionate about their teams and build their schedules around games, camping out to get tickets and tailgating enthusiastically for hours before the start of an event. You'll see evidence of students' devotion at these sports-happy schools in the form of banners, pennants, bumper stickers, T-shirts, etc. At other schools, athletics are an afterthought, and if you ask students about the football team they're likely to respond, "We have a football team?" If college athletics are important to you, you probably shouldn't attend such a school.

- *The neighborhood around campus and the school's hometown:* Try to save time to tour the town or city in which the school is located. If you can't, at least take a walk around the surrounding neighborhood to see what sort of off-campus housing, restaurants, clubs, and retail shops are easily accessible. If you visit enough schools, you'll probably notice that campus life is generally much more active in schools located in smaller towns. At big-city schools—in New York City, Boston, and Chicago, for example—students tend to seek their fun off-campus, and with good reason: Few schools could compete with all the options that a big city offers.

Keep in Mind:
Before you embark on a college visit, be sure to check out our comprehensive guide Best 378 Colleges and our website PrincetonReview. com to get some preliminary information about the schools you may want to visit.

WHEN IS THE BEST TIME TO VISIT COLLEGES?

There are two timing issues to consider in this question: the best time in the school's schedule, and the best time for you as a high schooler. Let's look at both.

Best Times To Visit During The College Academic Year

The best time to visit a school is when the school is in session. Yes, it's probably easier to visit during the summer when you're on vacation, but the trouble is that the school is on break then, too. You'll be able to see the campus and take a tour, but you won't be able to attend classes (summer classes are nothing like classes held during the regular academic year) and you won't get to see what the campus looks like when it's full of students. You won't get to see the students (or most of the professors and administrators, for that matter), so you won't be able to get a sense of how well you'll fit into the campus community. You won't get a good feel for the school and so will miss out on the most important part of your campus visit.

Be sure to check out the school's website and academic calendar to figure out which are the best days to visit.

During the school year, avoid visiting during school holidays such as Thanksgiving and Spring Break. Also, try not to visit during exam periods or reading periods (the few days or week of study time that precedes final exams, during which no classes are scheduled). It'll be difficult to attend a class during those times, and students will be preoccupied with exams and probably a little frazzled. They won't be in the mood to chat, because they won't have the time. Visit during these periods and you'll get a skewed impression of the school. You'll probably walk away thinking the students are all basket cases!

Fitting a College Visit Into Your High School Schedule

Exploit your vacation time and off days. When is your spring break? Use it to visit colleges that aren't on break at the same time. Check your school's calendar for three-day weekends; some colleges don't observe national holidays so you can use those weekends for a Sunday overnight visit and attend some college classes on Monday. Remember that overnight visits should be scheduled well in advance as they require extra planning both on your part and on the part of the school.

As for your own schedule, when is the best time in your high school career to visit colleges? The short answer is that, essentially, any time is good once you start seriously considering college choices. In practice this can depend on what your goals for the trips are, where you already are in the college application process and, of course, financial constraints.

Some students prefer to wait until they've already applied and have heard back from schools, using visits to help make their decision between schools where they've already been accepted. This can also help avoid spending money on visiting a school where they aren't accepted. In this case, you'd necessarily need to plan visits in the spring of your senior year.

In an ideal world, though, you could visit schools earlier in the process in order to decide where you want to apply. During your sophomore year and the autumn semester of your junior year, you should try to visit lots of different types of schools—big schools, small schools, urban campuses, suburban/rural campuses, private liberal arts schools, public universities—to see what options are available to you. Intensify your efforts during the spring semester of junior year and throughout senior year, and also intensify your focus; hone in on those schools about which you are most serious. While you're a junior and during the autumn semester of senior year, you should try to pay daytime visits to all the schools on your short list, while trying to schedule overnight visits for at least some of the schools that interest you most.

When you reach the end of your visits and it comes time to compare the schools you visited, remember to take into account the time of year you went. Most campuses are at their most alluring in the early autumn and late spring. Conversely, some schools can be pretty austere, even forbidding, in the height of winter. Don't let the season of your visit unduly influence your final decision positively or negatively.

HOW TO ASK THE RIGHT QUESTIONS

No matter how the information session is organized, at some point you'll get a chance to ask questions. Do so! It gives you a chance to learn about something that truly interests you and also provides an opportunity to impress the session leader with what an articulate and thoughtful person you are.

Lots and lots of questions are listed later, but here are a few rules of thumb when asking questions:

Ask about something that is of particular interest to you

Do you hope to study abroad in a particular country? Ask about the availability of international education programs. Are you interested in pursuing independent study in a particular field? Ask about the opportunities and resources that will be available to you. Would you like to get related work/internship experience while at school? Ask about available cooperative learning programs.

Don't ask about data and other information that can be easily found in the school's promotional material

Asking about average SAT scores, the number of volumes in the school library, the student:teacher ratio, etc., communicates that you are too lazy to find this readily accessible information yourself. It also suggests that you're asking a question simply for the sake of it, which fails to demonstrate genuine interest in attending that particular school.

If you are accompanied by your parents, politely suggest that they let you ask most of the questions

The school is considering you for admission, not your parents and those that ask long-winded questions designed mostly to show off how much they know about the school may think they are making a good impression, but their effect is actually the opposite.

Be polite

Present yourself well; don't slouch, don't chew gum, and speak politely. If your parents are with you, don't bicker with them. And for goodness' sake, don't tell the person conducting the information session that the school is your "safety" or that you'll only attend if you receive a monster scholarship (true stories). Remember: tact is key.

GUIDELINES FOR PARENTS

Be supportive, be positive and be patient: A college visit is a stressful time for everyone. Behave in a way most likely to minimize stress.

Schedule plenty of extra time in your itinerary

Nothing creates stress more effectively than running late for important appointments. Plan to spend at least three hours on each campus you visit. Build plenty of buffer time into your travel plans to and from campuses and to and from appointments on campus. Follow these guidelines and you shouldn't find yourself constantly rushing from one place to the next. Worst case scenario, you'll have some extra time on one of the campuses you're visiting—that's a win-win. Use the extra time to check out popular campus hangout spots.

Don't try to run the show

From the planning of the trip through its execution, consult with your child about the itinerary. Is he or she ready for on-campus interviews? How many campuses does he or she feel capable of assimilating in one day? Once on campus, resist the temptation to advocate for your child or to manage the on-campus experience. Give your child plenty of opportunities to explore on his or her own. And under no circumstances should you try to participate in your child's on-campus interview. It sends a terrible message to the school (i.e., our child is not self-sufficient enough to handle this experience) and almost always produces bad results.

Utilize your child's free time efficiently

While your child is exploring campus on his or her own, make your own inquiries. Check out the surrounding area to see whether it looks safe. Search for reasonably priced restaurants and shopping near campus. Visit dormitories, dining halls, computer labs, science labs, arts facilities, and whatever else might be of interest to your child.

Take pictures

Let's face it—this is way too embarrassing for your kid to be seen doing (your students will be focused on fitting in, not standing out!), but you, on the other hand, can snap away without any embarrassment. These photos will go a long way toward helping your child compare schools later.

Talk to other parents

Find out what other parents think about the school, what concerns they have, and what their questions are. Listening to them will help clarify some of your own concerns—you may even learn about a new scholarship, a new college financing program, or the name of another great school for your child to consider!

GUIDELINES FOR STUDENTS

Set goals in advance

What exactly do you hope to learn from your visit? Know before you go and you'll get a lot more out of it. Make a list of questions you want to answer during your trip (and check out the lists provided for you at the end of this book). You may not get to ask all your questions, but just having a list will help focus your observations while on campus.

Wear comfortable shoes but dress nicely

You'll be doing a lot of walking, so choose shoes that won't turn your feet into hamburger meat. Otherwise, dress nicely; remember, you're a guest in someone else's home and you should carry yourself accordingly. This doesn't mean you need to dress in a three-piece suit; wearing a tasteful shirt or blouse and clean pants (jeans or khakis) or a skirt is completely fine. A presentable outfit is especially important if you've scheduled an on-campus interview.

Don't be afraid to ask questions during your tour

Don't be shy. You're on campus to find out what you need to know; asking questions is the best way to get that done. Don't hog the tour guide's attention but don't be a wallflower either.

Don't be unduly influenced by the tour guide

Your tour guide may seem really cool, or may seem like a total dork. Either way, the guide is just one of many students who attend the school; don't judge the school based on this one person. Try to meet as many other students as you can to get a broad picture of the student body. Visit the student center and the dining hall. Introduce yourself to students and ask if they wouldn't mind answering questions. If possible, schedule an overnight visit with a stay in a host student's dorm room (many colleges offer this—just talk to the admissions office when you're scheduling your visit).

Keep a journal

We don't mean you actually have to take notes while you're visiting campus, although it's not a bad idea! At the very least, you should record your observations and insights about each campus you visit at the end of each day. You'll probably be visiting a lot of campuses and a journal will help you remember what you liked and didn't like about each school you visited.

Snap a few pictures. Maybe you can recruit your parents to be the "real" tourists, but even if not, take pictures of things about the campus that you really like so you can look back on the day when it's time to make decisions about which schools to take off your list.

9 STEPS TO A SUCCESSFUL VISIT

The logistics of organizing a multi-stop, multi-day trip can be a daunting task. Following the nine steps outlined below makes it a lot easier.

Step 1: Determine when you are free to take a trip

Check your school calendar to figure out when you have weeks off, three-day weekends, etc. If you plan to miss a day or two of school in order to accommodate your trip, figure out when your exams are scheduled and make sure you're not traveling during those days or during the week before.

Step 2: Identify all the schools you want to visit and then group them by geographic area

Collate the academic schedules of the schools you wish to visit with the dates of your planned trip. If possible, plan to visit the geographic region whose schools mesh best with your travel days. Try to avoid visiting campuses during holidays (e.g., Thanksgiving, Christmas, and Spring Break), reading periods, and exam periods.

Step 3: Create an itinerary

Map out the locations of the schools you plan to visit. If you have to fly to visit colleges, try to coordinate general geographic regions, and figure out

For help in identifying top colleges within a certain region, please visit PrincetonReview.com/ best-regional-colleges. aspx

if you'll be able to rent a car to drive between locations. If driving, try to map a course that connects the schools in a single loop in order to minimize driving time. Even if you're interested in three schools within a half-hour of each other, plan to visit no more than two schools per day.

Step 4: Tinker with the itinerary

Now that you know where you're going, look closely at the map. Are there other schools you might consider that are along your route? Make a note to squeeze in a quick visit to one or more schools. Also, take time to find out whether there are some fun sights to see along the way. Yeah, this trip is about seeing schools, but that doesn't mean you can't have a little fun, time permitting.

Step 5: Call the admissions offices of the schools you plan to visit

Schedule an interview if you choose to. Find out what time tours begin and end. If you're scheduling more than one campus visit per day, make sure to leave extra time at each school to wander around campus, talk with students, and explore the neighborhood and town surrounding the school.

Step 6: Create a daily schedule

Start with the appointments you've made and then figure out when you have to arrive and leave each school in order to make it to all your appointments. Use an online itinerary planner (such as Google Maps, Rand McNally, or Mapquest.com) to estimate your travel time between schools.

Step 7: Make your overnight arrangements

Find places to stay. If you're planning on staying on campus, make sure to contact the school and make arrangements at least two weeks in advance. Calling a month in advance is better; two months in advance, better still. If you travel with your parents, they will probably need to find a place to stay off campus. Contact the school to ask for recommendations. Schools sometimes have prearranged discount rates with local hotels and motels.

Step 8: Write out or print out your entire itinerary

Be sure it includes maps to and from schools and hotels, driving directions, all the phone numbers you may need, etc. Research any local dining and shopping establishments you're interested in visiting and print out their names, addresses, and telephone numbers.

Step 9: Write out a list of questions you want to ask at the schools

This is the only way to avoid that "Rats, I wish I'd asked about…" feeling that comes about an hour after you've left the campus. We have lists and lists of questions at the end of this book to help you make sure you get all the information you need—be sure to read them through, adding any questions particular to *you*.

When you finally hit the road, don't forget to enjoy yourself. Yes, college visits are important and should be taken seriously, but they are also wonderful adventures to new and exciting places. Soak it all in and be grateful that you're smart enough and capable enough to be looking forward to a college education. It's easy to take all that for granted, but you don't have to step back too far to gain some perspective and realize what a fortunate position you're in. So don't be afraid to have a little fun on your trip; you've earned it!

KEY PLACES TO VISIT

Remember to leave time after the tour/information session to walk around campus on your own. Although the promotional material, the tour, and the information session will all be helpful, they all represent an image of the school packaged by public relations professionals. You want to spend some time seeing the school without that filter. Visit whatever buildings you can access without school identification. High on your list of "must visit" places should be the main freshman dormitory (you'll probably be living there if you attend) and the dining hall (buy lunch and try to imagine eating this food every day of the week; also, try to work your way into a group of current students chatting among themselves on campus so you can ask them about the school); finally, make sure you visit the general information library (this is where books for required courses will be on reserve and thus is a place where you could spend a lot of your freshman year). You should also check out the student union, the athletic facilities, and any other facilities you expect to use. Are all these facilities up-to-date and well maintained? Can you imagine yourself happy in this setting? You should also spend some time exploring the neighborhood around campus.

You should try to attend at least one class while on campus. This will require some extra planning, as you will probably need to schedule your classroom visit in advance with the admissions office. Ideally, the school will send you to a class that's required for all freshmen. Unless the professor calls specifically on you, do not try to participate in the class. You are just there to observe, not to overwhelm your future classmates with your brilliance. Stay for the entire class no matter how boring it is; it's rude to get up and leave a class that's in session. And this may go without saying, but please remember to turn off your cell phone before you enter the classroom!

That's a whole lot of activity to cram into one visit, which is one of the reasons admissions professionals advise against visiting more than two campuses in one day. The other reason is sensory overload—visit more than two schools in a day and they all start to blend into one amorphous blob! Take notes during your visits (or immediately after) so that you can remember what you liked and disliked about each school. If you visit a lot of schools you will have a hard time remembering which details pertain to which school if you don't take notes.

Your campus visit presents an incredible opportunity to get the skinny on life at college from the real experts—the students in attendance. Don't be shy about going up to a student and asking them the tough questions—you'll be happy you did.

THE ESSENTIAL TIP LIST FOR GETTING THE MOST OUT OF YOUR COLLEGE VISIT

It's sometimes helpful to have everything boiled down to the basics, this section condenses our most essential tips for getting the most out of your college visit into one place. If your college visits are spread out over a long period of time and you don't have time to go back and re-read a section, or you want a quick reminder about what to look for right before you hit a campus, just visit this section for a refresher!

Visit as many colleges as you can

If possible, visit every college that you are strongly considering. Many students change their minds after a college visit. That's great—it means the visit has done its job. And this is obviously preferable to changing your mind after you enroll!

Mind the calendar

Schedule your visit while school is in session. You won't get a realistic idea of student life in August (or if you attend during a special event like Spring Fling).

Meet the experts

Talk to the current students—they may soon be your peers. If they have a problem or grievance, they will probably share it with you and if they love their school, they won't be shy about it either. Specific questions yield far more interesting (and helpful) answers. Here are a few questions to ask:

- What are the best reasons to go here?

- Why made you choose this school over others that you were considering?

- What do you do on weekends?

- What do you love about this college?

- What things frustrate you about this college?

- What do students complain about most?

- Did you have friends that were going here before you?

- Have you changed your major? (If so, why?)

- Are students friendly?

Meet the other experts

Stop by the admissions office and introduce yourself. Let them know what interests you about the school so they can direct you to the best place for further investigation. Collect contact information and send a brief, friendly email thanking them for taking the time to talk to you. If there is a sign-up sheet, add your name! Colleges do keep track of which applicants have demonstrated genuine interest in the school. Some schools will let you interview with an admissions rep during your campus visit. If this opportunity is available, don't pass it up.

Take the campus tour

Although it's the most obvious thing to do, the official campus tour is worth your while. (Find out if you need to register to get a spot.) It gives the school a chance to show its best face, like the brand-spankin' new theater or their rooftop planetarium. While you're walking around, check out the flyers and bulletin boards and pick up a school newspaper to get a sense of what's going on … then venture out on your own. The official tour will probably steer you clear of the school's less attractive features, like the shoddy dining hall or the tiny gymnasium. Take your own unofficial tour by wandering around campus. If there are any facilities that are important to you, find them and have a look for yourself. Make sure your destinations include the freshmen dormitories.

Be a student for a day (or night)

Some schools sponsor overnight programs in which you can stay with a current student. This is a great opportunity to get a deeper sense of campus life and interact with your potential future friends and roommates. Even if you don't stay over, most schools will allow you to sit in on lectures. Browse the course catalogue before you arrive, or ask the admissions office what classes are in session that day.

Save the best for last

You'll get better at visiting colleges with practice. As you compare schools, you pick up on the aspects you like and the aspects you're not so fond of. You also figure out the right questions to ask as well as the best campus spots to gauge student life. For that reason, visit your favorite schools last, so you'll be in the best position to make comparisons to the others on your list.

Don't rush to judgment

Be careful not to rush to judgment if the weather's bad or the class you attended is boring. There are bound to be sunny days and more interesting classes. At the same time, trust your gut. Sometimes it's love at first sight. Other times, something feels wrong (even if you can't put your finger on it).

Keep a record of every college visit

We recommend jotting down a few notes after every college visit. This may seem pointless, but trust us—after visiting the ninth or tenth school, you'll have a hard time remembering which one had the killer cafeteria or the great library. Keep track of the details you like and the stuff that you don't like, and when more questions arise (as they most definitely will) you can fire off an email for an answer rather than visiting a second time. Your notes will be helpful when you decide where to apply (and, after you're admitted, where to go). They should be candid and real. They're for you—not your parents or college counselor. Be honest with yourself and trust your gut.

CHEAT SHEET: THE MOST IMPORTANT QUESTIONS TO ASK WHILE ON CAMPUS

We've compiled some of the most useful questions to ask while you're visiting colleges and grouped them by subject. Some are no-brainers—you're going to need to know about dorms pretty much everywhere—but not all of these questions will apply for every school, and you may also already be familiar with the answers from a college's admissions brochure.

We encourage you to read through the lists below and use them both as checklists and as jumping-off points for thinking about the *specific* questions you might have. Your college-specific questions can be prompted either by the particular features of a school (for instance, is there a program that appealed to you in the college brochure that you want to know more about?) or about how you might fit in there (i.e., if your hobby is photography, do you want to know if there's a darkroom available on campus?).

Feel free to photocopy this list and take it with you when you're visiting schools. Use the space underneath each question as well as the sidebars to write in your answer. Even if you don't want to take actual notes while touring the campus, looking through it on your way back from a visit can help you recall what you saw and heard before it slips your mind.

Academics

- What are the most prominent majors and programs?

- Are those majors more difficult to get accepted into?

- Do they offer the major in my area of interest?

- How large or small are the classes?

- What is the student/faculty ratio (especially for the freshman class)?

- Are there freshman seminars?

- How much contact is there between students and professors?

- Are professors required to teach undergraduate courses or do they mostly focus on research?

- Are classes taught by graduate students, especially freshman classes?

- Are there research opportunities with professors?

- What is the Honors Program like?

- Is there a special winter or summer term?

- Who are the best professors?

- What is the quality of the student advising?

- Is there tutoring help on campus?

- How do we contact the office that helps students with learning disabilities?

- How do we contact the office that helps international students?

Administration

- How hard/easy is it to work with the administration?

- How hard/easy is it to work with the financial aid office?

- Does it seem like there is a lot of red tape or bureaucracy?

- How hard/easy is it to register for classes?

- How hard/easy is it to change classes/majors/departments?

- Is it easy to get face-time with administrators?

Dorm/Housing

- How many dorms are there?

- How are the dorms different from each other?

- What are the options (co-ed, suite-style, freshman, houses, honors)?

- Are students required to live on campus?

- Do most freshmen live on campus?

- Is there guaranteed housing for freshmen?

- What's the off-campus housing situation like?

- How are roommates paired up?

- What if that roommate doesn't work out?

- How many roommates per room for different dorms?

- What are the laundry facilities like?

- Are there curfews?

- What kind of security/entry is there for dorms?

- Are there refrigerators/microwaves/group kitchens?

- Are there dedicated study areas?

- Are there dorm events?

- Do the dorms close down during holidays?

Food

- What are the on-campus food options?

- What are the hours for the on-campus food options?

- What are the local/off-campus food options?

- Are there vegetarian/vegan options?

- How much of the food is bought locally?

- Is there a meal plan?

- How does the meal plan work (like debit card or per meal)?

- How much is the meal plan?

- How is the meal plan billed/paid for?

Extracurricular and Social Activities

- How many clubs, activities, and athletics are at the college?

- How do you sign up for clubs?

- What are the most popular student groups on campus?

- What is there to do on the weekends?

- Are there fraternities and sororities?

- How prominent are fraternities and sororities on campus?

- How prominent is drinking on campus?

- How prominent are drugs on campus?

- What activities are there that don't involve drinking and drugs?

- What kind of events are planned by the campus activities board?

- Are there lots of religious events?

- What kinds of events are school-sponsored?

- What kinds of speakers come to campus?

- What kinds of bands come to campus?

- Do students hang out on campus on the weekends or do they hit up local venues?

- Are there many student theater productions?

Athletics

- What kind of intercollegiate sports are prominent on campus?

- How do you purchase student tickets for sports events?

- What kind of intramural sports are prominent on campus?

- What kinds of sports facilities are available on campus?

- How much scholarship money goes to student athletes?

- What kinds of sports facilities and activities are there in the local community?

- Do athletes have special housing?

- Are admissions requirements different for athletes?

Technology

- How much of campus is Wi-Fi enabled?

- Are classrooms set up for laptops?

- Are there online classes?

- Do professors generally post class notes?

- How much of teacher-student interaction is online?

- How many computer labs are there on campus?

- Are computer labs open 24 hours?

- Are textbooks available as e-books?

Surrounding Town

- How well does the college get along with the surrounding town?

- What is the local social scene like?

- What is the crime rate in town?

- What are the job prospects like in the local town?

- What are the larger companies in town?

- Do they recruit interns from this college?

- What kinds of public transportation are available in town?

- Where is the local shopping center?

- Where is the closest grocery store?

- What other colleges are around here?

- What other towns/cities are around here?

Transportation

- Are freshmen allowed to have cars on campus?
- What is parking like?
- How much commuter parking is there?
- How much residential parking is there?
- How much does parking cost?
- Are there trolley or bus routes on campus?
- Is there transportation from campus to local areas?
- How late does that transportation run?
- Is there a bike-share program on campus?
- Is theft from cars a problem on campus?
- Is a car necessary to get around the town?
- How much will parking tickets cost?
- Is there a shuttle from campus to the airport?
- Are there late-night shuttles or taxis available?
- Is there a car-share program on campus (Zipcar)?

Study Abroad

- What percentage of students study abroad at some point during their four years?
- What countries do students go to?
- How do you sign up for study abroad?
- How do those credits count toward graduation?
- About how much does it cost?
- Does financial aid cover study abroad?

Financial

- How much is tuition?

- What other charges are there (room and board, fees, computers, etc)?

- What types of scholarships or financial aid is available?

- When are the deadlines for the forms?

- What do you need to do to apply?

- Are there jobs available on or near campus if you want to work? How easy or difficult is it to secure one?

Internships/Career

- What percentage of students receive jobs in their field of interest after graduation?

- Is there a job or career placement program?

- What internship programs or opportunities are available?

Politics

- Are students mostly conservative on campus?

- Are students mostly liberal on campus?

- Are students very politically active on campus?

Religion

- How actively religious are students on campus?

- What is the dominant religion on campus?

- How strict are the rules on campus?

- How tolerant are students of non-religious students?

Holidays/Festivities

- What is the holiday schedule for the school?
- Are the dorms closed over long holidays?
- Are there options for holiday housing?
- What are the Homecoming festivities like?
- What are holiday festivities like?
- What are some of the campus traditions?

Campus Media

- Is there a college radio station?
- Is there a campus newspaper or new website?
- Are there other student publications?

Students

- How happy are students?
- How nice are students?
- How much diversity is there on campus?
- Are students athletic-minded?
- Are students arts-minded?
- Are students involved in lots of clubs and activities?
- Is this mainly a commuter campus?
- Do students generally stay around campus on weekends?
- How tolerant are students of LGBT students?
- Where can I find the best food/coffee on campus?
- What is the school's best-kept secret?
- Can I get anything for free on campus?
- How often do you attend campus events?

Alumni

- How involved are alumni with students?

- How active is the alumni association?

- Are there alumni mentors for students?

Campus/Facilities

- Is the campus safe and secure?

- Is there a blue light system or a late-night escort system available?

- Is there a library on campus that is open 24 hours?

- How many bookstores are on campus?

- Is there a post office on campus?

- How accessible is the campus for students with disabilities?

TIPS FOR VISITING MILITARY ACADEMIES, WOMEN'S COLLEGES, AND HBCUS

Certain types of schools—such as all-women's schools, military academies, historically black colleges and universities, technical colleges, and sports-crazy schools—have readily identifiable distinguishing characteristics. You'll want to explore the issues associated with those characteristics during your visit; here's some information to get you started.

Military Academies

Federal military academies educate and train officers for the Army, Navy, and Air Force. These institutions require recommendation and appointment by members of Congress. There are certainly benefits associated with attending a United States military academy. In addition to free tuition, military academy students receive a top-notch education, a prestigious degree, and access to an unparalleled alumni network. Private and state supported military institutes, however, accept applications from students interested in attending. They all offer degree programs in engineering and technology with concentrations in various aspects of military science. When visiting a military academy, these are some of the things you should ask about:

- What is the length of the post-graduation commitment?

- What percentage of graduates receive their first choice assignments after graduation?

- What is the attrition rate for freshmen? How many leave because they "can't take it?"

- Is the campus coeducational? How fully are women integrated on campus? How are women treated by male classmates?

- Will the school accept your high school ROTC credit?

- To what extent do students get a "free ride?" Does the school charge tuition? Room and board? Other fees?

- What sort of extracurricular student activities are available? Does the average student have time to participate in these activities?

Women's Colleges

Women's colleges were originally founded in the nineteenth century to meet the educational needs of women—needs that had, up until then, largely been ignored. Independent nonprofit women's colleges were created as a counterpart to the liberal arts colleges that existed for men. Others were affiliated with religious denominations and open only to white women, while still others were founded as historically black women's colleges. While their numbers may not be as great as they once were, women's colleges have experienced a new popularity over the last several years. Competition is fierce at the most selective women's colleges, with many women choosing single-sex education not because it was the only option available to them, but because of the opportunities an all-women's college offers them.

Do you think you know all there is to know about women's colleges? Please take our Women's Colleges Quiz at inquiry. PrincetonReview.com/ ugrad/womenscollegequiz

According to the Women's College Coalition (WCC), students at women's colleges "report greater satisfaction than their coed counterparts with their college experience in almost all measures—academically, developmentally, and personally." In addition, the WCC states that women's college students "continue toward doctorates in math, science, and engineering in disproportionately large numbers." In fact, women's colleges confer a larger proportion of bachelor's degrees in traditionally male-dominated fields (mathematics, science, and engineering) than coeducational, private colleges do. Women's colleges also have a larger percentage of female faculty and administration. While many factors go into making a college choice, women's colleges are definitely worth considering. Here are some things to inquire about when you go visiting:

- What is social life like? Many women's colleges have relatively quiet campuses, which may or may not appeal to you.

- If you're interested in dating men, where are the closest men's and coed schools? Does the women's school traditionally have a strong social relationship with these schools?

- What are the advantages of attending a single-sex school? Your tour guide and the leader of your information session will be more than happy to tell you!

- Remember that most women's colleges are relatively small institutions. As with any small liberal arts college, check the availability of programs in areas that interest you. Does the school have extensive offerings in the liberal arts? Fine arts and performing arts? How about science and mathematics? Is cross registration at other schools available to make up for absences in the school's curriculum?

- Is there a visible LGBT population on campus? Are there organizations supporting these communities? Is there a visible heterosexual community on campus? Are there indicators of strained relations among these communities?

- What support and advising resources are available for students interested in graduate school and/or other pre-professional programs?

Historically Black Colleges and Universities (HBCUs)

An HBCU is, by definition, a school that was established before 1964 with the intention of serving the African American community. There are more than 100 HBCUs in the United States, and they come in all types and sizes—public and private, two-year and four-year, single-sex and coeducational. Few, if any of them, are all-black and some, such as Lincoln University of Missouri, actually have large white populations. The size and involvement of the African American community at any college is a factor you should weigh carefully before you apply. Dig beneath the perceptions and stereotypes to discover for yourself which environment is best for you. Visiting the schools you are considering is a great way to assess their environments. Start by asking these questions:

For a little more information about HBCUs, please visit PrincetonReview.com/college/historically-black.aspx

- Does the school have extensive offerings in the liberal arts? What about fine arts and performing arts? How about science and mathematics?

- Is cross-registration at other schools available to make up for absences in the school's curriculum?

- What is the social life like here?

- How strong is the alumni network? (This has historically been one of the great strengths of HBCUs.)

- How widely available is financial aid?

- How many companies recruit on campus? (HBCUs often excel in job placement for graduates.)

Part 4

The Right College for You

By The Staff of The Princeton Review

18 FACTORS THAT DO AND DON'T MATTER

Finding the right college for you is an exercise in matchmaking. You should begin with a thorough self-examination that will help you consider your options and keep track of those colleges that do and don't satisfy the various needs or wants you've identified. You can decide exactly how to build out your personal inventory—whether in spreadsheet, chart form or simply mentally—but you will find that in the course of your college search, you'll confront an amazing array of statistics and other data related to every college you consider. In order for all of this information to be helpful, you'll need to have some sense of how to interpret it, which is why a chart or table can play a helpful role in evaluation and comparison. Remember that choosing a college is a personal decision, so data is only one aspect of how a college should appeal to you. To get you started, we've listed eighteen factors that do and don't matter.

Money

A lot of colleges cost a lot of money. If your parents aren't rich, the cost will make a big difference. Even when colleges say they don't pay attention to applicants' financial need in accepting and rejecting students, they really do. How much money your parents can afford to spend on college is going to affect not only where you go to school but also what your life is like once you get there. Do you mind juggling a job (or several) with your schoolwork? Do you mind graduating with a heavy debt? Do you want to go to a school where virtually all of the students come from fairly wealthy families? There's a lot of financial aid out there, but few scholarships pay the entire bill, and most have strings attached. One of the important things you have to do is sit down with your parents and talk honestly about the bottom line. At the same time, don't rule out a college based on cost entirely—you haven't yet applied for financial aid, and grants and loans can make a big difference.

Distance

How far away from home do you want to be? Going away to school will definitely help you broaden your horizons, but you'll have to be outgoing enough to build a whole new social circle. And when you're calculating college costs, don't forget to add in the cost of transportation. Flying back and forth between school and home can cost a few thousand dollars a year, particularly if school and home aren't located on heavily traveled air routes. However, if the tuition somewhere further from home is much cheaper, then it might be a cost-savings to go "away" to school. Be realistic: Don't decide that you'll save money by staying at school during all your vacations. Students stranded on empty campuses during big holidays are among the most depressed people in the world. Spending holidays away from home may sound like a great idea to you now, but a rough first semester as a freshman could change your mind.

Location

Is there an area of the country you want to be in? City or country? Do you want to be in an urban setting? A rural setting? Something in between? Do you want access to mountains? A beach? Is there an outdoor activity you love to do that requires you to be in a certain geographical setting? Do you mind living in a town that has no good restaurants? These questions have nothing to do with education, but they are not frivolous. Again, you're selecting not only a school but also a place to live for the next few years. Be sure you want to (or at least can stomach) living there before you sign up to go. Also remember that if you're going to have to work your way through school, a big city will probably offer more employment opportunities than a small town. It will also make it easier to find jobs that won't bring you into constant contact with your schoolmates, if such a thing would bother you.

Climate

Does weather influence your decision? If you grew up in Florida, you may have trouble adjusting to winters in Maine. You're also going to have to buy a lot of new clothes. Weather can make a big difference to your state of mind. If rainy days make you feel gloomy, you may want to think twice about going to college in a place like Seattle. Though most schools aren't in places where you'll never see the sun, you'll still want to keep climate in mind.

Living Arrangements

How you live is just as important as where you live and colleges differ greatly in the housing they offer. Some offer none at all. Some don't permit off-campus living. Do you mind showering in a large bathroom with a dozen other people? Are single rooms available for freshmen? If it matters to you, find out. Your living arrangements will influence who your friends are, how you spend your free time, how early you have to get up in the morning, and how late you can stay out at night. Here's how one of our former students puts it: "The best thing about college for me isn't college, it's my apartment. After freshman year, you're allowed to live off campus. My parents give me what they would have spent on room and board, and I use it to pay my rent and buy my food. I sleep in a bed I bought for ten dollars, I make my own breakfast and my own coffee, [and] I feel like an adult. And my grades are better too." You might be a lot happier living in a dormitory around other students, but this particular student's college experience would have been much different if he had attended a school that didn't let sophomores live off campus. Life in virtually all freshman dormitories is alike in some respects: It's loud, messy, crowded, uncomfortable, and usually a lot of fun. There are important differences, though, and understanding them before you make a commitment can lead to a happier few years.

Where Your Friends Go

Going to college with high school friends can be great or terrible. On the one hand, going away to a college where you don't know anybody is one of the few opportunities you'll have in life to wipe the slate clean on the person you used to be. Even better, it comes at a time when many people are very eager to do just that. On the other hand, having a close friend nearby can make the first weeks of freshman year less frightening. Nevertheless, we feel you're probably better off on your own. You'll make more new friends if you don't have the old gang to fall back on. Feelings of freshman alienation usually don't last beyond the first couple of weeks. People also change at college. The kind of people you like to hang around with won't necessarily stay the same.

Where Your Girlfriend or Boyfriend Goes

A fair number of people marry their high school sweethearts but many more of them don't. Before you decide to attend a certain college to be with your current boyfriend or girlfriend, think through the consequences. Freshman year in college can put a huge strain on a high school romance. Dormitory life is fun and liberating. Even small colleges offer temptations that high schools don't. It takes a strong relationship to survive the dramatic change in lifestyle that freshman year in college means to most people. We knew two students who had been going steady since eighth grade. They ordered catalogs together, picked colleges together, filled out their applications together, and enrolled in the same school. Then, a week into freshman year, they broke up. They spent most of the first semester just trying to avoid each other on campus, which was hard because they were at a small school. He ended up transferring. Also, having a steady boyfriend or girlfriend nearby can limit your ability to make new friends of both sexes; you may want to consider attending college a few hours away from your significant other. You know the saying about if a relationship is meant to last, it will last; though that might not necessarily be true, a strong relationship will survive some distance.

Trends

Every year a few hot schools emerge to which everyone seems to apply. Hot schools are usually good colleges that are suddenly perceived as being easier to get into than the very best colleges or are schools that have seen a sudden increase in national exposure and attention. As a result, they attract a huge number of applications. But the more people who want to go to a school, the more people who are going to be rejected. This doesn't mean you shouldn't apply to a hot school; it just means you shouldn't depend on getting in, even if your credentials would ordinarily make you a strong contender. Use your judgment. If you decide to apply to a certain school because you read an interesting article about it in Time magazine, remember that millions of other people will have read about it too.

Student/Faculty Ratio and Average Class Size

While you should acknowledge these statistics in each college's information, course quality is much more important than class size (although it's also much harder to assess, unfortunately). Huge courses taught by great teachers are more rewarding than tiny courses taught by below-average teachers. In small classes, you could end up spending an excessive amount of time listening to the opinions of your classmates. Some professors who shine in big lecture courses are unbearable in small seminars. One of our students summed it up for us nicely: "I came from a big high school where there were never enough desks, and one of the things I cared about most when I applied to college was class size—I wanted them small. But the funny thing was [that] my very worst class freshman year was an English class that only had six students in it and that usually met in the professor's living room … and my favorite course was a freshman science course that met in an auditorium and had about 500 students in it. The professor was like a great actor, and every lecture was exciting." Also remember that student/faculty ratio and average class size mean even less if the courses you plan to take don't fit the usual pattern. If you are planning to major in Greek and the university to which you're applying only has seven Greek majors, many of your classes are going to be small no matter what the overall university statistics say.

Course Catalogs

Some students try to compare colleges on the basis of catalogs of course offerings. As college freshmen soon discover, course catalogs are works of fiction. Courses that sound great in a catalog can be very different in reality, and the course that makes you want to go to a certain college may be canceled by the time you get there. Who the teacher is usually makes more difference than what is being taught. Of course, if you have special academic interests, you need to be certain that the colleges you are considering can satisfy them. If you want to major in Russian, be sure the schools you apply to have Russian departments.

Campus Culture

Does the idea of Greek life frighten you, or is that something that you'd be interesting in participating in? Do you want an environment where students spend a lot of their free time in the library? Are lots of clubs and extracurriculars important to you? Do you want an active social life with large crowds gathering at a huge sporting event every weekend in the fall? Do most students live on campus and congregate in dorms, or are there a lot of commuter students? Do you want a campus that is a hotbed of political debate? Do you want to live in a place where students are focused on environmental initiatives? Do you enjoy a more artistic environment or a technical environment, perhaps? All of these things should be taken into account.

Viewbooks

Many colleges supplement their catalogs with viewbooks, brochures, and other publications. You can get some idea of what a campus is like by looking at the pictures, but no college in existence looks as good as it does in its viewbook. Let's face it: A viewbook is an advertisement. The college hopes it will put you in the mood to buy. You should be just as skeptical of a viewbook as you are of the claims in a television commercial. You will never find a college that has the same proportion of happy students, magnificent scenery, and beautiful weather that it depicts in its brochures. Colleges also use their viewbooks to spell out their educational philosophies. Most colleges have interchangeable philosophies—"a firm commitment to the liberal arts," and so on—but some colleges do have unusual programs or other specialized approaches to education. These will always be explained in the viewbook or other brochure. Colleges may have a five-year co-op program or an expanded Experiential Learning Programs that expose first- and second-year students to outside-of-the-classroom course work. There may be online courses or required study abroad so when you look at viewbooks, focus on the programs and not just the pictures.

What Your Parents Think

The truth is that you're probably going to need your parents' help in financing your education, so don't alienate them by saying that you don't care what they think. If you want to go to an Ivy League university but they want to economize by sending you to the local college, see if you can find a compromise. Try persuading them to at least let you apply to some local colleges and an Ivy League school or two. If you get into the school of your choice, your case will be strengthened, but if you don't, there's nothing to

SOME DOS AND DON'TS OF CHOOSING A COLLEGE

The college admissions process may seem like a minefield of advice. College counselors, parents, teachers, friends, and even representatives of the colleges themselves all have admonishments to "be sure to…" and "don't ever…" Unfortunately these tidbits, while intended to be helpful, can often contradict one another, giving students a picture of the process that looks more like a booby-trapped labyrinth than a map of a clear and straightforward path to success. In order to avoid adding to the confusion of the college selection process, here are just a few very important mistakes to avoid.

Get Started Now!

The biggest pitfall is probably the most obvious. Don't procrastinate! Getting started can be difficult, and there are plenty of places where you can get hung up or feel overwhelmed. Procrastinating can create undue stress and probably won't allow enough time to visit a campus so that you can get the most out of each college visit. And of course, there is also the ultra-last-minute procrastination of the applications themselves, which can cause you to make careless errors that could jeopardize your admissions chances. The bottom line here is that being prepared in advance for each step of the process can make the whole college admissions timeline much more manageable.

You have to take this project seriously. Which school you end up attending is the biggest factor that will shape your college experience, but many students don't put that much time or effort into this consideration. Don't make a decision without spending time researching colleges and finding out what you want. Because students don't often invest much time in exploring their options for different colleges, they can fall into the trap of assuming the best colleges are the most familiar ones. If you don't spend enough time thinking about the kind of person you are so that you can come up with a more appropriate "fit" instead of just getting in to some "brand name" institution, then you may not be able to realize your full potential, or you may just end up switching colleges after the first year because the experience wasn't what you dreamed it would be.

Schedule A College Visit

Part of taking this process seriously and doing your research properly is visiting as many colleges as you can. Often students and parents put this off, thinking it's either a waste of time or too expensive, but visiting at least a few schools is almost always worth it. Nothing can give you as much information about how a school "feels" and how you'll feel on it as actually walking around campus and getting a sense of its atmosphere. If you have the time and ability, visiting multiple schools early in your application process can help you narrow down which schools to apply to. If your candidate schools aren't local or you have limited means, it can be helpful to wait until you've received acceptances and weighed aid offers, and visit only your top two or three schools to aid in your final decision. We have multiple strategies and tips about planning an effective college visit in Part 3.

DOs	DON'Ts
Do it early, as soon as possible, or right now.	Don't procrastinate.
Do consider many schools you haven't heard of.	Don't choose a school based on name recognition alone.
Do listen to professional advice.	Don't neglect school visits.
Do it yourself!	Don't let your parents make all the decisions.
Do your research.	Don't let a school's "sticker price" scare you.

WOULD YOU RATHER?

Now that you know some of the key factors and some of the mistakes to avoid, it's time to really start figuring out what you want from colleges. Read through each question and write down your answer without thinking about it. You might be surprised what you learn about your college expectations.

Would you prefer a school that…

1. is big (10,000+ undergrads), medium (4,000–10,000 undergrads), or small (fewer than 4,000 undergrads)?

2. is close to home, or as far away as you can get?

3. requires you to live on campus, or off?

4. has an ivy-covered campus, or looks modern?

5. has a set, structured list of academic requirements, or grants total academic freedom for all four years?

6. is in a city, the suburbs, or a cornfield?

7. is warm and sunny 340 days a year, or cold and snowy from October to April?

8. has many of your high school friends as students, or is full of total strangers?

9. has plenty of fraternities and sororities, or no Greek scene at all?

10. has a dry campus, has somewhat of a social atmosphere, or is a party school?

11. has 400 students in lecture classes, or six kids in a small class?

12. is populated with liberal hipsters, or young Republicans?

13. has professors who will know your name, or will refer to you by your social security number (in paperwork, since they probably won't call on you in their large classes)?

14. has mostly students who live on campus all four years, or is mainly a "suitcase" school where people travel to and from campus?

15. assigns lots of homework and readings, or hardly any of the same?

16. is bureaucracy central, or a well-oiled machine?

17. has a politically active student body, or one that never reads a newspaper?

18. has tons of things to do off campus, or where the school itself is the center of all fun activities within a 20-mile radius?

19. has a diverse student body, or has a fairly uniform student body?

20. is very accepting of gay students, or has a "don't ask/don't tell" policy?

21. is a "jock" school, or is full of students who rarely participate in sports?

22. enrolls mainly pre-professional students, or kids who will "figure it out after we graduate"?

23. sends almost every junior abroad for a semester or year, or where everyone stays on campus all four years?

24. doesn't consider environmental issues as a top priority, or recycles everything possible?

There you have it: A few ideas about how to start your search for the college that will fit your needs. But you're not quite finished; we have a few more activities for you.

FINAL THOUGHTS

It's important to remember that most students end up liking where they go to college. The student who is crushed to have been rejected by Princeton ends up loving Oberlin and being happy that the fate kept her from being accepted by what had once been her first-choice school. In many ways, the most important thing about college is the one characteristic that virtually all colleges have in common: They are communities of young people living on their own without many serious responsibilities. You'll never get another chance to live this way, and you'll probably enjoy it almost anywhere you get the opportunity. In addition to determining where you spend the next four years of your life, where you go to school can determine where you work after graduation, whom you marry, where you live, and who your life-long friends are. A degree from Wharton really can make it easier to get a good job after graduation; however, spending four years in a sunny locale such as Hawaii really can be a lot of fun. You should make your college decision carefully and with a clear head. Don't make your decision simply to please (or infuriate) someone else. If you begin to think that you won't be able to go on living unless you get into Yale, get a hold of Yale's faculty directory and see where its professors went to college. You'll see that some of them went to Yale, some to Harvard, and some to other Ivy League schools, but that many of them went to exactly the sort of colleges that you may think are "beneath" you. If those colleges are good enough for Yale, might they not also be good enough for you? You should approach college selection thoughtfully, but not with a conviction that your entire life hangs in the balance.

Because, let's be honest, it doesn't. No matter the college, the education you will get out of it largely depends on what you put into it. No one can tell you what you want or need. Not your parents, not your guidance counselor, not your teachers, not your older brother or sister, not us. Students who end up enrolling in colleges based on the wants, needs, or expectations of others often regret it. You should certainly listen to the advice all these people have to give you, but you need to do your own soul-searching and research because only you can figure out what attributes of college are most important to you.

No matter where you go for your college research help or where you end up actually going to college, we sincerely hope that it's the right school for you. Best of luck!

NOTES